Town
Book of
Belfast

First published 1892
This edition 2008
First impression

ISBN: 978 1 906578 25 1 (softback edition)
        978 1 906578 30 5 (hardback edition)

This edition is a facsimilie of the 1892 edition.
Published by Colourpoint Books with the support of Belfast City Council.

Cover image: 1685 Phillips map of Belfast, courtesy British Library.

Layout and design: April Sky Design
Printed by: W&G Baird Ltd
Foreword to the 2008 edition ©2008 Ruairí Ó Baoill
Cover ©2008 Colourpoint Books. All rights reserved.

Colourpoint Books
Colourpoint House
Jubilee Business Park
Jubilee Road
Newtownards
Co Down
BT23 4YH

Tel: 028 9182 6339
Fax: 028 9182 1900
www.colourpoint.co.uk

TOWN BOOK OF
THE CORPORATION OF
BELFAST

1613-1816

FOREWORD TO THE 2008 EDITION BY RUAIRÍ Ó BAOILL

COLOURPOINT BOOKS 2008

ROBERT M YOUNG

BELFAST
MARCUS WARD AND CO., LIMITED
PRINTERS

The Town Book

of the

Corporation of Belfast

1613-1816

EDITED FROM THE ORIGINAL

WITH CHRONOLOGICAL LIST OF EVENTS, AND NOTES

BY

ROBERT M. YOUNG, B.A., C.E., M.R.I.A.

F.R.S.A.I. AND HON. LOCAL SEC.

HON. SEC. BELFAST NATURAL HISTORY & PHILOSOPHICAL SOCIETY

WITH MAPS AND ILLUSTRATIONS

BELFAST

MARCUS WARD & CO., LIMITED, ROYAL ULSTER WORKS

LONDON, NEW YORK, AND MELBOURNE

1892

New Seal of the City of Belfast.
1890.

TO THE RIGHT HONOURABLE

HARRIET,

COUNTESS OF SHAFTESBURY,

WIFE OF ANTHONY, EIGHTH EARL OF SHAFTESBURY,

AND ONLY DAUGHTER OF

GEORGE HAMILTON, THIRD MARQUIS OF DONEGALL,

This Volume,

CONTAINING THE RECORDS OF THE CORPORATION OF BELFAST,

FOUNDED AT THE INSTANCE OF HER FAMOUS ANCESTOR,

SIR ARTHUR CHICHESTER, BARON OF BELFAST,

IS,

WITH HER LADYSHIP'S GRACIOUS PERMISSION,

MOST RESPECTFULLY DEDICATED.

FOREWORD
TO THE 2008 EDITION

he original of the *Town Book of the Corporation of Belfast* is a 400 page manuscript recording decisions of the corporation and listing freemen from 1613 until the end of the eighteenth century. It is a key source for the history of the town, especially for the seventeenth and early eighteenth centuries, when other documentary materials are scarce.

Robert Magill (R M) Young was an architect and an antiquarian who edited the manuscript and published it in 1892 as *The Town Book of the Corporation of Belfast 1613-1816* through Marcus Ward and Co. Ltd., with the addition of his own explanatory. Young was born at Athlone in 1851, two years before the founding of the *Ulster Journal of Archaeology*, and educated at Queen's College, Belfast. He trained as an architect under his father (also Robert) and later joined the family firm in Belfast. Young was an active antiquarian during the first golden age of historians of Belfast, who included George Benn and William Pinkerton, and was a member of the Royal Irish Academy, a Fellow of the Royal Society of Antiquaries of Ireland and Honorary Secretary of the Belfast Natural History and Philosophical Society. In 1895 he became co-editor of the second series of the *Ulster Journal of Archaeology*. Amongst his other publications was the 1896 *Historical Notices of Old Belfast and its Vicinity*, based on the materials collected by William Pinkerton for a proposed history of Belfast. In 1878 he married Eleanor (also known as Nellie or Lally) Reid. They had four children and lived in *Rathvarna*, off the Antrim Road. Robert Magill Young died at the age of 74 in 1925, a year after his wife.

The Anglo-Normans established a settlement at Belfast in the late 12th or early 13th century. In the late medieval period there may also have been a small Gaelic presence, controlled by the Clandeboye O'Neills. Little is currently known about the nature, workings and precise location of these earlier settlements. It is only with the re-founding of the Town in the early 17th century that cartographic, documentary and archaeological evidence can be cross-referenced with any detail.

On the cessation of the Nine Year's War in 1603, the area around Belfast was one of a number of land grants made to Sir Arthur Chichester. Although Belfast was incorporated in 1613 with a sovereign (mayor), twelve burgesses and the commonalty (freemen) of the Town, in the early decades these had little real power. Belfast is unique amongst the major towns in Ireland in that its development was controlled by one family, the Chichesters (created earls post-1647 and later marquises), until the mid 19th century.

It is uncertain where the Corporation met in its early days. There is a reference in the *Town Book* to the *Towne Halle* in 1639, possibly located in Corn Market. In the later 17th century it appears that the Corporation met above the new Customs House, which was built in 1664. This building is illustrated on Thomas Phillips 1685 map of Belfast, and was sited close to the entrance to Belfast Castle.

The Town Book is a very important strand of primary information that helps chart the development of Belfast, describing the working of the Corporation with limited political power but still having an impact on peoples' everyday lives and business. It is in these aspects where there is detail and real interest. From the information contained within the *Town Book* we can get a picture the activities of Belfast's 17th and 18th century inhabitants of Belfast and what life was like.

The usefulness of the Town Book for archaeologists and historians is that it often discusses things that we have no other direct evidence for currently such as the early construction of houses and references to malting kilns. In 1638 it is directed that wooden chimneys were to be demolished to be replaced by ones constructed of brick, presumably to limit the dangers of fire. In the same year imports of salt, soap and *aqua vitae* (whiskey) are mentioned giving an idea of the essential commodities available to the town's people.

There are, however, other references in the *Town Book* to aspects of the 17th century town that it has been possible to investigate archaeologically. The only town defences ever constructed around Belfast were a bank and ditch erected in the 1640s. In 1645 there is reference in the

Town Book to *moweing the grass about the Rampier* (ditch). However, the defences appear to have been used primarily by the townspeople as a convenient place in which to dump rubbish because in 1671 there is a reference to the necessity of repairing a stretch of the defences *at the cost and charges of the Inhabitants of the said North Streete...* The repairs seem to have been unfinished for by the time of Phillips' map, 14 years later, the exact circuit of the town ditch is incompletely marked out. In recent times stretches of the ditch have been uncovered during excavations at Donegall Street, Gordon Street and Queen Street.

These are only a small sample of the many and varied and aspects of town life that are contained within the pages of the *Town Book*. The information is both informative and entertaining. The work of Robert Magill Young in compiling the *Town Book* and his other contributions to Belfast history, deserve to be celebrated.

The number of publications relating to the archaeology and early history of Belfast is growing, but the initiative of Belfast City council and Colourpoint Books in reprinting such an important and seminal source as *The Town Book of the Corporation of Belfast 1613-1816* is a boost to anyone interested in the story of Belfast.

Ruairí Ó Baoill
Centre for Archaeological Fieldwork,
School of Geography, Archaeology and Palaeoecology,
Queen's University Belfast,
Past chair of the Irish Post-Medieval Archaeology Group

TO THE READER.

ELFAST, *unlike many of the ancient boroughs in Great Britain and Ireland, possesses very few original documents illustrative of its early history. One of great importance, however, exists in the MS. containing the contemporary records of the old Corporation, now printed for the first time in the present work, by the kind permission of the owner, Mrs. Torrens, Edenmore, Whiteabbey.*

The painstaking historian of Belfast, the late George Benn, devoted a chapter of his well-known "History" to its contents, which he also referred to in his earlier volume, published in 1823. When the Municipal Reform Commissioners took evidence here in 1833, it was submitted for their inspection, together with a second book containing the later minutes, since lost. Henry Joy, the leading authority on local history, copied a few extracts about the end of the last century; while Dr. Kirkpatrick, in his work entitled "Presbyterian Loyalty Displayed," printed in 1713, made the first reference to it under the title of "Common Town Book of Belfast."

These writers only used such portions as suited their immediate purpose, and gave them, moreover, in a modernised form. The aim of the Editor has therefore been, as far as possible, to give a faithful reproduction of the original, with its solecisms and its peculiarities of spelling and punctuation, some unusual contractions in the earlier portion excepted.

The manuscript consists of four hundred leaves foolscap folio, of which one hundred and thirteen are blank pages. The paper is of excellent quality, with five separate watermarks, some foreign. A court hand is used for the earlier entries, many of which are very illegible in places, increased by the faded colour of the ink. Considerable difficulty was experienced in arranging the entries chronologically, partly because minutes had frequently been entered on blank portions of pages already written on, but mainly because the different sheets were kept loose for many years, and when subsequently discovered by the Marquis of Donegall in an old chest, were further disarranged by F. Bedford, who bound the existing volume.

In the printing of the work every effort was made to reproduce, by means of appropriate type, the quaint headings, &c., as originally written.

Preface.

The only additions are the ornamental capital letters and the woodcuts in the text. All the proofs were corrected by the Editor directly from the Town Book itself, a process which occupied the evenings of many months.

The words printed within brackets [] are struck through in the original with a pen, as corrections; and those printed in italics are interlineated in the manuscript. In the Notes the Editor has endeavoured to give fresh information from sources not hitherto accessible, supplementing Benn's and other well-known Histories. A Chronological List of Notable Events is prefixed to the work, in which will be found a number of interesting items not previously printed.

The Editor has been much encouraged in his labours (carried on in the intervals of professional duties) by the interest taken in the work by numerous friends. His best thanks are especially due to that most distinguished scholar, the Right Reverend William Reeves, D.D., President R.I.A., Lord Bishop of Down and Connor and Dromore, for his invaluable services in reading over and assisting in the correction of the proofs. The Editor's thanks are also tendered to the Countess of Shaftesbury, the Viscountess of Templetown, the Earl of Belmore, G.C.M.G.; The Belfast Harbour Commissioners, the Churchwardens of St. Anne's, Thomas H. Torrens, Esq., J.P.; C. H. Brett, Esq.; Lavens M. Ewart, Esq., J.P., M.R.I.A.; Samuel Black, Esq., Town Clerk; R. Meyer, Esq., Chief Clerk; Robert Day, Esq., J.P., F.S.A., M.R.I.A., Cork; Rev. G. Hill; Rev. A. Gordon, M.A., Manchester; Rev. James O'Laverty, P.P., M.R.I.A.; H. M'N. M'Cormick, Esq.; J. Henderson, Esq., M.A.; W. H. Patterson, Esq., M.R.I.A.; Classon Porter, Esq., Ballygally Castle; W. Swanston, Esq., F.G.S.; J. A. Rentoul, Esq., M.P., LL.D., London; Rev. W. Reynell, B.D., Dublin; J. W. E. Macartney, Esq., D.L., Clogher Park; Rev. Prof. G. T. Stokes, D.D., T.C.D.; John Vinycomb, Esq., F.R.S.A.I.; Talbot B. Reed, Esq., London; Rev. Charles Scott, M.A.; and to the Librarians at the British Museum, the Public Record Offices, London and Dublin, and the Bodleian Library.

Special thanks are also due to Miss Lewis, Nettlefield, for the use of the original Town Seal. Other friends will be found mentioned in the Notes.

CONTENTS.

LIST OF ILLUSTRATIONS.

The Frontispiece is based on the perspective drawing executed by D. Hanna, C.E., in 1883, of which only a few copies exist.

The quaint woodcuts used in the text are the work of James Smith, a local "engraver on wood, 30, Millfield" (Bradshaw's *Directory*, 1819). He worked for F. D. Finlay, whose books printed at the time contain many of the cuts. Permission to use them was kindly granted by the *Northern Whig Co.*, through their manager, Mr. W. Darragh.

A Chronological List of Notable Events connected with the History of Belfast to the present time.

[Extracted from STATE PAPER CALENDARS, REEVES' ECCLESIASTICAL ANTIQUITIES OF DOWN AND CONNOR, CLASSON PORTER'S MSS., &c.]

A.M. 3506. In the fifth year of the reign of Heremon, Loch Laogh in Ultonia (now Belfast Lough) broke forth.

A.D. 82. Agricola wintered at Stranraer, intending to cross by way of Belfast Lough and subdue Ireland.

160. Bresal, son of Brian, who reigned in Eamania 19 years, was drowned in Loch Laogh (now Belfast Lough).

667. The battle of the Ford (at Belfast) between the Ulidians and Picts, where fell Cathasach, son of Laircine.

1177. John de Curci held possession of the Castle of Belfast.

1210. King John passed Belfast on his way to Carrickfergus.

1306. The White Church (now Shankill), with the Chapels of the Ford, noted in the Irish Taxation Roll.

1315. The Scots under Edward Bruce wasted Belfast.

1333. William de Burgo, Earl of Ulster, murdered near the Fords of Belfast.

1476. O'Neill attacked and demolished the Castle of Belfast.

1489. Hugh Roe O'Donnell took the Castle.

1503. The Castle demolished by the Earl of Kildare.

1512. Retaken by the Earl of Kildare, and the spoils distributed amongst his soldiers.

1523. The Earl of Kildare wrote to Henry VIII. that he has "taken a Castle of Hugh O'Neill's called Belfast, and burned 24 miles of his country."

1537. A son of Con O'Neill taken prisoner at Belfast.

1551. Sir James Croft, Lord Deputy, repaired Castle of Belfast, and put there a garrison.

1552. Restored to Hugh McNeill Oge O'Neill by King Edward VI. "in the same state as when he first possessed it."

1553. Lord Chancellor Cusack writes, that Hugh O'Neill has two castles, an old one at Belfast, and Castell rioughe (Castlereagh).

1556. Lord Deputy Sussex encamped underneath the Cave Hill with his army.

1558. Belfast fortified and "the renowned Capt. Malbie" with 15 horsemen placed in it by Lord Deputy Sydney.

1568. An important agreement signed here by Lord Deputy Sydney and Sir Brian O'Neill.

1571. Queen Elizabeth granted the castle and town to Sir Thomas Smith.

1573. Belfast granted to Earl Essex, who "buildeth a forte neare Belfaste, whereby he commandeth the passages over certain rivers and waters, and cutteth downe wood quyetly to the great discouragement of the Irish." Earl Essex defeated Sir Brian O'Neill at Ballymacarrett.

1574. Earl Essex writes that the Brewhouse, Storehouse, and Mill are completed. Sir Brian O'Neill, his father and wife, seized by Earl Essex at a feast in the Castle.

1575. Earl Essex writes:—"I resolve not to build but at one place, namelie Belfaste, and that of little charge, a small towne there will keepe the passage." An engagement took place between Lord Deputy Sydney and MacNeill Brian Ertaugh at Belfast.

1583. Lord Deputy Perrot recommended Belfast to Queen Elizabeth as a fit place for shipbuilding, after visiting it.

1597. Shane McBrian took the Castle. As narrated by an eye-witness :—" One ensigne Pullen had the gyfte of Belfast castell, who in culler of this charge, robbed the people, and took their gudes round aboute hym, to mayntayne his drunkeness. And being drunck from his charge at Knockfergus, and a carswose sent hym by Shane M'Bryan, to loke to his chardges, wolde not forsake his wyne poots to serve her Maty; but lyinge still at Knockfergus, drinkinge, his owne man, named John Aloylon, gave the castell of Belfast to the enemye the xviiith daie June." Retaken 11th July by Sir John Chichester, who was killed in November by MacDonnell at Ballycarry. The Castle of Belfast a Government possession.

1598. The Castle of Belfast held by Sir Ralph Lane *in custodiam*.

1599. Sir Arthur Chichester appointed Governor of Carrickfergus and the two Clanneboyes.

1601. Cecil wrote to Lord Deputy Mountjoy suggesting Sir Arthur Chichester as governor of Ulster, but blaming his clemency to Con O'Neill of Belfast.

1603. Con O'Neill sent his servants to bring wine from Belfast to Castlereagh; they returning without it, explained that the English soldiers had taken it from them. He ordered them to revenge this insult, and in the fray a soldier was killed.

Accused of levying war against the Queen and imprisoned in Carrickfergus, he escaped by the help of Hugh Montgomery, Laird of Braidstane, by whom his pardon was procured in 1605 at the expense of most of his vast estates. The castle and estate of Belfast granted by King James to Sir Arthur Chichester, who wrote to Cecil :—"Albeit when I have it att best perfection I wyll gladly sell the whole landes for the wch others sell, five poundes in fee simple in these partes of the Kyngdome."   Sir Arthur Chichester appointed Governor of Carrickfergus and Admiral of Lough Neagh.

1604. Sir Arthur Chichester made Lord Deputy of Ireland, which office he held 10 years.

1605. Fairs and markets first established in Belfast.

1606. Numerous townlands in Malone and the Falls leased to Moyses Hill at £10 yearly.

1607. Town and Castle of Belfast declared forfeited by Sir Thomas Smith's descendants. Belfast mentioned as a suitable place for a Charter of Incorporation. The flight of the Earls, and the consequent Plantation of Ulster commenced.

1610. Sir Arthur Chichester writes to King James that he "would rather labour with his hands in the Plantation of Ulster than dance or play in that of Virginia."

1611. The Castle rebuilt and strengthened by Sir A. Chichester. "The towne of Bealfast is plotted out in a good forme, wherein are many familyes of English, Scotch, and some Manksmen already inhabitinge . . . and one Inn wth very good Lodgings wch is a great comforte to the travellers in those partes."

1612. Sir Arthur Chichester created Baron Chichester of Belfast. Castle built at Stranmillis by Moyses Hill.

1613. Lord Belfast resigned the office of Lord Deputy. Belfast constituted a Corporation by Charter on 27th April, with John Vesey as first Sovereign. Sir John Blennerhassett and George Trevillian returned as the two first M.P.'s.

1614. Lord Belfast again made Lord Deputy, when he caused the Irish Harp to be first quartered with the arms of England.

1618. Con O'Neill died at Holywood, and was buried at Ballymaghan.

1625. Lord Belfast died in London, Feb. 19. Buried in Carrickfergus Church, Oct. 24. Edward Chichester, brother and heir, created Viscount Chichester of Carrickfergus.

1630. The Chichester estate of Manor and Borough of Belfast valued at £400 per annum.

1635. Sir W. Brereton visited Belfast, and noted—"At Bell-fast my Ld Chichester hath another daintie House, wch is indeed the Glorye & Beautye of that Towne al-soe, where hee is most resident."

1636. A ship of 150 tons, called the "Eagle's Wing," built at Belfast, and 140 persons embarked for New England, but returned. Conference in Belfast Church between Bishop Leslie and five Presbyterian clergymen.

1637. Lord Deputy Wentworth abolished "the Carrickfergus privilege," thus freeing the port of Belfast.

1639. A detachment of the army raised by Wentworth to assist King Charles I. stationed in Belfast. The Town Hall fitted up to serve as a Court House.

1640. The Assizes held in Belfast for the only time till 1850. Maces, Arms, and Town Seal procured by the Corporation. A new grant of their estates given to the Chichesters by the King.

1641. A pestilent fever carried off about 2,000 in Belfast alone. "Not any that escaped this fever but lost all their hair." A letter sent King Charles at Edinburgh by Lord E. Chichester from Belfast giving the first news of the Rebellion. The town saved from the rebels by the bravery of Capt. Robert Lawson. Arms, including artillery, to defend Belfast, procured in Scotland by Cols. Chichester and Hill.

1642. The town fortified with a rampart and ditch by Col. Chichester. Gen. Robert Monro, with 2,500 Scotch soldiers, landed at Carrickfergus. The Earl of Leven brought over the remainder, 10,000 in all. Some billeted in Belfast. First Presbyterian congregation formed.

1643. Father MacCana visited Belfast, and wrote—"The town which is built there is no mean one." Col. Chichester appointed Governor of Belfast, and £1,000 given by the King to strengthen it.

1644. Belfast surprised and occupied by Gen. Monro on May 14. Thos. Theaker, Sovereign, states that all the free commoners, "except a very few," had taken the Covenant.

1645. The Parliament's Commissioners sent to Belfast refused possession by Gen. Monro.

1646. Owen Roe O'Neill completely defeated Gen. Monro at Benburb on June 5. Col. Arthur Chichester created 1st Earl of Donegall by King Charles. The Scotch forces in Belfast refused to admit the soldiers sent by the English Parliament.

1648. Gen. Monro arrested by Col. Monk at Carrickfergus, and Belfast surrendered to the English Parliament, who directed thanks to be offered by all their ministers in London for "the great mercy of surprising the said garrison, and taking the Scots prisoners." Lord Edward Chichester died at Eggesford, Devon, in July.

1649. John Milton made his famous attack on the Belfast Presbytery, as "that unchristian synagogue of Belfast," in his "Observations upon the Articles of Peace with the Irish Rebels, on the letter of Ormond to Colonel Jones and the Representatives of the Presbytery of Belfast." Lord Montgomery took Belfast for the King, and shortly afterwards Carrickfergus. Cromwell arrived in Ireland, and sent Col. R. Venables to Belfast, which surrendered on articles on 30th Sept. after four days' siege.

1651. The church converted into the Grand Fort and Citadel by Col. Venables.

1653. Belfast included in the proclamation of the Commissioners for Ulster removing certain Scots to the West of Ireland. In Belfast these were—"Lt. Thos. Cranston, Corporal Thos. M'Cormick, Hugh Doke, Robert Cluxton, George Martin, Alexander Lockard, Robert King, and Quintin Catherwood."

1654. Major Daniel Redmond returned as M.P. for Belfast and Carrickfergus. Essex Digby and William Dix appointed by the Government as the clergy of Belfast at £120 each per annum. W. Edmundson, the Quaker, mentions :—"At Belfast that town of great profession, there was but one of all the inns and public houses that would lodge any of our friends, which was one Widow Partridge who kept a public-house and received us very kindly."

1656. Henry Cromwell granted £100 to restore the church, after its use as a citadel.

1657. Col. Cooper, Governor of Ulster, wrote to Henry Cromwell that no Scotchman should be allowed in Belfast for some years. Population given by Petty as 366 English, 223 Irish.

1660. Great rejoicings at Restoration. Belfast contained 5 streets and 5 lanes with 150 houses.

1666. The Duke of Ormond, Lord Deputy, passed through Belfast on his way to quell a mutiny at Carrickfergus. 204 houses rated for Hearth money, the Castle for 40 hearths. Loaf sugar, 14d. per lb. ; butter, 20s. per cwt. ; meal, 7s. 6d. per barrel.

1667. Jeremy Taylor, Bishop of Down and Connor, died at Lisburn.

1672. De Rocheford visited Belfast, and wrote :—"Here is a very fine Castle, and two or three large streets as in a new built town." First Presbyterian Church built.

1675. Arthur Chichester, 1st Earl of Donegall, died in Belfast 18th March.

1681. Thomas Pottinger paid £20 rent for all Ballymacarrett.

1682. The foundations of the Long Bridge laid ; finished in 1688 ; cost £8,000.

1685. Thomas Phillips surveyed the town for the Government, and advised the building of a citadel at £42,000. The Corporation and inhabitants sent an address to James II. on his accession.

1687. A writ "Quo Warranto" served on Corporation, and the original Charter forfeited.

1688. The total amount of the customs and excise, £20,000. The chief place of trade was Rosemary Street. W. Sacheverell visited here, and noted :—"Belfast is the second town in Ireland, well built, full of people, and of great Trade." King James II. granted a new Charter, which became law 16th Oct.

1689. King William and Queen Mary proclaimed in Belfast. Belfast occupied for King James II. by "six companies of Colonel Cormack O'Neal's regiment and a troop of dragoons in Malone and the Fall, and they were kept to strict discipline." Duke Schonberg occupied Belfast 17th August. "Whilst the Duke staid at Belfast, there came a letter to him by a trumpet from the Duke of Berwick, but it was returned unopened, because it was directed For *Count* Schonberg."

1690. An Earthquake in Belfast. King William landed at Carrickfergus 14th June; drove from Whitehouse over the Strand, entering Belfast at the North Gate. A Royal Proclamation issued from "Our Court at Belfast," 19th June, prohibiting plundering by the army.

1692. In spring, seven arches of the Long Bridge fell in, "having been weakened by Schonberg's drawing his heavy cannon over it."

1694. W. Crafford, Sovereign, induced Patrick Neill and James Blow to start as printers.

1696. Corporation sent address to King William and Queen Mary. Swift made frequent visits to Belfast, where he proposed to "Varina," daughter of W. Waring.

1697. A violent storm threw down part of the Mill Gate and the vane of the Church.

1698. Butter, 30s. per cwt.; tallow, 44s.; salmon, 50s. per barrel ; beef, 14s. per cwt.

1699. Shaw's Bridge built. Ship "Loyal Charles," 250 tons, Hunter, master, launched.

1700. Only ten slated houses in Belfast. P. Neill printed first dated book in Belfast.

1704. James Blow printed the first edition of the Bible in Ireland. New sugar-house built.

1706. 3rd Earl of Donegall killed at the storming of Fort Monjuich, Barcelona.

1707. George Macartney, Sovereign, summoned before House of Commons, but acquitted. Greater part of Lisburn burnt. £54 collected here in a few hours for sufferers.

1708. The Castle burnt, April 25, three of Lord Donegall's daughters perishing in the flames. A company of militia raised, commanded by the Sovereign. Dr. Molyneux noted—"Belfast is a very handsome, thriving, well-peopled town ; a great many new houses and good shops in it." Second Presbyterian Church founded.

1709. The greatest flood remembered took place, carrying away Shaw's Bridge and many others. A public fast observed on account of great scarcity.
1712. Hanover Quay formed by Isaac Macartney on reclaimed ground.
1714. King George I. proclaimed "by 400 inhabitants on horseback, all pleased but a few."
1715. The first independent company of Volunteers formed.
1716. The fishing at Stranmillis let at £4 10s. od. and half the eels.
1717. Dr. W. Tisdall, vicar, cast in a suit to recover house-money from Corporation.
1720. All the houses in Bridge Street thatched.
1721. Third Presbyterian Church founded.
1723. Ships in Belfast—all craft included—370, carrying 9,180 tons.
1725. The Corporation petition for a Bill to improve Harbour. Houses in the Parish 2,093. Bleaching machinery first erected at Ballydrain.
1728. A year of great scarcity from failure of crops.
1729. The first Act to improve the Harbour obtained.
1731. The "Playhouse" first mentioned.
1732. The Barony of Belfast contained 4,532 Protestant and 340 R.C. families.
1737. *Belfast News-Letter* founded by Francis Joy. Yearly subscription—town, 4s. 6d. ; country, 6s. 6d. The Barracks built in Mill Street.
1738. Lord Donegall granted £1,500 to build a Linen Hall at Ann Street.
1740. A petition from merchants to improve Harbour sent Irish Privy Council. Regular trade between Belfast and West Indies commenced.
1745. *The Belfast Courant* printed by James Magee on paper made by James Blow.
1748. Primate Boulter wrote—"There are now 7 ships at Belfast carrying off about 1,000 passengers to America."
1750. The ancient stone coronation chair of the O'Neills of Castlereagh set up in Butter Market by the Sovereign, Stewart Banks.
1751. George Whitfield stayed some days in Belfast. [James] "Blow's Bible" printed.
1752. The first post chaise brought to Belfast. First Bank established by Thomas Bateson, James Adair, and Daniel Mussenden. Dr. Pococke noted—"Belfast is a considerable town of trade, especially in the linnen manufacture, in which they are all concerned. The town of Belfast consists of one long, broad street, and of several lanes in which the working people live. The church seems to be an old tower or castle, to which they have built, so as to make it a Greek cross."
1753. The first private lottery held to raise funds to build the Poorhouse.
1754. Donegall Street laid out. A Linen Hall built. 200 men start work on Lagan Canal.
1756. Serious riots caused by scarcity and distress. John Wesley first visited Belfast.
1757. First Census—1,779 houses, 8,549 inhabitants, 1,800 able to bear arms, 399 looms. 4th Earl of Donegall died.
1758. Capt. J. M'Cracken established first Ropewalk Company.
1759. James Blow, printer, died. 300 French prisoners kept in the Barracks.
1760. Thurot captured Carrickfergus, and requisitioned Belfast. Milewater fortified. 5,000 Volunteers enrolled. Splendid ball given by French and Swiss prisoners.
1763. Thomas Gregg sent first lighter to Lisburn with coals and timber. Customs, £32,900.
1764. A lump of ambergris weighing 1 cwt. found at Whitehouse shore. Lime first used in bleaching.
1765. Provisions very scarce ; £90 raised monthly for relief ; Lord Lieutenant gave £500. A Reading Society called the Belfast Library formed.
1766. A six-days post established between Belfast and Dublin.
1767. A Social Club met at Donegall Arms.
1769. Lord Donegall laid first stone of Exchange (now Belfast Bank) ; cost £4,000. The foundations of Chichester Quay, 320 feet long, laid by Mr. Thomas Gregg.
1770. The Farset River in High Street covered over.
1771. The Bachelors' Annuity Company of Belfast formed. David Douglas, of Templepatrick, rescued from Barracks by "the Hearts of Steel."
1772. Rev. James Saurin, vicar, died ; succeeded by Rev. W. Bristow. At the "Green" was a tenement held by those who managed the ferry-boat across the Lagan.
1773. Computed that "one-fourth of its manufacturing people and cash had emigrated to America from North of Ireland." Brown Linen Hall erected. 160 linen looms in town.
1774. The old Church in High St. taken down and St. Anne's begun. Poorhouse opened.
1775. Very high tide ; boats plying in High Street. *Belfast News-Letter* attacked by Dublin Press for its support of American Independence.
1776. Glass manufacture introduced. Arthur Young estimated value of the Chichester estate of Belfast at £2,000 per annum.
1777. Robert Joy and Thomas M'Cabe started cotton-spinning in the Poorhouse. No rain for 200 days.
1778. January 10. The raising of Volunteers suggested at a family party by Robert Joy. April 24. Paul Jones captured H.M.S. sloop "Drake" off Donaghadee. June 28.

"The first Belfast Volunteer Company paraded and marched to church in their uniform, which is scarlet turned up with black velvet, white waistcoat and breeches."

1779. John Howard visited the French prisoners confined here.
1780. The Amicable Society of Belfast protest against slavery on British soil. Lord Charlemont reviewed Volunteers for the first time.
1781. First Presbyterian Church, Rosemary Street, rebuilt ; Roger Mulholland, architect.
1782. The Tanners' Club commenced with 13 members.
1783. White Linen Hall erected on site granted in perpetuity by Lord Donegall. St. Mary's R. C. Church erected in Chapel Lane. *Belfast Mercury* issued.
1784. Nathaniel Wilson and Nicholas Grimshaw built first cotton mill in Ireland.
1785. A Harbour Board constituted by Parliament. The large glass-house at east end of Long Bridge built. Mrs. Siddons' first visit to Belfast. Population, 16,000.
1786. Vessels belonging to port, 772 ; tonnage, 34,287 ; revenue, £1,553. The old ford at foot of High Street removed by Harbour Board. The Belfast Academy founded ; Dr. Crombie, principal. Chief Baron Yelverton commenced a town in Ballymacarrett, but stopped by Lord Donegall. The third edition of Burns's poems printed in Belfast—the first and second having been printed in Kilmarnock and Edinburgh respectively.
1787. A Bank formed by John Ewing, John Holmes, John Brown, and John Hamilton. First Methodist Chapel erected in Fountain Street. Sovereign's Chain presented to Corporation by Lord Donegall.
1788. The Belfast Reading Society formed, now known as "The Linen Hall Library." The two Banks in Belfast issued notes payable in gold. First mail coach commenced to run between Belfast and Dublin.
1789. Nearly 300 houses built in Belfast during this year. A loyal address sent King George III. on his recovery. Mustard manufacturing started.
1790. Northern Whig Club instituted by Lord Charlemont. Francis Joy died, aged 93.
1791. First shipyard established by William Ritchie. Houses occupied, 2,209, by 18,320 people ; 8,932 males, 9,388 females. The Society of United Irishmen founded by S. Neilson, H. J. M'Cracken, T. Wolf Tone, and T. Russell. Theatre built.
1792. The first number of the *Northern Star* issued on 4th January. Famous meeting of harpers in Belfast, convened by Dr. J. McDonnell. Petition for Catholic Emancipation signed by Sovereign and principal inhabitants. Old Dispensary, now Royal Hospital, founded. First foundry started. David Manson died, aged 65.
1793. The Volunteers disbanded by Royal Proclamation. A Discount Office opened.
1794. Society of the New United Irishmen formed in Belfast. Lying-in Hospital opened. [H. Joy's] *Belfast Politics* printed.
1795. 72 delegates of United Irishmen at meeting in Belfast framed the "System of Committees." *The Gaelic Magazine*, by Miss Brookes, issued.
1796. Habeas Corpus Act suspended ; proprietors of *Northern Star* arrested. January 25. High tides commenced, which sometimes "ebbed and flowed 3 times in a tide ;" water 13 inches deep on south side of Arthur Street ; boats plied at south end of Bridge Street. First volume of E. Bunting's Irish Music printed.
1797. The Belfast Yeomanry formed. First Fever Hospital opened, with six beds. De Latocnaye notes—"Belfast has all the air of a Scotch town."
1798. May 7. Martial law proclaimed by General Nugent, followed by surrender of Volunteers' cannon. June 7. Battle of Antrim ; no one allowed in or out of Belfast except to market. June 12. Battle of Ballynahinch, the cannonading at which was heard in Belfast. June 18. Declaration of Loyalty by Belfast Yeomen. July 6. Henry Joy M'Cracken executed. Thermometer 21° this winter.
1799. 1st Marquis of Donegall died. Marquis Cornwallis presented with a Corporate Address at Lord Donegall's house. Great snowstorm ; for 7 days there was no post between Belfast and Donaghadee. Manufacture of vitriol introduced.
1800. Municipal Act obtained ; cost £1,260. Public Bakery opened. "The dear summer." 36 tan-yards at full work. Edward May, John Congreve, jun., M.P.'s.
1801. First Union Jack hoisted at Market House and Royal salute fired. Literary Society formed. Typhus very prevalent. Edward May, M.P.
1802. Population, 19,000 ; houses, 3,197. Mrs. Siddons' second visit, accompanied by Montague Talbot. Dr. Alexander H. Haliday, Lord Charlemont's friend, died.
1803. Two new corps of Yeomanry formed. T. Russel's abortive rising. Town guarded by sentinels. *Belfast Almanac* first issued. *Anna*, first novel written here, printed.
1804. Master Betty, "the Young Roscius," appeared at Belfast Theatre.
1805. *The Commercial Chronicle* issued by Drummond Anderson. Graving dock erected for two vessels ; cost £7,684. Valentine Jones died, aged 94.
1806. Belfast Medical Society inaugurated. The Galvanic Society formed.
1807. Population, 22,095; houses, 3,514; looms—cotton 629, linen 4, sailcloth 35, sacking 5. Irish Harp Society formed. The first *Belfast Directory* published.

1808. Rev. William Bristow, Vicar, died; Sovereign 10 years; his funeral was the largest ever witnessed here. *The Belfast Magazine* issued; it continued six years.
1809. House of Industry opened in Smithfield. First Ormeau Bridge built.
1810. Daniel Blow, printer and papermaker, son of James Blow, died, aged 92. Foundation-stone of Royal Academical Institution laid; architect, Sir John Soane. Belfast ships, 58 (28 armed); seamen, 742; tonnage, 8,335. Coasters, &c., 21; seamen, 44. A Night-Watch Society formed.
1811. St. Patrick's R. C. Church, Donegall Street, built; Protestant subscriptions, £1,711; total, £2,811. First Baptist Chapel built in King Street.
1812. St. George's Church erected on site of "Corporation" Church. James Sheridan Knowles had a school in Crown Entry. Old Market-house pulled down.
1813. Population, 27,832; 5,428 families in 4,416 houses. Montgomery's Market opened.
1814. Royal Academical Institution received Parliamentary grant. Customs duties, £450,498. Anacreontic Society formed. Sir Stephen May, M.P.
1815. Linen Hall Newsroom opened with 105 members. First stone of Hospital laid.
1816. First Stipendiary Magistrate, W. H. Ferrar, appointed. Savings Bank established.
1817. Frederick Street Hospital opened, August 1. Great dearth. Unprecedented outbreak of typhus fever. The House of Correction, Howard Street, erected, with the inscription, "Within, Amend; Without, Beware." [H. Joy's] *History of Belfast* published.
1818. *The Irishman* weekly newspaper commenced by John Lawless. A. Chichester, M.P.
1819. Jan. 27. In 36 hours 3 inches of water fell by rain gauge; barometer gave no warning. The first steamship, "Rob Roy," arrived from Glasgow. Steamship "Waterloo," 200 tons, 12 hands, registered here by A. Langtry, plied to Liverpool.
1820. William Drennan, M.D., died. Commercial Buildings erected; cost £20,000. Earl of Belfast, M.P.
1821. Belfast Natural History Society formed at Dr. J. L. Drummond's house by 8 persons.
1822. Population, 37,117; houses, 5,932. First stone of Gasworks laid by Lord Donegall.
1823. The town first lighted with gas. [G. Benn's] *Historical Account of Belfast* published.
1824. *The Northern Whig* issued by F. D. Finlay. *The Rushlight* published by son of James Hope, United Irishman. Cross-channel steamboat trade regularly begun.
1825. Mechanics' Institute founded. John Templeton, the famous naturalist, died at Malone, aged 60. Ardoyne Damask Factory started.
1826. Belfast Banking Co. established; capital, £500,000. Branch Office of Provincial Bank opened. The "Chieftain" steamship, built by Ritchie, and engined at Lagan Foundry, plied to Liverpool. Epidemic of typhus.
1827. Royal Botanic Garden formed. Fisherwick Place Church opened by Dr. Chalmers.
1828. The Manor Court Prison abolished, and debtors sent to County Gaol. May Street Church opened by Rev. Edward Irving.
1829. The Lunatic Asylum erected at a cost of £30,000. A. Mackay, jun., died.
1830. May 4. Foundation-stone of the Belfast Museum, College Square N., laid by Lord Donegall. The machine-spinning of linen yarn introduced by Messrs. Mulholland at York Street Mill. The Lying-in Hospital built.
1831. Population, 53,737; houses, 8,710. Third Presbyterian Church, Rosemary Street, rebuilt; cost £10,000. Sir A. Chichester, Bart., M.P.
1832. Bounties on exported linen discontinued. Epidemic of typhus fever and influenza. Cholera year, 2,870 cases; mortality only 16 per cent. owing to precautions taken. Sir A. Chichester, Bart., M.P.
1833. Oct. The Irish Municipal Commissioners held an inquiry into the Belfast Corporation.
1834. The manufacture of flax-spinning machinery introduced into Belfast. Lord A. Chichester and James E. Tennent, M.P.'s.
1835. Henry Joy, the greatest authority on Belfast history, and John M'Cance, elected M.P. with Lord A. Chichester in January, died.
1836. The Ulster Banking Co. established; capital, £1,000,000. Society for Prevention of Cruelty to Animals formed in Belfast. Association of Artists formed. J. E. Tennent and George Dunbar, M.P.'s.
1837. Act obtained to improve Harbour on Walker and Burgess's plans. Much typhus.
1838. 50 steam-engines of 1,274 horse-power in and about Belfast—12 erected in 1806-27, 10 in 1830-34, 17 in 1835-6-7, 11 in 1838. The first iron boat built at Lagan Foundry. Nov. 29. Very high tide. In Ann Street, water up to Corn Market; in Tomb Street, people escaped by boats. James Gibson and Earl of Belfast, M.P.'s.
1839. Ulster Railway opened to Lisburn—the first railway from Belfast. Music Hall built. *The Vindicator* issued—editor, Charles Gavan Duffy. J. E. Tennent and George Dunbar, M.P.'s.
1840. June 19. Belfast Water Commissioners incorporated by Act of Parliament.
1841. Population, 70,447; inhabited houses, 10,906. Daniel O'Connell, M.P., in Belfast. Belfast Union Workhouse opened. Rev. W. Bruce, D.D., died, aged 84.

1842. The first Town Council, under the Irish Municipal Corporation Act, elected for Belfast on 25th October. At first meeting, held on 1st Nov., George Dunbar elected Mayor; Town Clerk, John Bates. Francis M'Cracken, last survivor of the Belfast Volunteers, died; was enrolled 1788. *Banner of Ulster* issued. J. E. Tennent and W. G. Johnson, M.P.'s.

1843. Queen's Bridge, erected on site of old Long Bridge, opened Jan. 31; cost £28,000. Deaf and Dumb Institution erected. Union Club formed. David R. Ross and J. E. Tennent, M.P.'s. Geo. Dunbar, mayor.

1844. Amount of postage collected in Belfast, £4,625. 2nd Marquis of Donegall died. St. Malachy's Church consecrated. Alexander Mackay died; he was proprietor of *News-Letter* for nearly 50 years. John Clarke, mayor.

1845. County Gaol completed. New Belfast Bank built. Belfast and Ballymena Railway incorporated. Dr. James McDonnell died, aged 82. Andrew Mulholland, mayor.

1846. Co. Down Railway incorporated. Ulster Temperance Society formed by Dr. Edgar. James Young and G. Langtry died. Pilson's *History of Belfast* published. Lord J. Chichester M.P. in place of [Sir] J. E. Tennent. John Kane, mayor.

1847. New Harbour Act, changing title of Harbour Board to Belfast Harbour Commissioners. The "Swatara," emigrant ship, put in with fever on board, which was followed by 14,000 typhus cases. Reeves' *Ecclesiastical Antiquities of Down, Connor, and Dromore* published. John Harrison, mayor.

1848. April 11. Belfast and Ballymena Railway opened. Robert James Tennent and Lord James Chichester, M.P.'s. George Suffern, mayor.

1849. Queen Victoria and Prince Albert visited Belfast; gave £300 to Hospital. Queen's College opened. Victoria Channel completed. Second outbreak of cholera. Sir William G. Johnston, mayor.

1850. Assizes removed from Carrickfergus to Belfast. Albert and Queen's Squares formed on old Docks. James Sterling, mayor.

1851. Population, 100,301; houses, 13,965. *The Mercury* issued. Jas. Sterling, mayor.

1852. First British Association meeting here. Harbour Conservancy Act. Iron ship-building begun. New Northern Bank opened. Antiquarian Exhibition in Museum. W. Thompson, the great Irish naturalist, died. *Ulster Journal of Archæology* first issued. S. G. Fenton, mayor.

1853. Municipal boundary extended. Presbyterian College opened. Frederick Richard, Earl of Belfast, died at Naples. R. Davison and H. M'C. Cairns, M.P.'s. William McGee, M.D., mayor.

1854. New Harbour Office erected. Fred. H. Lewis, mayor.

1855. North-East Agricultural Association formed. Statue erected to Earl of Belfast. *Morning News* issued. John Bates died. Capt. James Verner, mayor.

1856. Vessels entered port, 5,394; tonnage, 772,127. St. Mark's, Ballysillan, consecrated. Dr. A. G. Malcolm, author of the *History of General Hospital*, died. Samuel Gibson Getty, mayor.

1857. New Custom House opened. Model School built. Ulster Club founded in the old "Donegall Arms" premises. Samuel Gibson Getty, mayor.

1858. Large extent of land reclaimed on Co. Antrim side of Lough. E. J. Harland took over Hickson & Co.'s shipyard. Samuel Gibson Getty, mayor.

1859. Burns' centenary celebrated. Victoria College founded. R. Davison and H. M'C. Cairns, M.P.'s. William Ewart, mayor.

1860. New Ulster Bank and Bank of Ireland opened. R. Davison resigned; S. G. Getty elected M.P. William Ewart, mayor.

1861. Population, 120,777; inhabited houses, 18,375. Royal Agricultural Show held. Great fire in Bedford Street. Sir Edward Coey, mayor.

1862. Ulster Hall opened by Lord Lieutenant. Large expansion of linen trade by American Civil War. Ulster Club new buildings erected. Chas. Lanyon, mayor.

1863. New Ormeau Bridge completed. Belfast Naturalists' Field Club formed. John Lytle, mayor.

1864. Corporation Indemnity Act. Great Riots, on which Commission sat in November. John Lytle, mayor.

1865. Increase of town unexampled. Serious scarcity of water. Rev. Dr. Montgomery died. John Lytle, mayor.

1866. Central Railway commenced. Lombard Street improvements made. Rev. Dr. Edgar died. Sir H. M'C. Cairns raised to Bench; C. Lanyon elected M.P. William Mullan, mayor.

1867. Hamilton Dock and Abercorn Basin opened by Lord Lieutenant. Social Science Congress; Lord Dufferin presided. S. G. Getty and C. Lanyon, M.P.'s. Sir David Taylor, mayor.

1868. New Town Reservoir made. Methodist College opened. Revs. Dr. Cooke and W. Bruce died. T. M'Clure and W. Johnston, M.P.'s. S. M'Causland, mayor.

1869. High tides caused flooding. Albert Memorial completed. Borough Cemetery and Ormeau Park opened. Sir J. E. Tennent died. Fred. H. Lewis, mayor.

1870. New Provincial Bank and Richardson's Warehouse opened. *Evening Telegraph* issued. Rev. Dr. Drew died. Samuel Browne, M.D., R.N., mayor.
1871. Town Hall opened. New Theatre built. Smallpox epidemic. Population, 174,412. Philip Johnston, mayor.
1872. Spencer and Dufferin Docks opened by Lord Lieutenant. Tramways opened. Robert Patterson, F.R.S., died. Sir John Savage, mayor.
1873. Trade much depressed. Peace Preservation Act in force. Rev. Dr. Morgan and W. Ewart died. Jas. Alex. Henderson, mayor.
1874. British Association met. Corporation Gas Act. Fitzroy Avenue Church opened. Marcus Ward & Co.'s new premises built. J. P. Corry and W. Johnston, M.P.'s. Jas. Alex. Henderson, mayor.
1875. Lepper's mill burnt down. *Ulster Echo* issued. Local trade depressed. Thomas G. Lindsay, mayor.
1876. Working Men's Exhibition in Ulster Hall opened by Lord Lieutenant. Cooke Statue completed. Sir Robert Boag, mayor.
1877. Disastrous fire following explosion in Castle Place. New R. C. Church of St. Patrick consecrated. Geo. Benn's *History of Belfast* published. Sir John Preston, mayor.
1878. Belfast Improvement Act. Court of Admiralty granted to Belfast. Townsend St. Church rebuilt. Samuel Black appointed Town Clerk. W. Johnston resigned ; W. Ewart elected M.P. Sir John Preston, mayor.
1879. Very severe winter. General Grant in Belfast. Young & Anderson's warehouse burnt. Workman & Clarke's shipyard opened. Associated Chambers of Commerce met here. John Browne, mayor.
1880. Corn Market improvement made. Foundation-stone of Belfast Academy, Cliftonville, laid. John Browne, mayor.
1881. Royal Avenue commenced. Presbyterian College granted Royal Charter. John Rea died. Population, 207,671. Sir E. P. Cowan, D.L., mayor.
1882. Harbour Act for new Docks and Channel. New Water Office built. Free Library Act adopted. Sir Joseph Napier, Bart., died. George Benn died. Sir E. P. Cowan, D.L., mayor.
1883. Visit of Sir Stafford Northcote. 3rd Marquis of Donegall died, when Irish estates devolved on his daughter Harriet, Countess of Shaftesbury. J. A. Henderson, proprietor of *News-Letter*, and Dr. James Moore, H.R.H.A., died. Sir David Taylor, mayor.
1884. Ormeau Avenue opened. Foundation-stone of Free Library laid by Lord Lieutenant. Meetings of Pan Presbyterian Council and British Medical Association held. James Torrens died. Sir David Taylor, mayor.
1885. Visit of T.R.H. the Prince and Princess of Wales ; latter cut first sod of Alexandra Graving Dock. Lord Hartington opened Ulster Reform Club. Lord O'Hagan, Earl Cairns, Dr. Thomas Andrews, F.R.S., and Rev. Classon Porter died. Sir W. Ewart, Bart. ; W. Johnston, E. S. W. De Cobain, and Sir James H. Haslett M.P.'s. Sir E. J. Harland, Bart., mayor.
1886. Albert Bridge collapsed. New Post Office opened. Lord R. Churchill's visit. Great riots. 8th Earl of Shaftesbury died. A. Nicholl, R.H.A., died. T. Sexton elected M.P. instead of Sir James H. Haslett. Sir E. J. Harland, Bart., mayor.
1887. Main Drainage Act obtained. Alexandra Park opened. John S. Brown died. Sir James H. Haslett, mayor.
1888. Free Library and Fine Art Loan Exhibition opened by Lord Lieutenant. Belfast created a city. Woodville Park opened. Local Bankruptcy Court formed. Rev. Dr. Bryce died. Robinson & Cleaver's new premises opened. Sir James H. Haslett, mayor.
1889. H.R.H. Prince Albert Victor opened Alexandra Graving Dock, and laid foundation-stone of Albert Bridge. "Teutonic" and "Majestic" launched by Harland & Wolff. 4th Marquis of Donegall died. Sir W. Ewart, Bart., M.P., and Sir Charles Lanyon, died. Sir E. J. Harland elected M.P. Charles Cunningham Connor, M.A., mayor.
1890. Corporation Bill to acquire White Linen Hall passed. New Albert Bridge opened by the Mayor. Jubilee of General Assembly. The Earl of Shaftesbury attained his majority. Joseph G. Biggar, M.P. for Co. Cavan, died. Charles C. Connor, M.A., mayor.
1891. Population, 273,055. Dr. George MacDonald delivered a series of lectures. New Victoria Channel opened. Dunville Park opened by Marquess of Dufferin and Ava. Site of Royal Hospital presented by Countess of Shaftesbury. M'Arthur Hall, Methodist College, opened. Soldiers' Home opened by H.R.H. the Duke of Cambridge. Grainger Collection of Irish antiquities, &c., presented to Corporation. Charles C. Connor, M.A., mayor.

Incorporation of Borough, April, 1613.

THE TOWN BOOK OF BELFAST.

Orders & Bylawes

Belfast tertio Die Augusti
Anno Dni 1632

Whereas Controversey hath growen w^{th}in this Corporacon touchinge the pam^t of Toungs to the Soveraigne by the Butchers inhabitinge same being made free of this Corporacon. Now for that it manifestlie appeares by good testimonie as well of the Antient Burgises as others that at the first Courte held within this Burrough after the first raisinge of this Corpo-

A Bylawe for the paieng of Tounges every weeke racon. It was agreed upon by the Soveraigne and Burgises of the said Towne and espeacially of the Butchers then made free That every Butcher being a ffreeman of the Towne should paie unto the said Soveraigne of the said Towne one toung weekely if the same Butcher should happen to kill anie Bullock *or Cow*, whereof due pam^t hath been made accordinglie every Thursday untill within one yeere or thereabouts which order we think fitt to be continued duly   And therefore in confirmaton and for the better strengthining thereof in tyme to come as well Wee the Soveraigne and Burgises of this Corporacon here assembled togither by a genrall consent and agreem^t as alsoe by and

B

with the consent of Henry Upton Esq. Agent for the right
Ho^{ble} the Lord Viscount Chichester doe make a By Lawe
from henceforth to be observed and kept That evrie Butcher
and Butchers within the Towne Libtie of this Corporacon
shall paie or cause to be paid unto the Soveraigne of this
Corporacon one Toung weekelie and evrie weeke soe long as
anie such Butcher or Butchers shall kill or cause to be killed
to his or their use anie Bullock of what kinde soever within
this Towne or Corporacon or within the Libities thereof.

Lewys Tomson Soveraigne

Jo: Vesey . Jo: Ayshe　　　　Henry Upton
　Cornelius Harman　　　　George Theaker
Robt ffoster　　　　Walterhouse Crimble
　　　　　　　　Thomas Bramstone
　　　　　　　　Gowen Bolby

Copia vera
Extus per me Clemt Osey Register

The Award of
Jno Wassher
gent concern-
ing the
Sovraigne &
Burgises of
Bellfast & the
Butchers of
the same

The Award of me John Wassher made and published the last day of August 1632 betweene Lewys
Tomson gent. Soveraigne of the Burrough of Belfast
& the Burgises of the same Burrough of the one p^{te}
and Rob^{te} Duninge Tho: Duninge, Ralph Dyson and
William Willson the younger of the same Towne
Butchers of the other p^{te}

The Award of
Mr. Wassher

Whereas Controversy hath arrisen betweene the said
pties touching the paim^t of a toung weekelie by evrie Butcher
inhabitinge and being made free within the said Corporacon
wch the said fower psons within named have of late tymes
refused to paie and espeaciallie to the said now Soveraigne.
Now for that I finde uppon full and due examinaton that
uppon the first errecton of the said Corporacon the Butchers
then made free did consent to a byLawe ppetually to be
stablished within the said Corporacon should weekelie and
evrie weeke soe long and soe often as the same Butcher and
Butchers should kill anie beefe theare paie unto the Soveraigne
for the tyme being one toung towards the Soveraignes hospe-
taletie wch byLawe was then agreed on and hath benn confirmed and established I doe therefore Order and Award
that the said fower Butchers shall paie unto the said Lewys
Tomson nowe Soveraigne for this psent yeere twentie toungs
apiece in satisfaccon of all the toungs arrearange **or growing**

due unto the said Soveraigne wch the said Soveraigne shall accept of in full paim.^t and satisfaccon for this p'nte yeere And that the said Butchers and everie of them after the expiraton of this yeere shall paie unto the next succeedinge Soveraigne yeerelie one toung weekelie and everie weeke soe long and soe often as he or they respectivlie shall kill anie beefe or beeves In witness whereof I have hereunto sett my hand the daie and yeere above said

Jo: Wassher

Copia vera per me
Clemt Osey Register
1632

20 Junii 1622

An order that noe free Burgis or free Comoner shall impleade one another out of ye Courte of Bellfast w.thout

[**It is ordered** and agreed by a genrall consent an assembly held for the Corporaton of Bellfaste that noe free Burgis nor free man of the said Towne or Corporacon shall sue or impleade anie other free Burgis or free Comoner of the said Towne for anie action or suite that the Court of the Corporacon maie heare without the consent of the Lo: of the Castle of Bellfast for the time being or Soveraigne of the same Towne then being first obtained unless such pson shall not have due p'ceedinge theire Everie p'son offending

xls

therein shall forfeite to the use of the Towne xls. and in default of paiment thereof uppon the Soveraignes warrant everie such offender is to be disfranchised and be dismissed of his ffreedom]

An order for such as refuse to come to divine Service

Att an Assembly held for the Burrough of Bellfast the XVth daie of October 1615 before James Burr gent. Soveraigne of the said Towne and before the free Burgises and Commalty of the same   It was ordered by the Soveraigne and Burgises and Commaltie of the same Towne That everie freeman and other Inhabitant w.thin the said Corporacon being of the age of xiii^{teene} yeeres or above that shalbe absent from Church or other place appointed for comon praier within the said Corporacon uppon the Sabboth daie or anie other daie appointed to be kept holy by the lawes or Statutes of this Realme without reasonable or sufficient cause to be allowed by the said Soveraigne there for the time being shall for everie default forfeit for the use of the Soveraigne free Burgises and Commaltie of the said Towne to the use of the

h. vs
W iis vid
S. xiid
C. xd

use (*sic*) of the Corporacon as followeth every vizt hous-
houlder for everie default vs. every woman that is married
iis. vi^d every servant man or woman xii^d every child dwelling
with his her or their father or mother x^d sterling for everie
default the same to be leavied by distresses to be taken upp
by the Church Wardens of the parish of Shankhill for the tyme
beinge by Warrant from the said Soveraigne out of the goods
& chattles of everie offender wch is or shalbe a househoulder
within the Libties of the said Towne of Bellfast   And all
other the forfeitures before mentned for the married woman
servants and children to be likewise leavied out of the goods
& chattles of the husbands fathers mothers and Masters of
the said offenders respectively as aforesaid   And if anie
resist or resistance shall happen to be made by anie of the
said offenders or others chargeable with the said forfeits
Then it is further ordered and established that the said
Churchwardens shall give notice to the Constables of the
said Towne for the tyme beinge and uppon such notice
given the said Constables and every of them shall assist the
Churchwardens in the leavieing and taking upp of the said
forfeitures and that everie of the said Churchwardens and
Constables wch shall refuse and not p'forme the contents of
this lawe or order shall for every default forfeit to the use

xxs

aforesaid xxs ster; to be leavied by the warrant of the said
Soveraigne for the time beinge the distresses soe to be taken
by vertue of this order or to be used and ordered in
all respects as distresses taken upp for rents and to be
ordered by the lawes or statutes nowe in force in this
Kingdome

An order
made for y^e
disfranchismt.
of R Dyson &
Tho Doninge
for not
p'forminge y^e
customes of
ye towne

Att an Assemblie held the eight day of October. 1630 it
was and is ordered and agreed uppon by a genrall Consent of
the Soveraigne and Burgeses of the Burrough of Bellfast then
assembled that for and by reason that Ralph Dyson and
Thomas Doninge have refused to obey & p'forme the customes and orders of the Towne and Corporacon of Bellfast
aforesaid That they and either of them shall be cleerelie and
absolutely disfranchised from the said Corporacon or otherwise the said Ralph Dyson shall paie for his offence the some
of xxvs Ster: and the said Thomas Doninge shall paie
xxs Ster: uppon paiment of wch said somes or uppon paiment of either of the said somes he or they soe paiege shall
stand and be free of the said Corporacon as before allwas
provided that they shall p'forme as well all such customes

and orders as have been heretofore made & ordered as all other customes and orders as shalbe hereafter made and agreed uppon by the Soveraigne and Burgises of the Corporacon aforesaid.

Walterhouse Crimble Soveraigne
Jo: Ayshe   Geo Theaker
Edw: Holmes   Lewys Tomson
Robert ffoster

Extus per me
Clemt Osey Register
1632

An order for selling ale

[**Att** an Assemblie held the seaventeenth day of October anno dni 1616 for the Burrough of Bellfast It was ordered and fullie agreed by the consent of the Soveraigne & free Burgises then assembled that no p'son free or forriner shall from henceforth have admittance to sell ale or other liquor within the said Burrough unless the same p'son be thought fitting for the same by the Soveraigne of the same Towne for the time being and the rest of the free Burgises there and enter into Recognizance if he be not free and without the spiall license of the then Soveraigne under his hand for the time being and appearing of record who is to observe all such statutes and orders as have benn in

iiis iiiid that behalf provided uppon paine of iiis iiiid everie time offendinge]

An order for not coming to Courte

Att an Assemblie held the fouer and twentieth daie of Aprill Anno Dni 1617 It was agreed by a genall consent That if anie Burgis or Freeman of this Corporacon shall at anie tyme refuse to come to the Courte of this Towne or before the Soveraigne warning being given him by the officer w^{th}out reasonable or sufficient cause to be allowed by the Soveraigne & Burgises shall for everie such default forfeict

xs to the use of this Corporacon xs for every such offence to be leavied as other ffines are lymitted in former orders

An order against ye selling of ale or other liquor at the time of divine Service

Att an Assemblie held the second daie of October Anno dni 1617. It was ordered that noe p'son within this Towne shall att anie tyme of Divine Service sell anie manner of wine ale or aqua vitae or anie thing vendible uppon its forfeiture to the Towne everie tyme convicted soe offendinge vis viiid

vis viiid ster to be leavied as other ffines

An order for attending the Soveraigne to Church

Att the same Assemblie It was also ordered that every Burgis and free Comner in this Towne shall every Sabboth daie or other day wherein there shalbe Sermon or other publique praier as often as Sermon and praier shalbe shall all repaire to the house of the Soveraigne for the time being and shall thence themselves in his Companie attending wth him to the Church or place of praier and from thence home againe or neere to his house uppon paine of

Everie Burgis iis freeman xiid

paiment by every Burgis iis and every freeman xiid unless some reasonable cause shalbe to the contrary shewed to the Soveraigne wch. moneys to be leavied as other fynes

An order for attending the Sovraigne to meete anie Lord &c

Att the same Assemblie It was likewise ordered that every Burgis and Comm^{r.} dwelling in this Towne of Bellfast or otherwise then resident shall whensoever occasion shall soe fall out for the Credit and grace of this Towne that the Soveraigne shall give them notice how short or soone soe ever it bee be readie to accompanie him to meete anie Nobleman Justices of Assyse or other state or p'son whatsoever that they shalbe all ready with the Soveraigne either horseback or ffoote either in the same Towne or the Libties thereof with him in the most decent sort the rest maie uppon paine either of comittall during the pleasure of the Soveraigne and Burgises for the time beinge uppon paine of paim^{t} by

Burgis xxs Comner xs

everie Burgis and everie free Comner [the wh to be levied as of the prevs.] such ffyne as in the suffrance of two or more of the Burgisses shalbe thought fitt soe as the said fyne doe not exceede xxs ster :

An order for all to be ready uppon warning to apprehend felons

Att the same Assemblie It was further ordered by a genrall consent that everie Burgis and ffreeman of this Towne uppon all houres shalbe ready either on horseback or ffoote as they are then p'vided and as occasion shalbe given for the service of the Kinge or good of this Towne for apprehending anie felons Rouges woodkernes or Craytes either within the Towne or anie the Libties thereof whensoever anie such notice shalbe given to them or anie of them by the Soveraigne for the time being uppon paine of Imprisonm^{t} during pleasure of the said Soveraigne Burgises and disfranchising anie such for refusing or careleslie neglecting the same from his or their ffreedome of this Towne ipso facto and paiment of such fine as shalbe laied uppon them or anie of them by the Soveraigne and Burgises of the said Towne for the time beinge and rest of the Burgises and to be leavied accordinge as other fines are to be paid   And also everie Burgis and free Comoner of this Towne uppon lawfull warninge by a daie to be limitted unto them Toties quoties occasion shall happen shalbe ready for the p'fitt of this Towne to accompanie the Soveraigne for the time beinge to anie place within the Libties of this Towne beinge three miles by a direct lyne from anie p^{te.} of the seytuacon of this Burrough to make anie lawfull seizure of goods or merchandize sould w^{th.}out leave or by anie not planted by the Lo: Chichester according to the grant and power of the charter granted to this Towne or for doing anie other lawfull act wch. maie be donn by vertue of the Kings grant in the said charter limitted unlesse he or they have some reasonable cause to alleadge to the contrary to be allowed by the Soveraigne for the time beinge and rest of the Burgises uppon paine of v^{li} ster: by everie Burgis and ls ster: by everie Comoner refusinge or neglectinge paiable as other ffines are lymitted

vli

Carew Harte

An order for not making ffences

[**Att** an Assemblie held the XIIIIth day of October 1619 by George Theaker Soveraigne and the rest of the Burgises that everie free Burgis and other Inhabitant wch. doo or shall hould anie land in Towne or ffeild within or belonging to this Corporacon who shall be found not to have their fences lawfullie made that of right he or they ought to have made shall paie for such default being lawfullie found after the first daie of Aprill next ensuinge 2s ster: to the use of the Soveraigne for the time being and soe from tyme to tyme who shall make or cause to make keepe and mainetaine all not such their ffences uppon warninge by the Surveyor to be appointed for that purpose shall paie as aforesaid ffive shillings ster:

vs

George Theaker]

An order for keeping of Inmates

Att an Assemblie held the 29th daie of June 1620 It is fully agreed uppon by George Theaker Sovraigne and the rest of the Burgises that noe Burgis nor free Cmner within this Corporacon shall take into their houses anie sub-tenant or Inmate without leave of the Soveraigne then for the time beinge under the paine of xs for everie such default to be leavied and paid in forme and manner as other ffines formerlie recorded

An order for
such as refuse
the office of
a Soveraigne

[**Whereas** at an Assemblie held for the Burrough of Bellfast uppon the xixth daie of July 1627 It was ordered by and with the consent of the Lord of the Castle the Soveraigne for the tyme beinge and free Burgises then assembled That in respect severall p'sons are not resident in the said Corporacon and doe not p'forme the duty thereunto belonginge either by takinge uppon them the office of Sufferaigne when they are elected or p'forminge such imposicons as are respectively laied uppon Inhabitants of the said Corporacon whereby those names are onlie filled upp and the burthen for the most pt^s. laid uppon the meane and disablest Inhabitants   We have therefore in redresse thereof thought fitt and soe doe accordinglie make it to be a bylawe to be henceforthe in this Corporacon observed and kept That the Burgises that shall from henceforth from time to tyme refuse or delaye to take uppon them respectively the office of Sufferaigne of the said Corporacon when they or anie of them shalbe thereunto required & duly elected not having a sufficient cause by the Soveraigne for the time beinge and the Burgises allowed of and during that time dwell and reside within or neere the Corporacon shall incurre and paie a ffyne of five pounds ster: to be imploied for the use and benefit of this Corporacon and shall also paie to the use aforesaid all such averages of Imposicons as shall justlie appeare hath been imposed in them otherwise to relinquishe their said places of Burgises and be dismist thereof by vertue of this order at the next assemblie to be held after such refusal]

vli

[**Att** an Assemblie held for the Burrough of Bellfast 29th die Junii anno dni 1620 It was fullie concluded and agreed uppon by the Soveraigne and Burgises of the said Burrough That noe Burgis nor free Cmoner shall take into their houses anie sub tennant or Inmate without leave of the Soveraigne then for the time being uppon paine of Tenn shillings sterlinge for every such default to be leavied and paid in forme and manner as other ffynes formerlie recorded]

An

Att an Assemblie held the eight daie of August 1633 It was concluded and agreed uppon by the Soffragan and Burgises their assembled That all the monies *hereafter* given (and bequeathed granted) by anie p'son to be free of this Corporacon and all ffynes imposed or to be imposed uppon anie Burgis or freeman for the breach of any ByLawe whatsoever and all other ffynes and p'ffitts that shall come and accrewe by the Sea or goods brought into this Towne from anie shipp or Barke and sould here or sett to sale by liberty of the Markett Provided that the liberty of the Markett be not given to anie fforriner without the consent of *the Constable of ye Castle* fouer or three of the Burgises at least with the consent of the Suffragan for the tyme beinge shall from tyme to tyme be wholy to the use of the Suffragan for the tyme beinge towards his hospetallety without rendring anie accompt for the same   And it is further agreed that no Burgis or ffreeman inhabitinge within this Corporacon shall paie anie Custome for anie kinde of graine or anie other wares or merchandise bought within this Corporacon or Libtie thereof unlesse it be for the Custome of Cowes and that onlie two pence for booking [there] of every Cow

Robt Foster Sovraigne

Henry Le'Squyre
      Cons^t Castle
George Theakir
Lewis Tomson
Thomas Bramston
Tho Chudleigh
G. B. Gowen Bolby

John Vesey
Walterhouse Crimble
Thomas Hannington

Att an Assemblie held for the Burrough of Bellfast the second daie of Aprill Anno dni 1635 in the p.^e sence and by the full and free consent of the right Ho^ble. Edward Lord Viscount Chichester Lord of the Castle——————

By lawes

Burgus de Belfaste

Att an Assembly held for the Burrough aforesaid the XXIX^te^ day of March 1638

Of Mault Kills in Town

Fforasmuch as by dayly experience it is founde that mault kills erected in the body of this Towne are very dangerous and enormious and may upon the least accident indanger the whole Towne to be consumed by fyre, It is therefore Ordered and established by the Sovraigne & Burgesses assembled by and with the consent of the Right Honble Edward Lord Viscount Chichester Lord of the Castle of Belfast, as a by Law p'petually to remayn That from henceforth noe p'son or p'sons inhabiting within the Burrough of Belfaste shall erect or make any mault kill, or make use of any mault kill already erected and built within the said Burrough, but in such convenient places as shalbe allowed of by the Lord of the Castle and the Soveraigne of the Burrough for the tyme beinge together with syxe of the Burgesses at the least upon paines of forfeiture of five pounds sterl : for every default to be levyed, that shall be presented

Edward Chichester
Henry Le' Squyre
Sovraigne
Jo: Leithes
Robt Foster
John Ayshe
John Wassher

Wood Chimneyes

Fforasmuch as it is founde that dayly inconvenyencies are likely to arise to this Towne and Burrough by reason of their woode chymneys It is therefore thought fit & soe ordered that the said Chymneys shalbe forthwth pulled down and Bricke Chymneyes made in steede thereof upon pain of forfeiture on every p'son that maketh default the some of forty shillings sterl: to be levyed as aforesaid

> Edward Chichester
> Henry Le' Squyre
> Sovraigne
> John Ayshe   Jo: Leithes
>   John Wassher
> Robt Foster

17th January 1639

The Information of Henry Sands gent : taken the day & yeare aforesaid before the Sovraigne & Burgesses

Who sayth that about the middle of October last past Robert Kile of Erwyn M'chant brought into this Towne 10 Hogsheads and 14 barrells of [white] salt & 12 ferkines of Soape & two bottles of Aqua Vitae the s^d salt beinge offered to the Towne to buy at ye rate of 7s. 3d. a barrell but ye Towne refused ye same at ye rate and thereupon ye s^d Robert Kile sould the said salt to John Gurley of Armagh w.hin this Corporacon for 7s a barrell and 3s 6d on upon the scoore and ye caske againe And ye said Gurley hath taken away 19 barrells of ye s^d. salt.   There *from* of ye s^d. salt five hogshedds & a barrell the s^d. Henry Sands hath seised on to ye use of ye Towne as beinge forrayne bought & fforrayne sould ye rest of the Comodityes he sould some to the Towne & some to strangers.

It is therefore ordered by ye s^d Soveraigne & Burgesses then assembled that ye said Robert Kile shall pay for & in consideracon of ye afores^d sale ye price of one barrell of salt or a barrell of salt itselfe to be disposed of to ye use of ye Towne & Burrough of Belfaste.

A Rate made and agreed uppon by the Sovraigne & Burgesses the 12th day of October 1639 for the fittinge of the Towne Hall wth p'titiones bench and a Barr & other necessaryes for the use of the Courts.

The Sovraigne	...	...	...	...	...	Xs
John Aish	...	...	...	...	...	IIs VId
Robert Foster	...	...	...	...	...	Vs
Thomas Hannington	...	...	...	...	Vs
Gowen Boltbey	...	...	...	...	...	IIs VId
John Haddocke	...	...	...	...	...	Vs
Thomas Bramstone	...	...	...	...	Vs
Thomas Theaker	...	...	...	...	...	Vs
John Washer	...	...	...	...	...	Vs
John Leithes	...	...	...	...	...	Vs
Mrs Bradely	...	...	...	...	...	IIIs IIIId
Sandy Thomson	...	...	...	...	...	IIIIs
Hugh Doake	...	...	...	...	...	IIIIs

William Leithes	...	...	...	...	...	IIIIs
John Love	...	...	...	...	...	IIIs
Richard Gately	...	...	...	...	...	IIIIs
James Anderson	...	...	...	...	...	IIs
Robert Neevans	...	...	...	...	...	IIIIs
Bryon M'Corry	...	...	...	...	...	IIs VId
John M'Murry	...	...	...	...	...	IIs VId
William Partridge	...	...	...	...	...	IIIs
William Richey	...	...	...	...	...	IIs
John Boyde	...	...	...	...	...	IIs VId
Quynton Catterwoode	...	...	...	...	IIs
Francis Radcliffe	...	...	...	...	...	IIs
Ralfe Dighton	...	...	...	...	...	IIs
John Wilkison	...	...	...	...	...	IIs
William Wilson	...	...	...	...	...	Is
John W Ratelocke	...	...	...	...	...	Is
John Johnson	...	...	...	...	...	IIIs IIIId
Robert Thompson	...	...	...	...	...	IIs VId
Alexander Johnson	...	...	...	...	IIs
Thomas Gill	...	...	...	...	...	Is
Richard Bayley	...	...	...	...	...	IIs
John Roye	...	...	...	...	...	Is
Robert Steevenson	...	...	...	...	Is
James Smith	...	...	...	...	...	Is
William Asmore	...	...	...	...	...	IIs
Dermott O'Kennan	...	...	...	...	Is
John Mankin	...	...	...	...	...	IIIs
Archy M'Caghan	...	...	...	...	...	O O
Henry Blackhurst	...	...	...	...	...	IIIIs
John Hudson	...	...	...	...	...	Is
Thomas Kerran	...	...	...	...	...	Is
Robert Partridge	...	...	...	...	...	Is
John M'Cullogh	...	...	...	...	...	Is

Wee have assented to this Rate & doe desire that the same may be levyd accordingly. Witness oᵗ hands the 12th day of October 1639.

Henry Le' Squyre
Robt Foster   Sovraigne
John Aishe . John Leithes
Thomas Theaker

A settled course agreed upon by the Right Honorable the Lord Viscount Chichester the Soveraigne and Burgesses of the Towne of Belfast for the Governement and regulateinge of the Market and the measures to be used therein, and in ye towne the first day of November 1639

Mr John Arnold Attáy at Law in Belfast fore me

First That the measures be reduced to the Winchester measure. That is to say, thirty two gallons to the Barrell and soe proportionably for wheat, Rye Oate—meale, Salt, Beanes, and Pease and the measure to be striked

Secondly That that Barrell for Mault, Barley and Oats be the double measure heapt,

Thirdly That the water measure for Corne Coles and salt comeinge by sea from other p^{ts} to be sould at the said Towne be forty gallons of the like measure to the single Barrell,

Ffourthly That the measure to sell Beere and Ale by be the London measure

Ffiftly That the measure for Wyne be five quarts to the Wynchester gallon and soe proportionably

Sixtly That to this purpose severall measures be made and kept in the Towne Halle to regulate all other measures by, And that none use any other measures to buy and sell by, but according to this p'porton and sealed by the allowed seale of the Towne and the yard and weights to be observed accordinge to the law in that case made and provided and sealed,

Seaventhly **iid for bookeing of a Cowe** That every freeman pay for the bookeing of a Cowe bought in the Markett or other day two pence

Eightbly **iiiid a Stranger** That every stranger pay foure pence

Nyntbly
for every
Sheepe Swyne
or Goate

That every freeman pay for every Sheepe, Swyne or Goate bought as aforesaid a farthinge,

Tentbly
of a Stranger

That every stranger pay a halfepenny

Eleaventbly
Mealemen for
the measure 1d
for ye Room 1d

That every meale man pay for the use of the measure for the day a penny   And for his Roome the day a penny

That forrayne Butchers that bringe meat to sell in the Market bringe the hide and tallow alsoe to the Market to sell and 1d to be paid for the custome of the hide

Twelftbly
for bookeinge
on horses vid

That every freeman and stranger pay for the Bookeinge of every horse bought in the Markett or other day six pence

13tbly
1d a loade for
al sorts of Vict

That every horse loade of Corne bread fish or other Victuall pay for the day a penny

14tb
for a horse
load of any
Comodity
of 1d

That every Butcher, Pedler or other standinge on the grounde or otherwayes with his wares in the Markett being a horse loade pay a penny

15tb

That none sell or buy in the Markett before the Bell doe ringe w.h is appointed to be att tenn a Clocke under the penalty of forfeiture of the thinge bought

16tb
for any beast
not standinge
in ye Pens to
be sould 6d

That no cattle horses sheepe hoggs or Goats stand in the places of the Markett to be sold but in the penns to that purpose sett up under the penalty for each Cowe or horse so standinge or other beaste as aforesaid Sixe pence

That those that have corne to sell doe bringe it to the Markett and that none buy out of the Markett

17tb
for every
horse standing
empty in ye
Markett
place 6d

That noe p'son whatsoever after the two next markett dayes doe pester the Markett place with an empty horse upon the penalty for each horse Sixe pence

18tb

That the Markett be kept rounde togeather and not scatteringe up and downe but all togeather in the Markett place

Provided always that these Orders and Customes shall in noe case extend to the Lord of the Castle for the tyme beinge nor to the standinge to be made about the walls of the Markett place

Edward Chichester
Henry Le' Squyre
Sovraigne
John Ayshe   Jo. Leithes
Rob: Foster   John Wassher

7 Jan 1640

It was then ordered by the Sovraigne and Burgesses then assembled that the Attorney shall take for his pleading only twelve pence fees at his first retayning & twelve pence every Court day after soe long as the action remaynes in Court undecided.

8th ffeb^r 1640.

The Informaton of Henry Sands gent: taken ye day & yeare afores^d. before ye Sovraigne & Burgesses then assembled

Sayth that upon or about ye 20th of November last John Warren brought into this Towne 13 barrells of salt & being not free of ye Corporaton exposed ye same to sale to one Mr. Gold not being free contrary to ye By Lawes & orders of ye s^d. Burrogh

It is therefore ordered by ye s^d. Sovraigne & Burgesses then assembled that ye said John Warren shall pay for & in consideraton of ye s^d. salt ye sum of forty shillings to ye use of the Burough afores^d.

Rob : Foster
Thomas Bramston
Tho : Theaker

John IH Haddocke
Sovraigne
Henry Le' Squyre
John Ayshe

8 ffebruary 1640

M. That ye eight day of ffebruary in ye yeare of o^r Lord God One thousand six hundred & fforty.

William Leithes of Belfast, marchant was by ye Sovraigne & maior pte of ye Burgesses elected Burges for ye sd Burrough in steed of John Willoughby gent deceased & being desired to take his oath accordingly utterly refused to take ye same but submitted himselfe to ye house for his fyne   John IH Haddock Sovraigne Henry Le'Squyre Robt Foster John Ayshe . Thomas Brampston.

8 ffeb 1640
M. That at ye Assembly aforesd, & by ye genrall consent of ye Sovraigne & Burgesses then assembled & upon ye refusall of William Leithes, Thomas Steephenson of ye said Burrough ffree comoner was elected Burges in steed of John Willoughby gen deceased, & is to be sworn on Thursday next accordingly.   John IH Haddock Sovraigne, Henry Le'Squyre
Robt Foster   John Ayshe
Thomas Bramston
Tho.⁵ Theaker

8 ffeb 1640
M. That at ye same Assembly for consideracons thereunto moving ye Sovraigne & Burgesses, & in respect to ye long absence of Gawen Boultby one of ye free burgesses of this corporacon it was thought fitt, that ye sd Gawen should be removed, wᶜh accordingly was done by consent of severall of his friends, and we doe make choice of Richard Gately to be Burgess in his steed.
This day sworn accordingly   John I. H. Haddock Sovraigne.   Robt Foster John Ayshe Henry Le' Squyre.

Thomas Steephenson sworne a free Burgess ye 25th day of February 1640

13 August 1640

At a Court then held it was concluded and agreed on that there shalbe an allowance of Tenn shill : a peece to two men that shall serve att the genrall Assize to be held for this County and 6s and eight pence to one man that shall serve at the Quarter Sessions for the Towne and Burrough of Belfaste and the same to be levyed accordinge as the Sovraigne for the tyme beinge shall direct.
Henry Le Squyre
Sovraigne
John Ayshe
Rob : Foster
Thomas Bramston
Thomas Hannington

13ᵗʰ August 1640

Whereas oath was made by Richard Duninge that William Roomeinge or his Servants did at or aboute the 8ᵗʰ day of this instant cast graines & other filth into the River that runeth through the middle of the Towne to the great annoyance of the neighbors and alsoe that John Whitelocke or his servants have comitted the like offence   It is therefore ordered that the fine or some of tenn shillings sterl shalbe imposed and levyed upon each of them for this offence

And Whereas alsoe the day & yeare afores.^d Thomas Hanington gent. made faith that John Leithes about the 6th of August last or his servants comitted the like offence he is therefore fined in the some of Tenn Shillings sterl

The charge of Candles for the Army for one moneth ended the 4th day of August 1640 & for one weeke ended the 11th of August 1640 is	1	19	6
More for Candles for 14 dayes ended the 25th of August 1640 ...	0	14	0
for ye Bridge at ye Milewater	02	10	0
More for the wodden horse for ye Souldiers	0	16	6
Sum	6	00	0

For the fees of the Cattle Custome^s through the Towne to be paid by Phelomy Coshnan	2	05	00
John Stewart for his freedome	1	06	08
Thomas Stevenson for his freedome	1	13	04
The Cattle Money for the yeare John Leithes gent was Sovraigne	2	05	00
	7	10	00

Att a Courte held the 13th day of August 1640 it was agreed and allowed that the money wthin disbursed should be paid & answeard by the Casualtyes wthin mentioned and the surplus thereof to goe to the further use of the Towne And the two Servants of the Towne wth the assistance of Ralfe Dighton Constable are forthwth to levy & take up the same to be imployed to the disbursemts afores.^d And the same brought into Court the next Court day

Signed   Henry Le Squyre
                       Sovraigne

     Jo Ashe
       Robt ffoster
       Thomas Bramston
       Tho Hanington

20th August 1640

Whereas Marryan the wife of John Wreight was pr̃sented for keepinge a disordered house It is therefore ordered ordered *(sic)* that the s.^d Marryan shall leave this Towne w^thin 12 weekes next after or receave such ponishm^t as shalbe thought fit to be inflicted upon her for a pr̃sentm.^t against her

24th Septembris 1640

Memorandum, that the customes of the cattle goeinge through the Towne is sett to farme to Thomas Postely and

c

Phelimy Cushnan for the *rent* [sum] of fforty shillings sterl: p'
Ann to be paid by them or either of them halfe yearely, that is
to say, at Lady day and Michaelmas yearely for and duringe the
terme of three yeares from the feast of St. Michaell the archangel now next ensueinge the date hereof. The same to be
paid and disposed of as the Sovraigne and Burgesses for
the tyme beinge shall direct

Henry Le' Squyre
Sovraigne
John Ayshe
Rob Foster
John IH Haddock
Tho: Theaker

24th Die Septembris 1640

Upon the humble petition of Roger Robins at an assembly
then held it was agreed that the said Roger Robyns shall be
Towne Clearke of the Burrough of Belfaste dureinge his
good demeanour & the pleasure of the Sovraigne and
Burgesses for the tyme beinge he onely takeinge the fees
allowed by the table of fees and both plt and Defend: not to
be admitted to any pleadinge but by their Attorney and
onely to drawe declarations for the plt

John IH Haddocke
John Ayshe
Rob Foster
Thomas Bramston
Thomas Hannington

A Rate made and agreed upon by the Sovraigne and Burgesses of the Burrough of Belfaste the 18th day of October 1640 for and towards the Sevrall uses hereafter expressed vizt.

For Fire and Candlelight for the Souldyers untill Candlemas alloweinge a barrell and halfe of char Coales & a pound of Candles a night wch at 8^d the Barrell char Coale and foure pence the pound Candles Cometh to untill Candlemas the Some of ... ... li 07 00 00

For Maces Armes and the Towne Seale for the Towne 26 whereof li Mr Squyre is pleased to pay six pounds thereof soe there to be paid by the Towne onely ... ... } 20 00 00

For charge of Candles before and since Michaelmas last ... } 03 10 10

For Phelomy Coshnans charge to serve at the Assizes and Sessions ... ... } 01 13 04

wch severall somes are applotted and are to be leavyed as followeth

Mr Sovraigne	XXVs	James Anderson	VIs
Mr Squyre	Xs	James Smith	Vs
Mr Wassher	Xs	Wm Postley	Vs
Mr Foster	XXVs	Edward Archer	IIIs VId
Mr Aysh	XXVs	Ralfe Dighton	Vs
Mr Bramstone	XXs	Quintin Catterwood	VIIs
Mr Hanington	XXVs	Alexander Thompson	VIIs
Mr Leithes	XXs	Hugh Doake	XVs
Mr Theaker	XXs	John Johnson	XIIIs
Wm Leithes	Xs	Robt Hollywoode	Vs
John Love	VIs	Richard Pitt	IIs
John Wilkison	Xs	Edward Sandsbury	Is
Leonard Thompson	VIs	John Moore	Vs
Bartholomew Longe	VIs	Edmond O'Harten	IIIs
John Sheeles	Xs	Thomas Kerran	VIIs
Ralfe Wall	IIIIs	Richard Partridge	IIs
John Sleeman	Vs	Wm Partridge	Xs
Francis Radcliff	Vs	Langely Carr	VIs
John Cottyer	IIIs	David Richy	IIs
John Roy	IIIIs	Wm Tomson	Vs
Thomas Barker	IIIIs	Wm Cottyer	Xs
James Dowdy	IIs	Wm Kelly	Vs
Willm Richy	IIIIs	Thomas Dobson	IIs
Mr Stevenson	XXVs	John Boyde	Xs
Walter Speede	IIs	Walter Baly	IIIIs
Thomas Remingham	iiiis	Jo: Huddlestone	IIs
Richard Carron ..	IIIs	Tho: Taylor	IIIs
John Hudson	IIIs	Bryan M'Corry	VIs
Henry Lorkham	IIIIs	Jo: Mathewes	IIIs
Mrs Boltbey	IIs	Alexander Johnson	Vs
Mr Gately	XVIs	Henry Sands	Vs
Robt Thompson	XIIIs	Marten Rattenbury	IIs
Willm Roominge	IIIs	Symon Spicer	IIIIs
Richard Cross	IIIIs	Thomas Gill	Vs
Wm Wilson	IIIIs	Richard Wall	IIs
Robt. Sponer	IIs	William Asmore	Xs

Andrew Croney ...	...	IIs	George Mankin and his		
John Wheath	...	Is	father	...	VIIs
John Tomson	...	IIs	Richard Duninge	...	IIIIs
John M'Murry ...	...	Xs	Edward Allen	...	IIs
Edward Morgan...	...	IIs	John Whatelock	...	IIIIs
John Handcocke	...	IIIs	James Russell	...	IIs
George Thomson	...	Vs	Richard Stafford	...	IIs
John M'Cullogh...	...	Vs	Hugh Hodge	...	IIs
John Hadden	...	IIs	David Elles	...	IIs
Thomas Thetford	...	VIs	Wm Lathom	...	IIs
Edward Moore ...	...	Xs	Wm Robson	...	IIIIs
Henry Blackhurst	...	XXs	Andrew Bell	...	IIIIs
Tho Becke	...	IIIIs	Stephen Mathewes	...	IIIs
Tho Groome	...	Xs	Thomas Moore	...	IIIIs
Symon Duninge ...	...	IIIIs	Donnell O'Hanan	...	IIs
John Pitt	...	IIIIs	Wright	...	IIs
John Stewart	...	Xs			
George Moore	...	Vs	Sum total XXXV^{li} ster		
Robt. Machett for his free-dome		Xs	£35 10 0		
Robt Batcheler for his free-dome		Xs			
Thomas Smith ...	...	Vs			

These are to will and authorize you Thomas Postely & Phelomy Coshnan Serjeants of Belfast to levy and take the sevrall somes to the names annexed of the p'sons named in this rate either by distresse or otherwayes beinge a rate agreed upon by us at an Assembly held to that purpose and this shalbe yo.r warr.t

Dated the 18th day of October 1640

And the same from tyme to tyme as it is collected to deliv.r to the Suffraine

Signed

John IH Haddock
Sovraigne
Henry Le' Squire
John Aysh
Rob.t Foster
Tho: Theaker

Belfast

M.d that the 30th daye of Januar 1642 upon the perusing of the Assessm.t for fire and candle light for the severall Guards w.th in this Towne it was found that many w.h the said assessm.t were not able to pay and many were Souldiers and could not bee compelled to pay whereby a great part of that asses.m.t was wantinge and 16li 6s 6d onely collected and that Mr. Sovraigne had fully disbursed that and 4li 5s 8d more of his owne money.   There was therefore a new assess.m.t made the saide 30th daye of Januar 1642 for to serve for the remainder of the said Winter Season vizt untill May next and to pay Mr

Sovraigne the moneys hee hath disbursed of his owne above that w.^h was collected of the last assess^{m.t} by Tho: Stephenson gent sovraigne of the Borrough and Towne of Belfast aforesaid. Rob^{te} Foster, John Ash, Tho: Theaker, Willm. Leythes gen: Burgesses of the said Towne and Hugh Doake and Will: Clugston M^{rc}hants & ffree staplers of the same w.^h assessm.^t is as followeth vizt.

James Anderson	3	0
Thomas Becke	2	0
James Smyth	2	0
Rob^{te} Grayson	2	0
Will: Steawart Se^r.	2	0
Hans Jackson	2	0
Will. Postley	3	0
Edward Archer	3	0
Jo: M'Golphin	2	0
Quintin Catterwood	4	0
Mr. Hanington	6	0
Hugh Doake	6	0
Rob^{te} Doake	4	0
Adam Leythes	3	0
Will: M'Kenna	4	0
Wid Thomson & her Sonne	4	0
Willm Clugston	3	0
Mr. Wm Leythes	6	0
Jo: Chesnutt	2	0
Thom Postley Junr	3	0
John Love	3	0
Thomas Roan	4	0
Mr. Theaker	5	0
Will: Ritchey	2	0
Ch^r. Gillett	3	0
George Dunkan	1	0
Rob^{te} Spooner	1	0
John Mitchett	2	0
John Hudson	3	0
Will Wright	2	0
Phil Coshnan	4	0
Henry Meade	2	0
The Butcher next unto Meads	1	0
The Brasier	4	0
Richard Gatcloy	6	0
Rob^{te} Thomson	3	0
Rob^{te} Dinninge	1	0
Will Wilson	3	0
John Cracken	2	0
John Thomson	1	0
Andrew Cromey	1	0
John M'Morrey	4	0
Edward Webb	2	0
John Hancock	2	0
Rinyan Watson	2	0
James Dowey	1	0
Nicholas Saxton	1	0
Thomas Waterson	2	4
George Moore	2	0
Mr. Foster	6	0
Tobias Courtney	2	0
Nicholas Garnett	2	0
Wid: Nevins	6	0
Mr. Squire	10	0
Mr Ash	5	0
Thomas Cooke	2	0
Leonard Hippie	2	0
Tho Gallopp	2	0
Will Kinninge	3	0
Franc Ratcliffe	3	0
John Cottier	2	0
Mr. Burkett	2	0
Franc Robinson	2	0
Samuell Dixson	2	0
Rob^{te} Matchett	3	0
Will Steawart	4	0
Thomas Barker	2	0
John Pitt	4	0
Edward Sandesberry	2	0
Ric Carron	2	0
Willm Sandsbrook	2	0
John Haddon	2	0
John M'Gill	2	0
Tho: Carron	3	0
Edm: Smyth	2	0
Richard Carter	2	0
John Sanders	2	0
Will: Patridge	3	0
Thomas Peeris	4	8
Thomas Bethe	1	0
David Ritchey	2	0
Willm Thomson	1	0
Wid Cottier	3	0
Wid: Boyde	3	0
Bryan M'Correy	2	4
John Mathews	3	4
Walter Baly	1	2
Andrew Bell Meale man	1	2
Allexan^r Johnston	2	4
Nevin Viccar	1	4
John M'Dowell	2	0
Tho: Gill	6	4
John Kennan	2	4
Rob^{te} Clugston	4	8
Mr John Leythes	4	8
Willm Asmore	4	0

John Steawart	...	...	4	8	George Mankin	...	...	4	8
Thomas Keningham		...	4	8	John Whitlock	...	...	2	0
Wid Thetford	...	...	3	0	Martin Goose	...	...	2	0
John Thomson	...	...	2	0	John Warring	...	...	6	0
John Browne	...	...	6	0			li	s	d

Sum total of this assess.^{mt} is [16 4 2]

15 7 0

Burgus de Belfast in Co Antrym Att a meetinge the seaventh daye of March Anno D'ni 1642 by the Sovraigne and Burgesses of the said Borrough and Towne of Belfast whose names are hereund.^{r} subscribed upon a plott by them laide downe & made for the makinge & erectinge of a Bulworke att the Strande side neare the house late of Bryan mcCorrey allotted for the said Sovraigne & Burgesses to erecte and make att their owne prop. costs & charges And the charge of the said worke now completed is found to amount to the some of thirtye pounds Sterl: It is therefore Ordered and mutually agreed upon by the said Sovraigne & Burgesses that they the said Sovraigne & Burgesses respectively shall pay and contribute towards the finishinge of the said worke fiftye shillings sterl: a piece and that evrye of the saide Burgesses shall pay in hand p^{r}sent the some of twentye shillings in parte and the resid: as the worke proceedinge on shall bee thought fitt

Thomas Stephenson Sovraigne		...	2	10	0
Henry Le Squire Esquire ...		...	2	10	0
John Ash Gentl:	...	...	2	10	0
Rob^{te} Foster Gentl:	...	...	2	10	0
John Leythes Gentl.	...	...	2	10	0
Thomas Theaker Gentl	...	...	2	10	0
Thomas Hanington Gentl:		...	2	10	0
John Haydock Gentl	...	...	2	10	0
Richard Gateley gentl:	...	...	2	10	0
John Davyes gen	...	...	2	10	0
John Mitchell gen	...	...	2	10	0
Willm Leythes gen	...	...	2	10	0
Walterhouse Crymble	...	...	2	10	0

24^r die Junii 1642

It is agreed that 20 loads of turfe shall bee allowed to the main Guard and by Guard evrye week for the space of halfe yeare w^h comes to 640 loads of Turfe att 4d a loade comes to 10li 13s 4d to w^h is to be added 2 Barrells of Sea Coles evrye week for the said tyme w^h comes to 8 Tuns of Coales att 4li 16s 0d. In all for fyeringe 15li 10s 0d

This is to bee made by an equall applott.ᵐᵗ upon evrye Inhabitant w.ᵗʰⁱⁿ the Towne and the lib'tyes thereof to bee brought in in Coales and Turfe before Lamas daye next or in defaulte thereof money to bee levyed and their pawnes taken upp for itt. The applott.ᵐᵗ to be made on Thursday next at the Assemblye

Itt is also desired that Collonell Chichester will be pleased to give Order that evrye Companye may bringe in fyeringe for their Captaines & Officers and not to charge the Towne w.ᵗʰ that p'ticuler

24° die Junii 1642

Itt is agreed that the Sovraigne shall bringe in a list of the men that are to be of the Traine Bande of the Towne on Thursday next and that they may be then enrolled as Souldiers. And itt is humbly desired that Collonell Chichester will supply the said Souldiers w.ᵗʰ armes soe many as shall be wantinge to be delivered to them. And an indenture to bee made and signed between the said Collonell and the Sovraigne to bind the Men and Armes may goe together from Sovraigne to Sovraigne whoe is to doe his best indevour for p'servation of the said Armes

24 die Junii 1642

It is agreed that the worke att the Bridge shall be finished att the charge of the Lo: Chichester whoe hath begun itt, the w.ᶜʰ his Lo.ᴾ.ˢ Officers have undertaken to do

24° die Junii 1642

It is agreed that for the finishinge of the Rampier about the Towne all such as have not paid their former rates shall presently pay them or bee distrayned for them. And that for a further addition to that worke The Lord Chichesters Officer in his Lo.ᴾᴾˢ behalfe is content to make the Drawe Bridge and pallisadoes and the Towne is content to give a thousand dayes worke with a man And itt is desired that in a further addition to soe necessary a worke that Collonell Chichester will take Order that each Companye of his Regim.ᵗ may worke three score dayes to the said worke And that hee will appointe their sevrall officers to see them p'form itt And alsoe to take Order that as many Souldiers as the Towne or other shall ymploy about the said worke may work for iiid a day ready money And that the said dayes worke uppon the Towne shall be applotted on Thursday next as the fyering is.

24° die Junii 1642

It is also agreed that such as have not paid their former assesses for Candles to Guards shall forth.ᵂⁱᵗʰ paye the same or be distrayned for itt And that there shall be money plotted for eight score pounds of Candles against the next winter

24° die Junii 1642

It is agreed that money shall be given to some man out of the levye moneys for the Toune to burye all the carrions w.ᵗʰⁱⁿ the Toune & libtyes thereof

24° die Junii 1642

It is agreed that Mr. John Ashe and Nicholas Garner shall have full power to levye moneys or worke w.ᵗʰⁱⁿ the Toune & lib'tyes thereof, viz.ᵗ:— from the Myle Water to the Gardners house in Malone as the worke shall require whereof they are to give an estimate on Thursday next

All these Orders aforesaide were agreed uppon by us att a meetinge for the whole Toune the said 24th daye of June

An Assessment made towards the mentaineinge of Garrisons in Belfast aforesaid in their sevrall Guards w.thin the same w.th fire & candle light the 29th of Septemb.^r 1642 for the winter season settled by Thomas Stephenson, gent!, Sovraigne of the Toune and Burrough of Belfast aforesaid.

Henry Le Squire Esqr. Rob^{te} Foster gen: Burgesses of the saide Towne, Rob^{ts} Nevins & George Martin mr'chants and free staplers of the same w.th the names of such as were assessed and what they were assessed in and what they have paid of the same.—Sum total collected 16 16   6.   *(154 names follow)*

Disbursed by Mr Soveraigne   }   Sum total disbursed

An Assembly.
John Davyes
gen. John
Mitchell g.^t
Wm Leythes
gent made
Burgesses

M.^d that the fourth day of December 1642 att an Assembly by the Sovraigne & Burgesses of the Borrough & Towne of Belfast then being vizt Thomas Stephenson gen: Sovraigne of the said Borroughe John Ashe gen: Rob^{ts} Foster gen: Thomas Hanington gen, Thomas Theaker gen: John Haydock gen: Richard Gateley gen: Burgesses of the said Towne   It was then thought meet and convenie.^t to ellect and chose three honest, sufficient discreete and understandinge gentlemen & Free Staplers of the said Borroughe & Towne of Belfast aforesaid to bee Burgesses of the said Corporacon and to fill upp the numb.^r of Burgesses in the places of such of the said Burgesses as were then deceased and wantinge of the said numb.^r vizt Lewes Thomson that hath absented & alienated himself out of this Kingdome for the space of six yeares last past.   John Washer gen: deceased. and Thomas Bramston gen: deceased   And therefore they the said Sovraigne & Burgesses afore-named by vertue of their Charter for this their Corporacon by one genrall & mutuall consent assent & agreement accordinge to the ancient use and custome of the said Towne and the Franchises and libtyes thereof have nomted ellected & chosen in the place & steed of the said Lewes Thomson John Davyes gen Free Stapler to be one of the Burgesses of the said Towne and in the place & steed of Thomas Bramston gen dec John Mitchell gen: Free Stapler to be an other of the said Burgesses and in the place & steed of John Washer gen dec.^d Willm Leythes gentl Free Stapler to bee an other of the said Burgesses of the said Borrough & Towne of Belfast aforesaid which said Johne Davyes John Mitchell and Willm Leythes gentl: and Free Staplers of the said Borrough were then willinge to accept of the said places of Burgesses and were then and there accordingly sworne & toke the oath of a Free Burgess of the said Towne before the said Sovraigne & Burgesses accordinge to the lawes use & custome of the said Towne and the Franchises and libtyes thereof

Burgus de
Belfast in
Com Antrym

Att a meetinge by the Sovraigne & Burgesses and the Cominalty of the said Borrough & Towne of Belfast for the provision of fieringe and candle for the sevrall Guards w.thin this Toune for this next yeare from the first of this pr.^{te} Maye there was an estimate made towards the same for the some of fiftye pounds sterl: to be forthw.th levyed of evrye each Inhabitant w.thin the said Towne and for an equall and indifferent assessm.^t thereof to be made Mr. Hanington Mr. John Leythes and Richard Gatcloy Burgesses of the said Towne Willm Clugston, Quintin Catterwood, Willm Patridge Franc: Ratcliffe & Thomas Beck were genrally ellected, pointed and chosen by the said

Burgesses & Cominaltye w.ᶜ Assessm.ᵗ by the said Burgesses & Cominaltye was accordingly made the 13th daye of Maye 1643 in manner and forme followinge vizt.

for the highe ways

Name	s	d	Name	s	d
James Anderson	4	8	Andrew Bell, Mealeman	3	o
John Postley	2	4	John M'Dowell	3	o
Robᵗᵉ Grason	3	o	Nevin Viccar	3	o
Lancellott Jackson	1	6	Alex Johnston	4	o
Willm Steawart	2	o	Artᵉ M'Holland	3	o
Thomas Beck	4	8	Ed Williamson	1	6
John Kennitye	2	4	Jo Johnston Merc	5	o
Thomas Addison Son	1	6	James Johnston	3	o
John Addison	2	o	John Lowden	2	o
Thomas Addison Junᵣ	3	o	Wid Thomson and her son	14	o
James Smyth	4	8	Willm Gryffyth	2	o
Thomas Whyteside	3	4	Nicholas Garnett	10	o
Willm Postley	4	8	Willm Chesnutt	3	o
Mr Mathews	6	o	Thomas Postley Junr	8	o
Edward Archer	5	o	John Love	3	o
John M'Golphin and his			Edm: Smyth	5	o
Mother	4	8	Richard Wall	4	8
Tho: Grome als Slye	5	o	Mr Foster	14	o
David Thomson	1	6	Robᵗᵉ Clugston	7	o
John Roye	1	6	John Clugston	5	o
Mr. Hanington	14	o	George Moore	4	8
Hugh Doake	14	o	Chr Marshall	4	8
Adam Leythes	5	o	Mr. Willm Leythes	14	o
George Smyth	2	o	Tobyas Courtney	4	o
Willm M'Kenna	5	o	Willm Thomson Mrchant	3	o
Robᵗᵉ Doake	5	o	George Stephenson Mrchant	2	4
Willm Clugston	5	o	Wid Nevins	11	4
Robᵗᵉ Taverner	3	o	George Martin	14	o
James Sheland	1	2	John Taverner	5	o
Robᵗᵉ Foster	1	2		li	
George Johnson	1	2	Mr. Squire	1 3	4
John Steawart	1	2	Mr Ash	14	o
George Wilson	1	2	Sa: Meeke	11	o
John Dowey	3	o	Sa: Johnson	11	o
John Bamber	4	8	Willm Conway	3	o
John Coates	3	o	John Sergantson	1	6
Robᵗᵉ Palmer	4	8	Rauff Pitt	1	6
Willm Coates	3	o	Edward Morley	1	o
Chr Thomson	1	6	Nicholas Thomson	1	2
Thomas Doughwood	3	o	George Davison	1	2
Patr M'Bryan	3	o	Thomas Yonge	1	2
James Hill	4	8	Mathew Sheppard	1	2
Robᵗᵉ Robinson	3	o	John Cottier	4	o
Ed Thomson	2	4	Franc Robinson	7	o
Tho. Cooke	3	4	Theophilus Newton	2	6
Willm Dunshee	3	o	Samuell Dixson	1	o
Willm Bryan	1	2	Mr Harrison	5	o
Nicholas Brookes	1	2	Robᵗᵉ Matchett	5	o
Robᵗᵉ Mettam	3	o	John Adamson	2	o

	s	d		s	d
Rob.te Fisher	3	o	Thomas Quin ...	3	o
James Rogers ...	1	6	L.t Dobbin	5	o
George Todd	2	o	Mr. Nearne	4	o
John Ransley ...	3	o	Chr Seaton	3	o
John Conway ...	3	o	Thomas Barker ...	3	3
Leonard Hippie ...	3	o	Ed Landsberry ...	3	o
John Lawell	3	4	Tho: Baker	5	o
Adam Aderson ...	2	o	John Pitt	4	8
Thomas Gallopp ...	3	o	Thomas Roan ...	10	o
Henry Marser ...	3	o	Mr Theaker	14	o
Wid. Sleminge ...	1	2	Thomas Waterson ...	3	o
Willm Kinning ...	5	o	Mr Hughes	2	4
Franc Ratcliffe ...	5	o	John Pitt Junr ...	1	6
Henry Simkins ...	3	4	Rob.te Walsh ...	10	o
James Ottiwell ...	3	o	John Walsh	5	o
Rauffe the Taylor ...	1	6	Mr Stephenson ...	14	o
Roger Farrell	2	o	Chr Gillett ...	4	o
Willm Thomson ...	2	o	George Dunkan ...	2	o
Art.e O Donnell ...	2	o	Walter Speed	1	6
John Norman ...	1	6	Rob.te Spooner ...	5	o
Willm Sannders ...	3	o	John Mitchell ...	3	o
Henry Blackhurst ...	9	4	John Hudson ...	5	o
Richard Gateley ...	14	o	Phil Coshnan ...	6	8
Isack Walsh	4	o	Henry Meade ...	2	o
Rob.te Burkett ...	3	o	Willm Davyes & his partner	6	o
Tho Haslipp ...	2	o	Edward Webb ...	3	o
John Pantley ...	3	o	Willm Patridge ...	5	o
Allex M'Collough ...	4	o	Thomas Peeris ...	6	o
Willm Wilson ...	5	o	Loughlin Carr ...	3	o
John Wheats ...	4	o	David Richey ...	3	o
Wid Wheats ...	2	o	Willm Thomson ...	2	o
Andrew Cromey ...	2	o	Wid Cottier	4	o
John Thomson ...	2	4	John Goddard ...	2	o
John M'Morrey ...	6	o	John Davison ...	1	6
Stephen Mathew ...	2	o	John Gryme	1	6
Richard Stafford ...	2	o	John Skerryes ...	1	6
Wid Hancock ...	1	o	Wid Boyd ...	5	o
James Dowey ...	2	o	Willm Taylor ...	1	6
Wid Wyer	1	2	Rinyan Watson ...	3	4
Nicholas Saxton ...	3	o	Pat.t M'Cawe ...	3	o
John M'Neisse ...	1	3	Archibald Caruth ...	5	o
Adam Burthick ...	2	o	Walter Correy ...	4	8
Tho: Florry ...	1	6	John Mathews ...	5	o
Mr. Allen	2	o	John Rigbie	5	o
Israell Christian ...	2	4	Walter Balye ...	3	o
Rob.te Kirke ...	1	6	Tho Stephens ...	2	4
Ric Carron	3	o	Allex the Scholemaster ...	3	o
George Wrybank ...	2	o	John Browne ...	14	o
Wid: Leythes ...	2	o	John Warringe ...	14	o
Wid Jeanes	2	4	Wid Thetford ...	5	o
Richard Johnston ...	3	o	John Barrowes ...	4	8
Wid Hudson	1	6	Martin Goose ...	3	o
John M'Gill	5	o	John Thomson, Butcher	3	o

	s	d			s	d
John Haddon	3	4	Wid: M'Collough	...	1	6
Tho Carron ...	7	0	John Whitlock	...	3	0
Richard Carter	4	0	Ed: Allen ...	...	1	6
Wid Clerkson	1	8	Morgan Joanes	...	1	6
Willm Thomson	1	6	Bernard Boskam	...	4	8
John Sannderson	2	0	George Mankin	...	7	0
Mr John Leythes	14	0	Tho Keningham	...	6	0
John Kernon ...	3	0	John Martin ...	...	3	0
James Taylor	2	4	John Steawart	...	5	0
Thomas Gill ...	5	0	John Cracken	...	3	0
Andrew Bill Serg^t.	2	0	Willm Asmore	...	5	0
Willm Hancocke	1	6	Wid Horner ...	...	3	0
Tho Postley Son	2	4	Willm Dunwithie	...	3	0
Chr Monncaster	1	6	Mr. Davyes ...	...	14	0
Willm Shaw ...	2	0	Mr Mitchell ...	...	14	0
Sandy Willy ...	1	6	Mr. Haydock	...	14	0
Walter Caruth	3	0		li		
Mr. George Bufore	3	4	50	0	0	
Rob^te Arthur ...	3	0				

A Second Sese mad the 22nd of December for 10 days provant for 400 Soulgers by those whose names are hereunder written

Mr Thomas Hanington	Nicholas Garner
Mr Hugh Docke	Quintin Catterwood
Wm Logston	George Mankin
John Stuard Marchant	Thomas Docke

A third Sesse being delivered the first of January 1644 Accordinge to the Sesse mad the 22 of December by

Mr Thomas Hanington	Nicholas Garner
Mr Hugh Docke	Quintin Catterwood
Willm Logston	George Mankin
John Stuard, March^t.	Thomas Docke

A Fourth Sesse made the 21 of January the same Sessers for 400 Soulgers for 10 days att 15d a man *(127 names)*

A Sess made ———— upon a troop of ye 20 . horse that is allotted for payment and for Colonell Home his use, ye 21st of January 1644 *(80 names)*

The ffift Sess made the 21st of January 1644 by ye last Sessers *(121 names)*

The 6° Sess made by ye former Sessers ye first of February for 104 men att 14d the man *(117 names)*

Ye 7° Sesse mad by ye former Sessers for men at 14d a man or 14^{lbs} of melle for every man this 11th day of February 1644 *(121 names)*

A Ses made by ye sworne Sessers for 6 of ye genall Magor troupe for every one 12ᵈm money & 3 bushels of ots   February ye 15 1644   *(94 names)*

Belfast February ye 21 1644 for 9 dayes for 415 men   *(130 names)*

Belfast

Att an Assemblye held before the Sovraigne Burgesses & Cominaltye of the Burrough & Towne of Belfast aforesaid the first day of March Anno dni 1644   It is ordered by one generall and mutuall consent assent & agreemᵗ   That yf anie p'son or p'sons whatsoevᵗ shall att anie tyme or tymes here-after bee refractorye or dissobedient to anie lawfull good and honest Lawe Order or Decree wᶜ shall be ordered decreed made & established for the good and peacable governemᵗ of this Corporacon and for the necessary affairs thereof or shall wittingly or willingly by acte or deed or by anie malignant or contemptuous words abuse and dissobey the Sovraigne or Burgesses or anie of theym or anie other p'son or p'sons wᶜ shall bee lawfully putt in Authoritye or in anie place or office for the affairs of this Towne shall suffer ymprisonmᵗ untill they submitt themselves by humble petition unto the Bench and shall forthwᵗʰ pay such Fyne and further ymprisonmᵗ as by the Sovraigne & Burgesses shall bee legally ordered and ymposed uppon them accordinge to the nature and quality of the offence

> Robᵗ Foster
> Sovraigne
> Thomas Hanington
> Willm Leithes
> Richard Gately
> Hugh Doake
> John Steward

Belfast

An Assessmᵗ made the first of March Anno dni 1644 for fifteene pounds two shillings and two pence sterl: wᶜ is due unto Mr Willm Leythes and in Arreares for fier and candle for six dayes provant to the Armye when they were out at the Leaguer and for twelve horses for the baggage at fourteene shillings a horse for thirtye six shillings wᶜ is due unto the Sovraigne and Wid: Patridge for bricks for the Court of guard and for Iron work for the gates for making of the bridgs at the gates and for the worke wᶜ is now in workinge about the rampier   *(134 names)*

Belfast the 14th of March 1644

A Sesse made for 6 of the generall marogers troop as followes *(102 names, Sum total 7 3 0)*:—

Belfast

An assessmᵗ made for the charge of makinge certaine Dams for the Trench and other charges about the same and for the remander of the moneys wᶜ was disbursed for provision that was to be taken upp w^{th}in this Towne for sixtie men and for the arreares w^s is behinde for fire and candle light the 19th of Octob^r 1644 *(135 names, Sum total 23 5 0)*

Belfast

Know all men by these presents that I Henrye lord Blaney Baron of Monaghan doo acknowledge and confess myselfe to owe and stand indebted unto John Mathews of Belfast merchant the some of eleven pounds sterl currant money of and in England due to bee paid unto the said John Mathews his Executors, Administrators or Assignes uppon demand to w^s pay^{mt} well and truely to be made & paid as aforesaid by the said Henrye Blaney doo bynde mee my heires, Executors and Administrators and everye of us firmly by these p^rsents.   In witness whereof I have hereunto sett my hand & seale the fifteenth day of Octob^r Anno dni 1644

Sealed signed and delivered
in the p^rsents of
Richard Wall

He Blayney 1644
vera copia concordat cū
original, et examinat, coram
Robt Foster
Sovraigne

Lisnegarvy 29 Octob^r 1644

Belfast

After thirtye dayes sight of this my first Bill my second not beinge paid I desire my worthy freind Mr John Davyes Comissarye of Victuall for the Ulster forces now at London to pay to Mr. John Mathew merchant or his Assignes the some of one & fortye pounds six shillings & eight pence ster^l and charge the same uppon account betwixt us or so much of it as shall not be otherwise sattisfyed by Col: Hill as p.' advice & soe I rest

Yo^r loveinge freind
Geo: Rawden
Vera copia concordat cū original,
et examinat, coram
Rob: Foster
Sovraigne

Lisnegarvy 29 Octob^r 1644

Belfast

After thirtye dayes sight of this my second Bill my first not being paid I desire my worthye freind Mr. John Davyes now at London and Comissary of Victuall for the Ulster forces to pay to Mr John Mathew Merchant or his assignes the some of one and fortie pounds six shillings and eight pence ster and charge the same uppon accounte between us or soe much of it as shall not be otherwise sattisfyed by Colonell Hill as p. advice and so I rest

Yo^r very loveinge freind
Geo: Rawden
Vera copia concordat cū original
& examinat coram
Rob: Foster

Belfast

Account made upp. this 29th of Octob^r 1644 at Lisnegarvy betwixt Mr. John Mathew and mee

In primis bought and recd of him 1 barrell of cut Tobacco
weyinge neat 150^{lb} at 3s. the pound 22 10 0

For the caske ...	...	...	...	...	...	00 02	0
For a dozen pounds more of the same tob rec by Mr Harrison ...						01 16	0
For a caske of hotte waters	...	...	...	...		01 12	0

For Druggs and a chest belonging to Mr James Renell lately dead
   & now bought for Mr Brookes for the use of the Lord Con-
   wayes Regim! & the Troope 20 00 00

                         Tot 46 00   0

Whereof paid in p!: for the Druggs towards paym! of Mr Renells
   debts 04 13   4
                        due 41 06   8

                                 Geo Rawden
                                 Rob: Foster
                                      Sovraigne

Belfast   The monthly assessm! concluded uppon the 14th of November 1644 by the maior parte of the Burgesses & Inhabitants of the Burrough and Towne of Belfast to be levyed of the saide Towne for the mantenine of six of the Generall Maior his Troop to begin the first of this Instante *(109 names, Sum total 7 10 0)*

         The charge of the Baggage horse w: have been ymployed for fetchinge the provant for Colonell Humes Regiment from Carrickfergus and alsoe the charge of boats w: was ymployed for the like service sinc the 29th of September last unto the 9th of December 1644

Imprimis for 4 Boats   ...   ...
Itm 3 tymes w! horses 02 5 0
Twice 18ᵈ horse and once 14ᵈ horse }
   threescore & ten horses everye tyme } 14 18 8
More uppon the Colonells service }
   fiftie horse at 14ᵈ a horse ... } 2 18 4
December the 12ᵗʰ for Provant for 400 men for 10 dayes
December the 22ᵗʰ for Provant for 400 men for 10 dayes more
Januar the first for Provant for 400 men for 10 dayes more
Januar the 11ᵗʰ for Provant for 400 men for 10 dayes more
Januar the 21ᵗʰ for Provant for 404 men for 10 dayes more
ffebruar the first for Provant for 404 men for 10 dayes more
ffebruar the 11ᵗʰ for Provant for 415 men for 10 dayes more
ffebruar the 21ᵗʰ for Provant for 415 men for 10 dayes more
March the 2ᵈ for fetching 10 dayes }
   Provant from Carr by horse } 4 14 6
March the 12ᵗʰ for one Boate fraight }
   of Provant for 10 dayes ... } 0 15 0

Belfast   **Att the Court houlden the twelveth of Decemb! Anno dni 1644 before the Sovraigne Burgesses and Cominalty of the Burrough & Towne of Belfast then p'sent these persons hereafter named by a genrall elleccon & consent of the said**

Sovraigne & Burgesses & Cominaltye were ellected nominated and sworne to plott assess & compose all assessmt^s wch are or shall be imposed uppon the said Towne for anie service to the releiffe of such of the Armye which are now charged uppon the Towne vizt

Willm Clugston Jnr
John Stewart Mercht Jnr
Georg Mankin Jnr
Nicholas Garner Jnr
Quintin Catterwoode Jnr
Thomas Becke Jnr

A 10 days proviant for 400 soulgers   *(113 names)*

The Second Sesse made the 14° of December 1644 accordinge to the keep for 6 of the Genarall Mayor Troupe

beinge	...	...	...	...	...	7li	9s	2d
p^d of this		...	...	...	...	5	17	9
						1	12	5

Belfast   An Assessm^t mad the 2nd of January 1645, for 7li 10s wch was laid on Mr Walcott, out of the last forty pounds wch was taken upp for the officers of Collonel Humes Regiment   Dated the 22nd of December. *(140 names)*

Belfast   An Assessm^t mad the 3d of January 1645, for provant for 400 of Collonel Houmes Regemt for 10 days *(145 names)*

Belfast   An Assessmt made the 13th of January 1645 for p'vant for 400 of Collonel Hoomes Regiment for ten days 12^d in money or 19^{lb} of meale each man *(135 names)*

An Assesmt the 23 of Jan: 1645 made for 400 of Collonel Hoomes Regiment 14^{lb} of meale or 12^d in money for 10 days *(132 names)*

A Ses for 6 of the generall Magors troupe the 14$''$ of Aprill 1645 *(99 names, Sum total 6 19 3)*

Belfast   Att an Assemblye houlden the fift day of May 1645 before the Sovraigne Burgesses and Cominaltye of the Burrough and Towne of Belfast aforesaid then p'sent those p'sons hereafter named by a genrall elleccon & consent of the said Sovraigne Burgesses & Cominaltye were ellected noiated and sworne to assemble and meet together when and soe often as they shall bee required and then and there shall plott compose

& make anie assessm! w.̣ shall bee given them in charge for the genrall service of the said Towne vizt

Mr Willm Leythes } Burgesses
Mr George Martin }

Thomas Postley Mrchant ⎫
Thomas Hardinge ⎪
Willm Thomson Mrchant ⎪
Tho Gillett ⎬ Cominalty
John Stewart Mrchant ⎪
Quintin Catterwood ⎪
Thomas Becke ⎪
Nicholas Garner ⎭

And these are to continue in the office of Assesso.ṛṣ dureinge the Sovraigntye of Mr Foster now Sovraigne

Belfast

An Assessm! made for the some of fourty eight pounds thirten shillings and two pence sterl for fire and candle for the Sevrall Guards w.̣ in this Towne from May day last untill May day next 1646 that is to say for one whole year the 10th day of May 1645 *(122 names, Sum total 48 13 2)*

Belfast

Whereas the Sovraigne Burgesses and Cominality of the Borrough and Corporaton of Belfast aforesaid have covennted and agreed w.̣ Mr Leythes one of the Burgesses of the said Towne That the said Mr Willm Leythes shall well and sufficiently furnish the severall guards w.̣in this Towne w.̣th fire and candle accordinge to the order & dirreccon given by L.̣ Colonell Maxwell unto the said Sovraigne & Burgesses untill the first daye of May now next ensuing and in consideracon thereof the saide Sovraigne Burgesses and Cominalitye have undertaken & promissed to pay or cause to bee paid unto the said Willm Leythes the just and full some of fourtye pounds sterl: in manner and forme following viz! ten pounds in hand and other ten pounds at and uppon the last daye of this p.̣sent May and other ten pounds at uppon the 24th day of June now next ensueinge and other ten pounds being the last paym.̣ of the said some of fourtye pounds at uppon the first daye of August then next followinge

In Testimonye whereof the said Sovraigne Burgesses and Cominaltye as also the said Willm Leythes have hereunto subscribed their names the fifteenth day of May Anno dni 1645

Alsoe the saide Mr Willm Leythes hath undertaken to deliver six score cash of Torfe at or before the 29th of Septemb! next w! shall be p!served and kept for the use of anie such Officer & Comander w! stands cheeff. Governor of this Towne & Garrison dated the 15th day of May Anno dni 1645 for w! he is to bee allowed out of his Sesse

Willm Leithes	Rob Foster Sovraigne
Tho Postley	Thomas Hanington
Quintin Catterwoode	Richard Gatlie
Christopher Gillett	Hugh H⊃ Docke
William Tomsonn	Marke

15th May 1645

That the daye and yeare aforesaid John Miller p
voluntarilye and freely referred to the
of Mr Willm Leythes & Willm Thomp
arbitrators indifferently ellected and chosen bet
the ending Order & determininge of all differen
betwixt them and that the said order and awar
by the said arbitrators betwixt the said ptyes
of this instant May and yf the said arbitr
said differencs Mr Hugh Doake is ellected
to make a final end & award in the same
the saide John Miller & Rob!e Clugston
their executo!s Adm!s & assignes either to
ten pounds sterl to bee paide uppon demand
shall refuse to p'forme observe & keep
award made by the said arbitrato!s
the Sovraigne hath subscribed his name

Rob Foster
Sovraigne

By verteu of a warrant dated the 15 day of May the sworne Sesors hath mad the Sesse for the mainting of six of the generall Majors Troop of the inhabetance of belfast *(63 names, Sum total 3 7 2)*

22d of May 1645

Rob!e Clugston of Belfast Merchant and John Miller of
aforesaid all contraversies betwixt them for money
all other demands whatsoever by their consents
and order of quarter Mr Leythes and Willm Thomp
st to make a full end thereof that that the
ore cause of champers for anie matter whatsoev!
begininge of the world unto this p!sent
day wherefore the above named arbitrato!s doe order the said
and John Miller shalbee good loveing freinds
for giveing either other anie passeages
this p!sent day and wee order and
sattisfaccon Rob! Clugston shall pay
unto John Miller. the full and just some
and fifteen shillings of currant money

D

that now passeth in paym⁺ betwixt man and man in Belfast at this pᵣsent and this money to bee paid the eigh day of June next to come and all their bookes for receipts and deilinges to be crossed and cleared and all other notes and Bills betwixt them to bee cancelled and torne and alsoe wee order that Rob⁺ Clugston shall pay unto John Miller the execucon for ten shillings wᶜ the charge recorded against him in Court and alsoe the money due to Willm Miller sonne of the said John Miller at the tyme it shalbee due and ———— 10ˡᵇ is spent at this pᵣsent to bee paid equally between them under this our order.   Witness our hands the day aforesaid

Willm Leythes
Willm Thomson

June 10th 1645. A Ses mad for the generall Major Troupe for this pᵣsent month *(70 names, Sum total 3 11 6)*

Belfast

The Affidavit of Thomas Postley of Belfast afo
Sergeants of Belfast aforesaid for and concerninge the
of an execucon uppon the body of Rob⁺ Clugston of
aforesaid merchant at the suit of Willm Bridge
Merchant for a certain debt of fourteen pounds and sixteen shillings sterl
wᵗ costs recorded against him in the saide Court by the saide Bridg

The said Thomas Postley uppon oath saith that after order given by the Generall Major for doeing of execucon uppon the said Rob⁺ Clugston accordinge to the judgm⁺ given in the saide Courte uppon the verdict given by the Jury wᶜ was then uppon the saide tryall and by warrant from the Sovraigne hee took and arrested the saide Robᵗᵉ and brought him in saufe keepinge before the said Sovraigne whoo uppon the same comitted him into sure custody of this deponent and soe remaineinge in custody as aforesaid the said Rob⁺ Clugston desired this deponent to goe with him along before Major Coughran and thereuppon the said Major Coughran desired the Sovraigne to comune furtᵣ wᵗ him who accordingly did   And some conference betwixt the saide Sovraigne and the said Major Coughran the saide Robᵗᵉ saide unto the saide Sovraigne (I did not take him before yoᵣ sergeant but now I will take him) and the Sovraigne saide (you may doo yoᵣ pleasure) and uppon that the Sovraigne went his way and the said Major then tok the said Robᵗᵉ Clugston away from this deponent

The saide Thomas Postley
sworn before me Robt Foster
Sovraigne of Belfast aforesaid   **Thomas Postley**
the 17 of June 1645

Rob⁺ Foster
Sovraigne

July ye 7° A Sesse mad for the Genarall Major troupe & for 4 horse from Knocvergus with provend at 9ᵈ ye horse 1645 *(94 names, Sum total 5 9 3)*

The 10th of July 1645

An assessment mad for 400 of Collonel Homes his Soulders for provant at 15ˡ of meall a man for 10 dayes as followes *(117 names)*

The 21 of July 1645.

An assessment mad for 400 men in guard as follows   *(129 names)*

The Sesse for Generall Majores Troope for 1 month ending the last of August 1645 for the month of September. payinge over againe   *(92 names Sum total 3 9 1)*

August 11th 1645

A Sesse mad for 400 Soulders att 15^l of mell or 14^d in money   *(127 names)*

August the 13th 1645

A Sses mad by the sworn Sessers for 26 bagage horses to goe out with the Regament

1	Mr. Harrington two third of a horse	...	...	$\frac{2}{3}$ parts
	Quintin Catterwood one third p^t ...	...	...	$\frac{1}{3}$ p^t
3	Mr. Thomas Walcot 2 horse	...	...	2 horses
4	Mr. George Martyn one horse ...	...	...	1 horse
5	Mr Hugh Docke one horse ...	...	...	1 horse
6	Thomas Waringe one horse	...	...	1 horse
7	Robt & John Clogston one hors ...	...	...	1 horse
8	Mr Laythes 2 third of a hors	..	...	$\frac{2}{3}$ p^t
	Willm M'Keney one third p^t		...	$\frac{1}{3}$ p^t
9	John Browne two 3 p^t ⎫ Timithy Milne 1-3 p^t ⎭	...	...	1 hors
10	Willm Tomson halfe horse ⎫ John M'Bryd halfe a horse ⎭	...	...	1 hors
11	Mr Sovraigne 2 third parts ⎫ Mr John Waringe 1 third pt ⎭	...	...	1 horse
12	John Stuard marchant halfe a horse ... Jo: Keningham halfe a horse ... John Pordon Loder & John Galpin halfe a quarter to helpe them ...			1 hors
13	George Mankin halfe a horse ⎫ George Tomson one quarter Willm Asmore one q^r. ⎭	...	...	1 hors
14	John Mathes halfe a horse ... John Rigby halfe a horse ... John Whitlocke halfe a quarter to helpe them		...	1 hors
15	Tho: Gill one quarter horse Walter Carouth one quarter Nevin Vicker 2 p^{ts} of a quarter Walter Baly one 3 of a quarter Andrw Bell & David Richey one quarter	...	...	1 hors
16	Edward Smith one third of a horse Mr Wall one 3 of a horse Nemia Richardson 2 p^{ts} of a third John Love one third p^t of a third	...	...	1 hors
17	Tho: Posell march^t halfe horse ⎫ Tho: Becke & Nickoles Garner halfe ⎭	...	...	1 hors

18	James Anderson one quarter James Smith one quarter Willm Posell 2 p^{ts} of a quarter John Kenedy 1-3 of a q^r Edward Archer 2 p^{ts} of a q^r John Tomson Tayler 1-3 p^t q^r	...	...	1 hors
19	George Simpson one quarter Widdow Tomson one q^r Robt Marke & Cristopher Marshall one q^r Cristopher Gillitt & Gorge Donkin 1 q^r	...	...	1 hors
20	Richard Gatley halfe a horse Ralph Huston 2 third p^{ts} of a quarter Willm Sands one thr: part of q^r Willm Wilson & Tho Gallop one q^r	...	...	1 hors
21	John Martyn one quarter of horse Andrw M'Ellroy & John Doey ¼ John M'Ellroy & Tho Cooke ½ dockter Nearne one quarter	...	...	1 hors
22	Mrs Lee Squire one halfe of horse John Tomson Castell 2 third of a q^r Willm Davis one 3 p^t of a q^r Mrs Stinson one quarter	...	...	1 hors
23	Robt Docke halfe horse George Smith one quarter Rinan Watson one quarter	...	...	...	1 hors
24	John M'Morey 2 p^{ts} of a quarter James Douey 1 third of a quarter John Hadden 2 p^{ts} of a qu John Michell one third of a quarter John Sanderson 2 p^{ts} of a quarter John Harden Smith one third of q^r Roger Haselden halfe a q^r Rch: Carran halfe a q^r	...	...	1 hors
25	Robt Spralle halfe a horse Robt Henderson one quarter John Anderson 2 p^{ts} of a quarter John Hugheson 1 third p^t of a qu^r	...	...	1 hors
26	Willm Rominge one quarter horse John Kenan & John Docke one q^r Willm Douthe & Willm Bryan halfe q^r Cristopher Cotes & Widdow Kyle halfe q^r Allexander Sinkler & Willm Corner 2 q^{rs} Henry Marston & Tho: Quin halfe q^r	...	...	1 hors

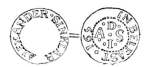

August 28   A Ses for 6 bagage horse

Mr Hanington, Mr Walcott, Mr Martyn and ther partners one horse	1 hors
Mr Dooke, Mr. Tho Waringe, Rob᷈ᵗ Clogston & Mr Laythes & ther partners	1 hors
Mr Browne, Willm Tomson, John Stuard & Gorge Mackin & ther partners	1 hors
John Mathews, Thomas Gill, Edward Smith & Tho Postell & ther partners	1 hors
James Anderson, Gord: Stinson, Mr Gatley John Martyn & ther partners	1 hors
Mrs Lee Squire, Robᵗ Dooke John McMoray Robᵗ Sprall & Willm Rominge & ther pᵗners one horse	1 hors

Agust the 28 1645

A Sesse made for the quante of biscet booter and cheese and two boates fraight for bringen upp proviant from Carrickfargus the Somme beeinge

	li	s	d
	11	12	4

				li	s	d
Mr Harrinton and his parterners				0	9	0
Mr Georg Martin				0	9	0
Mr Walcott				0	18	0
Mr Hough Dooke				0	09	0
Mr Tho: Warran				0	9	0
Mr Robt Clogston John Clogston				0	09	0
Mr Willm Laythes and his parterners				0	09	0
Mr Jo: Browne and his partners				0	09	0
Willm Thomson and his partners				0	09	0
John Steward and his partners				0	09	0
Georg Manking and his partneres				0	09	0
John Mathewes and his partneres				0	09	0
Tho: Gill and his partneres				0	09	0
Edward Smith and his partneres				0	09	0
Tho: Postley Marcht and his partners				0	09	0
James Anderson and his partners				0	09	0
Georg Steensonn and his partners				0	09	0
Mr Gatley and his partners				0	09	0
Jo: Martin and his partners				0	09	0
Mrs Lesquire and hir partners				0	09	0
Robert Dooke and his partneres				0	09	0
Jo McMorey and his partners				0	09	0
Rob Fyronall and his partners				0	09	0
Will: Kinard and his partners				0	09	0
Mr Soffrane and his partners				0	09	0

li   s   d
11 14   0

Mr George Martyn and Mr Hugh Doake sworne Burgesses

That att the Courte of Assembly houlden for the Borrough of Belfast aforesaid the third day of Octᵣ Anno dni 1645 in the tyme of Robᵗᵉ Foster Gentlman then Sovraigne Mr Ashe Mr Hanington Mr Theaker, Mr Gateley, Mr Willm Leythes

Burgesses then p.sent.   It was thought meete and convenient by the said Court to ellect and choose three honest sufficient discreet and understanding gentlemen Free Comoners of the said Towne to fill upp the numb.r of Burgesses in the placs of such of the Burgesses w.c. were then deceased, vizt (Mr Squire, Mr John Haydocke and Mr Thomas Stephenson) And therefore therefore (*sic*) they the said Sovraigne & Burgesses by vertue of their Chearter and accordinge to their ancient use and custome by one genrall consent & agreemt and by the well likeing and affeccon of the whole Cominaltye there present ellected and chose Mr George Martyn Mr Hugh Doake and Mr John Leythes sonne of Mr. Willm Leythes gentl. and Free Staplers of the said Towne Mr Martyn and Mr Doake then willing to undertake the same ymediatly were sworne and took the oath of a free Burgess and were then admitted into the said number of free Burgesses of the said Towne accordinge to the Lawes use and custome of the said Towne and the Franchises and Libtyes thereof but Mr John Leythes being then in England was respited for the taking of his oath until his next return out of England

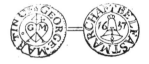 

Belfast

An Assessmt made the 13.th of October, 1645, for the monthly mantennce of six of Generall Maiors Troope for twentie shillings sterl for each horseman for this month according to Genrall Maiors order *(91 names, Sum total 3 3 0)*

Belfast

Rich.d Stafford appointed Sexton of the parish

Att the Court houlden the 16th day of October 1645   It is ordered by the Sovraigne and Burgesses together w.th the Cominaltye then p.sent that Richard Stafford beinge appointed Saxton for the parish Church of Belfast aforesaid hee shall receave for his yearly stypends and wages for his office & service of every howshoulder within the said parish and also of every other person or persons whatso.r. following anie trade or occupacon w.th.in the said Toune and parish though hee bee a single man and unmarryed though he bee noe howshoulder yet they shall pay everye one foure pence sterl: unto the said Richard Stafford yearly dureing the tyme hee shall contynue in the said office and that everye one as aforesaid shall pay p͞sent in hand foure pence a yeere sterl for a whole yeare now ending at May next. And alsoe the said Richard Stafford shall receave for every buryall at the said Parish Church hereafter foure pence sterl for makinge the grave. The said Richard Stafford takeing diligent care and charge for the decent keepinge of the saide Church and Church yard in decent order

Willm Leithes

Sov:

Hugh HD Doocke,   Rob: Foster
Quintin Q C Caterwoode   George Martin
                          John Stewartt
                          Robert Clugston
                          Jno: Becke

Belfast

WHEREAS it was formerly granted that the Inhabitants at Mr Ash his Trench should contribute w: Malone in all Sesses *for the Troope* for one yeare and now that the yeare is ended It is thought expedient and soe ordered by the Sovraigne & Burgesses together w. the Cominalty of the Borrough & Towne of Belfast aforesaid now assembled that the saide Inhabitants at the said Trench shall contribute noe further with the said Malone but w: this said Towne of Belfast as formerly hath been done

17th Octob: 1645

Belfast

An Assessm: made the 25th day of Octob: 1645 for foure Boate loads of provant from Carrickfergus, for one horse to Killwarlin, 4 horses to Eden Carrick and for moweing the grasse about the Rampier, the whole som is 2ꝉꝉ 16ˢ 0ᵈ *(24 names)*

Belfast

An Assessm: for 42ꝉꝉ w: is ypmosed upon the Inhabitants of Belfast for supply of the officers of Colonell Humes Regim: by order from the honor.ᵇ: his Mᵗ: Comissioners Governors of Ulster the first of Novemb: 1645 *(III names)*

The names of the Grand Jury of the Courte of Assembly houlden the second of Novemb: 1645, w: were then ellected by the Sovraigne Burgesses & Cominalty to bee Assessors uppon all occasions for the Towne w: shall be requisit for them and to continue in the same office untill the next Court of Assembly

Ch:. Bramston	Nicholas Garner
Thomas Wareing	John Mathews Tanner
Ch: Gillett	Willm Kinning
Ch: Marshall	Raufe Hughston
James Anderson	George Mankin
Edward Smyth	John Whitlock
John m Morrey	Willm Davyes
Willm Asmore	

Belfast

An Assessmᵗ made the fourth daye of Novembʳ 1645 for provant for foure hundred Souldiers of Colonell Hume his Regimᵗ for ten dayes at 15ˡ. of meale a man as followeth *(128 names)*

Belfast

An Assessmᵗ made the 15ᵗʰ dayes of Novembʳ 1645 for provant for foure hundred Souldiers of Colonell Humes Regimᵗ for 10 dayes *(128 names)*

Belfast

An Assessmᵗ made the 17th of Novembʳ. 1645 for the monthly mentennce of six of Generall Majors Troope for twelve shillings sterˡ and three Bushell of Oats for each horsman for this month according to Genrall Majors order the last winter *(113 names, Sum total 6 6 8)*

Belfast

An Assessment mad the 19ᵗʰ of November 1645 for 6 of Generall Majors Troopes at 12ˢ a man & three Bushells of Oates a man *(131 names)*

Belfast

An Assessmᵗ made the 26ᵗʰ of Novembʳ 1645 for a further supply of the Captanes of Colonell Homes Regimᵗ for 20£ 10ˢ 6ᵈ and for other occasions for the Townes service *(116 names)*

Belfast

An Assessmᵗ made the 26ᵗʰ of Novembʳ. 1645 for 400 of Colonell Humes Regimᵗ for provant for 10 dayes and 4 of the Canoneeres *(126 names)*

Belfast

An Assessmᵗ made the third daye of Decembʳ 1645 for provant for 400 Souldiers of Colonell Humes his Regimᵗ for 10 dayes *(125 names)*

The Assessors names

John Mitchell gen	John Steawart m
Robt ffoster gen	John mc Morroy
Richard Gately gen	Thomas Bork
Tho Bramston	

Belfast

The names of the Assessors ellected and chosen by the Sovraigne Burgesses and Cominaltye of the Borrough and Towne of Belfast aforesaid assembled and convened together the eight of Decembʳ 1645 and then sworne assessoʳˢ and to continue in the same office uppon all assesses unto the Court of Assembly next after Chrmas or otherwise untill they shall be discharged of the said office

Mr Harrington and ⎞
  Mr Doake   ⎠ Burgesses

Willm Clugston
Chr Marshall Junr
Quintin Catterwoodd Junr
George Mankin
Chr Gillett Junr
Tho: Beck Junr

Belfast

Money disbursed by Mr Willm Leythes Sovraigne for sevrall uses and Services for the Towne as followeth

Imprimis.	2 Tun of Coles for the Colonell Hume at 10ˢ 8ᵈ the Tun	...	...	1	1	4
	Mor for 2 Tun of Coles to him	...	...	0	18	0
Itm	One Tun of Coles for the Lᵗ Coᴸ Maxwell	...	...	0	08	0
Itm	for makinge up the hedge at the Strande to keepe upp the Rampier	...	...	0	18	8
	for mendinge the way to the Strand	...	...	0	08	8
	for mendinge the Guards	...	...	0	05	6
Itm	Paid downe for pᵗ of paymᵗ for the butter wᶜ the officers had when the went to the Feild	...	...	0	06	6
Itm	laide downe to maike up the pay for Daniell Monro his Troope	...	...	0	13	2
Itm	laid out for shingles to mend the Church wᵗ	...	...	0	05	0
Itm	laide out to make upp the money for the Officers in the last Sess	...	...	0	05	8
Itm	for 46 foott of bords to mend the Colonells windowes for nayles and worman shipp	...	...	0	06	7
Itm	for the Comon Charge of Souldiers Sessed in five houses for the Sessing of the Officers	...	...	1	3	4
	Sum total	...	...	7	0	5

Belfast

An Assesment mad ye 10ᵗʰ of December 1645 for 7ˡⁱ 7ˢ 6ᵈ ster wh Mr Soveraigne hath Disbursed for the Towne *(131 names, Sum total 7 10 0)*

Belfast

An Assesment mad the 13ᵗʰ of December 1645 for provant for 400 Souldiers of Collonell Humes Regement for 10 days. *(147 names)*

Belfast

An Assesment mad the 21ˢᵗ of December 1645 for the monthly maintenance of the Officers in Collonell Hums Regement for 30⁶ *(140 names)*

Belfast

An Assesᵐᵗ mad the 23ʳᵈ December 1645 for pʳvant for 400 men of Coˡˡ Houmes Regemt for 10 days *(144 names)*

O the right honor^ble Colonell Hume Governo^r of the Towne and Castle of Belfast &c

The humble petition of all ⎫ humbly sheweth unto yor
the Inhabitants of the Towne ⎪ honor that Mr Walcott
of Belfast Tennts unto the ⎬ cheeff Agent for the said
right honorb^le Edward lord ⎪ lord Viscount Chichester
Viscount Chichester ⎭ w^in the Barronye of Belfast
obtained an order from his Excellency Generall Lesley and
alsoe an other order from the Generall Majo^r Monrow for the
takinge upp of the Rents of each Tennt of the saide lord w^in
the said Barronye by vertue whereof hee hath duely receaved
the said Rents ev^r since   And now they will have a halfe
yeares Rent to pay Att the first of Novemb^r next.   Yo^r
humble petition^rs therefore in manifestinge their duety and
service unto yor hono^r and for the supply of yor honr^s Officers
for the p^rsent are and wilbee willinge to pay the said halfe
yeares rent unto yor hono^r for the said supplye   If yor hono^r
would bee pleased to procure an order from the Generall
Major where yor humble petitioners may be secured and
discharged and alsoe saved harmelesse from the said Lord
Viscount Chichester his Assignes and Agents whatsoev^r. in
payinge their said rent unto yor hono^r and they shall pray &c.

		Willm Leythes Sovraigne
Franc Ratcliff	Hugh Doak	Rob Foster
George Mankin	Richard Carron	Thomas Hanington
John Galphin	John Steawart	George Martin
John Pitt Senio^r		Richard Gately
Chr Bramston		

Belfast   At the Courte houlden the 4th of March 1646 Thomas
Carran Connstable of the Borrough & Toune of Belfast aforesaid being examined and sworne concerning the execucon of
a warrant given to him by the Sovraigne against John

Steawart of Belfast aforesaide merchant uppon oath saith
That hee went w.^t that warrant to attatch and arrest the saide
John Steawart and him saufly to keepe untill hee should find
Suertyes for the peace against all his Ma.^{ts} leidge people and
espiallye against Thomas Hanington gentl : one of the
Burgesses of this Toune whom hee had assaulted & beaten in
the oppen streets here in Belfast aforesaid and most scandal-
ously abused by scandalous words calling him p'jured knave
but the saide John Steawart desired the saide Constable to
see his warrant w.^c hee showed him and haveinge read it hee
in a most contemptuous manner and against his oath beinge
Sworne a Free Comoner tore the saide warrant and did throw
it into the fire and would not obey the Connstable at all,
againe the Sovraigne sent out another warrant for the saide
John Steawart for suertyes for the peace as aforesaid and to
answer for his contempt against the other warrant and the
saide Constable goeinge to execute second warrant directed
to him by the Sovraigne the saide John Steawart desired the
Connstable to see his warrant w.^c the said Connstable showed
him and the said Steawart when hee receaved the warrant
put it upp in his pockett and would not obey him at all

Burgus de Belfast in Com Antrym . **Whereas** at the Court houlden the 6th of March 1646 it
is made manifest by sufficient Testimony in oppen Court
That John Steawart of Belfast aforesaid Merchant had not
onely abused Thomas Hanington gentl : one of the Burgesses
of this Toune by scandalous words but alsoe had assaulted &
beaten the said Mr Hanington in the open Streets here in
Belfast aforesaid and alsoe in a most contemptuous manner
dissobeyed 2 sevrall warrants of the Sovraigne all w.^c beinge
against his oath of a Free Comoner and against an Order
made the first of March 1644 for w.^c offences of the said John
Steawart, wee the Sovraigne and Burgesses whose names are
hereund.^r written here assembled at this said Court doo dis-
franchisse the said John Steawart of all libtyes and privileidges
of this Corporacon

John Ayshe Sovrne

Richard × Gattley
marke
Hu.^h × Doake
his marke
George Martin

Rob. Foster
Thomas Hanington
Tho Theaker

Belfast

Att an Assembly houlden by the Sovraigne & Burgesses the eight daye of Novemb.ʳ 1647 the saide John Steawart M.ᶜʰᵗ in the order above menconed acknowledging his offence and submitting himself to the Bench uppon serious delibācon and uppon the good oppinion of the said Sovraigne & Burgesses & their good affeccon unto the said John Steawart they have not onely remitted the said John Steawarts offence but alsoe they the saide Sovraigne & Burgesses have receaved & admitted the said John Steawart to bee a Free Stapler & Free Comon.ʳ of this Toune according to the ancient libtyes privileidges & ffranchisses of the said Toune

Tho Theaker

Richard Gatlie.   Rob: Foster

George Martin

Willm Leithes   Thomas Hanington

To all Xtian people to whom this p.ʳsent writing shall come We the Sovraigne and Burgesses of the Borrough & Towne of Belfast in y.ᵉ County of Antrim within y.ᵉ Kingdome of Ireland send Greeting in our lord God everlasting Know yee that John Martin of Belfast aforesaid merch.ᵗ in y.ᵉ tyme of William Leathes gentlman now Soveraigne of the Borrough and Towne of Belfast aforesaid upon his humble peticon unto y.ᵉ said Soveraigne and Burgesses was admitted and sworne a Merchant Stapler and free Comoner of the Corporacon & Towne of Belfast afforesaid according to the Franchises libertyes previledges of the said Towne unto the said Soveraigne and Burgesses by his Ma.ᵗⁱᵉˢ Let.ʳˢ pattents granted In testimony whereof wee have caused the Common Seale of the said Towne to these p.ʳsents to be fixed the seaventh day of Apprill in the twoo and twentieth yeare of the Reigne of our Soveraigne lord Charles by the Grace of God of England Scotland France & Ireland Kinge Defend.ʳ of the faith Anno dni 1646

WILLIAM LEATHES
Sover

Richard Wall Towne Clerke
of the Borrough afforesaid

Att an Assembly houlden the 18th day of June Anno dni 1646 Willm Leythes gen Sovraigne, Mr Foster Mr Hanington Mr Gateley Mr Martin Mr Doake Burgesses of the Borrough aforesaid then p.ʳsent together w.ᵗ many of the Cominaltye John Leythes Gentl sonne of the saide Mr Willm Leythes was sworne one of the Burgesses of the saide

Toune according to the elleccon & order by the Assembly at the Court houlden the third of Octob.ʳ 1644 and toke the Oath of Burgess according to the use and custom of the said Toune

Willm Leythes

Sov.ʳ

George Martin   1646
Rob Foster
Thomas Hanington
Richard Gateley
Hugh Doake

Att an Assembly held for the Burrough of Belfast the 20th day of March 1643. Wheras there were two of the Burgesses of the said Burrough Deceased vizt Henry: L:: Squire Esqʳᵉ and John Haddock gent: Therefore in the pᵣ̇sence of Thomas Theakir Suffran thence—the major part of the Burgesses whose names are hereunder written Major George Rawden and Captain Roger Lyndon were elected to be made free Burgesses of the said Burrough

Tho Hannington
John Mitchell
John Leithes
Tho Stephenson
William Leithes
Richard Gately

Att the Assembly 18 Junnii 1646 it was proclaimed by the said assembly concerninge the said order that it was proved by the said assembly that the said order was not legall but fained

Willm Leathes Sov
1646

Thomas Hannington
George Martin
Rob.ᵗ Foster

Att an Assemblye houlden the 18th of June 1646 it was thought meete & expedient that the order above specified for the ellection of Roger Lyndon Esqʳᵉ and George Rawden Esqʳᵉ to be Burgesses as aforesaid shall be repealed and utterly revoked

Willm Leathes, Sov.ʳ

Thomas Hannington   Rob.ᵗ Foster
Richard Gatlie   George Martin
Hughe Doake

Belfast

ATT the Court of Assembly houlden the 13th of Januar 1647 It was moconed by the said Courte That an honest discreet and und'standing man well learned in the law shall bee ellected and chosen to bee a constant Toune Clerke of this Courte of the Borrough of Belfast aforesaid and to have a patent for the due execucon of his office *during his good behavior* according to the auncient use and custom of this Towne and according to the libtyes and privileidges as hath been used in other Courts and this elleccon to be made by the Sovraigne and Burgesses at the next Court to be houlden for this said Burrough to the end that all records belonging to the said Court and for the publique service of the said Towne may be kept in due forme & p'petuity

ИD Hugh Doak Sovraigne
W Crymble
Thomas Hannington
Willm Leithes
1647
Richard Gately
George Martin

29 die Januar 1647

At the Courte then houlden wee the Sovraigne & Burgesses by the experience and good oppinion wee have had & doo beare unto Richard Wall have ellected & chosen him to bee our Toune Clerke during his honest carriage & upright behavio͛ in the said place and that he shall have a patent for the same und͛ our hands and the Comon Seale of this Towne

ИD Hugh Doak
Sovraigne
Thomas Hanington   Rob͛ Foster
George Martin

Belfast

M͛ that the 15ᵗʰ daye of February Anno dni 1647 M͛ Foster and M͛ Leythes being called before the Sovraigne to testify their knowledge concerning an agreem͛ made betwixt Widowe Anderson late wieffe of John

Anderson deceased on the one p.te and **Thomas Smyth** of Belfast aforesaid Blackesmyth on the other p.te That about June last they were chosen to bee Arbitrators by the saide Widdow Anderson and the saide Thomas Smyth for the ending and determining of a certain difference then depending betwixt them uppon the same the said M.r Foster and M.r Leythes did draw both the saide ptyes to this Agreem.t as followeth viz.t First the said Thomas Smyth should have hould possess and enjoye one shoppe or Smythie w.ch was late Willm Patridge her former husband deceased whereof half was given unto him in marriage w.th her daughter and alsoe all the worke Tooles w.ch the saide Willm Patridge had at the tyme of his death halfe of w.ch said Tooles was likewise given unto him bye his said marriag and alsoe all the houses and buildings w.ch standeth betwixt the saide Smythie and the dwelling house of the saide Willm Patridge and a parte of a garden w.ch once John Sanderson had in possession during the naturall lieffe of her the saide Widdow Anderson and for w.ch saide p.rmisses the saide Thomas Smyth should well and truely paye or cause to bee paide unto the said Widdow Anderson dureing her lieffe yearely and from yeare to yeare the some of fourtye shillings ster.l at two times in the yeare viz.t at May daye and the first of Novemb.r by even and equall porcons and that his tyme should begin att May then past and his first rent daye to bee the first of Novemb.r w.ch is now past and that hee should have the remaind.r of an apprentishippe of one boy called Francis Barden w.ch was an apprentis w.t the said Willm Patridge besides all w.ch the saide Thomas Smyth was to have the half of a Cowehouse w.t the said widdow And.r son during her lieffe.

Rob Foster
Willm Leythes

15th of Februar 1647

(margin: Belfast)

John Harden Smyth being sworne and examined at what tyme hee delivred possession of the shoppe w.ch hee had from Widdow Anderson late wieffe of Willm Patridge saith that hee delivered possession of the saide shopp unto Thomas Smyth the second of May last.

Vicesimo die Marcii Anno dni 1647

(margin: Belfast)

M.d That the daye and yeare aforesaide James Lynsay of Belfast aforesaide hath acknowledged and confessed himself well contented sattisfyed and paid of and by the hands of John Whyte of Antrym m.r. as well for one debte of fiftye pounds ster.l w.c was heretofore due unto the saide James Lynsay by bill as above for all other debts reckenings and accompts whatsoev.r w.ch hath been betwixt us for anie cause matter or thinge whatsov.r since the begininge of the world untill the daye of the date hereof and thereof and everye p.t and p.rcll thereof doe for mee the saide James Lynsay my heres Execut.rs and adm.rs and for evrye of us clearly acquite exonrate and discharge him the saide John Whyte his Execuo.rs and adm.rs for ever by these pr.nts In witness whereof I the said James Lynsay have caused this my discharge and acquittance on the p.t & behalf of the said John Whyte to be registered in the book of record w.t in this Towne and hereunto have subscribed my name the daye and yeare first above written

James Lindsay

Intrat' et inroll' in die
  & Anno super
  ad instance p.rd Johis Whyte
  p.rd Jac Linsay

sub manu
per me Richardū Wall
Clericum curiæ Burgi sive
ville p.rde

Att an Assembly by the Sovraigne and Burgesses the eight daye of Novemb.ʳ Anno dni 1647 uppon the takinge an Accompte of the money w.ᶜ hath beene given by certaine charitable and well disposed people now deceased to the future releiffe of the poore distressed Inhabitants of the Borrough of Belfast vizt by Mr Edward Holmes deceased sometymes Sovraigne of this said Towne the some of fourtye

£40 o o

pounds sterl the interest whereof was to bee distributed yearely to the said poore   Now itt appeares upon takinge

7 o o

of this said accompt that [this] *there* was [ten] *seaven* pounds put into the hands of one Mr John Washer nowe deceased whose Estate w.ᵗin this Towne since the tyme of the begining of the Rebellion is laid wast nor posteritye of him left here wherebye the said [ten] *seaven* pounds w.ᵗ the interest thereof is left desparat yet yf there bee *anie* meanes left whereby the said [ten] *seaven* pounds or anie interest now dew may bee obtained ; It shalbee p.ʳsently thought *uppon* & put in execucon, And whereas there is other ten pounds thereof put into the hands of Gowen Boltye and Sibbye his wieff late wief of the said Edward Holmes for the w.ᶜ Mr Richard Gateley is bound   It is ordered that the said Gowen Boltbye shall paye in lieu of the interest w.ᶜ is in arreare for the tyme past fourtye shillings att or uppon the 24th of Decemb.ʳ next and for the tyme to come shall give *new* bonnde but the same securitye and whereas there is other ten pounds of the said fourtye pounds in the hands of ffranc Ratcliff it is ordered likewise that the said ffranc Ratcliffe shall pay in lieu of the interest w.ᶜ is in arrear for the tyme past fourtye shillings sterl at or uppon the said 24th of Decemb.ʳ and shall give new bonnde   And whereas likewise there is other ten pounds of the said fourtye pounds in the hands of Mr Thomas Theaker one of the Burgesses of this Towne it is ordered that the said Thomas Theaker shall paye in lieu of the interest w.ᶜ is in arreare for the tyme past fourtye shillings at or uppon the 24th daye of Decemb.ʳ next and shall give new bonnd for ye principall   And yf anie of the said ptyes vizt Gowen Boultbye, ffrancis Ratcliffe and Mr Thomas Theaker shall refuse to p'forme this order or to give securitye for the principall somes according to the Tenor hereof   It is ordered that they shall paye the whole interest now in arreare for the tyme past and shall give security for the

E

principall somes not w.^t standing, or otherwise they shall
bee proceeded against by due course of Law

HD Hugh Doake

George Martin   Soveraigne

Rob Foster

Thomas Hanington

Tho : Theaker

Richard Gatlie

Willm Leithes

1647

Belfast

WHEREAS likewise att the said Assembly by the
Sovraigne and Burgesses the eight daye of Novemb.^r
1647.   Itt did appeare uppon Information by Mr
Rob.^{te} Foster one of the Burgesses of the said Toune that hee
had disbursed to Mr Nearne for a house for to bee a Courte of
Guarde iiii^{li} sterl out of his owne purse for sattisfacon whereof
unto himself hee was pleased to accept iii^{li} whereof he hath
receaved xxxixs and viiid sterl of the free Comon.^{rs} made in
the tyme when he was Sovraigne and hee is to have from
Rob.^{te} Clugston xxs sterl w.^c is ordered by the Bench for the
said Rob.^{te} Clugston to pay to the use of the Toune for his
ffreedom and soe the saide Mr Foster is cleared of all accompts
whatsoever w.^c can or may bee exacted for the tyme of his
sovraignety.

Hugh Doake

HD

Sovraigne

Richard Gatlie

Rob Foster

George Martin

Willm Leithes

1647   Thomas Hanington

Belfast

Whereas likewise att the saide Assemblye   Itt doth
manifestly appeare that Mr Thomas Hanington one of
ye Burgesses of this Towne in the tyme of his Sovraignty
had disbursed of his owne purse for sevrall uses for the
Towne sevrall somes of money for w.^c the Sovraigne &
Burgesses have made composicon w.^t him and are agreed to
give him fiftye shillings sterl w.^c is to bee paid unto him out
of some moneys w.^c is due unto the saide Toune by such
p'sons w.^c heretofore have beene admitted ffree w.^tin the said

Toune and soe the said Mr Hanington is absolutely clear for all accompts during the time of his Soveraignty

Hugh ⊢D Doake

Sovraigne

Richard Gatlie, Tho Theaker.

Rob Foster

Belfast   Likewise Mr George Marten is to bee allowed [foure payable] xxs sterl for meale w^c was taken from him to give to some poore people w^c was sent over for England in the begininge of this Rebellion

Hugh ⊢D Doake

Sovraigne

Richard Gatlie
Willm Leithes   Rob Foster
1647
George Martin   Thomas Hanington
     Tho Theaker

Belfast   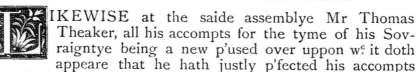IKEWISE at the saide assemblye Mr Thomas Theaker, all his accompts for the tyme of his Sovraigntye being a new p'used over uppon w^c it doth appeare that he hath justly p'fected his accompts for all receipts & disbursm^{ts} whatsoev^r and that there was due unto him by his disbursm^{ts} for the Toune use more than his receipts iii^{li} xv^s x^d sterl for w^c hee hath beene allowed him out the assessm^{ts} ymposed uppon him at sevrall tymes since May last iii^{li} iii^s vi^d and the rest to bee allowed him out of his Sess untill it bee fully sattisfyed and soe the saide Mr Thomas Theaker is cleared of all his accompts both for his disbursm^{ts} & receipts for the use of the Toune from the begininge untill this p'sent daye

⊢D Hugh Doake

Tho Theaker   Sovraigne

George Martin,   Richard Gatlie,   Rob Foster

Willm Leithes

1647   Thomas Hanington

Belfast

Likewise att the saide Assemblye Mr Willm Leythes one of the [Sovraign] Burgesses of this Toune although hee had formerly p'fected his accompts for all his disbursm⟨ᵗˢ⟩ & receipts for the use of the Toune in the tyme of his Sovraigntye yet nowe desiring that his saide accompts might bee cleared before this assemblye and soe recorded   It doth appeare manifestly that hee hath made a nise and p'fect accompt and that hee hath disbursed of his owne accord for the good & welfare of the said Toune in work done in the Church yarde and about the Church and in some other services for the use of yᵉ Toune iiiˡⁱ sterl wᶜ hee *doth* gratisly clear the Towne of and therefore the saide Mr Leythes is cleared of all his accompts both for his disbursmᵗˢ and receipts for the tyme of his Sovraigntye

Hugh Doake

Willm Leithes HD Sovraigne
1647 Robt Foster
Thomas Hanington Richard Gatlie
Tho Theaker George Martin

Belfast

Att the said Assemblye houlden by the Sovraigne & Burgesses the eight daye of Novembᴿ 1647. Itt is ordered and thought fitting and convenient for the decency in the placinge of the Burgesses in the Church att the assemblinge of the Congregacon for the publique worᴾᴾ of God eyther uppon the Lords daye or anie other daye appointed for publique worᴾᴾ (that the twoe Seats wᶜ heretofore was allotted and sett aparte for the Burgesses for their ease next adjacent to the Sovraignes seat) because that there is a greater concourse & assembly of the people nowe for the p͏ᵗsent by reason of the twoe Regimᵗˢ remaining in this Towne one of the saide seats during these tymes may bee verye well reserved and kept for the saide Burgesses notwᵗstanding the great Assembly   Itt is therefore ordered that one of the saide seats shalbee constantly kept and p͏ᵗserved for the said Burgesses from tyme to tyme and that noe person or persons whatsoev^r eyther ye fforraigner or ffree Comon^r shalbee admitted into the said Seat and that noe Free Comon^r or Inhabitant of this Toune or parish shall intrude himselfe into the said seat from hencforth w^c yf anie doe contrarye to this order they shall pay xii^d a piece for evrye offence they shall give herein and that Mr Sovraigne [shall] for the tyme [levyed] beinge shall see the same levyed w^tout unnecessary delay w^c xii^d shall goe towards the reparing of the Church, And after that it may please God to give a more peacable tyme amongest us and that the parish may bee eased of the multitude of offic^rs and Souldiers w^c remaines amongst us, That then the saide twoe seats shall be solely to & for the ease & seats of the said Burgesses and noe other.

HD Hugh Doake Sovraigne

Willm Leithes   Rob Foster   Thomas Hanington
1647   Tho Theaker   Richard Gatlie
George Martin

Decimo nono die Marcii——

Noverint omnes per presentes nos Jacobum Nisbitt de Ladytowne infra Regnum Scotie generosum Johan Paule et Jacob.ⁿ Rogers de Glascho infra Regnum pdct Mercatores teneri et firmiter obligari Jacobo Maxwell de Carrickfargus infra Regnum Hibernie Mercator in ducentis libris legalis monete de et in Anglia solvendis eidem Jacobo Maxwell aut suo certo attorn Executor vel assignat suis ad quam quidem solucionem bene et fideliter faciendam obligamus nos et quemlibet nostrum per se pro toto et in solid' heredes Executores et administratores nostros firmiter per presentes sigillis n'ris sigillat dat vicesimo nono die Novembris anno dni 1647.

The condicon of this obligation is such that if the above bound James Nisbitt John Paule and James Rogers or any of them or the Executors administrato.^{rs} or assigns of them or any of them doe well and truly pay or cause to be payed unto the above named James Maxwell his Execuo.^{rs} administrato.^{rs} or assigns The some of one hundred pounds current and lawfull money of and in England At one entyre payment upon the first daye of May next ensuing the date above written w.^tout further delay Att or w.thin the now dwelling house of the said James Maxwell in Carrickfargus above written That then this obligacon to bee void and of none effect or else to stand in full strength & vertue

Signed sealed and delivered
    in the presence of
    Val : Savage
    Ja : hamilton
    Tho : Houghton
    Edward Morton

    Ja Nisbitt
    Johne Paull
    James J R Rogers
    his deed :

Belfast

M.^d That the eightenth daye of Decemb.^r Anno dni 1647, at the convening of the Sovraigne and Burgesses Willm Thomson of Belfast aforesaid Mr^{te} made his composicon for his monethly assem.^t dureinge the tyme that these Burthens lyeth uppon the Inhabitants of the said Towne for the Officers mantennce, provant for the Souldiers for Genrall Major.^s Troope for fier and candle to the Guards and for repairing the Rampier That hee the said Willm Thomson shall well and truely paye or cause to bee paid from moneth to moneth dureinge the said tyme the some of twentye and five shillings sterl: everye moneth, and so payinge the same the said Willm Thomson shall shall bee clearly acquitted from all other Sesses levyes taxes and imposicons whatsoev.^r w.^c shall or might bee imposed laide or assessed uppon the saide Willm Thomson for anie cause whatsoev.^r excepting quarters for Souldiers As witness their hands hereunto subscribed the daye and yeare first above written

                    Hugh HD Doake
Willm W T Thomson   Sovraigne
W L   Willm Leithes   Rob Foster
       1647   Thomas Hanington

The sixt of Apprill Anno dni 1648 this order above written is repeald and revoked by consent of the whole Bench

HD

Rob Foster
Thomas Hanington
Willm Leithes
1648

Belfast

HEREAS att an Assembly houlden the eight day of Novemb.^r 1647, it was ordered that those persons w.^c had the money w.^c was given by Mr Holmes to the use of the [Towne] poore being in arreare for the use of the said money should in lieu of all arrears past pay onely the some of fourtye shillings a peece nowe at Chrmas according to w.^c order ffranc Ratcliffe doth now come heare and payes for his par.^t twentye *shillings* and by reason of the scarsity of these tymes daye is given him untill May daye next for the paym.^t of the remand.^r Lt Theaker is come likewise and hath paid likewise twentye shillings and hath like tyme given him for the paym.^t of the remand.^r of the fourtye shillings Mrs Boltbye hath paide likewise twenty shillings of her p.^{ts} and by reason of her necessitye is remitted and acquitted for the rest Richard Gateley being suertye for the said Mrs Boltbye is cleared by this order for all arreares past untill this p.^rsent this 23rd of Decemb.^r 1647

HD
Rob Foster
Thomas Hanington
Willm Leithes
1647
George Martin

Belfast

    Att the Court houlden the 30th of Decemb^r 1647 uppon the advisem.^t by the said Court for the Searchinge and Sealing of Leather here w.^tin this Towne   It is ordered by the saide Court that by reason of this winter season Leather cannot conveniently bee dryed in it right season as it ought to bee according to the Statute. Therefore it shall and may bee lawfull to and for the Searchers and Sealers of Leather that yf they bee required to seale anie Leather during this winter season untill the first of March, yf anie such Leather bee sufficiently tanned though not throughly dryed they shall seale the same otherwise not, and after the said first daye of March noe Tanner shall not offer to put to sale anie Leather whatsoev: except the same bee sufficiently Tanned and throughly dryed and searched and sealed according to the Statute in paine of such forfeture as is lymitted in and by the said Statute

Hugh HD Doake
Sovraigne
Rob Foster   Willm Leithes
Thomas Hanington   1647

Belfast

The 11th of Januar 1648

At the Courte of Assembly houlden the daye and yeare aforesaid   It is agreed uppon by the genrall consent of the Sovraigne and Burgesses then p.ʳsent that there shalbee a constant yearely stipend of xˡⁱ sterl allowed by the saide Toune for the myntenence of a schole master for the educacon & bringinge upp of youth wᵗin this Toune and meanes made for a convenient howse or chambʳ for the said schole master to inhabit in and also a convenient schole howse to teach in and that for the raiseing of the saide yearly stipend of xˡⁱ and the meanes for the dwelling howse & schole howse dureing these troublesome tymes,   That there be from Quarter to Quarter a Sesse ymposed uppon each Inhabitant wᵗin this Toune accordinge as their abilityes shalbee justly found by the Sessoʳˢ and that the Sovraigne of the Toune for the tyme beinge shall from Quarter to Quarter cause such a Sessmᵗ to bee made and duely levyed accordingly

Rob Foster
Sovraigne

Fra: Meeke
 Constable of the Castell
Thomas Hanington
Tho Theaker

Willm Leithes
1648
Richard Gateley
Hugh HD Doake
George Martin

Bee it knowne unto all men by these p.ʳsents that I Thomas Smyth of Dublin m'chnt doo owe and am indebted unto Joseph Harries of Carrickfergus the full and just some of fourtye and twoe shillings sterl to bee paid to the said Joseph Harries his Executoʳˢ admʳˢ or assignes uppon the last daye of this instant September to the p'formnce whereof I binde me my Executoʳˢ admʳˢ and assignes firmely by these p.ʳsents   As witness my hand the second day of September, 1648.

Witness hereunto
 Hugh Lyndon
 Edmond Yeo

per mee Thomas Smyth.

Inrotulatur et Examinatur concordat cum originali per me Ricum Wall clericum curiæ Burgi sive Ville de Belfast 30 die Januarij 1648

More   I doe acknowledge to have recᵈ at the hands of Joseph Harris m'chant the number of fiftye Barrells and a halfe of barque of wᶜ I doe promise to give him a true account of the proceed att Carrickfergus upon demand   As witness my hand the 2ᵈ Septembʳ 1648.

per me Tho: Smyth

Witness hereunto
 Hugh Lyndon
 Edmond Yeo

Inrotulatur et examinatur concordat cum originali per me Ricum Wall clericum curiæ &c 30 die Jan. 1648

Bee itt knowne unto all men by these p{r}sence that I Thomas Smyth of Dublin mchant doe stand and am justly indepted unto Joseph Harris of the County of the Towne of Carrickfergus m'chant in the Some of eleven pounds and ten shillings currant and lawfull money of and in England to bee paid to the said Joseph Harris his Executo{rs} adm{rs} and assignes uppon the thirtieth daye of September next ensueinge the date hereof at his now dwellinge house in the Towne aforesaid to w{c} paym{t} truely to bee made I binde me my Executo{rs} adm{rs} and assignes firmly by these p{r}sents As witness my hand and Seale this 25th day of July 1648

per me Tho Smyth

Witness
 Clem{t} Bashford
 Michaell Savadge

Inrotul' et examinat' concordat cum originali per me Ricum Wall clericum curiæ & 30 die Januar. 1648

15° die Septembr 1648

Belfast Bee it knowne unto all men by these p'nts that I John Clugston of Belfast merchant doe owe and am indebted unto Captain Robert Lawson of Londonderrye m'rchant the some of fourtye eight pounds eighte shillings and seaven pence currant money of England to bee paid to the said Captane Rob{t} Lawson his heres Executo{rs} administrato{rs} or assignes in or uppon the tenth daye of Novemb{r} next ensueinge the date hereof to the w{c} paym{t} well and truely to bee made I doe bynde mee and my heires Execut{rs} and administrato{rs} firmly by these pnts. In witness whereof I have hereunto set my hand and Seal the twentie sixt daye of Octob{r} 1647 in the yeare of the raigne of our Sovraigne Lord Kinge Charles &c

John Clugston

Sealed and delivered in
 the presence of
 Ja. Coningham
 John Burneside

HD Hugh Doak
 Sovraigne
vera copia concordat cum originali et Examinatur per me Ricardum Wall Clericum curiæ ibidem

M.ᵈ That the thirtieth daye of Novemb.ʳ in the foure and twentieth yeare of the raigne of our Sovraigne Lord Charles by the grace of God of England Scotland France and Ireland Kinge defender of the faith &c Anno dni 1648 Robert Foster of Belfast aforesaid gentl. nowe Sovraigne of the said Towne, Thomas Rigbye sonne of Richard Rigbye late of Clough Castle wᵗʰin the parish of Belfast aforesaid husbandman deceased came before the said Sovraigne and of his own Accord and free will and by and wᵗ the consent assent and good likeinge of all his freinds and kinsfolke then being and liveinge wᵗin the said Towne of Belfast put himself an Apprentice and covenant servant unto John Rigbye of Belfast aforesaid Tanner his brother for the full Terme tyme and space of seaven whole yeares fully to bee compleat & ended three yeares of wᶜʰ saide Terme the saide John Rigbye acknowledgeth were ended at and uppon the first daye of Novemb.ʳ last past before the date hereof and were well and faithfully served and imployed in the Service of the saide John Rigbye his said Master and by him acknowledged and taken to bee part of the saide Thomas Rigbye his apprenticeshippe And the said Thomas Rigbye doth covennt promisse and grannt to and with the said John Rigbye his Executoʳˢ administratoʳˢ and Assignes and to and wᵗ evrye of them by these prsents That hee the said Thomas Rigbye shall and will dwell wᵗ and well and faithfully serve the said John Rigbye his said Master dureinge the remaindʳ of the said term of seaven yeares the tyme of his saide apprentishipp as his apprentise and covennt servant after the forrme and maner of an apprentice according to the Statute in that case made and provided as well in the arte crafte trade science mistery and occupacon of a Tanner as alsoe in all other the facultyes labors workes necessarye occasions and businesses of the said John Rigbye wᶜʰ are and shalbee honest just and lawfull dureinge the said Terme And that the said Thomas Rigbye shall not in aniewise waste destroye put away or otherwise unlawfully ymbesill anie the goods, wares, merchandize or other commodityes of him the said John Rigbye his said master or knowe or cause the same or anie of them to bee wasted destroyed or put awaye or unlawfully ymbesilled dureing the said Term but shall to the uttermost of his power staye lett and hinder the same or else ymediatly give notice and warning thereof unto the said John Rigbye his said master And further alsoe that hee the said Thomas Rigbye dureing the said Terme shall not haunte use frequent or otherwise pracktise anie unlawful games comon alehouses Tavernes bawdye houses or anie evil lewd or dishonest companie to the loss prejudice or hinderance of his saide master nor by any meanes or by or uppon anie occasion of his owne absent or wᵗ·drawe himself out of or from the worke labor service or businesses of his said Master by day or by night wᵗhout the licence libtye or privileidge of his said Master And alsoe that hee the said Thomas Rigbye shall not dureing the said Terme buye sell or exchange anie goods wares merchandize or comodityes to the use benefitt or profitt of himself or of anie other pʳson or pʳsons whatsoevᵗ save onely to the use benefitt or profitt of his said Master dureinge the said Terme wᵗhout the speciall lycense of his said Master The Secretes and Counsell of his saide Master lawfull juste and honest dureing the saide Terme hee shall well and faithfully keepe secrete and conceale Matrimonie hee shall not contract or comitt fornicacion to or wᵗ anie woman dureing the said term And lastly hee the said Thomas Rigbye shall and will from tyme to tyme and at all tymes hereafter dureing the said Terme order behave rule govern and behave himself towards the said John Rigbye his said Master in all things as aꞟ obedient just true and faithfull Apprentice and covennt servant ought to doe and behave himself In consideracon of wᶜᵉ said dutye, obedience good and civill behaviour and faithfull service in manner and forme as aforesaid to bee done and faithfully p'formed unto the said John Rigbye his said Master   The said John Rigbye for himself his Execut[ors] and administrat[ors] and for evrye one of them doth covenant promise and grant to and w[t] him the said Thomas Rigbye his Executo[rs] Administrato[rs] and Assignes and to and w[t] evrye of them by these p'sents that hee the said John Rigbye shall and will at all and evrye tyme and tymes hereafter and from tyme to tyme dureing the said Terme instructe teach and informe or cause to be instructed taught and informed him the said Thomas Rigbye his said Apprentice as well in the arte trade craft science misterye and occupacon of a Tanner as alsoe in all other artes trades crafts sciences misteryes and occupacons w[c] the said John Rigbye his said Master now useth exerciseth or pracktiseth or hereafter shall use exercise or pracktise dureing the said terme as well in the best sort maner and forme as the said John Rigbye his said Master can instructe teach and informe by his dilligent instrucion & informacion and as the capacity and understandinge of the said Thomas Rigbye can or may attaine unto   And alsoe   And alsoe (*sic*) that hee the said John Rigbye his Executo[rs] adm[rs] or Assignes shall well and truely pay or cause to bee paid unto the said Thomas Rigbye his Apprentice and covenant servant the some of twentye six shillings sterl. yearely dureing the said Terme and alsoe shall give and allowe his said Apprentice the Tannery of half a deacre of Leather evrye yeare dureing the said Terme towards the mantennce of him the said Thomas Rigbye w[t] apparrell and other necessaryes   And alsoe yf the said Thomas Rigby shall dilligently obediently and faithfullye serve & staye w[t] the said John Rigby his said Master dureinge the said Terme   That then the said John Rigby his Execut[ors] or admin[rs] shall well and truely paye or cause to bee paid unto the said Thomas Rigbye the some of five pounds sterl. in money or comodityes at the end and expiracon of his said Terme of Apprentishippe   In witness whereof both the said John Rigbye and Thomas Rigbye came before the said Sovraigne and mutually acknowledged this said Agreem[t] and desired the same to bee enrolled & registered uppon Recorde and have hereunto subscribed their names the day and yeare first above written.

Burgus de Belfast in Com Antrym

M[d] That the 23th of Decemb[r] Anno dni 1648 ffrancis Ratcliff haveinge in his hands & custody the some of ten pounds sterl. given to the Towne by M[r]. Edward Holmes for the use of the poore of the saide Towne and now beinge behinde for the yearely interest thereof the some of fourtye shillings sterl. the w[c] for the tyme p'sent hee is not able to pay yet to give satisfaccion for the same and for the yearely interest thereof for the tyme to come dureinge these troublsome tymes The saide ffranc Ratcliffe for himself his Executo[rs] Adm[rs] and Assignes and for evrye of them [by these prstes] doth covenant promise and Grant to and w[t] the Sovraigne and Burgesses of the Borrough and Towne of Belfast aforesaid and their Successors That they the saide Sovraigne and Burgesses shall receave yearely and from yeare to yeare from and by the hands of some Tenant or Inhabitant w[t]in some cottage standing uppon the land of the saide ffranc Ratcliff lyeing and being w[t]in Belfast aforesaid betwixt the Miln port and the Miln untill the said ffranc Ratcliffe or his assignes shall finde other securitye for the fourtye Shillings nowe in arrear   The

Rec from Tho Cook by Mr ffoster of the 10[s]. hee was to pay in hands 5[s]. from W Dunshee 3[s]. 4[d]. W[m] Bryan 3[s]. 4[d]. Jo: Martin 5[s]. o[d] Rob ffoster

said ffranc Ratcliff is to pay xx[s] sterl in hand and xx[s] sterl at May next ensueing and afterwards there is xx[s] to bee paid at and uppon the [24th of December] *first of Novemb[r]* then next followinge   And afterwards twenty Shillings yearely to bee paid at *May* [Easter] and the [24th of December] *first of Novemb[r]* by these persons Tenants and Inhabitants of the said land in manner and forme followinge vizt. Thomas Cook x[s] in hand and afterwards x[s] pr Anm at *May* [Easter] and the [24th of December] *first of Novembe[r]* by even and equall porcions Willm Dunshee 3[s]. 4[d] in hands and afterwards vi[s] viii[d] yearely at the dayes and tymes as aforesaid Willm Bryan 3[s]. 4[d] in hand and afterwards vi[s] viii[d] yearely as aforesaid John Martin v^s in hands and afterwards x^s yearely as aforesaid And they the said Thomas Cooke Willm Dunshee Willm Bryan and John Marten their Executo^{rs} Adm^{rs} & assignes and for evrye of them doe covennt promisse and undertake to and w^t the saide Sovraigne & Burgesses of the Burrough and Towne of Belfast aforesaid and their Success^{rs} well and truely to pay or cause to bee paid unto the said Sovraigne and Burgesses and their Successors the said sevrall somes aforesaid in maner and forme as aforesaid dureinge the tyme aforesaid untill the said ffranc Ratcliff shall give other security   In witness whereof they the said ffrancis Ratcliff Thomas Cook Willm Dunshee Willm Bryan and John Martin the daye and yeare first above written have subscribed their names

ffrancis Ratcliffe

2nd die Octob^r 1649

M^d That the daye and yeare aforesaid Thomas Haward Mr John Bullin-brooke Chiorgeon Henry Cook Master of the Fellowshipp John Bedwell and John Pickton did personallye come before mee George Marten Mr^t nowe Sovraigne of the Burrough and Towne of Belfast and did sevrally Testifye uppon their Corporall oathes That John Blacke and Rob^{te} Black and most of the Inhabitants of Groomsporte (except Willm Stephenson) together w^t severall Inhabitants of Bangwell w^t some of the cuntrye *there* next adjacent w^t sevrall officers & souldiers vizt. Ca: Willm Young Ca: Ja. Steawart, Cornet Rob^{te} Purdye &c uppon Thurdsdaye the 11th, of this instant w^t force and Armes surprise the Barque called (the Katherine of Belfast) and did surprise and take Major Westmorland and sevrall other officers and passengers of sevrall degrees, and Thomas Haward above named and Robbed and spoyled him of goods and Merchandize to the value of 110^{li} and 10^s sterl or thereabouts.

Tho Haward	John Bedwell
John Bullinbrooke	John Pickton
Henry H Cooke	

Burgus de Belfast in Com Antrym

Att the Courte of Assembly houlden the 9th daye of Januar Anno dni 1650 Whereas Willm Thomson late an Inhabitant wthin this Towne was arrested by vertue of an order from the honorble the Commission^{rs} for the Revenues in Ulster for arreares of Sesse for the tyme as hee hath absented himself out of this Towne according to the said order uppon his petition unto the Sovraigne Burgesses and Cominaltye s'mitting himself unto the order of the said Courte for the said arreares   It is ordered by the saide Courte That the saide Willm Thomson shall p^rsently pay unto the Sovraigne for the use of the Towne for discharge of the arreares of his Sesse wch was due unto the Towne as aforesaide the some of ten pounds sterl xl^s for Mr. Sovraigne his charge and the Marshalls Fees in the same and upon p'formance hereof the said Willm Thomson shalbee clearly and fully discharged

Afterwards uppon greate importunity and supplication by the above named Willm Thomson Itt is ordered that hee shall paye in hand five pounds sterl' and other five pounds at and uppon the first day of Apprill next ensueing for paym^t whereof Willm Thom of Belfast Mchant hath engaged himself unto the Sovraigne at the day lymitted and for the xl^s the said Willm Thomson shall bring a free discharge unto the Sovraigne from the provost Marshall

Will: Thom

Willm W T Thomson, marke

M^d that the 24th daye
of Apprill 1651 the
ten pounds in the Order
above mencioned is acknowledged
by the Sovraigne & Burgesses to

be fully sattisfyed and paid by the above named Willm Thomson & Wm Thom according to the said order.

And how the same hath beene wholy disbursed and ymployed for the Townes use and occasions by the Sovraigne & Mr Willm Leythes   It hath beene made manifestly appeare in oppen Courte the said 24th daye of Apprill 1651, and therefore the said Mr. Sovraigne & Mr. Leythes are clearly discharg of that accompt

Thomas Hanington
Sovraigne

To the right honorble the Lord President wth the rest of the honor[ble] the Comission[rs] of the Revenues for the province of Ulster

The humble Petition of the Sovraigne Burgesses and Inhabitants of Belfast

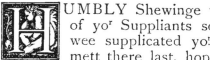

UMBLY Shewinge unto yo[r] hono[rs] that by reason of yo[r] Suppliants soe greate and heavy burdens wee supplicated yo[r] hono[rs] at Colrane when you mett there last, hopeinge for some ease or reliefe as wee still doe but as yet have had none w[ch] inforceth us yo[r] suppliants, to acquaint yo[r] honor[s] that wee reaped small benefitt by the honor[ble] Col Venables order,   And that now of late there is fallen defects and noewayes able to make paym[t] of their monetly Assess, the numb[r] of eight or ten w[ch] paide monethly the summ of five pounds the w[ch] being summd unto our former defects make upp nere thirty pounds monethly All w[ch] being added unto yo[r] petitior[s] Cesses inforceth this their Supplication.

> May it therefore please yo[r] hono[rs] in tender consideration of their deplorable condicon as to take away part of their saide monethly assesses or helpe yo[r] supplicators by adding some other quarter to bee their assistants or by granting unto them some custodim lande and Tythes whereby they wth their wth their (*sic*) poore familyes may not bee totally ruined and they as bound shall pray &c

Carrickfergus March the 13th 1650

Mr Teag O'Hara is hereby ordered to pay unto the petitioners the twenty twoe pounds wch hee is to pay p Anm towards the easing of their contribution and yf the petition^{rs} can finde out anie other way to their advantage and not to the publique Revenues p^{r}judice it shalbee granted them

Cha: Coote
R. Venables
Chidley Coote

| An Order uppon Teag O'Hara for paying the xxii ponds wch hee was ordered to pay to Belfast for the Tyethes of his owne Crates | Whereas Mr Teag O'Harah desires to bee freed from paying or contributing anie thing wth the protected people in the Baroni of Loughinsolin but to reside in the County of Antrym and to be a distinct Crat by himself   Wee are very well content therewth Provided he pay five pounds ten shillings quarterly or more yf it come to his xpation of what is contracted wth the said protected persons for wch some of 5^{li} 10^s he is to pay unto the Sovraigne of Belfast towards their helpe in the Sess & contribution of that Towne |

Cha: Coote
R: Venables
Chydley Coote
Rob Baron

Receaved by the Sovraigne by vertue of the order aforemencioned from Teag O'Harah for the first quarter since the said order ended the 10th of May 1651 the some of 5^{li} 10^s and disbursed by him as followeth.

li	s	d		
3	0	0	In primis to Mr Willm Leythes for sevrall ymploym^{ts} and disbursm^{ts} of money wch hee had about the works of the Towne 3^{li}	
1	16	0	Item paid to Mr Theaker for quarters for Mr Shamba for three monethes 12^s the monethe ended the tenth of June 1651 1^{li} 16^s	
0	09	0	Item to Jacksons sonne for mending the Strand way over the water 9^s	
			Some total	5 5 0
			Remaineinge in Mr Sovraigne's hands of the 5^{li} 10^s 0^d the some of } ··· ··· ···	5 0

ARMS OF DUBLIN.   ARMS OF IRELAND.   ARMS OF KILKENNY.

Ireland

By the Commission^rs of the Parliam^t of
the Comon wealth of England for the
Affairs of Ireland

It is ordered that the respective Tresurers of the Revenue in the respective
p.cincts in Ireland doe not from and after due notice hereof yssue out anie
money arising from the receipt of the customes or excise w^thout warrants
und^r the hands of three or more of the Commission^rs of the Parliam^t of the
Comon wealth of England.   Kilkenney March 19th 1650

H: Ireton Edm: Ludlow Miles Corbet
Jo: Jones   John: Weaver

Imprinted at Dublin Anno d'ni 1650

It is ordered That the Comissioner^s of the Revenue in each p.cinct in Ireland
doe take view and survey of all houses and lands in and about evrye City and
Garrison Towne w^thin evrye respective p.cinct and doe take especiall care that
all materialls belonging to the same bee p.served from waste : And doe let
and set the saide houses and lands for one yeare to the best advantage for the
Comon wealth,   And where anie p.son shall undertake to build a new, finishe
or repaire anie howses or other buildings w^thin anie of the saide Cityes or
Townes : The said Comission^rs have hereby power and authority to make such
contracts on the behalf of the Comon wealth wth such p^rson & p.sons and
therein to take due consideration of the charge that every such whoe shall
contract wth them shalbee at in the building finishing or repairing the p.mises
and to allow conditions suitable and proportionall thereto.   Provided that the
Comission^rs of the Revenue shall not grant anie of the p.mises soe to be built
finished or repaired for above the Terme of seaven yeares w^thout espiall warrant
from the Comission^rs of Parlm^t

Kilkennye March 19 1650
Miles Corbett
Hr: Ireton, Edm: Ludlow, Jo: Jones John Weaver

Whereas great spoile and waste hath lately beene and is dayly made of Oak
Ash Elm and other Trees in or neare the sevrall garrisons and Townes in
Ireland and the Plankes, Rafters, Beames, doores, and other materialls belonging to diverse vacant and ruined howses have been taken away burnt or wasted
whereby much damage doth arrise to the Comon wealth and a great want of
wood and Timber is likely to ensue for p.vention therefore of the like mischiefes
hereafter and that all yong Timber trees and other wood fitt for building,
plow Timber or other uses of Husbandry may bee for the future better
p.served and mantained.   It is hereby ordered that noe Governor of Garrison

Souldier or other person or persons, whatsoev.ʳ shall have after publication hereof in the respective Countyes and Garrisons fell cut down or otherwise destroy anie Timber tree oak ash elm or other tree (of what growth soev.ʳ) or quick sett hedges groweing or being uppon anie grounds belonging to the Comon wealth or uppon anie grounds belonging to anie person that hath been in armes or assissted or p.ʳmoted the warr in Ireland against the Parliam.ᵗ of Comon wealth of England w.ᵗʰout s'piall lycenses from the Com.ʳˢ of the Revenues of the respective p.ʳcincts first had and obtained in writing   And the said Com.ʳˢ and Governo.ʳˢ respectively are hereby authorised to yssue out such licenses in all such cases where they find the same to bee of publique profitt & advantage and not otherwise   And that noe Souldier or other p.ʳson doe take burne or otherwise wast anie Timber or other materialls belonging to anie ruinous empty or other house   And the saide Com.ʳˢ for the Revenue or Governors of the next Garrison in their respective p.ʳcincts are hereby authorised and required to yssue out their warrants, or otherwise to app.ʳhend such persons as shall (after publication hereof) comitt anie waste or spoile uppon anie howse Timber or other woodd afore in contempt of this order and uppon proofe made thereof comitt such p.ʳson or persons to prison untill full reparacon bee made for the same or such punishm.ᵗ bee inflicted on the offenders as the saide Com.ʳˢ or Governo.ʳˢ respectively shall judge agreable to justice   And to the end that this order bee put in due and speedy exeecucion All Governors of Countyes Cityes and Garrisons and other officers are hereby authorised and required to cause the same to bee published and to endevo.ʳ to restrain the mischieffes aforesaide and severely to punish all Transgressors against the intent hereof   And all and evrye Governo.ʳˢ of Cityes and other Garrison is hereby required to take speciall care that the woods w.ᶜʰ shalbee necessaryly used for fuell in his respective Garrison bee cut at seasonable tymes and in husbandlike manner and noe more bee felled than shall bee necessary to be spent in the said Garrison and according to the Establishm.ᵗ shortly to be made

Kilkennye 22 March 1650

Hen Ireton   Edm Ludlow   Miles Corbet
Jo Jones   John Weaver
Imprinted at Dublin Anno dni 1651

Memorand

    That M.ʳ Essex Digby preacher of the Word of God at Belfast in the County of Antrym came unto mee Richard Wall gent. Towne Clerk of the Borrough of Belfast aforesaid this p.ʳsent day being the first of March 1651 and desired that hee might have enrolled uppon Record Letters of Administration w.ᶜʰ were granted him of the goods and Cattells w.ᶜʰ were the lady Lettice Langford late of Carrickfergus whoe dyed intestete by Alexand.ʳ Colvill Doctor of Divinitye ut Sequitur in hec verba viz.ᵗ Allexander Colvill Sacrae Theologicæ Docto.ʳ Comissarius legitimê Constitutus dilecto in Christo Essex Digby, de Collshell in Comitatu Warwick in Insula Angliae Clerico fratri dominæ Laeticiæ Langford de Carrickfergus

Alsoe the above named M.ʳ Essex Digby desired the enrollm.ᵗ of an Assignm.ᵗ made by James Tracey and John Orpin Executors of the Last Will and Testament of Dame Anne Langford the widow and relict of S.ʳ Hercules Langford late of Carrickfergus Kn.ᵗ deceased the Tenor of w.ᶜʰ Assignm.ᵗ is as followeth :—

    To all christyian people to whom these p.ʳsents shall come   Know yee that wee James Tracey and John Orpin Executors of the last Will and Testament of Dame Anne Langford the widowe and relict of S.ʳ Hercules Langford late of

F

Carrickfergus Kn^t deceased doe hereby for and in consideracon of the some
of twoe hundred pounds bequeathed as a legacy by the said Will & Testament
of Dame Anne Langford bearing date the fifte daye of Apprill 1647 unto Dame
Lettice Langford late wife unto Sr Roger Langford of Carrickfergus aforesaid
Knight deceased freely assigne unto the saide Dame Lettice[digby]Langford one
Bond or Bill wherein the honor^ble Captane Arthur Chichester now Earle of
donnagall stands bound unto the said Dame Anne Langford bearing date the
26th daye of Febr 1639 for the paym^t of fiftye pounds in and uppon the last
day of May following as alsoe one other bond of Two hundred pounds like
money bearing date the fift day of July 1641 wherein Robt Foster and Rich:
Foster of Belfast in the County of Antrim gent stand bound unto the said Dame
Anne Langford for the paym^t of one hundred pounds at and uppon the first day
of Novemb^r Anno dni 1642 as alsoe one other bond of *thirti* [fifty] pounds sterl
bearing date the 24th day of Januar 1637 wherein Mathew Johnston Humphrey
Johnston and John Davyes of Carrickfergus Alderman stande bound unto the
said Dame Anne Langford to sattisfy and paye unto her the full some of
fifteene pounds at or uppon the the first daye of Novemb^r following as alsoe one
other Bond of thirtye pounds sterl wherein the said persons stand bound unto
the aforesaid Dame Anne Langford to sattisfy and paye unto her the some of
fifteene pounds like money wch Bond beareth date wth the former and payable
at May 1638 as alsoe one other Bond of thirtye pounds sterl wherein the said
Mathew Johnston Humphrey Johnston and John Davyes stand bond unto the
saide [John] Dame Anne Langford wth the former and paym^t of fifteene pounds
at or uppon the first day of May Anno dni 1639 and lastly one bill bearing date
the 23th of Januar 1637 wherein Humphrey and Mathew Johnston stand bound
to sattisfy and pay unto the said Dame Anne Langford the full some of seaven
pounds and ten shillings like money att or uppon the first day of August 1639.
All wch some and somes of money contained mentoned and expressed in the
aforesaid sevrall bonds amounts unto the (*sic*) of two hundred twoe pounds and
ten shillings sterl &c   In witness whereof wee have hereunto put our hands
and Seales the tenth day of Apprill Anno dni 1650

Sealed signed and delivered   James Tracey
    in the p^rsence of   John Orpin
        Edmond Yeo
    George Woodencroft
        Rob^te Russell

        Alsoe the said Mr Essex desired the enrollm^t of three sevrall bonds
und^r hands and seales wch could not bee done verbatim and in due form by
reason of his sudden departure from henc for England yet the substance of
the Bonds are as thus

        Matthew Johnston Humphrey Johnston and John Davyes of Carrick-
fergus doe stand bound unto Sr Hercules Langford Knight in the Some of
thirtye pounds sterl by their bond und^r their hands & seales bearing date the
24th day of Januar 1637 to pay or cause to bee paid unto the said Sr Hercules
Langford his Executo^rs Adm^rs or Assignes the Some of fifteene pounds sterl at
and uppon the first day of May 1638.

                                                    Mathew Johnston
Sealed signed and delivered   Hum: Johnston
    in the presence of   Jo Davies
        Ri Shukburgh
        Tho Whitaker

Mathew Johnson Humphrey Johnson and John Davyes of Carrickfergus doe stand bound unto Sr Hercules Langford Knight in the Some of thirtye pounds sterl by their bond und^r their hands and Seales bearing date the 24th daye of Januar 1637. to pay or cause to bee paid unto unto the said Sr Hercules Langford his Execut^{rs} adm^{rs} or assignes [at and uppon] the some of fifteene pounds at and uppon the first day of No: 1638.

Sealed signed and delivr^d
in the prsce of
  Ri: Shukburgh
  Tho: Whitaker

      Mathew Johnson
      Hum: Johnson
      Jo: Davyes

Matthew Johnson Humphrey Johnson and John Davyes doe stande bond unto Sr Hercules Langford Knight in the some of thirtye pounds sterl by their bond und^r their hands and seales bearing date the 24th of Januar 1637 to pay or cause to bee paid unto the said Sr Hercules Langford his Execut^{rs} adm^{rs} and Assignes the some of fifteene pounds at and uppon the first daye of May 1639

Sealed signed and delivered
in the p^rsence of
  Ri. Shukburgh
  Tho Whitaker

      Matthew Johnson
      Hum Johnson
      Jo Davyes

These three sevrall bonds were produced and shewed by the aforenamed Mr Essex Digby unto mee in due forme und^r hand and seale by Mathew Johnson Humphrey Johnson and John Davyes aforenamed dated as aforesaid and attested by the said witnesses Richard Shukburgh Tho Whitaker the materiall substance thereof inrolled as aforesaid

      By mee Richard Wall
       Towne Clerke

M^d That the 26th of Decemb^r 1650 at the Courte houlden and by the meetinge of the Sovraigne & Burgesses then and there p^rsent uppon consideracon of the poore estate of Sibbye Boltbye it could not in conscience bee otherwise adjudged but that the arreares of the [x^{li}] use for the x^{li} wch was left in her hands for the use of the poore by Mr Holmes her form^r husband shee beinge in great necessitye and not now able to paye the same shalbee clearly remitted & acquitted untill this p^rsent

  Richard Wall
  Towne Clerke

    Thomas Hanington
      Sovraine
    Rob Foster

M^d that the 26th of Decemb^r 1650 Lt Theaker came into Courte and paid xx^s of the arreares wch hee is behynde of the use and interest for the x^{li} wch was put in his hands of the money given by Mr Holmes for ye use *of y^e* poore

    Thomas Hanington
      Sovraine
   Rob: Foster

16 Mar. 1651

Sciant presentes et futuri nos Richardum Hunte de Henerichellym in comitatu Surrie yoman et Johannem Hunte filium et heredem proximum mei dicti Richardi Hunte dedisse concessisse et hac presenti charta nostra confirmasse Johanni Helhows de Walton super Thamses in comitatu Surrie predicto yoman pro quadam pecuniarum summa nobis per dictum Johannem Helhowse ad sigillationem presentium plene solutam et contentatam totam illam parcellam sive peciam terre nostram vocatam Buryguston jacentem et existentem in Walton predicto que quidem parcella siue pecia terre per estimacionem continet sex acras terre sive majus aut minus et abuttat super quandam clausuram cujusdam Richardi Bernardi ex parte austriali et super communiam de Walton predicto ex parte orientali habendum tenendum gaudendum predictam parcellam siue peciam terre cum suis pertinenciis prefato Johanni Helhowse heredibus et assignatis suis in perpetuum tenendum de Capitalibus Dominis feodum illius per servitia inde debita et de jure consueta.   Et nos vero prefati Richardus et Johannes Hunt predictam parcellam terre cum suis pertinentiis prenominato Johanni Helhowse heredibus et assignatis suis contra omnes gentes warrantisabimus imperpetuum defendemus per presentes Noueritis insuper nos prefatum Richardum et Johannem Hunt fecisse ordinasse constituisse et in loco nostro posuisse dilectum nobis in Christo Thomam Mowld yoman nostrum verum et fidelem ac legittimum attornatum ad intrandum pro nobis vice et nominibus nostris in predictam parcellam sive peciam terre cum pertinentiis ac legalem et pacificam possessionem et seisinam sic seisinam inde capiendum post hujusmodi possessionem et seisinam sic inde captam et habitam.   Deinde pro nobis vice et nominibus nostris ad deliberandum plenam legalem et pacificam possessionem et seisinam de et in premissis cum pertinentiis prefato Johanni Helhows heredibus et assignatis suis imperpetuum secundum tenorem vim formam et effectum hujus presentis charte nostre ratum gratum presens et habituri totum et quicquid dictus noster Attornatus fecerit aut fieri procurabit in premissis   In cujus rei testimonium huic presenti charte nostre sigillum nostrum apposuimus Datum vicesimo sexto die martii annis regnorum Philippi et Marie dei gratia Regis et Regine Anglie Hispanie Francie Utriusque Cicilie——et Hibernie Fidei defensoris Archiducis Austrie ducis Burgundie Mediolani Brabantie Comitis Haspurgi Flandrie et Tirrollis tertio et quarto inde quod predictus   Johannes Helhowse heredes et assignati sui imperpetuum solvent seu solui faciant prenominato Richardo et Johanni Hunt heredibus et assignatis suis imperpetuum annuatim ad festum Michaelis Archangeli sex denarios legittime petitum.

Status et seisina ac legalis et pacifica possessio capte et deliberate fuere die et Anno ut infra secundum tenorem vim formam et effectum hujus presentis charte in presentia
Richardi   Woodclerk   Tristram Woodclerk   Thome   Woodclerk Thome Dalley Thome Greenetree Richardi Clerici Johannis Clerici et aliorum fide dignorum

The Deed it self whereof this is a true Copie was at this present in the custodie of Captan John Ellis of Ballygarmarton

Enrolled by mee Richard Wall Towne Clerke of Belfast the day and year first above written

M^d   That whereas Willm Postley Carpenter late of Belfast deceased by and
wth the consent of Katherine his wiffe in his lieffe *tyme* did give unto John
ffrancis in marriage wth Mary Duninge widow their daughter all his tenem^t and
dwelling howse in Belfast aforesaide whereof the had possession Nowe the
said ffrancis and Mary his wieffe have sould ye said dwelling howse [and tene^mt]
to the use of the State for the some of twelve pounds sterl. whereof they have
acknowledged to have receaved full sattisfaction and paym^t   In witness whereof
they have hereunto subscribed their names the 7th day of Apprill 1651.

John francis
Mary ffrancis × marke
Katherine Postley × her marke

M^d.
      That whereas Andrew Mabrey had a Cottage or dwelling howse standinge
15^s.   nere the place where the great Fort is errected pulled downe for enlarginge of
a highwaye thereby and by apprisement of Mr Willm Leythe and Thomas
Postley M^rc the said Mabrey was adjudged to receave in full sattisfaction for
his damage the some of fifteene shillings sterl the said Andrew Mabrey doth
hereby acknowledge the receipt thereof   As witness his hand the 12th of
Apprill 1651

Andrew × Mabrey
his marke

M^d.
      That I John Quiggin have receaved full sattisfaction for the damage of
12^s.   my howse wch was pulled downe nere the Grand fort accordinge to the
appraisem^t of Mr Leythes and Thomas Postley M^rt beinge the some of xii^s sterl
as witness my hand the 12th of Apprill 1651.

×
John Quiggins marke

M^d.
      That wee Thomas Grome als Slye and James Smyth have receaved full
8^li   sattisfaccion for our dwellinge howse wch was standinge here at Belfast and
in all 21^li 7^s   pulled downe for the erectinge of the Grand fort accordinge as it apprised and
valewed by Mr Foster and others beinge the some of eight pounds sterl as
witness our hands this 18th of Apprill 1651.

Tho: × Grome als Slye
Jane I Smyth wieff of Ja:
Smyth her mrke insteedd
of her husband being now sick

Att the Courte of Assembly houlden the 26th of June 1651   It is ordered uppon Mr Steawarts petition unto the Sovraigne Burgesses and Cominaltye of this Borrough and Toune of Belfast uppon serious consideracon of his weake estate that hee shall onely paye what Sesse hee is behind and in arreare and for the tyme to come hee is to pay foure shillings the moneth untill the first of May next and to bee freed from all other and contributions whatsoev. for anie estate hee hath in this Towne   These Burgesses hereund. named subscribed the said order

Tho Hanington Sovraigne

Hugh Doake Geo Martin John Leythes Junr Fr Meeke Robt Foster Tho Theaker Willm Leythes Richard Gateley

ARMS OF CARRICKFERGUS.

ARMS OF IRELAND.

ARMS OF CLONMEL.

Ireland   By the Com.^{rs} of the Comon Wealth of England for the affaires of Ireland &^c

It is ordered that the Com.^{rs} of applotm.^t in each respective Barronie in Ireland bee authorised & required to app.^rhend or cause to bee app.^rhended examined and ymprisoned sturdie Beggars Rogues and Vagabonds Idle persons out of service and to erect & keep stocks in oppen convenient places for such offend.^{rs} and to send such as they shall see cause together w.th their Examinaccons taken to the Comand.^r of the next Garrison that soe they may bee sent to the cheif Garrison in each respective Countye and there proceeded against accordinge to their severall demerritts   And it is further ordered that the said Com.^{rs} of Applot.^{mt} be impowered w.thin their severall prcincts as aforesaid to ascertaine Servant wages to ord.^r and moderate the hyer of laborerers accordinge to lawe, and to p.^rvent the abuses and excessive rates of in Tawing Tanning and brogues likewise.   Likewise to cause watch and ward to bee duely kept & pursued by Hu and Crye accordinge to lawe : and to appoint in each parrish some fitt persons to see the said watch duely kept and observed   And the Governors of Garrisons as aforesaid and others that have power for the administration of Justice are to cause such offend.^{rs} sent as aforesaid to bee punished accordinge to lawe
Clon Mell 15 May 1651.

It is ordered the Com^{rs} of Applotm^{t} in their sevrall p^{r}.cints doo put in execution all the acts & ordinances of Parliam^{t} against drunkeness profane swearinge and cursing and profanacion of the lords day by travellinge or by sports pastimes and unlawful games or frequenting Alehouses and to bringe the offend^{rs} to due punishm^{t} as by the said acts lawes and ordinances is required   Dated at Carrickfergus 3 Decr 1651.   Signed by

> R Venables Geo Rawden G Blundell
> Jas Waite Tobias Norrice

The Oath of the Sovraigne of Belfast as it was ministred the 30th of Septemb^{r} 1650 and the 29th of Septemb^{r} 1651.

You shall sweare that you shall well and truely serve in the office of Sovraigne of this Corporacion and Towne of Belfast from this tyme forward untill the feast of St Michaell the Archangell now next ensueinge that is to saye for one whole yeare yf you soe long live and continue in the said Office

Comonwealth   You shall acknowledge the power and authorytye of the Parliam^{t} of England and Governem^{t} by States to bee just honorable and lawfull and shall to the uttermost of yor power mantaine and uphould all the rightes libtyes Interests and privileidges of the same   You shall in all things execute the office of a Justice of Peace w^{th}in this Corporacon and the libtyes thereof dureinge the tyme of yor sovraignetye   You shall alsoe to the uttermost of yor power see the peace of the Comon wealth of England and Ireland well and faithfully p^{r} served and kept. both in yor owne person and in all other person & persons whatsoev^{r} w^{th}in yor jurisdiccon and libertyes.   You shall see equall justice done as well to the poore as to the Rich dureinge the tyme of yor office accordinge to yor power skill and understandinge

You shall keep yor Courts in due order accordinge to the Franchises libertyes and privileidges of this Towne and Corporacion and as they have beene formerly kept and therein shall doe equall and indifferent justice to all persons whatsoev^{r} to the best of yor knowledge skill and understandinge

You shall likewise keep the Clerk of the Markett Courts w^{th}in your libertye and Jurisdiccion and therein see that there bee just weights and measures observed and kept by all persons and that you see unto the correccion of victualls w^{th}in the Towne and the libertyes thereof that is to saye of bread beare Ale wine fish and flesh

You shall see unto the searchinge and Sealinge of leather w^{th}in this Towne accordinge to the Statute   And alsoe shall truely and carefully see unto the severall crafts trades & occupacions wch are w^{th}in you^{r} libertye and Jurisdiccon and shall justly and duely correct and reforme the same according to the Statute

You shall fairly and gently entreat the people of this Towne und.r yo.r power and authoritye w.th equall right and justice to yo.r best endevo.r power skill and und.rstandinge and to the uttermost of yo.r power and endevo.r mantaine and uphould all the rights libtyes privileidges Jurisdiccons lawes and ordinances of this Corporaccon w.ch are granted unto the same by lawfull authoritye for the peaceable quiett & civill governem.t of the same

All these points and articles you shall dilligently carefully and truely observe & keep to the uttermost of yo.r power skill knowledge and und.rstandinge   Soe helpe you god in Christ Jesus

By the Commission.rs for Administration of Justice and for probatts of last Wills and Testam.ts at Dublin

Whereas administration of all & singular the goods and chattells debts and creditts of Archibald Moore late of Lisnegarveye merchant deceased is by the said Commission.rs comitted and granted unto Jane Moore widow y.e Relict of the said Archibald   These are therefore to require and authorise yo.u John Stuart of Belfast merchant Willm Tom and Geo: M.cCartney of the same merchants or anie twoe of you to valew and appraise uppon yo.r corporall oaths all such goods and chattells debts and creditts as were of the said Archibald Moores as shall come unto yo.r hands sight or knowledge and to retorne a true & perfect Inventory thereof unto the said Com.rs und.r the hands of you or anie twoe or more of you containinge the sevrall p'ticulars and true valewes thereof together w.th this Comission close sealed upp w.th all convenient speed and at the furthest by the last daye of Maye next ensueinge [this] together with this Comission dated at Dublin the xvi.th daye of this instant March 1652

This is a true copie   Gerrard Lowther, Edw: Bolton
of the originall by mee   Ja: Donelan
examined   Tho Dongan
         Richard Wall   Willm Sandes R.t

d   That the 14th of [December] July 1652 it did appeare before Mr Reynalds Mr George Marten & Mr Wareinge being assembled together that L.t Theaker did pay unto Mr Sovraigne at Chrmas last the some of xx.s w.ch is for interest of x.li put into his hands of the money given by Mr Holmes deceased for the use of the poore w.ch xx.s was paid by Mr Sovraigne unto Jane Whitlock for takeinge of a poor wench prentice and Jane Whitlock acknowledged the receipt thereof at this p.rsent

Edw Reynell
George Martin
Thomas Waring

[M.d that whereas one Willm Erwin of Banshaw in the parish of Annandell in Scotland was authorised by one David Erwin of Mowisknow in Scotland aforesaid by his letters of Attorney under his hand & seale bearing date the 24th August 1652]

M̶ᵈ

That Whereas one John Armstrong of the Maine Water [was] in the County of Antrym was authorised by one David Erwin of Mowisknowe in the parish of Kirkpatrick in Scotland by his Letter of Attorney undᵗ his hand and Seale bearing date the 24ᵗʰ of August 1652 to aske demand and receave of Thomas Foster of Drommall neare unto the Maine Water in the Countye of Antrym aforesaid all such some & somes of money as hee the said Thomas Foster was in aniewise due unto the said David Erwin by anie bond bill or specialty or by letter of assignation made & subscribed by Chr Foster (*sic*) father of the said Thomas Foster or anie other debt whatsoevʳ due uppon anie bargain reckening or accompt and the saide John Armstrong one debte of ixˡⁱ viˢ viiiᵈ sterl by one Bill dated the 28ᵗʰ of Decembʳ 1626 Now the said Thomas Foster this pᵣˢent day the first daye of Januar 1652 came before Tho Wareinge gen: Sovraigne of the Borrough and Towne of Belfast in the County of Antrym and produced one Edwᵈ Purdy of Ballydollaghan in the Countye of Downe husbandman of seaventy yeares of age of good and perfect memory who upon his oath before the said Sovraigne lawfully administered did testify and declare that hee was pᵣⁱˢent by when as hee the said Edward Purdy did see the said Thomas Foster at his howse in Ballydollaghan aforesaid about twentye years since deliver unto the said David Erwin twoe baye maires in discharge and full sattisfaccon for all debts reckenings and accompts whatsoevʳ wᶜʰ then the said David Erwin could in aniewise claim challeng or demand of the said Tho Foster eyther for himself or his said father And uppon receipt of the said twoe bay maires the said David Erwin then promissed eyther to send the said Thomas Foster a full discharg for all things whatsoevʳ betwixt him the said David Erwin and the said Thomas Foster and his father then liveinge wᵗʰⁱn eight weekes then next after or else he would burne the said Bill of ixˡⁱ viˢ viiiᵈ

Thomas Waring

Edward ✕ Purdy mrke

Sufraine

Alsoe at this Courte houlden the 16th of Septembʳ 1652 Sibbye Boltbye came and desired that the xxˢ wᶜʰ shee was to pay at Chrmas last to the poore for the use of xˡⁱ left by Mr Holmes her former husband might bee allowed her beinge in great necessitye wᶜʰ being considered by the said Court is allowed her

Richard Wall
Towne Clerk

Thomas Hanington
Sovraine
Jo: Leithes
Rich: Gaytleye

The xxᵗⁱᵉ shillings wᶜʰ is due by Mrs Boltby of the poores money for the yeare 1653 and the xxᵗⁱᵉ shillings in arreare this yeare 1654 is allowed her for her relieffe being in great necessitye by consent of the Courte this 25th of Januar 1654

At the Courte houlden the 6th of July 1654 paid by Lᵗ Thomas Theaker xxtie Shillings sterl for the use of the poore beinge for interest of 10^{li} sterl given as a legacie by one Mr Holmes deceased for the use of the poore of the Towne

Likewise paid by ffrancis Ratcliffe the 6th of July 1654 the sum of xxtie shillings sterl for the use of the poore as aforesaid

Paid by Mr Willm Leythes for the use of ffrancis Ratcliffe vi^s viii^d being for his rent due at Hallontyde last wch is for the use of the poore this 25th of Januar 1654.

Paid by ffrancis Ratcliffe ye sum of twenty shillings st^r being for ye poore left by Mr Holmes for y^e. yeare endinge ye 25th of Decr 1661

Paid by John Allsinor ye sum of six shill^s and eight pence by ye Annuall rent of Fortye shill^s st^r ending [of] at ye 25th of Decr 1661. left by Thomas Chepline att his death for ye use of ye poore of Belfast Parish

Paid by William Cordiner ye sum of twenty shill' st^r unto ye Soffraigne [of the] for y^e. use of ye poore of Belfast being his rent ending at ye 25th of December 1661

I Robert Jackson Church Warden doe acknowledge to have receaved from Mr John Rigby Sofferaigne y^e. sume of two pound six shill^s and eight pence ster to bee paid to ye poore of Belfast as witness my hand this 2^d January 1661

Robert Jackson

I Nicholas Gardiner *Church Warden* doe acknowledge to have rec^d from Sampson Theaker ye some of twenty shill^s ster for y^e. use of ye poore for his rent ending ye 25th of Decr 1661

Witness my hand
Nicholas Garnett

Paid by Sampson Theaker ye sume of twenty shill^s st^r for ye use of ye poore for ye yeare ending ye 25th Decr 1662 by us Church wardens

Paid by ffrancis Ratcliffe ye sume of twenty shill^s st^r for ye use of ye poore for ye yeare ending ye 25th Decr 1662 by us Church wardens

Paid by Wm Cordiner ye sume of twenty shill^s st^r for ye use of ye poore for ye yeare ending ye 25th of Decr 1662 by us Church wardens

Paid by Jo Ellison ye sume of foure shill st^r for ye use of ye poore ending ye 25th of Decr 1662 by us

Nicholas Garnett
Lawrance Whiteside

Whereas I John Shorte of Dublin M^{r}chant am justly indebted unto John Rigby of Belfast in the County of Antrim Tanner the full & just summe of twenty & foure pounds 18^s & 6^d sterl curr^t lawfull money of England and for paym^t thereof have assigned him to receive (uppon her bond deliver^d to him) of Mrs Prudence Povey of the said Belfast in the County afores^d ye full summe of twenty & foure *pounds* eighteene shillings & six pence sterl' like curr^t money

of England at or uppon y.ͤ last daye of May 1655   Now yf the saide Prudence
Povey doe not paye or cause to bee paide unto y.ͤ s.ᵈ John Rigby his Execuṭoᵖˢ
admᵖˢ or assignes the saide summe of twenty and foure pounds eighteen
shillings & six pence at yͤ tyme aforesaid I doe hereby in default thereof
promisse & engage to pay or cause to bee paid the said summe of twenty &
foure pounds eighteene shillings and six pence unto the said John Rigby at or
before the last day of June next ensueinge   As witness my hand & Seale this
[last] first of M.ͬ.ch 1654

Signed & sealed per John Shorte

This former bill undͬ the hand & seale of the said John Shorte in the said bill
named was thus

Signed sealed & delivr.ᵈ (and
these words (unto ye s.ᵈ John
Rigby) in the 18ᵗʰ line inter-
lined before the delivery in
the presence of

This Bill enrolled the 25ᵗʰ of Apprill
1656 is accordinge to the originall
Examined by mee

Tho Wareinge
Nicholas Garnet
Hercules Hillman

Richard Wall
Towne Clerk

Be it knowne unto all men by these pͬ.sents that wee S.ͬ David
Cuningham of London Knight and Baronet William Moorehead
of Farnham in the Countye of Surrey gent and S.ͬ David Cuningham
of Robertland in the Countye of Ayre in Scotland Knight and
Baronet doe owe and are bound unto the Right Honorᵇˡͤ James
Lord Viscount of Claneboy in Ireland and James Traill of the
Countie of Downe in Ireland gent the some of Twelve hundred
pounds of good and lawfull money of England to bee paid unto the
said James Lord Viscount of Claneboy and James Traill or either
of them their Execuṭoᵖˢ Administraṭoᵖˢ or assignes unto wͨʰ paymͭ
well & truely to bee made wee bind and oblige us and everie one of
us for himself for the whole joyntly and sevrally and evrie one of
our heires execuṭoᵖˢ and administraṭoᵖˢ firmly by by (*sic*) these pͬ.sents.
[and] Sealed wͭʰ our Seales Dated the twoo and twentith day of July
in the yeare of our Lord God one thousand six hundred fiftie and
twoo

£1,200
Bond for

1652

The Condicion of the obligacion above written is such that whereas the above
named James Lord Viscount Claneboy and James Traill together wͭʰ the
bounden S.ͬ David Cuningham of London Knight and Baronet and William
Moorehead wͭʰ one Ronnan Cuningham of London gent by an obligacon
undͬ their hands & seales bearing date the third daye of June Anno dni 1644 in
the twentith yeare of the late Kinge Charles stand joyntly and severally bound to
Edward Stretchley of the Citie of London gent in one thousand pounds of lawfull
money of England wͭʰ condicon for true paymͭ of the some of five hundred
[pounds] and twentie pounds of like money on the fift daye of December next
ensueinge the date of the same obligacon as by the same more largely
appeares In and by wͨʰ obligacon the said S.ͬ David Cuningham of London
and the said S.ͬ David Cuningham of Robertland and the said William
Moorehead stand bound as aforesaid for the propͬ debt and at the request of
the saide James Viscount Claneboy   And Whereas the said James Viscount
Claneboy for the satisfaction of the said debt costs damage and indepnifyeinge

the said Sr David Cuningham Sr David Cuningham and William Moorehead have deposited in the hands of the saide Sr David Cuningham Sr David Cuningham and Willm Moorehead the six hundred pounds for the use of the said Edward Stretchley Yf therefore the said *S^r* David Cuningham of London William Moorehead and Sr David Cuningham or either of them their or either of their heires executo^{rs} administrato^{rs} or assignes doe well and truely pay or cause to bee paid to the said Edward Stretchley his executo^{rs} adm^{rs} or assignes all the said sum of six hundred pounds of lawfull money of England wth all damage or interest wch either is or shall growe due uppon the same Att the dwellinge house of Henry Arnost situate in Bow lane London uppon or before the fift daye *of* [or before] December next ensueinge the date *hereof* And shall thereuppon alsoe clerely discharge and make voyd the said obligacon and at all tyme and tymes hereafter free the saide James Viscount of Claneboy and James Trayll their heires Execut^{rs} and administrato^{rs} of the same and all hurte damage danger or expence they or anie of them shall or may sustaine thereby And yf the said Sr David Cuningham William Mooreheade and Sr David Cuningham shall on or before the said fifth daye of December next ensueinge deliver or cause to bee delivered the said before recited obligacion to the saide James Viscount Claneboye and James Traill or to Hugh Cuningham gent^l or whom they or anie of them shall appoint to receive cancell and make voyde the same And alsoe yf that untill the true paym^t of the said six hundred pounds and interest & damages & costs of suite as aforesaide to the said Edward Stretchley his Executo^{rs} administrato^{rs} or assignes in manner aforesaide and untill the deliverye upp of the saide bond as aforesaide the said Sr David Cunnigham of Robertland his Executo^{rs} & adm^{rs} shall forbear to aske demand or sue for anie debt or some of money that is or may bee due unto him by or from the said James Viscount of Claneboy his Executo^{rs} or admo^{rs} but shall suffer the same to remaine in his hands untill he bee discharged of and from the said debt due to the said Edward Stretchley & deliverye of the saide bond as aforesaid wthout fraude or covin. That then this p^rsent obligacion shalbee voyde & of none effect or else it shall stand & remaine in full force & vertue

Sealed & delivred in the	D: Cuningham
p^rsence of to the use of	Willm Moorehead
the above named Lord	D: Cuningham
Claneboy & James Traill	
Phineas Tooker	Enrolled & examined by the true copie
Phillipp Rawlens	of the originall the 8th of Octob^r 1656

To All Christian People to whom these p^rsents shall come or may concerne These are to certifie That Thomas Williams Master of the good shipp called the Angell Michall of Dublin came this p^rsent day before me Thomas Wareinge gentl now Sovrane of the Borrough and Towne of Belfast in the Countye of Antrim and did voluntarily take his oath and depose That hee the saide Thomas Williams comeinge from Rochell in France for Ireland wth his said shipp laded wth certaine goods and merchandize belonginge unto one George McCartney of Belfast aforesaid Marchant bound for the said place about the nintenth of Novemb^r last about foure leagues to the southward of Sillye was surprised and taken by a man of warr whose name hee this Depon^t knoweth not but as hee doth conceave by his best Intelligence hee did belonge to Oastend, And hee this Depon^t with his men shipp and goods beinge in restrainte & keepeinge wth the said Man of warr the said Man of Warr tooke out of this Depon^t shipp one pakett of Ribbons one hatt and one hogsheade of wine amountinge to the valew of sixtie seven pounds sterl' or thereabouts wth other goods & merchandize   But the said Master p^{r}tendinge his shipp was of Amsterdam in Holland hee got cleare from the said Man of Warr onelye wth the losse of the goods & merchandize to the valew aforesaid And the said Master beinge arrived wth his said shipp here at Belfast aforesaid charged wth the said goods & merchandize hath voluntarily deposed uppon his oath as aforesaid.   In Testimonie whereof I have hereunto caused the Comon Seale of this saide Towne to be fixed & subscribed my name the fourteenth day of December in y^{e} yeare of our Lord_____

M^{d} that I Richard Wall of Belfast in the Countye of Antrim Towne Clerke of the saide Borrough at the instance and request of Rob^{te} Nevin of Belfast aforesaid Merchant and by the power given unto mee by his letter dated the eightenth day of this instant gave warninge unto John Clugston of Belfast aforesaid Merchant That hee the saide John Clugston should remove out of his now dwellinge house in Belfast aforesaide and delivr upp all his possession in anie shopp backside or backside howses warehowse storehowse garden or anie other buildinge thereunto belonginge wch hee had or enjoyed by lease from Mr John Steawart and Jenet his wief lately called Jenet Nevin widowe relict of Rob^{te} Nevin late of Belfast aforesaide Merchant deceased wherein or unto the saide Rob^{te} Nevin in his life tyme had propright and tytle and wch since his death did acrew and of right belonge unto Rob^{te} Nevin his sonne at and uppon the first daye of Maye wch shall bee in the yeare of our Lord God one thousand six hundred fiftye and eight at wch tyme the saide Clugstons tyme and Terme of in & unto ye p^{r}mises would bee expired ended & determined And the Answer of the saide John Clugston was unto mee that hee the saide John Clugston had had sufficient warning of that before and that it was sufficient warning These persons beinge p^{r}sent ffirst before James Robinson of Belfast aforesaid butcher and the wiefe of Josias Marter of Belfast aforesaid Merchant and afterwards came there in p^{r}son at the tyme of the saide warninge John Correy of Belfast aforesaid Merchant and John Biggart of Belfast aforesaid Merchant whoe did *heare* mee the said Richard Wall give to the saide John Clugston the like warninge again in the behalf of the said Rob^{te} Nevin now liveinge to remove as aforesaide and the saide John Clugston gave answer as aforesaide This was done by mee the_____

Richard Wall
Towne Clerke

M^{d} That at the Court of Assembly 1658   It is ordered by the Sovrane and Burgesses then p^{r}sent   That all such persons whoe have heretofore beene admitted & sworne ffree staplers & ffree Comon^{rs} of the Corporacon and whose Fines were ordered and adjudged accordinge as is expressed in the

Margent unto their names annexed at the saide Court shalbee collected levyed & paid w.thout delay

Willm Leithes 1658 Sov.^r

Jo Leithes Tho Theaker TT Tho Waring John Rigbee

Belfast

　　　　Att an Assembly houlden 1659. William Leathes gentl Sofferaigne, Lt Thomas Theaker Mr George Martin Mr Hugh Doake & Capt Francis Meeke & Burgesses of the Borrough afforesaid then p.^rsent George M'Cartney gent was sworne one of the Burgesses of the said towne according to ye ellection and order at y^e Court houlden the 17th of Septr 1659 and toke y^e oath of a Burgesse accordinge to y^e use and custom of the said Towne and Corporation

Willm Leithes 1659 Sovr.^e

Jo: Leithes

Tho Theaker TT George Martin
Hugh Doake ᕼᕲ his marke

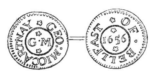

　　　I John Allsinor of the Parrish Yeoman doe acknowledge myselfe to be indebted unto y.^e Soffraigne of the Borrough of Belfast afforesaid ye sume of Forty Shill str to be p.^d upon demand and I doe by these p.^rsents likewise ingage to pay ye anuall Rent of ye said Forty Shill to ye said Soffraigne for ye use of ye poore of ye said parrish for soe long time as ye Forty Shill shall remaine in my hands it being ye will and testam.^t of Thomas Cheaplin whoe left ye same to ye use of ye poore afforesaid at his death In wittness whereof I hereunto sett my hand this 25th of Decr 1659

	his
Witness	John × Allsinor
Robt Leathes	marke

3 Novr 1659　　　　　The oath of a Sargent of ye Mace of Bellfast
　　　　　　　　　　　　　in ye County of Antrim

　　　Yo^u shall sweare that yo^u shall well and truely serve in ye office of a Sargent to this Corporation and all such warrants and p.^rcepts as shall be issued from ye Sofferaigne for ye time being and therein doo yor duty in all and every thinge that belongeth to ye office of a Sargent to ye best of yor skill knowledge and understanding [So help yo^u God] You shall also make due returne of s^d warr.^{ts} & Precepts and not keep the same or any of them in y.^r hands but you shall use y.^r best Endeavour to execute the same & every of them without protraction of time & without fav.^r or affection mallice or evil will

Verses p͟sented to Generall Monck

Advance George Monck & Monck S͟t George shall be
Englands Restorer to Its Liberty
Scotlands Protector Irelands President
1660   Reduceing all to a ffree Parliam͟t
And if thou dost intend the other thinge
Goe on and all shall Crye God save y͟e Kinge

R	R doth Rebellion Represent
V	by V nought els but Villainyes is meant
M	M Murther signifyes all men doe knowe
P	P Perjuryes in ffashion growe
	Thus R and V with M & P
	conjoyn'd, make up our miserie.

The oath of a ffree man
of Belfast in the Countye
of Antrim

Burgus de
Belfast in
Com Antrym

I.   A: B: doe hereby promise That from henceforth I will not doe nor suffer to bee done anie thinge that may bee to the hurte and hindrance of this Corporacon But will advance the profitt and good of the same by the best I may   And that I will from henceforth well and faithfully keepe the secret Counsell of this Towne and Corporacon   And that I will not Conceale or Keepe in my hands or Custodye anie Goods or Merchandize of anie fforrainer or Alien that is not Free within this Corporacon whereby to hinder the good and benefitt of this said Towne   And that I will obey the Sovraigne of this Towne for the tyme beinge and anie other Officer under him att his appointem͟t and comand doeinge their office lawfully.   And that I will bee subject and obedient to such lawfull by Lawes Statutes and Orders w͟c are now legally and orderly established and sett downe for the good and wellfare of the said Towne and w͟c hereafter may bee established for the good and Civill Governm͟t of the same consentaneous and agreeinge w͟t the lawes

[Comon-
wealthe]

and Statutes of this Kingdome.   And that I will not from henceforth sue or ymplead anie Free Burgesse or Free Comon͟r out of the Jurisdiccon of this Court for anie cause this Courte may beare and hould plea w͟t out license of the Lord of the Castle or the Sovraigne of this said Towne for the tyme beinge as longe as I may have indifferent and equall justice and due proceedings in the said Court   Soe helpe you God &c.

The Oath of a ffree Burgess
of Belfast 1660

Yoᵘ are ellected and chosen to be one of the Burgesses of this Borrough and Towne of Bellfast dureing yoʳ good behaviour and civill carriage in the said place.

Yoᵘ shall therefore be readie at yᵉ Comandemᵗ of the Sofferaine of the said Towne for the time being either by himselfe or upon notice given unto yoᵘ by anie his Officers to attend upon the said Sofferaine and him assiste with yoʳ best advice and Councell in anie doubtfull cause or in anie other cause tending to yᵉ good benefitt and proffitt of the same and alsoe for the good and welfaire and peaceable and civill governemᵗ thereof and to yᵉ uttermost of yoʳ Power endevoʳ to defend maintaine and uphould all the ffranchises libtyes and pʳviledgs whatsoever wᶜʰ are now or hereafter shall or may bee by lawfull authority given or granted unto this said Towne and Corporation soe longe as yoᵘ shall continue one of the number of the said Burgesses.

Yoᵘ shall alsoe further doe and execute all other things whatsoever belonging unto yᵉ place of a ffree Burgess of this Corporacon to yᵉ best of yoʳ experience witt and knowledge so helpe yoᵘ God &c.

Memorandum. That yᵉ 24th of January 1660 Capt Meeke then Soveraigne who keept Court that day with severall Burgesses and free Comoneʳˢ of the Corporacon then assembled

there being then a difference depending in y.ᵉ said Courte Between John Stewart March.ᵗ and William Taylor Mercht Whereupon y.ᵉ Court was proceeding and send for y.ᵉ said William Taylor to make answer to yᵉ said suite who retourned answer to yᵉ said Court he would not come unless he was caused by order and thereupon yᵉ Court ordered Tho Bankes sargent to bringe him as may appeare by yᵉ anexed warrant und.ʳ yᵉ Soveraignes hand bearinge date aforesaid by force of wᶜʰ ye said William Taylor appeared and beinge demanded to *enter his* appeare.ˢ & make answer to yᵉ said suite and proceed to a legall tryall he alltogether refused but slighted and contemned yᵉ Court sayeing he had nothing to doe with yᵉ Court nor yᵉ suite with many peremptory and uncivill expressions with threatenings of what he would doe to yᵉ Judges of yᵉ said Court by Law all wᶜʰ he accted in the face of yᵉ said Court whereupon yᵉ Soveraigne & the Burgesses there assembled ordered y.ᵉ said William Taylor to be disfranchised of his freedome in to and of yᵉ said Corporacon and from that time forward to *be* taken as a stranger or allien to yᵉ said Corporacon

Signed by ordʳ
Robᵗ Leathes

Memorandum. That George M'Cartney Burgesse Robert Smith William Reainold Waynwright of London marchant came before me this 18ᵗʰ day off ffebruary 1660 and desired to have enrolled a Letter of Attorney the tenior whereof is as ffolloweth. Know all men by these p̓sents that I James Waynwright of London Esquire have made ordained and in my place putt and constituted And by these p̓sents doe make ordain and in my stead and place putt and constitute my Loving Brother Reginald Waynwright of London marchᵗ my true and Lawfull Attorney for me and in my name and to my use to ask demand leavy sue for recover and Receive by all Lawfull ways and meanes whatsoever, of and from all such person and persons whom it doth shall or may concerne within yᵉ Nations of Scotland and Ireland all such summ and summes of money debts claymes and demands whatsoever wᶜʰ they or any them are indebted and doe truly owe unto me by bond bill specially booke Accompt or by any wayes or meanes whatsoever Giving and by these p̓sents granting unto my said Attorney his substitutes and assignes All my full Power and Authority in exercise of yᵉ premisses All such p̓son or p̓sons doth shall or may concerne their executors Administrators and goods if need shalbee to sue arrest attach seize sequester imprison and condeyme and out of prison to deliver, And to appeare before all and all manner of Judges Justices and Ministers of yᵉ Law, and to compound compromise conclude agree recover and receive & upon recoveries and Receipts or upon and composition other agreemts acquittances or any other Lawfull discharge for me and in my name to make seale and as my deed to deliver And one Attorney or more under him to make substitute and revoke And generally to doe execute prosecute and determine all and every act and acts thing and things whatsoever which in or aboute the premisses shall be needful necessary or convenient as ffully

G

and effectually as I myselfe might or could doe personally holding and allowing for firme and stable all & whatsoever my said Attourney his substitutes and assignes or any of them shall lawfully doe or cause to be done in or about the premisses by virtue of these presents. In witness whereof I the said James Waynwright have hereunto sett my hand and seale this twelvth day of October in ye yeare of our Lord one thousand six hundred ffiftie and nine,

Sealed and delivered in the presence of

John Leman
John Morris
John Burton serv^t

Enroled and Examined agreeing with the originall by me Rob: Leathes cler of the Borrough of Bellfast the day and yeare above said.

James Waynwright

This is acknowledged to be a true copy of the letter of Attorney Witnesse my hand this 8 of March 1660

Reginald Waynwright

Att an Assembly holden ye 17th of Apprill 1660 William Leathes gent Sofferaigne John Leathes Thomas Warring Hugh Doake John Leathes Senior and John Ridgby Burgesses of ye Borrough afforesaid then present William Warring gent *sonn to Thomas Warring* was sworne one of ye Burgesses of ye said Towne according to ye ellection and order at ye Court holden as afforesaid and tooke ye oath of a Burgess according to ye use and custome of ye said Towne and Corporacon

Willm Leithes Sover

Jo: Leithes Tho Waring Hugh HD Doake John Leathes John Rigbee

Att an Assembly holden the fift of May 1660 William Leathes gent Sofferaigne John Leathes his deputy George Martin Thomas Waring Hugh Doake John Leathes senior John Ridgby George M'Cartney and William Warring Burgesses of the Borrough afforesaid then present Edward Reynalls gent was sworne one of the Burgesses of ye said Towne according to ye ellection and order at ye Court holden as afforesaid and tooke ye oath of a Burgesse according to ye use and custome of ye said Towne and Corporacon

Jo Leithes Soveraigne

Hugh HD Doake Geo M'Cartney John Leathes Will: Waring George Martin Tho Waring John Rigbee

Att an Assembly holden the 25th of June 1660 Capt Francis Meeke Sofferaigne John Leathes George Martin Thomas Warring Hugh Doake John Ridgby George M'Cartney

Wm Warring and Edward Reynell Burgesses of yᵉ Borrough of Belfast afforesaid then pᵣ̇sent and upon consideracon had of yᵉ want of a Burgess to make up yᵉ numbᵣ in yᵉ Roome and place of Mr William Leathes deceased Mr Thomas Wallcott was ellected and and (*sic*) sworne one of yᵉ Burgesses of yᵉ said Towne according to yᵉ ellection and order of yᵉ sᵈ assembly afforesaid and tooke yᵉ oath of a Burgesse according to yᵉ use and custome of yᵉ said Towne and Corporacon

Fra Meeke Sufraine

George Martin Hugh HD Doake Tho Waring Geo M'Cartney Willm Waring Edw: Reynell

BY the Sofferaigne and Burgesses of the Borrough

Whereas wee the Sofferaigne and Burgesses by vertue of Letters Pattens to us and our Successors for ever granted by the late Kinge of ever Blessed memory Kinge James have power (at our discretion) upon yᵉ longe absence Misdemenor or death of any Burgess or Burgesses to disfrancis him or them of his or their Burgessᵖ and of any liberty or priviledge he or they may or could enjoye thereby, And whereas wee have seriously considered that Walterhouse Crimble one of the Burgesses of this Corporacon hath removed his habitacon and ben absent from this Corporacon dureing yᵉ time of sixteen yeares last past to yᵉ dammage of [the] of the (*sic*) Corporacon neither is he intended to live amongst *us* and he is likewise Impotent by reason of old age therefore wee doe order and it is hereby enacted that yᵉ said Walterhouse Crimble from and after the day of the date hereof be disfranchised from his Burgesseship and from all rights and previledges thereunto belonging and hereafter to be taken

and deemed as none of the Brotherly Society of this Corporacon and that his place be p^rsently supplied by one of
an honest life and conversation understanding and resident
amongst us   That out of respect and affection wee have and
beare to Gilbert Wye Esqr Stewart to the R^t Honor^{ble} ye Earle
of Donnegall a person qualliffied in all respects as afforesaid
wee have ellected and chossen him the said Gilbert Wye to
be one of the Burgesses of this Corporacon in place and stead
of the said Walterhouse Crimble   Given und^r our hands this
18th day of September in the fourteenth yeare of the Raigne
of our Sofferaigne Lord Charles the Second by the Grace of
God Kinge of England Scotland France and Ireland defend^r of
the faith &c 1662

John Rigbee Soferaine

> Jo: Leathes George Martin Edw Reynell Tho Waring
> Tho Walcot Geo M'Cartney

Att an Assembly held the eighteen day of September in
the fourteenth yeare of the raigne of our Sofferaigne Lord
Charles the Second by the Grace of God Kinge of England
Scotland France and Ireland defender of the faith &c John
Rigby Esqr Sofferaigne, John Leathes George Martin
Thomas Warring Edward Reynells Thomas Wallcott George
M'Cartney William Warring Burgesses of the Borrough of
Belfast afforesaid then p^rsent Gilbert Wye Esq was sworne
one of the Burgesses of the said Towne in the stead and place
of Walterhouse Crimble (who is deposed by order for causes
therein menconed beareing date the day of the date hereof)
according to ellection and ord^r. at y^e Court held afforesaid and
tooke the oath of a Burgesse according to the use and custome
of the saide Towne and Corporacon

John Rigbee Soferaine

> Geo M'Cartney George Martin Jo Leathes Tho
> Waring Edw Reynell Tho Walcot

His Majesties Gracious Letter and Declaration sent to the House of Peers by Sr John Greenvil K^t from Breda and read in the house the first of May 1660

To the Speaker of the House of Peers and to the Lords there assembled
Charles R

Right Trusty and Right well beloved Cosins and Right trusty & well beloved Cosins and trusty and Right well beloved wee greet yo^u well : Wee cannot have a better reason to promise ourselfe an end of our comon sufferings and calamities and that our own just power and authority will with God's Blessing be restored to us, then y^t wee heare yo^u are again acknowledged to have that authority and Jurisdiction which hath allwayes belonged to yo^u by yor birth and the Fundamentall Lawes of the Land : and wee have thought it very fitt and safe for us to call to yo^u for yor help in ye composing the confounding distempers and distractions of ye Kingdome in wch yor sufferings are next to those wee have undergone ourselfe : And therefore yo^u cannot but be the most proper Counsellors [from] for removeing those mischiefs and for preventing the like for ye future How great a trust wee repose in yo^u for the procuring and establishing a Blessed peace and security for ye Kingdome will appeare *to yo^u* by our enclosed Declaration which trust wee are most confident you will discharge with that Justice & and wisdom that becomes yo^u and must allwayes be expected from yo^u and that upon yor experience how one violation succeeds another when ye known Relations and Rulers of Justice are once transgressed yo^u will bee as as (*sic*) Jealous for the Rights of the Crown and for the Honno^r of yor King as for yor selfes and then cannot but discharge yor trust with good success and provide for and establish the Peace Happiness and Honno^r of King Lords and Comons upon that foundation which can only support it and wee shall be all happy in each other : and as the whole Kingdom will blesse God for yo^u all so wee shall hold our Self obliged in a speciall manner to thank yo^u in particular according to ye affection yo^u shall express towards us wee need ye less enlarge to yo^u upon this subject because wee have likewise writ to ye house of Comons wch wee suppose will communicate to yo^u : And wee pray God to blesse yor joint endeavours for ye good of us all and so wee bid yo^u very heartily farewell Given at our Court at Breda, this day of Aprill 1660———————

CHARLES : R

CHARLES, by the Grace of God King of England Scotland France and Ireland defender of the faith &c to all our loveing subjects of what degree or quallity soever, Greeting if the generall distraction and confusion which is spread over the whole Kingdom doth not awaken all men to a desire and Longing that those wounds which have so many yeares together been kept bleeding may be bound up all wee can say will be to no purpose : However after this Long silence we have thought it our duty to declare how much we desire to contribute thereunto and that as we can never give over the hope in good time to obtaine the possession of that R.^t which God and nature hath made our due so wee doe make it our dayly suit to ye divine providence that hee will in compassion to us and our subjects after so long misery and sufferings comitt and putt us into a quiet and Peaceable possession of that our Right with as little blood and damnage to our people as is possible, Nor doe wee desire more to enjoy what is ours than that all our subjects may enjoy what by Law is theirs by a full and entire administration of Justice throughout the Land and by extending our marcy where it is wanted and deserved.

And to ye end that the fear of punishment may not engage any conscious to themselves of what is passed to a p.^rseverance in guilt for the future by opposing the quiet and happiness of their Country in the Restoration both of King Peers and people to their Just Ancient and Fundamentall Rights wee doe by these presents declare that wee doe grant a Free and Generall pardon which wee are ready upon demand to pass under our Great Seal of England to all our subjects of what degree or quallity soever who within fourty days after the publishing hereof shall lay hold upon this our grace and favor and shall by any publick act declare their doeing so. And that they retourn to the Loyalty and obedience of good Subjects (excepting onely such persons as shall hereafter be excepted by Parliam.^t) those only excepted. Lett all our loveing subjects how faulty soever relie upon ye word of a Kinge solemnly given by this present declaracon that noe crime whatsoever committed against us or our Royall Father before the publication of this shall ever rise in Judgment or be brought in question against any of them to the least endamagement of them either in their lives Liberties or Estates or (as far forth as lies in our power) so much as to the prejudice of their Reputations by any Reproch of term of distinction from ye rest of our best subjects wee desireing and ordaining that henceforward all notes discord separation and difference of Parties be utterly abolished among all our subjects whom wee invite and conjure to a perfect union among themselves under our protection for ye resettlement of our Just Rights and theirs in a free Parliam.^t by which upon the word of a Kinge wee will be advised

And because the Passion and uncharitableness of the times have produced severall opinions in Religion by which men are engaged in Parties and animosities against each other which when they shall hereafter unite in a freedom of conversation will be composed or better understood wee doe declare a Liberty to tender Consciences and that no man shall be disquieted or called in question for differences of opinion in religion which doe not disturbe the peace of the Kingdom And that wee shall be ready to consent to such an Act of Parliament as upon mature deleberation shall be offred to us for ye full granting that indullgence.

And because in the continuall distractions of so many yeares and soe many and great Revolutions money grants and purchases of Estates have been made to and by many officers Soldiers and others who are now possessed of the same and who may be lyable to actions at Law upon severall titles wee are likewise willing that all such differences and all things relating to such grants sales and purchases shall be determined in Parliament which can best provide for the just satisfacon of all men who are concerned.

And wee doe further declare that wee will be ready to consent to any Act or Acts of Parliament to ye Purposes afforesaid and for y.^e full satisfaction of all arrears due to y.^e officers and y.^e Souldiers of y.^e Army under y.^e command of Generall Monck and that they shall be retained in our service upon as good pay and conditions as they now enjoy.

Given under our Sign Manual and Privy Signet at our Court at Breda this $\frac{4}{14}$th day of April 1660 in the twelfth year of our Reign

DUBLIN

Reprinted by William Bladen by Special Order Anno Domini 1660

Know yee that I John Leathes of Rathnewgent. in y^e County of Westmeath and one of the Burgesses of this Borrough this seaven and twenyeth day day (*sic*) of May 1660 make claime to ye benefit of y^e exceeding great grace and Mercy held out by his most excellent Majesty Charles y^e Second by y^e Grace of God Kinge of England Scotland France and Ireland defender of y^e Faith &c to all his loving subjects by a declaracon under his signe Manual and privy signett at his Court at Breda $\frac{4}{14}$ of Aprill 1660 and in y^e 12th yeare of his Majestys Reigne and sent to y^e Houses of Peers and Comons in England and Published by order of y^e first of May 1660 and doe with thankefullnesse and Joy of hart lay hould embrace and accept of his Majestys Grace and favour offered therein and doe humbly pray the benefitt thereof. And that this my prayer and acceptance may be recorded as a publiqe Act of mine and entred amongst the Records of this Court And likewise doe owne and acknowledge his Majestie to be Soveraigne Lord and Kinge and Promise to yeald all constant and faithfull obedience to his Majesty As witness my hand

Acknowledged before
Capt ffrancis Meeke
Soveraigne of this
Borrough and Entred
per Robt Leathes
        Towne Clk

Memorandum that I Roger Humphreys of Bellfast afforesaid this fifth day of June 1660 make claime to ye benefitt of y^e exceeding great Grace and Mercy held out by his most excellent Majesty Charles y^e Second by y^e Grace of God King of England Scotland France and Ireland defender of y^e faith &c to all his loveing subjects by a declaracon under his signe Manual and privy signett at his Court at Breda $\frac{4}{14}$ of Aprill 1660 and in y^e 12th yeare of his Majestys Reigne and sent to y^e house of Peers and Comons in England and published by order of y^e first of May last past and doe with thankefullness and Joy of hart lay hold imbrace and accept of his Majestyes Grace and favour offered therein and doe humbly pray the benefitt thereof And that this my prayer and acceptance may be recorded as a publique act of mine and entred amongst the Records of this Court. And likewise doe owne and accknowledge his Majestie to be my Soveraigne Lord and Kinge and Promise to yeald all constant and faithfull obedience to his Majestie As witness my hand

Acknowledged before
Capt ffrancis Meeke   Roger Humfreys
Sofferaigne of this Borrough
and entred per
        Robt Leathes

Memorandum That I William Dix of Bellfast in ye County of Antrim this eight day of June 1660 make claim to ye benefitt of the exceeding great grace and marcy held out by his most excellent Majesty Charles the Second by the Grace of God Kinge of England Scotland France and Ireland defender of y^e Faith &^{c} to all his loveing Subjects by a Declaration under his Signe Manuall and privy signett at his Court at Breda $\frac{4}{14}$ of Aprill 1660 and in y^e 12th yeare of his Maj^{ties} Raigne and sent to y^e houses of Peers and Comons in England and published by order of the first of May last past and doe with thankfullness and Joy of harte lay hould embrace and accept of his Maj^{ties} grace and favour offered therein and doe humbly pray the benefitt thereof And that this my prayer and acceptance may be recorded as a Publique act of mine and entered amongst the records of the Court And Likewise doe owne and acknowledge His Matie to be my Soveraigne Lord and Kinge and promise to yeald all constant and faithfull obedience to his Majestie

As witnesse my hande.

Accknowledged before Capt
ffrancis Meeke Sofferaigne
of ye said Borrough
and entred per me

    Robt Leathes
        Town: Clk

Memorandum That I Robert Leathes of Bellfast in ye County of Antrim this eight day of June 1660 make claime to ye benefitt of y^e exceeding great grace and Marcy held out by his most excellent Majesty Charles y^e Second by y^e Grace of God King of England Scotland France and Ireland defender of y^e Faith &c to all his loveing subjects by a Declaration und^r his signe Manual & privy signett at his Court at Breda $\frac{4}{14}$ of Aprill 1660 and in ye 12 yeare of his Majestyes Raigne and sent to ye house of Peers and Comons in England and published by order of y^e first of May last past and doe with thankfullness and Joy of heart lay hold embrace and accept of his Majesties grace and favour offered therein and do humbly pray the benefitt thereof And that this my prayer and acceptance may be recorded as a publique act of mine and entred amongst the records of this Court And likewise doe owne and accknowledge his Matie to be my Soveraigne Lord and Kinge and Promise to yeald all constant and faithfull obedience to his Majestie

As witness my hand

        Rob Leathes

Accknowledged before
Capt ffrancis Meeke
Soff^{rne} of ye said Borrough
& entred by myselfe

        R. L.

Att an Assembly held for ye Borrough of Belfast the 24th of June 1660 before Captn ffrancis Meeke gent Sofferaigne of ye said Towne and before ye Burgesses of ye same It was ordered by the Sofferaigne and Burgesses afforesaid with ye consent of Arthur Lord-*Visct* Chichester of Carrickfargus and Earle of Donegall (Lord of ye Castle of Bellfast

afforesaid) that no Burgess of yᵉ said Borrough from and
after yᵉ date hereof that is or shall bee ellected and sworne
Sofferaigne of yᵉ Borrough afforesaid dureing the time of
his Soveraigneship shall sell by retaile in his house any
Wines of what kinde soever or any Beere Ale or Aquavite or
keepe entertainemᵗ in his house *dureing* his office afforesaid
upon paine of one hundred pound to be levied upon his goods
or chatles to and for yᵉ use of yᵉ Corporacon and yᵉ said
Burgesse soe offending to be disfranchised of his Burgessᵖ?

Fra Meeke Sufraine   I consent to this
                                Donegall

Tho Waring Geo M'Cartney Will: Waring Edw:
Reynell George Martin Hugh Doake HD his marke
Tho Walcot

Memorandum that James Smith of Ballyvally in yᵉ Parrish of Sea Pattrick
and County of Downe and Gilbert McGarragh of yᵉ Bellfast afforesaid
came before me and desired to have enrolled a bargaine of saile of his yᵉ said
James Smiths and Jane his wiffe right in [his] *all their* houses lands and
tennemᵗˢ in Bellfast made to yᵉ saide Gilbert McGarragh as follow in these
words.   Memorandum That I James Smith of Ballyvally in yᵉ parrish of
Seapatrick in yᵉ County of [Antrim] Downe yeoman for divers good causes and
consideracons me thereunto moveing but especially for and in consideracon of
ye sume of thirty three pounds sterling to bee paid as followeth by Gilbert
McGarragh of ye Towne and parrish of Bellfast and County of Antrim have
and doe by these presents for me my Executors Administrators and Assˢ by
and with yᵉ consent of Jane my wife whoo doth hereunto subscribe bargained
sould assigned and sett over unto him yᵉ said Gilbert McGarragh his
Executors Administrators and Assˢ all our Right title interest claime and
demand wee have had or should have in and to ye Lands tenemᵗˢ hereditamᵗˢ
and appurtenances to them belonging Now in ye hands of him the said
Gilbert, Thomas Postley and John Thomson of Bellfast and all other claymes
and demands whatsoever I or my wife have to any tenemᵗ or professions
whatsoever in Bellfast afforesaid from this time forth and for ever he yᵉ said
Gilbert m'Garragh his Executoʳˢ Administratoʳˢ and Assˢ Yealding and payeinge
unto me my Executors Administrators or Assˢ ye sume of thirty and
three pounds ster. aforesaid whereof I accknowledge to have received in
part paymᵗ ye sume of five shillˢ and six pence in Gold and yᵉ remainder
to be paid at two severall paymtˢ viz yᵉ sume of sixteen pounds tenn
shillˢ to be paid [as afforesaid] to me or my assˢ upon demand and
ye other part being ye sume of sixteen pounds tenn shillˢ str to be
paid as afforesaid at or before ye fourth day of August next ensueinge the
date hereof wᶜʰ in ye whole makes ye sum of thirty three pounds afforesaid
being ye full consideracon afforesaid and I and my Executors to leave him ye
said Gilbert his Executors Administrators and Assˢ free from all rents arrears
of rents & dutys due to yᵉ Lord Chichester out of yᵉ premisses   Provided
allways that ye said Gilbert and his Assˢ make good those tennents interest
that now live on ye premises they makeing their said interest good to clayme ye
same   And it is further agreed between me yᵉ said James and the said Gilbert

McGarragh that I doe engage that upon ye payment of ye first sume specified herein to deliver to him ye said Gilbert or his Ass^s ye grand Lease under ye hande and seale of Edward Lord Chichester of ye premisses and all other writings concerning ye same he ye said Gilbert giveing a Bond for ye last paym^t of ye said money accordinge [to ye said Bargain and to do or endeavour with ye Land Lord to Procure a Reversion for ye said Gilbert and for his Ass^s of ye Premises. In witness whereof I have hereunto set my hand and seal this 21st of May 1660

Enrolled and Examined according   James Smyth
to the originall this 10th of August 1660
by Mee Rob Leathes Town Ck] to these p^r.sents and I doe engage to goe with him ye said Gilbert before the Lord Chichest^r and thereto accknowledge ye said Bargaine and to doe my Indeavour with ye said Lord to procure a Reversion for ye said Gilbert and his Ass^s of ye premisses   In witness whereof I have hereunto sett my hand and seale this 21st day of May 1660

Signed sealed and delivered   James Smith
  in ye p^r.sents of   Jane Smith
John Stewart
James Stalker
Robt Leathes

  Enrolled and examined
  according with the originall
  10th of August 1660

      Robt Leathes

      Know all men by these p^r. sents That I Thomas Christian of Liverpoole in ye County of Lancaster Marchant doe owe and Promise to pay unto Thomas Warren of Belfast in ye County of Antrim March^t the full and Just sume of fifty and six pounds of currant and Lawfull money of and in England to be paid to the Said Thomas Warren his heirs Executors administrators or ass^s upon demand for paym^t whereof I the said Thomas Christian afforesaid doe firmely by these p^r.sents bind myselfe my heirs Executors Administrators or Assignes in ye above said sume of fifty and six pounds   Witness my hand and Seale the seaven and twentyth day of May one thousand six hundred sixty and one In the thirteenth yeare of the Raigne of our Soveraigne Lord Kinge Charles the Second

      The condicon of this obligacon is such that if the above bounden Thomas Christian his heirs Executors Administrators or Ass^s doe pay or cause to be paid unto Thomas Warren his heirs Execut^{ors} Administrat^{ors} or Assignes upon demand the sum of eight and twenty pounds of Lawfull English money then this obligacon to be voyd otherwise to stand in full power force and vertue Witness my hand and Seal the seaven and twentieth day of May 1661

Signed sealed and delivered   per me Thomas Christian
  in ye p^r.sence of us

      William Stacley   Enrolled and exam, agreeing
Daniel DC Christians marke   with ye originall by me

                                             Robt Leathes
                                          this 22^d of ffeb^r 1661

M.ᵈ That William Stacley and Daniell Christian came before me John Rigby Sofferaigne of this Towne and Borrough of Belfast where was produced to them a bill obligator und.ʳ ye hand and seale of Thomas Christian to wᶜʰ they were witnesses (the above enrolm.ᵗ being a true and p'feict coppy examined as afforesaid of yᵉ said Bill) and they declared upon their corporall oaths that they did see ye said Thomas Christian signe seale and deliver ye said Bill to ye above said Thomas Warring for his use ye
of ffeb.ʳ 1661   John Rigbee
                                                              Sofraine

Know all men by these p.ʳsents that I John Egelsham of Bellfast in ye County of Antrim within ye Kindom of Ireland M.ʳchant doe owe and stand Indebted unto Lawrance Breeres of Liverpoole in the County of Lancast.ʳ Marc.ᵗ the sume of thirty one pounds fifteene shillings six pence due to be paid unto yᵉ said Lawrance Breeres his heires or assignes att or before the first of May next ensuinge for wᶜʰ payment well and truely made I bind mee my heirs Execut.ᵒʳˢ And administrat.ᵒʳˢ firmely by these p.ʳsents in the sume of sixty one pounds ster   Asse witnesse my hand and seale the 16ᵗʰ of ffebruary Anno Dni 1660

Signed sealed and delivered   John Egelsham
   in ye p'sence of us

     Tho Christian
     Jo.ⁿ Starkie
     George Stewart

Mr Eglesham I pray pay the within sume unto Mr Tho Warring I havinge Received the vallue in goods pray faile not to pay him upon demand the bond being due the first of May   I doe not doubt of yo.ʳ p'formance I rest

                    Yo.ʳ loveing friend
                                            Tho Christian

I doe hereby oblidge myselfe my Execut.ᵒʳˢ Administrat.ᵒʳˢ or ass.ᵗ to pay unto Laurance Breeres of Liverpool mar.ᵗ att or upon first of May next ensue-ing the sume of foure pounds tenn shills str as wittness my hand and seale the 18th day of ffebruary Anno Dni 1660

Signed sealed and delivered   John Egelsham
   in ye p.ʳsents of
     Thomas Buck

Mr Eglesham I desire to pay the above some according as beefore desired and Mr Warrings receipt shall be yo.ʳ discharge from yo.ʳ loving friend

                                            Tho Christian

Enrolled and examined
according to the originall
by me Rob.ᵗ Leathes
   This 22nd of ffeb.ʳ 1661

Att an Assembly of yᵉ Soveraigne and Burgesses held for the Corporacon this 24th day of January 1662   Peirce Welsh shoomaker one of yᵉ ffreemen of this Corporacon being called

before yᵉ said Soveraigne & Burgesses to make answer for
his misdemeanor comitted agˢᵗ yᵉ Soveraigne where upon
debate of yᵉ matter yᵉ said Peirce Welsh was found guilty of
yᵉ said misdemeanor that is to say that he yᵉ said Peirce
Welsh being before yᵉ Soveraigne yesterday yᵉ 23rd instant
about some differance between him yᵉ said Peirce and his
man where yᵉ said Peirce by his words slighted and contemned
yᵉ Soveraigne and his officers and their authority saying he
would not yeald any obedience to him or them casting at
nought yᵉ oath he had *taken* upon his admition to his ffree-
domship wherein he became bound by the said oath to yeald
all obedience to yᵉ Soveraigne & his officers and although
yᵉ Law of this Kingdom is strickt in those cases for punishing
of offendʳˢ yett yᵉ Soveraigne hath remitted yᵉ strictness of it
and only have disfranchised him yᵉ said Peirce Welsh of his
Freedom and prevellidges of this Corporacon and ordered
that he shall be comitted to Prison there to remaine 24 hours
or to pay for yᵉ use of the Corporacon yᵉ sume of tenn shills
ster   Therefore it is hereby ordered & enacted by yᵉ Soveraigne and Burgesses now assembled that he yᵉ said Pierce
Welsh shall be disfranchised of his Freedom & previledge
aforesᵈ and to undergoe yᵉ Imprisonmᵗ or pay yᵉ sume afforesaid and this undᵣ our hands the day & yeare afforesaid.

Geo M'Cartney
Soveraigne

Tho Warring

Jo Leathes
Hugh ᴴᴰ Doake

this 5th of Febᵣ 1662

It is this day ordered by yᵉ Soveraigne & Burgesse upon
yᵉ peticon & humble [peticon] submission of him yᵉ said
Peirce Welsh that he the said Peirce be restored to his
former priveleidge of this Corporacon notwithstanding our
former order

Memorandum That whereas Andrew Loyd of Dublin marcht did putt
aboard ye Mary of Greenock in Scotland Thomas Macombe Master eighteen
barrells and firkins and eight boxes directed to Mr. Thomas Warring of Belfast
wᶜʰ accordingly was delivered to ye said Thomas Warring but upon weight of
ye boxes of Tabbaco and other Caske there was found wanting ye number of
seaventeen pound and twelve ounces of neat Tabbaco according to ye bill of
particulars sent to ye said Thomas Warring of yᵉ goods afforesaid   Therefore
at ye desire of yᵉ said Thomas Warring ye said Thomas Macombe and Robert
Wilson both of ye Vessessell *Company* afforesᵈ made[the] oath before John Rigby
Esqᵣ Sofferaigne of the Borrough afforesaid that they nor any belonging to

ye said Vessell did to their Knowledge deminish or imbessill any of y.ᵉ said Tobacco above y.ᵉ vallue of six pence str but as they rec.ᵈ ye same aboard so they delivered ye same to ye said Thomas Warring w.ᶜʰ ye Thomas Warring desired might be recorded this 8th of Apr 1662

Entered by

Rob.ᵗ Leathes Towne Clerk

TT an Assembly of y.ᵉ Sofferaigne and Burgesse held for y.ᵉ Corporacon this 24th day of June 1662 it was ordred and is hereby established   Whereas there have been sessed & applotted upon y.ᵉ Inhabitants of the Towne and quarters of Bellfast severall sumes of money for severall uses of y.ᵉ said Towne and quart.ʳˢ as may appeare from y.ᵉ time that ffrancis Meeke entred into y.ᵉ office of Sofferaigne of this Corporacon to this day and that by y.ᵉ retourne of y.ᵉ Collect.ᵒʳ [are in arreare] severall of y.ᵉ said Inhabitants are in arreare [of] y.ᵉ said Sesses   That y.ᵉ said severall sessesse soe in arreare *be* by distresse or otherwise collected and brought into y.ᵉ hands of y.ᵉ Sofferaigne for y.ᵉ time being and that y.ᵉ Sofferaigne for y.ᵉ time being by his warrant und.ʳ his hand from time to time cause y.ᵉ said assessem.ᵗ to be collected and brought in as afforesaid for y.ᵉ use afforesaid

John Rigbee Sofraine

Fra: Meeke Tho Walcot Edw Reynell Hugh ᚼD Doake Tho Waring Geo M'Cartney

Yo.ᵘ and every of yo.ᵘ shall sweare that [yo.ᵘ and every of yo.ᵘ] for y.ᵉ terme of one whole yeare begining from y.ᵉ 9th of Oct.ʳ 1662 *yo.ᵘ if yo.ᵘ soe long* ———— shall duly and truly execute y.ᵉ office of overseers of y.ᵉ Markett [on the Mark]

accordinge to such Rules Articles and Instructions as shall be given yo.ᵘ in charge according to yo.ʳ best skill knowledge and understanding Soe help yo.ᵘ God in Christ

Daniell Christian
John Martin Marchᵗ. } Overseers of ye Markett sworne
Arthur Houghton

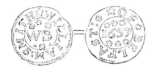　　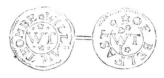

    Know all men by these pʳsents that I John Chrichton marcht in Belfast doe by vertue of one Comission to me granted by Mr. John Hudson, marcht owner of ye Unicorne of Wirewatter sell and dispose unto William Smith William Thombe Hugh Eccles and Michaell Biggar marcht in ye afforesaid Corporacon all and wholy the afforesᵈ Shipp with tackell furniture and other necessaryes conform to an Invoyce produced and doth oblige myselfe my heires Executors and Assˢ to warrant and harmlesse keep the fforesaid Buyers free from all taxes claimes rights or titles or any other trouble whatsoever that any person or persons may alledge after the delivery of the said ship and further obleidge myselfe as afforesaid to make delivery of her at or before ye first day of november next ensueing the date hereof inconveeniencie of wind and weather and all hassards whatsoever being exceipted, for wᶜʰ Ship the fforesaid marchants doth oblige themselves joyntly and severally their heires executᵒʳˢ or Assˢ to thankfully pay or cause to be paid unto John Hudson and partners their heires executᵒʳˢ or Assˢ ye full and just sume of six hundreth and eighteen pounds sterling currant money of England at two severall paymᵗˢ it is to say the one moyetye thereof at or before yᵉ first day of March next ensueing the date hereof the other halfe or moyetye at or before ye first day of July next following wᶜʰ will be in the yeare of our Lord one thousand six hundred and sixty three yeares to which promisses both parties hath Interchangeably sett their hands and seales this second of October Anno Dom 1662

Witnesse pʳsent
  John Stewart
  James Biggar

                                       William Smith
                                       William Thom
                                       Hugh Eccles
                                       Michaell Biggar
                                       John Creichton

    Enrolled and examined according to the originall per Robᵗ Leathes this 24th of Octʳ 1662 R.L.

            By the Soveraigne of the Borrough of Bellfast and one of His Majᵗⁱᵉˢ Justices of the Peace for yᵉ County of Antrim

    These are to certifie all whom it may concerne that the Bearer hereof John Creichton marcht and part owner of ye good ship called the Unicorne of Belfast afforesaid is a ffree Dennisson of this Kingdom of Ireland borne in ye County of Tyrone and is an Inhabitant and free comoner and Marchant of the Staple of the Borrough of Bellfast afforesaid all wch I certifie   as witnesse my hand and seale of ye said Corporacon this 26th of December 1662.

Enrolled and Ex: George M'Cartney
    per Robt Leathes   Soveraigne

By George m'Cartney Esqre Soveraigne of the Borrough of Belfast and one of
    his Mat^{ies} Justices of Peace for the County of Antrim

These are to testifie to all whom it may or shall concerne that William
Harwood quarterpart owner of the ship called the North Star of Bellfast came
before me the day of the date hereof and in ye p^rsence of William Smith
William Thom and William Moore of Bellfast afforesaid Marchants and there
freely declaired and accknowledged (notwithstanding he the said William
Harwood in his owne name had bought from Claies Pieters Wittepart of
Amsterdam in Holland one vessell or shipp called a Buÿs shipp with masts
yards sailes rops cables and ancors and all other things to her belonging
burden about fourscore tunn as may more at large appeare by ye anexed
Instrum^t of writing Subscribed by John Van Wyning notary Publique in
Amsterdam afforesaid) that there doth but belong and of right appertaine to
ye said William Harwood only one quarter parte of ye said ship now called
ye North Star of Bellfast,   And the other three quarter parts of ye said
ship is properly and doth belong unto William Smith William Thom and
William Moore afforesaid whoe were and are part owners with the said
William Harwood in bueying the said ship and by their factor according to
their severall and respective shares and proporcons furnished him with money
soe to doe and likewise ye said William Harrwood with ye afforesaid owners
desired and requested yf it might be certified he the said William Harrwood
hath but right and title to one quarter part of ye said vessell or ship and noe
more and that he neither can or will claime any other interest or title in y^e
said ship but ye said quarter part all wch I testifie to be true   As witnesse my
hand and comon seale of the Corporacon afforesaid this thirtyth day of
October Anno dom 1662

                                                      Geo : m'Cartney
Enroled and examined   Soveraigne
according to ye originall
per Robt Leathes
        Towne Clerke

Know all men by these p^rsents :   Whereas William Harwood late Master
of ye good shipp called ye Golden Star als the North Star of Bellfast hath for
and in consideracon of ye sume of three score and eight pounds st^l. to him
paid sould ye quarter part of ye said shipp to William Smith William Thom
and William Moore of Belfast afforesaid marcht^s and whereas by vertue of y^e
annexed letter of Attourney made to me James Sparkes of Bellfast afforesaid
march^t to sell and dispose of ye fourth parte of ye said quarter part wch doth
belong to Cornelis Vander Vere and Thomas Prettyman of Amsterdam   I
therefore in pursuance of ye said letter of attourney and for and in consideracon of ye sume of seaventeen pounds ster to me in hand [had] paid by
William Harwood afforesaid doe by these p^rsents for me and the said Cornelis
Vander Vere and Thomas Prettyman and their ass^s allow condisend fully
agree and confirme ye saide bargaine and saile made by ye said William
Harwood of ye quarter part afforesaid the fourth of ye quarter part afforesaid
(included) to ye said William Smith William Thom and William Moore affore

said and doe hereby ingage myselfe to save indempnifie and keepe harmlesse the said William Harrwood and his ass⁵ of and from yᵉ said Cornelis Vander Vere & Thomas Prettyman and their executoʳˢ administratoʳˢ and ass⁵ for or by reason of ye saile of ye said sixteen part of ye said *shipp*   In witness whereof I have hereunto sett my hand and seale the thirteenth day of December in yᵉ. yeare of our Lord God one thousand six hundred sixty two 1662

Signed sealed and   James Sparkes
delivered in yᵉ pᵗsence of

    Geo : m'Cartney
       Soveraigne
       Mic Bigger
       Robᵗ : Leathes

      Enroled and Examined according
        to ye originall per Robᵗ Leathes

Att an Assembly held this 7th January 1663 by the Soveraigne and Burgesses of the Borrough afforesᵈ it is this day ordered That if William Taylor marchᵗ who for offences by him comitted agsᵗ ye Sovʳᵉ & Burgesses was disfranchised of his freedomeˢᵖ. of this Corporacon doe not before ye next Court of assembly to be held for ye Corporacon afforesᵈ submitte & confesse his error that he hath comitted agsᵗ them shall for ever hereafter be disenabled to be admitted a Comoner & free marchᵗ of yᵉ staple of this Borrough

              Signed by order

                  Robᵗ Leathes

Stet

TT an Assembly held for ye Burrough of Bellfast this 7th day of January 1663 & by and with y.ᵉ consent of the Rt Honno^{ble} the Earle of Donnegall Lord of the Castle of Bellfast before George m'Cartney Esq Soveraigne of the Borrough of Bellfast and before ye free Burgesses of the same   That whereas dayly complaintes [is] are made by severall Inhabitants of the said Borrough that great anoyance is comitted by the Butchers of this Towne by killing and slaughtering of Catle they suffer the Blood and Garbage of their slaughter houses, some to lye in ye streets & other parte to run into severall channells and ditches of this Towne to the corruption and putrefaccon of the River and anoyance of their neighbours by reason of the stinke and evill and infectious smell (that if not timely prevented) will by all likelyhood bringe some Ruinous and pestellentiall desease amongst yᵉ Inhabitants, which for the future that care may be taken and such enormityes cured,   It is ordered and by and with the consent affores^d it is hereby enacted that if any Butcher or Butchers or any other person whatsoever shall from and after the date hereof slaughter or kill or cause to be slaughtered or killed any catle of what kinde soever within this Towne of Belfast without they or any of them soe doeing shall carry or cause to be carryed the same day all yᵉ Blood and Garbage of such beasts or catle soe killed or slaughtered twenty yards beyon ye full sea marke every such Butcher or other person offending herein shall for every offence pay twenty shillings sterling to be levied imediatly by distresse or otherwise as is accustomed &c

Will: Waring

Geo M'Cartney Sovraigne
Tho Walcot   Edw Reynell   Tho Waring   Gill^t
Wye   George Martin   John Leathes   Joh Rigbee
Jo Leythes   Hugh ᚻD Doake

Stet   7 Jan 1663

Att the Assembly held yᵉ 7th of January affores^d for the Corporation afforesaid by and with yᵉ consent of the R^t Honor^{ble} yᵉ Earle of Donegall it is ordered and enacted that if any person or persons shall from and after yᵉ date hereof incumber leave or cause to be left upon any of the Streets and Laÿns of this Towne of Bellfast any timber carts, cars,

H

hoggsheads barrells or other caske full or empty or any other thing of what quality soever without leave first had and obtained from yᵉ Sovraigne of yᵉ Borrough afforesᵈ for yᵉ time being soe to doe and that to be granted in cases of necessity as yᵉ Sovraigne shall allow of every such person or persons offending herein shall pay for every offence tenn shillˢ ster   And it is further ordered that all person or persons within the Towne being Masters of familyes or tennants liveing in any house or houses or that useth or occupieth any shopp, seller, warehouse, storehouse, or any place or ground (though waste) fronting upon any of the Streets or Lanes afforesaid shall every week twice that is to say on Wednesday and Saturday sweepe and make clean or cause to be swept and made clean, his or their part or porcion of the street that belongeth to such house or houses shopps sellers warehouses storehouses or any other place or places respectively and if any such person or persons shall neglect or refuse soe to doe every such person [shall] shall pay twelve pence ster for every offence

A bye Law

Geo: mᶜCartney Sovraigne

George Martin   Tho Waring   Tho Walcot   Edw: Reynell   Hugh ᕼD Doake   John Leathes   John Rigbee   Jo: Leathes   Gillᵗ Wye   Will: Waring

1663

TT ye assembly held ye 7th January afforesᵈ for ye Corporacon afforesaid by and with ye consent of ye Rt Honorbˡᵉ ye Earle of Donegall it is ordered that every person or persons shall build up or cause to be builded up and topt ye bankes of yᵉ River of this Towne of Bellfast with brick or stone and lime above yᵉ streets or Pavemᵗˢ such hight as some parte of yᵉ said River wall *is*[are] allready made and ye same to be compleated and finished before the last day of June next ensueing ye date hereof and every person or persons that is or shall be concerned to build up ye Banke of yᵉ said River and that shall neglect or refuse soe to doe shall pay tenn shills ster for every offence to be imediatly levyed by distresse or otherwise as is accustomed &c

George: M'Cartney Sovraigne

George Martin   Jo: Leathes   Tho Waring   Tho Walcot   Edw: Reynell   Hugh ᕼD Doake   John Leathes   John Rigbee   Gillᵗ Wye   Will: Waring

ATT an Assembly held for yᵉ Corporacon this 14th of April 1664 by yᵉ Sovraigne and free Burgesses by and with yᵉ consent of ye Rt Honorᵇˡᵉ yᵉ Earle of Donegall it is ordered that Hugh Eccles marct shall have liberty to make a Bridge over ye River of Belfast before his new howse soe broad as a coach or a wheel car may go over without molestacon hinderance or interuption of any person or persons whatsover and further it is enacted that any person or persons inhabitants of this Towne shall and may have Liberty to build and erect bridge or bridges over ye River afforesaid first haveing and obtaining ye consent afforesaid

Geo: MᶜCartney Sovraigne

Edw: Reynell Hugh Doake ꟼD his mark Gillᵗ Wye Will Warring Jo: Leathes Tho Walcot John Leathes

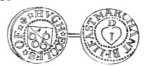

Know all men by these presents That I Robert Barrow of ye Cittie Dublin esqʳ doe owe and stand justly indebted unto Rebecca Parkinson of Bellfast in ye County of Antrim widdow the just and full sume of two hundred pounds of current money of and in England to be paid unto the said Rebecca Parkinson or to her certaine Attourney her Executoʳˢ Administatʳˢ or assˢ for ye paymᵗ whereof well and truly to bee made and performed I binde myselfe my heirs executors and administrators in ye whole and every part firmly by these pʳˢents Signed with my hand and sealed with my seale this eight and twentieth day of September one thousand six hundred fifty and seven

The Condition of the above written obligacon is such That if the above bounden Robert Barrow his heirs Executᵒʳˢ and Administratᵒʳˢ and every of them their and every of their *(sic)* heirs executᵒʳˢ and Administratᵒʳˢ shall well and truly content sattisfie pay or cause to be well and truly contented sattisfied and paid unto the above named Rebecca Parkinson or to her certaine attorney her Executoʳˢ administrators or assˢ the full and just sume of one hundred pounds of good and lawfull money att ye now dwelling house of Mr. Will *Dix* in Bellfast att or upon the twenty ninth day of September wᶜʰ shall be in ye yeare one thousand six hundred fifty and eight att one whole and entire payment without fraude or further delay That then this present obligacon to be voyd and of none effect or else to remaine in full fforce power and effect in Law

Signed sealed and delivered in ye pʳsence of us
  Sam Bonnell ⎫
  John Benson ⎬
  Wm Dix ⎭

Rob Barrow

Enroled and examined according to ye originall this 11th June 1664 per Robᵗ Leathes

By the Sovraigne and Burgesses of the Corporacon
of Bellfast Assembled yᵉ 25th June 1664

HEREAS there hath benn for a longe
time past great want of a Court House
or Towne Hall for this Corporacon
whereby the decency Authority and well
Governing of this Burrough hath received
prejudice and determᵗ. both in ye body
Corporate and Politique [even to yᵉ
anihillating of that Antiquity Splendor
and Majesty wherewith it has been adorned] wherefore
wee have in Councell determined and decreed that such
decayes and ruins shall be repaired and to that end [did
place] *have* given in charge to ye Grand Jury in Hillary
Terme 1663 to [present] inquire and present ye yearly
charge and repaire of ye Court House Lett unto ye
Corporacon by ye now Soveraigne wᶜʰ Jury by their
pʳsentmᵗ ye 23rd of March 1663 hath thought fitt &
determined under their hands that ye sume of five pounds
per annum be paid to ye Sovraigne for ye said Court House
soe longe as it shall be for ye Towns use and ye sume of
be likewise paid him to putt it in repaire wᶜʰ

afterwards he is soe to maintaine Therefore wee doe
hereby order that a warrant doe imediately issue from ye
Soveraigne for Applotting and leving of ye said sume
of Tenn pounds being for two years rent ending att
Michaellmas next ensueing as alsoe for ye sume of
in consideracon of ye repairs with ye sume of
for his Maj^{ties} Armes to be in ye said Courthouse wch said
severall sumes is to be applotted and levied only of and
from ye [ffree] Soveraigne ffree Burgesses free Comoners
and march^t staplers of this Borrough and if any person or
persons shall refuse to pay his equall proporcon of ye said
severall sumes according to his or their capacity and
abilityes that then ye Soveraigne for ye time being is
hereby Authorised and Impowered by warrants from time
to time to levy ye said assessm^t by way of distresse or
otherwise of each person soe refusing and the same to
apprize and sell and convert to ye uses afforesaid retourning
ye overplus to ye owner if any be and that ye said sume of
five pounds yearly be continued to ye said Soveraigne for
ye said Court house soe long as ye same shall be for ye use
of this Corporacon to be assessed levied and paid as
afforesaid dated ye 25th of June 1664

By George M'Cartney Esqr Soveraigne and ye free Burgesse of ye Borrough of Bellfast

HEREAS there hath benn a longe time past great
want of a Court House or Town Hall for this
Corporacon of Bellfast whereby the decency of
this Borrough hath rec^d prejudice and determ^t
both in ye body Corporate & Pollitique wherefore wee have
in councell determined and freely consented that whereas
George M'Cartney now Soveraigne of Bellfast affores^d hath
procured leave and p'mission of ye R^t Honor^{ble} ye Earle of
Donegall that ye upper parte of those Sellers next ye
Markett place wch ye said Soveraigne now rents of ye said
Earle and hath rented for some years last past shall be
made use of as a Court house as it hath benn in ye yeare
1663 and this p'sent yeare 1664 dureinge his Lorp^s pleasure
and whereas ye said Soveraigne hath upon his own Charge
made a paire of Stayres to ye said House and adorned it
with his Maj^{ties} Armes and caused Seats both necessary and
convenient for ye affores^d use of ye s^d Corporacon wee doe
therefore according to ye p'sentment of ye Grand Jury

dated ye 23rd March 1663 & ye Judgem^t of workmen at ye charge wch. ye said Soveraigne hath disbursed for his Maj^ties Armes and ye p'ticulars affores^d y^t ye sume of twenty pounds sixteen shill^s & nine pence str to be forthwith levied upon ye Soveraigne free Burgesses and Comonality of ye s^d Corporacon and paid to ye s^d Soveraigne and that ye Roofe of ye s^d Court house to be repaired at ye charge of ye said now Soveraigne [chargd] dated ye 30th. of June 1664

Geo: m'Cartney Soveraigne

Edw: Reynell   John Leathes   Hugh Doake HD his mark   Will: Waring   Gill^t Wye   Jo: Leithes   John Rigbee

A By Law for y^e Erecting and keepeing in Repaire
y^e Court or Markett house or Towne Hall

Att an Assembly held the   day of   1665, Edward Reynells Esqr then Soveraigne of the Borrough of Bellfast By and with the Consen^t of the R^t Honble Arthur Earle of Donegall Lord of the Castle of Bellfast and by the Soveraigne and Burgesses of ye Borrough afforesaid it is ordered and for a By Law for ever to continue   In consideration that ye Inhabitants of Mallon ffall and dunmury and part of the parish of Coole by their representatives the Grand Jury at a Court Leete for the said mannor consente to pay towards the Erecting and building up a Court house and Markett house in this Corporation as by ye p^r.sentm^t may appeare the said Inhabitants of Mallon ffall and Dunmurry with part of the parish of Coole haveing allready paid part of theire proporcion and paying the Remainder according to yᵉ Sesse made thereupon That ye Inhabitants of the said Mallon ffall and dunmurry with part of the parish of Coole soe many of them as are within the mannor of Bellfast shall have their owne proper goods brought into the Towne, Tole and Custome free usually paid att ye gates of the said Towne and noe other   Provided allwayes that noe person an Inhabitant of any of the places afforesaid by pretence or coloure of the liberty afforesaid shall at any time owne any fforriners goods whereby the Custome of the said Towne be Lessened That then any person against whom any such thinge shall be proved before ye Soveraigne of the said Borrough for the time being by the oath of one wittnesse shall loose the benefitt of the freedom afforesaid and forfeit ye sume of forty shills ster to be levied upon the goods and chatles of the person offending and to be imployed as afforesaid And Provided allwayes that all persons inhabiting of any of the places afforesaid shall yearely and every yeare pay their severall and respective proportions of money towards the repaire of the said [house] Court house and Markett house from time to time as often as the same *shall* be needful and Necessary

Stet

At an Assembly of the Soveraigne and Burgesses held for the Corporacon of Belfast the fourth day of January 1665 Edward Reynell Esqʳ the Soveraigne by and with the consent of the Right Honoᵇˡᵉ Arthur Earle of Donegal Lord of the Castle of Belfast. It is ordered established and enacted that whereas from time to time several sumes of money have heretofore been received by the Soveraignes from ffree Comoners of this Corporacon and by the late Rebellion and other revolucions hapening for severall yeares last past noe accompt hath beene given of the same   And forasmuch as Mr John Rigby George MꞆCartney Esqʳ and Mʳ William Waring for and on the behalfe of his father late deceased are ready to give an Accompt of w.^{t.} moneys were received in their times.   That from henceforth every Soveraigne that shall succeed in the place and office of Soveraigne of the Borrough of Belfast aforesayd shall have full power and authority with the assistance of the major part of the Burgesses (within one month after he shall be sworne Soveraigne) to call the p.^rceeding Soveraigne to an accompt of all such sumes of money as were received in his time of and from any ffreeman or given by any other person to be employed for the good of this Corporacon and how disbursed and disposed to the use aforesayd.   And if that any Soveraigne shall happen to dye within the time of his being sworne Soveraigne that then it shall and may be lawfull to and for the succeeding Soveraigne to call and cause the Executors or administrators of the Soveraigne that shall soe happen to dye as aforesayd to give a true and just accompt of all and every such sume or sumes of money as shall be received or disposed of as aforesayd any act order or by Law of this Corporacon at any time or times heretofore made published or established to the contrary in anywise notwithstanding

Edw Reynell Sovraigne
Sovraigne

John Leathes	Tho Walcot	George McCartney
Jo Leathes	George Martin	George : McCartney
John Rigbee	Gill.^t Wye	

Stet

Att an Assembly of the Soveraigne and Burgesses held for the Corporacon of Belfast the fourth day of January 1665 in the time of Edward Reynell Esqr then Soveraigne by and with the assent and consent of the Right Hono.^{ble} Arthur Earle of Donegall Lord of the Castle of Belfast aforesayd   It is hereby ordered and established the dayly

growing charge of the poore and other wayes of disbursing
moneys being considered and the great want of a Town Stock
to defray any emergent charge and the number of ffree
Comoners dayly encreasing rather to the hurt and detriment
of this Corporacon than to the creditt or advantage thereof
It is ordered by and with the consent aforesayd that the
Soveraigne for the time being and every Soveraigne for the
time being to come shall not admit any person to be a ffree
Comoner of the Corporacon aforesayd without reserving
the full moyety of such sume or sumes of money (as shall
be agreed upon for the making of any person ffree) to and
for the use of the sayd Towne And that noe ffreeman
hereafter shall be admitted and sworne a ffree Comoner in
noe other place and at noe other time but in open Court three
or two at the least of the Burgesses beside the Soveraigne
being present   Any Act order use custome or By Law of the
Corporacon heretofore made used,or done to the contrary in
anywise notw^{th.}standing.

A by law to be made for prentises to come w^{t}hin 3 months after their time is out or to lose their freedome

Edward Reynell Sovraigne
Soveraigne

John Leathes	Tho Walcot	George McCartney
Jo: Leathes	George Martin	Geo: McCartney
John Rigbee	Gill^t Wye	

Att the same Assembly and by and wth the consent of
the Right Honble Arthur Earle of Donegall and Lord of the
Castle of Belfast   It is ordered and enacted and to remaine
as a By Law for ever that noe Inholder Aleseller or
Victualer w^{th}in the Burrough of Belfast shall not from
henceforth suffer any person or persons unlesse lodgers in
their houses to drink or play at any Game whatsoever after
the houre of Nyne at Night and that every person that shall
offend as abovesayd shall pay to the Soveraigne for the
time being the summe of Three shillings and four pence
ster to be levyed by distress or otherwise and every person
that shall be found drinking or playing after the time
aforemencioned shall pay to the Soveraigne the sum of One
Shilling ster

Edw Reynell Sovraigne

John Leathes	Tho Walcot	George McCartney
Jo: Leithes	George Martin	Geo: McCartney
John Rigbee	Gill^t Wye	

The first day of December in the Yeare of our Lord God one thousand six hundred sixty and five Att an assembly of the Soveraigne and Major part of the Burgesses of the Borrough of Belfast for the Ellection of Two Burgesses in the vacancy of Mr Thomas Waringe and Capt ffrancis Meeke deceased upon deliberate and mature consideracon ffrancis Thetford and George McCartney Gentle^m free Comoners of the Borrough were Ellected and then sworne ffree Burgesses of the said Corporacon of Belfast in the stead and place of the said Thomas Waringe and ffrancis Meeke as aforesaid Edward Reynalds Gentleman then being Soveraigne of the said Borrough

Edw Reynell Soveraigne

Geo: M'Cartney   John Leathes   Nethaniel Byrt

Memorandum that William Montgomery came before mee the fifth day of Aprill [and] in the yeare of our Lord 1666 and did declare that one James Akin of the parish of Templepatrick in the County of Antrim did [at March last] ye 30th day of October 1665 engage under his hand and Seale to deliver to Alexander Alen Cuningham of Erwin in the Kingdome of Scotland Merchant Threescore Boles of oate meale wth one peck to the Bole each Bole to be of Belfast measure to be delivered to the said [Alexand] *Alen* Cuningham or his Assignes at or before ye first day of March thence next following   And further that the sayd [Ja] Alexanders Vessell sent to receive the sayd meale hath lyon upon demurrage for want of the meale 28 dayes before the date hereof and much damage the said Alexander hath received over and above the said demurrage the meale being not delivered as aforesayd

MEMORANDUM That at a meeting of the Soveraigne and Burgesses of the Borrough of Belfast the 15th day of October 1666 wth the consent of the Right Honble the Earl of Donegall have unanimously agreed (by reason of a proclamacon from the Ld Leiuten^ant and Councill for the calling in of all charters granted to Cityes and Townes and for the renewing of them) at their owne charges will from time to time advance such sume or sumes of money as shall be required for the renewing of the Charter of this said Borrough And for the present undertaking the sayd worke doe Agree that every Burgesse shall forthwith deposite 1^l ster and that if any Burgesse *or Burgesses* shall at present or for the future refuse to pay such sume or sumes as shall proportionably come to *his or* their share or shares that then [the] every such Burgesse or Burgesses soe refusing wth the consent of the Lord of the Castle and major part of the Burgesses shall be Disfranchised of all his libertyes as a ffree Burgesse of this Corporacon

Donegall

Edw Reynell Sovraigne

John Leathes   Gill^t Wye   Fra: Thettford   George M'Cartney   Geo M'Cartney   Jo: Leithes   John Rigbee   George Martin

At an assembly of the Soveraigne and Burgesses of the Borrough of Belfast the eighth day of November 1666 it is enacted and ordered by the Soveraigne and Burgesses aforesayd that John Worthington shalbee from henceforth disfranchised of his freedome and priviledges as a free Comoner of this Corporacon by reason of his the sayd Johns concealing the goods of fforrainers and aliens not being free contrary to the ffreemans oath in that case made and provided

Edw Reynell Sovraigne

Geo: M'Cartney   George Martin   Will: Waring John Rigbee   George M'Cartney

That the 13th of December 1666 John Worthington prefferred his peticon to ye Cott and upon due consideracon thereof the sayd John was admitted a Free Comoner of the Borrough of Belfast being the 8th day of November last past disfranchised of and from his freedome in the Corporacon

Edw Reynell Soveraigne
Soveraigne

Mich: Harrison   John Leathes

Omnibus et singulis Justiciariis et Costodibus pacis ac majoribus Aldermanis Superioribus Ballivis Constabulariis officiariis Ministris ae fidelibus Legeis Domini Regis nunc ad quos hoc presens scriptum pervenerit Robertus Bindlos Baronettus Major Burgi siue ville Lancastrie in Comitatu Lancastrensi Willelmus Townson et Egidius Hoysham generosi Ballivi eiusdem Burgi siue ville salutem in Domino sempiterno Sciatis quod Villa et Burgus Lancastrie predicti est antiquus Burgus et quod omnes Burgenses illius Burgi habent gaudent et fruuntur et a tempore quo memoria hominum in contrarium non existit habuerunt gavisi et fructi sunt libertate privilegio et immunitate esse exonerati et quieti de omni Theolonio passagio pontagio stallagio pannagio Tunnagio et Lastagio ac etiam de omnibus aliis exactionibus et demandis quibuscunque pro omnibus rebus et merchandisis suis emptis siue venditis per totum regnum Anglie necnon per quascunquas portus Maris et Insulas Civitates portus et Villas Hiberniæ Walliæ et Manniæ et quod Dominus Jacobus nuper Rex Anglie Scotie ffrancie et Hibernie per Litteras suas patentes sub magno sigillo suo Anglie concessit et confirmavit Burgensibus suis Burgi sui predicti et successoribus suis in perpetuum Libertates privilegia et immunitates predictas secundum tenorem diversarum Chartarum progenitorum et predecessorum dicti Domini Regis et iisdem Burgensibus et predecessoribus suis Concessarum a tempore Regni Johannis quondam Regis hujus Regni Anglie et per Excellentissimum principem Dominum Nostrum Carolum Secundum Nunc Regem Anglie Scotie ffrancie et Hibernie et iisdem Burgensibus et successoribus suis per Litteras suas patentes tam sub sigillo magno suo Angliæ quam sub sigillo Ducatu sui Lancastrie nuper confirmatarum prout in eisdem Litteris patentibus et Chartis penes predictos Burgenses remanentibus plenius continetur—et Apparetur Quæ quidem premissa non solum vobis tenore presentium Testificamur necnon quod quidem Willelmus Yeates Burgensis est admissus et Juratus et per Spatium Tredecim Annorum iam ultimo elapsorum admissus et iuratus fuit ad Libertates eiusdem Burgi siue ville Lancastrie Videlicet admissus et iuratus fuit ut prefertur in et super nonum diem Octobris Anno Millessimo sexcentesimo quinquagessimo secundo Quapropter nos prefati major et Ballivi specialiter Rogamus quatenus cum dictus Willelmus Yeates aut Servientes sui venerint ad civitates villas portus seu alia loca infra Regnum Anglie seu ad portus et Insulas Hibernie Wallie seu Manne cum bonis rebus seu merchandisis suis quod ipsi sint exonerati et quieti de omni Theolonio passagio (Anglice Through Toll) pontagio stallagio pondagio Tunnagio Lastagio et aliis exactionibus et demandis quibuscunque Secundum Concessionem dicti Domini Regis ac progenitorum suorum ut prefertur In cujus rei Testimonium presentibus sigillum Burgi siue Ville predicti apposuimus Quinto die ffebruarii Anno regni Domini domni nostri Caroli secundi dei Gratia Anglie Scotie ffrancie et Hibernie Regis fidei Defensoris decimo octavo, Anno Domini 1665

Robt Bindlos,	William Townson
Major Lancastrie	Gyles Heysham
	Ballivi Lancastrenses

This Certificate enrolled ye 29th January 1667 is according to the originall examined per me

Sam Downes
Towne Clerk

Noverint Vniversi per presentes nos Willelmum Molloy de civitate Dublin Armigerum et Arthur Ardagh de Civitate Dublin predicta generosum teneri et firmiter obligari Timotheo Taylor de Grange in Comitatu Antrim generoso in ducentis libris sterlingorum soluendis eidem Timotheo Executoribus Administratoribus et assignatis suis ad quamquidem solucionem bene et fideliter faciendam obligamus nos et utrumque nostrum per se pro toto et in solido heredes Executores et administratores nostros firmiter per presentes sigillis nostris sigillatas datos undecimo die Martii Anno Dom. 1666

The condicion of this obligacion that if the above bounden William Molloy and Arthur Ardagh or either of them their Executor^s Administ^{rs} or Assignes or the Executo^{rs} Admo^{rs} or Assignes of either of them shall well and truely content satisfy and pay or cause to be well and truely contented satisfyed and payd unto the above named Timothy Taylor his Execut^{ors} Administ^{rs} or Assignes the just and full sume of one hundred pounds ster currant and lawfull mony of and in England at or upon the eleaventh day of September next ensueing the date hereof that then the above obligacion to be voyde otherwise the same to remaine in full force and vertue in Law

Signed sealed and delivered in the presence of us	Wm Molloy Arth: Ardagh

Ja Nixon
Nicho. Pudsey
Charles Molloy
Laur. Quicke
Theo. Taylor

Enrolled and examined wth the originall the 15th day of October 1667

per me   Sam Downes
Towne Clerk

TT an Assembly of the Soveraigne and major part of the Burgesses of the Borrough of Belfast [for] the second day of December 1667 for the eleccon of a Burgesse in the vacancy of John Davis Esqr deceased upon deliberate and mature consideracon Hugh Eccles one of the Free Comoners of this Borrough was elected and then sworne a Free Burgesse of this place in the stead of him the sayd John Davis Esqr deceased as aforesayd   Given under our hands the second day of December 1667

Geo McCartney Soveraigne

Jo: Leithes   Hugh HD Doake   John Leathes   Will: Waring   Edw: Reynell   Tho: Walcot   ffra: Thettford George McCartney

21th January 1668

Att an Assembly of the Soveraigne and Burgesses of the Borrough of Belfast by and with the consent of the Right Honor^ble the Earle of Donegall Lord of the Castle of Belfast   It is ordered and established and to remaine as a By Law for ever that noe Inhabitant of the Borrough aforesayd *from ye date hereof* shall take to apprentize any boy or Girle but that the Indentures to be made in such cases shall be made by the Towne Clerck of the Corporacon and by noe other person   And the names of the Apprentize [to] and Master acordaine shall be by him recorded in a Booke for that purpose wth the time of such apprentize

serving   And the sayd Towne Clerck shall not take above
the sume of five shillings ster for each payre of Indentures
and enrolling them   And if any person shall serve an
Apprentishipp by any other Indentures made otherwise
then above sayd hee shall have noe benefitt but be looked
upon as an Alien & forrainer provided that if any person
shall bring their Indentures in writing and that they shall
be allowed of by the Soveraigne to be[the]in forme then there
shall be but one shilling allowed for the enrollm! to the
Town Clerck

Geo: M'Cartney Soveraigne

Gillt: Wye   Jo: Leythes   George Martin   Edw:
Reynell   John Leathes   George M'Cartney   Hugh:
Eccles

The Porters oath as it was administred [on] the
Sixth day of ffebruary to some and agreed
to be administered to the rest ye 11th of this
Instant ffebruary 1668

I A: B: Admitted and Allowed of by the Soveraigne
and Burgesses of the Burrough of Belfast to act therein in
the employm.t of a Porter w.th.in the Towne and Libertyes
aforesayd doe hereby sweare during my employm.t as porter
or in anything thereunto belonging from time to time and
at all times to receive Coales Salt or any other goods
measurable of and from any Shipp Vessell Barque Boate or
Gabbart full measure to which my horse or carr may come
to receive w.th.in the Dock or Key or other place of discharge
belonging to this Borrough and the same soe received by
my selfe or ordered to be received by any person within the
Towne and Liberty aforesayd to deliver to noe other person
than appointed w.th.out any embezelling or lessening thereof
And that I will not being employed by any merchant or
other Inhabitant of this Borrough with its Liberty either by

night or day by deed or word doe or cause to be done any losse damage or p.judice   Soe helpe mee God

Wee John Black and Michaell Biggar merch.t doe acknowledge Ourselves our Executo.rs & Admo.rs to be endebted to the Soveraigne & Burgesses of Belfast for the time being Joyntly & sevrally the sume of forty pounds ster if the sayd John Black Porter shall not observe fullfill and keepe the aforesayd in every clause

Witnesse our hands y.e eleaventh
     day of ffebruary 1668

Know all men by these p.r.sents that wee Cuthbert Studholme William Hutchinson Joseph Nicholson and Robert Jackson gen.t Administ.rs of all and singular the goods Chattles debts and creditts w.tsoever w.ch Richard Scott of the Citty of Carlile in the County of Cumberland merch.t late deceased dyed seized of have assigned ordained and in our stead and place appointed and by these p.r.sents doe assigne ordaine authorise appoint and constitute our trusty friend William Woods of Carlile our true and lawfull attorney for us in our names and to our owne proper use as Administ.rs of the sayd goods and chattles to aske demand sue for levy require recover and receive of and from any person or persons w.tsoever w.th.in the Kingdome of Ireland all and singular such debts goods chattles sume and sumes of money as they or any of them were owing and indebted unto the sayd Richard Scott at the time of his death or w.ch then did appertaine or belong to him the sayd Richard Scott giving and hereby granting unto the sayd William Woods our full power and lawfull authority for us in our names and to our use as aforesayd to sue arrest implead condemne and imprison all or any of the debtors aforesayd and at his pleasure the same persons out of prison to deliver or cause to be delivered and upon the receipt of any such debts sume or sumes of money or other goods or chattles as aforesayd to our use to be received of any of the sayd persons Acquittances or other lawfull discharges for us and in our names to make seale and deliver as our act or deedes and Attorney or Attorneys for the purpose aforesayd under him to substitute and appoint and at his pleasure to revoke and all and every other thing or things w.ch shall be needfull or necessary to be done in or about the premises the same for us and in our names to doe as fully and effectually as wee ourselves might doe if wee were personally present Ratifying allowing and confirming by these presents w.tsoever our sayd Attorney shall lawfully doe or cause to be done in or about the execucon of the premises   In witness whereof wee have hereunto sett our hands and seales the Twenty seaventh day of Aprill in the Twentyeth yeare of our Soveraigne Lord King Charles the Second of England &c Anno Dom 1668

Sealed signed and
delivered in y.e
p.r.sence of us
    William James
    ffr: Woods
    William Jackson

Cuth: Studholme
W.m Hutchinson
Jos: Nicholson
Rob.t Jackson

This Letter of attorney Enrolled the Eighth day of June 1668 and according to the originall Examined by me

        Sam Downes
8 June 1668   Towne Clerk

Memorand the Last Will and Testam^t of Richard Scott of Carlile merc^t bears date ye second day of October 1667 by wch Will the said Richard Scott did appoint Mr Thomas Craister Mr Joseph Nicholson Mr Cuthbert Studholme and Mr Robert Jackson Tutors and guardians to his children John Scott Nathaniel Scot Mary Scot Sarah Scot and Elizabeth Scott and to have the whole managem^t of his reall & personall Estate for his childern's use making his childern joynt Executors wch sayd Will bearing date as aforesayd was signed and sealed in the p^{r}sence of

Rich: Gilpin.   Jos: Jackson
Tho: Stainebanke

Probat of the sayd Will of Richard Scott and Letters of administracon was made and granted the 16th day of January 1667 to Cuthbert Studholme of Carlile merc^t and to William Hutchinson of New Castle upon Tyne merc^t Joseph Nicholson Clerk Rector of Plomblaine and Robert Jackson of ye City of Carlile aforesay^d gent of all the goods and chattles belonging to ye said Richard Scott deceased to and for ye use of his children afore named during their minority   All this appeares to be true the copy of the Will Letters of administracon wth the probate under the Seale of office and signed by Phil Broome in the p^{r}rogative Court of Yorke were all examined [by me] the 8th day of June 1668 by mee

Sam Downes Towne Clerk

And this brevitate enrolled at the request of Richard Page & Mr Wm Woods

Sam Downes

AT an Assembly of the Sovraigne and Burgesses of the Borrough of Belfast [it] held the 9th day of July 1668   It is agreed that the sume of foure pounds ster shall be levyed by way of Sesse upon this Corporacon for the making of a new *plush* Cushion for ye Towne Hall

Entred by order

per me   Sam Downes
            Towne Clerck

HE foure and twentyeth day of April 1669   Att an assembly of the major part of the Burgesses of the Burrogh of Belfast and by the consent and in the presence of the Right Hono^ble Arthur Earle of Donegall S^r. Hercules Langford Knight and Barronett was elected and sworne a free Burgesse of the Corporacon of Belfast aforesaid in the roome and stead of Mr John Rigby late deceased

   Donegall   Geo M'Cartney Soverainge

      HD John Leathes Will Waring Tho Walcot Gillt Wye George M'Cartney

   Know all men by these p^rsents that I Petter Cassainge doe hereby Acknowledge and confess myselfe to have received of and from the hand of Mr Thomas Owen March^t in goods and moneys to the full valeiu of two hundred and ninty four pounds six shillings and five pence ster wch is for the use and accompt of my Master Mr Henry Lauie and for his partner Mr Edward Thompson both mercht^s in Burdeaux and that by vertue of my order by them to have granted as also by their Letter to the foresaid *Mr* Thomas Owen bearing date the thirtieth day of March last in the yeare of God 1665 the wch sume I doe hereby acknowledge to have receaved   In Witness whereof I have heirunto set [to] my hand and seale the 21th day of June   Ano dom 1665

                         P: Cassaing
                         my Mr. Henry Lauye X
                         Mr Thompson

Signed Sealed and
Delivered in the p^rsents
of us

                         Will: Thomb James Monttgomery
                         Josia Martin not publicus

   This acknowledgm^t enrolled the 3rd day of June 1669 and was examined wth the originall per me

                         Sam Downes
                         Towne Clerck

   Know all men by these presents that I Petter Cassaigne doe hereby acknowledge and confess^e my selfe to have received from Mr Thomas Owen Merch^t in Belfast one Bill of Exchange upon Mr James Cuninghame March^t in Cadis of the sume of five hundred peices of eight and that to be payd to my Mr Henry Leuie or to his order wch bill was of the date of the 9th of June and uppon payment of the sume to him the aforesayd Henry Lauie or his order that then the sayd Henry Lauie deductinge out of the same nine pounds ster and odd moneys wth the Ballance of the Acc^tt to him sent and that the full remainder shall be in his Masters hands and to be payd upon demand to the sayd Thomas Owen March^t or order Witnesse my hand and seale the 21st of June 1665

P Cassaing
for my Mr Henry Lauie

Signed Sealed and
delivered in the
p^rsence of
    Will Thomb
    Ja Monttgumbrey
    Josia Marten   not publicus

The above acknowledgm^t was enrolled the 3rd day of June 1669 and was examined with the originall per me

Sam Downes
Towne Clerck

HE six and twentyeth day of August one thousand six hundred sixty and nyne at an assembly of the major part of the Burgesses of the Burrough of Belfast and by the consent of the Right Hono^ble Arthur Earle of Donegall Captaine Robert Leathes one of the free Comoners of this Burrough was elected and sworne a free Burgesse of the Corporacon of Belfast aforesayd in the roome and stead of Mr Hugh Doake late deceased

Geo: McCartney Sovraigne

Jo: Leithes   Will: Waring   Edw Reynell   George
M'Cartney   Hugh: Eccles   Her: Langford   John
Leathes   Gillt Wye

Att an Assembly of the Sovraigne and Burgesses of Belfast the sixth day of July 1671 by and with the consent of the Right Honble Arthur Earle of Donegall Lord of the Castle of Belfast It is ordered and enacted for a By Law for ever that noe ffree Burgesse ffree Comoner not residing within the Towne and Libertyes of the Corporacon shall have any benefitt or priviledge of the Customes and dutyes usually payd for any goods or wares brought in at the gates of Belfast But shall pay for every horse Loade or carr the Comon due or to be proceeded ag^t as other Forrainers unless the sayd persons Free Burgesses and Comoners aforesayd shall be from time to time [be] assessed wth the Inhabitants of the Towne and pay proportionablie accordinge to their Trade driven here that then this By Law shall not extend to them This By Law being grounded upon a

presentm^t made by the Grand Jury the thirteenth of
October 1670 rehearsed in the words aforesayd

Will Waring Sovraigne

George Martin   John Leithes   Edw Reynell   Tho
Walcot   Fra Thettford   George McCartney   Hugh
Eccles

Att the same Assembly It is ordered by the Soveraigne
and Burgesses wth the assent and consent aforesayd that there
be made forthwith [made] at the charge of the Corporacon
foure Hogsheads of a full Bourdeaux Gage to be lodged in
the hands of foure persons by the appointm^t of the Soveraigne for the time being in the most fitt places in the
Towne for the good of the Corporacon   And all persons
selling Turffe to be delivered here in any part of the Towne
the party buying requiring the party selling to be tryed by
the Towne measure the sayd Buyer shall pay to the Keeper
of the Hogshead one penny for every hundred as alsoe
foure Barrells to be made as aforesayd Winchester measure
for the measuring of Lime to be appointed as aforesayd the
Keeper shall have of the Buyer two pence for every score
of Barrells or proportionably for a lesser quantity

Will: Waring Sovraigne

George Martin   John Leathes   Edw Reynell   Tho
Walcot   ffra: Thettford   George M'Cartney   Hugh:
Eccles

TT an Assembly of the Soveraigne and Burgesses of this Burrough of Belfast and by and with the consent and assent of the Right Hono^{ble} Arthur Earle of Donegall and Lord of the Castle of Belfast the sayd Soveraigne and Burgesses taking into consideracion the presentm^t of Three severall Grand Juryes the one bearing date the seaventh day of April in the Yeare of our Lord God 1670 another dated the thirtyeth day of June in the said yeare the last dated the seaven and twentyeth day of April 1671 all urging the necessity of repayring the course of the backwater belonging to the Miln and the same to be brought to the Rampyer nere the north gate and from thence on the backside of the North Streete as low as the house of Henry Thetford in the sayd street and from thence all along to the present Soveraignes new plantacion And the same to be repayred and maintained from time to time at the cost and charges of the Inhabit^{ts} of the said North Streete It is ordered and enacted by and wth the consent aforesayd (finding a great necessity of doeing the sayd worke and the use it may be of in time of necessity and otherwise) that the sayd worke be forthwith repayred and made up by the sayd Inhabitants of the North Streete and for the future to be maintained and kept from time to time at their only costs and charges this to stand and remaine for a By Law for ever   This ordered and enacted the eight and twentyeth day of September in the yeare of our Lord God one thousand six hundred seaventy and one

Will Waring Soveraigne

Jo: Leithes   Tho Walcot   John Leathes   Robt Leathes

ROPOSALS for renewing and altering the Charter of Bellfast by consent of ye R^t Honble Arthur Earle of Donegall 1671

1 That the Charter be Renewed with Augmentacion of Preveliges.

2 That y^e stile of Soveraigne and Burgesses Be Mayor and Aldermen with a Comon Councell consisting of 24 Burgesses.

3 That ye R^t Honble ye Earle of Donegall Lord of the Castle of Bellfast be preserved in all his priviledges and Libertyes as formerly in ye Charter.

4 That ye By Laws acts and ordinances of the Corporacon with the consent of the Lord of the Castle of Bellfast be only made by ye Mayor Alldermen & Comon Councell.

5 That ye Court of Record held for ye Borrough to have power to trye actions [without repetition] of 50^{li} ster.

6 That they may have Quarter Sessions or Assemblyes with Grand Juryes to inquire into present and correct all misdemeanours & Trespasses whatsoever comitted or done in ye Corporacon and to mend all faults and breaches in Bridges streets lanes & highwayes ffences and watercourses in ye said Borrough by ffine or other punishm^t.

7 That [all] the through Tole Customes of the gates and Tongues be continued as formerly

8 That ye Precint and Libertyes *& Limitts* of the Borrough and Corporacon of Bellfast *as formerly* extend itselfe three mile distant on every side of the Towne by a straight line with power to sett up markes in every convenient places upon the meares thereof.

9 That ye Mayor for yᵉ time being be Justice of the Peace [at large] for ye County of Antrim & County of Downe

10 That all fforraigne Boates Vessell or shipps wᶜʰ belong not to ye Corporacon be lyable to pay three pence ster per Tunn towards ye repaireing ye key or wharfe and clensing the River or dock.

11 Whereas the Corporacon of Bellfast have neither lands Tenemtˢ hereditamtˢ Comons, Towne Stocke or pursse to pay or defray any Publique Charge or Contingences of the Corporacon neither is their any maintenance arriseing or growing due out of the Corporacon for ye Magistrate and Officers thereunto belonging that supplycation be made to have it granted that all fforran shipps and marchants not free in ye Corporacon pay wharfeage and Keage & *Cranage* to ye use of the Corporacon according to ye Rules and methods of other Corporacons & Cittyes especially Droheda.

12 That all ye present members of the Corporacon be continued in their privelidges libertyes and freedoms unlesse such who shall refuse ffreely willingly and readly contribute according to their Estates to ye charge of getting ye new Charter and in order thereunto that a speedy way be laid downe to raise money for defraying the charge of [getting] the said Charter.

ARMS OF DROGHEDA.

ARMS OF GALWAY.

ARMS OF CORK.

By George M'Cartney Esqr Soveraigne
of the Borrough of Bellfast

By vertue of ye power given me from ye R! Honnor.ᵇˡᵉ
Arthur Earle of Donegall to execute ye office of water
Bayliffe place for ye Creeke or Harbour of ye Borrough of
Bellfast and to receive all dues dutyes Customes fees and
p'quisitts thereunto belonging and for ye more better
Keepeing ye Channell of ye said Harbour with markes or
pearches to ye Convenience of all shipps barkes boats
Gabbarts and Lighters to transport themselves from ye
poole of Garmoyle to ye Towne of Bellfast without danger
of grounding upon ye bankes of ye said Channell I doe
heereby sett and to farme lett unto John Dean of Bellfast
Mariner for one whole yeare comenceing from ye nine and
twentieth day of September instant ye office of water Balife
of ye said harbour to execute all & every thinge thereunto
belongeing especially in setting and keepeing pearches upon
ye said River in usuall places thereof and to receive for
his service therein only ye ffees of Anchoridge accustomed
due for ye same in consideracon whereof ye said John
Dean shall pay to me or my Assˢ yᵉ full sume of fforty shills
halfe yearly by equall proporcions hereby requireing ye said
John Dean from time to time and at all times to give me
account of all misdemeanours transactions and accedentes
that may happen in ye said office of water Bayliff especially
to give me a true account of all Vessells Barkes and Boats
comeing into ye said harbour with coles salt ffish Corne
or other Victualls or any other lading out of wᶜʰ any
custome doth or may arise to ye sᵈ office for ye comon use
thereof   Witness my hand and seale this 9ᵗʰ day of October
1672

George M'Cartney

Y the R! Honor.ᵇˡᵉ Arthur Earle of Donnegall Visct
Chichester of Carrickfargus Governor of the same
Barron of Bellfast and one of His Majᵗⁱᵉˢ Most
Honor.ᵇˡᵉ Privy Councell of Ireland.
Whereas I have given and granted unto Michaell Harrison
Esqr my Seneschall yᵉ office of water Balife for yᵉ Creeke
or Harbour of yᵉ Borrough of Belfast during my plesure
with all yᵉ ffees and perquisitts thereunto belonging Yet
neverthelesse out of my good will and affection to yᵉ Sove-
raigne of yᵉ said Borrough for his better incouragement in

ye governm^t of ye said Towne which generally consists of marchant and maryten affaires I have thought fitt that ye said office of water Baylife should be granted to ye Soveraigne of ye Borrough aforesaid for the time being under a yearly accknowledgement rendered to ye said Michaell Harrison   Pursuant thereunto ye Soveraignes of ye Borrough afforesaid for many yeares last past have and still do execute ye said office or place of water Bayliffe   Now whereas John Dean my Water or Bargeman is imployed by George M'Cartney now Soveraigne of ye Borrough afforesaid in the said office for this two years last past receiving only for ye service ye fees and perquisitts of ancoridge in consider whereof he paid a yearly rent to ye said George M'Cartney as appeares by agreement und^r their hands between them and for as much as ye said John Dean to my certaine knowledge is the Most fitt able and skillfull person to pearch out the Chanell from Bellfast afforesaid to the pool of Garmoyle the better to   all ships Vessels Boats Gabots and Lighters Loaden and unloaden to navigate to and againe in the said channell for ye good and wellfare of Trade in ye wch imployment ye said John Dean hath behaved himselfe honestly skilfully and dilligently as I am credibly informed by ye said George M'Cartney and others. Therefore I do hereby recomend the said John Dean to the Soveraigne of ye Borrough afforesaid for the time being and to all others whome it may concerne that the said John Dean may be contained and imployed in the said office or place of water Bayliffe as heretofore he hath been during my pleashure with full power to execute all warrants propperly belonging and appertaining to the said office he   of the same in consideration whereof he is to pay the accustomed rent to the Soveraigne for the time being   Provided allways and it is my will and pleasure y^t the said John Dean from time to time and at all times necessary and needfull sett markes and pearches upon the River of Laggan up to Stand Millis as also upon the new Dock or River up to the sluces of Castle Wharfe and for his better incouragem^t and duracon in the imployment I this instant of writing together with ye agreem^t of the sade George M'Cartney made with the sade John Dean as allso ye confession of the said Soveraigne hereunto may be recorded amongst the records of the Borrough of Bellfast   Given under my hand and seale at Belfast this eight day of September Anno Dom one thousand six hundred seventy four 1674   Donegall

TABLE of the office and duty of a Water Bayliff to the lord Admirall with the fees and perquisites belonging to the same established in the 4th yeare of King Edward the sixth by Thomas Lord Seymore then Lord High Admirall of England & Ireland and ever since continued and observed accustomably in England by the said Water Bayliffes in right of the admirall

1 The Water Bayliff is to enquire and find out as much as in him lyeth all such rights and duties as do any wayes belong unto the admirall and seize them unto his uses and to certifie and be accomptable for the same

2 The Water bayliff is to search any navigable River Port or Haven within the Admiralls Jurisdiccion where any danger may be and to Beacon buoy or perch the same that no barque ship or vessell sustaine any damage either by rock shelve or quick sand by defect thereof every barque ship or vessell to pay accordingly as they pay in London towards the maintainance of them, Anno 4° Hen 4°

3 The Water bayliff is to have a speciall regard of the afores[d] Rivers or streames that there be no stakes obstacle or impediment either by anchor, timber, weares, stakes, riddle, or such like, which may prejudice or disturb the passage of any boate barque or ship in their way to or from any towne wharfe key or Creaney and to certifie who are offenders in this to be punished according to the statute in that behalf either by imprisonment or fine or both if it be thought fitt, Anno 4° Hen: 4° Cap 11° Anno 12° Hen: 4° Cap 7°

4 The Water bayliff upon any difference in contracts for marine Cause for any fact or offence within the admiralls Jurisdiccion comitted is to arest or attatch any merchant Owner of Shipp proprietor or any other p'son or p'sons malefactors or other adherents as well within liberties and franchises as without, taking such fees as in right doth belong to the same, Ex Officio

5 The Water bayliffe is to search all passengers suspected to be Jesuit, Seminary Priest, comeing into the Realme, or fugitives out of the Kings Dominions for seditious books, p'dons bulls or such like and for letters of advice to or[for]from any the Kings enemies and to stay all such suspected p'sons until they shall be examined and shall obtain licence for their further passage. Stat:

6 The Water bayliffe is to enquire and search what p'son or p'sons do cast out of any Ship Cracer or any other Vessell within any haven or river Creek or Channell flowing or running to any towne Citty or burrough within any of the Kings Dominions any manner of gravell ballast rubbish or any other wreck or filth whereby the River may any way be annoyed or clogged the party so offending shall forfeit for every such offence 5 pounds, the one halfe to the King the other half to him that will sue for the same, Anno 34° Hen 8° Cap. 9°.

7 The Water bayliff is to make stay of any that be in office or in the Kings pay or any other p'son of what quality or condicion they be which shall be suspected privily to go about to convey themselves out of the Kings dominions without licence first obtained excepting such p'sons as are limitted so to do by the statute and whatsoever Master or owner of ship shall carry any such p'son or p'sons not having licence as afores? shall forfeit his said shipp barque or vessell, Anno 9° Ed. 3°

8 The Water bayliff is to search for the good and increase of the Navy of the Kings Dominions that no p'son or p'sons do lade or cause to be laden in any shipp, bottom, or bottoms, whereof any stranger, or strangers borne be proprietor shipp Masters or partners any ware, merchandize, victuall or other things of what kind or nature soever they shall be to any forraigne Kingdome or region or from any port or creek of this Realme to any port or creek of the same Realme upon pain to forfeit all the goods so laden or carried or the value thereof unless they shall obtain a certificate under the seale of the Admirall his deputy or Deputies or from the customer or controuler if neither the Admirall or his deputy be resident at *or*

in the said port or creek, that there may be not any English shipp or shipps of the Kings leidge people sufficient to transport the said goods wares and merchandize within the port where they are to be shipped   Anno 5° R 2nd Cap 3°

9 The Water bayliff is to enquire and search that no merchandize entring into the Realm or goeing out of the same shall be charged or discharged in a creek, water place, or small arrivall except it be by the coertion of the tempest at sea, but in the great parts and places where the King may be satisfied of his customes upon pain to forfeit to the King all the merchandize so charged or discharged,   Anno 4° Hen. 4 Cap. 20°

10 The Water bayliff is also to enquire and find out what p'sons unlawfully do fish with netts or engines so that thereby the fishes are destroyed and to certifie the same unto the Conservator and also app'hend and attatch all such p'sons that they may receive condigne punishm^t according to the statute in that behalf, Anno 13° E 1° Anno 13° E 3°

11 The Water bayliff is to search and enquire of those that in the entry or mouth of any River or in any port or haven do forestall and engrosse any victuall fewell or other goods before such things shall be brought to the Key or Markett to the detriment of the Common people next adjoining, Anno 25° E. 3^d Cap. 2^d

12 The Water bayliff is to find out and app'hend those w^{ch}[ith] in their shipps wittingly receive rebells, fellons, murderers, piratts, banished men, outlaws or their goods and do convey them away privily from being app'hended to answer the laws in that case provided.   Communis Lex.

13 The Water bayliff is to enquire whether any p'son hath taken in the sea, or within any other place within the admiralls Jurisdiccion any whales, sturgeons, porpusses, balens, grasps, or any other great or overgrown fish and hath not satisfied the L^d admirall for the same.   per litteras patentes.

14 The water Bayliff is to press all manner of shipps barques hoÿes or any other vessell for the service of

the King or for carrieing any victuall or Munition to any of the Kings Storehouses shipps Castles and fforts and also to press Marriners or seafearing men for the furtherance of the s^d service and shipp so often as need shall be.   virtute Officii.

15 The Water bayliff is also to forbid all people to build any wharfe, key, or house upon the shore of any of the ports, havens, rivers or creeks within the high water and low water marke without licence first had and obtained of the Lord admirall for the time being his deputy or officers.

16 The Water bayliff is to have the custody of the water measure and weights and to [weigh] measure and weigh all and singular goods, & merchandizes wch are to be weighed or measured within the ship board to be laden, carried, transported, or brought over, that thereby the King be not deceived in his customes nor none of his subjects either in false measure or weights, and also size and seale every water weight & measures, the water bushell to contain ten gallons in measure and to be sealed or marked with the seale of the Admiralty & the weight to contain six[ty] *score* pounds of Averdupoiz beams sealed or marked accordingly   Anno 11° Hen 7°

17 The Water bayliff is also to build and keep a Crane for the lading and unlading merchants goods and also to have a wharf or key to which all merchants goods are to be brought & landed, there to be weighed and measured and to certifie the quantity to the Customers according to the entry and the King not deceived by false and short entryes and to pay the Cranage and wharfage as is accustomed where Cranes and wharfes are already builded.   virtute Officii.

18 The Water bayliff is to keep the ferryes for carrieing of passengers over any river in the admiralls Jurisdiccon or aboard or from any shipp or barque and to suffer none to undertake the ferrying of passengers over any the Kings streams afores^d or aboard or from any shipp only such as shall be licensed by the Ld Admirall or his officers or shall be free so to do by his service and the oath of allegiance and supremacy to be taken before the officers or masters of Trinity House appointed for that purpose.

19 If any merchant or proprietor do sell any barque or shipp to any merchant or other man of a contrary port, the seller shall pay to the Water Bayliff for alienation of the s^d shipp 6^s 8^d toward the maintainance of the Buoys and Beacon of the same Harbour from whence the shipp is carried, Secundum Curiæ advtus.

20 The Water *bayliff* is also to have of every Boat a fish, as coddling, hake, plaice, mullett, haddock or any other wett or dry fish, one cheif fish, and also for any drying of their s^d fish netts upon the sea, beach, or shore, as is accustomed to be paid where any such fisher netts are usually dryed.

21 The Water bayliff is to have of every barque shipp or vessell that taketh ballast of sand gravell or stone both within the flowing and reflowing of the sea or salt water upon any of the shores within the admiralls Jurisdiccion for castage of every Tunn of the said ballast 3^d sterl, per Litteras patentes

22 The Water bayliff is also to forbid all Inhabitants dwelling upon or neare the shore of the ports Havens rivers or creeks beneath the bridges to cast out of their houses, yards, wharfes *or* Keys, any rubbish Soyle seacole dust or morttar whereby the River or any of the afores^d place may be cloÿed annoyed or the fishings of the s^d place prejudiced or driven away the parties so offending are to forfeit for every such offence 3^s 4^d and to receive such other punishm^t as shall be thought fitt by the Lord Admirall or by his deputy per litteras patentes et consuetudines et antiquo spectand et p'tinent Coronæ Regis

23 The Water bayliff is to have for anchorage of every
shipp with two topps   ...   ...   00 : 01 : 00
Of every Barque or Shipp with one topp 00 : 00 : 06
Of every small boate that beareth
anchor   ...   .   00 : 00 : 03
Of every strange bottom   ...   ...   double duties
And which soever of their barques shall cast ancor not having a buoy therto in any of the navigable rivers shall forfeit to the Water Bayliff 00 : 03 : 04

24 The Water Bayliff is to have for grounding
every anchor   ...   .   00 : 00 : 06
and of every stranger   ...   ...   00 : 01 : 00

25 The Water bayliff is to have of every barque ship or
vessell laden with corn, cole, or salt, one measure
wherewith they do usually measure, of the s^d corn,
cole, or salt; and every vessell laden with iron,
timber, freestone, hard stone, clap boards, dale
boards, masts, mill stones or green stone, for bally-
age, for every one of these 1^s per litteras patentes et
consuetudines &c

26 The Water bayliff is to have for beaconage of every
shipp that crosseth the sea at her entrance into any
port toward the maintenance of such beacon

00 : 00 : 09

And of every barque and boate along ⎫
  the coast so long as they enter ⎬ 00 : 00 : 03
  these ports and take benefitt of ⎪
  the beacon, but only ⎭

27 The Water bayliff is to see that the fishermen in the
time of herring fishing do keep the orders prescribed
according to the statute in that behalf, and upon
every misdemeano^r as the trespass is so the punishm^t
and also that they do not sell their fish at Sea,
before they come into the haven and the capell of
the ship to be drawn upon land upon paine of
forfeiture of all their fishes so taken, and imprisonment at the Kings will and the s^d Water Bayliff is
to have of every boate of herrings, fresh or salted
for the fishing line one hundred of herring, be they
either handled or barrelled.

28 The Water bayliff is to p^rsent all such persons as do
wrongfully exact and take by colour of their office
any manner of Customes or duties not allowable in
any of the ports of this Realm upon any manner of
goods or merchandize whereby the merchants are
constrained to forsake the s^d port to the hindrance
of his Maties subjects and the Common profitt of the
Realm

To the Right Wopp^full Georg McCartney Esqr
Sovraigne of the Burrough of Bellfast and the
Wopp^full Bench his brethern

THE Humble petition of the Tailors ffreemen
of y^e s^d Burrough Humbly sheweth that
your pett^rs being by you^r wo^pps favo^r
admitted and sworne ffree Commoners;
have uppon all occassions given their
dutifull obedience in watch warde: assesses;
and all other Incombant taxes; Impossed
on them, by order as afforesaid and still are Redy uppon all
occassions to manifest their compliance as ffarr as their
abilities extends unto: now soe itt is, that notwithstandinge
good & wholesum Lawes were established; by ye Common
Councell of ye said Burrough; and confirmed by you^r wo^pps
consent for the Incurradgm^t of ffreemen Inhabitants of this
Towne, yett a nuemorous sort of Idell vagabond Tailors
Daily resort hither and Reapes the Benefitt of the said
Towne, out of you^r pett^rs Mouths not soe much as paieinge
one farthing towards ye deffrayinge of any Publique Chardge
whereby ye ffrequent usse off ye same: you^r pett^rs with their
families wholy, are allmost Ruined and undoubtly will bee
unless relieved

Tho: Lightfoot, James Reed
John hudllston, Francis Cox
John Reynalds William Gibb,
William Crakan, Obadiah
Grove, Jo^n Fisher, Robert
White, John Johnston,
Robert Hunter, Tho
M'Clune, James Allex^r,
Andrew Smith, Jo^n M'Cuden,
Allex^r Latimer, Thomas
Hanna, Edward Marshall,
John Nobell

May it therefor please you^r
wo^pps to consider the p^rmises
& graunt you^r order that all
such loose persons as abovesaid may bee compelled by
you^r authority afforesaid to
depart to their severall
residentces & straight to
leave ye Towne Otherwaies,
that you^r officers uppon
notice first given may attatch
any such person soe found
to bring them or anie of
them befor you^r wo^pps or
success^rs to pay ye fine and
paine Impossed on; him;
them or any of them (by
the by Lawe) and they as
bound shall ever pray &c

Haveing taken due Inspection into ye above Pettition wee ffind ye Request to bee Reasonable, & pursuant to their desire doe hereby require & comand the Sergeants att Mace them and Either of them; uppon notice to them or any of them first given to apprehend any such loose Tailor working in Towne & not being ffree & being soe apprehended to bring before mee or other Sovraigne my success.ʳ from time to time & att all and every time to bee dealt with according to yᵉ purport of our by Lawe in that case made & Provided: Given under our hands & his Maᵗⁱᵉˢ seall of our said Borrough ye 5ᵗʰ January 1673

Georg M'Cartney Sov

William Waring   Georg M'Cartney

N the name of God Amen I Arthur Earle of Donnegall being at ye pr.sent in perfect memorie Judgement and understanding tho frail & weake through bodily sickness & distemper accounting it spirituall prudence & Christian wisdome to ease myself of all outward & worldly cares that thereby I may be more free to lay down my earthly tabernacle and render up my soul to God who gave it me do make this my last will and testament

And first I solemnly and sencearely render up my soul to God my most mercifull Father and Creator believing in yᵉ alone meritts and rightousness of Jesus Christ my most gracious Saviour and Redeemer for everlasting salvation and eternall life and my Body to be decently interred att Carickfergus in ye buriall place of my Ancestors And for my worldly Goods and Estate I doe order & appoint as followeth

And first I doe nominate and appoint my dearly beloved wife Lettitia Countess of Donegall my sole Executrix of this my sole last Will & testament and my Brother in law Sʳ Michaell Hicks Knight, and Arthur Upton Esqʳ whome out of yᵉ speciall confidence I have on them I appoint to be overseers to see all yᵉ following particulars of this my last Will to be truely timely and punctually pr.formed

Imprimis   I leave and bequeath to ye Poor of ye parish of Belfast Two hundred pounds to be disposed of in such manner and form as my said Executrix or Overseers shall think fitt

Item   I leave and bequeath to ye Poor of ye Parish of Carickfergus ffifty pounds sterling to be disposed of in manner and form as my said Executrix or overseers shall think fitt.

Item   I bequeath to my Grand-child Arthur St Leger all my Lands and tenements in ye County of Waterford and one thousand pounds ster: to be paid him w.thin one year after my decease.

Item   I leave and bequeath to my two grand daughters sisters to ye said Arthur St. Leger one thousand pounds ster: a piece to be paid within one year after each of their Marriage respectively

Item   I leave & bequeath to John Wrey ye son of Christopher Wrey deceased one hundred pounds ster per Ann.^m for seaven years comencing ye next quarter after my death

Item   I leave and bequeath to my severall Nephews Capt John Chichester Quarter Master John Chichester Mr Charles Chichester and Mr Arthur Chichester one hundred pounds ster: yearly to each of them for four years ye first payment to comence within one month after my death

Item   I leave and bequeath to each of my severall servants that are actually in my service at ye p'sent time and hath served me above one whole full year to each of them respectively one whole years wages or salary over and besides what is realy due to them for their past service and wages and to Ann Ogelby my servant that constantly attended me ten pounds ster: yearly for [her] four years

Item   I leave and bequeath to Mr Samuell Bryan my household chaplain as a testimony of my sincere love to him fifty pounds ster: over and above his years salary for four years to comence within two months after my death

Item   I leave and bequeath to Mrs Elizabeth Cornwall Ten pounds ster: a year for four years to comence within a year after my death

Item   I leave and bequeath to Richard Cannon Ten pounds ster: a year for four years to comence within a year after my death

Item   I leave and bequeath unto Arthur Upton of Castle Norton Esqr fifty pounds ster: a year for four years to comence within a year after my death

Item   I leave and bequeath to my Brother in law Sr Michael Hicks aforesaid one hundred pounds ster: a year for four year to comence within a year after my death.

Item   I leave and bequeath unto Doct^r Hugh Kenedy who hath been Phisitian to my self and family these severall years past fifty pounds ster: a year *for four years* to comence within a year after my death

Item   To Mr Claudius Gilbert Ten pounds ster: yearly for four years to comence within two years after my death

Item   To my Honble Father in law Sr William Hicks I leave and bequeath a piece of plate to ye value of forty pounds ster:

Item   I leave to my god sons Arthur Upton and Chichester M'Cartney to each of them ten pounds ster: a piece yearly for four years to comence within two years after my death

Item   I leave and bequeath out of my tenderly and fatherly affection to my dear daughter Ann Chichester as a testimoney of my owning her dutyfull beheaviour to my self and Dear Mother over and above what I have given her by deed of settlement ye sume of two thousand pounds ster: to be paid out of the Lands of Ennishowen in ye County of Donegall

Item   Out of a farther testimoney of my respect and perticular kindness that I have to my Dear wifes Brother Sr Michael Hicks I will and bequeath to him ye Castle town & eleaven Quarters of Land of Bart lying in ye Barrony of Ennishowen in ye County of Donegall for sixty one years comencing at All Saints last ye years undetermined in ye p^{r}sent Lease he hath being included therein And whereas ye said Sr Michael stands oblidged by vertue of his said p^{r}sent Lease to pay fifty pounds ster yearly for ye said lands my will now is and soe I declare and appoint that he my said Brother in law Sr Michael Hicks his Ex^{rs} adm^{rs} & assignes pay only ye just sume of twenty pounds ster yearly henceforward out of ye said lands and premisses aforesaid untill ye end and expiration of ye sixty one years aforesaid

Item   My will is and so I declare appoint and order that ye severall Legacies aforesaid be truely thankfully timely and punctually paid out of that and those parts of my Estate that is not settled by Deed or Deeds upon my aforesaid dear wife and daughter it being none of my intention to charge any part of my Estate that I have settled upon my said wife & Daughter with any of ye aforesaid Legacies

Lastly I do hereby revoke and disanull all former and other Will or Wills whatsoever provided always that this be not construed or intended to prejudice or invalidate any deed or Deeds formerly made to ye use benefitt or behoofe of my aforesaid dearly beloved wife and Daughter preceding ye date of these p^rsents In Witness whereof I have hereunto put my hand and seal ye seventeenth day of March one thousand six hundred seventy & four 1674

Wittness hereunto David Kenedy Henry Upton Geo: McCartney	Memorandum before y^e signing & sealing hereof y^e word Chichester was interlined [&] and he willed and bequeathed a years salary to his steward Mr Patrick Mortimer

Burgo de Bellfast   18 Oct 1674

WHEREAS it is a publique greivance in this
Corporation complained of; That those persons,
who daily bring turff to y^e Towne of Belfast to bee
sold; not only commits a great injury in makeing
their turffe in their size to longe thereby to hinder
ye close packing of them in their sacks or Common measure
by wch they are to bee sold but Likewayes that ye quantity of
each horse Load coms farr short of ye common hogshead or
measure of ye Corporation to ye great abuse and p'judice of
ye Inhabitants of ye same; Therefore to prevent such disorders for ye future in soe gennerall affaire; At an Assembly
held for ye said Burrough ye 18th day of October 1674 before
Hugh Ecckles Esqr Sovraigne of ye said Burrough Bee it
enacted & ordained as a by Lawe for ever by and wth y^e
consent of ye Right Honno^ble Arthur Earle of Dunegall L^d of
ye Castle of Bellfast, And ye said Sovraigne Burgesses and
Comminallity, from & after ye 20th day of October Instant that
doo sell or put to sale any Turffe to ye Inhabitants afores^d;
either by ye horse Load or otherwayes shall cause or make
each load to containe one full Hogshead of wine measure
according to ye Ancient Custome of ye said Corporation,
uppon ye penaltie of forfeiting each Load that shall be
wantinge in ye s^d measure the one halfe to ye use of y^e
Corporation and ye other halfe to such persons as shall
discover ye same. The lyke abuse is committed in y^e
Common saile of Lime, for ye p^rventing of wch be it lykewaies
enacted by ye Assembly Afores^d that all Lime sould to y^e
Inhabitants afores^d; by ye Barrell Load or otherwaies doe
containe ye full measure of ye Bristowe Barrell under y^e
pennalty of forfeiting each Barrell or load of Lime that shall
bee wanting of ye measure aforesaid & all forfeitures to bee
converted to ye uses affores^d.

Att an Assembly held this 20th day of Jany 1675 before
George M'Cartney Esqr Soveraigne of ye Burrough of
Bellfast it is ordered that the p^r.sent Soveraigne *y^e*
Soveraigne for ye time being shall have full power forthwith
to call all persons whatsoever in whose hands or Custody
any of ye poores money wch were left by Will or otherwise
to reliefe of ye poore distressed Inhabitants of this Corporacon that are Fallen into decay and poverty and ye said
p'sons soe haveing such money to compell them by suite of

Law or otherwise to give a Just & true account of yᵉ same for yᵉ uses afforesaid and for the future to have yᵉ same moneys well secured by bonnds with security

Geo : M'Cartney Soveraigne

Mich. Harryson Tho. Walcot George Martin Joh Leathes George M'Cartney Edw Reynell Gillᵗ Wye Robᵗ Leathes

ATT an Assembly held this 20ᵗʰ day of January 1675 for ye Corporacon of Bellfast before George M'Cartney Esqr Soveraigne with ye Burgesses and Comonality of said Burrough Thomas Knox Marchᵗ Foreman of ye Grand Jury ([cum] sosius) amongst other things considering ye great prejudice donn to Marchants in theire Trade and shipping for want of a good large kea or wharfe upon ye River and dock of Bellfast did present it as a thinge most necessary for ye good of Trade and wellfaire of this Corporacon that ye old kea or wharfe be inlarged and built up upon ye strand on ye south side of ye river of ye Towne of Bellfast & next adjoineing to ye old kea afforesᵈ. or ye new stone houses of George M'Cartney & Henry Thomson and for ye better effecting whereof they have desired that supplycation be made to ye Rᵗ Honnoᵇˡᵉ ye Countis Dowager of Donnegall & ye Lady Ann Chichester to gaine their consent and supply towards ye building of ye same as well as that money may be levied of ye said Corporacon to ffinish ye said worke Wee therefore considering ye necessity of ye worke and ye good desire of ye Grand Jury doe this day order that ye said kea or wharfe shall be made and inlarged from ye said new stone house to ye lagan River at low water marke as shall be thought fitt and [in or] pursuant thereto ye Soveraigne for ye time being shall give order from time to time to applott and collect from the Inhabitants afforesaid such moneys as shall be needfull for ye said worke & for ye confirming hereof this order shall be made into a by Law to remaine

Geo M'Cartney Soveraigne

George M'Cartney Gillᵗ Wye John Leathes Robᵗ Leathes Mich Harryson George Martin Edw Reynell

Burrough of }   Att a Court of Assembly held the
  Belfast   } eighteenth [day] day of Apprill In the
yeare of our Lord God 1676 Before the Corporation of the
Burrough afores.ᵈ the ffreemen Backers of this Corporation did
[admitt] prefer a petition to the Soveraigne and the Burgisses
his bretherin And upon due consideration had thereof by
the Soveraigne and Burgesses itt is ordered that imeadiatly
from and after this 18th day of Apprill 1676 noe stranger
or Allien that is not free of the burrough afores.ᵈ shall put
to saile or sell either in Publique or privatt any bread of
what kinde soever within the Towne of Belfast afores.ᵈ without it be upon the Markitt day from Nine a Clock in the
morning to three in the afternoone

HE nineteenth day of October one thousand six
hundred seaventy six being at an Assembly
held for ye Corporacon of Belfast ye Soveraigne
and major parte of yᵉ Burgesses of ye Borrough
afforesaid James M'Cartney gentleman one of ye
ffree Comoners of this Borrough was ellected and sworne a
ffree Burgesse of ye Corporacon of Bellfast afforesaid in ye
roome place and stead of William Warring Esqʳ late
deceased

Geo M'Cartney Soveraigne

Tho Walcot George Martin John Leathes George
M'Cartney Hugh: Eccles Edw Reynell John
ʰⁱˢ I L ᵐᵃʳᵏ Leathes Fr Thettford Rob Leathes

The 14ᵗʰ day of June 1677 being at yᵉ Assembly held for
yᵉ Corporacon of Bellfast yᵉ Soveraigne and major parte of
yᵉ Burgesses of yᵉ Borrough affores.ᵈ Henry Thetford
gentleman one of yᵉ free Comoners of this Corporacon was
ellected and sworne a free Burgesse of the Corporacon of
Bellfast afforesaid in yᵉ Roome and place and stead of John
Leathes gentl late deceased

Geo: M'Cartney Soveraigne

Edw Reynell Tho Walcot George M'Cartney
George Martin John Leathes Fr. Thettford
Robᵗ Leathes

Burrough of Belfast } Att a Court of Assembly held for ye Borrough affores^{d} this 26th of July 1677 by y Soveraigne and Major pte of ye Burgesses then assembled *it was ordered* that ye sume of six pounds sterl be forthwith assessed and applotted upon ye Inhabitants of ye Towne of Bellfast for ye Furnishing and buying of twelve good substantiall halberts for ye use of ye said Towne ye better to arme and [their] strengthen the night watch of ye s^{d} Towne in order to ye good security and safety of ye said Towne and Inhabitants thereof wch said twelve halberts are to be preserved and made forthcomeing for y^{e} use afforesaid by y^{e} Soveraigne of y^{e} said Borrough for y^{e} time being

Geo: M'Cartney Soveraigne

John Leathes Edwd Reynell Tho Walcot Robt Leathes Ja: M'Cartney Henry Thettford

Att an Assembly held for the Borrough of Belfast with the consent of the Right Honno^{ble} the Countess Dowager of Donnegall this twenty fifth day of Aprill one thousand six hundred seaventy eight. It is ordered by the Soveraigne and Burgesses then and there assembled; That upon p^{r}sentment of the Grand Jury then given in, and alsoe from complaint of severall of the said Burrough, And the suburbs thereto belonginge that the Mastive dogs belonginge to Butchers, Tanners, and other the Inhabitants dwelling in this Corporation and the suburbs and fields thereunto belonginge, have Barbarously ffallen upon horses in carrs, upon the Street, And alsoe horses out of carrs, And have violently Torne and abused them, That some of them have beene in hazard to die, And alsoe ffallen upon severall cattell both upon the Streets and in the ffields, Insomuch that severall cattell are mightily abused, and some of them killed to the great losse of many of the poore Inhabitants of this Corporacon. And also that the said Dogs have ffallen upon severall men and boyes upon the Streets and Lanes of this Towne and suburbs thereunto belonginge, and have pult them to the Ground, Torne their cloathes and Torne some of their fflesh and eaten the same Insoemuch that many Inhabitants feare their lives to walke the streets or laines either by night or day for the said dogs and Bitches. IT IS THEREFORE Enacted by the consent aforesaid to endure for ever for A By Law of this Corporation That if any Butcher, Tanner, or any person whatsoever Burgess or ffreeman, or any other Inhabitant within the said Corporation, suburbs, or Liberty thereof, shall keep any Mastive Dog or Bitch walkinge in the streets, or in the fields after this day, unlesse they bee Sufficiently muzled and collored soe that they bee fully secured from any danger of doeinge harme either to man or beast, every such [such] person Shall for every such offence, of dogg or Bitch wanderinge unmuzled and secured as aforesaid, pay the sume of Forty Shillings sterlinge; To bee Levyed of their goods and chattels by distress or otherwise for the use of the Corporation; Besides their actions at Comon Law which shall and may be comenced against every such offender And for want of money or distresse for sattisfieinge the said Fine, that such persons shall bee comitted to prison by the Soveraigne for the time beinge dureinge pleasure. And Lastly it shall be Lawfull for any person whatsoever findeinge any of the said Dogs or Bitches offeringe or doeinge any Injury to kill them notwithstand of this former Fine

Geo M'Cartney Soveraigne

John Leathes Fr Thettford Hugh Eccles George M'Cartney Tho Walcot Rob Leathes

At an Assembly houlden for the Borrough afforesaid

The 25th day of July in the yeare of our Lord God one thousand six hundred seaventy and eight beinge at the Assembly held for the Corporacon of Belfast   The Soveraigne and major parte of the Burgesses of the Borrough aforesaid Lewis Thomson and John Hamilton gentlemen ffree Comoners of this Corporation were ellected and sworne ffree Burgesses of the Corporacon of Belfast aforesaid in the Roome place and stead of Henry Thetford and George Martin gentlemen late deceased

Geo: M[c]Cartney Soveraigne

Mich Harrysone (John)   Tho Walcot   George M[c]Cartney   Hugh Eccles   Ja: M[c]Cartney   John Leathes   Edw Reynell   Fr Thettford   Rob[t]: Leathes

Borough of Belfast   By George M[c]Cartney Esq[r]
Soveraigne

WHEREAS many complaints from time to time have been made of y[e] great want of good and wholsome water to supply y[e] dayly necessary occations of y[e] Inhabitants of this Towne of Bellfast for y[e] River that runs through y[e] said Towne is very much defiled and greatly abused by all manner of sinks falling into y[e] said River and other nusances corrupting y[e] same whereby ye water is made altogether unfit for ye use of man in meats and drinks   And whereas for y[e] better supply of y[e] said Inhabitants with good and wholsome water y[e] springes neere y[e] said Towne have ben viewed and an estimate thereof taken by George M[c]Cartney Burgesse and Capt Rob[t] Leathes w[ch] will cost neere two hundred and fifty pounds ster to bringe y[e] said water in pumps or wooden pipes from y[e] Upper or Tuck Mill Dame to y[e] great bridge of y[e] said Towne (contayneing aboute 200 pearch in Lenth) a place most convenient to supply y[e] whole Towne with water by a Comon Conduit   Therefore I doe hereby recomend y[e] said worke (soe well designed by y[e] said George M[c]Cartney & Capt Leathes and feasable to be don) to all y[e] Inhabitants of y[e] Towne of Bellfast to give their free will offeringe to defray y[e] said charge as verely believing every p'son that has a regard to his owne health will be moste ready and willing to further y[e] said worke notwithstanding it may be carryed on by y[e] Legislative power of y[e] Corporation dated y[e] 29th of July 1678

Geo M[c]Cartney

To George M[c]Cartney
March[t]

Soveraigne

Capt Rob[t] Leathes Pat[k] Hamilton gent Henry Cheads, W[m] Reyney John White, John Stewart James Stewart, James Buller and Robert Humphreys March[ts]

These to manage ye Subscription

agreed with y[e] workemen the 8th of August following to w[ch] agreement Mr Soveraigne signed

To all Christian people to whom these p^rsents shall come I John Biggar of Belfast in ye County of Antrim Marchant send Greeting   Whereas I am by Leasse bound to p^r.forme severall rents dutyes buildings improvem^ts. and reservations unto ye Rt Honble Arthur Earle of Donegall Visct Chichester &c on my part as by ye said Leasse dated ye first day of Aprill in ye Yeare of our Lord God one thousand six hundred sixty and eight and in ye nineteenth yeare of ye Reigne of our Soveraigne Lord Charles ye second by ye Grace of God Kinge of England Scotland ffrance and Ireland &c appeares, And whereas there is Severall Sumes of money due unto William Biggar in ye said Leasse named for arreares of rent of his part of ye said lands and tenem^ts wch I doe owe and am indebted unto him amounting to ye sume of seaventy pounds ster and unto my well beloved freinds James Gregg of Ballycopland in ye County of Downe and Thomas Biggar of Erwin in ye Kingdome of Scotland the sumes of fforty pounds ster wch I owe and am indebted unto them ye said James Gregg and Thomas Biggar by bonds which Rents dutyes Covenants Bargains and engagem^ts unto ye said Rt Honble Earle of Donegall and sumes of one hundred and tenn pounds to ye above said William Biggar James Gregg and Thomas Biggar I cannot fullfill p'forme satissfie nor make paym^t of as ye said noble Earle and they ye said William Biggar James Gregg and Thomas Biggar desire and doe demand of me by reason of many debts are owing unto me Know yee that I the said John Biggar for and in consideration of ye severall obligacions on my part to be p'formed in ye said Leasse as may be made appeare ; Relacion being had thereunto at more large, and for and in consideration of ye above mencioned sume of one hundred and tenn pounds debts, have given granted and by these presents doe give Grant and make over unto ye said William Biggar James Gregg and Thomas Biggar their heirs execut^rs administrato^rs. & ass^s all and singular my part interest, claime title and right unto ye said Leasse and all things therein contayned given and granted by ye Rt Honble Earle of Donegall afforesaid unto ye above named William and me ye said John Biggar (vizt.) one Tenem^t or halfe Burgage share of land scituate and being on ye south side of High Street in Bellfast afforesaid contayneing in ffront to high Street fforty two foote and six score and six ffoote backwards on ye east in Scoolhouse Lane together with three acres and a quarter of land in ye ffields be it more or lesse next Gills Land and allsoe ye plott of ground without north gate Street in Bellfast afforesaid and next adjoyneing to ye Grass of ye Rampier scituate on ye north side, of ye high way Leading from ye Towne to Pett^rs Hill called Goose Lane Contayneing thirty ffoote in ffront and extending backwards to a field of ground belonging to me ye said John Biggar all w^ch [said] demised premisses with all and singular my part and parcell thereof and of all houses Lands buildings Graftings plantings and improvemt^s with every thinge proffits and effects whatsover to me belonging or in anywise appertaining To have and To hould receive take and enjoye the same allwayes without any manner of prejudice of what is Covenanted reserved and excepted in ye said Leasse unto ye said Rt Honble Earle of Donegall his heirs and [assignes] successors unto ye said William Biggar his heirs Execut^ors administrat^ors and ass^s and they the said James Gregg and Thomas Biggar their heirs Execut^ors administrat^ors and ass^s as their and every of their own proper goods Lands and houses and Chatles for ever absolutely without any Reclaime Challenge or Contradiction whatsoever, and I have sett and putt to ye said William Biggar James Gregg and Thomas Biggar in full and peaceable possession of all and every of ye premisses by ye delivery unto them of a peece of coyned

money comonly called six pence fixed to ye seale heereof   In Witnesse of ye premisses I ye said John Biggar have heerunto sett my hand and seale this twenty two day of March in ye yeare of our Lord God one thousand six hundred sixty and eight and in ye twentieth yeare of ye reigne of our Soveraigne Lord Charles the second by ye Grace of God Kinge of England Scotland ffrance and Ireland &c   John Biggar.
Signed sealed and delivered
in ye presence of us
        John [Jamy] Erwin
        George McNaght
    Recorded and examined agreeing with ye originall this 11th day of March 1680 at ye desire of James Biggar Brother and Executor to ye above said William Biggar late deceased

                        Robt Leathes
                        Towne Clk

THE Table of Fees belonging and taken in the Borrough Court of Bellfast from the first time of Mr. Henry Lesquire Soveraigne [and before] Anno 1635

To the Judge of the Court.

	li	s	d
For every Judgemt undt twenty nobles	oo	o1	oo
For every Judgemt above twenty nobles for every pound four pence ster.	oo	oo	o4
For allowance of every writt out of the higher Court five groats	oo	o1	o8
For every Bayle	oo	oo	o4
For signing every Warrant	oo	oo	o4

To the Towne Clarke

	li	s	d
For entering of every [Bayle] action	oo	oo	o4
For entering of every Bayle	oo	oo	o4
For every Writ of Sumons Attachment Capias or distringas	oo	oo	o4
for every Venirefac alias Ad Plures and Writt of execucion	oo	o1	oo
for filling every declaracion plea and other pleadings and afidavits &c	oo	oo	o4
for ye coppy of declaracions pleas and other pleadings whatsoever for every sheete containing 12 lines ...	oo	oo	o4
for every apearance	oo	oo	o4
for every pledge of prosecucion where ye plaintiff is not a freeman and an Inhabitant in ye Jurisdiction of the Court	oo	oo	o8
for every imparlance, continuance warrant of Attorney and Joyeneing of issue	oo	oo	o4
for every peremtory day	oo	oo	o4
for entring every verdict.	oo	o1	oo

	li	s	d
for entring every Speciall verdict.	oo	o2	oo
for entring every Judgem^t by default confession dismisse Composition or satisfaction	oo	o1	oo
for taxing cost	oo	oo	o4
For entring every Writt out of ye Higher Court	oo	oo	o6
For certifieing every Record into the Higher Courts by Writt of Error habeas Corpus or writt of priveledge for every Role	oo	o6	o8
The fees of every person ellected sworne and recorded Burgesse twenty shill^s	o1	oo	oo
The fees of every Freeman recorded Marchant or gentleman five Shillings ster	oo	o5	oo
The fees of every person sworne freemen and recorded by their handy craft	oo	o2	o6
For every Burgesse tickett und^r the Seale of ye Corporacion tenn Shill	oo	1o	oo
For every March^t freemans and other freemans Tickett und^r ye Seale	oo	o5	oo
For every writing Certificate Bill of health for Shipping *or passe* wch may require to have ye Seale of the Corporacion affixed to it	oo	o2	o6

ffees agreed upon by ye Soveraigne and Burgesses to be taken by ye Towne Clarke 14th of Octob^r 1680

		li	s	d
1680	for entring every Submission or Travers upon a presentm^t	oo	oo	o6
	and for all ye rest of the fees upon ye Travers as in other actions			
	That no Fines be remitted without payeing twelve pence to ye Clarke or six pence ster if the fine exceed not two shills and six pence ster ...	oo	o1	oo
	For all Corporacion Warrants for mending of Bridges highwayes aprisends distresses Sesses or applotm^{ts} or any other kinde whatsoever and for pannells of Grand Jurys for each two shills and six pence ster to be paid outt of the readyest and sufficient fines ———	oo	o2	o6
1680	For entering the presentm^t of a Grand Jury in a Booke to be paid out of the fines of the said presentmen^t five shill^s	oo	o5	oo
	For recording every By Law Act and Ordnance of Corporacon to be ut supra five shill^s ster ...	oo	o5	oo

To the Sergeants at mace

		li	s	d
1635	For serving and executing of every Sumons Attachm^t or distringas	oo	oo	o6
	For ye Fees of every person that is comitted for want of Bayle or any other causes	oo	oo	o4
	for every Bayle	oo	oo	o2
	for sumoning every Jury between party and party	oo	oo	o6
	for every Judgem^t	oo	oo	o6
	for serving every execucion	oo	oo	o8
	The fee of every person that is comitted upon an execucion for his Irons	oo	o1	oo

		li	s	d
for every Writt from the higher Court		oo	oo	o4
1635	For sumoning of the Grandury (*sic*) and Freemen to Attend a Court of Assembly to be paid out of y⁰ Fines of the presentmᵗ two shills ster ...	oo	o2	oo
	For y⁰ fees of every Burgesse admitted	oo	1o	oo
	for y⁰ Fees of every freeman *marchant* admitted ...	oo	o5	oo
	for every macanick	oo	o2	o6
	for every oath in Court	oo	oo	o4

Attourney Fee

		li	s	d
1635	his retaining Fee	oo	o2	o6
	For drawing every Declaracion	oo	o1	oo
	For drawing every plea or other pleading	oo	o1	oo
	his Fee upon the tryall of the cause and on every Judgmᵗ	oo	o2	o6

THROUGH Tole and Customes taken at y⁰ Gates and passages into y⁰ Towne of Belfast for y⁰ use of the Soveraigne for y⁰ time being

ffor every horse Load of goods or marchandize being a fforriner or any sort of Timber	one halfepeny
for *every* wheele car Load of goods afforesaid	one penny
for every cart Load of goods drawne by more beasts than one for every beast	one halfepeny
for every Bull or Bullock ox cowe heifer brought into y⁰ Towne are driven through y⁰ Towne being fforraine one halfepeny	one halfepeny
1635 & for horsses and mares driven through one halfepeny	one halfepeny
Every fforrainer that slaughters or causes to be slaughtered any catle in y⁰ Towne and libertys of the same all y⁰ tongues of y⁰ said catle to be given to y⁰ Soveraigne to whom of ancient right and custome they belonge or to pay fower pence ster for each Tongue at y⁰ discretion of y⁰ said Soveraigne or ellection	a Tongue or fower pence ster for each at y⁰ election of y⁰ Soveraigne
Every ffreeman Butcher in y⁰ Towne & Corporacon or other ffreeman killing or cause to be killed one or more catle for saile or to be sould *in y⁰ markett* the Soveraigne is to have one neat Tongue from every person as afforesaid every weeke soe often as they or any of them shall kill as afforesaid	a Tongue each weeke
For every standing *place* or standing sett up in y⁰ Markett place or streets in Bellfast Towne by any person whatsoever to sell or retayle any goods or marchandize whatsoever shall pay for such place or standing every pedlar or Gray marchᵗ two pence ster & every other person one penny	Gray Marchants & pedlars 2ᵈ & others 1ᵈ
Out of every Sack of Meale sould in y⁰ Towne of Bellfast by retaile or wholesaile one standard quart dishfull	one quart dish full

Out of every Barrell of Wheat Rye Masslin Barley } one quart
Pease Beans and Oats &c one quart dishfull } dish full
affores.ᵈ

All vessells or shipps Loaden with coals or part pay
halfe a barrell of coales to yᵉ Sargnt.ˢ

Out of every Sack of Turffe to take two turffe for
Custome

except ye ffees established in 1680 not then in being

The afforesaid Table of fees are yᵉ whole fees taken in yᵉ Borrough
Court of Bellfast and allsoe all yᶜ petty customes and through Tole taken at
yᶜ gates and Markett of the Towne and Borrough of Bellfast a copy whereof
was *sent* up to yᶜ Parliamᵗ at Dublin yᶜ 5ᵗʰ of Feby 1665 by Edward Reynell
then Soveraigne and were approved of and confirmed

Entᵈ & examᵈ   Edward Reynell
  per Rob Leathes   Soveraigne

HIS 27ᵗʰ day of August in yᵉ yeare of our Lord
God one thousand six hundred [seavant] and
eighty being at yᵉ Assembly held for yᵉ Corporaccon of Bellfast the Soveraigne and Major
parte of yᵉ Burgesses of yᵉ Borrough afforesaid
Capt Edward Harrisson a ffree Comoner of this Corporacon
was ellected and sworne a ffree Burgesse of the Corporacon
of Bellfast afforesaid in yᵉ roome place and stead of Sʳ
Hercules Langford Kᵗ & Barronett who surrendred [who]
his Burshipp to yᵉ Corporacon and desired it to be given
to yᵉ said Edward Harrisson

Geo M'Cartney Soveraigne

Michˡ Harrisson   George M'Cartney   Fra Thettford
Lewes Thompson   John Hamiltone   Tho Walcot
John Leathes   Ja M'Cartney   Robᵗ Leathes

A Coppy of a Lettᵗ from my Lady Langford to Capt Harrisson as ffolloweth

Sʳ I am desired by Sʳ Hercules Langford to accquainte you that he cannot be
in yᵉ north as hee intended and writt to yoᵘ in his last by reason he is so
disinabelled by sicknesse that he cant travill but he is well content that yoᵘ have
his place of Burgesse of Bellfast. he knows its not in yoʳ power to putt another in
his place without his consent but since yoᵘ desire it and to doe you a kindesse he
quitts it to yoᵘ. and wishesses it may doe yoᵘ much good he has such weaknesse
in his right hand that he cannot write nor make any use of his hand wᶜʰ is yᵉ
cause that he doth not write to yoᵘ himselfe wᶜʰ is all at present from yoʳ friend &
humble servᵗ

Mary Langford

This 27ᵗʰ day of August in yᵉ yeare of our Lord God
one thousand six hundred and eighty being at yᵉ Assembly
held for ye Corporacon of Bellfast The Soveraigne and

major parte of ye Burgesses of ye Borrough afforesaid Thomas Knox Gentleman and a ffree Comoner of this Corporacon was ellected and sworne a ffree Burgesse of ye Corporacon of Bellfast afforesaid in ye roome place and stead of Gilbert Wye Gentleman who surrendered his Burgisship as by ye underwriting.

Geo M'Cartney, Soveraigne

Tho Walcot   Mich^l Harrisson   Fra Thettford   Ja M'Cartney   E Harrison   Robt Leathes

A coppy of parte of Lett^r from Coll. Hill to George M'Cartney Esqr Soveraigne of Bellfast bearing date at London ye 31 of July 1680 in these words following (Mr Wye offered me to resigne to me his Burgesse sh^p [place] my Lady is willing to have it for Mr Knox & soe am I

John Hill

Memorandum the 24th of June 1684. Sr William ffranklin produced to ye Soveraigne and Burgesses assembled at ye house of Mr John Hamilton then Soveraigne a writting und^r ye hand and seale of Mr. Gilbert Wye one of the Burgesses of this Corporacon wherein he resigned up his Burgesship to ye said Corporacon in whose place Mr Thomas Knox was ellected aud sworne as afforesaid notwithstanding some of the Burgesses where (*sic*) disatisfied that Mr Wye should have ben putt out of his place without a fault or a resignation appearing *contrary to Charter* but now all are satisfied by y^e said resignation

ROPOSALLS made to ye Soveraigne & Burgesses at a Court of Assembly held for ye Borrough of Bellfast ye 14th Octob^r 1680 to be debated and disgested into By Laws Acts and Ordinances for ye good of the Corporacon

1 That the Poores money be secured on Lands or in good hands and suff^ct security to be passed by Indenture from Soveraigne to Soveraigne yearly; and the Table where ye benifacto^rs for ye poore are incerted may be fairly drawne over and the Earle of Donegall's name may be entered in Lett^rs of Gould with the sume blanke in its collume till ye 200^li left by his will be paid for ye use of the said poore and allsoe ye names of all other persons with their sumes may be entered that have given that others when they see what is left and soe well secured may be induced to ffollow their good example for ye good of the decayed Inhabitants of this Corporacon.

agreed on & to be don accordingly.

2 That all Inmates and Beggars who come into and secrettly convey them selves into ye Towne and beggs to releive beggars may be dilligently sought after and a speedy course taken to discharge ye Towne of such.—Agreed on to be donn

3 That ye Orphant children left on ye Towne such as are fitt to be bound apprentices may be sett to Masters and ye Towne eased of the burden—agreed to be donn.

4 That *all* the waights and measures used in ye Corporacon be tryed ajusted and sealed by a Court of Clarke of the Markett heire every yeare and the due ffees paid for ye same—agreed on

5 That Lights in Lanthorns be hunge at every other house doore or window time aboute in ye Dark Nights from ye houres of six to tenn from ye 29th of September to ye 29th of March ffollowing to give lights to ye Streets and Lanes of ye Towne for the benefitt of ye Inhabitants and passingers and to prevent disorders and mischeife—agreed on

6 That all freemen of this Corporacon be minded of their oath (at Assemblys) not to sue or implead any ffreeman in any other Courte than the Borrough without Leave first had and obtained in writing und.^r ye hand of the Soveraigne

7 That a rate be sett upon porters either with carridge of horsse or without proportionable to all ye Streets and Lanes of the Towne to where they shall carry any goods and that noe such shall be admitted to ride their horsse when in a Carr or Cart in any of the Streets and Lanes afforesaid to prevent disorder and mischeife wch have thereby usually happened— agreed to and the rates to be considered

8 That a rate be putt upon salters and packers of Beefe und.^r a penalty if they doe not salt and packe faithfully and that none salt or pack Beefe for sale but such as shall be allowed and approved of—agreed on & ye persons and number to be considered on

9 That all persons presented by ye Grand Jury shall have to ye next Court or that seaven night to submitt or Travis to their p^rsentm^{ts} & to pay not above six pence ster for entring their Travis and if the party submitts or found guilty by a Jury upon his Travis then the fine to be agreed on by the Soveraigne with 3 or more of the Burgesses or the Bench be they more or lesse and such fines levied for ye use of the Corporacon—to be considered on that a right method be taken for doeing of this

10 That ye By Law Impowering the Soveraigne of the said Corporacon to have and receive to his use ye ffines may be repealed—agreed on

11 That a Treasurer may be appointed to receive the fines and all other moneys of the Corporacon and not to issue the same for any use whatsoever—particular warrant—agreed on

12 That all such warrants be signed by the Soveraigne for the time being and three or more of the Burgesses [at ye Least]

13 That noe ffine be remitted without twelve pence ster be paid the Clarke for his ffees cleereing ye said fine upon ye Role, p^rsentm.^t or otherwise—agreed on

This 27th of Janry 1680 (1)

This day being a Courte of Assembly held for the Borrough of Bellfast it was agreed on by the Soveraigne

and major part of the Burgesses That the Soveraigne
for the time being Lewis Thomson John Hamilton and
Thomas Knox Burgesses have power to reduce all the
above proposalls into a certaine method for rates number
and place where such are required and the rest to be
drawne up in such order as upon a Generall view and
debate of us all or major parte they may be made By Lawes
for yᵉ good of the said Borrough

Signed by order

R L Clk

HEREAS there was a by Law made by
Authority of yᵉ Corporacon yᵉ 19ᵗʰ day of
October 1667 for ye granting all fines upon
p'sentmᵗ of Grand Jurys and petty Customes
not exceeding Tenn Shill stᵣ to yᵉ use of yᵉ
Soveraigne for yᵉ time being towards his house keepeing
wᶜʰ By Law have ben from time to time very much
complained of by ye generallity and major parte of this
Corporacon as grevious to ye people and a takeing away of
ye Revenue of this Towne by wᶜʰ they are disinabled to
pay Severall Contingent charges of the said Towne and
particular that ye Grand Jury for ye Borrough held at a
Court of Assembly ye 27ᵗʰ day of Jany 1680 complained of
ye said By Law and presented their desires to ye Bench that
ye said By Law might be repealed and yᵉ ffines and
Customes retourne to ye use of ye said Corporacon and soe
managed hereafter that a stock or Towne pursse may
effectually be raised for ye Generall Good of ye said Towne
Therefore it is hereby ordained and enacted as a By Law
for ever By the Soveraigne and Burgesses at ye Court of
Assembly held for ye said Borrough the 21ˢᵗ day of Aprill
1681 and by the Authority of ye said Corporacon That ye
said By Law shall be and are heereby wholly taken away
made voyd and null and fully repealed as if ye same had
never ben.   Provided allways that it shall be in ye power
and major part of yᵉ Burgesses at any time to allow to yᵉ
Soveraigne for ye time being such sume or sumes of money
out of ye said ffins and petty customes as they ye said
Soveraigne and major parte of ye Burgesses shall thinke

fitt towards his hospitallity and house keeping dated ye 21ˢᵗ of April 1681

George MᶜCartney Soveraigne

George M'Cartney Thomas Walcott ffra Thetford
John Leathes Robert Leathes Lewis Thomson
John Hamilton Tho Knox Sampson Theaker
Copia Vera Rob Leathes Town Clk

Entᵈ & exᵈ

This 24 of June in ye yeare of our Lord God one thousand six hundred and eighty one being at ye Assembly held for ye Corporacon of Bellfast ye Soveraigne and Burgesses of ye Borrough of Bellfast Sampson Theaker Gentleman and free Comoner of this Corporacon was ellected and sworne a free Burgesse of ye Corporacon of Bellfast afforesaid in ye Roome and place and steed of Hugh Eccles Gentl late deceased

George MᶜCartney Soveraigne

Geo M'Cartney Tho Walcot John Leathes Robᵗ
Leathes Lewes Thompson Tho Knox ffra Thettford Ja M'Cartney John Hamilton L Harrison

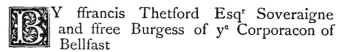

Y ffrancis Thetford Esqʳ Soveraigne and ffree Burgess of yᵉ Corporacon of Bellfast

An ordᵗ for yᵉ Sessing of 135ˡⁱ for watter pipes

Whereas George M'Cartney of Bellfast Marchᵗ and Capᵗ Robᵗ Leathes ye 8th of August 1678 by and with ye Consent of ye Soveraigne and Burgesses and major parte of ye Comonality of this Corporacon did agree with workemen for ye conveyeing cleane wholsome water in wooden pips undᵗ ground ye lenth of 200 pearches into ye Towne of Bellfast for ye supply and generall good of ye Inhabitants of ye said Towne according to wᶜʰ agreement ye said worke was made and performed and water brought to ye said Towne Runing at three severall conduits standing in ye streets whereof all ye Inhabitants are partakers of ye benefitt of ye same att ye proper cost and charges of ye said George M'Cartney to ye vallue of one hundred seaventy five pounds whereof ye Rt Honb^le Leticia Countis Dowager of Donegall voluntary to incourage soe good a worke has paid and promised to pay ye sume of forty pounds ster & whereas ye remaining sume [of] being one hundred thirty ffive pounds ster could not be raised by subscriptions Therefore the severall Grand Juryes of this Corporation vizt at assembly held the 14th of October 1680—20th Aprill 1681—ye 28th July 1681 have p^rsented that ye said George M'Cartney should be reimburssed his costs and charges of ye said worke by assessm^t from the Inhabitants of Bellfast, Pursuant thereunto wee ye Soveraigne and Burgesses this day assembled doe order by vertue of ye power of ye said Corporacon That ye Soveraigne for ye time being issue out warrants from time to time to ye Severall Sessers that were and are now chosen since ye 8th of August 1678 requireing them or any three or more of them equally to applott and Sesse on ye Inhabitants of Bellfast accordinge to their severall Estates and abillityes the said sume of one hundred thirty five pounds ster and that ye same may be forthwith lieved (*sic*) and paid to ye said George M'Cartney to reimbursse himselfe ye charges of ye said worke Provided allwayes that all those persons who have freely contributed and paid to ye said worke be allowed the same in their respective Sesses Dated ye 11th of May 1682

ffra: Thettford, Soveraigne

Lewes Thompson	Robt Leathes	Tho: Walcot
Tho: Knox	George M'Cartney	John Hamilton
John Leathes	Fra: Theaker	

Borrough of Belfast

BY ffra Thetford Soveraigne Borrough of Bellfast Whereas the Towne of Belfast for many yeares last past has been very defective of good clean and wholsome water to ye prejudiceing ye health of the Inhabitants which grevance and want was in or about ye 29th of July 1678 by George M'Cartney Esqr. then Soveraigne of the said Borrough und^r his hand recomened to ye Inhabitants to raise money by a ffree will offring to defray ye charge in bringing clean ffresh water to ye said Towne through pipes two hundred pearch as it was

then projected by George M'Cartney March^t & Captn
Robert Leathes att an estimate charge of two hundred and
fifty pounds ster wch recomendacion was freely imbraced by
the said Inhabitants and many of them subscribed to ye
said worke and that so good a designe (wch was liked and
much recomended by all sorts of people) should not goe
back or want incouragem^t ye R^t Hono^rble Leticia Countis
Dowager of Donegall gave forty pounds ster to ye
same and thereupon and by a general consent ye said
George M'Cartney and Capt Robert Leathes agreed with
workemen begun and perfeicted ye said worke in wooden
pipes bound with Iron contayneing in lenth two hundred
Irish pearch with water house and three conduits (runing)
at ye charge of one hundred seaventy five pounds ster w^ch
was expended and laid out att ye proper cost and charges
of ye said George M'Cartney wch sume is not repaid unto
him notwithstanding the said subscription and to remedy
ye remissness of the said Inhabitants therein severall Grand
Juryes of this Corporation (vizt) att Assembly held for ye
same ye 14th of October 1680 ye 20th of Apl 1681 ye 28th of
July 1681 [have] did all of them amongst other things for ye
good and benefitt of this Towne p^r.sent that one hundred
thirty five pounds ster should be raised by way of assessm^t
on ye Inhabitants of Bellfast wch with ye sume of fforty
pounds given by ye said Countis of Donegall should be
paid into ye hands of ye said George M'Cartney with
thankes to reimburse himselfe ye afforesaid charge of one
hundred seaventy five pounds conveying ye water in ye
Towne of Bellfast and forasmuch as ye money allready paid
ye said George M'Cartney by moste of the subscribers doe
not satisfie ye charge for that there is still due him a considerable sume of money wch by an order of ye Soveraigne
and Burgesses ye 11th of May 1682 was appointed to be
raised by way of assessm^t as by ye said order may more at
large appeare These are therefore by the authority afforesaid
and pursuant to ye severall p^r.sentm^ts of ye Grand Juryes
afforesaid to will and require you uppon sight heereof to meete
together in some convenient place and before yor departure
to applott and Sesse upon ye Inhabitants of Bellfast equally
accordingly to their severall Estates and abillityes ye sume
of one hundred thirty five pounds ster. and ye same fairely
drawne und^r yor hands subscribed retourne to me that a
warrant may be issued out for ye collecting and bringing in
ye said 135^li att or before ye 1st day Septr next that the said

George McCartney may be thankfully paid and that such p'sons as have allready paid by free will offering shall be allowed ye same in their respective Sesses and heereof yoᵘ are not to faile as yoᵘ will answer ye contrary and for yoʳ soe doeing this shall be yoʳ warrant dated yᵉ 17ᵗʰ of July 1682

ffra Thetford Soveraigne

To Capᵗ *Robᵗ* Leathes
Mr Lewis Thomson
Cornett John Hamilton
Mʳ Tho Knox
} Burgesses or any two or more

Will Lockert Marchᵗ
Quarter Mastʳ Wᵐ Craford
Wᵐ Reyney Marchᵗ
James Stewart Marchᵗ
Henry Cheads Marchᵗ
John Adam Marchᵗ
Andrew Maxwell Marchᵗ
Richard Ayshmore
James Gambell
} or any three or more of them

HE six day of September one thousand six hundred eighty two ye Soveraigne and major parte of ye Burgesses assembled together in ye markett or Courthouse for ye chusing and ellecting a Burgess in ye place of Mr Edward Reynalls who departed this life ye 29ᵗʰ of August last att wᶜʰ meeting Lᵗ John Tooley was ellected and chosen and sworne a free Burgesse of ye Borrough of Bellfast in ye roome and place of ye said Mr Edward Reynalls

ffra Thettford Soveraigne

John Leathes　　Tho Walcot　　George M'Cartney
Lewis Thompson　Tho Knox　　Fra Theaker

Ad Curiam Publicam tentam Vicesimo die Maii anno Regni Domini nostri Caroli secundi &ᶜ Tricesimo Quinto Annoque Domini Sexcentesimo Octogesimo Tertio Coram Ludovico Thomson Superior villae pʳᵈ W:E: armiger Electus et constitutus fuit m— ejusdem Villae ex mutuo assensu totius curiae. In cujus Testimonium Idem Superior presentibus subscripsit et sigillum comune Villae pʳᵈ apponeficit die et anno Supradic

HE twenty fourth day of March one thousand six hundred eighty six the Soveraigne and major part of the Burgesses assembled together for the chusing and electing a Burgesse in the place of Mr Jno Hamilton who departed this life the twentyth instant, at which meeting Mr Willm Crafford merchant was elected and sworne a free Burgesse of the Burrough of Belfast aforesaid in the roome and place of the said Mr Jno Hamilton.

Robt Leathes Soveraigne

Will ffranklin   John Hill   John Leathes   Geo M'Cartney   ffra Thetford   George McCartney   Ja McCartney   Lewes Thompson   Tho Knox   Fra Theaker   Joh: Tooley

At an Assembly held 22nd Octob^r 1686 for the Borrough of Bellfast certaine rules and orders were established & made for ye preventing unnecessary delays in ye proceedings of the Court of Record held for ye said Borrough

HE plaintiff is to enter his action with ye Towne Clarke or his deputy and take from him an attachment directed to ye serjeants or one of them and signed by ye Soveraigne for the time being to arrest ye body or goods of the defendant to answer his plaint next Court upon executing of wch writt ye defendant may give any substantiell freeman Bayle and no other then such at the will of the Clarke or Serj^ts who are to answer such Bayle to ye Court and all such Bayle to be recorded with ye action in ye Court booke

2 That after ye attachment is executed if the defendant be in custody for want of Baile and the [deft] plaintiff charge him not with a declaracion next Court he shall be nonsuited and pay costs and if Baile be taken the plaintiff is next Court after such arrest made to file his declaracion and for want thereof a Rule to be entered that the plaintiff declaire ye next Court ffollowing or to be nonsuited and if no declaracion be then filed the plaintiff to be nonsuited according to ye Rule & pay costs.

3 If the plaintiff file his declaracion according to ye rule then a rule to be entered that ye defendant plead next Court or Judgem^t & for want of wch plea judgem^t to passe by default with costs of Court & soe of other pleadings the above methods to be observed.

4 If any ffreeman sue another ffreeman then he is to repaire to the Towne Clarke or deputy & enter his action & from him receive a summons to ye defendant to appeare next Court to answer ye plaintif wth if he appeare to the rules to be entered as in the case of attachm^t above is mencioned. if he doe not appeare upon ye Sumons then attachment is to be taken out in manner afforesaid and ye rules and proceedings to be entered in maner and forme as afforesaid

5 That noe forraigne plea to be received into ye Court or filed as a record without the oath of the party or his Attorney who tenders the same.

6 That demures in inferior Courts and upon smale actions tend more to delay them justice and therefore not to be allowed in the Court without being signed by Councell and if the Court suspect the reality of its being signed while perhaps such Councell lives remote the Demurrer not [being signed] to be accepted unlesse ye party produceing the same or his Attorney make oath that it is really signed by such Councell

7 That upon every Judgm.ᵗ by default confession by verdict or non pross that ye party for whom such judgment passes shall come to ye record and by the Clerk have his [Judgm] execucion drawne up and signed by the Soveraigne to leavy the sume awarded by such Judgm.ᵗ with ye costs of the party and for want of his body or goods ags.ᵗ the Bail or manucaptor if he be defendant or agst the pledge if plaintiff. the same to be on one writt for ye more speedy proceeding.

8 It is allwayes provided that notwithstanding the afforesaid Rules the Soveraigne hath liberty to continue ye same upon affidavett made or for such other reasons as to him shall appeare : the said Rules being chiefly designed to bound the litigious delayes of the Attorneys who are hereby ordered to be concluded by ye said Rules or to be debarred from practice in ye Court or have such other cheques as the Soveraigne judges convenient.

9 That upon all fines at Courts of Assembly for non appearance or other fines whatsoever then inflicted if the Court think fitt to mitigate or remitt such fines that notwithstanding the party amerced shall pay twelve pence ster to ye Clerk for cleareing the said ffine upon ye Record Role according to a former order of the Soveraigne and Burgesses in ye year 1680

𝕭y, lawes

Borrough
Belfast

Att an Assembly held the 4ᵗʰ day of November one thousand six hundred eighty six 1686 with the consent of the Honor.ᵇˡᵉ S.ʳ William ffrancklin Lord of the Castle of Bellfast it is ordered by Robert Leathes Esqr Soveraigne and the Burgesses then and there assembled.

Butchers to repaire to ye new Shambles 12ᵈ fine

That whereas dayly complaints are made of the inconvenience of the Butchers keepeing their meate upon the streets without shambles w.ᶜʰ not only is undecent of itself but much straitens that part of the street which is designed and alotted for publique markett. and whereas for the publique good there is an apartment prepared within the new buildings on ye south side of Castle Streete that all Butchers inhabitants of this said Towne shall repaire to ye said Apartment and furnish themselves with shambles Convenient at or before the 25ᵗʰ day of March next upon pain of forfeiting twelve pence sterl toties quoties found in the streets with stales and that the said stales shall be removed the said fine to be levyed by distresse or otherwise by warrant from the Soveraigne for the time being and the same to be imployed for ye good and benefitt of this Corporacon

a barrell of Lime to be 32 gallons Winchester

Att ye same Assembly by the authority afforesaid Ordered that whereas there is great fraud comitted dayly by the selling of Lyme by unjust and undue measures, That from and after the first day of May next every barrell of

Rock or unfallen Lyme brought to be sould or sould within this Corporacon shall containe thirty two gallons Winchester measure upon paine makeing default of six pence sterl per barrell toties quoties the same to be levied &c ut supra.

ye Turfe hogshead to be 70 gallons 2ᵈ fine

Att ye same Assembly by the authority afforesaid Ordered that all horsse Loads of Turfe brought into this Corporacon to be sold shall be of the full measure of one Burdeaux wine hogshead of Seaventy wine gallons upon paine of two pence sterl for every faulty Load and that there be at the publique charge of the Borrough sealed hogsheads prepared for measureing the same and Lodged in some convenient place in ye Towne to be found on all occasions by wᶜʰ debates of that nature are to be decided to be levied ut supra.

Lanteren & candle light to be hunge out 6ᵈ fine

Att the same Assembly the 4ᵗʰ of November 1686 Ordered that to prevent the dangers to which persons walking in the night about their lawfull occasions are incident to, every Inhabitant in every Street and Lane of this Corporation shall from henceforth in every yeare from the 29ᵗʰ of September to ye 25ᵗʰ of March hang out at their respective doores or shops one Lanthorne and candle lighted from ye houre of seaven oClock till ten at night when it is not moon-shine in ye said houres, upon paine of 6ᵈ ster per night toties quoties to be levied &ᶜ.

Beefe barrells 30 wine gallons 12ᵈ fine

Att ye same Assembly Ordered that whereas it is known that the reputacion of the Trade in this Towne abroad is much impaired by the insufficiency of Beefe barrells for several yeares past every Beefe Barrell made by any Cooper in Bellfast or by him them or any person sold in ye said Towne after ye first day of May shall be made of good well season timber well hooped and stanch and to be of the measure of thirty wine gallons on paine of twelve pence ster for every faulty barrell to be levied &ᶜ.

Bucketts Ladders & hooks poles provided 4ˢ 6ᵈ fine

Att the same Assembly ordered that for the better secureing the houses of this Corporacon from the casulty of ffire and in imitacion of the laudable practice of other Towns and Borroughs every Inhabitant of sixty pounds str free substance shall at or before the first day of May next at his own proper cost furnish one Leathern buckett and the same deliver to ye Soveraigne for the time being to be lodged in some place ready on all exigences and that the Soveraigne at the publique charge do compleat the Ladders wᶜʰ now are to be fower in number and provide a cupple of poles with hooks and chaines for pulling downe houses on such occasions the said Bucketts to be delivered to ye Soveraigne for the use afforesaid against the next quarterly Assembly for this Borrough on pain of fower shills and six pence ster forfeiture each person to be levied &ᶜ

I consent to these By Lawes
& orders & that they be duly
recorded

    Will ffranklin

To all ye anexed orders and By Lawes made the 4ᵗʰ of Novembᵣ 1686 the Soveraigne and Burgesses then assembled doe here subscribe to

           Robᵗ Leathes Soveraigne

Jo Hill   John Leathes   Lewis Thomson   Geo: M'Cartney   Sa: Theaker   George M'Cartney John Tooley   Edward Harrisson   Arthur Upton

John Younge Com Sergᵗ
10 ffeby 86 (7)

ACOBUS Secundus Dei Gratia Angliæ Scotiæ Franciæ et Hiberniæ Rex fidei defensor &ᶜ Vice-comiti Antrim salutem precipimus tibi quod non omittas propter aliquam libertatem in Ballivia tua quin eam ingrediaris et per probos et legales homines de Ballivia tua sciri facias Superiorem liberos Burgenses et Communes Burgenses de Bellfast in comitatu predicto quod sint coram Barronibus de Scaccario nostro apud le King's Courts Dublin in quindeno Paschæ proximo futuro ad reddendum nobis quo Warranto jure sive titulo clamant habere uti & gaudere libertates privilegia et francisia sequentia videlicet fore de seipsis unum corpus corporatum et politicum in re facto et nomine per nomen Superioris liberorum Burgensium et Communii Burgensium de Belfast et per idem nomen placitare et implacitare respondere et responderi ac habere potestatem mittendi duos Burgenses ad attendendum parliamentum et tenere Curiam de Recordo quæ quidem franchesia libertates et privilegia predicti Superior liberi Burgenses et communitas Burgensium predicti per spatium vinus anni jam ultimo elapsi et amplius usurpaverunt et adhuc usurpant in nostri contemptum et regii nostri prerogativi grave dampnum et prejudicium manifestum prout in quadam informacione versus prefatos Superiorem liberos Burgenses et communes Burgenses de Belfast in comitatu predicto exhibituros per attornatum nostrum generalem qui pro nobis in hac parte sequitur plenius liquet et apparet, et ulterius ad recipiendum quid Barrones nostri superinde fieri faciant quod de jure et secundum leges et consuetudines dicti regni nostri Hiberniæ fuerit faciendum et habeas ibi tunc nomen et per quos eis jura faciant et hoc breve

Jone Henrico Hene nostro capitali Barroni Scaccarii nostri predicti apud Le King's Courts predictum xii. die Februarii anno regni nostri tertio

Barry

Johannes Nethercott

deputatus Rememorator Thesaurarii

Copia vera of what by Michael M'Cormick was given the Soverain the 9th April 1687

Aprile 11th 1687

At an Assembly of the Soveraign and major part of the Burgesses then had touching the s^d Quo warranto

RESOLVED That we the Soveraign and Burgesses of this Burrough are unanimously agreed to defend our charter by all legall means whatsoever, and in order thereunto will give our best assistance with advice and money to retaine Councell, Attorneys, Solicitors & other Agents for carrying on a Legall Defence in what Courts soever the said Charter shall hereafter be legally impeached.

Robt Leathes Soveraigne

Tho: Knox   Sa: Theaker   Joh: Tooley   Wm Crafford Geo M'Cartney Joh Hill Tho Walcot George McCartney Ja: M'Cartney Lewis Thompson

The seventh day of May one thousand six hundred eighty seven, the Soveraign and major p^t of the Burgesses assembled together for the chusing and electing a Burgesse in the room of L^t. John Tooley who departed this life

the sixth instant, at which meeting M͏ʳ William Lockhart Merch͏ᵗ was elected and sworne in the place of said L͏ᵗ Tooley

Rob͏ᵗ Leathes Soveraigne

Joh: Hill   Sa Theaker   W͏ᵐ Crafford   Geo: M͏ᶜCartney   John Leathes   Tho Walcot   ffra: Thetford   George M'Cartney   Ja: M'Cartney   Lewis Thompson

At an Assembly of the Soveraigne & Burgesses on Saturday the 14ᵗʰ of May 1687

RESOLVED

That whereas by M͏ʳ Martins letter of the 12ᵗʰ instant (who solicites the affair about the charter) there is hazard of Judgm͏ᵗ being entered up ag͏ˢᵗ it for not sending up the originall pattent to be p'duced to the Attorney Genrall as a voucher to the plea filed pursuant to a peremptory rule of Court of ye 9ᵗʰ instant It is now resolved that the s͏ᵈ charter be forthwith sent up to Mr Martin our s͏ᵈ solicitor by Hugh Crafford an expresse, that Mr Martin may use all possible meanes to p͏ʳvent or retrieve what contempts Judgments or other misavencincies may be placed upon us for the reason aforesaid & it is now accordingly sent up

Rob͏ᵗ Leathes Soveraigne

The enrolment of the charter is dated 11ᵗʰ Jac: primus of Engl͏ᵈ & 46 of Scotl͏ᵈ

Geo: M'Cartney
Lewis Thompson
George M'Cartney
Wm Crafford

JAMES the Second by ye Grace of God of England Scotland ffrance & Ireland King Defend͏ʳ of ye ffaith &c To all to whom these our Lett͏ʳˢ Pattents shall come Health, Whereas the Town or Borrough of Belfast in ye County of Antrim hath been an antient Borrough & ye Soveraign ffree Burgesses & Cominality of the Town or Borrough aforesaid have had used & enjoyed very many liberties priviledges and ffranchises within ye Towne or Borrough aforesaid or to have use and enjoy did pretend & to be one body politick & corporate by ye name of Soveraign ffree Burgesses and Comonality of ye Borrough afores͏ᵈ: all w͏ᶜʰ ffranchises liberties & priviledges into our hands by Judgm͏ᵗ of our Court of Excheq͏ʳ: of our Kingdom of Ireland were seised   YET wee are willing that ye Town of Belfast in ye County of Antrim afores͏ᵈ in ye Province of Ulster be & remain a ffree Borrough & that within ye Borrough afores͏ᵈ from hence for ever there be had a sure and undoubted custom of for and in keeping of our peace & ruling & governing of ye same Borrough & our people there dwelling and

The Grant

1687

Liberty for
choosing
men for
Parliam.ᵗ

others therein accustoming KNOW YEE that wee of our speciall Grace & of our certain Knowledge & meer Motion with ye assent & consent of our well beloved and very faithfull Kinsman & Councellᵗ Richard Earl of Tyrconnell our Deputy Generall & Generall Governor of our Kingdom of Ireland according to ye tenor & effect of our certain Letters signed with our hand & under our seal bearing date at our Court at Windsor ye twentieth day Septembᵗ in ye third year of our Reign & inroled in ye Roles of ye Chancery of our Kingdom of Ireland for us our heires & Successors have granted appointed ordained & declared that ye said Town of Belfast & all & singular Castles Messuages Tufts mills houses edifices structures Curtillages gardens waters Rivers Lands & Tenemᵗˢ whatsoever with their appurtenances lyeing and being in or within ye same Town or village or pᵗcints of ye same from henceforth bee & for ever hereafter shall be one entire & ffree Borrough of itself by ye name of ye Borrough of Belfast & from henceforth shall be named mentioned and called ye Borrough of Belfast & them all in one entire & ffree Borrough of itself by ye name of ye Borrough of Belfast wee erect constitute make & ordain by these pᵗsents And that ye Borrough *of Belfast* & ffranchises of ye same themselves extend & pretend & may & can be extended & pretended as well in lenth & bredth as circuit & pᵗcint to ye same & accustomed bounds & metes to wᶜʰ & such as ye late Borrough of Belfast & ye circuit & pᵗcint of ye same and ye jurisdiction & liberty thereof at any time heretofore were extended or pᵗtended or to extend or pretend were accustomed AND further wee will ordain & appoint by these pᵗsents for us our heires & Successors that wᵗʰin ye Borrough aforesᵈ there be one body Corporate & Pollitick consisting of one Soveraigne thirty five ffree Burgesses & Comonality & that all ye Inhabitants within ye said Town Liberty & franchises of ye same from henceforth for ever are & shall be one new Body Corporate & politick in substance deed & name by ye name of Soveraign ffree Burgesses & Comonality of ye Borrough of Belfast and them by ye name of Soveraign ffree Burgesses & Comonality of the Borrough of Belfast one new Body Corporate & politick in substance deed & name really & to ye full for us our heires & Successors wee erect make ordain & constitute by these pᵗsents And that by the same name they have pᵗpetual Succession & that *they* by ye name of Soveraign ffree Burgesses & Comonality of the Borrough of Belfast are & shall be for ever hereafter persons fitt & capable by ye law to have seek receave & possess ye lands tenemᵗˢ Liberties priviledges jurisdictions ffranchises & hereditamᵗˢ wᵗsoever of wᵗ degree nature or form soever they be to themselves & their Successors in ffee & perpetuity or for term of years & also ye goods & Chattles & all other things of wᵗ kind nature or form soever they be and also to give grant lett & assign ye lands tenemᵗˢ & hereditmᵗˢ goods & chattles & to do and execute all other acts & things by ye name aforesᵈ And that by ye name of Soveraign ffree Burgesses & Comonality of ye Borrough of Belfast they may & can plead & be impleaded answer and be answered defend and be defended before us our heires & Successᵗˢ or elswhere wheresoever of & in all & all manner of accounts suits pleas complᵗˢ & demands wᵗsoever against them or by them by any manner of way to be pᵗsented or brought & that all ye Inhabitants of ye Town aforesᵈ & who hereafter are admitted into ye Liberties thereof are & shall be ye Comonality of the said Town AND further for us our heires & Successᵗˢ wee grant to ye Soveraign ffree Burgesses and Comonality of ye Borrough aforesaid & their Successᵗˢ & for us our heirs and Successᵗˢ wee do ordain and declare that they ye said Soveraign ffree Burgesses of the Borrough aforesᵈ for ye time being and their Successᵗˢ or the major pᵗᵉ of them for ever have and shall have full power & authority of choosing sending & returning two discreet & fitt men to serve and attend in every Parliamᵗ in our said Kingdom of Ireland hereafter to be held & that such men so chosen sent and returned have and shall have full power and authority to handle and consult of things and matters wᶜʰ to them and others there shall be expounded or declared and thereupon their vote and consents freely to give and to do and execute all other things wᵗsoever as fully and freely as any other Burgess of any other Borrough in our said Kingdom of Ireland or in our Kingdom of England in Parliamᵗ there *to* do and execute have been accustomed Wherefore wee will & by these pesents for us our heires & Successᵗˢ wee give &

grant to ye said Soveraign free Burgesses & Comonality of ye Borrough afore-said & their Successⁿ & also wee command & firmly for us our heirs & Successⁿ comand all our Sheriffes officers and Ministers of our heirs & Successⁿ wᵗˢoever wᵗʰin our County of Antrim for ye time being to whom any of our writt or writts of our heirs & Successⁿ for electing Burgesses in Parliamᵗ within ye said County of Antrim at any time shall be directed that every such Sheriffe officer or Minister to whom any such writt or writts so as aforesᵈ shall be directed shall make his pʳcept to ye Soveraign & ffree Burgesses of ye said Borrough of Belfast for ye time being and to their Successors for electing & returning of those two Burgesses according to ye form and effect of ye said writt or writts and that these our Letters Pattents or Inrolᵐᵗˢ of ye same shall be as well to the said Soveraign & free Burgesses of ye Borrough aforesᵈ for ye time being & to their Successⁿ as to all & singular our Sheriffs officers & ministers of our heirs & Successᵒʳˢ wᵗˢoever a sufficient warrant & discharge in this behalfe WITH that intent that in future time it may appear that this new Incorporacon be now at first composed of honest men for us our heirs & Successⁿ wee make constitute & name Thomas Pottenger to be Ruleing Soveraign of ye said

Sovereign appointed } Borrough to continue in ye said office untill ye feast of Sᵗ Michaell ye Arch Angell next after ye date of these pʳsents and afterwards untill another of ye Burgesses of ye said Borrough in ye office of Soveraign of ye Borrough aforesᵈ shall be named and sworn except in the interim he be removed whom and every other Soveraign in ye Borrough aforesᵈ to be chosen for evill

Burgesses appointed } behaviour in his office wee will may be removed by yᵉ Burgesses of ye Borrough aforesᵈ or the greater pᵗᵉ of them and likewise for us our heirs & Successⁿ we make constitute and nominate Neil O'Neil Barrt: Mark Talbott Esqʳ: Daniell O'Neil Esqʳ: Charles O'Neil Esqʳ: ffelix O'Neil: Esqʳ John O'Neil Esqʳ John O'Neil de Balliboran Esqʳ: Daniel MᶜNaten Esqʳ: James Wogan Esqʳ: James Netervile Esqʳ: John Savage Esqʳ: Marten Gernon Esqʳ: John MᶜNachten Esqʳ: Æneas Moylin Esqʳ: George MᶜCartney Esqʳ: John O'Neil gentˡ: *Tonᵗ O'Neil gentˡ*: Patrick Moylin Physit: Charles Mulhollen Gentˡ: Abraham Lee gentl: George MᶜCartney Merchᵗ : Tho: Knox James Shaw William Lockard Will: Dobbin Edward Pottenger Peter Knowles John ffletcher John Eccles William Craford Henry Chads Humphrey Dobbin David Smith Hugh Eccles & John Chambers to be prime and first thirty five Burgesses of ye Borrough aforesᵈ to continue in their offices of ffree Burgesses of ye same Borrough dureing their respective naturall lives except in ye interim by Reason of some proviso in these pʳsents they be removed or any of them be removed or except in ye interim for evill behaveing of themselves or for any reasonable cause by the Soveraign & ffree Burgesses of ye Borrough aforesᵈ for the time being or ye major part of them from their offices aforesᵈ shall be removed or any of them shall be removed of wᶜʰ every *one* and every Burgess hereafter in ye Borrough

The oath } aforesᵈ to be chosen for ye like cause from Soveraign & ffree Burgesses of ye same Borrough for ye time being or from ye major part of them we will to be removed AND further wee will that ye said Tho: Pottenger whom by these pʳsents we have made Soveraign of ye Borrough aforesᵈ before he exercises his office he came before the last Soveraign of ye Towne aforesᵈ or

The oath } before any Justice to keep our Peace within ye County of Antrim or before ye Constable of ye Castle of Belfast & shall in due manner take *as well* ye Corporall Oath following (vizt) I do hereby acknowledge profess testifie & declare in my conscience before God & ye world that our Soveraign Lord King James is Lawfull & Rightfull King of this Realme & other his Majᵗⁱᵉˢ dominions & countries & I will bear faith & true allegeance to his Majᵗʸ his heirs & Successors & him & them will defend to the utmost of my power against all conspiracies and attempts wᵗˢoever wᶜʰ shall be made against his or their Crown and Dignity and do my best endeavour to disclose & make known unto his Majᵗʸ his heirs and Successⁿ or to ye Lord Deputy or other cheife Governer or Goveʳⁿᵉʳˢ of this Kingdom for ye time being all Treasons & treaterous conspiracies wᶜʰ I shall know or hear to be intended agᵃᵗ his Majᵗʸ his heirs and Successⁿ or any of them And I do make this precognicion & acknowledgmᵗ heartily willingly & truely upon ye true faith of a Christian so help me God &ᶜ And I do also declare & belive that it is not Lawfull upon any pretence wᵗˢoever to take arms agᵗ ye King and that I do abhor that treaterous position of takeing arms by his authority agᵗ his person or ag‘ those that are Comissioned by him so help me God &ᶜ As his Corporall Oath antiently used to ye office of Soveraign of ye Borrough afores⁴ well and faithfully in all things and by all things to his office belonging to execute to whom respectively for us our heirs & Success™ we give power of administering that oath AND further wee will that ye Soveraign of ye Borrough afores⁴ be annuall & elective & therefore we will & by these p'sents for us our heirs & Success™ we grant to ye said Soveraign ffree Burgesses & Cominality of ye Borrough afores⁴. & their Success™ that ye said Soveraign & free Burgesses of ye Borrough afores⁴ for ye time being for ever yearly on ye feast of ye nativity of St John Baptist if it be not ye Lords day then ye next day following may & have have power to gather themselves togather in any place convenient within ye Borrough afores⁴ & that ye said Soveraign & ffree Burgesses so gathered together or ye greater pᵗᵉ of them for ye time being before their departure then and there have power to elect one of ye ffree Burgesses of yᵉ Borrough afores⁴ whom they judge most fitt to exercise ye office of Soveraign of ye said Borrough for one year from ye feast of St Michael ye Archangel then next following and from thence untill one other of ye ffree Burgesses of ye Borrough afores⁴ to his office shall be in due form elected & sworn & that every Soveraign so elected before he be admitted to execute ye said office or be Soveraign or so accounted he shall take as well his corporall oath antiently used to ye office of Soveraign of ye Borrough afores⁴ well and faithfully in all things and by all things to his office belonging to execute as another oath of fidelity afores⁴ on ye feast of St Michaell ye Archangell next after such election before ye p'sent Soveraign of ye Town afores⁴ then liveing or before ye Constable of ye said Castle of Belfast or two Burgesses of ye Borrough afores⁴ for ye time being to whom respectively for us our heirs & Success™ wee give full power & authority to administer these oaths AND more over of our like speciall grace & of our certain knowledge & meer motion wee will & by these p'sents for us our heirs & Success™ wee grant to ye said Soveraign ffree Burgesses & Comonality of ye sᵈ Borrough & their success™ that if & as often as it shall happen ye Soveraign of ye sᵈ Borrough of Belfast for ye time being after election & before he shall be sworn or within one year after he shall so as afores⁴ be elected & sworn to the office of Soveraign of ye Borrough afores⁴ to dye or ye office afores⁴ by any means wᵗsoever be vacant that then & so often ye Soveraign & ffree Burgesses or ffree Burgesses of ye Borrough afores⁴ as ye case shall happen & their success™ for ye time being or ye greater pᵗᵉ of them may & have power within ten days after such vacancy or death to elect one of discreetest of ye ffree Burgesses of ye Borrough afores⁴ to execute ye office of Soveraign of ye Borrough afores⁴ for ye year following or for ye remainder of his year as ye case shall happen & from thence untill another of ye ffree Burgesses of ye sᵈ Borrough be in due form elected & sworne to ye office & that every person so as afores⁴ elected and chosen in ye office of Sovereign of ye Borrough afores⁴ may & can execute that office for ye year following or for ye residue of his year as aforesd and from thence untill another of ye ffree Burgesses in that office shall be made & sworn so as every one so elected first take his corporall oath antiently used to ye Sovereign of ye said Borrough well and faithfully to execute & ye other oath of fidelity afores⁴ before ye p'cedent Sovergⁿ of ye Borrough afores⁴ then liveing or before two ffree Burgesses of ye said Borrough for ye time being to whome wee respectively give for us our heirs & Success™ power of administring these oaths and that ye Sovereign of ye Borrough afores⁴ for ye time being when he shall depart from his office be Burgess of ye Borrough afores⁴ dureing his naturall life except in ye interim he be removed by reason of some proviso in these presents AND further wee will & by these presents for us our heirs & Success™ do grant to ye sᵈ Sovereign ffree Burgesses & Comonality of ye Borrough afores⁴ & their Success™ that if any of ye ffree Burgesses of ye Borrough afores⁴ so as afores⁴ in these presents named or any other or others of ye ffree Burgesses of ye same Borrough hereafter to be elected shall dye or from his office be amoved by reason of any proviso in these presents that then ye Sovereign & ye rest of ye ffree Burgesses of ye Borrough afores⁴ for ye time being or ye greater part of them within ten days next after such ffree Burgesses death or amoveing may and have power to gather themselves together in any convenient place within ye Borrough afores⁴ & that ye sᵈ

Margin notes:

Choosing ye Sovereign

In case of death or removall to choose a new Sovereign

for choosing of new Burgesses

Sovereign and ffree Burgesses so gathered together or ye greater p^{te} of them before they depart one or as many as they shall want of ye s^d number of ffree Burgesses of ye better and more honest of ye Comonality of ye Borrough afores^d into ye place or places of such ffree Burgess or ffree Burgesses so dead or from his office or their offices amoved to choose may & have power to continue in their offices dureing their respective naturall lives Except in ye meantime by reason of some proviso in these presents or for evill Governm^t or for evill carrying themselves in that behalfe be amoved or any of them be amoved & that every new Burgess in these presents named and every person so into ye office of ffree Burgess of ye Borrough afores^d to be elected before his office to execute he be admitted take his corporall oath antiently used ye office of ffree Burgess of the Borrough afores^d well & faithfully to execute & ye other oaths of fidelity afores^d before ye Sovereign of ye Borrough afores^d for ye time being to wch Sovereign for ye time being for us our heirs and Success^{rs} we have given and granted power to administer these oaths and so as often as ye case shall so happen

for making
By laws AND further of our greater speciall grace & of our certain knowledge & meer motion & by these presents for us our heirs and Success^{rs} we give & grant to ye s^d Sovereign ffree Burgesses & Comonality of ye Borrough of Belfast & their Success^{rs} that they & their Success^{rs} from time to time so oft as to them shall seem expedient they may and have power themselves to gather & assemble in any convenient place within ye Borrough afores^d and at their meeting there to make decree or and establish such and such like acts ordinances & Statutes called Bylawes for for (*sic*) ye good & safe government of ye Borrough afores^d & the Inhabitants of ye same as to them or ye greater p^{te} of them shall seem necessary & that they have power & authority by ffines & pecuniary mulcts to punish chastize and correct all manner of p'sons delinquent ags^t such acts ordinances & statutes & ye same fines amercem^{ts} mulcts & pecuniary punishm^{ts} they may & have power to levy & have to ye use & behoofe of ye s^d Sovereign ffree Burgesses & Comonality of ye Borrough afores^d & their Success^{rs} without any account thereof or any other thing to be rendered or made to us & our Success^{rs} All & Singular such Laws Acts Statutes & Ordinances so as afores^d to be observed wee will under to keep a
Court of
Record ye pains therein contained   PROVIDED allways that ye said Laws Statutes & Ordinances be not contrary or repugnant to ye Laws Statutes & Ordinances of our Kingdom of Ireland   AND moreover of our more ample & speciall grace & of our sure knowledge & meer motion wee will & by these presents for us our heirs & Success^{rs} wee have granted to ye s^d Sovereign free Burgesses & and Comonality of ye Borrough afores^d and their Success^{rs} that they & their Success^{rs} for ever may have & hold & to have & to hold may have power one Court in any convenient & open place within ye Borrough afores^d to be held before ye Sovereign of ye s^d Borrough for ye time being & ye s^d Court to hold pleas every Thursday from week to week of all & singular Accounts debts Covenants trespasses detinue contracts & demands p'sonall w^{t}soever not exceeding ye sume of fifty pounds ster happening or arising in or within ye s^d Borrough of Belfast or ye Liberties thereof   And that that Court be reputed & The Sovereign
a Justice of
Peace taken a Court of Record for ever   AND further of our more ample & speciall grace & of our certain knowledge & meer motion wee will & by these p'sents for us our heirs & Success^{rs} grant to ye said Sovereign free Burgesses & Comonality of ye Borrough afores^d and their Success^{rs} for ever that ye Sovereign of ye Borrough afores^d for ye time being and his Success^{rs} as soon as he shall have taken ye usuall oath well & faithfully to execute ye s^d office of Sovereign & ye other oath of fidelity afores^d in form as above in these p'sents is specified in very deed be a justice & keeper of our peace of us our heirs & Success^{rs} and also to enquire hear & determine all things [concerning] concerning our peace in or within ye s^d Borrough or ye liberties of the same & as soon as ye s^d Sovereign hath taken his corporall oath antiently used of well & faithfully executing & exercising ye office of a justice of ye peace as before before (*sic*) ye Sovereign p'cedent or any justice of ye peace within ye County of Antrim afores^d or before two of ye Burgesses of ye Borrough afores^d to whom respectively for us our heirs and Success^{rs} wee give power to administer these oaths   AND further wee will & by these presents for us our heirs

and Success" we grant to ye Sovereign free Burgesses & Comonality of

Liberty for a Town Hall & Seale

ye s^d Borrough & their Success" for ever that they may have a merchant Hall within ye s^d Borrough & comon seale in such form insigned & inravened as to them shall seem best to serve for ye business of ye s^d Borrough for ever & that they may & have power for ever from time to time as often as need shall require of themselves to elect constitute & ordain two Serjeants at mases & other inferior officers & ministers necessary for ye better governing of ye Borrough afores^d & ye Inhabitants of ye same & every person so from time to time so elected constituted & ordained wee make constitute & ordain for us our heirs & Success" to be Serjeants at mases & other inferior officers & ministers

Election & turning out Sergeants

of ye s^d Borrough respectively & in their offices may continue dureing their good behaviour or at ye will & pleasure of ye s^d Sovereign ffree Burgesses & Comonality of ye Borrough afores^d & that every such Sergeant officer & minister before he be admitted to execute his office shall take before ye Sovereign of ye s^d Borrough for ye time being his usuall Corporall oath for his well & faithfull behaveing in his s^d. office & ye other oaths of fidelity afores^d to whom for us our heirs & Success" wee have given power to administer these oaths AND

Sovereign made Clerk of ye Markett

furthermore for us our heirs & Success" wee grant that ye Sovereign of ye Borrough afores^d for ye time being for ever be Clerk of ye Markett within ye Borrough afores^d & ye liberties of ye same & from time to time may have & will have full power & authority to do & execute all & Singular things to ye office of clerk of ye markett within ye Borrough afores^d belonging or appertaining so that no clerk of our markett of us our heirs & Success" ye Borrough afores^d or ffranchises of ye same shall enter ye office of clerk of ye markett or anything to ye s^d office belonging or appertaining there to do or execute nor in any office of clerk of ye markett within ye Borrough afores^d or ye Liberties

For a Wharfe or Key

of ye same touching in anywise himself Lett in WEE will further & of our speciall grace & of our certain knowledge & meer motion wee grant to ye s^d Sovereign ffree Burgesses & Comonality of ye Borrough of Belfast & their Success" that hereafter it may be Lawfull & shall be Lawfull for ye Sovereign Burgesses & Comonality of ye Borrough afores^d & their Success" to choose establish and have within ye ffranchise of ye s^d Borrough one wharfe or Key in any place convenient upon ye Bay or Creek of Belfast afores^d & also that it may be lawfull & shall be lawfull to all and Singular Merchants as well natives as Aliens & all other our subjects & Leige people with what ships or boates soever to come & have access to ye s^d wharfe or Key & thereto discharge & unload And from thence to carry away & convey all and all manner of merchandize or wares without *our* hindrance of us our heirs & Success" of any of our customers searchers or any other our officers of us our heirs or Success" in our port of Carrickfergus resideing PROVIDED allways that ye said Merchants & ye rest of our leige people & subjects pay or cause to be paid to us our heirs & Success" all and Singular customes as well great as small subsidies of poundage and impositions due & payable to us our heirs & Success" for all and Singular merchandize comeing in or carried out as is afores^d AND further for us our heirs & Success" wee will ordain & declare that for ye future in ye Borrough afores^d there be one skillfull in ye Law who shall be ye Record^r of ye Borrough afores^d & also another discreet man who shall be clerk or prothonator of ye Court of Record afores^d & Comon Clerk of ye Borrough afores^d and whensoever ye Sovereign & ffree Burgesses of ye Borrough afores^d for ye time being in ye Recordery of ye Borrough afores^d they constitute or ye greater p^te of them for us our heirs & Success" wee have assigned and constituted to be our Recorder of ye Borrough aforesd and also do constitute Ralph Booth Gentl to be the new prothoatory (*sic*) & Clerk of ye Court of Record afores^d & Comon Clerk of ye Borrough afores^d to continue in those offices dureing his naturall life respectively exerciseing by

for electing A new Clerk in case of death or Removall

himself or his deputies except in ye interim by reason of some proviso in these p^r.sents or for his evill behaviour ye s^d Sovereign and free Burgesses of ye Borrough afores^d for ye time being or ye greater p^te of them they be amoved or any of them be amoved every one whereof & every Record^r or clerk for ye future in ye Borrough afores^d to be chosen for their evill behaviour by ye Sovereign & free Burgesses of ye Borrough afores^d or ye greater p^te of them for ye time being wee will to be amoved And further for us our heirs & Success" wee give & grant to ye s^d Sovereign ffree Burgesses & Comonality of ye Borrough afores^d

& their Success^{rs} that ye Record^r of ye Borrough afores^d for ye time being or ye said new prothonatory or Comon Clerk of ye Borrough afores^d for ye time being should depart or any of them shall depart or from their respective offices be amoved or their offices shall be vacant that then it shall be lawfull for ye Sovereign & ffree Burgesses of ye Borrough afores^d for ye time being another discreet man skilled in ye Law & another discreet & skillfull man into those offices respectively to name & choose & in them respectively to continue dureing their naturall lives & to exercise by themselves or their deputies except in the interim for ye causes afores^d they be amoved or any of them be amoved so as every such Record^r & new Prothonotary & Comon Clerk of ye Borrough afores^d & all other Record^{rs} & Prothonotarys & Comon Clerks of ye Borrough afores^d hereafter to be elected & their deputys before they respectively exercise their respective offices they take their Corporall oaths antiently used well & faithfully to exercise their offices & ye other oath of fidelity afores^d before ye Sovereign of ye Borrough afores^d for ye time being to w. Sovereign for the time being for us our heirs & Success^{rs} wee give power to administer these oaths And further for us our heirs & Success^{rs} wee give & grant to ye s^d Sovereign & ffree Burgesses & Comonality of ye Borrough afores^d & their Success^{rs} that ye Sovereign & ffree Burgesses of ye Borrough afores^d for

To make freemen }

ye time being & ye major pte of them have full power & authority to admitt men & persons to be ffreemen of ye Borrough afores^d wch s^d ffreemen so to be admitted & every of them shall take their corporall oath used for ffreemen & ye other oath of fidelity afores^d before the Sovereign for ye Borrough afores^d for ye time being to wch Sovereign for ye time being for us our heirs and Successors wee give power to administer those oaths.

To make a Deputy Sovereign

And that it shall be Lawfull for ye Sovereign of ye Borrough afores^d for ye time being from time to time to make & constitute one of ye ffree Burgesses of ye s^d Borrough to be deputy Sovereign & that such Deputy may & have power to do & execute all things wch to that office do appertain or belong so as every such Deputy before he exercise ye office of Deputy Sovereign take as well his Corporall oath used well & faithfully in all things ye office Deputy Sovereign of ye s^d Borrough to exercise & ye other oath of ffidelity afores^d before ye Sovereign of ye Borrough afores^d for ye time being To whom for us our heirs and Success^{rs} wee give power to administer those oaths

This is to be placed after ye power granted to make freemen

Grant of Toll and Customes }

And further for us our heirs and Success^{rs} wee give & grant for ye maintainance & sustenance of ye Borrough afores^d & for mending of ye Street walls gates Bridges & Keys there and of other publique work of ye Borrough afores^d for ye time being to ye Sovereign ffree Burgesses & Comonality of ye Borrough of Belfast afores^d & their Success^{rs} so many such like & so much ye same & such like Castles messuages houses Tofts gardens Lands & Tenem^{ts} Comon of pasture reversion remainder rent service custome petty duttys murage pavage anchorage gateage wharfeage Tollage powers authorities merchant Key customes exemptions return of writts Jurisdictions ffranchises Liberties & priviledges & other hereditam^{ts} w^tsoever & ye goods & chattles so many such like & soe much & wch to ye Sovereign ffree Burgesses & Comonality of ye Borrough of Belfast at any time before ye Judgem^t afores^d given had occupied used or enjoyed by reason of any Charters Lette^{rs} Pattents Comissions p^rscriptions Customes or other Lawfull title w^tsoever or to have occupied use & enjoy they were lawfully accustomed or any of them have accustomed to bee held from us our heirs & Success^{rs} as of our Castle of Dublin in ffree & Comon soccage for ye rent & service therefore accustomed Saveing always & out of this Charter or grant to us our heirs & Success^{rs} excepted & reserved all title power right rent service custome subsidie poundage excise debt Jurisdiction disposition Liberty priviledge & demand w^tsoever wch wee before ye Judgm^t afores^d given have had held or occupied in right of our Crown in or wthin the Borrough afores^d & ye ffranchises & liberties thereof otherwise then by reason of ye discontinuance fforfeiture or dissolution of ye liberty and ffranchises so as before into our hands seized PROVIDED always & full power & authority for us our heirs & Success^{rs} wee reserve & give by these p^rsents to our Deputy Gen^{ll} & other Chiefe Govern^r or Govern^{rs} of us our heirs

Liberty for
ye L^{d.}
Deputy to
remove
either
Sovereign or
Burgesses

& Success^{rs} of our Kingdome of Ireland for ye time being by order of ye private Councell of us our heirs & Success^{rs} of our Kingdom of Ireland und^{er} their hands write to the Sovereign or any other or other of ye ffree Burgesses or other officer of ye Borrough afores^d by these p^rsents named & constituted or hereafter to be elected & constituted at ye will & good pleasure of our Deputy Genr^{ll} or other our Chiefe Govern^r or Govern^{rs} of us our heirs and Success^{rs} of our Kingdom of Ireland for ye time being by any such order of our privy Councell of us our heirs and Success^{rs} of our Kingdom of Ireland to them respectively signified to be amoved & removed or declared to be amoved and as often as our Deputy Gener^{ll} or other our Chiefe Govern^{r.} or Govern^{rs} of us our heirs and Success^{rs} of our Kingdom of Ireland from time to time by such order of our private Councell of our Kingdom of Ireland shall declare or they shall declare such & such like Sovereign or any other or any other (*sic*) of ye ffree Burgesses or other officers of ye town afores^d for ye time so to be amoved or be amoved that then & from thenceforth every such person or persons so amoved or declared to be amoved from their respective offices in very deed without any further process is amoved & shall be amoved & are and shall be amoved & the same so often & as often as ye case shall happen anything to ye contrary notwithstanding

Admirality
excepted
hereafter

Saving & out of this Charter or Grant to us our heirs & Success^{rs} excepted & reserved all & all manner of Jurisdiction of our great Admirality of us our heirs and Success^{r.} and by these p^rsents for us our heirs and Success^{rs} do prohibite every person & persons from ye execution of any Jurisdiction of the Admirality

this Charter
to be taken
for ye best
advantage
of ye
Corporation

afores^d by vertue colour or pretence of this present Comission anything to ye contrary thereof notwithstanding   AND   that these our Letters Pattents or ye Inrollm^t of ye same shall be construed interpreted & adjudged to ye best advantage benefitt & favour of ye s^d Sovereign ffree Burgesses & Comonality of ye Borrough afores^d & their Success^{rs} ag^t us our heirs & Success^{rs} as well as in all our Courts of us our heirs & Success^{rs} within our Kingdom of Ireland as anywhere else wheresoever without any confirmacion licence or tolleration hereafter to be procured or obtained notwithstanding that our writt of ad quod Dampn hath not issued to enquire of ye premisses or any inquisition hath not been had of our title to ye premisses before ye makeing of these our Letters Pattents And notwithstanding the Statute of Lands & tenem^{ts} in Mortmaine not put AND notwithstanding ye statute made at Limerick in ye thirty third year of ye Reign of King Henry ye eight for for lands given by ye King and any other statute defect or any other thing cause or matter w^tsoever to

The L^d
Deputy to
approve of
ye Clerk

ye contrary notwithstanding Saveing & reserving to our chiefe Govern^r or Govern^{rs} of us our heirs & Success^{rs} of our Kingdom of Ireland for ye time being power of [approving] aproveing of every Record^r or Comon Clerk hereafter to be elected within ye Borrough afores^d so that no such Record^r or Comon Clerk exercise his office untill he be approved of by such Govern^r or Govern^{rs} under their hand or hands writeing   PROVIDED always that these our Letters Pattents be Inrolled in ye Roles of our Chancery Court of our Kingdome of Ireland within six months after ye date of these p^rsents   In Testimonie whereof these our Letters wee have made pattents   WITNESS our Ld Deputy Gen^{rll} Govern^r of Ireland afores^d at Dublin ye sixteenth day of October in ye fourth year of our Reign 1687

Domvile

Examined by Andrew Bunbury Deput' Clerk of ye Inrolled in ye Roles of ye pattents of ye Chancery of Ireland ye twenty ninth day of October in ye fourth year of ye Reign of James ye Second & examined by Andrew Ram Clerk in ye office of ye Master of ye Rolls

PPLICA^N being made to his Ex^{cy} by the Roman Catholique officers Garrisoned in that town, that there is no convenient or fitt place appointed for their hearing Masse and Divine Service on Sundays and Holy-Days, but an old ruinous house; his Ex^{cy} taking it to consider^n directs me to desire and require you to lett the said officers and Sould^{rs} make use of, either the Town house or School house or some other decent & fitt place for the said divine service, as in all other Corpora^{cns} of the Kingdom the Magistrats do freely allow, and is expected you will likewise do, and not doubting of yor complyance herein,

   I am

     Yo^r humble Ser^t

       Pat^k Clogher—Secrety

Chappel Izod ye 7th 7b^r 1688.

To the Mayor Sherriffs Aldermen & Burgesses of the Town of Belfast.   Copia Vera

R   Belfast 7b^r 12. 1688
I have comunicated yo^{rs} of the 7th inst to my brethern the Burgesses of this Corporacon, we have considered of the Contents thereof, and are heartily sorry that his Ex^{cy} should happen to desire of us what is not in our power to grant. As for the Schoolhouse it being of the foundation and free gift of the Lorde Donegall deceased and now repaired and supported by his heirs, 'twere presumption in us to dispose of what we have only a comon interest with all others His Maties Subjects. And for the town house it being the onely place purchased and sett apart by the Lord and Inhabitants of the Manor & Corpora^n of Belfast, for keeping Courts, holding of Sessions, and frequent meetings of the Sovereign and Burgesses for regulating and dispatching the affairs of the Corporacon, we canot (wthout great injury to the Town, and depriving ourselves of those conveniencies necessity forced us to provide for) comply wth what His Ex^{cy} desires of us. We doubt not but the officers and Souldiers you speak of,

may if they please meet wth a conveniency in town, but the poverty of our Corporacon & uncertainty of its continuance is such, no revenue Lands tenements nor salary belonging to it, it seems a little hard to expect that the charge of such provision should be laid wholy on ye Sovereign and Burgesses especially now enjoying the liberties of our charter only ex gratia. Since our circumstances are such, we hope S^r you will become our advocat to his Ex^{cy} to assure him what is realy true that our noncomplyance proceeds not from any peevish perverse humour but only want of ability and opportunity to gratify his Expections whose demands shall always be observed to the utmost of our power.

I am

S^r   Yo^r most humble Servant

Robt Leathes

To the B^{is}p of Clogher.

The twenty fifth day of ffebruary one thousand six hundred eighty nine (styl'angl') the Soveraigne & Burgesses then assembled for chusing and electing a Burgesse in the room & place of Mr Thomas Walcoat who died the twentyth of ffebry instant did choose & unanimously elect James Buller taner in the room of the said Mr Walcoat who was accordingly sworne to the office of Burgesse.

Robt Leathes Soveraigne

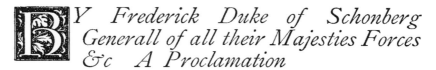

Y Frederick Duke of Schonberg Generall of all their Majesties Forces &c A Proclamation

WHEREAS wee are fully satisfyed that there has been great Invasion made upon the propriety of the Protestant subjects and Antient Charters of the respective Corporation in this kingdom and that severall Protestant Justices of the Peace have ben removed from their Places of Trust, whereby great disorders such as Burglaries, Robberies, Fellonies, and other out Rages have been committed in this kingdome And wee, being desirous to redress the said grieveances do hereby think fitt to Publish and declaire, that the said Protestant subjects be and hereby are restored to their former proprieties and the respective Corporacions to their

Antient Charters, and the severall protestant Justices of the peace to their respective Trusts, hereby Impowering them to doe and execute all and every act matter and thing as they might or could *doe* by vertue of their respective Charters or any Commission of the peace formerly granted dureing their Majesties pleasure, the said Justices of the Peace in their respective Stations are hereby required to take care that no Land Lord exact on any Tenant not being able to pay his rent presently or on demand they takeing it into their Consideration that it is a yeare of Warrs and devastation but that when the Lawes is open to take their Course by the Law   Given at our Headquarters at Dundalk the 14th of September 1689   In the first yeare of their Majesties Reigne   Schonberg

ARMS OF DUNDALK.

 N the twenty sixth day of May one thousand six hundred and ninety the Soveraigne and Burgesses then assembled for chuseing a free Burgesse in place of Mr Francis Thetford Burgesse who departed the twenty third of this instant May did elect and unanimously choose Mr David Smith Mercht to be a free Burgesse in the room of the said Mr Thetford who was accordingly sworn to the said office

Robt Leathes Soveraigne

Intd per Tho Craford
    d. clerc vill

8br 1mo 1690

Then delivered to Mr Wm Lockart Soveraigne for the year next ensueing these things belonging to the Towne, that is, a Copy of the Charter, the parchment Schedule of By Laws, one Bond wth warrant of Attorney rent charge and counterpart of a defeasance for 300li str of the poors money *due by the Lady Marchionesse of Antrim* a bond of ten pounds of the poors money due by Mr Sampson Theaker, a bond of ten pounds of the poors money due by Mr Lewis Thompson a tin qrt standard pint standard half pint & knogin, a brasse fourteen pound wht a seven pnd weight a four pnd a *two* pnd a pnd half pnd quarter two ounces & ounce:

the brasse quart standard Jno Griffen the Sergeant hath; & the brasse standard gallon Wm Ratcliffe the water bailiffe hath. also delivered then the Town seall. the originall Charter Capt McCartney hath.

The above particulars mencioned to be delivered to me, I have rec^d

William Lockhart

N the seventh day of March one thous^d six hundred ninety one the Soveraign and Burgesses then assembled for chuseing a free Burgesse in place of Mr Sampson Theaker who departed

they did elect & unanimously choose the Rt Honb^le Arthur Earle of Donegall in room of the said Mr Theaker

Ja: M'Cartney Soveraign

Rob Leathes   Lewis Thompson   Tho: Knox
Wm: Crafford   William Lockhart   James Buller
Arthur M'Cartney L: Harrison

On the first day of June one thousand six hundred ninety one the Soveraigne and Burgesses then assembled for chuseing a free Burgesse in place of George M'Cartney Esqre Burgesse who departed the twenty third of May last, they did elect & unanimously choose Mr Arthur M'Cartney M^rt son of the said Geo M'Cartney to be a free Burgesse in the room of his said father, who was accordingly sworne to the said office.

William Lockhart Soveraigne

Robt Leathes Ja: M'Cartney Sa: Theaker Wm: Crafford David Smith

Memorandum that by the unanimous Consent of the Soveraigne & Burgesses of this Burrough Francis Cordner formerly established Sergeant at Mace in room of Tho: Whitlock (and who had been sworne to the office) was confirmed in the said employ; and this day John Beck was placed Serg^t (and duly sworne) in the room and place of John Clugston serg[t] who was from the office amoved for his unfitnesse to serve the Corporac[n] in that capacity.

Dated Sept[br] 26th 1692

Signed by ord[r]

Tho: Craford d. cl vill

On the eighth day of April one thousand six hundred ninety three the Soveraigne and Burgesses then assembled to choose a free Burgesse in the room of Ensign John Leathes Burgesse deceased (who was buried at Whitehaven on the 3rd instant as by his wifes letter to M[rs] M[c]Cartney appeers the copy whereof is underwritten) did unanimously elect Jno Chalmers Mercht a free Burgesse in room of the said Ensign Leathes

W[m] Crafford Soveraigne

Lewes Thompson   William Lockhart   James Buller
David Smith

Whitehaven April 5th 1693

Mrs M'Cartney

These is to desire you in your husbands absence, to buy me five dozen of clift boards and send them by the bearer John Hodgson; and I shall satisfy you at our meeting, w[ch] I intend very speedily if the Lord permitt. My dear husband hath finished his course and I hope has entred in to eternal joy, he was inter'd the 3rd of this instant, so I take leave humbly begging that the Lord will fitt us all for our change, w[ch] is all from yo[r] real friend

Jane Leathes

It would do us a great
kindnesse for here we shall
want to clear us, & and it would
be better yn Irish money   Copia vera per
To Mr Geo M'Cartney   Tho Craford
    Mrt Belfast   d. cler vill

Know all men by these presents that I Francis Ratcliffe cloathier have remised released and for ever quit claimed, and by these presents do remise release and for ever quit claime unto my brother Richard Ratcliffe of Belfast cloathier his heirs Exo[rs] and admo[rs] all and all maner of acion and acions sutes bills bonds writings obligatory debts dues duties accompts sum & sums of money Judg[ts] executions Extents quarrels controversies trespasses damages and demands whatsoever both in Law and Equity or otherwise howsoever w[ch] against the said Rich[d] Ratcliffe I ever had & which I my heirs Ex[rs] & adm[rs] shall or may have claime challenge or demand for or by reason or meanes of any matter cause or thing whatsoever from the beginning of the world unto the day of the date of these presents. In witnesse whereof I have hereunto sett my hand & seal the eighteenth day of december one thous[d] six hund ninety three. at perfecting this Release my bro Rich[d] paid me six pounds ster

Signed sealed & d[d]   ffrancis Ratcliffe
    in the presence of us

Wm Crafford Soveraigne   Rob[t] Leathes   Lewes Thompson
Tho: Craford   d. cl vill

AT an Assembly held the sixth day of Sept.ʳ 1694 at the Tholsell of Belfast in and for the Burrough Town and Corporacon of Belfast Willm Crafford Esqʳ being Sovereign. Forasmuch as it is found by comon experience that many persons who have not been bred merchants within the Town nor elsewhere, have of late for their private lucre and gaine used to buy great quantities of butter hides and tallow as ye same was coming to the said Towne of Belfast, to be sold, and have ingrossed the same into their hands wᵗʰ designe to sell it dearer to the Merchant adventurers Exporters and traders inhabiting the said Town of Belfast, than he who brought the same to be sold: For the remedy whereof and for pᵣ.venting the great abuses and sinister practices comitted and done in buying and selling as aforesaid, It is Ordered and declared by the Soveraigne and Burgesses and free Comonalty of this Corporacon and by authority of the same, by and wᵗʰ the consent of the Right Honble the Earle and Countesse of Longford Lords of the Castle of Belfast that the market for the sale and purchase of butter *hydes & tallow* wᵗʰin the Towne and Borrough of Belfast is & hereafter shall be wᵗʰin Castle Street or some part thereof between the uper Castle gate and Church Lane & Skiper Lane on either side of the River & in Bridg Street between the [upper Castle gate and Church Lane] Bridg called the Stone bridg and the corners turning down to broad street and Rosemary Lane and that hereafter no butter hydes nor tallow coming to the Town of Belfast to be sold shall be bought or caused to be bought or sold directly or indirectly by any person whatsoever before the said butter hides and tallow shall be brought or come within the streets aforesaid limited and appointed for the market and sale thereof under the penalty of being by law prosecuted as unlawfull ingrossers and forestallers of the mᵣᵏᵗ

Wm Crafford Soveraigne

William Lockhart   L Harrison   David Smith
Tho: Knox   Jno Challmers   George M'Cartney
Robᵗ Leathes   Lewes Thompson   James Buller
Will Arthur cum Sociis   Tho Craford d. cl vill

PUBLIQUE ORDERS.

Ordered, to prevent the undue throwing out of Ballast into the Lough & chanell, that the masters of all ships & vessells shall from time to time and at all times hereafter bring up all their ballast whether stone or gravel in Lighters, and the same putt out at such place on the Key as the water Bailiff shall appoint, the same to be disposed of for the public use of the Corporacon, and no person to take the same for his private use of which all persons are to take notice as they will answer the contrary at their perills
Dated 8^{br} 19th 1694

Edwd Harrison Sovereigne

By the Sovereign of Belfast

Pursuant to an order of Court upon P^{r}sentment of the Grand Jury for regulating the abuses in keeping watch in this Burrough you are req^{red} duly to sumon by turns the persons whose names are hereunto annexed to serve as Captains of the watch with the number of twelve substantial men every night; and such Captains you are to sumon to be wth me every night before setting the watch to receive the word and orders, & let them know that they are to continue from nine a clock at night to six in the morning and to go the grand round at twelve a clock at night, and that you yourself see due care taken that the Top Tee & Trevally be beaten every morning and evening. Hereof fail not at yor perills and this is yor warrant.
Given und^r my hand and seal 8b^r 20 1694

Edwd Harrison Sovraigne

A COPPY of the Charter of Bellfast granted the 11 year of King James the first 27th April 1613

AMES by the Grace of God of England Scotland ffrance and Ireland King defender of the faith &c To all to whome these presents shall come greeting Know yee that wee as well at the humble petition of the Inhabitants of the Town of Belfast in our County of Antrim within our province of Ulster in our Kingdome of Ireland as also for the Inhabiting and planting of those Northern parts in the same our Kingdome depopulated and wasted according to the established form of the Common wealth in our Kingdome of England excellently setled And for the more better proceeding and perfection of that new plantation of late there happely begun of our especiall grace and of our certain knowledge and our meer motion by the consent of our well beloved and faithfull Councellor Arthur Lord Chichester of Belfast our deputy Generall of our said Kingdome of Ireland And also according to the intent and effect of our Letters signed with our own proper hand and under our own signet Dated at our mannor of ffarneham the last day of July in the year of our raigne of England ffrance and Ireland the fifth and of Scotland the two and fortieth and now inrolled in the rolls of our Chauncery of our Kingdome of Ireland aforesaid

Wee do appoint ordaine and declare by these presents that the aforesaid Towne of Belfast and all and Singular Castles Messuages Tofts Mills houses Edefices buildings curtilages gardens wast places the foundation of Watter Courses and Tenemts and hereditamts whatsoever with their appurtenances lyeing or being in or within the same Town or Townland or precincts [thereof] *of the same* (the Castle of Belfast together with the curtilages gardens orchards and edefices whatsoever to the said Castle belonging [duely] *onely* excepted) are and shall be of the rest in perpetuall times to come one sole and free Burrough of itself by the name of the Burrough of Belfast and they shall be named nominated and called from others the Borrough of Belfast and wee doe erect constitute make and by these presents ordaine all those in one sole and free Burrough of itself by the name of the Borrough of Belfast And further more we will ordaine and by these presents appoint that within the Borrough aforesaid there be one body Corporate and pollitick consisting of one Soveraigne Twelve ffree Burgesses and of the Comonality and that all the Inhabitants within the aforesaid Town and lands aforesaid are and shall be for ever in present force [one] from others one body Corporate and pollitick in deed fact and name by the name of the Soveraigne ffree Burgesses and Comonality of the Burrough of Belfast And wee erect make ordain and by these presents constitute these by the name of Soveraigne ffree Burgesses and Comonality of the Burrough of Bellfast aforesaid one body Corporate and pollitick in deed matter and name really and to the full for us our heirs and successors and that by the same name they may have perpetuall succession And that they by the name of the Soveraigne ffree Burgesses and Comonality of the Burrough of Belfast aforesaid are and shall be for ever in time to come of a fitt person and capable in the Law to have [seek] *perceave* receave and possess the Lands Tenemts Liberties previledges Jurisdictions ffranchises and hereditaments whatsoever of what kind nature or forme they have been to them and their Successrs in ffee and perpetually and also the goods and chattles and whatsoever other things of what kind nature or quality they have been And also to give grant lett and assigne the Lands Tenemts and hereditamts goods and chattles and to doe and execute all and singular other deeds and things by the name aforesaid And that by the name of Soveraigne ffree Burgesses and Comonality of the Burrough of Bellfast they may plead and be impleaded answer and to be answered defend and to be defended before us our heirs and Successors and before whatsoever our Justices and Judges of our heirs and Successors and others whatsoever in whatsoever our Courts of our heirs and Successors and to and other whatsoever of and in all and all manner of actions suites pleas plaints and demands whatsoever to be prosecuted or brought against them or by them

And that they the aforesaid Soveraigne *and* ffree Burgesses of the Burrough aforesaid and their Successors for ever may have full power and authority to chuse send and returne two discreet and fitt men to serve and attend in every parliament in our said Kingdome of Ireland hereafter to be held and that such men so elected sent and returned may have full power and authority to handle and consult upon those things and matters which to them and others shall be there expounded and declared and thereuppon freely to give their voyces and opinions and to do and execute other matters whatsoever soe fully and freely as any other Burgisses of any other antient Burrough in our said Kingdome of Ireland or in our said Kingdome of England have been accustomed to doe and execute there in Parliament.

Wherefore wee will and by these presents for us our heirs and Successors doe give and grant to the aforesaid Soveraigne and free Burgesses of the Burrough and to their Successors And also wee doe charge and firmly command for us our heirs and Successors all high Sheriffs officers and Ministers of our heirs and Successors whatsoever of our said County of Antrim for the time being to whome any of our writt or writts for the chusing of the Burgesses of the Parliament within the said County of Antrim in any time shall be directed That

To send two members of Parliament.

The High Sheriffs power

every such high Sheriff officer or Minister to whome any such Writt or Writts shall be directed soe as aforesaid shall make their precept to the Soveraigne and ffree Burgesses of the said Burrough of Bellfast for the time being for the election and returne of these two Burgesses according to the forme and effect of the same Writt or Writts And these our Letters Pattents or the Inrolement of the same shall be as well as the said Soveraigne and ffree Burgesses of the Burrough aforesaid and their Successors as also to all and singular high Sheriffs officers and Ministers whatsoever of our heirs and Successors a sufficient warrant and discharge in that behalfe And for that intent as may appear in time to come that this new incorporation may first of all be composed of approved and honest men wee make constitute and name

The first Sovereign and 12 Burgesses

John Vesey to be the ffirst *and moderen* Soveraigne of the said Burrough continuing in the said office untill the feast of St Michaell the Archangell next after the date of these presents And likewise wee make constitute and name Sr ffulke Conaway Knight, Thomas Hibbotts, Esqr, Moses Hill Esqr, Humphry Norton Esqr, William Lewsly, John Willoughby, Cary Hart, John Aysh, Samuell Boothe, James Burr, Walterhouse Crimble, and John Burr to be the first twelve ffree Burgesses of the aforesaid Burrough to continue in those offices of ffree Burgesses of the same Burrough dureing their severall lives unless in the meantime by behaveing themselves evill or for any reasonable cause they shall be removed from the offices aforesaid or any one of them shall be removed And all the Inhabitants of the Twone aforesaid and such and soe many other men whom the Soveraigne and ffree Burgesses of the same Burrough for the time being shall admit into the Liberty of the Borrough aforesaid wee will constitute and ordaine to be of the Comonality of the Burrough aforesaid And moreover wee will that John Vesey whome by these presents wee have made Soveraigne of the Burrough aforesaid shall before the eighteenth day of May next following after the date of these presents come before Sr ffulke Conaway Knight now Lieut Governor of the Towne of Knockfergus and in due manner shall take as well the oath of Supremacy as alsoe his Corporall oath well and truly to execute the office of Soveraigne of the Burrough aforesaid untill the feast of St Michaell the Archangell next coming as is aforesaid And that the Soveraigne of the Burrough aforesaid may be elective and therefore wee will and by these presents for us our heirs and Successors wee

The election of a Sovereign yearly

doe grant to the aforesaid Soveraigne ffree Burgesses and Comonality of the Burrough aforesaid and to their Successors that the aforesaid Soveraigne and ffree Burgesses of the Burrough aforesaid for the time being yearly for ever upon the feast of the nativity of St John Baptist if it happen not to be on the Sabbath day and if the aforesaid feast doth happen to be upon the Sabbath day then upon the next of the same feast they may be able and may assemble themselves in any convenient place within the Burrough aforesaid and the Soveraigne and ffree Burgesses soe assembled together wee will and grant that the aforesaid Arthur Lord Chichester of Bellfast his heirs and assignes remaining Lords of the said Castle of Bellfast shall nominate three discreet and sufficient men remaining ffree Burgesses of the said Burrough and shall present the names of them to the aforesaid Soveraigne and ffree Burgesses of the Burrough aforesaid of whome the aforesaid Soveraigne and ffree Burgesses so assembled or the greatest part of them before they shall depart may then and there chuse one whome they shall judge most fitt to exercise the office of Soveraigne of the said Burrough for one year from the feast of St Michaell Archangell next next following and until one other of the Burgesses of the same Burrough shall be in due manner elected made and sworne to that office And in defect of such nomination by the aforesaid Lord Chichester his heirs or assignes made in manner and form aforesaid wee will and grant that the said Soveraigne and ffree Burgesses of the Burrough aforesaid then and there may freely chuse one of the discreetest ffree Burgesses of the said Burrough to execute the office of Soveraigne for one year as aforesaid

And that every Soveraigne soe elected before he shall be admitted to execute the office aforesaid either the Soveraigne may be or may have as well the oath of supremacy as his corporall oath well and truly to exercise the office of Soveraigne of the Burrough aforesaid upon the feast of St Michaell Archangell next after such election he shall take before the aforesaid Arthur Lord Chichester of Bellfast or the heirs or assignes of the Lord of the said Castle of Bellfast or in his or their absence before the Constable of the said Castle of Bellfast for the time being

And wee doe grant full power and authority to the aforesaid Arthur Lord Chichester of Belfast and to his heirs and assignes aforesaid and to the Constable of him or them of the Castle of Bellfast aforesaid for the time being to take the aforesaid oath of every such Soveraigne newly chosen And moreover of our like especiall grace certaine knowledge and meere motion we will and by these presents for us our heirs and Successors wee grant to the aforesaid Soveraigne free Burgesses and Comonality of the said Burrough and to their Successors that if and as often as the Soveraigne of the said Burrough for the time being shall happen to die or void by any manner of means from the office aforesaid within one year after he shall be elected and [serve] sworne as aforesaid to the office of Soveraigne of the Burrough aforesaid that then [the] and so often the aforesaid Arthur Lord Chichester of Bellfast his heirs or assignes aforesaid shall

Election on the death of Sovereign

nominate three discreet and sufficient *men* of the aforesaid number of free Burgesses of the Burrough aforesaid and shall present their names to the said ffree Burgesses of the Burrough aforesaid for the time being [otherwise] of which the said free Burgesses may chuse one most fittest in the office of Soveraigne of the said Burrough for the residue of that year within ten days after such vacancy and in defect of such nomination or presentation by the aforesaid Lord Chichester of Belfast his heirs or assignes to be done in manner and forme aforesaid wee will and grant that the said Soveraigne and ffree Burgesses of the said Burrough then and there may chuse one of the discreetest ffree Burgesses of the said Burrough to execute the office of Soveraigne for the residue of that year as is aforesaid And that every person and persons in the office of Soveraigne of the Burrough aforesaid soe as aforesaid elected to the office of Soveraigne of the Burrough aforesaid may be able to execute untill the feast of Michaell Archangell next following after such election the oath of supremacy aforesaid and alsoe the aforesaid oath for the due execution of his office of Soveraigne of the Burrough aforesaid so as aforesaid first to be taken

And moreover of our especiall grace meere motion and certaine knowledge wee will and by these presents for us our heirs and successors doe grant to the aforesaid Soveraigne ffree Burgesses and Comonality of the Burrough aforesaid and to their Successors that if any one or any of the aforesaid ffree Burgesses of the Burrough aforesaid so as aforesaid in these presents named or any one or any of the ffree Burgesses of the same Burrough hereafter to be chosen shall die or shall be removed from that office which ffree Burgesses and every one of them or any one not behaveing himself well in that office wee will to be amoved at the pleasure of the Soveraigne and the major part of the ffree Burgesses of the same Burrough for the time being that then the Soveraigne and the rest of the ffree Burgesses of the Burrough aforesaid for the time being may within seaven days after the death or removeing of such ffree Burgesses assemble themselves into any convenient place within the Burrough aforesaid And that the said

Election of a Burgess

Soveraigne and free Burgesses soe assembled or the major part of them before they shall depart one or so many as shall be wanting of the aforesaid number of ffree Burgesses of the best and most approved Inhabitants of the Burrough aforesaid in the place or places of that free Burgess or of those free Burgesses so dead or from that office removed they may chuse to continue in the same office during their naturall lives unless in the meantime for their evill Govermt or for behaveing themselves evill in that behalf shall be removed or one or any of them shall be removed

And that every person soe in the office of ffree Burgess of the Burrough aforesaid elected before he shall be admitted to execute that office shall take his corporall oath well and faithfully to execute the office of ffree Burgess of the Burrough aforesaid within seaven days next after such his election before the Soveraigne of the Borrough aforesaid for the time being or before such other ffree Burgess of the same Burrough then liveing and remaining in that office or the major part of them to which Soveraigne for the time being or to which ffree Burgesses or the major part of them for the time being wee give and grant by these presents full power and authority to take the aforesaid oath of every ffree Burgess newly chosen and soe as often as the case shall so happen

The Lord of ye Castle & the Constable to be Burgesses

And further more of our especiall grace certaine knowledge and meere motion wee will and grant that as well the Lord of the said Castle of Bellfast for the time being and his heirs as alsoe the Constable of the said Castle for the time being are and shall be ffree Burgesses and every one of them may and shall be a ffree Burgess of the said Burrough of Bellfast and shall enjoy soe many such and soe great Liberties previledges and Imunityes how many soe many and as great as any other Burgess or any other Burgesses of the said Burrough of Bellfast by vertue of these our Letters pattents may have use and enjoy

Assemblys for By Laws

And further more of our more especiall Grace certain Knowledge and meere motion we will and by these presents for us our heirs and Successors wee doe give and grant to the aforesaid Soveraigne ffree Burgesses and Comonality of the Burrough aforesaid and to their Successors that they and their Successors from time to time as often as it shall seem best expedient unto them they may gather and assemble themselves in any convenient place within the Burrough aforesaid and in their meetings there by the advise and consent of the aforesaid Arthur Lord Chichester of Bellfast his heirs and assignes aforesaid being Lords of the said Castle of Bellfast to make appoint and ordain and establish such acts ordinances and Statutes called By Laws for the good ruling and sound Government of the Burrough aforesaid and the Inhabitants of the same such as and which shall seem necessary to them or the major part of them And that they may have power and authority to punish chastise and correct by fines and penalties of money all persons delinquent against such acts ordinances and Statutes and those fines amercements and penalties of money they may levy and have to the use and behoofe of the aforesaid Soveraigne ffree Burgesses and Comonality of the Burrough aforesaid and of their Successors without our hindrance our heirs and Successors and without any accompt or any other thing thereof to be rendred or made to us our heirs or Successors All and Singular which Laws Acts statutes and ordinances so as aforesaid to be made wee will to be observed under the pain in them contained Provided allways that the said Laws statutes and ordinances are not against or repugnant to the Laws and statutes of our said Kingdome of Ireland

Not to Plead out of the Borrough Court

And moreover of our especiall grace certain knowledge and meere motion wee will and grant by these presents for us our heirs and Successors to the aforesaid Soveraigne ffree Burgesses and Comonality of the said Burrough and to their Successors that noe Inhabitants of the Burrough shall implead or be impleaded out of the said Burrough of or for any Lands Tenements Rents or other hereditamts within the said Burrough or within the meares ffranchises Liberties Limitts or precincts of the same or of or for any Trespasses detainews covenants debts demands accompts contracts or any other causes demands or controversies whatsoever within the said Burrough or within the ffranchises Liberties or meets of the same made or to be made arrising or to arise without the especiall licence of the said Arthur Lord Chichester of Bellfast his heirs or assignes being Lord of the Castle of Bellfast aforesaid unless it concerns us our heirs or Successors or the right or interest of the Soveraigne and ffree Burgesses or their Successors in the right or pollitick capacity of them or unless it concerns the Soveraigne in his own right.

The Borrow Court a Court of Record to try cases not exceeding £20 Irish

And moreover of our more especiall grace certain knowledge and meere motion wee will and by these presents for us our heirs and Successors doe grant to the aforesaid Soveraigne ffree Burgesses and Comonality of the Burrough aforesaid and to their Successors that they and their Successors may for ever have and hold and may be able to have and to hold one Court in any place convenient and fitt within the Burrough aforesaid to be held before the Soveraigne of the same Burrough for the time being and in the same Court to hold pleas every Thursday from week to week of all and Singular accounts debts Covenants Trespasses detaines contracts and demands personall whatsoever not exceeding the sum of Twenty pounds currant money of Ireland happening or arising in or within the aforesaid Burrough of Belfast or the Liberties of the same and that that Court may be reputed and esteemed a Court of Record for ever

And furthermore we will and by these presents firmly injoining wee charge and command that noe person nor persons from henceforth hereafter shall sell or expose to sale nor shall cause to be exposed by retale any marchandize

Extent of s^d Borrough

comodoties whatsoever by way of merchandize within the space of three miles by a direct line on every part of the said Burrough of Bellfast measured round about unless such person or persons have been or shall be planted or placed by Arthur Lord Chichester his heirs or assigns being Lord of the Castle of Bellfast in or within the aforesaid Burrough of Bellfast or Liberties of the same or there dwellers residents or Inhabitants or shall be or have been dwelling resident or Inhabiting under the paine or forfeiture of all and Singular such marchandize and comodoties so against the Tenor and intention of these our Letters pattents sold or putt to sale   And moreover of our more especiall grace certaine knowledge and meere motion wee will and by these presents for us our heirs and Successors doe grant to the aforesaid Soveraigne ffree Burgesses and Comonality of the Burrough aforesaid and their Successors for ever that the Soveraigne of the Burrough aforesaid for the time being and his Successors in very deed and as soon as he shall receave and take his oath of the aforesaid office of the Soveraigne well and faithfully to be executed in the

The Sovereign a Justice of Peace

forme aforesaid before in these prsents specified shall be a Justice and Keeper of the Peace of our heirs and Successors within and through the whole Burrough of Bellfast and in and within all and Singular Liberties Limitts and meets thereof and that the same justice may have full power and authority to keep and conserve our peace our heirs and Successors and also to enquire hear and determine all things concerning our peace in or within the aforesaid Burrough or Liberties of the same

And moreover we will and by these presents for us our heirs and Successors doe grant to the aforesaid Soveraigne ffree Burgesses and Comonality of the

a Town hall

said Burrough and to their for ever that they may have a Marchant Hall within the Burrough aforesaid and one Comon seale in such forme and as shall seem best unto them to serve for ever for the businesses of the same Burrough

And that they may be able for ever from time to time as often as it shall be

Two Sergeants att Mace & other Ministers

needfull of themselves to chuse constitute and ordaine two serjeants at mace and other inferiour officers and necessary ministers for the better government of the Burrough aforesaid and the Inhabitants of the same   And wee make constitute and ordaine every person soe from time to time ellected constituted and ordained to be the serjeants at mace and other inferior officers and Ministers of the same Burrough respectively and in their offices to continue dureing their good behaviour or at the Will and pleasure of the said Soveraigne ffree Burgesses and Comonality of the Burrough aforesaid and that every such serjeant officer and minister before they shall be admitted to exercise their office shall take before the Soveraigne of the said Burrough for the time being his Corporall oath for the well and truly bering his office Moreover wee grant that the Soveraigne of the Burrough aforesaid for the time being for ever shall be Clark of the Markett within the Burrough aforesaid and Libties of the same and from time to time they may have

Sovereign Clerk of the Market

full power and authority to doe and follow all and singular to the office of the Clark of the Markett belonging or pertaining so that noe other Clark of our Marketts our heirs or Successors shall enter into the Burrough aforesaid or the ffranchises of the same there to doe or execute the the (*sic*) office of the Clark of the Markett or anything to the said office belonging or appertaining neither shall he enter himself in any office of the Clark of the Markett any ways tuching the Burrough aforesaid or the Libties of the same ffurther more wee will and of our especiall grace certain knowledge and meere motion doe grant to the aforesaid Soveraigne ffree Burgesses and Comonality of the Burrough *aforesaid* that hereafter it may and shall be lawful to all freemen of the Burrough aforesaid and their Successors to chuse and establish within the ffranchises of the

Wharffe or Key

said Burrough one wharffe or Key in any convenient place uppon the Bay or Creek of Bellfast aforesaid And also that it may and shall be Lawfull to all and Singular Marchants as well Twonsmen (*sic*) as strangers and to all other our subjects and Leige people with whatsoever shipp or Barque to arrive or bring to the said Wharffe or Key and there to discharge and unlaid and from thence to carry and convey all and Singular Merchandizes and Mercionaries without our hindrance our heirs and successors or any Customer Controwler or any other our officers of our heirs or successors resident in our port of Carrickfergus, Provided always that the said Merchants and the rest of our Leige people and Subjects doe pay or cause to be paid to us our heirs and Successors all and

N

Singular Customes as well great as small subsidyes of poundage and impositions due or payable in the said port of Carrickfergus or Bay or Creeke of the same for all and singular Merchandizes brought in or carryed forth as aforesaid

And moreover of our more especiall Grace certain knowledge and meere motion wee grant unto the aforesaid Soveraigne ffree Burgesses *and Comonality* of the Burrough aforesaid and their Successors for ever that these our Letters pattents and every article and clause in them contained or the Inrolment of them are to be construed interpreted and adjudged towards the greatest advantage benefitt and favour of the aforesaid Soveraigne ffree Burgesses and Comonality of the Burrough aforesaid and their Successors towards and against us our heirs and Successors as well in all our Courts as otherwise wheresoever without any confirmations Licenses or Tollerations hereafter to be secured or obtained notwithstanding that our Writt of ad Quod Dampñ hath not issued first to enquire of the premisses before the makeing of these our Letters Pattents And notwithstanding any other defect or any other thing cause or matter whatsoever to the contrary notwithstanding we will and also grant to the same Soveraigne ffree Burgesses and Comonality of the Burrough of Bellfast aforesaid and to their Successors that they may have and shall have these our Letters Pattents under our great Seale of Ireland and sealed and to be made in due manner without any fine great or small therefore to be made & paid to us our heirs or Successors in our hamper or otherwise to our use soe that express invention be not made of the true yearly worth or of the certainty of the premisses or any one of them or of any gift or grant by us or by any of our progenitors to the said Soveraigne ffree Burgesses and Comonality of the Burrough before this time made remaining in these presents any Statute Act ordinance or proviso or any other thing cause or matter whatsoever made contrary to these presents in anything notwithstanding In Testemonie of which thing wee have caused these our Letters pattents to be made Wittness our aforesaid Deputy Generall of our Kingdome of Ireland at Dublin the seaven and twentieth day of Aprill in the Year of our Reigne of England ffrance and Ireland the Eleaventh and of Scotland the six and ffortieth

Edgworth

VILLA SIVE DE BELFAST **Burgus**

At an Assemblie there holden the seaventeenth day of October in the nineteenth year of the Raigne of our Soveraigne Lord Charles the Second of England Scotland ffrance and Ireland King Defendor of the ffaith &c Anno Domini 1667

WHEREAS in the year of our Lord God 1635 by the full and free consent of the Rt Honble Edward Lord Viscount Chichester the Lord of the Castle of Belfast severall good and wholmsome Acts orders and By Laws were *then* made and established for the due ordering and better Regiment of this Corporation for the further and more fully confirming of which the Rt Honoble Arthur Earl of Donegall now Lord of the Castle aforesaid hath fully consented and freely agreed wth the now Soveraigne Burgesses and Grand Jury Representatives of the Comonality of ye said Corporation and by them hereby enacted and ordered and for ever to stand and be in force and power as By laws of this Corporation to all intents and purposes as by the following words they are exprest and at large sett down

1ᵗ For Burgesses and Soveraigns

IN THE PRESENCE and by ye full and free consent of the Rt Honoble Edward Lord Viscount Chichester Lord of ye Castle of Belfast It is ordered by the Soveraigne and Burgesses then and there assembled & ordained as a By Law for ever to indure that if any freeman of the Corporation being elected Burgess by the Soveraigne & Burgesses of the same or the more of the same refuse to take upon him the place of a Burgesse and to take his oath accordingly he or they soe refuseing shall forfitt the sume of five pounds ster And if any free Burgess of this Corporation which hereafter shall be elected Soveraigne within the said Borrough shall refuse to take the office upon him and be sworn accordingly he or they so refusing shall forfeit and loose Ten pounds ster the same to be levyed by warrant of the Soveraigne for the time being and to be employed for the good and benefitt of this Corporation

2ᵈ For repairing fences

IN THE PRESENCE and by the full and free consent of the Rt Honble Edward Lord Viscount Chichester Lord of the Castle of Belfast It is ordered by the Soveraigne and free Burgesses then and there assembled and ordained as a By Law for ever to indure That every free Burgesse free Comoner and other Inhabitants of this Town wᶜʰ now doe or hereafter shall hold or possess any house or land in Towne or fields within the precints of this Corporation shall within one month now next coming well and sufficiently repaire all and every ye fences and inclosures he or they ought to repaire And ye same from time to time shall maintain and keep upon pain of forfeiture of five shillings ster for every default to be levyed and employed as aforesaid

3ᵈ For keeping of swine

IN THE PRESENCE and by the full and free consent of ye Rt Honble Edward Lord Viscount Chichester Lord of ye Castle of Belfast It is ordered by ye Soveraigne and Burgesses then and there assembled and ordained for a By Law for ever to endure That no free Burgess free Comoner nor any other Inhabitant dwelling within this Corporation shall suffer any horses mares Garrons cows or other cattle swine or Geese wᶜʰ he or they shall keep to go at large in ye Streets or highways to the annoyance of their neighbours upon pain of forfeiting for every fault they shall be taken in ye sum of ten shillings ster to be levyed and employed as aforesd

4ᵗʰ Agᵗ leaving of Dung hills

IN THE PRESENCE and by and with ye full and free consent of ye Rt Honble Edward Lord Viscount Chichester Lord of ye Castle of Belfast It is ordered by ye Soveraigne and Burgesses then & there assembled and ordained for a ByLaw for ever to endure That no free Burgess free Comoner or other Inhabitant dwelling or Inhabiting within this Corporation shall make or cause to be made any dunghills in ye open streets before their doores to continue there above three days or cast any Carrion dyeing stuffe or any other loathsome thing into ye River coming through ye said Town of Belfast to ye annoyance of ye water and hurt of their neighbours upon pain of forfeiting for every such default ye sume of five shillings ster Provided that such as have any dunghills before their doors shall have such convenient time for ye removing of ye same as ye Soveraigne for ye time being shall think fitt ye said fines to be levyed and employed as aforesaid

5ᵗʰ For sueing in ye Courts

IN THE PRESENCE and by ye full & free consent of ye Rt Honble Edward Lord Viscount Chichester Lord of ye Castle of Belfast It is ordered by ye Soveraigne and Burgesses then and there assembled that noe free Burgess nor free Comoner of this Corporation shall sue or implead any of ye free Burgesses or free Comoners of ye same Town for any action that ye Court of this Corporation may heare without ye consent of ye Lord of ye Castle of Belfast for ye time being or Soveraigne of ye same Town then being first obtained unless such person shall not have due proceedings there every person so offending therein shall forfeit forty shillings ster: for every default ye same to be levyed & employed as aforesaid

6th No malt killns to be built without ye consent of ye L⁴ Castle

AT AN ASSEMBLY held the 29th of March 1638 in the presence of the Rt Honble Edward Lord Viscount Chichester Lord of ye Castle of Belfast and with his consent It is ordered and established by ye Soveraigne and Burgesses as a By Law for ever to remaine That from henceforth no person or persons inhabiting within ye Borrough of Belfast shall erect or make any Malt Kilnes or make use of any Malt Kilnes already built within ye said Towne but in such convenient places as shall be allowed of by the Lord of ye Castle and Soveraigne for ye time being wᵗʰ six of the Burgesses at least upon pain of forfeiture of five pounds ster for every time he shall be presented for the same to be levyed & employed as aforesaid

7th Agᵗ Wood Chimneys

AT THE SAME ASSEMBLY by and wᵗʰ ye Consent aforesaid It is ordered (daily inconveniencys likely to arise to this Towne & Borrough by reason of wood Chymnies) That ye said Chymnies wthin ye Rampier of this Town be forthwith pulled down and brick Chymnies to be made instead thereof upon pain of forfeiture on every person that maketh default ye sume of forty shillings ster to be levyed and employed as aforesaid

8th No Sovⁿ to sell ale or any liquor during his Sovᵗʸ repealed in the year 1716 Mr Gurner Soveraign

AT AN ASSEMBLY held the 24th of June 1660 Capt ffrancis Meeke Soveraigne It was ordered by the Soveraigne and Burgesses with the consent of the Rt Honble Arthur Earl of Donegall Lord of ye Castle of Belfast That no Burgesse of ye Borrough of Belfast from and after ye date hereof that is and shall be elected and sworn Soveraigne of ye Borrough aforesaid dureing ye time of his Soveraignty shall sell by retaile in his house any wine whatsoever or any beer ale or aqua vitæ or other strong waters or keep entertainmt in his house dureing his office as aforesaid upon forfeiture of one hundred pounds to be levyed upon his goods and chattles to & for ye use of this Corporation.

9th ffreemen refusing to appear being summoned

IN THE PRESENCE and by the full and free consent of the Rt Honble Edward Lord Viscount Chichester Lord of the Castle of Belfast It is ordered by the Sovereign & Burgesses then & there assembled That if any free Burgesse or free Comoner of this Corporation shall att any time refuse to come and appear at ye Court held within this Corporation or before the Soveraigne for ye time being warning being given unto him or them by ye officers without reasonable or sufficient cause to be allowed of by the Sovereign and Burgesses shall for every such default forfeit to ye use of this Corporation Tenn shillings Ster for every such offence ye same to be levyed and employed as aforesaid

10th Agᵗ selling Wine &c time divine service

IN THE PRESENCE and by and with the consent of the Right Honble Edward Lord Viscount Chichester Lord of the Castle of Belfast It is ordered by the Sovereign and Burgesses then and there assembled That no person or persons whatsoever shall sell any manner of ale wine or aqua vitæ or anything vendible within this Corporation at ye time of divine Service or sermon time upon forfeiture for every time that he or they shall be convicted thereof six shillings and eight pence ster to be levyed and employed as aforesaid

11th to accompanying the Sov^r to Church

IN THE PRESENCE and by the full and free consent of the Rt Honble Edward Lord Viscount Chichester Lord of ye Castle of Belfast. It is ordered by the Sovereigne and Burgesses then and there assembled That free Burgesse and *free* Comoner in this Corporation shall every Sunday or other day wherein there shall be a sermon or other publique prayers as often as it shall so happen to be shall all repaire to the house of the Sovereign for ye time being and shall attend in his company to ye Church or place of prayer and from thence home again or neer to his house upon pain of payment by every Burgess two shillings ster and every free Comoner twelve pence ster unless he or they so neglecting shall show to ye Sovereign for the time being some reasonable cause to ye contrary the same to be levyed and employed as aforesaid

---

12th to attend the Sov^r to meeting Judges

IN THE PRESENCE and by the full and free consent of the Rt Honble Edward Lord Viscount Chichester Lord of ye Castle of Belfast It is ordered by the Sovereign and Burgesses then and there assembled That every ffree Burgess and ffree Comoner dwelling within this Corporation or otherwise then resident shall whensoever occasion happens for the Credit and grace of this Corporation notice being given unto them how short or soon soever it be shall be ready to accompany the Sovereign for ye time being to meet any nobleman Justices of Assize or other state or person w'soever that shall come into this Town and that they shall be likewise ready either on horseback or foot wth ye Sovereign either in ye said Town or ye Liberties thereof in ye most decent manner they may or best can upon pain either of comittmt dureing the Sovereigns and Burgesses pleasure for ye time being or upon pain of paymt by every free Burgess and free Comoner such fine as by ye Sovereign and two or more of ye Burgesses shall be thought fitt so as ye fine do not exceed twenty shillings ster: the same to be levyed and employed as aforesaid

---

13th Butchers to carry their blood and garbage into the sea

AT AN ASSEMBLY held there the seventh day of January 1663 with ye consent of the Rt Honoble Arthur Earl of Donegall Lord of ye Castle of Belfast It is ordered by (George M'Cartney Esqr) Sovereign and the Burgesses then and there assembled That whereas daily complaints are made by severall Inhabitants of ye said Burrough that great annoyances are done by the Butchers of this Town by Killing and slaughtering of Cattle suffering ye Blood and garbage some to lye in ye Streets and other parts to run into severall channells and ditches of this Town to ye corrupting of ye River and other annoyances to the neighbours for the avoyding the same for ye future that if any Butcher or Butchers or any other person whatsoever shall from and after ye date hereof slaughter or kill or cause to be slaughtered or killed any cattle of what kind soever within this Town of Belfast wthout they or any of them so doing shall carry or cause to be carryed ye same day all ye blood and Garbage of such beasts or cattles so killed or slaughtered twenty yards beyond ye full sea marke every such Butcher or other person offending herein shall for every offence pay twenty shillings ster to be Levyed [by distresse] and employed as aforesaid

---

14th Of leaving timber carts or carrs in the streets & for cleaning the streets

AT THE SAME ASSEMBLY by and with the full & free consent of the Rt Honble Arthur Earl of Donegall It is ordered and enacted that if any person or persons shall from and after ye date hereof encumber leave or cause to be left upon any of ye Streets and Lanes of this Town any Timber Carts Carrs Hoggsheads barrells or other Caske full or empty or any other thing of w^t quantity soever without leave first had and obtained from ye Sovereign for ye time being so to do and to be granted in case of necessity as ye Sovereign shall allow of every such person or persons offending herein shall pay for every offence ye sume of ten shillings ster: And it is further ordered that all persons within this Town being masters of families or tenants living in any house or houses or that useth or occupieth any shopp cellar warehouse storehouse or any place or ground though waste fronting upon any of ye Streets or lanes aforesaid shall every week twice that is to say on Wednesday and Saturday sweepe and make cleane or cause to be swept or made cleane his or their part or portion of ye Street that belongeth to such house or houses shopps cellars warehouses storehouses or any other place or places respectively And if any such person or persons shall neglect or refuse so to do every such person or persons so offending shall pay twelve pence ster for every offence to be levyed and employed as aforesaid .

15th Liberty to erect Bridge over River

AT AN ASSEMBLY held the fourteenth day of Aprill 1664 wth ye consent of ye Rt Honoble Arthur Earl of Donegall Lord of ye Castle of Belfast It is ordered by ye Sovereign and Burgesses then and there assembled That any person Inhabiting in the High Street shall have liberty against his house to erect and build over ye River a Bridge for coaches or carrs to goe over without any lett or hindrance from any person leave being first had from ye Lord of ye Castle or ye Sovereigne for ye time being

---

16th Sovn to call preceding Sovn to an acct for what money recd for the benefit of the Corporacon

AT AN ASSEMBLY held ye fourth day of January 1665 Edward Reynells Esqr then Sovereign by and wth ye consent ye Rt Honoble Arthur Earl of Donegall It is ordered established and enacted that whereas from time to time severall sumes of money have been received by ye Sovereignes from free Comoners of this Corporation and by ye late Rebellion and other Revolutions happening for several years last past noe accompt hath been given of ye same And forasmuch as Mr John Rigby George M'Cartney Esqr and Mr William Waring for and on ye behalfe of his father late deceased are ready to give an accompt of what moneys were received in their times that from henceforth every Sovereign that shall succeed in ye place and office of Sovereign of ye Borrough of Belfast aforesaid shall have full power and authority wth ye assistance of ye major part of ye Burgesses within one month after he shall be sworn Sovereign to call ye preceding Sovereign to an accompt of all such sumes of money as were received in his time of and from any freemen or given by any other person to be employed for ye good of this Corporation and how disbursed and disposed to ye use aforesaid And if that any Sovereign shall happen to dye within ye time of his being sworn Sovereign that then it shall and may be lawful to and for ye succeeding Sovereign to call and cause ye Exrs and admrs of ye Sovereign that shall so happen to dye as aforesaid to give a true and just accompt of all and every such sume or sumes of money as shall be received or disposed of as aforesaid any act order or By law of this Corporation at any time or times heretofore made published ordered or established to ye contrary in anywise notwithstanding

---

17th All ffreemen to be made free in Court 3 or 2 of the Burgesses present one moiety of the money to be for the use of the Court

AT THE SAME ASSEMBLY by and with ye full and free consent of ye Rt Honble Arthur Earl of Donegall Lord of ye Castle of Belfast It is ordered by ye Sovereign and Burgesses ye daily growing charge of ye poor and other ways of disbursing moneys being considered and ye great want of a Town Stock to defray any emergent charge and ye number of free Comoners daily increasing rather to ye hurt and detrimt of this Corporation than to ye credit or advantage thereof It is enacted by ye consent aforesaid that ye Sovereign for ye time being and every Sovereign for ye time to come shall not admitt any person to be a free Comoner of this Corporation without reserving ye full moyety of such sume or sumes of money as shall be agreed upon for ye making of any person ffree to and for ye use of ye said Town And that no ffreeman hereafter shall be admitted and sworn a ffree Comoner in no other place and at no other time but in open Court three or two at ye least of ye Burgesses beside ye Sovereign being present any Act Order use or custome of this Corporation heretofore made used or done to ye contrary in anywise notwithstanding

18th noxious Games &c

AT THE SAME ASSEMBLY by and wth ye full and free consent of ye Rt Honble Arthur Earl of Donegall Lord of ye Castle of Belfast   It is ordered and enacted and to remaine as a By Law for ever that no Inholder Aleseller or Victualer within ye Borrough of Belfast shall [not] from henceforth suffer any person or persons unless Lodgers in their houses to drink or play at any game w'soever after ye hour of nine at night and that every person that shall offend as abovesaid shall for every offence pay to ye Sovereign for ye time being ye sume of three shillings and four pence ster to be levyed by distress or otherwise and every person that shall be found drinking or playing after ye time afore-mentioned shall pay to ye Sovereign for ye time being ye sume of five shillings ster for every default to be levyed and employed as aforesaid

19th for keeping up ye river wall

AT AN ASSEMBLY holden for ye Borrough aforesaid by ye consent aforesaid ye seventeenth day of October 1667   It is ordered by ye Sovereign and Burgesses that every person Inhabiting or that hereafter shall inhabit in ye Street called ye High Street shall build with lime and stone or brick so much of ye wall of ye River as shall front to his or their house or houses in ye same manner and form as the most part thereof is now built and ye same so built shall from time to time repair and keep up every person neglecting so to do shall for every default forfeite ye sume of ten shillings ster to be levyed and employed as aforesaid

20th No person to be admitted free as an apprentice unless within 3 months after he has completed his time

AT THE SAME ASSEMBLY by and wth ye consent aforesaid   It is ordered and established as a By Law for ever   That w'ever person or persons that shall serve as an apprentice wth any master wthin ye Liberty of this Corporation and shall not wthin three months after ye compleating of his apprentiship by his Indenture or otherwise make it appear to ye Sovereign for ye time being that he hath served his time wthin ye Liberties aforesaid shall utterly loose ye benefitt of being made a free Comoner of the Borrough according to ye custome in that case formerly used but shall be accounted an alien and foreiner and compound for his freedome as aliens and foreiners notwithstanding any act custome or use to ye contrary made or used at any time heretofore provided this law shall not extend to any persons beyond ye seas

21st Against harbouring inmates

AT THE SAME ASSEMBLY by the full and free consent of ye Rt Honoble Arthur Earl of Donegall Lord of ye Castle of Belfast   It is ordered and ordained for a By Law for ever to continue   That no cheife Tenant or sub-tenant living wthin ye Town and Liberties of Belfast w'soever shall from hence-forth take into their houses to inhabite any persons either marryed or single wthout every such cheife tenant as shall bring in any do first secure ye Towne from any charge that may ensue or such tenants shall obtain leave from ye Lord of ye Castle or ye Sovereign for ye time being under their hands in writing nor shall any Tenant wthin ye said Liberty divide his dwelling house or other his houses into more Tenemts than formerly they have been used or enjoyed for ye taking in or harbouring Inmates wthout leave obtained as aforesaid   Any Burgess free Comoner or other person offending in ye premisses shall forfeit for every default ye sume of forty shillings ster to be levyed and employed as aforesaid   And any person or persons that shall be brought in as Inmates aforesaid shall upon knowledge thereof by warr from the Sovereign imediately be turned out of ye Town and Liberties thereof

22th to pay the Customes

AT THE SAME ASSEMBLY by and with ye full and free consent of ye Rt Honble Arthur Earl of Donegall Lord of ye Castle of Belfast and by ye Sovereign and Burgesses of ye Borrough of Belfast   It is ordered and for a By Law for ever to continue in consideration that ye Inhabitants of Mallon ffall and

Dunmurry and part of ye parish of Coole by their representatives ye Grand
Jury at a Court Leete for ye said *manner* consent to pay towards ye erecting
and building up a Court house and Markett house in this Corporation as by ye
presentmt may appear ye said Inhabitants of Mallon ffall and Dunmurry wth
part of ye parish of Coole having already paid part of their proportion and
paying ye remainder according to ye assesse made thereupon That ye
Inhabitants of ye said Mallon ffall and Dunmurry wth part of ye parish of Coole
so many of them as are within ye manor of Belfast shall have their own proper
goods brought into ye Towne Tole and Custome free usually paid at ye gates of
ye said Town and no other provided allways that no person an Inhabitant of any
of ye places aforesaid by pretence or colour of ye Liberty aforesaid shall at any
time owne any forreiners goods whereby ye Custome of ye said Town may be
Lessened   That then any person against whome any such thing shall be proved
before ye Sovereign of ye said Borrough for ye time being by ye oath of one
witnesse shall loose ye benefitt of ye freedome aforesaid and forfeit ye sume of
forty shillings ster to be levyed upon ye goods and chattles of ye person offending
and to be employed as aforesaid   And provided allways that all persons
Inhabiting in any of ye places aforesaid shall yearly and every year pay their
severall and respective proportions of mony towards ye repair of ye said Court
house and Markett house from time to time as often as ye same shall be needfull
and necessary

23th Butchers to pay Tongues

AT THE SAME ASSEMBLY   Whereas it hath been an ancient custome
of this Corporation that every Butcher free of this Borrough killing or
slaughtering any Bullocks or Cows of what kind soever wthin this Town or
Liberty thereof to pay every week he so killed to ye Sovereign for ye time being
one tongue of ye Beast or Beasts he should slaughter   It is ordered by ye
Sovereign and Burgesses then assembled and by and with ye consent aforesaid
and to stand for ever as a By Law of this Corporation   That every Butcher
free as aforesaid shall every week so long as he shall kill or cause to be killed
and slaughtered any Bullock or Cow within ye said Town and Liberties thereof
shall observe ye aforesaid custome   And that every other person that is not free
of this Corporation but a forreiner and alien to ye same shall not slaughter or
kill any Bullock or Cow of w^t kind soever within ye said Town or Liberties
thereof but shall pay to ye Sovereign for the time being for every Bullock or
Cow that he shall kill or slaughter ye sume of four pence ster and none to kill
within ye said Town of Belfast without license first had and obtained from ye
Sovereign for ye time being Excepting allways ffree Comoners every person that
shall refuse to pay ye four pence aforesaid for every beast he shall slaughter as
aforesaid shall for every default forfeit ye sume of one shilling ster for every
Bullock or Cow he shall kill or cause to be killed ye same to be levyed and
employed as aforesaid

24th Ships not to hinder Gabbords to discharge

AT THE SAME ASSEMBLY   Upon complaint of ye daily annoyance
hindrance and stoppage made of and to Gabbords and Boates plying in and out
of Dock belonging to this Town by shipps Barkes and other vessells coming up
into ye same and lyeing there to discharge their loadings by which much
damage hath and may for ye future accrue to merchants and others employing
Boates and Gabbords   It is ordered thereupon by ye Sovereign and Burgesses
of this Corporation then assembled by and with ye consent aforesaid to endure
for ever for a By Law of this this (*sic*) Corporation   That no shipp or Barke of
w^t Burden soever shall come into ye said Dock to lighten or discharge their
loading or to take in their loading but at such times as there may be no
hindrance for Boates and Gabbords to pass to and fro and those that shall so
come in after publishing of this By Law to be licensed by ye Sovereign or ye
Water Bayliffe for ye time being and to fall down out of ye said Dock
whensoever thereunto required by the Sovereign or Water Bayliffe every person
that shall offend herein for every fault that shall be made appeare before the
Sovereign for ye time being shall forfeit ye sume of forty shillings ster to be
levyed and employed for ye repaire of ye Key or Dock as shall be thought fitt

25th Presentments & petty customs to be for the use of Sov^a

AT THE SAME ASSEMBLY by and with ye consent aforesaid It is ordered and to stand for ever a By Law of this Corporation that all fines upon presentments made by ye Grand Juryes from time to time not exceeding Ten shillings ster and that all petty customes shall be to ye use of every Sovereign dureing his time of being Sovereign of ye Borrough of Belfast for and towards his house keeping without giving any accompt for ye same notwithstanding any By Laws to ye contrary provided no petty customes be exacted from any Burgesse or free Comoner of this Corporation

26th Sovⁿ to sell distresses

AT THE SAME ASSEMBLY by and with ye consent aforesaid It is ordered that every Sovereign of this Corporation for ye time being shall have power to apprize and sell within fourteen days time all distresses taken from any person or persons within this Town and liberties thereof refuseing to pay any pecuniary mulct or assesse made layed or imposed upon him or them and the overplus if any be shall be returned to ye person offending or owner thereof

I doe allow and freely consent to these By Laws being twenty and six in number and think them fitt and necessary for ye good governmt of this Corporation

The Grand Jury.	Donegall
Michaell Biggar	George M'Cartney Soveraigne
Alexander Smithe	John Leathes senior Gilbert Wye
Charles Whitlocke	John Leathes Junior
George Snoden	Thomas Walcott
John M'Cartney	Edward Reynalls
John Shankes	George M'Cartney niger
Thomas Lightfoote	Hugh Doake
Mathew ffarrell	William Waring
John Christian	ffra Thetford

27th Butchers to sell their meat in ye shambles

AT AN ASSEMBLY held ye fourth day of November 1686 with ye consent of ye Hono^{ble} Sr William ffrancklin Lord of ye Castle of Belfast It is ordered by Robert Leathes Esqr Sovereigne and ye Burgesses then and there assembled That whereas daily complaints are made of ye inconveniency of Butchers keeping their meat upon the Streets wthout the Shambles wch not only is indecent of itselfe but much straitens that part of ye Street which is designed and allotted for Public Markett and whereas for ye public good there is an apartmt prepared wthin ye new buildings on ye South side of Castle Street That all Butchers Inhabitants of this said Town shall repair to ye said apartment and furnish themselves wth shambles convenient at or before ye 25th day of March next upon pain of forfeiting twelve pence ster: toties quoties found in ye Street wth Stalls and that ye said Stalls shall be removed ye said fine to be levyed by distresse or otherwise by warrant from ye Sovereigne for ye time being and ye same to be employed for ye good and benefitt of this Corporation

28th Every barrell Rock Lime to contain 32 galls Winchester measure

AT THE SAME ASSEMBLY by ye authority aforesaid ordered That whereas there is great fraud comitted dayly by ye selling of Lime by unjust and undue measures That from and after ye first day of May next every Barrell of Rock or unfallen Lime brought to be sold or sold wthin this Corporation shall contain thirty two gallons winchester measure upon pain making default of six pence ster: per Barrell toties quoties the same to be levyed ut supra

29th Every load of turf to fill a Wine hhd

AT THE SAME ASSEMBLY by ye authority aforesaid ordered that all horse Loads of Turfe brought into this Corporation to be sold shall be of ye full measure of one Bordeaux hhd of seventy wine Gallons upon pain of two pence ster for every faulty load and that and that (*sic*) there be at ye Publick charge of the Borrough sealed hoggsds prepared for measuring the same and lodged in some convenient place in the Town to be found on all occasions by which debates of that nature are to be decided to be levyed ut supra

30th to put out Lights

AT THE SAME ASSEMBLY ordered that to prevent the dangers to wch persons walking in ye night about their Lawfull affairs are incident to every Inhabitant in every Street and Lane in this Corporation shall from henceforth in every year from ye 29th of September to ye 25th of March hang out at their respective doors or shops one Lanthren and candle lighted from ye hour of seven at night till ten when it is not moonshine in ye said hours upon pain of six pence ster: per night toties quoties to be levyed ut supra

31th Beef Barrells to be made of good seasoned timber & contain 30 wine galls

AT THE SAME ASSEMBLY ordered that whereas it is known that ye reputation of ye trade in this Towne abroad is much impaired by ye insufficiency of Beefe Barrells for severall years past every Beefe Barrell made by any Cooper in Belfast or by him them or any person sold in ye said Town after ye first day of May shall be made of good well seasoned Timber well hooped and staunch and to be of ye measure of thirty wine gallons upon pain of twelve pence ster. for every faulty barrell to be levied ut supra

32th to furnish bucketts

AT THE SAME ASSEMBLY ordered that for ye better security of ye houses of this Corporation from ye casuality of fire and in imitation of ye laudible custome of other Towns and Borroughs every Inhabitant of sixty pounds ster: free substance shall at or before ye first day of May next at his own proper cost furnish one leathren bucket and ye same deliver to ye Sovereign for ye time being to be lodged in some place ready on all exigences and that ye Sovereign at ye public charg do compleat ye Ladders wᶜʰ are to be four in number and provide a couple of poles with hookes and chains for pulling down houses on such occasions ye said Bucketts to be delivered to ye Sovereign for ye use aforesaid against ye next quarterly assembly upon pain of forfeiture of four shillings and six pence ster: of each person to be levied ut supra

33th Butter Hydes & Tallow to be sold in the middle of ye town

AT AN ASSEMBLY held ye sixth of September 1694 at ye Tholsell of Belfast in and for ye Borrough Town and Corporation of Belfast William Craford Esqr Sovereign For as much as it is found by comon experience that many persons who have not been bred marchants wᵗʰin ye Town nor elsewhere have of late for their private lucre and gain used to buy great quantities of Butter Hydes and Tallow as ye same was coming to ye said Town of Belfast to be sold and have engrossed ye same into their hands wᵗʰ design to sell it dearer to ye merchant adventurers exporters and traders inhabiting ye said Town of Belfast than he who brought ye same to be sold For ye remidy whereof and for preventing ye great abuses and sinister practices comitted and done in buying and selling as aforesaid It is ordered and declared by ye Sovereign and Burgesses and free Comonality of this Corporation and by authority of ye same and by and wth ye consent of ye Rt Honoᵇˡᵉ ye Earl and Countess of Longford Lords of ye Castle of Belfast that ye markett for ye sale and purchase of Butter hydes and Tallow within ye Town and Borrough of Belfast is and hereafter shall be wᵗʰin ye Castle Street or some part thereof between ye upper Castle Gate and Church Lane and Skiper Lane on ye other side of ye River and in Bridge Street between ye Bridge called ye stone Bridge and ye corners turning down to broad street and Rosemary Lane and that hereafter no butter hydes or Tallow coming to ye Town of Belfast to be sold shall be bought or caused to be bought or sold directly or indirectly by any person wʰsoever before ye said butter hydes or Tallow shall be brought or come wᵗʰin ye Streets aforesaid limitted and appointed for ye markett and sale thereof under ye penalty of being by Law prosecuted as unlawfull ingrossers and forestallers of ye markett

Gabbards &c to pay tunnage

AT AN ASSEMBLY of the Sovereigne and Burgesses held ye 22nd day of October 1696   It is enacted as a By Law of this Corporation pursuant to a presentment of ye Grand Jury this day given in for Keeping cleane ye Docke and for a fund to make a sluce for keeping clean ye said Docke by scowring that all vessells ships barkes or boates belonging to forreiners that will have liberty to discharge at ye Key of Belfast w^thin ye said Docke shall pay two pence for every tun that such vessell ship or bark shall be of burthen and ye same rate upon every vessell which shall take in any loading outwards and all such Gabards vessells or lighters as belong to freemen of ye Borrough which goe to England Scotland or elsewhere or along ye coast shall pay one penny per tun for their burthen at discharge and ye same rate on loading outwards and all such gabards and Lighters as only pley to garmoyle and in ye Lough shall pay ten shillings per annum to be paid at 2s 6d quarterly ye said severall sums to be received by such person as ye Sovereign and Burgesses or ye major part of them shall appoint to be applyed for making good and preserving ye said Dock and ye superplus of what can be saved from ye necessary disburse that way to be preserved for a fund for erecting a sluce in ye River from Skiper Lane to Church Lane which sluce hath by severall Grand Jurys been represented to be made and had been done before now had it not been for ye interruption of Civill affairs in ye warr

No Vessel to Lye at anchor the South ward of the Dock

AT THE SAME ASSEMBLY ordered upon presentmt of ye same Grand Jury for preventing ye doing damage on ye new Bridge that hereafter no vessell ly at anchor to ye southward of ye Dock and that such as are on ye north side of ye Dock be well mored on pain of forty shillings a tide fine for ye preservation of ye Bridge for ye future

River to be cleaned once every yeare

AT AN ASSEMBLY held ye 21st of January 1696 upon a presentmt of ye Grand Jury ordered that ye River be cleaned once every year to prevent overflowing and every person bordering on ye River from Mr Chades *bridge* to ye neer mill on both sides that do not every year clear ye River before their holding between ye beginning of May and midsumer shall pay 5/- fine each pearch.

At an Assembly March 30 1696

RDERED
That whereas some late Sovereigns of this Corporat.ⁿ have *not* because of the late troubles paid the moyety of the freemens money received upon admitting persons to their freedom of this Corporat.ⁿ w.ᶜʰ is contrary to a By-Law heretofore made. We the Sovereign & Burgesses are of opinion that it is very fitt that the said By Law be recontinued, & do appoint and agree that no person be hereafter admitted a freeman of this Corporat.ⁿ w.ᵗʰout paying the sum of ten shills ster to the use of the Corporat.ⁿ the same to be lodged in the hands of Thomas Craford Town Clark or such other person as shall be appointed to receive the same by the Sovereigne & Burgesses, unlesse the Sovereigne & major part of the Burgesses present when such freeman is made dispense w.ᵗʰ and remitt the paym.ᵗ of the s.ᵈ ten shils or any part thereof.

Lewes Thompson Sovereign

L Harrison   George M'Cartney   Rob.ᵗ: Leathes
Ja: M'Cartney   Wm: Crafford   William Lockhart
David Smith   Willm: M'Cartney

The humble addresse of the Sovereigne Burgesses
& principal Inhabitants of the Corporat.ⁿ of Belfast
Mar 30 1696

AY it please yo.ᵣ most Excell.ᵗ Ma.ᵗⁱᵉ We yo.ᵣ Ma.ᵗⁱᵉˢ most dutifull & Loyall Subjects do humbly begg leave heartily to congratulate yo.ᵣ Ma.ᵗⁱᵉ upon the happy and providential discovery of that most barbarous & hellish plott lately designed & carried on by papists and Jacobites against your Ma.ᵗⁱᵉˢ most sacred person & Government, & sincerely give thanks to almighty God for the great mercy vouchsafed to us & all Protestants, in confounding their devices, & bringing the intended villanous Executioners thereof to condign punishm.ᵗ and we take this occasion to assure yo.ᵣ Ma.ᵗⁱᵉ that we are fully satisfied that yo.ᵣ Ma.ᵗⁱᵉ is our rightful & lawfull King, and as we of this Corporat.ⁿ were early assertors thereof in this Kingdom, so we still by Gods Grace persevere therein, & will to the utmost of our power defend yo.ᵣ Ma.ᵗⁱᵉˢ Person right & Government against the late King James, the pretended Prince of Wales and all their adherents, wishing yor Matie a long and prosperous Reigne over us & a continued successe agst yor Maties & our Enemies.

Lewes Thompson Sovereign

Copia vera   & signed by 81 more hands

T an Assembly of the Sovereigne and Burgesses held the twenty second of Oc^{br} 1696 it is enacted as a By Law of this Corpora.ⁿ pursuant to a P^rsentm.^t of the Grand Jury this day given in for keeping cleane the dock and for a fund to make a sluice *for keeping clean the said dock by scouring* that all vessels ships barks or boats belonging to forreigners that will have liberty to discharge at the Key of Belfast wthin the said dock shall pay two pence for every tun that such vessel ship or bark shall be of burthen, and the same rate upon every vessel which shall take in any lading outward; and all such gabards vessels or lighters as belong to freemen of the Burrow which go to England Scotland or elsewhere or along the coast shall pay one penny per tun for their burthen at discharge, and the same rate on lading outward: & all such gabards or lighters as only ply to Garmoyle and in the Lough shall pay ten shils per annm to be paid at 2. 6^d quarterly; the said severall sums to be received by such person as the Sovereigne and Burgesses or the major part shall appoint to be apply'd for making good and p^rserving the said docke, and the superplus of what can be saved from the necessary disburse that way, to be preserved for a fund for erecting a sluice in the River from Skiper Lane to Church Lane which sluice hath by severall Grand Jurys been p^rsented to be made and had been done before now had it not been the interruption of civil affairs in the warr, At the same time ordered upon a P^rsentm.^t of the same Grand Jury for preventing the doing damage on the new Bridge that hereafter no vessel ly at anchor to the southward of the Dock, and that such as are on the north side of the dock be well mored on pain of fourty shils a tide fine. *for ye preservation of ye Bridge for ye future*

  Ordered upon p^rsentm^t of the Grand Jury 21. Jany '96 that the River be cleaned once every year to p^rvent overflowing, and every person bordering on the River from Mr Chad's bridg to the [upper] near mills on both sides that do not every year clear the River before their holding between the beginning of May & midsumer shall pay 5ˢ fine *for* each pearch

Robᵗ Leathes Soveraigne

Longford A Longford James Buller Ja M'Cartney
David Smith   L Harrison   Arthur M'Cartney
Lewes Thompson Jno Challmers Wm Crafford

We Mary Mathews widow and Charles Mathews both of Dromore in the County of Down Exʳˢ to Michael Mathews late of Dromore deceased, ourselves our Exʳˢ admʳˢ and assigns do hereby acknowledge to have received from Matthew Betts James MᶜCreery and Joseph Dixon full satisfacion of all bills bonds debts dues Reconings and accounts and demands whatsoever that was or hath been due to the aforesaid Michael Mathews or us his Exʳˢ from the beginning of the world to the day of the date hereof as witnesse our hands and seales this 14ᵗʰ day of June one thousand six hundred and ninety seven. [Sig] Memorandum that the said Betts discharges Mʳˢ Mathews and Mʳ Charles of all accounts due to him, and them

Signed sealed and delivered in the pʳsence of us

Derb: Blacker   his   Mary Mathews   ⓧ
Mʳˢ Linch   Simon × Dixon
                     mrk
                                 Charles Mathews ⓧ

Whereas I have now changed the place of my Residence. And removed from Belfast to Dungannon. where I cannot be so usefull nor serviceable to the Corporatione, as my Inclinations doe leade me. & my place of a Burgess doeth require I Doe therefore Resigne my place of Burgess of the Burough of Belfast into the hands of the Right Honᵇˡᵉ Arthur Earle of Donegalle Present Soveraigne of the said Burough; & to the Rest of the Burgesses of the same. To be by them disposed off as in Justice and Equity they shall think fitt As witness my hand the 17ᵗʰ Xber. 1697

Tho Knox

PON the above resignation of Mʳ Thomas Knox the Sovereign & Burgesses assembled this 23ʳᵈ of xbʳ 1697. did unanimously choose & elect Capt Edwᵈ Brice a free Burgesse of the Burrough of Belfast in room of the said Mʳ Knox who was accordingly sworn

Donegall Sovereign

William Lockhart   James Buller   David Smith
Arthur M'Cartney Jno: Challmers Cha: Chichester
George M'Cartney Robᵗ Leathes Lewes Thompson
L: Harrison   Wᵐ: Crafford

ORASMUCH as by free elecion of the Sovereigne & Burgesses of Belfast I was the 7th day of March 1691 Chosen a free Burgesse of the Burrough of Belfast I do hereby resign the said office into the hands of the Sovereign and Burgesses as aforesaid: decr 23rd 1697

Donegall

Upon the above Resignan of the Rt Honble Arthur Earle of Donegall the Sovereigne & Burgesses this day assembled did unanimously elect and choose the Honble Charles Chichester Esqr brother to the said Earle to be a free Burgesse of the Burrough of Belfast in room of the sd Earle who accordingly was sworne this 23rd of Decbr 1697

Donegall Soveraigne

George McCartney Rob Leathes Lewes Thompson L: Harrison Wm Crafford William Lockhart James Buller   David Smith   Arthur: McCartney Jno: Challmers

Upon the sixth day of September one thousand six hundred ninety eight the Sovereign and Burgesses did assemble to choose and elect a free Burgess in the place & roome of Willm Lockhart mrt. deceased and did unanimously choose the Honble Capt John Chichester a free Burgess in the room of the said Wm Lockhart & he was sworne according to the said elecion.

Rob Leathes Sovereigne

Ja: M'Cartney   Lewes Thompson   Wm Crafford James Buller   David Smith   Arthur: M'Cartney Jno Challmers   Cha: Chichester   Edwa Brice   Ri: Willoughby Constl. Castl.

October 9. 1698

HAVE recd from Capt Robt Leathes dep: Sovereigne—the Rt Honble the Earle of Donegall, the Town Charter in English & Latine, the By Laws, the Lady Marchioness of Antrim's Bond & Rent Charge 300li of the poor—Mr Theakers Bond for 10li of the same, Wm Kerr bond of 10li of the same, Lord Donegalls bond 10li of the same, Lady Longfords letter for 100li of the same   Witness my hand the day & year aforesaid,

Also the standard measures ly in the Court house

[lying in]   David Smith Soveraigne

Copy of an order to Mr Jemmett July 29. 1697

Sir, what money you have received for the Towns use toward building a Sluice out of the tunage, after deduction of your own allowance pursuant to the orders to you granted, please to pay the same to me Thomas Craford the Town chamberlane whose receipt will be sufficient to you.   I am Sir yor humble servt

R. L. Sovraigne

To Warham Jemmett Esqr Com^r of Belfast.

I have rec^d this 5th ffebry 1698/9 a Comission from the Sovereign and Burgesses of Belfast to receive the dock fees according to the w^{thin} By-Law of which I do hereby oblige myself my Ex^{trs} and Adm^{trs} in the penall sum of fourty pounds ster to give acct & make paym^t of my receits from time to time to the s^d Sovereign and Burgesses & their successors when thereunto required. Witness my hand & seall ye day & year aforesaid

    Rc^d   Tho: Craford not Pub°   Nath: Bÿrtt

Upon the fourteenth day of October one thousand seven hundred the Sovereign and Burgesses did assemble to choose and elect a free Burgesse in the place and room of Capt Edward Harrison Burgesse deceased, and did unanimously choose David Buller m^{rt} a free Burgess in room of the said Capt Harrison, & he was sworn accordingly

George M'Cartney Soveraigne

Robt Leathes   Lewes Thompson   Wm Crafford
James Buller   David Smith   Arthur: M'Cartney
Jno Challmers

UPON the twenty sixth day of April one thousand seven hundred and one the Sovereigne and Burgesses did assemble to choose and elect a free Burgesse in the place and room of the Honble Capt Charles Chichester Burgesse deceased, and did unanimously choose Isaac M'Cartney m^{rt} a free Burgesse in room of the said Capt Charles Chichester and he was sworne accordingly.

George M'Cartney Soveraigne

Donegall   Robt Leathes   Lewes Thompson   W^m
Crafford   James Buller   David Smith   Jno
Challmers   David Buller Ri: Willoughby Cons^t Cast

Burgus de   At an Assembly held the 8th of May 1701
Belfast   Geo: McCartney Esqr Soveraigne

Whereas it is found by experience that merchants as well strangers as Inhabitants of this town have been of late and dayly are imposed upon by the Porters or Carmen in exacting extravagant rates for drawing of goods, for the preventing whereof in time to come it is hereby ordered and enacted as a By Law of this Corpor^t by the Soveraigne Burgesses & Comonality by and with the consent of the Right Honble Arthur Earle of Donegall Lord of the Castle of Belfast that the following rates & no other be taken by the severall carmen, upon pain of being suspended from their employ, disfranchised of their freedom and amerced & fined as extortioners viz:

1 for every tun of coals salt or goods portable in bags from the Wharf to the Barracks or without miller gate and to Peters hill or without north gate twelve pence per tun & no more.

2 for every Tun of coals salt &c from the Key to any place above the bridg opposite to James Arbukle's house to any street lane or place within north gate & mill gate 2ᵈ per Load being eight pence per tun & no more.

3 for every tun of coals or salt &c below the said Bridg opposite to James Arbukle's house six pence per tun.

4 for every hhd of wine vinegar or other liquor 2ᵈ per hhd.

5 for every butt or pipe of wine Brandy or other liquor drawn on the slade and cellard by the carmen eight pence to any place within the gates.

for every hogshead of Muscovado Sugar six pence.

6 for every ten firkins of butter, being a car load from peters hill or any part wᵗʰout Mill gate or from any other street or lane in town two pence.

7 Every carman standing next to any goods to be laded shall sett to work at the aforesaid rates wᵗʰout pʳtending any new or other bargain for his work than the above rates and every merchant may choose and make use of such carman as he thinks fitt.

8 Every carman shall be ready on all occasions by turns upon the sumons of the Constables to do all publick services for the King upon mᵗching of the Army or otherwise.

And for the encouragement of a certain number of Porters to do all the work at the rates aforesaid and that straglers do not intrench upon their privileges the licensed porters for work are reduced to the number of 30 whose names follow viz Arch Tod Tho Wallace Jno McGown Ja Campbel Jno Tod Gilbt Tod Ja McDowel Tho Smith Jno Shaw Tho Slope Jno M'Crath And: Jamison Jno Taggart David Harman Wm Boyd Gilb Robison Al Robison Jno Gardner Rob Maxwell Gilb Tod Junr Jno Thomson Ja Murray Charles Ramage Matthew Leath Wm Neilson Tho Neilson Jno Neilson Tho McLearn Jno Neill & Thom Easton

And all other labourers are hereby discharged to work wᵗʰ any horse & carrs and it is hereby ordered that no person shall be licensed as a Carman till the death or superanuacion of some of the aforesaid persons; and such as then makes applicaⁿ to succeed in the said office shall repair to the said Corporacⁿ of carmen, without consent of the major part of whom the Soveraigne & Burgesses are not to inlist any such new carman or carmen

Intrᵈ per Tho Craford d clk Vill

Upon the sixth day of ffeby one thousᵈ seven hundred and two the Sovereigne & Burgesses then mett to choose a free Burgesse in the place & room of James Buller Burgesse deceased did unanimously choose & elect Neil Macneil apothecary a free Burgesse in the room of the said James Buller and he was accordingly sworn in the said office

David Buller Sovereigne

Lewes Thompson Wᵐ Crafford David Smith
Jno Challmers Edwa Brice

The Oath of the Sovereign of the Burrough of Belfast

You swear, that you shall well and truly serve our Sovereign Lady Queen Ann by the space of one whole year ending at Michaelmas next : and untill one other of the Burgesses be duly elected made and sworn to your office as Sovereign of the Burrough of Belfast (if God grant you so long life) with your best endeavour according to the power given unto you ; by Her Majties Letters Patents. You shall according to the best of yr knowledge and discretion do equall justice, as well to the poor, as to the Rich. You shall truly fairly and gently treat the people of this Town and Burrough. You shall use yr best endeavour to uphold and maintain the Rights and Liberties Jurisdictions, Priviledges, and Lawfull ordinances, of this Burrough ; Correction of Victualls that is to say bread beer ale wine fish and flesh, You shall truly and carefully see or cause to be seen into ;

Craftsmen, Artificers, and Labourers, You shall truly enquire of and the faulty Justly correct and duly reforme Widdows and orphans you shall succour and defend : and in all other things that shall or may concern the Town and your office You shall faithfully and uprightly demean yourself for the most quiet benefit worsip credit and advancement of this Burrough and the Inhabitants thereof

So help you God
in Christ Jesus

Upon the sixteenth day of October one thousand seven hundred and two the Soveraigne & Burgesses then mett did administer the oaths of allegiance & fidelity and oath of a Burgesse to George McCartney Esqr Counsel-at-law who had bin on Thursday the 8th 7br elected & chosen a free Burgesse of Belfast in the room of Mr Black George M'Cartney Mrt Signed by the said Soveraigne Burgesses and the Constable of the Castle

David Buller Sovereign

Pa: Duff Constable of the Castle. Robt Leathes
Lewes Thompson Wm Crafford David Smith
Arthur: Macartney Edwa Brice Isaac M'Cartney

County Antrim	Att ye Generall Qr Sessions of the Peace held for the County afforesaid at Ballymenagh the 10th of January 1704

Inter alia prsented as ffolloweth

Whereas many Sheep are stolne in ye County of Antrim the fflesh sould in open markett and the skins concealed soe that the theives cannot be discovered Wee therefore present that all Mutton that shall hereafter be brought into any markett within this County that the Skin or Skins of such Mutton with the markes of the same shall soe be brought along with it that the marke of such sheep may be Known whether ear marked or otherwise

Towards Execucion whereof It is ordered by the Court that all such Mutton that shall hereafter be brought to be exposed to sale without the skin or skins and the markes as afforesaid, the said mutton shall be forfeited for the use of the poor where the same is sould whereof all persons concerned are to take notice. dated as aforesaid

This order to be proclaimed and
fixed up in open markett (Belfast)

Signed by order
Hugh Smith dep clk

July 29. 1704

Gentlemen
By a late Act of Parliament disabling disentors to serve in public office I find it convenient for me to demitt the exercise of Sovereigne in yor Corporaⁿ; & therefor as a clause of yor Charter inables you I desier you'l please to convene

next Thursday (for the weakness of my brother makes me necessarily absent) and elect one of yor number to act as Sovereigne till Mich.^s that Mr Macartney comences pursuant to the elecion at midsumer, he is a gentleman if you think fitt may enter upon the trust now.

I am

To the Burgesses of Belfast.   Yo.^r most humble serv.^t

David Buller Sovereign

July 31. 1704

Burgus de } Pursuant to the above Instrument of
Belfast   } dimission from the Sovereigne,

We the Burgesses subscribing did conveene and having consulted our Charter what is to be done upon the death of a Sovereign or when the said office by any means whatsoever is vacant, did unanimously elect George M'Cartney Esqr to serve as Sovereign during the residue of this currant year and he was duly sworne to the s.^d office in the Castle before the Constable or his deputy the day afores.^d

Arthur: Macartney Lewes Thompson Edwa Brice, Jno. Challmers Wm Crafford Neil McNeile Robt Leathes David Smith

On Monday the sixth day of August one thousand seven hundred & five the Sovereign and Burgesses mett in choose a free Burgesse in room and place of Mr David Smith Burgess deceased, and did unanimously elect Michael Harrison Esqr Comissary General of the Musters, a free Burgess in room of the said David Smith, & he was accordingly sworn

Geo: Macartney Sovereign

Pa: Duff Constable of the Castle   Rob Leathes Lewis Thompson

KINGE CHARLES [K] OF SPAINE LETT^R TO HER MA^{TIE} ANN QUEEN OF GREAT BRITTAIN &c IN THE YEAR 1706

MADAM my sister, it is allwaies with the uttmost sattisfacion that I doe justice to those worthy persons who signalize themselves by their conduct and valour in their Maj^{ties} service and mine, My Lord Donegall was remarkably so when alive; and more particularly the last siege of my Citty of Barcelonie; both in his quicknesse in succouring it from Girona, and the long valliant defence he made in fort Mountjouy where he lost his life, att the assault; it is in a great measure to his memory that I am indebted for the preservation of that capital; and it may be for all the possions I now have in Spain I shall injure yor Majesties usuall generosity by offering to recomend to yor ffavour the family of soe worthy a gentleman for I know yor Maj^{ties} inclynacions go to it I will only add that I shall place all yor markes of favour and acknowledgem.^t wch yor Maj^{tie} will please to bestow on ye ffamily to my own account as well as the remaining obligacions I am with the sincere respect gratitude and love &c

To ye Queen of Great Brittain &c

On Saturday the twenty first day of December one thousand seven hundred and six the Sovereign and Burgesses mett to choose a free Burgesse in room & place of Arthur Macartney Burgesse deceased, and did unanimously elect the Honble Jno Chichester Esqr second son of the Right Honble the late Earle of Donegall a free Burgesse in room and stead of the said Arthur Macartney.

Geo: Macartney Sovereign

Pa: Duff Constaple of the Castle   Robt Leathes
Lewes Thompson

On the seventeenth day of Feby one thous^d seven hundred and seven The Soveraigne and Burgesses then assembled for choosing a free Burgesse in place of Mr Lewis Thompson Burgesse who departed this life on Wednesday the eleventh of this instant They did elect and unanimously choose Mr Nicholas Thetford of Belfast a free Burgesse in place and room of the said Mr Lewis Thompson and at the same time the said Mr Thetford took the oath of a Burgesse and other oaths as usuall

Geo Macartney Soveraign

Henry Ellis   James Gurner   Roger Haddock
Robt Leathes John Hallridge Nath Byrtt Richard
Wilson   George Portis

On Thursday the twenty fourth day of April one thousand seven hund^d. and seven there was produced to the Sovereign & Burgesses an Instrum^t und^r hand and seal of Isaac McCartney one of the free Burgesses of this Burrough resigning the said office in favour of John Hallridge Esqr upon wch the said Sovereign & Burgesses did elect and choose the said John Hallridge a free Burgesse of the s^d Burrough in room and place of the s^d Isaac McCartney & he was sworne accordingly.

Geo Macartney Soveraign

Robt Leathes   Lewes Thompson

On the 24th day of June one thousand seven hundred and seven being the day by Charter for electing a Sovereigne of Belfast to serve for one year from Michaelmas next ensuing, Pa^t Duff Esqr p^r.sented to the Sovereign & Burgesses a letter from the R^t Honb^le the Countess of Donegall containing a list of Burgesses for the said office dated 19th June who were Michael Harrison Esqr. Capt Edward Brice and Mr John Chambers & the said elecion fell upon Capt Edwd Brice.

The Corporation of Belfast hath power to make By Laws & punish offenders by ffines with ye generall proviso that nothing shall impower them to act contrary to ye Law of this Kingdom By colour of which within seven years past they have raised a yearly shipmoney tax, by charging two pence per tunn on all vessells that carry loading out of their dock notwithstanding ye Dock of Belfast is a free landing place by Act of Parliament. They have also raised several summs of money to oppose ye Establisht minister in ye prosecution of his just right, and compelled his parishoners to bear large proportions by distraining & selling ye goods of those that refused to join in so unlawfull an undertaking

Their presentments are generally made by persons that have little or no Estate or free rents who are Dissentors from ye Church of England their Applotters are seldom if ever sworn equally to assess ye money great part of wch they charge on ye free rents of those that have interest in Belfast and liberty thereof even gentlemen that are neither freemen nor trade wth them & who are not concerned in their Corporation whether they dwell in ye City of Dublin or elsewhere. They refuse coppies of their presentments & disbursements to such as are willing to pay any Rate that can be demanded for ye same & thereby prevent their making it publickly appear how unjust their levies are and how oft they raise money for pretended works & necessaries wch is never applyed to ye same and also have extravegantly they dispose of ye said money. They have long prevented any endeavours to redress these grievances by threatning to humble all that oppose them.

Resolved

On the question that by ye act to prevent ye further growth of popery ye Burgesses of Belfast are obliged to subscribe the Declaration & receive ye Sacrament according to ye usage of ye Church of Ireland.

Resolved

That ye Burgess ship of such Burgesses of Belfast who have not subscribed ye Declaration & received ye Sacrament pursuant to ye said act are by such neglect become vacant.

A further Question being proposed that ye takeing two pence per tunn by ye Corporation of Belfast for every ship that comes to ye key of Belfast is arbitrary and illegall and a debate arising thereon

Ordered

That ye Debate be adjourned till to morrow at 12 o'Clock & nothing to intervene

Mercurii 29° Die. Octr 1707

Ordered

That ye said debate be further adjourned till Saturday next.

Jovis 30th Die Octr 1707

Ordered

That ye Charter Books of Belfast remaining with ye Clerk of this House be delivered to ye respective persons who brought in ye same

On the twenty eighth day of November one thousand seven hundred and seven Pat Duff Esqr produced an authority of the 11th instant from the Earle of Donegall & the Countess of Donegall his mother and Guardian constituting him Constable of the Castle of Belfast, Pursuant to wch he took the oath of a Burgess he being as Constable of the Castle one of the Burgesses by the Charter having at the same time taken the oaths of fidelity & abjura^n & repeated the Declaration.

Geo: Macartney Soveraign

Robt Leathes   Lewes Thompson   John Hallridge

In pursuance of a late vote of the Honble House of
Comons of Ireland last Session of Parliament the Sovereigne and Burgesses of Belfast Burrough did assemble on
the 29th of November one thousand seven hundred and
seven to chuse six free Burgesses in the rooms of W^m
Crafford & Edwd Brice Esq^rs David Buller Neil Macneile
Jno Chalmers and the Honble Jno Chichester Esqr brother
to the R^t Honble the p^rsent & fourth Earle of Donegall,
which said Burgesses have qualified themselves according
to the late act of Parliament ag^t the growth of popery; and
the said Sovereign & Burgesses did elect Nicholas Thetford
Nath Byrt Richd Willson George Portis Henry Ellis and
James Gurner free Burgesses in room of the aforesaid six
who were accordingly sworn except Nich. Thetford who
was absent   Geo: Macartney Soveraign

    Robt Leathes   Lewes Thompson   John Hallridge

Whereas Mr Nicholas Thetford was at an assembly of
the Soveraigne and Burgesses on the twenty ninth of
November last elected and chosen a Burgesse of this
Corpor^n and he the said Nicholas Thetford did not take
the oath of Burgess^sp. to the said Corporation within seven
days as is required by the said Charter, nor has not within
the time limited by the late act of Parliament to prevent
the further growth of Popery in taking the oaths [and did
not receive] as by the said act is required whereby the said
Burgesse place is become vacant, In pursuance of the
Charter of Belfast now the Sovereign and Burgesses of
Belfast aforesaid did this day assemble themselves being
the seventeen

Whereas Mr Nicholas Thetford was at an assembly of
the Soveraigne and Burgesses on the twenty ninth day of
November last past elected and chosen a Burgesse of this
Corporation and he the said Nicholas Thetford did not
take the oath of Burgesse to the said Corpora^n within seven
days as is required by the said Charter nor did not within
the time limitted by a late act of Parliam^t to prevent the
further growth of Popery Record himself to have taken
the Sacrament acording to the Church of Ireland or take
the oaths at the next quarter Sessions as in & by the said
act is required whereby the said Burgess-ship is become
vacant In persuance of the Charter of Belfast the Soveraign
& Burgesses did assemble themselves together on the

seventeenth day of Feby one thousand seven hundred and seven and did then and there elect and choose Rodger Haddock of Carren Bane & Malone gen one of the free Burgesses of this Corporat^n in the room and place of the said Nicholas Thetford and he accordingly at the same time tooke the oath of office of Burgesse of Belfast other oath usuall

Geo: Macartney Soveraign

Henry Ellis   James Garner   Robt Leathes   John Hallridge   Nath Byrtt   Richard Wilson   George: Portis

December the 4th 1707

On Thursday this day in open Court Rich^d ffinley Junr was chosen by the Soveraign Burgesses & Comonality to serve as sergeant at mace in room of Jno ffisher deceased one of the Sergeants and was accordingly sworne to the said office in public Court

Geo Macartney Soveraign

Rob Leathes   Lewes Thompson   Richard Wilson Henry Ellis

Councellor Macartney *Soveraigne* [his]
Speech to ye Duke of Ormond at his comeing to [of] Belfast 1707

May it please Yo^r Grace there [can] *is none can* be [more] more senciable nor have a higher esteeme of this great honor conferred upon us by Yo^r Grace than the members of this Corporation are. and what wee want in words to expresse wee assure Yo^r [Maj^tie] Grace wee have in inclynation and it shall ever appeare in our accions of Loyalty to her Maj^tie by a constant and firme adherance to ye Crowne of England and the Succession as by Law established; as allsoe in our dutyfull affection to yor graces person and Governm^t: this parte of the Country has not ben happy in ye presence of a Chieffe Governor this many Yeares and I make noe doubt but it is the forerunner of a blessing to it indeed; when by Yo^r Graces observation wisdom and great authority, wee may hope for such advantages as may make us as well able as wee are loyall subjects and ready upon all occations to serve her Maj^tie it is no small misfortune to us, this soe criticall a Jounture to have our Patron absent from us butt when I consider that his person and courage is soe generously and well Imployed in her Maj^ties service abroad I cannot tell how to bewaile it and I hope yor Grace will exceipt of these assureances of our fidellity from me wch wood have ben much better and strongly inforced from were wee soe happy as to had him amongst us.

A Power given to Robert Leathes of Bellfast Esqr to be Constable of the Castle of Bellfast | Know all men by these p^rsents That I Arthur Earle of Donegall and with the approbation and consent of Catherine Countesse Dowager of Donegall my mother and Guardian doe hereby constitute and appoint Robert Leathes of Bellfast in the County of Antrim Esqr Constable of the Castle of Bellfast for and untill the first day of November next and do hereby give and grant to ye said Robert Leathes full power and authority to exercise the office of Constable for and dureing the aforesaid term and to doe and performe all matters and things appertaining to the office of Constable of the said Castle and to receive and take the ffees and proffits thereto of right appertaining and belonging   In witness whereof the said Catherine Countess Dowager of Donegall and Arthur Earle of Donegall have hereunto affixed their hands and seals this thirtyeth day of August one thousand seaven hundred and eight   1708

Sealed and delivered   K. Donegall
in the presence of
   William Westgarth
   Peter Ward   Donegall
   John M'Neill   Copia vera

 HEREAS the Key of the Port of Bellfast is greatly out of repaire and ye dock almost closed up with sluch and dirt their being no fund to repaire or cleanse ye same   Wee the Soveraigne Burgesses & Commonality of Bellfast afforesaid being very sensible that unlesse some fund or other be procured the same will every day become more ruinous which will greatly impaire the trade as well as p^rjudice and Lessen Her Maj^ties Revenue in this place doe make it our request that Samuell Ogle William Craford George McCartney and Edward Brice Esqrs will be pleased to Apply themselves to this present Parlem^t for obtaining an act to lay two pence a tun upon all goods imported and exported by freemen and three pence a Tun upon all goods imported and exported by fforeigners from of the said Key to be a fund for cleansing the Dock and harbour afforesaid and for the more effectuall makeing and keepeing in repaire the said Key   Given und^r o^r hands at Bellfast April 27 1709
Signed by ye Soveraign Burgesses and Commonality

   Wee the Collector Survey^r and other the officers of the port of Bellfast att the request of the Soveraigne Burgesses and Commonality of the Corporacon of Bellfast afforesaid doe hereby certify that ye Key and Docke of this port is greatly out of repaire and the Docke very much Gorg'd with sluch and dirt wch obstructs Vessells and Lighters to gett in and out of the same and we are of opinion that if some fund be not procured to keepe in repaire and cleanse the same in some little time the Docke will be so choked up that Lighters will scarcely gett in and out to load and unload their goods upon the Key wch will be a great discouragm^t to ye trade of this place and may lessen Her Maj^ties Revenue therein   dated at Bellfast this 28 Aprill 1709

On the seventh day of May 1709 the Soveraign and Burgesses then assembled for chooseing a free Burgesse in place of Michael Harrison Esqr deceased Burgess who departed this life in England the twenty third day of Aprill 1709 they did elect and unanimously choose Mr George Macartney attorney a free Burgesse in place and room of the said Michael Harrison and at the same time the said Mr George Macartney took ye oath of a Burgesse as usuall

   Robt Leathes   Geo Macartney   George Portis

HEADS of A Bill for ffinishing the Key and Clensing and Keepeing in repaire the harbour and dock of Belfast Anno 1709

Whereas the port of Bellfast in ye Province of Ulster hath by longe experience been found to be of great Importance to her Maj^ties Revenew Trade in generall and to the benefitt and advantage of all the Countyes adjoyneing thereunto

And Whereas the Soveraigne Burgesses and Comonalty of Bellfast have for many yeares at great expences maintained and repaired the Key on both sides the River and by continuall cleansing and scouring the Dock and in [repaireing] keepeing up perches on the sides of the Chanell of the harbour there have preserved a free and open passage for boats [lighters] Gabbards Lighters and other vessells to come up and discharge their Lading at the same Key wch expenses they were enabled to defray by a certaine Tunnage wch the Merchants and Traders there voluntarly consent and agree to pay for that end and purpose

And whereas the said paym^ts for want of the authority of Parliament has ben of late discontinued and the great unavoidable charge wch is dayly necessary for preserveing the said port is become unsupportable by the said Soveraigne Burgesses and Comonality who have not nor ever had any Lands or Revenew belonging to them whereby the saide Key is become ruinous and the Dock and Channell choaked up to such a degree as that the said port and harbour so beneficiall must inevitably in a little time become Inaccessible to ye determ^t of her Maj^tie the great prejudice of Trade and the utter ruine and Impoverishing of the Inhabitants and adjacent Countyes

ffor Remedy whereof may it please your most Excellent Maj^tie at the humble request of the said Soveraigne Burgesses and Commonality of Bellfast that it may be enacted and wee pray it may be enacted by the Queen's most Excellent Matie by and with the consent of the Lords Spirituall and Temporall and Comons in this *present* Parliament Assembled and by Authority of the same that from and after the first day of August in this present yeare of our Lord one thousand seaven hundred and nine all Brittish and Irish ships Imployed or made use of to import or export any goods or merchandizes out of or into the said port of Bellfast (Ships in pay of Her Matie her heirs or Successors only exceipted) shall pay to the said Soveraigne Burgesses and Comonality of Bellfast and their Successors or to such person or persons as shall be by them appointed to receive the same for theire use Two pence per Tunn for every Tunn such ship or ships shall be burthen and for every Foreigne ship or ships so imployed or made use of to import or export any goods or merchandizes out of or Into the said port of Bellfast shall pay as afforesaid three pence per Tunn for every Tunn such shipp or ships shall be burthen wch Tunnage as well in Brittish and Irish shipps as in foreign ships shall be computed by outward gageing of the said shipps respectively and not otherwise and ye person or persons for ye time being appointed to receive the said Tunnage is and are hereby Impowered to make such outward gauge of all and every such ship or ships as they shall have occation for the doeing thereof

And to the end that the said respective dutyes of Tunnage wch shall become due by vertue of this Act may be effectualy levyed and paid as afforesaid wee pray that it may be further Enacted by the authority afforesaid that noe officer of Her Maj^ties Customhouse in Bellfast from and after the said first day of August one thousand seaven hundred and nine shall cleare or discharge any ship or ships or permitt any ship or ships outward bound to saile till the Comander or Master thereof shall have brought a discharge from the officer for the time being appointed to receive the said dutyes of Tunnage, Testifiinge such ship or ships to have paid their Tunnage wch discharge on paying the said Tunnage shall be immediately granted and made without fee or reward fraud or delay and in case of refusall or delay the officer refuseing or delaying shall forfeit five pounds sterl for every such refusall or delay to the Master or Comander of such ship to be recovered in a summary way before the Soveraigne of

To pay 2^d per tun tunage foreigners 3^d per tun by outward guage

The ship to be cleared out until pay^t of tunage

the said Towne of Bellfast for the time being to be levyed by distresse to be made by warrant of the said Soveraigne and by a sale of the goods and Chatles of such officer so refuseing or detaineing to give such discharge

And wee pray it may be further Enacted by the Authority afforesd that all and every the summ and summs of money arising growing due or levyed by

(marginal note) to be applied in mending yᵉ Kay & scowering yᵉ dock & channel & keeping up Perches

vertue of this Act (the sallary and necessary expences of the officer appointed as afforesaid to receive the said Tunnage only excepted) shall from time to time and at all times hereafter be applyed to and laid out in mending finishing [the] and keepeing the said key of Bellfast on both sides the River in good and sufficient repaire and in scowering the said Dock and keeping it passable at all times for boats Gabbarts Lighters and other vessells to come up and discharge at the said key and in cleansing the Channel of the harbour and keeping Perches therein for the ease safety and conveniency of shipps resorting to the said port.

And to the end the money wᶜʰ shall be received by vertue of this Act may be duly applyed to ye intent and purposes herein and hereby before mencioned and intended wee pray it may be further Enacted by the Authority afforesaid

(marginal note) Soveraign to call a meeting of yᵉ Corpⁿ & Commonality in Nov & summon yᵉ Collector &c to account & inspect them from time to time

that the Soveraigne of Bellfast for the time being shall every year summon an assembly of all the Burgesses and Commonalty of the said Corporacon of Bellfast to meet on Thursday ffollowing the first day of November And the said Soveraigne Burgesses and Comonalty so assembled shall summon or call before them the Collector and Receiver of the dutyes of Tunnage hereby granted and all and every other person or persons who shall be Imployed in the disbursemᵗ of the same or otherwise in the Execution of this Act and require them to give and render upon oath a Just and true account of all the money wᶜʰ shall be soe received and of the disbursemᵗˢ and application thereof from time to time and the said Soveraigne Burgesses and Commonality or such persons as they shall *appoint* for that purpose shall from time to time inspect such accounts and cause them to be entered fairely in a booke wᶜʰ shall be kept among the Publick records and writings belonging to the said Corporacon of Bellfast And the said Soveraigne Burgesses and Comonalty of Bellfast so Assembled afforesaid are hereby empowered to adjourne themselves from time to time and to

(marginal note) and to give directions for yᵉ application of yᵉ money

make and give such orders Rules and directions for the due application of the moneyes afforesaid to the ends and purposes Intended by this act as to them or the major part of them shall seem reasonable and convenient And in case the said Soveraigne for the time being shall refuse or neglect to call and appoint a Generall Court of Assembly to be held as afforesaid or the Collector or Receiver

(marginal note) The collector or Soveraign neglecting or refuseing to account to forfeit £100 each

of the said dutyes of Tunnage or any other person or persons who shall be imployed in the disbursemᵗ of any of the moneys wᶜʰ shall be soe received shall neglect or refuse to give in their accounts as afforesaid the Soveraigne and person or persons soe makeing default shall respectively shall forfeit and pay the sume of one hundred pounds sterl one moyety thereof to such person as sue for the same the other moyety to ye said Soveraigne Burgesses and Comonalty for the uses above mencioned to be received by action of debt in any of her Maᵗⁱᵉˢ Courts of Record in this Kingdom

(marginal note) the Soveraign out of yᵉ first profits to pay yᵗ expenses of this act

Provided allwayes and wee pray it may be further enacted by the authority afforesaid that the said Soveraigne Burgesses and Commonalty [aforesaid] of Belfast shall out of the first profitts payable and ariseing out of or from the saide dutyes of Tunnage hereby granted pay or cause to be paid all such sumes of money as shall be necessary to defray the expences of passing this bill.

(marginal note) The Soveraign not to exact any sum or sums for Kayage or wharfage after passing yᵉ act

Provided allwayes and we pray it may further enacted by the Authority afforesaid that from and after the said first day of August one thousand seaven hundred and nine that the said Soveraigne Burgesses and Comonalty shall not exact or demand any sum or sumes of money for Keyage or Wharfage on the said Kea of Bellfast from any Marchant or Trader for any goods or Marchandizes to be shippt of or Landed on ye said Key of Bellfast but that all Marchants and Traders there shall in lieu and consideration of the said duty of Tunnage hereby granted be at all times hereafter freed and exempted from paying Keyage or Wharfage for any goods to be exported or Imported into the said port of Bellfast

(marginal note) Sovereign to plead & use yᵉ act as a public act

And we pray it may be further enacted by the Authority afforesaid that the said Soveraign Burgesses and Commonalty of the Corporation of Bellfast and the officer or officers by them imployed to receive the dutyes hereby granted shall be at liberty to plead and make *use* of this Act in all or any of Her

Majties Courts of Justice in like manner as if the same were a publick Act of Parliam' and the same as a publique Act shall be esteemed deemed and taken in all Courts of Justice in this Kingdom

Surplus after finishing Kay & clearing yᵉ harbour to be applied to Bridges pavements water pipes & other public works

Provided Allwayes that if their shall be any surplus of money arrising from or by such Tunnage after ffinishing the Key and clearing the said Dock or Harbour the same shall be applyed for ever hereafter in ye first place towards the support and repaires of the Publick Bridges Pavements and water pipes within the said Towne of Bellfast and repaireing the Markett house within the said Towne the remainder thereof if any shall be to be applyed by the said Corporacon with the consent and approbation of the Earle of Donegall Lord of the Castle of Bellfast and his heires or such other person or persons as be Lord or proprietor of the Castle of Bellfast or the guardian of such Earle or proprietor if he be under age such consent appearing by Instrument under his or their hands and seales to other publick workes and uses within the said Town of Bellfast

to prevent misapplication of money Earl of Donegall & his Heirs may inspect and examine accts persons misapplying to forfeit treble yᵉ sum one moyety to yᵉ poor the other to yᵉ person suing

And for the more Effectuall preventing of all missapplication of the said money ariseing by such Tunnage as aforesaid wee pray it may be further enacted that it shall and may be Lawfull to and for the Earle of Donegall and his heires or other Lord or Proprietor of the Castle of Bellfast or the Guardian of such Earle or proprietor if hee shall bee under age And he and they are hereby Impowered and Authorized by vertue of this Act once every yeare to Inspect and examine the Accounts of such Receipts and disbursemᵗˢ as have ben made of the money ariseing by such Tunnage as afforesaid in the preceding year And if any person or persons who by the Act is or are impowered have received or disposed of any part of the said money otherwise than to such uses as by this Act is directed and appointed he or they shall forfeit the treble value of such money so misapplyed to be sued for by Civill bill or by plaint or Information in any of her Majᵗⁱᵉˢ four Courts at Dublin in wᶜʰ no Essoỹgn Protection nor wager at Law nor more then one Imparlance shall be allowed the one moyety thereof to goe to the use of the poor of the Parish of Bellfast the other moyety to go to such person as shall sue for the same in manner afforesaid And if any of the persons or bodyes Politick afforesaid shall refuse or neglect when required yearly to lay the said Accounts before the said Earle of Donegall or other Proprietor of the said Castle of Bellfast or his or their guardian when under age as aforesaid he and they shall forfeit and pay the sum of one hundred pounds to be sued for and recovered and to be applyed in manner aforesaid and the defᵗ or defᵗˢ against whom such recovery shall be had shall pay treble costs.

AN Act for finishing the Key and Cleansing and Keeping in Repair the Harbour and Dock of Belfast

Its great importance

Whereas the port of Bellfast in the Province of Ulster hath [ben] by long Experience *ben* found to be of great Importance to her Majᵗⁱᵉˢ Revenue Trade in Generall and to the benefitt and advantage of all the Countyes adjoyneing thereunto

An Whereas the Soveraigne Burgesses and Commonalty of Bellfast have for many yeares at great expences maintained and repaired the key on both sides the River and by continuall cleansing and scowering the Dock and in keeping up perches on the (*sic*) of the Channell of the Harbour there have preserved a free and open passage for boats Gabbards Lighters and other vessell to come up and discharge their Lading att the said Key wᶜʰ Expences they were enabled to defray by a certaine Tonnage wᶜʰ the Marchants and traders to and from the said port did voluntarily consent and agree to pay for that end and Purpose

and Whereas the said payment for want for want (*sic*) of the Authority of Parliamt to levy and raise the same has benn of late discontinued the great unavoidable charge wᶜʰ is dayly necessary for preserveing the said Port cannot be borne by the said Soveraigne Burgesses and Comonalty who have not nor ever had any land or certaine Revenue belonging to them whereby the said key is become Ruinous and the Dock and Channell chocked up to such a degree as that the said Port and Harbour so benefitiall must Inevitably in a litle time become Inaccessable to the determᵗ of her Maᵗⁱᵉˢ the great prejudice of Trade and Impoverishinge of the Inhabitants and adjacent Counties

For Remedy whereof may it please yo' most Excellent Majestie at the humble request of Arthur Earle of Donegall Lord of the Castle and Proprietor of the Towne and Libertyes of Bellfast and allsoe at the request of the said Soveraigne Burgesses and Comonalty of the said Towne that it may be enacted and be it enacted by the Queen's Most Excellent Majestie and by and with the advice and consent of the Lords Spirituall and Temporall and Comons in this present Parliamt assembled and by authority of the same that from and after the first day of September in the present yeare of our Lord one thousand seaven hundred and nine all shipps of the built of Great Brittan or of this Kingdom Imployed or made use of to [trans]*im*port or Export any goods or marchandizes of or into the said port of Bellfast (ships in pay of her Maj^{tie} or heires or Successors only excepted) shall pay to the Soveraigne Burgesses and Commonalty of the said Towne of the said Towne (*sic*) the same to be received by such person or persons as shall be appointed to receive ye same in manner and forme hereinafter mencioned

2^d per tun foreigners 3^d per tun

and to and for the uses herein after directed two pence per Tunn for every Tunn such ship or ships shall be burthen and for every Forreigne Ship or Ships so Imployed or made use of to Import or Export any goods or Marchandize out of or into the Port of Bellfast shall pay afforesaid three pence per Tunn for every Tunn wch ship or ships shall be be (*sic*) Burthen wch Tunnage as well of the built of great Brittain or of this Kingdom as in fforeigne ships shall be computed by

by out^d guage

outward gageing of the said shipps respectively and not otherwise and the person or persons for the time beinge appointed to receive the said Tunnage is and are hereby Impowred to make such outwarge Gage of all and every such ship or ships as the shall have occasion for the doeing thereof.

not to be cleared until payment

And to the end that the said respective dutyes of Tunnage wch shall become due by vertue of this Act may be effectually Leavyed and paid as afforesaid Be it further enacted by the Authority afforesaid that noe officer of her Maj^{ties} Custom house in Bellfast from and after the first day of September one thousand seaven hundred and nine shall clear or discharge any ship or shipps or permitt any ship or shipps outward bound to saile till the Comander or Master thereof shall have brought a discharge from the officer for the time being appointed to receive the said *duty of* Tunnage testifying such ship or shipps to have paid their Tunnage wch discharge or paying the said Tonnage shall *be* Imediatly granted or made without favor Reward fraud or delay and in case of refusall or delay the officer refuseing or delaying shall forfeit five pounds sterling for every such refusall or delay to ye Master or Comander of such ship to be recovered in a sumari way before the Soveraigne of the said Towne of Bellfast for the time being to be leavyed by distresse to be made by warrant of the said Soveraigne or in his absence by warrant of some of the Justice of the Peace in or neere the said Towne who is hereby Impowered and required to issue such warrant and by sale of the goods and chatles of such officer so refuseing or delaying to give such discharge

to be applied in finishing & mending the Kay scowering ye dock & harbour & keeping perches

And be it further Enacted by the Authority afforesaid that all & every the sume and sumes of money arriseing or growing due or levyed by vertue of this Act the sallary and necessary expences of the officer apointed as afforesaid to receive the said Tunnage and gauge the said ships not exceeding in the whole twenty five pounds per Ann onely excepted) shall from time to time and at all times hereafter be applyed to and laid out in mending finishing and keeping the said Key of Bellfast on both sides the River in good and sufficient repaire and in scouring the said Dock and keeping it passable at all times for boats Gabbards Lighters and other Vessells to come up and discharge at ye said Key and cleansing the Channell of the Harbour and keepeing perches therein for the ease safety and conveniency for shipps resorting to ye said Port

And to the end the money wch shall be received by vertue of this Act may be daily applyed to the Intents and purposes herein and hereby before mentioned and Intended Be it further Enacted by the Authority afforesaid that the Soveraigne of Belfast for the time being shall every yeare summon an asssembly of the said Corporation of Bellfast to meet on thursday following the first day of November and the said Soveraigne Burgesses and Commonalty so Assembled shall sumon or call before them the Collector or Receiver of the duty of Tunage hereby granted and all and every [the] other person or persons who shall be imployed in the disbursemt of the same or otherwise in the execution of this Act and require them to give and Render upon oath and Just and true account of all the money wch shall be soe received and of the disbursemts and application thereof from time to time and the said Soveraigne Burgesses and Comonalty or such person as shall be apointed for that purpose shall from time to time inspect such accounts and cause them to be entered fairely in a booke wch shall be kept amonge the publique Records and writings belongeing to the said Corporation of Bellfast.

And the said Soveraigne Burgesses and Commonalty of Bellfast soe assembled as afforesaid are hereby Impowered to adjourne themselves from time to time and to make and give such orders Rules and directions for the due application of the money afforesaid to the ends and purposes intended by this act as to them or the major part of them shall seem Reasonable and convenient   And in case the said the said (*sic*) Soveraigne for the time being shall refuse or neglect to call and appoint a Generall Court of Assembly to be held as afforesaid or ye Collector or Receiver of the said duty of Tunage or any other person or persons who shall be Imployed in the disbursemt of any of the money wch shall be so received shall neglect or refuse to give in their accounts as afforesaid the said Soveraigne and person or persons soe makeing default shall respectively forfeit and pay the sum of one hundred pounds sterl one moyety thereof to such person as shall sue for the same the other moyety to ye said Soveraigne Burgesses and Comonalty for the uses above mencioned to be recovered by action of debt in any of her Maties Courts of Record in this Kingdom

Provided Allways and be it further enacted by the Authority aforesaid that the said Soveraigne Burgesses and Commonalty of Bellfast shall out of the first money and profitts payable and arriseing out of or from the said duty of Tunnage hereby granted pay or cause to be paid all such sumes of money as shall be necessary to defray the expences of passing this Act.

after 1st Sept 1709 Soveraign not to enact or demand kayage or wharfage but merch^{ts} to be exempted from it

Provided allwayes and be it further enacted by the Authority afforesaid that from and after the said first day of September one thousand seaven hundred and nine that the said Soveraigne Burgesses and Commonalty shall not exact or demand any sume or sumes of money for Keyage or wharfage on ye said Key of Bellfast from any Marchant or Trader for any goods or marchandizes to be shipt of or Landed on the said Key of Bellfast but that all marchants and Traders their shall in leiu and consideration of the said duty of Tunnage hereby granted be at all times hereafter freed and exempted from paying keage or wharfage for any goods to be Exported or Imported into the said [dock] *Port* of Bellfast

And be it further Enacted by the Authority afforesaid that the said Soveraigne Burgesses and Commonalty of the Corporation of Bellfast and the officer or officers Imployed to Receive the dutyes hereby granted shall be at Liberty to plead and make use of this Act in all or any of her Maties Courts of Justice in like manner as if the same were a publick Act of Parliament and the same as a Publick Act shall be esteemed and taken in all Courts of Justice in this Kingdom

Provided Allwayes that there shall be any surplus of money Ariseing from or by such Tunnage after finishing the Key and clensing the said Dock or harbour the same shall be Applyed for ever hereafter in the first place towards the suport and Repaire of the publick Bridges Pavements and water pips within the said Towne of Bellfast and repaireing the Markett house within the said Towne of Bellfast the Remainder if any shall be applyed by the said Corporation with the consent and approbation of the said Earle of Donegall Lord of the Castle of Bellfast and his heires or such other person or persons as shall be Lord or proprietor of the Castle of the Castle (*sic*) of Bellfast or the guardian of such Earle or proprietor if he be under age such consent appearinge by Instrum^{t} under his or their hands and seales to and for the publicke workes and uses within the said Towne of Bellfast

And for the more effectuall preventing of all misapplication of the said money arriseing by such Tunnage afforesaid   Be it enacted by the authority afforesaid that it shall and may be lawfull to and for the Earle of Donegall and his heires or other Lord proprietor of the Castle of Bellfast the Guardian of such Earle or proprietor if he shall be under age and he and they are hereby Impowred and Authorized by vertue of this Act once every yeare to inspect and examine the Account of such receipts and disbursements as have ben made of the money arriseing by such Tunage as afforesaid in the preceding yeare.

And if any person or persons who by this Act is or are impowred or have received or disposed of the money thereby raised or any part thereof shall have imployed or disposed of any part of the said money otherwise then to such uses as by this Act are directed and apointted he or they shall forfeit the treble vallue of such money so misapplyed to be sued for by action of debt Bill plainte or Information in any of her Maties foure Courts at Dublin in wch no Esseigne Protection or wager at Law nor more than one Imparlence shall be allowed the one moyety thereof to goe to and be paid to the Minister and Churchwardens for the use of the poore of the Towne of Bellfast the other moyety to goe to such person as shall sue for the same in manner afforesaid and if any of the persons or Bodies Poletick afforesaid shall refuse or neglect when required yearly to lay the accounts before the said Earle of Donegall or other Proprietor of the said Castle of Bellfast or his or their Guardian when under age as afforesaid he and they shall forfeit and pay the sume of one hundred pounds to be sued for and recovered and to be applyed when Recovered in manner afforesaid and the Defendant or Defendants against whom such Recovery shall be had shall pay treble costs Provided allwayes and be it further Enacted by the Authority afforesaid that the Collector or Receiver to be appointed for receiving the duties arriseing by such Tunnage as afforesaid shall be annually chosen in manner ffollowing and not otherwise that is to say the said Lord or Proprietor or Proprietors of the Castle of Bellfast for the time beinge his her or their guardian in case he she or they shall be under age shall and may by Authority of this Act nominate three of the Burgesses of the said Corporation of Bellfast and present them every thursday next after the twenty fourth day of June to the Soveraigne Burgesses and Commonalty of Bellfast out of wch said Burgesses soe named as afforesaid the said Soveraigne Burgesses and Comonalty of Bellfast shall and may and the are hereby Required annually on the said day to chuse one to be Collector of the said dutyes for the ensueing yeare to enter into office on the ffeast day of St. Michaell the Archangell next ensueing such Ellection and be accountable for his Receipts and paymts thereout as well to the Lord or to the Proprietor or Proprietors of the Castle of Bellfast for the time being his her or their Guardian (in case of minority as likewise to the Soveraigne Burgesses and Commonalty of Bellfast in such manner as in and by this Act is prescribed

Provided Allwayes and be it Enacted by the Authority afforesaid that Nathaniell Byrtt one of the Burgesses of Bellfast shall by the Authority of this Act be and is hereby declaired to be Collector of the duties afforesaid and soe shall continue till the twenty ninth day of September which shall be in the yeare of our Lord God one thousand seaven hundred and tenn and be accountable in manner afforesaid unlesse in case of death or removall in wch case &^c as often as that shall happen from time to time it shall and may be lawfull to and for the said Lord or to or for the Proprietor or Proprietor of the Castle of Bellfast for the time being his her or their Guardian in case he shee or they shall be under age within twenty dayes next after the death or removall of any Collector or Receiver of the Dutyes of Tunnage afforesaid to nominate three other Burgesses of the said Town of Bellfast out of wch the said Soveraigne Burgesses and Comonalty of Bellfast shall and may and they are hereby required to name a Collector to receive the duties arriseing by such Tunnage for and untill a new Collector shall be nominated and chosen in such manner as by this Act prescribed in his place and shall take upon him the execution of his office as abovesaid which new Collector shall be accountable in such manner to the Lord or to the Proprietor or Proprietors of the Castl of Bellfast for the time being his her or their Guardian in case of Minorities and likewise to the Soveraigne Burgesses and Commonalty of Bellfast as the deceased or removed Collector or Receiver should or ought to have been and is by this Act prescribed

Provided Allsoe and be it further Enacted by the Authority afforesaid that in case the Lord or the Proprietor or Proprietors of the Castle of Bellfast or his her or their Guardian in case of minority shall not on every thursday next after the twenty fourth day of June nominate three Burgesses of the said Corporation of Bellfast or shall not within the space of twenty dayes after the death or Removall of any receiver or Collector so nominated and Ellected nominate

All this is
added

three *other* Burgesses of the said Corporation of Bellfast or shall not within the space of twenty days after the death or Removall of any receiver or Collector soe nominated and Ellected nominate three other Burgesses of the said Corporation as afforesaid that then in such case and as often as shall soe happen it shall and may be lawfull to and for the Soveraigne Burgesses and Comonalty of Bellfast in default thereof to proceed to (*sic*) a Collector or Receiver of the said Duties of Tunnage to continue for and untill another Collector or receiver of the said duties of Tunnage shall be nominated by the Lord Proprietor or Proprietors of the Castle of Bellfast his her or their Guardian in case of minority and Ellected by the Soveraigne Burgess and Commonalty of Bellfast and take upon him the execution of his office wch Collector or receiver soe to be Ellected by the Soveraigne Burgesses and Comonalty of Bellfast shall be accountable in such manner and to such persons as any Collector nominated by the Lord or by the Proprietor or Proprietors of the Castle of Bellfast his *her* or their Guardian in case of minority should or ought to have been And *in* case such Lord or [by the] Proprietor or proprietors of the Castle of Bellfast his her or their Guardian (in case of minority) should or ought to have been (*sic*) and in case such Lord or Proprietor or proprietors his her or their guardian in case of minority shall neglect to make such nomination to the said Sovereigne Burgesses and Comonalty within the respective times hereinbefore limitted for such nomination That then *in* [and] every such case upon every such neglect the said Soveraigne Burgesses and Commonalty are hereby authorized to nominate and Ellect such person to be Collector and Receiver of the said Duties as they shall think fitt who shall continue therein untill the time for the annuall nomination and Ellection of such Receiver or Collector his hereby appointed and directed respectively with the same power and Authority to collect and receive the said Dutyes as [to] the annuall Collector and Receiver of the said dutyes should have don

And in case of the death or removall of any such Receiver or Collector that ye Collector of her Maties Revenue in Bellfast shall be and is hereby required Authorized and Impowered to receive the said severall duties untill a new Collector and receiver thereof shall be nominated and Ellected as afforesaid.

And in case the Soveraigne Burgesses and Comonalty shall neglect to— to make choice of a Collector or receiver of the said severall duties within three dayes after such nomination the said Lord or by the Proprietor or proprietors of the Castle of Bellfast his her or their Guardian (in case of minority out of the said three Burgesses so to be nominated by such Lord or Proprietor or Proprietors of the Castle of Bellfast his her or their Guardian as afforesaid then and soe ofteen and in every such case upon every such [case] neglect   It is hereby Enacted that it shall and may be lawfull to and for the Lord or Proprietor or proprietors of the Castle of Bellfast his her or their Guardian as afforesaid under his her their hand and seale to nominate and appointe such one person of the said Burgesses to be Collector and receiver of the said severall dutyes hereby granted and to continue therein from the time of such appointm^t until the time for the annuall nominacion and Ellection of such Collector and receiver shall next happen

And every such Collector or receiver are hereby Enacted to be accountable for the said severall duties to such person and in the same manner as the Annuall Collector and receiver thereof are hereby directed and required

Provided [that] Allwayes that this Act shall continue and remaine in force for the space of twenty one yeares and to the end of the next Session of Parliam^t and noe longer

BRIEF in Behalfe of the Corporacon of Bellfast
The designe of this Bill is to supply the Inconveniences that the Towne of Bellfast lyes under in being deprived of the Tunnage the heretofore had by vertue of a Bylaw made by consent of the Lord of the Castle for keepeing the Key the Dock and harbour in repaire.

This duty is in a maner a Tax upon the Tradeing men of the Corporation wch they are willingly to pay for the incouragem^t of their Trade soe as it may be in such hands as they may be assured will applye it for the advantage of Trade.

In all grants for the benefitts of Corporacons the grant is made and the managem[t] thereof is intrusted to the care of the Corporation who are to reape the benefitt thereof and to suppose they will misapplye it as it layes a great imputation on them, soe it is without president to place it into any other hand

The Corporation have hitherto given sufficient Testimony of applying that duty to the repaire of the Key and since it is not in ye power of any person to show that ever there was one farthing misaplyed there no reason to doubt their care therein for the future.

The Lord of the Castle have ben heretofore allwayes inclynable to incourage the trade thereof and never interposed in any affaire relating to their Trade And as the Lords of the Castle can never be supposed to be connsant in affaires of Trade soe they never interfered with the marchants therein

The person to receive ye money and the method of layeing it out was allwayes intrusted to ye Corporation and the late Lord Donegall nor any of his predisessors Lords of the Castle never had ever desired to have any hand in the managem[t] thereof.

The Corporation is willing to live easly mind their businesse and to have a good correspondence with the Lord of the Castle and they apprehend to Lett the Lord of the Castle have any hand in the managem[t] of this duty will be means to creat misunderstanding between the Castle and them.

Its proposed as amendm[t] to the Bill that the Lord of the Castle doe yearly present 3 Burgesses and the Corporation to chuse one of them to collect and be accountable to the Lord of Castle and the Corporation

Wee doe apprehend that is to give the intire disposall of the duty to the Lord of the Castle [& doe yearly present 3 burgesses of the Corporation to chuse one of them to be collector & to be accountable to ye said Lord of the Castle & the Corporacon] for by this means none can be Collector but by favour of the Castle and consequently will be intirely under his Governmt

if the Lord of the Castle should have the nameing of 3 Burgesses whereof the Corporacon is to chuse one the Corporacon will have no choice for by the Charter the Lord of the Castle make whom he pleaseth Constable of the Castle and he by vertue of his office is allwayes a Burgesse the Constable of the Castle is allwayes the Lords sarvant

They have named Mr Byrt to be Collector & hereafter they may name him and Capt John Chichester one of the family who is above attending such an office and the Constable of the Castle who are Burgesses or they name two with one whom they have a mind should be Collector what ellection then have the Corporation

Suppose the Lord of the Castle name Burgesses who are insolvent and Imbessell the money who shall answer it to the Corporacon besides people wont dare to call him strictly to account or to prosecute him for any mismanagem[t] being the creature of a great man for feare of disoblidgeing

The nameing of 3 to be Collectors will be like the nameing of 3 to be Soveraigne the Lord of the Castle putt a marke upon the one he would have chosen Sovereign and whoe ever votes for any other is ill look'd upon by the Castle this wee have found by experience and may reasonably expect the like treatment for the future

The cause of the present misunderstanding between the Castle and the Towne is because the Towne would not consent to give up the intire managem[t] of the Corporacon in making Burgesses chusing a Soveraigne and ellecting such persons to serve in Parliam[t] as were recomended to them by the Castle.

As to ye Limitacion of 21 yeares its altogether unreasonable to make Temporary provission when the charge of keeping up the Key and cleansing the Dock and Channell will be perpetuall.

The clause w[ch] requires the Collector to account before the Lord of the Castle and the Corporacon may create great confusion for by this meanes if the Lord of the Castle and the Corporacon doe not both of them approve of the Accounts the Collector who is lyable to penaltys cannot be discharged and good men will be freightned from serveing.

Wee have complimented the Lord of the Castle with haveing the Accounts layed before them one every yeare by w[ch] they will have an oppertunity of [sueing for the penalty and taking care] seeing whether there be any mismanagemt or misapplicacion and thereby have an oppertunity of sueing for the penalty and takeing care that the intent of the Act be pursued and noebody will dare to tripp when they know they are to undergo such an Inquisition.

Wee had severall meeting upon this occassion before the Bill passed the house of Comons and this business of the Collector was looked upon soe unreasonable that they did thinke fitt soe much as to putt it into the Clause the brought into the house but they expressing some Jealousey as to the surplus if there should be any that the Corporacon might make a fund of it and *att* some time or other perhapps make use of it against the family to convince that that wee had nothing in our view butt a publick good wee complimented them with leaveing it in my Lord Donegalls power to putt a negative upon the applicacion of the surplus money, if they are not content with this the Corporacon will not consent to under the Tax unlesse they may be at liberty to dispose of it for the benefitt of their trade.

Nota,

That there can be no parity of reason because the Lord Donegall has a power by the Charter to name 3 to be Soveraigne that he should here have power to name 3 to be Collector because the Soveraigne is the principall person in the Corporacon and that was a trust reposed in him by the Crown when there was not above 3 or 4 houses in the Town and the protestant Interest was not well established in that part of the Countrey to keepe Corporacon stanch in their allegiance and in the Intrest of England but even the Crown did not thinke fitt to grant any larger power for the election of the Burgesses and the chooseing of all the Inferiour officers and Sarvants of the Corporacon such as this Collector must be is left intirely to ye Corporacon without the Castle and therefore to grant him this power now would be giveing him more then every any of his predecessours Lords of the Castle [and therefore] ever claimed or had and would be an Innovacion upon ye Corporacon

If it be objected that ye Corporacon cannot make a by Law without the consent of the Lord of ye Castle it is true they cannot but when it is once made a by Law the Lord of the Castle as nothing to doe further with it or any power in the execucion of it nor did any of the Lords of the Castle ever interfere in ye execucion of the by Law which is now proposed to be confirmed by an Act of Parliamᵗ. Soe the single question is whether the Lord of the Castle or rather indeed now whether the Legislature do thinke this is a reasonable law and will be for the advantage of trade and her Maᵗⁱᵉˢ Revenue if so the Lord of the Castle ought to have no more to doe with it upon any pretence of any power from the Charter then he has in the execucion of any other of the by Lawes or then any other of his predecessors ever had.

HIS is to certifie all whom it may concern that I John Jay now Residenter in Belfast in yᵉ County of Antrim in yᵉ Kingdom of Ireland aged about seventy eight or seventy nine years born att Scabee in Yorkshire in England am yᵉ son of George Jay yᵉ Elder brother of Sucklin Jay who gott into yᵉ Estate of Helveston four miles from Norwich in yᵉ County of Norfolk after my fathers death and in my minority and I afterwards growing to be about sixteen years of age listed myself a souldier in Croumwells army came for this Kingdom and am here settled and finding myself antient and uncapable of travell and knowing had Justice and Equity took place yᵉ Estate of Helveston aforesᵈ should have fallen to me and being sencible of my negligence and knowing my Brothers son yᵉ Bearer hereof to be lawfull heir of yᵉ said Helveston after my decease thinks myself bound in conscience I haveing no children to make knowen to him yᵉ Reallity of yᵉ said concern as by letters from me he hath received and cannot but declare and testifie that yᵉ said Bearer George Jay is yᵉ Lawfull begotten son of my Brother George Jay born in London in yᵉ little Mineris in yᵉ year one thousand six hundred seventy and two and have therefore on that account given yᵉ said George Jay my nephew full power and Authority as by a letter of Attourney in his Custody doth more fully appear to sue for yᵉ said Estate of Helveston dureing my life and I do further testifie and declare that no person or persons whatsoever recᵈ from me or by my order any writings to recover yᵉ premisses for yᵉ certainty whereof I have sett to my hand and seal the 18th day of May one thousand seven hundred and ten 1710

John Jay

Burrᵒ de }   We ye Sovereign Burgesses and ffreemen of ye Burrough
Belfast }   aforesᵈ in ye County of Antrim in Ireland

Do hereby certifie to all whom it may concern that yᵉ above John Jay an antient and honest Inhabitant of this Borrough has signed sealed and delivered to his Brothers son George Jay yᵉ above contentts wᵗʰ a letter of Attourney to sue for yᵉ right of yᵉ sᵈ John Jay.

Given under our hands and seale of yᵉ sᵈ Burrough this 18th day of May 1710

Roger Haddock Soveʳⁿ

John Craford   Hen: Shads   Rob: Leathes   James Gurner   Nicholas Thettford   George Portiss

Know all men by these presents that I John Jay of Belfast in yᵉ County of Antrim in yᵉ Kingdome of Ireland do hereby nominate constitute ordaine and appoint George Jay (my Brothers son) of Belturbett in yᵉ County of Cavan in yᵉ aforesᵈ Kingdome my true and Lawfull attourney for me and in my name stead and place to enter into and take possession of all that messuage Lands tenemts and hereditamts (or Estate) called Helveston for (*sic*) miles from Norwich in yᵉ County of Norfolk in England & also for me & in my name to sue forth and prosecute against any person or persons whatsoever any writt or writts action or actions as to him shall seem meett for yᵉ recovering or obtaining the possession or seazing of yᵉ premisses or any part thereof & further do & execute all & every such act or thing tending to yᵉ recovery of my Estate & right in yᵉ said messuage & lands or any part thereof and further I do hereby give and grant unto my said attourney full and whole power & authority from me & in my name stead & place to make and conclude wth any person or persons any agreemt whatsoever tuching ye premisses in as full & ample manner as I myself could do in my own person & I will ratifie & confirm whatsoever my said attourney shall Lawfully do in persuance of these presents   In witness whereof I have hereunto sett my hand & seal this 18th day of May 1710

John Jay

Signed sealed & delivered in presence of

Roger Haddock Soveʳⁿ

Rob Leathes   John Craford   James Gurner   Nicholas Thettford
George Portiss   Hen: Shads

On the eigth day of December one thousand seven hundred and Eleven the Sovereign and Burgesses then assembled ffor chooseing a free Burgess in place of Mr Richard Willson Burgess who departed this life on Sunday the second day of December Instant they did elect and unanimously choose Hans Hamilton Esqʳ a free Burgess in his place and room And at the same time the said Mr Hamilton took the oath of a Burgess as Usuall

Roger Haddock Soverⁿ

Rob Leathes   Geo Macartney   John Halridge
Nicholas Thettford   George: Portis   James Gurner
Geo: Macartney

To the Soveraigne & Burgesses of the Corporation of Belfast

Whereas I Roger Haddock of Carranbane in the County of Downe one of the Burgesses of the s⁰ Corporation am by my own private affairs and by other business in which I am engaged prevented from giveing due attendance or doing such service to the s⁰ Corporation as I am inclined to doe   Now I the said Roger Haddock doe for the reasons afores⁰ by these presents Surrender & give up to the s⁰ Soveraigne & Burgesses my Burgeship which I desire they will be pleased to accept of & dispose of the same to such person as they shall think most capable to serve the s⁰ Corporation   In witness whereof I have hereunto putt my hand & seale the 14th day of Novembr 1713

Roger Haddock   Ja: Wallace   Ter: Dogherty   John Murray   Copia vera

We the Sovereign and Burgesses having been assembled to Elect and choose a free Burgess to serve in the room of Mr Roger Haddock of Carranbane who resigned his place of Burgess which resignation did first come to our hands the seventh of December one thousand seven hundred and thirteen We did unanimously choose Mr. Robert Le Byrtt of Belfast a free Burgess of this Corporation in his room the same day   And whereas the said Robert Le Byrtt hath been hitherto hindered from taking the oath of a Burgess by reason of his being detained in Dublin he haveing been sent thither to the Parliam⁺ with the Records of this Corporation by the Sovereign of this Burrough we do therefore now confirm the said Election and he hath this day accordingly taken the oath of a Burgess before us   As witness our hands this twenty eigth day of December one thousand seven hundred and thirteen

Robert Leathes Soveraigne

Nath: Byrtt   Henry Ellis   George Portis   James Gurner   Nicholas Thettford   Thos: Banks

This day at an Assembly of the Sovereign and Burgesses of the Burrough of Belfast Mʳ Thomas Banks was sworn [Burgess] *as being* Constable of the Castle of Belfast before us as witness our hands the twenty eigth day of December one thousand seven hundred & thirteen

Robᵗ Leathes Soveraigne

Nath: Byrtt   Henry Ellis   George Portis   James Gurner   Nicholas Thettford

29ᵗʰ day of January 1714

Att a Court then holden wee the Soveraign and Burgesses by the experience and good opinion wee have had & do

still have unto Robert Lebyrtt a Burgess of this Burrough
have elected & chosen him to be our Town Clerk during
his honest carrying and upright behaviour in the said place
and have given him a pattent for the same under our hands
& the Comon Seal of Town

James Gurner Sovereign

Rob.ᵗ Leathes   Nath: Byrtt   George Portis   Henry
Ellis   Nicholas Thettford   Tho.ˢ: Banks Constable
of the Castle

We the Sovereign and Burgesses having been assembled
to Elect and chose a free Burgess to serve in ye Room of
James Macartney Esq.ʳ one of the Judges of his Maj.ᵗⁱᵉˢ Court
of Common Pleas in Ireland who resigned his place of
Burgess (which resignation came to our hands the sixteenth
day of August 1715 and dated the said day) we did unanimously choose Edward Clements Esq.ʳ a free Burgess of this
Corporation in his room same day and the said Edward
Clements hath this day accordingly taken the oath of a
Burgess   Wherefore we do confirm the said Election
und.ʳ our hands this said 16 day of August 1715

James Gurner Sovereign

Robt   Leathes   Jn°   Ech: Chichester   Geo:
Macartney   John Hallridge   Nath: Byrtt   Henry
Ellis   George: Portis   Nicholas Thettford   Geo:
Macartney   Robt: Lebyrtt

At an assembly held in the Burrough of Belfast
by the Sover.ⁿ and Burgesses of the said Burrough
the twenty fifth day of June 1716   James Gurner
Esq.ʳ then Sovereign

Whereas there was a By Law made the twenty fourth
day of June 1660 prohibiting any Burgesse after being
Elected and sworn Soveraign of the Burrough of Belfast to
sell by Retail in his house any wine, beer, ale aqua vitæ or
other strong waters or keep entertainment in his house
dureing the time of his being Sovereign of the said
Burrough on forfeiture of one hundred pounds   And
whereas it is the opinion of the Sovereign and all the
Burgesses now present that whoever is admitted a Burgess
of the said Corporation ought to be qualified to serve as

Sovereign when Elected and also that the said By Law is useless and inconvenient   It is therefore ordered by the said Sovereign and Burgesses that the said By Law be and is hereby Repealed annulled and made void to all intents and purposes whatsoever and the same is accordingly hereby declared to be from the date hereof annulled Repealed and made void to all intents and purposes whatsoever

James Gurner Sovereign

Robt Leathes   Henry Ellis   George: Portis   Hans Hamilton   Robt Lebyrtt   Thos: Banks

This day at an assembly of the Sovereign & Burgesses of the Burrough of Belfast the Revd Doct^r William Tisdall was sworn as being Constable of the Castle of Belfast before us   As witness our hands this fifth day of Aprill 1717

Henry Ellis Sovereign

This day at an assembly of the Sovereign and Burgesses Capt Robert Leathes was sworn as being Constable of the Castle of Belfast before us   As witness our hands this 29 June 1717

Henry Ellis Sovereign

Nicholas Thettford   Robt Lebyrtt   Nath: Byrtt George Portis   James Gurner

We the Soveraign & Burgesses haveing been assembled to Ellect and choose a Free Burgess to serve in the Room and place of Edward Clements Deceased we have unanimously chosen Thomas Hewetson a ffree Burgess of this Corporation in his Room this 27th day of May and the said Thomas Hewetson hath this day accordingly taken the oaths of a Burgess whereof we do confirm the said Ellection under our hands this said 27th day of May 1718

Jo: Carpenter Sovereign

Henry Ellis   James Gurner   Robt: Lebyrtt   Robt Leathes

The 10th Day of November 1720

At a Generall Assembly of the Sovereign and Burgesses and free Commonalty of the Towne and Corporation Edward Hall was duly elected and chosen to serve the

Corporation in the office of Serjeant at Mace in the room and place of John Brooks Deceased

Robt: Byrtt Sovⁿ

Isaac McCartney　Robt Hamilton　Mich^l Wood Lewes Smith　Thos Miller　Rober^t M'Calpin　Tho: Warnock　Geo: Macartney　Nath Byrtt　James Gurner　Nicholas Thettford　Ja^s Macartney

Belfast September the 28th A^o Dni 1721

At a Court then held we the Soveraigne & Burgesses have administred the oath of a ffree Burgess to Robt Green Esqr Constable of the Castle of Belfast and do hereby allow he hath a Right to all the priviledges and Libertys wch any Constable of the Castle heretofore has enjoyed & which by the Charter of the said Town are allowed

Robt: Byrtt Sovⁿ

John Hallridge　Henry Ellis　George: Portis　James Gurner　Nicholas Thettford　Ja^s Macartney

Belfast the 24th day of October An^o. Domini 1723

At an [court] *Assembly* then held Wee the Burgesses have administred the oath of A free Burgess to Thomas Banks Gent Constable of the Castle of Belfast and doe hereby allow he hath a Right to all the priviledges and Liberties which any Constable of the Castle heretofore has Enjoyed & which by the Charter of the said Town are allowed

Burrough of Belfast 20th Septr 1725

At an Assembly of the Sovereign & Burgesses then mett together the underneath bonds and papers were Delivered over by Arthur Byrtt son to the late Nathl. Byrtt Esqr Sov^m of the s^d Burrough to James Macartney Esqr the p^rsent Sov^m thereof　The Right Honble The Earl of Donnegalls bond for 200^l dated the 26th March 1702 & payable to Jno Chalmers Esqr then Sov^m for the use of the poor　Sampson Theakers Bond for 10^l dated the 25th Decr 1676 & payable to George Macartney Esqr then Sovⁿ.　John Carpenter Esqr his Bond 150^l dated 1st Decr 1720 & payable to Robt Byrtt Esqr then Sovⁿ　Mr Isaac Macartneys promisary note for 242^{ll} ster Dated the 8th day of Septr 1718 & payable to George Macartney Esqr then Sovr^m　The Lady Longfords Letter dated 29th Decr 1692 -owing the rec^t of 100^l for the use of the poor　Robt Leathes Esqr his rec^t to Clotworthy Upton Esqr for 32^{ll} dated 4th June 1714 A Rec^t from Robt Leathes Esqr to Geo McCartney Esqr Sov^m for sev^{ll} bonds & papers therein mencioned to be Delive^d to him Dated 28th May 1714　Clothworthy Upton Esqr his acco^t for Interest Due to the

poore   Roger Haddocks Rec^t to Clotworthy Upton Esqr for 96^l dated
Jany 3rd 1710   Ditt^{os} Rec^t to Ditto for 32^{ll} Dated 10th June 1712   James
Gurner Sov^{rn} his Rec^t to Ditto for 32^{ll} Dated 19th November 1714
Dittos Rec^t to Ditto for 32^{ll} Dated 9th July 1715   A Letter from Thos
Banks to the Sov^{rn} & Burgesses dated 18th August 1718 giving an acco^t of
32^{ll} by him paid to Captn Leathes on acco^t of Interest due by Ld Donnegall
to the s^d poor   A List of the poor & the *money* paid them to the year
1719 A paper of orders of an assembly dated the 22^d Aprill 1725 in relacion to
the poors money   Memo^{rn} a Rec^t given same day by the Sov^{rn} for the above
papers

　　　　　　　　　　　　　　　　　　　　　　James Macartney Sover^n

Burrough of }   At an Assembly of the Sovereign Burgesses & Comonality of
　Belfast　}   said Burrough Arthur Byrtt Esqr Sovrn held the eight day ot
November 1744 at the Market house of said Burrough and continued from time
to time by adjournment to the 15th of said month as appears by the List of
voters hereunto annexed to choose a Sergeant at Mace for said Burrough in the
Room & place of Edward Hall who for his mismanagement in his office as also
that he is at present confined in Jeal at Carrickfergus for Debt and not Likely
to be relieved by which means he is rendered incaple of doing his duty as Town
Serjeant Clement Monepenny was elected Chosen & sworn same day Serjeant
at Mace for said Burrough by the majority of said assembly in the Room &
place of said Edward Hall so disqualified   Dated this 15th day of November 1744

　　Entered by Robt Byrtt Town Clerk　　　　　　Ar: Byrtt Sovern

CANDIDATES

No	Clements Monepenny	No	Arthur Hall
1	James Archbald	1	Roger Haddock　7
2	Thomas Banks Esqr　1	2	And^w M'Comb　8
3	Hugh Donaldson　2	3	Alex^r M'Kyle　9
4	John Sharp　3	4	James Greerer
5	Thomas Beatton	5	Wm Wallace
6	Alex^r Young　4	6	Ja^s Holmes　10
7	John Stewart	7	Duncan Taylor　11
8	John Gordon	8	John ffleming　12
9	Danl Blow	9	Robt Stewart　13
10	John Brown	10	John Beggs　14
11	Alex^r Stewart　5	11	John Potts　15
12	Ben^m Legg　6	12	Hugh Lynn　16
13	Henry Blair　17	13	John Ashmere
14	Margetson Saunders　18	14	John Scott
15	John Johnston　19	15	John M'Munn　35
16	And^w Gelaspie	16	Saml Moffett
17	Sm^{ll} Wilson　20	17	John Ballentine Barber　36
18	Robt M'Mullan	18	Robt Gaskin
19	Robt Caulfield	19	Charles Ramage
20	Robt Clark	20	Jas Adair Senr.　37
21	John Black	21	And^w Hannah　38
22	Isaac Read　21	22	Sam^{ll} Brown
23	Edward Mitchell　22	23	John Cunningham　39
24	James Carmichael	24	Richd Coleman　40
25	Hugh Martin　23	25	Wm Paterson
26	Thos Lowry	26	Geo Walls
27	Willm Miller	27	Saml Boyd　41
28	Hugh M'Kitrick　24	28	Thos ffife　42
29	John M'Nish　25	29	John Cowden　43

No	Clements Monepenny	No	Arthur Hall
30	Robt Wills 26	30	John ffife Barber 44
31	Sam^{ll} Smith 27	31	John Whitlock 45
32	John Gregg	32	Wm Cross 46
33	Wm Gregg 28	33	Geo Sharp 47
34	John Coheran	34	John Stevenson 48
35	Sam^{ll} Joy	35	Wm Sharpley 49
36	Wm Stott 29	36	Mathew Douglass 50
37	Jam^s Peacock 30	37	Michael M'ffall 51
38	Gilbert M'Cully 31	38	Tho Whitnall 52
39	Walter Wilson 32	39	Tho Servise 53
40	Jam^s Smith 33	40	Alex^r Mugerlane
41	Geo Ashmere 34	41	Jam^s Boyd 54
42	Wm Archibald	42	Thos Johnston
43	Chas Hamilton	43	John M'[Cleary]Creery
44	ffra Kirkland 55	44	Robt M'Creery
45	Wm Hannah	45	John Dorment
46	John Taylor	46	John Lowden 69
47	John M'Donald 56	47	Geo M'Creery 70
48	Jas Bell	48	David Jukes
49	Thos Anderson	49	Thos Warnock 71
50	John M'Murray	50	Wm M'Cleary 72
51	Val Thetford 56	51	Thomas Smalshaw 73
52	Wm Holmes 57	52	John Ratclife
53	John Millwright	53	John Peart 74
54	Jas Blow 58	54	Michl Ratclife 75
55	Henry Duncan 59	55	Geo M'ffarson
56	Ed^d M'Donald 60	56	John Miller
57	John Leech 61	57	John Smith
58	Hugh Boyd	58	John Brown
59	John Jemison	59	Alex^r Ward 76
60	John Knox	60	John M'ffadden
61	Chas Walsh 62	61	Jas Ramsey
62	John Duff Burgess 63	62	Wm Nutt
63	Wm Simpson 64	63	Moses Hill
64	Jas Ross 65	64	Jas Anderson
65	Wm Boyd 66	65	Wm Worthington Junr 77
66	Henry Kelso	66	Wm MaGofolk 78
67	James Weir 67	67	Wm Mathews
68	Wm Dick 68	68	Robt Black
		69	Thomas Gregory 79
	Adjourned to Saturday	70	Richd Whitford 80
	the 10th of Novr 1744	71	ffra Beaty
		72	Wm Wha 81
69	Alexr Spawin 82	73	Saml Galloway
70	Tho Whiteside 83	74	John Jakson
71	Revd Geo Robertson 84	75	Robt Corbitt
72	John Gibson	76	Alex^r Mears 102
73	Neile Patten	77	Robt Gutry
74	Ralph Charley 85	78	Jas Lemon
75	John Leith 86	79	Tho Coulter 103
76	Jas Wilson 87	80	Hh^u Haven
77	Tho Jones 88	81	David Stevenson
78	John Ross 89	82	Michl Ratcliffe Senr 104
79	Wm Worthington Senr 90	83	Mathw King 105
80	Wm Lawson 91	84	Pat Gibson
81	John Holmes	85	Wm Cambell
82	Dav^d Lyons	86	Wm Beck
83	Wm Biggar	87	Wm Caruthers

No	Clements Monepenny	No	Arthur Hall
84	Robt Aldrich	88	Saml Allen 106
85	John Jones 92	89	Robt Henderson
86	Hugh Beaty	90	Geo Magee
87	Ed⁴ fforsyth	91	John Herd 107
88	John fforsyth 93	92	Richd Coulter 108
89	Henry Charley 94	93	Israel Burns 109
90	Martin Worthington 95	94	John M'ffarran
91	Henry Linn	95	Arthʳ Clark
92	Adam Addidle	96	George Cork 110
93	James Chads 96	97	Hen Vernett
94	ffra Bowell 97	98	Tho Graham 111
95	Wm Kirkwood 98	99	Isaac Hall 112
96	Jas Woods 99	100	John Hall 113
97	Wm Legg 100		
98	John Stewart		Adjourned to Saturday
99	Thos M'Connell 101		the 10th of Novr 1744
100	John Wilson		
101	Cha M'Neily	101	Andw Sloan 127
102	Obedʰ Grove 114	102	Cha Moor 128
103	Cha Young 115	103	John Brown
104	Jas Charley 116	104	Thos Heming
105	James	105	Neile Magee 129
106	Wm Brown	106	Hugh Holmes 130
		107	John Dorment
	Adjourned to thursday	108	John Riggs
	the 15th of Novr 1744	109	Andw Trimble
		110	Davᵈ Mote
107	Geo Macartney Esqr	111	Robt M'ffall 131
108	Revd Barnard Ward	112	Wm Watt 132
109	Val Jones Junr	113	Gawen Davison
110	Thos Gregg	114	Samˡ Read 133
111	Vincent Mercy	115	Davᵈ Logan 134
112	John M'Kedy 117	116	John Bole
113	Saml Stanton 118	117	Wm Pettycrewe
114	Robt Wallace		
115	John Hay		Adjourned to thursday
116	Hen: East		15th Novr 1744
117	John Rice 119		
118	Jas Dixon		
119	Wm Johnston Landwʳ		
120	Saml M'Teer		
121	John Armstrong 120	133	Wm Hamilton
122	John M'Cahee	134	John Clark 138
123	John Bennett 121	135	Wm Culbert 139
124	Hen M'ffadden	136	Jas M'Donald 140
125	Saml Macartney 122	137	Phi: Coats 141
126	Robt Hay 123	138	Robert ffoothey 142
127	Archd Miller 124	139	Nathl Morrison 143
128	Gilbert M'Dowell 125	140	Michl Addidle 144
129	Jas Law 126	141	Jas Young 145
130	ffaithfull Wilson 135	142	Thos Sturgeon 146
131	Randall Pettycrew 136	143	Michl Mears 147
132	Isaac Agnew 137		

Att the adjournmt to this day at the Close thereof the said Arthur Hall gave up having no more to poll nor offering any more votes & the said Clements Monepenny being 26 votes more than said Hall the Election was declared publickly in Court in the favour of the said Monepenny who was then & there sworn into the office of Serjeant at Mace for the Burrough of Belfast aforesaid in the Room & place of the aforesaid Edwd Hall

Entd this 15th day of Nov 1744 upon   Ar: Byrtt Sovn
Record by Robt Byrtt Town Clark

For Clements Monepenny	143	
For Arthur Hall	117	
	26	Majority for C Monepenny
	260	Gross amount

Bur: of ⎰   At an Assembly of the Sovereign & free
Belfast ⎱ Burgesses of this Corporation this day held in order to chuse a burgess in Parliament in the room of David John Barry Esqr deceased & in pursuance of a precept from the Sheriff of this County We doe unanimously Chuse & Elect the Honble John Chichester to represent us in Parliam^t in the room of s^d Mr Barry

Dated this 14th November 1745   Ar: Byrtt Sov^n.

Copy of the freedom presented to his Grace the Ld Primate in a gold Box the 2nd Septr 1748

Be it Remembered that an assembly held at ye Town Hall of the Burrough of Belfast the 2^d day of Septr in the year of our Lord *1748* Margetson Saunders Esqr Sovereign of s^d Burrough his Grace the most rev^d father in God George Lord ArchBpp of Ardmagh Primate & Metropolitan of all Ireland & one of the L^ds Justices thereof was unanimously admitted into the Liberties & franchises of ye said Burrough as a singular mark of our Esteem & affection for him   In Testimoney whereof we have caused the Common Seal of ye s^d Burrough to be hereunto affixed the day & year afores^d

Margetson Saunders Sov^n.

Constables for ye Town *1748*

James Tough	John Steele	Hugh Marron	Charles Walsh
James Baird	Hugh Barnet high Const.		

Burrough of ⎰   At an Assembly of the Sovereign and
Belfast ⎱ free Burgesses of this Corporation this day held in order to chuse a burgess in Parliament in the room of the Honble John Chichester dec^d and in pursuance of a precept from the Sherriff of this County We doe unanimously chuse and Elect William Macartney of the Town of Belfast Esquire to represent us in Parliament in the room of the said John Chichester

Dated this 14th day of October 1747 forty seven
Margetson Saunders Sov^n.

Names of the Sworn Measurers 1738 & 1754

1 Robt Huey	8/9 Jo^n McClealan
[2 Pat M'Bride]	9/10 Richd Campbell
[3 Mich Wood]	[11 Ja. Dickson]
4 Arch^d Whiteford 2	[12 Arch^d Vickar]
5 Alex^r Johnston 3	[13 Arch^d Taylor
6 Ivar M'Intosh	12-14 Jo^n Brown
7 Dougall M'Gregor 5	13-15 Duncan Stewart
8 John Campbell 6	*14 Henry Mullan*
Robt Hamilton	

Constables for the year 1753 for the Town of Belfast

Wm Wilson high constable
Wm Turner In Ann Street
Geo: Mitchell old Quay
Jo^n Harvey weaver Mill Street
Wm Taylor N: Street
Arch^d Scott   do

Constables for the year 1754 for the Town of Belfast

James M'Watters High Constable
Wm Brown in Bridge Street
Wm Stewart in North Street
Wm Henderson in New Key
Edwd Harrison in Mill Street
Gaun Wallace in Bridge Street

Belfast Wednesday Oct 28 1767

At an Assembly of the Soveraign Free Burgesses & Freemen of this Corporation this day held at the Market House Nathaniel Boddle was unanimously chosen one of the Sergeants at Mace of this Borough in the Room of George Murray deceased

At the same time the said Nathl Boddle took the oath of a Sergeant at Mace before me   Geo Macartney
Ent^d Henry Joy D. T. Clke

The Oath of the Sovraigne

You shall sweare that yo^u shall well and truly serve our Soveraigne Lord the Kinge by the space of one whole yeare now next ensueing as Sovraigne of the Burrough of Bellfast (If God grant you soe long life) *&* *untill a successor be sworne wth yor best endea^vr.*] according to the power given unto you by his Maties Lres Pattents and [that] you shall according to the best of yor knowledge discrecion doe equall justice as well to the poore as the rich and truly fairly and *gently* [litely] intreate the people of this Burrough *you* [and] shall use yor best endeav^rs to uphold maintayne the rights Libties jurisdiccions and [all] Lawfull ordinances of this Towne and Burrough correccion of victualls (That is to saie) breade wine beare Ale ffish and fleshe you shall truly and tenderly see *or cause to bee seene* unto craftsmen Labourers and Artificers you shall *truly enquire of and those that shall* be found guilty faulty and trespassinge therein you shall justly correct and duly reforme, widdows and orphans you shall succour and Defend   And finally in all other thinges that shall or may concerne yor office you shall therein faithfully and uprightly demeane yor self for the most quiet benefitt worshipp honesty [and] creditt *&* *advancem^t* of this yor Burrough and *the* Inhabitants thereof.   Soe help yo^u God in Jesus Christ,

The Oathe of Supremacy

I doe *hereby* [utterly] testefie and declare in my conscience that o^r Soveraigne Lord King Charles his highnes is the only supreme Governo^r of this Realme and of all other his highnes's Dominions and Realmes as well in all Spirituall & ecclesiasticall thinges or causes as in causes and matters temporall and that noe forraigne Prince person prelate state or potentate hath or ought to have any Jurisdiccion power superiority preheminence or authorety ecclesiasticall or Temporall within this Realme and therefore I doe utterly renounce and forsake all furraigne Jurisdiccions powers superiorityes and authoretyes and doe promise that from henceforth I shall beare faithe and such [truth] true alleagiance to the Leige highnes his heires and Lawfull Successors and to my power shall assist and defend all Jurisdiccions priviledges power and authorety granted or belonging to the King's highnes his heires & Successors & enrolled and annexed to the Imperiall Crowne of this Realme   Soe help me God &c

The Oath of the Overseers of the Markett

You shall sweare that you will serve in the office of overseer of the Markett in this Towne untill Easter next if you soe long live dureing wch time you shall well and truely looke into ye wholesomnesse of all sorts of flesh meate corne graine meale Butter and Bread that shall come into the Markett, and see that noe corrupt victuall be brought and sold into the Markett, and if any you are to take it away and from time to time to acquaint ye Soveraigne for the time being of the same and that you shall observe such orders and By Lawes of the Corporacon relateing to the Markett (agreeing wth the statute in that case made and provided) as shall be given you in charge from time to time by the Soveraigne aforesayd and all other things relating to the office of an overseer of the Markett according to your skill and knowledge you shall observe Soe helpe you God

[The Oath of a Market Juror per stat 27 Geo. 3. to be sworn one by one in] open court [at Assizes] [You shall well, truly,] and Diligently exercise the office of a Market juror in the Borough of Belfast without favour or affection malice or ill will, to any person or persons whatsoever So help you God

The oath of a free Burgesse

You shall sweare that yo^u will be ready as one of the Twelve Burgesses of this Towne and Burrough of Belfast to doe yor best endeav^rs for the publique good thereof and that you come uppon due warning given you by or from the Suffran of this Towne and Burrough for the tyme being or any by him appointed to give your true advice and best Counsell in any thing that you shall be required touching the ffranchise weale and the good rule and government of this Towne as oftentymes as cause and occasion shall require And that from henceforth you shall attend & assistant to ye Suffran of this Towne for ye tyme being And that you will keepe the Councell and ordinances made by the Suffran and the major parte of the Burgesses by and wth the consent of the Lord of the Castle or in his absence the Constable thereof These and all other things wch belong to a Burgesse of this Towne to doe or to be done you shall well and truly keepe & performe So helpe you God in Christ Jesus,

ARTHUR *LORD CHICHESTER BARRON of BELLFAST* in y^e County of Antrim in y^e Province of Ulster in y^e North of Ireland was a younger son of Sr John Chichester of Rawley near Barnstable in Devonshire where he attained to Capacity for ye University he was sent to Oxford and was of Exetter College he was only a Gramer Scholler and being very active strong and ingenious took affection to a Millitary Course he went first into Ireland takeing with him for Companion Bartholomew Fortescue my fathers youngest Brother whom he *much* loved he being as I have often heard his Lord^sp say very good Company a valient strong man and one of ye best wrestlers in those times they stay'd a while with Sr George Bourchiers who was then Master of ye Ordinance in

Ireland and son of yᵉ Earl of Bath and father of this Earl a Noble Gentleman they had been Actors with other young gentlemen of a youthfull rash trick in England for which they fled into Ireland and when their friends had obtained their pardon of Queen Elizabeth they returned to England soon after my Lord Chichester who was then but Master Chichester adventured abroad for advancement and ffortescue turned sea Capᵗ and died in that employment   Chichester was afterwards made Capᵗ of one of yᵉ Queen's best ships under yᵉ command of yᵉ Lord Sheffeild at yᵉ Sea fight with yᵉ Spanish Armado in 1588

He had yᵉ comand of one of yᵉ Queen's ships with 500 men in Sʳ ffrancis Drakes last voyage to yᵉ west Indies.   Sʳ francis Drake died there at that time   He was a volunteer in yᵉ Earl of Essexes voyage to Spain and at Cales Captain Paul Chichester who was an able darring man being slayn with a bullett yᵉ Earl of Essex gave him his Company.

He was Sergeant Major Generall of yᵉ Queen's Army in Pickardy under yᵉ comand of Sʳ Thomas Buskervill and at yᵉ seige of Ameans was shott in yᵉ shoulder and for his couragious good service then and in those warrs was there knighted by King Henry yᵉ fourth.

When those civill warrs were ended he went into yᵉ Low Countries where he had a Company of 200 men which then was his subsistance but Sʳ Rob: Cicell Secretary of State to yᵉ Queen being very much his noble friend telling her Majᵗⁱᵉ what pitty it was so able a gentleman should bury his time in that Country with a single Company she haveing Imployment for him in Ireland where his Brother Sʳ John Chichester was slayn with a bullett; got Leave of yᵉ Queen to send for him, he being then garrisoned at Ostend, and to employ him in yᵉ service of Ireland with a Regmᵗ of 1200 men, with which command he was sent thither and according to his commision landed them with himself at Dublin Sʳ Adam Loftus of Rathfernam Lord Chancellor and Sʳ Rob: Gardiner Lord Chief Justice being Lords Justices in yᵉ intervals Between yᵉ death of yᵉ Lord Barrows Lord Deputy who dyed at Newry and yᵉ coming of yᵉ Earl of Essex Lord Lievtent from Dublin he was sent with a Regmᵗ to garrison at Tradath within a short time after yᵉ Earl of Essex arived at Dublin with yᵉ Gallantry of England and hearing much in praise of Sʳ Arthur Chichester and perfection of his Regmᵗ made a journey purposely with his Gallants to see him and Sʳ Arthur haveing drawn his Regmᵗ up in a most fair field and exercised them perfectly at which he was excellent they being in close order yᵉ Earl thinking to put a sully on them by breaking throw them charged at them with his Gallants Cavallry but yᵉ Collonell not being used to receve foyles had so ordered his Pikes as they forced yᵉ Earl to a Corry Coale and upon his wheele a saucie fellow with his Pike prickt his Lordˢᵖ saveing your reverence in yᵉ Rear and made him bleed; so he haveing enough of that smarting sport, he retreated giving yᵉ Collenell and his Regmᵗ high praise. his Lordˢᵖ stayed but a short while in Ireland then came Sʳ Charles Blunt Lord Mountjoy Lord Deputty and was after Earl of Devonshire who within few months made Sʳ Arthur Chichester Serjeant Major Generall of yᵉ Army he well knowing his strong Abillityes in ffrance and yᵉ Low Countries where they had been intimate friends Sʳ Harry Danvers who was afterwards made by King James Lord Danvers and Earl of Danby was before Major Generall: about six months after he was made Governor of Carrickfergus and those parts which being so far off from yᵉ Lord Generall: as he could not attend to receive and distribute his orders Sʳ John Barkley was made Major Generall: who about a year after was slayn with a bullett at yᵉ takeing of an Island in a logh called Maherlecoo

in yᵉ County of Ardmagh then was Sʳ Arthur Chichester made Major
Generall again and at lenth had that office by patent dureing life and after
his invading yᵉ County of Tyrone by boats over Logh Neagh from
Maserine in yᵉ County of Antrim and raiseing a ffort at his landing place
which was after named Mountjoy he was made Governor thereof and yᵉ
adjacent countries by Pattents and Admirall of Logh Neagh by yᵉ name of
Logh Chichester yᵉ next year yᵉ Queen dying King James made yᵉ Lord
Deputy Mountjoy Lord Lieutenant of Ireland and Sʳ Arthur Chichester
Sʳ Harry Docwray and Sʳ Wᵐ Godolfin Privy Councellors of Ireland which
was when they were upon their March with yᵉ army in Munster to reduce
yᵉ Citty of Watterford Cork and Limrick that rebelled and would not
proclaime King James as their King but they were forced to it and some
of yᵉ Chief actors hanged at Cork yᵉ next Spring yᵉ Lord Lievtenᵗ: went for
England all being at Peace in Ireland so did Sʳ Arthur Chichester and Sʳ
George Carry of Cockinton in Devonshire who was then Treasurer in
Ireland was for ye pʳsent left Lord Deputy and about two years after or less
it being in 1604 Sʳ Arthur Chichester was made Lord Deputy which he
held twelve years which was longer than Ever any did before or since and
towards his end of that Governmᵗ he was made Barron of Belfast his own
Town and after his rendering up of yᵉ King's sword was made Lord High
Treasurer of Ireland then he retired to his Estate and Governmᵗ in
Ulster and about three years after was by Lettʳ from King James called
into England and imployed Ambassador to yᵉ Princes of yᵉ Union in
Germany and in short time after his return was made one of yᵉ Councell
of Warr and within few months one of yᵉ Lords of yᵉ Privy Councell of
England and in few years after dyed in London much lamented by all that
knew him he was buried at Carrickfergus where he had built yᵉ noblest
brave house in yᵉ Kingdom and had prepared a neate Tomb to receive
him when when (*sic*) God should please to send him to it.

He was one so farr from ambition and coveteousness that he nether by
friends nor of himself [would] *moved* for advancmᵗ Millitary or Civill but
still it was confered on him unsought as all those commands and honours
were wᶜʰ he had by favour of Sʳ Rob: Cicill Earl of Salisbury yᵉ Earl of
Devonshire and Lastly from King James so likewise was his Knighthood
by ye King of ffrance all wᶜʰ certainly would not have been lay'd on him
had he not been a very meriting man and of such deportmᵗ as gained a
generall good opinion and Love.

To my Knowledge yᵉ Earl of Devonshire in time of his being Lord
Deputy said he wondered at Sʳ Arthur Chichester for others prest him for
many things but he for nothing but grumbled like a right western man and
that he had twice made him Major Generall and given him two Governmᵗˢ
those of Carrickfergus and Tyrone and knew not what more to do for him at
pʳsent but make him Lievtenant Generall: of yᵉ Army which he would do if
he found him grumbling still and then unless he could make him Generall: and
Lord Deputy he had done as much as was in him to do for him at lenth
he made him both Loveing him very much. He never sought yᵉ honour
of Barron nor knew it was comeing to him untill yᵉ first Lord Caufield
who was then S. Toby Caufield brought him a Patent for it from yᵉ King
as a present from Sᵗ Humphrey May who had in England yᵉ mannage and
disposall of all Irish affairs and procured it for him Loveing him heartly
they being ancient acquaintances and friends.

I well know that King James by his Lettʳˢ of favour and grace called
my Lord Chichester into England in 1613 he being then Lord Deputy
Sᵗ Humphrey May who had strong power with ye King offered to get him

made an Earl and as I heard Knight of yᵉ Garter if he would but court a little yᵉ then Favorite yᵉ Earl of Sumersett which he said he could not do and that he had more honour by being a Barron then his Estate could becoming a nobleman support.

He moved not to be a Privy Councellor of England King James knowing well his abillityes his well deservings and his discreet and honorable manage of his negotiations in his Embassage in Germany did it of himself.

He was no very good Orator but had a singular good expression with his pen sublime and succinct according to yᵉ subject whereof he wrote and yᵉ Person to whom his Lettʳˢ to King James were so acceptable as he gave him encouragmᵗ and command to write often to him and once when yᵉ King received a Lettʳ from him he gave it to his ffavorite Sumersett biding him learn it without book saying he had not received such a Lettʳ since he was King of England and yᵉ secretary of State yᵉ Earle of Salisbury and Lords of yᵉ Councell would give his lines high praise he was a great statesman and good comon wealths man and as knowing able a souldier as any of our nation in those times ; he was a carefull performer of his mannagmᵗˢ and keeper of his word no man knew his composition and disposition better than myself Therefore I may with confidence and truth say this that he was a man of great honour Piety prudence justice bounty and valour very hospitable charitable affable and excellent good company within and without doors being a Lover of all Civill becoming sports games and recreations.

His Estate was all of his own acquisition by fair purchase only yᵉ King gave him Sʳ Cahier O'Doghertyes County it being by his rebellion Escheat to yᵉ Crown and he with his adherents being cutt off by yᵉ Industry and activity of my Lord Chichester that land was then worth about 1000ˡⁱ per Ann: within those times of Largis and in that Kingdom and at yᵉ furthest point north was no great gift or reward from a King to a Subject that had been 12 years his Vice Roy and so well a Deserver

His Estate being about 8000ˡⁱ per Ann: he left to his good Brother Sʳ Edward Chichester who also inherited his honour of Barron of Belfast and in short time after was made Viscount of Carrickfergus and Governor of that Town and Country and 3 or 4 years before his death his Son was made by King Charles Earl of Dunnagall in yᵉ north of Ulster in which County he hath 20 miles of Land at Least he was bred with and by his noble uncle Arthur Lord Chichester and in much is a good coppy of that originall upon the grand horrid Rebellion in Ireland he advanc't at his own charge a Regmᵗ of horse and a Regmᵗ of ffoot for yᵉ service of the King and did very acceptable service he being a gallant gentleman couragious steddy Just and noble hearted

With the first Lord Chichester that man of great honour and noble Endowmᵗˢ I had from my coming young from School my Education and by him yᵉ foundation of my Advancemᵗˢ and fortune acquired in Ireland

ffayth: ffortescue

Sʳ Josias Bodleys Annagram upon Arthur Chichester

Cares hurt yᵉ Rich
Riches cure yᵉ hart
They care great Lord in wealth and honour Rich
They name transposed doth show cares hurt ye Rich
Yet in those Riches Richer then thou art
Still strive to be for Riches cure ye hart

Translated out of ffrenche

HENRY by y^e Grace of God King of ffrance and Navarre to all p^rsent and to
come Greeting   Whereas there are Differences of Qualities vocations and
exercises between the servants of Kings and princes some being for the Councell
and Ministry of matters of State of ye Justice and of Civill governm^t ye others
for deeds of Armes Conduct and execution of warr and the others for matters fitt
and necessary for ye Pe[a]rson of ye Prince tending all indifferently to a like end
wch is to perform all of them their dutyes and charges to content their said
Prince who in the doing thereof (as not ungratefull in ye acknowledgeing of
their good and Loyall services) ought not to be spareing toward them of his
Graces favours and Liberalities and specially to honour and make their names
and memory perpetuall [doth] wth honourable titles and dignities agreeable to their
vertues and des[a]erts to ye end that in giveing them occasion to continue and
persevere many may take example by them and indeavour to imitate and follow
them to ye end to yield their services acceptable and commendable Wherefore
considering ye vertues deserts and laudable parts wch are in ye person of our
dear and well beloved Arthur Chichester Capt of one of ye Companies of English
Soldiers serving on foot wch the Queen of England our Right dear and Right
beloved Good sister and cousen hath sent for our succour considering that y^e
said Capt Chichester hath worthely beheaved himself in ye siege which we have
layd before ye Town of Amiens and in The Encounter wch wee have had with our
Enemies wch were come to succour this said Town wherein he hath made good
proofe not only of a Singular affection to our service But also of a great courage
and valour haveing voluntarily exposed himself to all kinds of perills and dangers
It hath seemed unto us that it were very meet that ye said Capt Chichester
should receave the like grace and favour wch wee have accustomed to bestow and
distribute to our good and zealous servitors wch are to be comended as he is
for ye honour and praise of their persons.   Therefore and for other good con-
siderations us thereunto moveing have wee in ye p^rsence of certain Princes of

our blood of our Right dear and beloved cousins the Duke of Montmorancy Peer and Constable of ffrance and of Monsu' de Biron Marshall of ffrance and of sundry great and noble Lords and Captains made and created, do make and create ye said Capt Chichester Knight And we have given and granted, do give and grant unto him y° order of gyrted warlike Knight and have with our hand Imbraced him even as for y° obtaining of such a degree it is required and accustomed to y° end y° said Cap' Chichester may from henceforth injoy and use ye Rightes honours and authorities of Knight, priveledges, prerogatives, and preheminences, w°ʰ thereunto do belong as well in matters of warr arms and assembles as in Judgm' Court and without and in all places elsewhere it shall appertain and need shall require cheefly to bear y° armes furniture and weed appertaining to y° degree of Knighthood even so and in such form and manner as other Knights made and created by our Predecessors Kings and by us are accustomed to do and bear Wee do also will our beloved and faithfull [Provosts Judges Captaynes Cheeftains and Conductors] y° Persons Keeping our Courts of Parliam' and all   generall Marshalls of ffrance Governors Baylifs Seneshalls Provosts Judges Captaines Cheeftaines and Conductors of men of warr Ban and ariereban Mayors Aldermen Counsells Councellors and magistrates of our Townes and Cittys and all others our other Justices and officers to whom it shall appertain that they cause suffer and permitt y° said Capt Chichester fully and peaceably to enjoy and use y° said rights of Knighthood honours prerogatives priveledges and preheminences w°ʰ thereunto do belong even so and in y° form and manner as is aforesaid Ceasing and causing to cease all troubles and hindrances to the contrary for such is our pleasure notwithstanding wʰsoever orders decrees or prohibitions to y° contrary hereof ye w°ʰ in this behalfe and without prejudice thereunto in other things we have derogated and do derogate also the derogatory of y° derogatory therein contained and to the end it be a thing firm and stable for ever we have caused our seale to these p'sents to be putt y° right of us in other things and of others in all reserved we do also pray y° said Lady Queen of England our dear and well beloved good sister and Cousin to permit y° said Capt Chichester to injoy and use y° favours which we have granted unto him in this behalfe even so and as wee should or could do in like occasion for those wᶜʰ shall be recommended unto us on her behalfe Given in ye Camp before Amiens in y° month of September Anno one thousand five hundred four score and seaventeen And in ye ninth year of our Raign Subscribed thus=HENRY=And upon ye fold by ye King DENEUFVILLE VISA=And sealed with a seale in Green wax under appending.

CHICHESTER EARL OF DONEGAL.

This family seems anciently to have born the name of Cirencester and was one of the most eminent in the County of Devon for its antiquity, Estate and Employmt⁵ & alliances having flourished for several generations at South Poole not far from Kings Bridge where their most ancient habitation was they have a right to quarter the arms of the Ralieghs, the Beaumonts, the Willingtons, & many other noble familys. The 1st of the name to be met with is Walleran de Cirencester, to Walleran succeeded John his son, & to him Sʳ John, Sir Thomas, Sir John, Richard, who leaving the name of Cirencester alˢ Chichester fixed upon the latter, to him succeeded John, Sir John, Richard Edward, and Sir John, who married a Daughter of Sir William Courtneys in Devonshire by whom he had 5 sons and 8 Daughters

1ˢᵗ Sʳ John, Ancestor to Sʳ John Chichester Bart:

2 Arthur whose abilitys and Services raised him to the peerage of Ireland

4 Sʳ John, who sought glory in Ireland where his services were rewarded wᵗʰ y° post of Serg' Major and y° honour of Knighthood, he was distinguished from his Broʳ by ye name of Sʳ Joⁿ the younger, he lost

his life on an Enterprise ag[t] James MacSourley MacDonnell
(after Earl of Antrim) about 4 miles Distant from Carickfergus

3. Edward, Ancestor to ye Earl of Donegal

5 S[r] Thomas to whom K: James granted a Lease in ye Co: of Wicklow
and gave to him and his heirs ye Lands of Radonnell containing
1000 in Co: of Donegal

Sir Arthur Second Son of S[r] John   In 1599 commanded 200
foot at Carickfergus and did signal services   In 1603 he was made a
Privy Counsellor & Governor of Carickfergus wth all other forts wth Lough
Neagh & y[e] Commoditys thereof Coll! & Govern[r] of the forces stationed at
Carrickf[s], Kilwarling, The little Ards, the Clanaboyes, the Duffraine, Killultagh, The Route & the Glynnes In Ulster, & of all the Inhabit[ts] thereof, to
attend upon him & be at his Direction, also Admiral of Lough Sidney
otherwise Lough Neagh wth the fishing thereof as far as the Salmon Leap on
the River Banne, Governor of fort Mountjoy   By patent 1st feb 1603 he
was made L: D: of Ireland & that year established 2 new Circuits, sending the
1st Justices of Assize into Connaught & retrieving the Circuit of Munster,
w[ch] had been discontinued for near 200 years, the former Circuits only
Encompassed the English Pale.   In Consideration of his great Services the
King granted to him the territory or Country of Inishowen, otherwise
called O'Dogherties Country, wth all the Hereditaments thereof, possessed
by S[r] Jo[n] O'Dogherty, or his son the late Traytor Caher O'Dogherty
(Except such lands as were to be allotted to y[e] Bishop of Derry & 1000
acres to the city of Derry) together with the custody of Culmore Castle
for Life, he had a grant thereof by Patent 22nd feb 1609 to hold by
Fealty, and the yearly rent of £86 : 12 : 8 Eng! making Irish £115 : 10 : 2½
wth a power of holding 4 several courts Leets, within the Island of Inch, the
territory of Tuogh Croneine, & Tuogh Clagh, the manor of Greencastle,
otherwise New Castle and the Island of Malyne a fryday market & 2 fairs
on the last days of August & April at Bancranocha, a Munday market & 2
fairs on 30 Sep[r] & 1st Ap[r] at Greencastle, a fair 20th Oct[r] at Drange.   To
Divide the territory into Precincts, wth free warren.   This was again confirmed by Letters Patent dated 6th July 1610 he was made Culmore Fort
w[ch] he surrendered.   On 14th Jany 1610 he had a grant of the Castle of
Dungannon & 1320 acres of Escheated Lands within that precinct   In
consideration of his surrender of certain fishings granted to ye City of
London his Majesty granted to him during his life and the life of his
nephew Arthur, & Ar: Langham, the Entertainment by ye Day ——— as
Captain & 9[sh] for 9 horsemen, to Employ them where he should think fit
during his life & afterwards to be Resident in the territory of Innishowen,
the pay to commence 1[st] Oct[r] 1611 w[ch] was renewed 29[th] August 1616
without che[c]que   The K: the 8[th] of Augt 1620 ordered an Effectual grant
to be made by Patent confirming all his former grants & accordingly 2
Distinct Patents were passed dated 20[th] Nov[r] 1621,   By Letters Patent
bearing date 22[rd] feb 1612 he was created Baron Chichester of Belfast,
Entailing the honour on his Issue male, he continued in the Government 10
years Successively in the last of w[ch] he had occasion for all his great abilitys,
the manage the most stubborn Parliament that ever was in Ireland w[ch] met
ye 18th May 1613   On 27th July 1614, he was again made L:D: In w[ch] year
the Harp was first marshalled wth the arms of England.   On the 29th Nov[r]
1615 the K: was pleased to disburthen him of that charge On the 13th July
1616 he was constituted Lord High Treasurer of Ireland & whilst he continued In Ireland resided at Carickfergus, where in 1618 he built a
magnificent house called Joymount,   On 2nd May 1622 he was sent

Ambassador to the Palatinate, & thence to treat of a peace w.th ye Emperor he returned in October to England, & 31.st Decr was sworn of his Majestys Privy Councel. He Departed this life (in as great honour as any English-man of that age) In London *19 feby 1624 & Interred* 24.th Octr 1625 In the Church of St Nicholas In Carickfergus, under a stately monument of marble & alabaster A handsome monument is also erected to his memory in the Cathedral Church of Exeter And in a little Oratory adjoining to the Church of Eggesford He married Letitia the Daughter of Sir Jo.ⁿ Perrott to whom he was ye 3.^d husband his only son Arthur born the 26.th Sept 1606 dyed on the 30.th of the next month, so that Sir Edward his next Bro.^r Succeeded him in his large Estate and the honour being limited only to his Issue male, K: Charles ye 1.st conferred it anew on Sir Edward & added to it the title of Viscount Chichester of Carickfergus, dated at Westm.^r 1.st Ap.^r 1625 & constituted him that year Governor of Carickfergus Admiral of Lough Neagh, Governor of Culmore & that same 12.th of Octr he was sworn of his Majestys Privy Council he had also a Confirmation of the Estate 22.nd Sepr 1640 for the fine of £467 : 17 : 6 was made joint Com.^r of ye treasury w.th Lords Grandison & Ormond 12.th Octr 1632 he commanded a Regim.^t on the breaking out of ye rebellion in 1641, he sent an express to the K: & was commissioned by him to raise forces, he was a worthy and Eminent person well accomplished both for war & peace he dyed 8.th July 1648 his children Arthur, John, Edward, Elizabeth & Mary Arthur the eldest was born 16.th June 1606, 25.th Augt 1625 he was appointed to the command of a troop of horse, in 1639 he represented the County of Antrim in Parliam.^t On the breaking out of the rebellion he did considerable service, the 14.th feby 1643 he was constituted Governor of Belfast & the territory of Inneshowen & for the better fortifying of the town of Belfast, his Majesty directed the Ld Lieu.^t to advance 1000.^{ll} to him forthwith, the K: on the representation the Marquis of Ormond was pleased by Privy Seal 15.th Jany 1646 & by Patent at Dublin 30.th Mar 1647 to create him Earl of Donegal w.th limitation of honour to the Issue Male of his father, In 1647 he was one of the 4 hostages sent by Orm.^d to the Eng.^l parliam.^t, 2.nd Mar 1660 he was made Captain of a troop of Horse & ye 12.th Custos Rotulorum for the Countys of Antrim & Donegal & 22.^d May 1662 one of the Trustees for the satisfaction of ye personal arrears of the commissioned officers, for Service in Irel.^d before 5.th of June 1649, was Governor of Carickfergus & in 1668 Established a Math.^l Lecture in the Univ: of Dub: & for its maintenance granted to s.^d College for ever the annuity of 30.^{li} Issuing out of the territory of Magherimore &.^c the Lecturer to read Lectures every term & to Instruct all desirous to learn the Mathematicks especially such as should be brought up in ye Schooll of Belfast, Erected by him wherein he made a provision for poor schollars to be brought up in Learning. He dyed at Belfast 18.th March 1674, was buryed at Carickf.^s 20.th May 1675, he bequeathed to the poor of ye parish 50.^{li} & to those of Belfast £200 :—he married 3 wives, his 1.st Dorcas Daughter of Jo.ⁿ Hill Esqr his 2.nd Mary Daugh.^t of Jo.ⁿ Digby 1.st Earl of Bristol & by her had 6 sons & 2 daughters who all dyed young, his 3.rd Letitia Daugh.^r to Sir Wm Hickes, who after marryed Sir Wm Franklyn, he had Issue Wm Ld Chichester, & 3 Daugh.^{rs} who all Dyed young Except the Lady Ann, who became heiress to 2000.^{li} a year, who marryed 1.st Jo.ⁿ Butler Earl of Gowran who leaving her a widow without Issue, she next marryed Francis Aungier Earl of Longford by whom she likewise had no Issue, she dyed ye 14.th Novr 1697. In Eggesford Church there is a most sumptuous Monum.^t Erected to his L.^dships memory where he stands in Just & full proportion in pure alabaster finely polished between his Ladys in Effigy on each hand. His L^d^ship was succeded by his Nephew Sir Arthur Chichester, Eldest son of his Bro^r^ John & was 2nd Earl of Donegal, He married Jane Daughter to John Itchingham of Dunbrody in the Co: of Wexford Esqr who afterward married Richd Booth Esqr [who] She became sole heir to that Estate wch by Act of Parliam^t^ 10th Geo 1st was settled on ye Honble John Chichester Bro^r^ to ye present Earl & his heirs for Ever, He had Issue 4 Sons & 3 Daugh^rs^ vizt Arthur his Successor, John, Edward a clergyman father to the rev^d^ Ar Chichester born 5th Jany 1716 after his decease, Charles, Lady Jane marryed to Davies Lennard Barrett Esq [Mary] Catherine to————Taylor Esqr, Mary to Sr Robt Newcomen. Arthur 3rd Earl of Doneg^l^ commanded a Regim^t^ of foot in the Reign of K: Willm wch being disbanded he had 8^sh^ per diem in consideration of his services

On the 28th June 1701, he was again promoted to a Regim^t^ of foot raised in Ireland, he was sent to Spain to Defend the rights of the house of Austria, he & Baron Palanck were the 1st who set foot on shore wth 12 Grenadiers In Feb^ry^ 1704 the Prince of Hesse conferred on his L^d^ship the Commission of Major Genl of the Spanish forces, & on the 16th & 22^d^ of Augt 1705, he was of the Council of war held on Board the Brittannia concerning the siege of Barcelona for wch he gave his voice, & in Novr was made Governor of the Fortress of Gironne on the River Fer, 15 miles distant from the Sea, & 45 from Barcelona, after many glorious services he lost his life 10th of Ap^r^ 1706 at the fort of Monjuick was buryed at Barcelona, he marryed 1st Lady Barbara Boyle Daughter to ye Earl of Orrery, by whom he had a son Charles who dyed young & she dyed the 20th Novr 1682 & was buryed in St Patricks Dublin, he marryed 2dly in 1685 Lady Catherine Forbes only daughter to Arthur Earl of Granard who dyed at her Seat at Abinger in Surrey wth a large Character 15th June 1743, & was Interred in the vault at Carickfergus, had Issue 2 Sons & 6 Daughters Arthur his successor 4th & present Earl of Doneg^l^. John who was marryed 13th Sepr 1726 to Elizabeth Eldest Daughter to Sr Richd Newdigate of Arbury in Warwickshire, She died at Abinger 15th feby 1747, he was member of Parliam^t^ for Gowran & Belfast in the Reign of K: Geo ye s^nd^, for the latter of wch he was again chosen 14th Novr 1745 & dyed at Bath 1st June 1746 left 2 sons Arthur born 13th June 1739 *created Baron Fisherwick June 19th 1790* John Born 26th Decr 1740 *and died feby 6th 1783 unmarried* & a Daughter. Daughter Lady Catherine born in 1687 was marryed 9th Sepr 1713 to Clotworthy Ld Viscount Massereene. Ladys Jane, Frances, & Henrietta were unfortunately burnt In the house of Belfast by ye carelessness of a serv^t^ who put on a large fire of wood, to air a room she had washed. Lady Mary dyed unmarryed. Lady Ann marryed 12th July 1716 to James Earl of Barrymore

His Lordship was born the 28 Mar: 1695, & 3rd of Octr 1716 Marryed the Lady Lucy Ridgeway, Elder Daugther & Co heir to Robert Earl of Londonderry who dyed 16th July 1732 at Bromfield In Essex, his Lordship had no Issue his Titles are Arthur Chichester, Earl of Donegal, Visc^t^ Chichester of Carickfergus, & Baron Chichester of Belfast, his arms are quarterly, the first & fourth chequce, Topaz and Ruby ; a Chief, Vair ; the Second & 3^d^ Sapphire, Fretteé, pearl—Crest, on a wreath, a Stork, Proper, holding in its Beak, a Snake, pearl, the head gold, supporters, two Wolves Ruby, Ducally gorged & chained Topaz. Motto Invitum Sequitur Honos. or, Honor Sequitur fugientem.

The paper underneath, and that on the other leaf, were taken out of the Belfast News-Letter Dated the 6th of October 1794 by Will Atkinson Town Clerk of the Borough of Belfast.

LIST of the VOLUNTEER COMPANIES and MILITIA that marched to BELFAST to oppofe the French : fet down in the Order of time in which each refpective Corps arrived, from Friday the 22d to Tuefday the 26th of February, 1760.——Thofe marked thus (*) did not accept of pay from the town of Belfaft.

COUNTY OF ANTRIM.

Places where raifed.	Commanders Names,	No. of Men.	Time of Arrival, &c.
*Antrim Volunteers	Lieut. James Finifton, commandant—4 fergeants, 4 corporals, 2 drums.	96	Marched into Belfaft on Friday evening ; all uniformly cloathed, and compleatly armed, with 25 rounds of cartridges.
*Lifburn Volunteers	Edward Smith, Efq. Captain, (who being at Parliament) Lieut. Abraham Crommelin Commandant	130	Received the French prifoners on Thurfday eveng (being then under arms ready to march to Belfaft) guarded them all night, went off with them on Frid. morning to Moyra & Dromore, and came to Belfaft about 5 the fame evening, after a march of 21 miles.
*Killulta	(Thefe and Lifburn Comp. Lord Hertford's tenants.	198	328 Arrived in fevaral parties at different times, and incorporated with Lifburn co. on Saturday. (68 received pay).
Templepatrick Volunteers.	Arthur Upton, Efq. Captain, (who being at Parliament) Henry Shaw, Efq. 1ft Lieut. Commandant.	70	Arrived on Saturday at nine in the morning, and continued till the French failed.
Shane's-Caftle Volunteers.	Charles O'Neil, Efq. Captain, (who being at Parliament) Kenedy Henderfon, Efq. 1ft Lieut. Commandant	94	Arrived on Saturday night, well armed, with 9 rounds of cartridges ; and followed next day by 7 pieces of fmall cannon from Shane's-s-Caftle, which were planted on the breaft-work at Mile-water.
*Carrickfergus Carmoney	Mr James Mc. Ilwean, Captain. Mr. Henry Langford Burleigh, do.	40 55	Guarded the French prifoners from that town to Belfaft. Arrived in Belfaft early in the morning after the French landed.
*Killead	Roger Moore, Efq. Capt.	40	Arrived on Friday, all armed.
In and near Antrim	Mr. Thomas Thompfon, Capt.	133	Volunteers, formed on the occafion, (of which 81 armed) arrived on Saturday—But one ½ recd. pay.
Ballymena—two Companies.	Hugh Campbell and Blainy Adair, Captains.	108	Arrived on Saturday ; and on Tuefday a party of them were fent down the water to reinforce Capt. Dingey, where they remain'd until the French fail'd
Broughfhane	Mr. John White, Capt.	42	Arrived on Saturday night ;—nine of them with fcythes fixed on poles.
*Ballymoney	Charles O'Hara, Efq. Captain (received pay but for 30 men)	76	Arrived on Sunday at 2 in the afternoon, after a march of 38 miles in 24 hours—Mr. O'Hara could have marched 500 brave men had there been arms for them.
Ditto	John Henry, Efq. Capt.	60	Arrived on Monday.
Donegorr	Rev. Patrick Bennett.	28	Arrived on Sunday.
*B:Caftle Volunteers	Hugh Boyd, Efq. Col. Commandant	200	Arrived on Monday, all armed ; & were afterwards join'd by upwards of 150 more, in feveral parties.
Rafharken	John Rowan, Efq. Captain	75	Arrived on Tuefday.
*Belfaft Town, three Companies	James Rofs, Efq. — 82 Stewart Banks, Efq. — 189 Mr. John Brown — 98	369	Marched to Three Mile Water on Saturday morning ; as did all the Companies that were then arrived.

The Corps that affembled at Ballahill, 1¼ mile N. E. of Carrickfergus ; under the care and direction of Robert Dalway, Efq.

Iflemage, Raloo, Glen, Templecorran, Killroot, Ballahill, and C:Fergus liberties	Marriot Dalway, Efq. Capt. Rev. James Dunbar, Mr. Patrick Allen, Lts. Mr. Edward Hudfon, Part of Lord Antrim's Regiment,	200	Affembled on Friday, &c. moft part well armed.
Larne	Adam Johnfton, Efq. Capt. Mr. James Agnew, Lts. Mr —— Blair,	115	435 Arrived at Ballahill on Friday.
Glenarm	—— Myars, Efq. Capt. John Mitchell, Lts. William Higginfon, Rev. Thos. Reed, Enfign.	120	Arrived at Ballahill on Sunday, all in a good uniform, and well armed ; with three pieces of cannon mounted on carriages.

TOTAL Co. ANTRIM. 2249

COUNTY OF DOWN.

Lord Hillfborough's Regiment.

Place	Officers	No.	Notes
*Purdy's Burn	James Willfon (for his father Hill Willfon, Efq. appointed paymafter to the K's forces on that occafion) Captain. Alexander Legg and Thomas Stewart, Efqrs. Lieutenants	195	Arrived in Belfaft on Friday morning, well armed; being the firft confiderable body that came in: entered forthwith on duty, and continued fo until the French failed.
			459
Caftlereagh	Thos. Pottinger, Efq. Capt.	80	- - - Arrived on Friday forenoon.
Hillfborough	Lieut. Dan. Hull, Commandant	184	- - - Arrived on Friday evening at four o'clock.

Lord Rawdon's Regiment.
(under his Lordship's command.)

Place	Officers	No.	Notes
Moyra	His Lordfhip's company 95 / John Stothard, Efqr's ditto 40		- - - Arrived on Friday forenoon.
Dromore, two companies	Coflet Stothard, and James Waddell, Capts. 183	498	Guarded the French prifoners to Banbridge, and arrived in Belfaft on Saturday; 60 of thefe armed with back-fwords and pikes.
Gilford	Achefon Johnfton, Efq. Capt. 90		Arrived Saturday morning; only one half had guns.
Warringftown	Samuel Waring, Efq. Capt. 60		Arrived on Sunday.
Maghralin	Charles Douglas, Efq. Capt. 30		Arrived fame day.

Bernard Ward, Efqr's. Regiment.
In his abfence (being at Parliament) Jno. Echlin, Efq. L.C. Commandt.

Place	Officers	No.	Notes
From Downpatrick, Caftleward, Bangor, Newtown, the Ards, Lecale and Gillhall	Henry Waring / Charles Echlin / Steele Hawthorne / David Caddell / John Magill Efqrs. Capts	350	Thefe, with the Lieutenants and Enfigns of each refpective company, arrived on Saturday.
Waringsford	A Company joined faid regiment	50	Arrived fame day.

James Stevenfon, Efqrs. Regt.

Place	Officers	No.	Notes
Killileagh	In his abfence (he being at Parliament) Robert Blackwood, Efq. Lieut. Col. Commandant 167	349	Arrived on Saturday.
Cumber & Ballybeen	Robert Gillefpie, James Patterfon, and Robt. Kyle, Capts. 135		Thefe three companies arrived on Friday forenoon.
Cumber	John White, Capt. 47		Arrived on Saturday.

Matthew Forde, Efq. Colonel Commandant.

Place	Officers	No.	Notes
Seaford	14	194	
Saintfield	Henry Savage, Efq. Lieut. 50		Arrived on Saturday.

Place	Officers	No.	Notes
Ards Regiment	Francis Savage, Efq. Colonel Commandant.	220	Arrived on Monday at noon, divided into three companies, raifed at Portaferry, Greyabby and Ballywalter; and fame day marched to Bangor to guard the coaft.
Newtown	Arthur Kennedy, Efq. Captain	85	Arrived on Friday forenoon.
Holywood	James Hamilton, Efq. Captain	80	Arrived fame day at 2 in the afternoon.
Donaghadee Volunteers	Hugh Boyd, Efq. Captain	133	Arrived on Saturday; and on Monday marched with feveral other companies, to guard the coaft between Holywood and Donaghadee.
Downpatrick—3 companies Volunteers	John Trotter, Charles Johnfton and Wm Hamilton, Efqrs. Capts.	130	Arrived on Saturday.
*Newry Volunteers	Captain Thomas Braddock	30	Arrived fame morning, on horfeback.

Total from C. DOWN.   2578

COUNTY OF ARMAGH.

Place	Officers	No.	Notes
Lurgan Volunteer Troop of Dragoons	William Brownlow, Efq. Captain; who left Dublin on the firft advice, and put himfelf at their head on Tuefday	140	Received an account at 10 on Thurfday night of the French being landed; marched off a quarter after 12, and arrived at 11 on Friday forenoon, under the command of Jas. Forde, Efq. ift Lieut.
Lylo Volunteers	William Robinfon, Efq. Captain	70	Arrived on Saturday morning.
Rich-hill Volunteers	Thomas Roe, Efq. Captain	114	Arrived on Sunday, on horfeback.
*Armagh Volunteers	Thomas Mc. Cann, Efq. (as Sovereign of Armagh) Captain	100	Set out from Armagh on Saturday evening, on horfeback, all armed, and arrived in Belfaft on Sunday morning at ten o'clock.
*Tandragee	Samuel Blacker, Efq. Captain. (In whofe abfence, being in Dublin) Rev. Geo. Cherry, lieut. Commandt	101	Marched on Saturday morning, and arrived at Belfaft on Sunday morning, led all the way by Mr. Cherry, on foot, after a march of 25 miles.
	Total to ARMAGH	525	(Total of the Three Counties 5352.)

THE Names of the Burgesses who have represented this Borough in the Different Parliaments of this Kingdom from the year 1613

Years	Names
1613	Sir John Blennerhasset K^t 2^d Baron of Exch^r
	George Trevilian Esqr
1639	Sir Willm Wray K^nt & Bar^t
	George Rawdon Esqr
1661	Willm Knight Esqr Counsellor at Law
	Henry Davys Esqr
1692	James MacCartney Esqr
	Geo MacCartney Esqr
1695	Honble Charles Chichester
	James MacCartney Esqr
1703	Willm Crawford Merchant
	Willm Cairnes Merchant Dublin
1707	Willm Crawford Merchant
	Samuel Ogle Esqr
1713	Robt Moore Esqr
	Anthony Atkinson Esqr
1715	The Honble Capel Moore } lost their seats.
	Geo MacCartney Esqr
	by another Indenture
	The Honble Jno Itchingham Chichester } and made their election good
	Geo Macartney Esqr
1721	Geo Macartney Esqr Senr
	Geo Macartney Esqr Junr
1725	The Honble John Chichester
	Geo Macartney Esqr
1727	The Honble David John Barry
1745	Geo Macartney Esqr
	The Honble John Chichester
1747	Geo Macartney Esqr
	Willm Macartney, Esqr
1757	Willm Macartney Esqr
	The Honble Arthur Barry
1761	The Honble John Chichester
	John Ludford Esqr
1768	Honble Henry Skeffington
	Alexr Crookshanks Esqr Judge
1784	Honble Henry Skeffington
	Honble Joseph Hewitt
1790	Honble Henry Skeffington
	Sir Willm Godfrey
1797	Right Honble Lord Spencer Chichester second son to the Marquis of Donegall
	Geo Crookshank Esqr
1798	Alexander Hamilton Esqr in place of Lord Spencer Chichester
1800	Edward May Esqr Father-in-Law to the Marq^s Donegall in place Alex^r Hamilton Esqr

Nota Burgensī de Burgo Belfast

Resignavit	John vesey gent	*mort*	
mort	Sr Tho: Tibbots Kt	*mort*	
mort	John willougby gent	*mort*	1652
mort 13 1	John Asshe gent	—— 1 —— 1	
12 2	Walterhowse Crimble gen	—— 2 —— 2	
mort	George Theaker gent	*mort*	
mort 3	Henry Squire gent	—— 3 *mort*	
mort	Lewys Tomson gent	—— 4 *extr mort*	
mort 4	Robert ffoster gent	*mortuus*	
mort	Thomas Bramston ge	*mort*	
extr	Gowen Bolby gent	*extr mort*	
xs 11 5	John Leithes gent		
mort 6	Thomas Hanington gent	*modo Supr* 1652	
mort	John Wassher gen	*mort*	
10 7	Thomas Theaker gen	*mort*	
mort 8	John Haddock gent	*mort*	
9	Thomas Stephenson gen	*modo Superior mort* 25 Feb 1640	
mort 10	Richard Gately gen	*mortuus* 8th ffeby 1640	
9 11	John Davyes gen	*extr* 1652	1642 elected
8 12	John Mitchell gen	*extr* 1652	1642 Burgesses 4 Dec
7 13	Willm Leythes	decr ffeby 1640 *mort superiorum mort*	
o 6	George Martyn	*ext* 1652	
o 5	Hugh Doake		
o 4	John Leythes junr gen		
mort 3	Thomas Wareinge gen	Ellected and sworn the 24th June 1652	
o 2	John Rigby gen	*mortuus*	
mort	ffrancis Meeke gen	*mortuus*	
o	George M'Cartney gent	& sworne the 17th of Sep 1659	

The names of the Burgesses of the Borrough of Bellfast

x s	William Warring gen ellected and sworne ye 17th of [May] *Apll* 1660
	Edward Raynalls gent ellected and sworne ye 5th of May 1660
x s	Thomas Wallcott gent ellected and sworne ye 24th of June 1660
	Gilbert Wye Esqr elected & sworne a Burgesse of this Corporacion the 18th of September 1662
x s	Francis Thetford gent was elected & sworne a Burgess of this Corporacion the 1t of December 1665
o	George M'Cartney niger was elected and sworn a Burgesse of this Corporacion 1mo Decembris 1665
	Hugh Eccles was elected and sworne a Burgesse of this Corporacion the 2nd December 1667
	Sr Hercules Langfford elected and sworn ye 24 of Ap 1669
	Capt Robert Leathes [gent] was elected and sworne a Burgesse of this Corporacon on the 26th of August 1669
	James M'Cartney Councellor at Law was sellected and sworne a free Burgess ye 19th October 1676
	Henry Thetford gent was elected and sworne a free Burgesse yt 14th of June 1677
	Lewis Thomson gent was elected and sworne a free Burgess ye 25th July 1678
	John Hamilton gent was elected and sworne a free Burgesse ye 25th July 1678
	Capt Edward Harrison was elected and sworne a free Burgesse ye 27th August 1680
	Thomas Knox gent ye 27th August 1680 sworn a free Burgess
	Sampson Theaker gent was elected and sworne a free Burgesse ye 24th June 1681
	Lt John Tooley was elected and sworne ffree Burgesse ye 6th September 1682
	2nd Mar William Crafford was elected and sworne ffree Burgesse the 4th of March 1686
	William Lockart Marcht was elected and sworne free Burgesse the 7th May 1687
	James Buller tanner was elected and sworn a free Burgess ffeb 25-89
	David Smith was elected and sworne a free Burgesse May 26 1690
	Arthur M'Cartney mercht was elected and sworn a free Burgess 1st June 1691
	The Rt Honble Arthur Earle of Donegall was elected and sworn March 7, 1691
	Jno Chalmers mercht was elected and sworn a free Burgesse April 8 1693
	Capt Charles Chichester was elected and sworn a free Burgess 23 December 1697
	23 Dec 1697 Cap Edward Brice was elected & sworne a free Burgess 1697
	Capt John Chichester was elected and sworne a free Burgesse 6th September 1698
	David Butle marchant was elected and sworne a free Burgesse ye 14th October 1700
	Isack M'Cartney marchant was elected and sworne a free Burgesse ye 26th day of Aprill 1701
	George Macartney Esqr councel at Law was sworn Burgess 8br 16 1702
	ffeby 6 1702 neil mcneil apothecary was sworne Burgess

KING JAMES THE FIRST upon the humble Peticion of the Inhabitants of the Towne of Belfast by the consent of Arthur Lord Chichester Barron of Bellfast and Lord deputy Generall of Ireland by his Maj^{ties} Lett^{rs} adated at the Mannor of ffarnegham the last [the last] day of July and of his Raigne of England ffrance and Ireland the fift and of Scotland the 42 & inroled in the Chancery of Ireland Granted a Charter to ye said Inhabitants to make the Towne and precincts of Bellfast one ffree Borrough by the name of the Borrough of Bellfast and within the said Borrough there be one body Corporate & politique consisting of one Soveraigne twelve free Burgises and of the Comonaltie in deed fact and name by the Name of the Soveraigne ffree Burgises and Comonaltie of the Borrough of Bellfast and that by the same name they may have perpetuall Succession the Patten passed ye 27th Ap^l in ye eleaventh of his Raigne.

The names of the first Soveraigne and Burgisses named in the Charter and the rest that succeeded to ye year 1698.

Names		The Time when made Burgises		The time when they were Soveraignes beginning at Michaelmas *& ending* in ye year anexed to their names
John Vesey Gent				first Soveraigne 1613
Sr ffulk Conway Kt				
Sr Thomas Hibbetts Kt Stewart to Arthur Chichester Lord Deputy of Ireland				
Sr Moses Hill Kt				
Humphrey Norton Esqr		Burgesses by Charter 27 April 1613		
William Lewsley:	gent			
John Willowbye:	gent			1614
Carew Hart:	gent	The Lord of the Castle		1627, 1617, 1618
John Assh:	gent	of Belfast for ye time		1646
Dannill Booth:	gent	being and his heires		
James Burr:	gent	& the Constable of y^e		1615. 1616
Walterhouse Crimble:	gent	said Castle for y^e		1630 removed for 16 years absences anno 1662
John Burr.	gent	time being are ffree Burgesses by Charter		
Edward Holmes	gent			in ye years 1622. 1623
left 40l ster to ye poore being ye first money left in ye kinde				
George Theaker	gent			1619: 1620
Lewis Thomson	gent			in 1631. 1634, removed for being alienated out of this Kingdom 6 years
Skyte	gent			
Henry Le Squire	gent			
Stewart and Constable to Ld Edward Chichester				1635. 36: 39
Robert ffoster	gent			1632: 44: 48
Thomas Bramston	gent			1633.
Lewis Thomson	gent			1634
Gawen Boltby	gent			removed for absence
John Leathes Senior	gent			1638: 55
Thomas Hanington	gent			1641: 50: 51
John Wassher	gent			1637:
Seneschall to Ld Edward				
Thomas Theaker	gent			1643: 54
John Haddock	gent			1640:
In place of Gawen Boltby Richard Gatley	gent	8	ffeby 1640	
In place of John Willoughby Thomas Bradley	gent			
Thomas Stephenson	gent	8	ffeby 1640	1642
In place of Lewis Thomson John Davis	gent	4	December 1642	

	The Names			The time when made Burgisses			The yeares when they were Soveraignes
In place of Thomas Bramston	John Mitchell	gent	4	Dec^r	1642		
In place of John Wassher	William Leathes	gent	4	Dec^r	1642		in 1645-57-58 & 59 and dyed in May 1660 Captain Meeke served the remainder
In place of Henry Le Squire	George Martin	gent	30	Octo^r	1645		in 1649
In place of John Haddock	Hugh Doake	gent	30	Octo^r	1645		in 1647
In place of Thomas Stephenson	John Leathes Junior	gt	18	June	1646		
	Thomas Warring [after] high Sherrife of the County Antrim	gent	24	June 1652 chosen Soveraigne ye same day that he was chosen Burgess			in 1652-53-56-65-66 & in that year dyed. Edward Reynell served ye remainder
In place of Thomas Hannington	John Ridgby ye first Soveraigne made Justice of Peace of the County Antrim wch still continues to ye Soveraigne for the time being	gent	17	Sep^r	1655		in 1661 for ye year ending 1662:
In place of Richd Gately	Capt ffrancis Meeke Constable of the Castle of Bellfast		13	June	1657		in 1660
In place of John Ash who dyed May 16 1658: vide Church Registry	Capt George M'Cartney Justice of the County of Antrim & High Sherriffe of the same		17	Sep^r	1659		in 1663-64-68-69-76-77 & 78 79 & 80.
	William Warring Justice of Peace & High Sherriffe of ye Co Antrim	gent	17	April	1660		in 1670-71
	Edward Reynell[s]	gent	5	May	1660		in 1667
In place of William Leathes	Thomas Wallcott Steward to Lord Edward & Arthur ffirst Earle of Donegall	gent	25	June	1660		in 1672
In place of Walterhouse Crimble	Gilbert Wye gent Stewart to Arthur first Earle of Donegall		18	Sept^r	1662		resigned anno 1680
In place of Thomas Warring	ffrancis Thetford	gent	1	December	1665		in 1681
In place of Francis Meeke	George M'Cartney *niger* high Sherrif of the Co Antrim	gent	1	Dec^r	1665		in 1673-74 & 1701
In place of John Davies	Hugh Eccles high Sherrife Co Downe	gent	2	Dec^r	1667		in 1675
In place of Jno. Rigby	Sr Hercules Langford Justice of Peace and High Sherrife of the County of Antrim		24	Aprill	1669		resigned in favour of Capt Edward Harrison
In place of Hugh Doake	Capt Robert Leathes Justice of Peace of the County Antrim Seneschall of the Mannor of Bellfast & Constable of the Castle of Bellfast		26	Augt	1669	The word blotted is five dayes	in 1686-87-88-89-90 & 97 and in 1714: resigned anno 1717. ye 14 of June [his Roy] 1690 [his] his Royall Majesty Kinge William landed at Carrickfergus & that day came to Bellfast & received with great aclamacions of Joy & stayed *five* dayes in Bellfast ye Soveraigne & Burgesses had ye honor of kissing his Maj^{ties} hand, he stayd 5 five dayes:
In place of Wm Warring	James M'Cartney Councellor at Law, Justice of Peace of ye County Antrim & Seneschall of the Mannor of Bellfast memb^r of Parliament for ye same and at lenth one of ye Justices of ye Kings Bench		19	Octob^r	1676		in 1692 resigned anno 1715
In place of Jno Leathes Senior	Henry Thetford	gent	14	June	1677		
In place of Henry Thetford	Lewis Thomson	gent	25	July	1678		in 1682: 1696:

	The Names		The time when made Burgisses		The yeares when they were Soveraignes
In place of George Martin	John Hamilton gent	25	July	1678	in 1683-84
In place of Sr Hercules Longford	Capt Edward Harrission *(sic)* High Sherrife and Justice of Peace of the County Antrim	27	Aug⁸ᵗ	1680	in 1695
In place of Gilbert Wye	Thomas Knox Justice of Peace and high Sherrife of the County Antrim and Member of Parliamᵗ	27	Aug⁸ᵗ	1680	in 1685 resigned his Burgess ship Anno 1697
In place of Hugh Eccles	Sampson Theaker gent	24	June	1681	
In place of Ed: Reynalls	Lt John Tooley	6	April	1682	
In place of Jno Hamilton	William Craford gent Parliament man for Belfast	4	May	1686	in 1693:94 removed for not being qualified according to yᵉ Statute
In place of John Tooley	William Lockhart gent	7	May	1687	in 1691
In place of Thos Walcoat	James Buller gent	25	ffeby	1689	
In place of Francis Thetford	Capt David Smith	26	May	1690	in 1699 & 1700
In place of George M'Cartney	Arthur M'Cartney gent	1	June	1691	
In place of Sampson Theaker	The Rt Honoᵇˡᵉ [The third] Arthur *the third* Earle of Donegall	7	March	1691	in 1698 resigned anno 1697
In place of Jno Leathes	John Chalmers gent	8	April	1693	in 1702 removed for not being qualified according to the Statute
In place of Arthur 3d Earle of Donegall	The Honoᵇˡᵉ Capᵗ Charles Chichester brother to yᵉ said Earle [who] was made Burgesse in his Lordships place who resigned being then Lord of the Castle of Bellfast	23	Decʳ	1697	for yᵉ yeare ending Micalmas 1700 but being absent at Michaellmas in London Mr David Smith continued Soveraigne for that yeare
In place of Thomas Knox	Capt Edward Brice gent Member of Parliament	23	Decʳ	1697	removed for not being qualified according to the Statute
In place of Wm Lockhart	The Honoᵇˡᵉ Capt John Chichester brother to yᵉ said Earle Member of Parliament for Bellfast & Col of Militia	6	Sep	1698	for yᵉ year 1712 but being in England Roger Haddock continued Sovereign for yᵉ year
Pat Duff	Richard Willowby gent Constable of the Castle wᶜʰ made him Burgesse by Charter Patrick Duffe gent Constable of the Castle Burgesse by Charter				
In place of Capt Edward Harrison	David Buttell gent	14	October	1700	in 1703 & 1704 surrendered up the rod yᵉ 29 of July 1704 by a late Act of Parliamᵗ disabling dissenters to serve in publique office and succeded for the remainder of that yeare by George M'Cartney Esqʳ Councellor at Law
In place of Capt Charles Chichester Colonel of Militia	Isacke M'Cartney gent	26	Aprill	1701	resigned anno 1707 in favour of Jno Hallridge Esqʳ
In place of Geo M'Cartney niger	George M'Cartney Esqʳ Councellor at Law and Justice of Peace of the County of Antrim	16	October	1702	part of yᵉ yeare 1704 in Mr. Buttles place & for yᵉ yere 1705 and 1706 and 1707 & 1708
In place of James Buller	Neile McNeile gent	6	ffeby	1702	removed for not being qualified according to the Statute
In place of David Smith	Capt Michael Harrison Comissary Generall of the Musters	6	August	1705	
In place of Arthr M'Cartney	The Honoᵇˡᵉ John Chichester yᵉ second sonn to yᵉ Rt Honoᵇˡᵉ Arthur the 3d Earle of Donegall	21	December	1706	removed being a minor and not capable of qualifying under the Statute

The Names		The time when made Burgisses			The yeares when they were Soveraignes
In place of Isaac M'Cartney	John Haltridge Esqʳ High Sheriff of Down & Justice of the peace & membʳ of Parliamt	24	Aprill	1707	
In place of Wm Crawford	Nathaniell Byrtt gent yᵉ place of William Craford Esqʳ not qualyfied according to act of Parliamt	29	Novemʳ	1707	1725: dyed in his year yᵉ remainder served out by Doctor James M'Cartney
In place of Edward Brice	Richard Willson gent in place of Edward Brice Esq not quallified &c	˙9	Novʳ	1707	1709
In place of David Butle	Ensigne George Portis in place of David Buttle not qualyfied &c	29	Noveʳ	1707	
In place of Neal M'Neal	Lᵗ Henry Ellis in place of Neile McNeile not quallyfied &c	29	Noveʳ	1707	1717: 1720: 1722: dyed in this yeare no Sovereign for yᵉ remainder of his year nor for yᵉ following yeare 1723 vide page 279
In place of Jno Chichester Esq	James Gurner gent in place of John Chichester Esq brother to yᵉ 4th Earl of Donegall not quallyfied	26	Novemʳ	1707	1715: 1716:
In place of Jno Chalmers	Roger Haddock gent in place of John Chalmers not quallyfied &c	17	ffeby	1707/8	1710:1711:1712: resigned his Burgess-ship anno 1713
In place of Lewis Thomson	Nicholas Thetford gent in place of Mr Lewis Thomson	17	ffeby	1707	on yᵉ 29th of November he was chosen in place of Wm Craford not qualified according to Statute, But refusing a Burgess ship coming in such manner; He was again chosen yᵉ February after anno 1707 in place of Lewis Thompson deceased.
In place of Michael Harrison	*Major* George Macartney gent Atturney in *place* of Capt Michaell Harrison ellected and sworne yᵉ 7 day May 1709 He was Justice of yᵉ peace and Parliament man for Belfast	2	May	1709	1724: dyed in his year ye remainder served out by Nathaniel Byrt Esqᵣ
In place of Richard Willson	Hans Hamilton gent in yᵉ place of Richard Willson ellected and sworne the 8th day of December 1711 High Sheriffe of yᵉ County of Ardmagh and Down Justice of the peace and member of Parliament	8	Decemb	1711	1713:
	Tho Bankes gent Constable of the Castle of Belfast & tooke yᵉ oath of a Burgess	8	Decemb	1711	
	Robert Le Byrtt gent Constable of the Castle of Belfast & tooke the oath of a Burgess	24	June	1712	As to yᵉ office of Constable of the Castle It is so changeable ·& so many successions that were they entered regularly, as often as new appoynted, They would fill up of themselves several pages.
In place of Roger Haddock	Robert Le Byrt gent	28	Xbʳ	1713	1721:1734-1735-1739-1740-1743
	Thom Hewitson	27	May	1718	
In place of Judge McCartney	Edward Clements Esqr High Sheriff of yᵉ County of Antrim and Justice of yᵉ peace for sᵈ County and Major of Militia	16	August	1715	
In place of Edwd Clements	James M'Cartney				pᵗ 1725 & 1726
In place of Captn Robert Leaths	Jno Carpenter gent	13	April	1717	1718:1719:
In Room of Harry Ellis Deceas'd	John Clugstone Honᵇˡᵉ Jo Skeffington	12	Novr	1723	pᵗ of 1726 & 1727-1728-1732-1733

	The Names	The time when made Burgisses.			The yeares when they were Soveraignes
Mich Thetford Deceas'd	Gen¹ Nich⁵ Price	12	Novʳ	1723	
Jas Gurner Deceas'd	Chaˢ Macartney	12	Novʳ	1723	
Geo Portis Deceas'd	Jaˢ Read	12	Novʳ	1723	
Geo Macartney Junr Deceas'd	Honbˡᵉ John Chichester	11	Augᵗ	1724	*Mort*
John Haltridge Deceas'd	Crom¹ Price	16	febʳʸ	1724	*Mort*
Nathl Byrtt Deceas'd	Ezek¹ Davis Wilson	27	Sepʳ	1725	*Mort*
Dr Jas Macartney Deceas'd	John Duff	18	Sepʳ	1727	1730-1741-1742-1747 pᵗ of 1753 dyed in the office
Jas Read Deceas'd	Thoˢ Banks	18	Sepʳ	1727	1729
Hans Hamilton Deceas'd	Arthur Byrtt	12	May	1729	1731-1744-1745-1746-1752-[1754] 1757 *Mort*
Jon Carpenter Deceas'd	Arthur Thetford	20	May	1729	*Mort*
Ar Thetford Deceas'd	Margetson Saunders	17	May	1733	1736-1737-1738-1748-54 *Mort*
Genl Price Deceas'd	Wᵐ Montgomery of Rosemount	30	July	1735	*Mort*
Ezek Da Wilson Deceas'd	Valentine Jones of Lisburn	2	May	1738	*Mort*
John Clugston Deceas'd	Davys Wilson	4	May	1738	*Mort*
Honble John Skeffington Deceas'd	Honbˡᵉ Arthʳ Skeffington	27	Sept	1742	*Mort*
Robt Byrtt Deceas'd	Wm Macartney	17	febʸ	1745	resigned in July 1770
Thos Banks Deceas'd	Stewart Banks	26	May	1746	1755-1758-1762-1766-1771
Honble John Chichester Deceas'd	Geo Macartney Mercht	22	Sepʳ	1745	1749-1750-1751-1756-1759-1763-1764-1765-1767-1768 *Mort*
Honble Arthur Skeffington Deceas'd	Jos Green	6	8ber	1747	*Mort*
John Duff Deceas'd	Honbˡᵉ Arthʳ Barry	31	Octbr	1753	*Mort*
Wm Montgomery Deceas'd	John Gordon	6	June	1755	Resigned
Margetson Saunders Deceas'd	Stephen Haven	6	Sepᵗ	1757	1760-1770 *Mort*
Jos Green Deceas'd	Jaˢ Hamilton	6	Sepᵗ	1757	1761-1769 *Mort*
George Macartney Deceas'd	John Ludford	3	Decʳ	1757	Resigned in July 1775
In place of Charles Macartney Esq deceased	Thoˢ Ludford Esqr	15	March	1759	Resigned in July 1770
In place of Davys Wilson Esqr deceased	The Honbˡᵉ John Chichester Brother to yᵉ present Right Honbˡᵉ Arthur 5ᵗʰ Earl of Donegall	17	July	1760	*Mort*
In place of Valentine Jones Esqr deceased	James Lewis	1	April	1761	Sovʳⁿ for 1773-1777 *Mort*
In place of John Gordon resigned	The Honbˡᵉ Hungerford Skeffington	8	Sept	1767	*Mort*
In place of Honble Hungerfd Skeffington Deceased	Revd Jams Saurin	30	Sep	1768	*Mort*

	The Names	The time when made Burgisses.		The yeares when they were Soveraignes
In place of Wm Macartney resigned	George Portis	26	July 1770	
In place of John Ludford resigned	George Black	26	July 1770	Sov^n for 1774 1775 1776 1782 1783 1785
In place of Tho Ludford resigned	Shem Thomson	26	July 1770	Sov^n for 1772 *Mort*
In place of James Hamilton deceased	Rev Wm Tisdall Justice of peace for the County of Antrim	26	July 1770	*Mort*
Hble Arth: Barry	The Honble Henry Skeffington	18	July 1774	Justice of peace for the County of Antrim
Revd James Saurin	Rev Will: Bristow: Justice of peace for the County of Antrim	18	July 1774	1786-1787-1788-1790-1791-1792- 1793-1794-1795-1796-1798
Arth Byrt	Samuel Black	18	July 1774	Sov for 1779-1780-1781-1784-1789
Shem Thompson	Henry Joy	1	May 1781	*Mort*
Crom Price	Edward Patterson	1	May 1781	resigned in Sept 1793
John Chichester	Edward Kingsmill	28	Octr 1786	Justice of the peace for the Counties of Down and Antrim
James Lewis	Robt Apsley M D.	28	Octr 1786	
Stephen Haven	Chichester Skeffington	29	Sept 1792	
George Macartney	John Brown	29	Sept 1792	1797-1799-1800-1801 *Mort*
Henry Joy	E D Wilson	21	April 1796	
Will Tisdall	Rev Geo Macartney LLD	21	April 1796	carried to page 187

	Names continued from page 236	The time of their being made Burgesses		The time when they were Soveraigne Magistrate
In place of Saml Black deceased	Geo Bristow	2	Decem^r 1797	
In place of Revd E Patterson resigned	Rev Snowden Couples	2	Decr 1797	
E Kingsmill	Ld Spencer Chichester	18	Ap^l 1799	*dead*
Geo Portis	Ed^d May	18	Ap^l 1799	24 Septr 1802 *Dead*
Thos Saunders	Art, Chichester			resigned
Geo Black	Sir Wm Kirk Kt	17	feby 1801	*dead*
Honble Chichester Skeffington resigned	Art Chichester	15	June 1801	1802
Art Chichester	Honble Chichester Skeffington	15	June 1801	*dead*
Jno Brown	Thos L Stewart	5	May 1802	
Stewart Banks	E May Junr	24	June 1806	30th October 1806 *dead*
R Apsley	Rev^d R Wolsely	1	Augt 1806	
Revd W Bristow	Thomas Verner	16	March 1810	24th June 1812
Earl Massereene	And^r Alexander	22	Novr 1811	
Sir Ed May	Sir Stephen May	23	Sept 1814	13 March 1815

Electo Superiorum

1632 **Robert ffoster** gent one of the Burgesses of the Burrough of Bellfast was by Lawfull p'sentacion from the right Honble Edward Lord Viscount Chichester the 24th day of June Anno d^ni 1632 elected and chosen in the office of a Sovraigne of the said Burrough and to take his oathe uppon the ffeaste of St Michaell tharchangell next ensueinge for the due execucion thereof for one whole yeare from thence to be compleate and ended according to the tyme in and by his Maj^ties Charter granted to the said Burrough lymitted

1633	**Thomas Bramston**	⎫
1634	**Lewys Tomson**	
1635	**Henry Le=Squire**	
1636	**Henry Le=Squire**	
1637	**John Wassher**	
1638	John Leythes	(A similar entry to the one above
1639	**Henry Le Squire**	occurs after each name followed by
1640	**John Haddocke**	periods, but is here omitted for
1641	Thomas Hanington	brevity.)
1642	Thomas Stephenson	
1643	Thomas Theaker	
1644	Robt ffoster	⎭

Juratio Superiorium

1632 **Robert ffoster** gent one of the Burgisses of Bellfast was the XXIXth daie of September Anno Dni 1632 sworne in the office of a Soveraigne for the Burrough aforesaid before John Wassher gentleman Constable of the Castle for the tyme being and so continued in the said office for one whole yeere from thence next ensueinge

1633 **Thomas Bramston** . . . . sworn before John Wassher (A similar entry to the one above occurs after each name followed by periods.)

1634 **Lewys Thomson** . . . . sworn before Henry Le Squire Constable of the Castle

1635 **Henry Le=Squire** . . . . sworne before John Wassher

1636 Henry Le Squyre . . . . sworne before the R^t Honble Ld Viscount Chichester

1637 John Wassher . . . . sworne before Henry Le Squire Constable of the Castle

1638 John Leathes . . . . sworne before Henry Le Squire Constable of the Castle

1639 Henry Le Squyre . . . . sworne before the Rt Honble Ld Viscount Chichester

1640 John Haddock . . . . sworne before the R^t Honble Ld Viscount Chichester

1641 Thomas Hanington . . . . sworne before the R^t Honble Ld Viscount Chichester

1642 Thomas Stephenson . . . . sworne before the R^t Honble Ld Viscount Chichester

1644 Robte ffoster . . . . sworne before ffrancis Meeke Captane Constable of the Castle

1645 Willm Leathes gentl one of the Burgesses of the Borrough and Towne of Belfast by lawfull p'sentacion from Captain ffrancis Meeke Constable of the Castle of Belfast in the absence of the right hono^ble Edward Lord Viscount Chichester upon the 24th day of June 1645 was elected and chosen in the office of Sovraigne of the said Borrough and to take his oath upon the 29th day of Septemb^r next ensueinge for the due execucion thereof for one whole yeare from thence to be compleat & ended according to the tyme in his Ma.ᵗ Charter granted to the said Borrough lymitted these Burgesses hereafter named being uppon the Elleccion

Robte ffoster Sovraigne

ffrancis Meeke Constable

John Ash gen [whose name & hand was written hearunto without any consent of mine witness my hand   John : Ayshe : sovran]

Thomas Hanington gen   Richard Gately gen   John Mitchell gen   George Martyn gen   Hugh Doak gen

> This writing above defaced was found to be indiscreetly writen by Mr Ash and therefore ordered to be raced by the Sovraigne & Burgesses

Richard Gatlie   Thomas Hanington HD   George Martyn Tho Theaker   Rob Foster

Willm Leathes gentleman one of the Burgesses of the Borrough and Towne of Belfast uppon the 29ᵗʰ day of September 1645 was sworne in the office of Sovraigne of the said Borrough wᵗⁱin the Castle of Belfast before Major Coughran then Comander in Cheefe there and from him did receave the staffe for to continue in the said office for one whole yeare yf hee soe long live

[this oath was given by maior Coughran contrary to our Charter and Improperly taken by Mr Leathes]

Likewise this entry of Mr Ash ordered to be raced by the Sovrainge & Burgesses

Hugh HD Doake   Rob Foster   Thomas Hanington   Tho Theaker   Richard Gatlie George Martyn

1646 John Ash gentleman one of the Burgesses of the Burrough and Towne of Belfast by lawfull pʳsentacion from Captain ffrancis Meeke Constable of the Castle of Belfast aforesaide in the absence of the right Honoble Edward lord Viscount Chichester uppon the 24th daye of June 1646 was ellected and chosen in the office of Sovraigne of the said Borrough and to take the oath of [the] a Sovraigne uppon the 29th of Septembr next ensueinge for the due execucion thereof for one whole yeare from thence to be compleat and ended accordinge to the tyme in his Maties letters patents granted to the saide Borrough lymitted.   These Burgesses hereafter named being uppon the Elleccion

Willm Leithes Sovr 1646

Thomas Hanington   Richard Gately   George Martin   hew doak   John Leese ffra: Meeke   John Michell   Rob Foster   Jo: Leithes

1646 John Rigby gent one of the free Burgesses of ye Borrough and Towne of Belfast uppon the 24th day of September 1646 was sworne in the office of Soveren in the Castle of Bellfast before Capt ffrancis Meeke Constable of the Castle of Bellfast and to continew in the said office for one whole yeare yf he so long live

John Ayshe Sovern

1647 Hugh Doake gent one of the Burgesses of Belfast uppon the 29th of September 1647 was sworne in the office of Soveraigne of the said Borrough wᵗⁱⁿ the Castle of Belfast before Caᵗ ffrancis Meeke Connstable of the Castle in the absence of the right honorble Edward Lord Viscount Chichester and to continue in ye said office for one whole yeare yf hee soe long shall continue in the said office

1648 Robert ffoster . . . . (A similar entry to the one above occurs after each name followed by periods.)

1649 George Marten . . . .

1650 Thomas Hanington . . . sworn before Ca: ffrancis Meeke by authority and order from Col Robert Venables commander in cheiff wᵗʰin these parts of Ulster

1651 Thomas Hanington . . . . sworne before Capt ffrancis Meeke

1652 Thomas Warringe . . . . sworne before Capt ffrancis Meeke

1653 Thomas Wareinge . . . . sworne before Capt ffrancis Meeke

1654 Thomas Theaker . . . . sworne before Capt ffrancis Meeke

1655 John Leythes sen . . . . sworne before Capt ffrancis Meeke

Att an Assemblye by the Sovʳane and major pᵗˢ of the Burgesses the 17th daye of Septembʳ 1655 upon the Ellection of a Burgess in the place and roome of Mr Thomas Hanington deceased late one of the Burgesses by consent of the right honorᵇˡᵉ Arthur Lord Viscount Chichester and by the Elleccion of Mr Thomas Theaker then Sovʳane of the Borrough of Belfast and the major pᵗˢ of the Burgesses then beinge Mr

John Rigby was ellected and sworne a ffree Burgesse of the said Borrough in the rome of the said Mr. Hanington according to the libtyes & privileidges of the said Towne wch said Sov^rane & major p^{te} of Burgesses then p^rsent uppon the said Elleccion have hereunto subscribed their names the daye and yeare above said

Tho Theaker Sov^raine

Willm Leithes 1655   George Martin   Richard Walle Towne Clerk   John Leithes
John Michell   Tho Waring   × Richard Gateley m^{rke}

1656   Thomas Wareinge elected and sworn as Sovereign . . . .

1657   Att an Assembly houlden the 13th of June 1657 by the Sov^rane & Burgesses for the Ellection of a Burgess in the rome of Mr Richard Gateley late Burgess deceased Captane ffrancis Meeke was ellected and sworne in the office of a Burgess of the said Borrough of Belfast in the p^rsence of the Sov^rane & Burgesses whose names are as hereafter followeth

Tho Wareing Sov^rane

Willm Leythes   George Marten   Hugh Doake   John Leythes Senr   Tho Theaker

1657   Willm Leathes elected and sworn as Sovereign . . . . (A similar entry to the one above occurs after each name followed by periods)

1658   William Leathes elected and sworn as Sovereign . . . .

1659   William Leathes gent was sworn in ye office of the Sofferaigne of the Borrough of Bellfast the 29th day of September 1659 according to the use and custome of the said Towne for the due execucion of his said office before Capt ffrancis Meeke Constable of the Castle of Bellfast in ye absence of the right honor^{ble} Arthur Lord Viscount Chichester of Carrickfergus and Earle of Donnegall and is to continue in the said office for one whole year according to ye time limitted by the Charter if he shall soe longe live but on ye 6th day of May 1660 he departed this life in Bellfast where great Lamentaⁿ. was made for ye Losse of soe honest just and upright man and eminent in his place being ever a support to ye needy fatherlesse and widdows ye next day following appointed for his buriall was carryed by eight of his surname payr^d in Brothers accompannyed by ye R^t Honnor^{ble} ye Earle of Donnegall & ye Marquisse of Antrim with ye greatest part of ye Inhabitants of Bellfast and many others, there was placed on his hearsse eight Scuchens of his Armes with ye white rod of Justice and ye two Maces of ye Corporacon mourning Ribbon was dealt [in] plentyfull all performed by his sonns and after he was interr'd and his funerall sermon preached Capt ffrancis Meeke one of the Burgesses of ye Corporacon by ellection with consent of ye R^t Honno^{ble} ye Earle of Donnegall was sworne in ye office of Soveraigne of ye Borrough afforesaid to continue till ye ffeast of St Michaell ye Archangell next following

1660   Capt ffrancis Meeke . . . . (see preceding note) Elected and Sworn as Sovereign before Thomas Walcott Constable of the Castle

1661   John Rigby elected and sworn as Sovereign before the Right Honourable Arthur Lord Viscount Chichester he was allsoe made Justice of peace for ye County of Antrim as he was Soveraigne of Bellfast and the Soveraignes for ye time being successively are to be Justices of Peace as afforesaid

1662   George M'Cartney . . . . elected and sworn as Sovereign before Capt Meeke Constable of the Castle

1662   George M'Cartney gent was sworne and made Justice of peace for ye County of Antrim by vertue of ye Comission of ye peace und^r ye great Seale of Ireland and to continue dureing his Soveraignty of ye said Borrough

1663   George M'Cartney . . . . elected and sworn as Sovereign before Thomas Walcott Constable of the Castle

1664   Tho Warring . . . . elected and sworn as Sovereign before Michael Harrison Constable of the Castle

1665   Thomas Waring . . . . elected and sworn as Sovereign before Michael Harrison

1666   Thomas Waring . . . . But on the three and Twentyeth day of November following he departed this life in Belfast

And Edward Reynell gent one of the Burgesses of this Corporacon was the first day of December next following by elleccion and with the consent of the Right Hono^{ble} the Earle of Donegall sworne Soveraigne of the said Borrough and to continue in the sayd office untill the feast of St Michaell next following

1666   Edward Reynell Esqr aforesayd one of y^e Burgesses of Belfast on y^e 24th of June 1666 by Lawfull p^rsentacon from y^e R^t Hono^{ble} Arthur Earle of Donegall & was elected and chosen to y^e office of Soveraigne of Belfast afforesaid for one whole yeare from y_e 29th of September next following

R

1667 Edward Reynell Esqr afforesaid . . . . sworn before the Rt Honble the Earl of Donegall

1668 George M'Cartney . . . .
1669 George M'Cartney . . . .
1670 William Warring . . . .
1671 William Warring . . . .
1672 Thomas Wallcott . . . .
1673 George M·Cartney . . . .
1674 George M'Cartney . . . .
1675 Hugh Eccles . . . .

(A similar entry to the one above occurs after each name followed by periods)

1676–81 George M'Cartney Esqr a Burgess of this Corporacon was elected and sworne Soveraigne for yᵉ yeare ending Michaellmas 1676. After elected and sworne from yeare to yeare successively till yᵉ end of yᵉ yeare 1681

1682 ffrancis Thetford Burgesse ellected and sworne Soveraigne for yᵉ yeare end Michaellmas 1682

1683 Lewis Thomson Burgesse was elected and sworne Soveraigne for the year end Michaelmas 1683

1684–1685 John Hamilton gent one of the Burgesses of the Corporacon of Bellfast was elected and sworne Soveraigne for the yeare ending Michaellmas 1684 and after was ellected and sworne Soveraigne for yᵉ yeare end Michaellmas 1685

1686 Thomas Knox Burgess was elected and sworne Soveraigne for the yeare end Michaellmas 1686

1687–1688–1689–1690 Capt Robᵗ Leathes Burgesse was elected and sworne Soveraigne for the yeare end Michaellmas 1687 afterwards ellected and sworne from yeare to yeare successively till yᵉ end of yᵉ yeare at Michaelmas 1690. That Thomas Pottinger a marchᵗ & ffreeman *of Bellfast* without yᵉ consent of the Lord of the Castle Soveraigne Burgesses and Comonallity of the Borrough of Bellfast procured a new Charter from King James then in Ireland in yᵉ yeare 1689 *upon* and yᵉ said Thomas Pottinger was made yᵉ first Soveraigne and thirty five Burgesses vizᵗ Neil oNeil Barrᵗ Marke Talbott Esqʳ Daniel ôNeil Esqʳ Charles ôNeil Esqʳ ffelix ôNeil Esq John ôNeil de Ballyboran Esqʳ Daniell M'Naten Esqʳ James Wogan Esqʳ James Netervile Esqʳ John Savage Esqʳ Martin Gernen Esqʳ John M'Nachton Esqʳ Æneas Moylin Esqʳ George M'Cartney Esqʳ John oNeil gent Toul oNeil gent Patrick Moylin Phisicⁿ Charles Mulhollan gent Abraham Lee gent George M'Cartney merchᵗ Thomas Knox James Shaw William Lockard William Dobbin Edward Pottinger Peter Knowles John ffletcher John Eccles William Craford Henry Chads Humphrey Dobbin David Smith Hugh Eccles and John Chalmers in which Charter there is a proviso that yᵉ Lord Deputy generall or other Cheife Governors of Ireland with yᵉ Privy Councell have power to amove or remove the Soveraigne or Burgesses or any of them or any other officer in yᵉ said Borrough *att their* will and good pleasure from their respective offices and places of trust & that noe Recorder or Towne Clerk of the Borrough afforesaid that shall be elected and chosen by yᵉ Soveraigne & Burgesses afforesaid for the Borrough afforesaid [shall not] be admitted till he or they be approved of by the Cheife Governor or [Cheife] Governors afforesaid soe that it appeares plainly by the said proviso that the Soveraigne and Burgesses Recorder Towne Clarke Sargents at Mace and any other officer of the said Borrough without any fault comitted or offence given may at any time be laid asside or removed at the pleasure of the Cheife Governor or Governors & privy Councell of Ireland afforesaid anythinge to the contrary thereof notwithstanding O brave Thomas Pottinger who did not consider the sollem oath of a freeman he had taken to maintaine all the rights and privelidges of the Corporacon granted by the old Charter by wᶜʰ the Corporacon was governed by a Soveraigne and twelve Burgesses beside yᵉ Earle of Donegall Lord of the Castle of Bellfast and the Constable thereof who are Burgesses by yᵉ old Charter That upon Landing of their Majᵗⁱᵉˢ Army at Bangor in yᵉ County of Downe yᵉ fifteenth day of August one thousand six hundred and eighty nine undeʳ comand of his Grace [ffrederick Duke] ffredrick *Duke of* Sconberg genᵣall of their Majᵗⁱᵉˢ fforces when he came to Bellfast he issued a Proclamacion bearing date yᵉ fourteenth September one thousand six hundreḍ eighty nine impowring and comandinge all Protestant subjects to retourne to their severall and respective propertyes and their respective Corporacons to their antient Charters and the severall Protestant Justices of the peace to their respective trust impowring them to doe and execute all things they might or could doe by vertue of their Charters and Comissions of the peace pursuant to wᶜʰ proclamacion Capt Robert Leathes the last Soveraigne of the old Charter at yᵉ time when yᵉ new one was brought to Bellfast Tooke upon him againe yᵉ Governmᵗ and magistracy of the Corporacon as formerly & continued therein till

Michaellmas one thousand [seven] *six* hundred and ninety 1690 in wch yeare ye fourteenth day of June one thousand six hundred and ninety his most gracious and Puissant Maj^{tie} Kinge William Landed at Carrickfargus & that same day his Maj^{tie} and Duke Sconberge in a Coach came to Bellfast (the Towne at that time being full of his Maj^{ties} Army and Traine of Artillary besides many hospitalls of sick sold^{rs} from ye Camp of Dundalke) was received at ye entrance of the Towne by the Soveraigne Burgesses and Inhabitants of the Corporacon and that part of the Armey then in their best formallitys with acclamacions of great joy and rejoyceing and was conducted to ye Castle where he graciously received the Soveraigne & Burgesses where ye Soveraigne upon his Knee humbly presented the Rod of authority wch his Maj^{tie} received bidding him rise and gave it back againe and ye Soveraigne againe kneeling presented an addresse of the Soveraigne Burgesses and Comonality wch was [red] *read* before his Maj^{tie} and after received it and the Kinge put it in his Pockett and then the Soveraigne and Burgesses had the honor of Kissing his Maj^{ties} hand That his Maj^{tie} stayed five nights in Bellfast and was very *well* pleased with the Inhabitants and the Towne and its cittivation and said (when within the Castle and the doors being open to ye garden) that was litle Whitehall—it cannot be omitted to tell that the Soveraigne intended to acquainte his Maj^{tie} that the Corporacon had neither Lands Tenem^{ts} hereditam^{ts} Rents or Comons to maintaine and support the authority of the same or for discharging any publiqe Taxes or charges of the Towne Though by its Trade it was considerable in customes and Excise in ye Exchequer to ye vallue of about Twenty thousand pounds str per Ann—humbly to pray his Maj^{tie} that he would be pleased to grant out of the enemyes Estates (he was goeing to subdue) such a proporcion as his Maj^{tie} in his gracious favour should think fitt butt the Burgesses were altogethur against it (amongest severall of their argum^{ts} saying it would be a great shame to begg of his Maj^{tie} at his comeinge to Towne though they were tould such an oppertunity (if lost) might never againe be had ; It was certainly reported by a gentleman of good creditt and reputacion that when ye Kinge was in ye West of Ireland discourceing of the Kingdom in [genell] generall this gentleman being present heard *his Maj^{tie} say* that he liked the north part where his Maj^{tie} had been especially Bellfast and the Country thereabouts and said likewise that if the Magistrates and people of Bellfast had asked anything of him he would have given it them the losse is irrepaireable till a King or Queen comes to Bellfast wch may never be but if it should happen their inclynacions may not be soe kinde to Bellfast *as* his Maj^{tie} King William designed ye old Proverb holds a dum man getts noe land time was and now [it] is Past.

1691 William Lockart Burgesse was elected and sworne Soveraigne for the yeare ending Michaelmas 1691

1692 James M'Cartney Esqr Councellor at Law & Burgesse was elected and sworne Soveraigne for the yeare ending Michallmas 1692

1693–1694 William Craford Burgesse was elected and sworne Soveraigne for the yeare ending Michallmas 1693 and allsoe elected and sworne for the yeare end Michallmas 1694

1695 Capt Eward (*sic*) Harrison Esqr Burgesse was elected and sworne Soveraigne for the yeare ending Michallmas 1695

1696 Lewis Thomson Burgesse was elected and sworne Soveraigne for the yeare ending Michaellmas 1696

1697 Capt Robert Leathes Esqr Burgesse was elected and sworne Soveraigne for the yeare ending Michaellmas 1697

1698 The Rt Honble Arthur Earle of Donegall was elected and sworne Soveraigne for the yeare end Michallmas 1698

Captain Robert Leathes served Deputy for ye yeare ye Lord Longford and Lady Ann then Lords of the Castle of Bellfast

1699–1700 David Smith Burgesse was elected and sworne Soveraigne for the yeare ending Michallmas 1699 Capt Charles Chichester being ellected for ye yeare ending Michallmas 1700 but after went to London & came not to Bellfast at Michallmas to be sworne soe David Smith continued Soveraigne for that yeare according to Charter

1701 George M'Cartney Burgesse was elected and sworne Soveraigne for ye yeare ending Michaellmas 1671

1702 John Chalmers Burgesse was elected and sworne Soveraigne for the yeare ending Michaelmas 1672

1703 & parte of 1704 David Buttle Burgesse was elected and sworne [Soveraigne] for the yeare ending Michallmas 1703 and againe elected and sworne Soveraigne for ye yeare ending Michallmas 1704 but surrendered the Rod the 29th of July 1704 by a late Act of Parliam^t disabling dissenters to serve in publiqe office and succeded for ye remainder of that yeare by George Macartney *Esqr* Councellor at Law part of 1704   George M'Cartney Esq.ʳ Councellor at Law & Burgesse was ellected sworne Soveraigne for that parte of yᵉ yeare viz from yᵉ 29ᵗʰ July 1704 to Michaellmas ffollowing wᶜʰ time Mʳ Buttle yₑ former Soveraigne surrendered up into yᵉ hands of the Corporacon disabling dissenters to serve in publiqe office by vertue of an Act of Parliamᵗ in that case made and Provided

1705   George Macartney Esqʳ Councellor at Law & Burgesse was ellected and sworne Soveraigne for the yeare ending Michaellmas 1705

1706   George M'Cartney Esqʳ Councellor at Law & Burgesse was ellected & sworne Soveraigne for the yeare ending Michaellmas 1706

1707   George M'Cartney Esqʳ Councellor at Law and Burgesse was ellected and sworne Soveraigne for the yeare ending Michaellmas 1707

1708   George Macartney Esqʳ Councellor at Law and Burgess according to former ellection for yₑ yeare 1707 continues Soveraigne for the yeare end Michaellmas 1708 because according to yᵉ Charter [Capt Brice being upon] yᵉ Leete sent downe to yᵉ Soveraigne & Burgesse undᵗ ye hand of yₑ Rᵗ Honᵇˡᵉ yᵉ Countis Dowager of Donegall and yᵉ Rᵗ Honᵇˡᵉ yᵉ Earle of Donegall had 3 Burgesse named one of wᶜʰ was Capt Edward Brice who was ellected and chossen for that yeare but would not quallifie himselfe according to the Act of Parliamᵗ soe that he disabled himselfe from takeing yᵉ office of Soveraigne

1709   Whereas the Rᵗ Honᵇˡᵉ Arthur Earle of Donegall did in pursuance of the power to him given by the Charter send us Leete this day in wᶜʰ Leete were named Michaell Harrison Esqr Richard Willson gent and James Gurner gent Wee the Soveraigne and Burgesses in pursuance of the power to us given by said Charter have elected and chosen said Richard Willson one of the three named in said Leet to serve as Soveraigne of the said Borrough for the yeare ensueing from Michaellmas 1708 to Michaellmas 1709 as wittness our hands the 24th of June 1708   Geo Macartney Soveraign

Robt Leathes   Nathl Byrtt   Richard Willson   George Portis   Henry Ellis   James Gurner   Roger Haddock   Nicholas Thettford

1710   (A similar entry occurs after each year, followed by periods, but is omitted for brevity)   .The Leet, James Gurner Roger Haddock and Nathaniel Byrt who was chosen as Sovereign   Richard Wilson Sovereign

Robt Leathes   Nathl Byrtt   George Portis   Henry Ellis   Nicholas Thettford   Roger Haddock   James Gurner

1711   .   .   .   .   The Leet Roger Haddock present Sovereign, James Gurner James Portis Roger Haddock chosen   Roger Haddock Sovern

Robt Leathes   Geo Macartney   Nathl Byrtt   Richard Wilson   George Portis   Henry Ellis   James Gurner   Nicholas Thettford

1712   .   .   .   .   The Leet Roger Haddock present Sovereign, the Honble John Chichester & James Gurner the Honble John Chichester chosen

Roger Haddock Soverⁿ

Robt Leathes   Geo Macartney   John Haltridge   Nath Byrtt   George Portis   Henry Ellis   James Gurner   Nicholas Thettford   Geo Macartney

Whereas Cap John Chichester was ellected Soveraigne of the Borrough of Bellfast for the yeare 1712 but he being in England and came not to Bellfast at Michaellmas following to be sworne according to yᵉ charter So Roger Haddock yᵉ present Soveraigne continues for that yeare

1713   .   .   .   .   The Leet Roger Haddock present Sovereign, Hans Hamilton James Gurner Hans Hamilton chosen   Roger Haddock Sovern

Henry Ellis   James Gurner   Nicholas Thettford   Rob Le Byrtt   Robᵗ Leathes   Nath Byrtt   George Portis

1714   .   .   .   .   The Leet Hans Hamilton Robert Leathes James Gurner Robert Leathes chosen

Hans Hamilton   Nath Byrtt   George Portis   Henry Ellis   James Gurner   Nicholas Thettford   Robᵗ Lebyrtt

1715   .   .   .   .   The Leet Robert Leathes James Gurner Henry Ellis James Gurner chosen   Robᵗ Leathes Soveraigne   Nath Byrtt   James Gurner   Robᵗ Lebyrtt   Tho Banks

Whereas yᵉ Right Honᵇˡᵉ yᵉ Earl of Donegall did send a Leet in pursuance to yᵉ power given him by yᵉ Charter for electing yᵉ Soveraign of Belfast for yᵗ ensueing year commencing from Michaelmass next and upon yᵉ said Election yᵉ Sovereign and Burgesses met this day in yᵉ Town Hall commonly called yᵉ Markett house of Belfast that in yᵉ said Leet James Gurner Esqr Robert Leathes Esqr and Robert Le Byrtt Gent were nominated by the said Earl of Donegall That upon y[e] said Election the Hon[ble] Capt John Chichester George Macartney and John Haldrick Esqrs Mr George Portis Mr Nicholas Thetford and Mr George Macartney Gents in y[e] said Election give their votes for y[e] said Robert Leathes Esqr To Succeed as Sovereign for y[e] year commencing at Michaelmas next the votes for y[e] said Robert Leathes being y[e] six Gents above mentioned and at y[e] same time James Gurner Esqr present Sovereign Nathaniel Byrtt Robert Leathes Robert Le Byrtt Mr Henry Ellis four of y[e] Burgesses in y[e] Corporation of Belfast and Mr Thomas Banks Constable of the Castle gave their votes for y[e] Election of Mr Robert Le Byrtt The said James Gurner Sovereign did not give two votes but decided that if he had two votes he gave them for the said Robert Le Byrtt Witness our hands this 24th June 1715 James Gurner Sovereign

Nicholas Thettford   Rob[t] Lebyrtt   Geo Macartney Jun[r]   Tho[s] Banks   Jno Rich: Chichester   Geo Macartney   John Haltridge   Nath Byrtt   George Portis   Henry Ellis

N B Gurner continued Sovereign y[e] said year of this Election

1717 (see note p 244) . . . . The Leet James Gurner Hans Hamilton Henry Ellis Henry Ellis chosen   James Gurner Sovereign

Rob[t] Leathes   Henry Ellis   George Portis   Hans Hamilton   Rob[t] Le Byrtt Tho[s] Banks

1718 . . . . The Leet Henry Ellis John Carpenter James Gurner John Carpenter chosen   Henry Ellis Sovereign

Rob Leathes   Nath Byrtt   George Portis   James Gurner   Nicholas Thettford Rob[t] Lebyrtt

1719 · . . . The Leet John Carpenter Henry Ellis Robert Lebyrtt John Carpenter chosen   Jo[n] Carpenter Sovereign

Nath Byrtt Henry Ellis   George Portis   James Gurner   Nich Thettford   Rob[t] Lebyrtt   Tho Hewesson   Rob Leathes.

1720 . . . . The Leet Robert Lebyrtt Henry Ellis James Gurner Henry Ellis chosen   Jo[n] Carpenter Sover[n].

Geo Macartney   John Haltridge   Nath Byrtt   Henry Ellis   George Portis   James Gurner   Rob[t] Lebyrtt   Nicholas Thettford   Geo Macartney   Jas Macartney

1721 . . . . The Leet Henry Ellis present Sovereign Robert Lebyrt James Gurner Robert Lebyrt chosen   Henry Ellis Sove[n]

Geo Macartney   Nath Byrtt   Geo Portis   James Gurner   Nicholas Thettford   Geo Macartney   Jas Macartney   John Clugston

1722 . . . . The Leet Robert Byrrt present Sovereign, Henry Ellis James Gurner Henry Ellis chosen   Robt Byrtt Sov[n]

Geo Macartney   Nath Lyrtt   Geo Portis   James Gurner   Nicholas Thettford   Geo Macartney   Henry Ellis   Jas Macartney   John Clugston

Whereas the R[t] Hon[ble] Arthur Earl of Donegall did in pursuance of a power to him given by y[e] Charter send us a Leet this day in w[ch] Leet were named Hans Hamilton Esqr Robert Byrt and John Carpenter Wee the Free Burgesses of the Burrogh of (There being no Sovereign of y[e] said Towne sworne) in pursuance of y[e] power to us given by y[e] s[d] Charter have unanimously Elected & chosen y[e] s[d] Hans Hamilton Esq[r] one of y[e] three Burgesses named in y[e] s[d] Leet to serve as Sovereign of this Burrough for one year to comence from Michaelmas next

Witness our hands this twenty fourth day of June 1723

N B. From y[e] death of Mr. Ellis and during y[e] year 1723 Throw contests between y[e] Burgesses and Family there was no Sovereign nor did Mr Hamilton tho Elected as above for 1724: But by agreement George Macartney Jun[r] Esq[r] did serve for that year

Geo Macartney   Nathl Byrtt   George Portis   Geo Macartney   Robt Byrtt   Jas Macartney   John Clugston

1725 (see note p 244) . . . . The Leet Nathaniel Byrt Doctor James Macartney John Clugston Nathaniel Byrt chosen

George Macartney   Robt Byrtt   Jas Macartney   John Clugston   Chas Macartney Tho[t] Banks Constable of the Castle

1726 . The Leet Doctor James Macartney John Clugston the Honble Nicholas Price Doctor James Macartney chosen   Nath Byrtt Sovereign   Robert Byrtt James Macartney John Clugston Cha Macartney Tho Banks Constable

1727 The Leet John Clugston, Honble John Skeffington Nicholas Price John Clugston chosen.   Geo Macartney Robt Byrtt John Clugston Chas Macartney Ezek Davys Wilson

THE ROLL OF THE FREEMEN

Belfast 21° January 1635 *mort*	Sampson Styles was made free Stapler of the Burrough aforesaid the day & yeere aforesaid
mort	The same day John Dickson was made free of the same
22° January 1635	John Langtree was made free Stapler the day aforesaid of the same
[*mort*]	The same day Thomas Hodgkins was also made free Stapler of the same
	Thomas Hodgkins venit in propria persona sua 23 die Maij 1648 per quod satis liquet comparuit hic adhuc superstes testis Edwardus Bell de Malone per me Ricardum Wall
Mr Jo: Wassher *mort*	The same day Willm Walsh was made free of the same
Soveraigne 1637	James Wooddroffe gent made free Stapler of the Burrough of Bellfast
mort	the fift day of October Anno dni 1637
mort	Nicholas [Tomson] Tomas gent made free Stapler the same day and yeere
	Henry Sands gent made free Stapler of this Burrough the seaventeenth day of October 1637
	Ellys ffogg merchant made free Stapler the same day & yeere & gave to the towne xx⁸
7° Die December	Thomas Bradley gent made free Stapler the same day & yeere
1637 *mort*	Humphrey Beare *gent* made free *Stapler* the same day & yeere
mort	Symeon Spier made free *Stapler* the day & yeere
sexto ffebruary 1637	Robt Gibson made free Stapler & gave to the towne x⁸
Octavo febᵣ 1637	George Martyn was made free Stapler & gave to the towne iijˡⁱ
	William Cluggeston was made free Stapler & gave to the towne 30⁸
5° Aprilis 1638	John Hodges gen was made free Stapler
	John M'Cullogh the same day was made free Stapler & gave to the Towne x⁸ & is to give to the Church x⁸ :
24 May 1638	Thomas Burton shoemaker was made free of this Corporacon
28 Junii 1638	James Russell was made free of this Corporacon
[16 July]	Edmond O'Hartan carpenter was also made free
16 August 1638	Richard Vicary merchant was made free [of]
12° Septr 1638 *mort*	John Lane Clothyer was made free
mort	Robt Booth whelewright was alsoe made free
20 Sept 1638	Thomas Cuningham was made free and is to pay to the towne x⁸
	The same yeere
	Henry Larkham weaver was made free
	James Carr Taylor was made free
xxvi Sept 1638	Henry Symkins chandler was made free & is to give x⁸ to the towne
Burgus de supradic- to Belfast in Comi- tatu Antrim	Tempore John Leithes generosi Superioris Burgi sive ville de Belfast communes et liberi homines Burgi sive ville predicte factum et admissum apud curiam Assemblicionis tunc ibidem decimo die Januarii Anno regni Domini Regis Caroli nunc Anglie &c decimo quarto 1638

Richard Carron of Belfaste in the Countye of Antrim Webster was admitted a free man & Commonᵣ within the said Towne accordinge to the ancient lawes libtyes and privileidges thereof and receaved the oath of a free Comonᵣ the daye and yeare aforesaid

John OHadden of Belfast aforesaide shoemaker was admitted a free man & Comoner within the said Towne accordinge to the ancient lawes libtyes and privileidges thereof and receaved the oath of a ffree Comonᵣ the daye and yeare aforesaide and did then promise to give five shillings for a gratuity to the use of the Towne

The sixt daye of June Anno dni 1639 Tho Godffrey Taylor was admitted a ffreeman & Comoner within the saide Towne accordinge to the ànncient lawes libtyes and privileidges thereof and receaved the oath of a ffree Comon' the daye and yeare aforesaide and did then promise to give five shillings to the use of the Towne for a gratuity

The eighteenth daye of Julye Anno dni 1639 Thomas Bayley Clothier was admitted a ffreeman and Comoner within the saide Towne accordinge to the anncient lawes and libtyes thereof and did take the oath of a ffree Comoner the day and yeare aforesaide and did then promise to give five shillings for a gratuity to the use of the Towne

The eighteenth daye of July Anno dni 1639 John Cottier Clothier was admitted a ffreeman and Comon' within the saide Towne accordinge to the anncient lawes libtyes and privileidges thereof and did take the oath of a ffree Comon' the day and yeare aforesaid and did then promise to give five shillings for a gratuity to the use of the Towne

The twelvth day of September Anno dni 1639 Thomas Rorke gentl was admitted a ffreeman & Comoner within the saide Towne accordinge to the ancient lawes libtyes and privileidges thereof and did take the oath of a ffree Comon' the daye and yeare aforesaide and did then promise to give five shillings for a gratuity to the use of the Towne

The neenteenth daye of September Anno dni 1639 Robte Whiteside feltmaker was admitted a ffreeman & Comon' wthin the saide Towne accordinge to the anncient lawes libtyes and privileidges thereof and did take the oath of a ffree Comon' the daye and yeare aforesaide and did promise to give five shillings for a gratuitye to the use of the Towne

The said neenteenth day of September 1639 Thomas Gilpatricke merchant was admitted a ffreeman & Comon' within the said Towne accordinge to the anncient lawes libtyes and privileidges thereof and did take the oath of a ffree Comon' the daye and yeare aforesaide and did promise to give five shillings for a gratuity to the use of the Towne

The neenetenth daye of September Anno dni 1639 Willm Lythom glasier was admitted a ffree man & Comon' within the saide Towne accordinge to the anncient lawes libtyes and priviledges thereof and did take the oath of a ffree Comon' the daye and yeare aforesaide and did promise to give five shillings to the use of the Towne

The neententh daye of September Anno dni 1639 Robte Spooner shoemaker was admitted a ffree man & Comon' within the saide Towne accordinge to the anncient lawes libtyes and priviledges thereof and did take the oath of a ffree Comon' the daye and yeare aforesaid and did promise to give for a gratuitye to the use of the Towne v⁸

The xxviijth daye of September Anno dni 1639 John Lawe merchant was admitted a ffree man & Comon' within the saide Towne accordinge to the anncient lawes libtyes & privileidges thereof by and wᵗʰ the full assent consent & agreem' of the Sovraigne & Burgesses of the saide Towne and hath promised to give

The xxvjth daye of September Anno dni 1639 Richard Wall clerke of the Borrough & Towne Courte of Belfast was admitted a ffreeman & Comon' within the saide Towne accordinge to the ancient lawes libtyes and privileidges thereof and did take the oath of a ffree Comon' the daye and yeare aforesaid

The daye and yeare aforesaide John Goye Joyner was admitted a ffreeman & Comon' of this Towne of Belfast and did take the oath of a ffree Comon' the daye and yeare aforesaide and did promise to give five shillings for a gratuitye to the use of the Towne

The day and yeare aforesaid Edmund Barnes blacksmyth was admitted a ffreeman & Comon' of this Towne of Belfast and did then take the oath of a ffree Comon' and did promise to give v⁸ for a gratuitye to the use of the Towne

The daye and yeare aforesaid Hughe Boothe Smyth was admitted a ffreeman & Comon' of this Towne of Belfast and did then take the oath of a ffree Comon' and did then promise to give v⁸ for a gratuitye to the use of the Towne

The daye and yeare aforesaide Matthew Westfeild glasier was admitted a ffree man & Comon' of this Towne and did take the oath of a ffree Comon' and did promise to give v⁸ for a gratuitye to the use of the Towne

The xxviijth daye of Septembr Anno dni 1639 Willm Thom merchant was admitted a ffree man & Comon' of This Towne and did take the oath of a ffree Comon' and did promise to give v⁸ for a gratuity to the use of the Towne

The xxviijth day of September Anno dni 1639 George Austen servante to Mr *John* Leithes Sovragne was admitted a ffree man & [Comon'] *Stapler* of this Towne and did take his oath the daye and yeare aforesaid

The daye and yeare aforesaide John Gausley Clothier was admitted a ffreeman & Comon' of this Towne and did then take the oath of a ffree Comon' and did promise to give v⁸ for a gratuitye to the use of the Towne

The xxviijth of September Anno dni————George Bradshawe merchant was admitted and made a ffree Stapler within Towne accordinge to the anncient lawes libtyes & priviledges thereof by and wᵗʰ the full Assent consent and agreem' of the Soveraigne and Burgesses of the saide Towne

The daye and yeare aforesaide John Barnes servant unto Mr Willm Leithes was admitted a ffreeman & Comon^r of this Towne and did take the oath of a ffree Comon^r the daye and yeare aforesaid

The daye and yeare aforesaide Nivens Viccar Shipp Carpenter was admitted a ffree man & Comon^r and did then take his oath and did promise to give v^s for a gratuitye to the use of the Towne

The daye and yeare aforesaid Joseph Walker Shoemaker was admitted a ffree man and Comon^r and did then take his oath and did then promise to give v^s for a gratuitye to the use of the Towne

The daye and yeare aforesaid Alexander McKesney husbandman was admitted a ffreeman and Comon^r and did then take his oath and did promise to give v^s for a gratuitye to the use of the Towne

The daye and yeare aforesaid Thomas Charles butcher was a ffree man & Comon^r and did then take his oath and did promise to give v^s for a gratuitye to the use of the Towne

The daye and yeare aforesaid Richard Christopherson butcher was admitted freeman and Comon^r and did take the oath and did promisse to give v^s for a gratitute to the use of the Towne

The xxviijth daye of September Anno dni 1639 Willm Richey merchant Burgesse in Aire was admitted and made a ffree Stapler within the Towne accordinge to the anncient lawes libtyes and privileidges thereof by and wth the full assent consent and agreem^t of the Soveraigne and Burgesses thereof and did take his oath and then promise to give v^s to the use of the poore of this Towne

The daye and yeare aforesaide Hughe Leithes glover was admitted a ffree man & Comon^r of this Towne and did take his oath according to the order and custom of this Towne

The xxixth daye of September Anno dni 1639 Henry Blackhurst merchant was admitted and made a ffree Stapler within this Towne and did take his oath accordinge to the anncient lawes libtyes and privileidges thereof

The daye and yeare aforesaid John Leithes Eldest sonne of m^r Willm Leithes merchant was admitted & made a ffree Stapler within this Towne and did take his oath accordinge to the anncient lawes libtyes & privileidges thereof

By Henry Squyre Esqre

30° January 1639

Burgus de Belfast *mort* — Leonard Thompson of Belfast marchant was made a free Stapler, att an Assembly then held before the Soveraigne of the sd Burrough and Burgesses then keepeinge Session, and tooke the Oath accordinge to the Anntyent Custom

31° Aprilis 1640

Att a genrall Assembly then held Sr William Wray Knite and Barronett was made a ffree Stapler of this [of this] Burrough wth a genrall consent.

Danyell mcNeale gent the day and yeare above said and at the Assembly aforesaid was made a ffree Stapler of the afore said Burrough.

the 30° of July 1640

mort Upon the humble peticion of Thomas Stevenson att a genrall Assembly then held with the genrall consent of the Sovraigne and Burgesses then Assembled The said Thomas Stevenson was made a ffree Stapler of the aforesaid Burrough for wch he gave Thirty three shillings & four pence to be imployed for the good of the Towne.

Burgus de Belfaste 30° July 1640

Upon the humble peticion of John Stewart att genrall Assembly held for the Burrough aforesaid the day & yeare aforesaid The sd John Stewart was made a ffree Comoner of the aforesaid Burrough for wch he hath given the some of Twenty six shillings & eight pence for to be imployed for the good of this Corporacon

Burgus de Belfaste 17° Septembris 1640

Upon the humble peticion of * * * Edward Moore at an assembly then held for the Burrough aforesaid the day & yeare aforesaid was with a genrall consent of the Burgesses then Assembled made for a freeman of the aforesd Burrough for wch he gave 6s 8d sterl to be imployed for the use of the sd Burrough

Burgus de Belfaste 13° Augusti 1640

Mort Att an Assembly then held for the aforesaid Burrough Sr Charles Coote Knight and Barronett Corronell of one of his Mat^s Regimt^s was made a ffree Stapler of this Towne and Corporacon By and wth the genrall consent of the Soveraigne and Burgesses then assembled.

The day and yeare abovesaid Leiuetenant Corronell Theobald Taffe att the Assembly aforesaid and wth the genrall consent aforesaid was made a free Stapler of this Towne and Corporacon

The day and yeare aforesd and wth the consent aforesaid Sr James Dillon Knt was made a free Stapler of this Towne and Corporacon

The day and yeare aforesaid and wth the consent aforesaid Sr John Jefford Leiuetennt Coronell of one of his Mat^s Regymts was made a free Stapler of this Towne and Corporacon

mort The day and yeare aforesaid Capt George Peasely was wth the genrall consent aforesaid made a free Stapler of this Towne and Corporacon

24° Septembris 1640

At an Assembly then held wth the consent of the Burgesses then Assembled Henry Billingsby gent was made a free [Stapler] *man* of the Towne and Burrough of Belfaste

Burgus de ⎱
Belfast ⎰

By John Haddock gent
6° Octobris 1640

wch sd two sumes ⎱ were to be levyed ⎸ in a rate for fyre ⎸ & Candell for the ⎰ army then beinge ⎸ here ⎰	Robert Machett a free Comoner & *promised to* give to the Towne x^s Robt Bacheler the same day made a free Comoner and [gave] *promised* likewise x^s for the good of the Towne
15° Oct	William Blake *Cooke* was made a free Comoner
8° ffebr	Richard ffoster was made a free Comoner
4° Juni	Phillipp Wenman Esqre was made free of the Corporacon being elected a Burges for the parliam^t in steed of Sr Wm Wrey Knt & Baronett
	John Davyes gent the same day was made a freeman
22° Junii	[Henry Anderson was made free of this Corporacon]
8th July 1641	James Haddock was [made] sworne a free Comoner
15th July 1641	Edward Thunger was made a free Comoner
	William Griffith the same day was sworn a free Comoner
	[James Miller the same day was sworn a free Comoner and was to give to the use of the Towne 13s 4d]
29° July	Patrick Starling sworne a free Comoner & Thomas Theaker bound to discharge the Towne for 3 years
	Thomas Postley Junr sworne a free Comoner
	Adam Leithes sworne a free Comoner
	George Duncan sworne a free Comoner
mort	Gilbert McGarragh sworne a free Comoner
	John Tomson sonne of Alex^r Tomson free Comoner
	James Clogh the same day [a] sworn a free Comoner
23° Sept 1641	William Downeman sworne a free Comoner
	Edward Woods the same day sworne a free Comoner
24°	William Wheaton the same day sworne a free Comoner

Belfast Burrough

By Thomas Hanington gen Sr

7° octob John Speed sworne a free Comoner & promised to give 2^s presently & x^s when he keepes a shopp [for]

The last of June 1642 John Browne merchant admitted & sworne a ffree Stapler w^thin the Burrough & Towne of Belfast aforesaid and submitteth himselfe to the lawes orders & Customes of the same

Tempore Thome Stephenson Superioris Burgi
sive Ville de Belfast in Com Antrym 1642

The fourth daye of December 1642 John Mitchell gen was admitted and sworne a free Stapler w^thin the Burrough & Towne of Belfast aforesaid

Md. that at the Courte holden the fourtenth daye of September 1643 John Steawart gen uppon his petition to the Soveraigne & the Burgesses then present was admitted & sworne a ffree Stapler w^thin the said Towne and hath promised to give xx^s for a gratuitye to the Towne

John Clugston merchant sworne and admitted as aforesaid to give xx^s

Thomas Wareinge Tanner sworne & admitted in like maner and to give xx^s

John Pentland merchant sworne & admitted in like maner a free Comoner and to give 9s 4d.

Thomas Waterson Shoemaker sworne and admitted a free Comoner as aforesaid and to give 9s 4d.

Bernard Boskam brasier sworne and admitted a free Comoner as aforesaid and to give 9s 4d.

John Ash gen Robt ffoster gen John Leythe gen Thomas Hanington gen Thomas Theaker gen Richard Gately gen and Willm Leythes gen ffree Burgesses of the said Towne was present at this Courte

Burgus de Belfaste

In Tempore Thomæ Theaker gen Superioris Burgi prd. An° Dni 1643

Mem^m that upon the 13th day of October an assembly Courte being then held John McCrakan was then admitted a free Comoner of the Corporacon for wch he gave 5s sterl for the use of the Corporacon

26° Octobr An° 1643

mort Mem that the day abovesaid att an assembly then held Nicholas Garnett was admitted a free Comoner of this Corporacon for wch he was to give 9s 4d ster for the use of this Corporacon

30 die December 1647 Nicholas Garner referd himself to the order of ye Bench what hee shall give to the use of the Towne in consideration of his ffreedom

The same day Edward Smith was made a free Comoner for wch he gave 9s 4d sterl

The same day John Rigby was admitted a free Stapler and gave 9s 4d

30 die December 1647 Apud Cur John Rigby toke his oath that he hath paid unto Mr Theaker 6s 8d of the 9s 4d for the use of the Towne

2° Novembr 1643

mort The day abovesaid att an assembly then held Marten Gose was admitted a free Comoner of this Corporacon and was to give 5s sterl for the use of the Corporacon

9° Novembr An° Supra Dict

The day and yeare abovesaid att an assembly then held William Sambrooke was admitted a free Comoner of this Corporacon and is to give 6s 8d sterl for the use of this Corporacon

The same day was Wm Davyes admitted a free Comoner and is to give 6s 8d for the use of the Corporacon

The day aforesaid Patrick Gough was admitted a free Comoner of this Corporacon and gave 6s 8d for the use of this Corporacon

John Ash gent Robert ffoster Thomas Hanington gent and Richard Gately *gent* beinge then present and Assembled wth many other freemen

16° die Novembris 1643

The day above said Thomas Barker was admitted a free Comoner of this Corporacon and is give vis viijd sterlinge for the use of this Corporacon

11° die Januarii 1643

The day above said at an Assembly then held Tymothy Miller was admitted a ffree Stapler of this Corporacon and is to give vis viijd sterl for the use of the Corporacon

The same day Christopher Marshall was admitted a ffree Stapler of this Corporacon and is to give vis viijd ster for the use of the Corporacon

The day aforesaid

ffrancis Robison of Belfast was admitted a free Comoner of this Corporacon for wch he is to give vis viijd sterl for the use of this Corporacon

25° die Januarii 1643

The day aforesaid Wm Tomson was admitted a free Comoner of this Corporacon for the wch he is to give 5s sterl for the use of the Corporacon at an Assembly in presentia John Ash Thomas Stevenson Thomas Hanington

19th die [Januari] Marcij 1643

George Stevenson the day abovesd was admitted a ffree Comoner of this Corporacon for the wch he gave 4s 8d sterl for the use of this Corporacon

30 die December 1647 George Stephenson toke his oath that he hath paid the 4s 8d to Mr Theaker to the use of the Towne

9° die Maij 1644

10th of ffebr 1658 John Martin paid 4s 6d to Mr Will Leythes Sovrne

Christopher Gillett & John Martin the day and yeare abovesd were admitted free Comoners of this Corporacon for the wch they are to give by Michmas next for the use of ye sd Corporacon one Ryall a peece which is in all 9s 4d

June the 26th 1644

John Wareing John Sanderson and John Mitchell the day and yeare above said were admitted free Comoners of this Corporacon for the wch they are to give by Michaelmas next for the use of the said Corporacon

Julij the 20th 1644

John Coupland the day above sd was admitted a ffree Comoner of this Corporatione

Tempore Robti ffoster gen Superior Burgi sive Ville de Belfast Anno dni 1644

Edward Leythes sonne of Willm Leythes gen one of the Burgesses of this Towne was admitted and sworne a ffree merchant Stapler of this said Towne according to the Orders & Customes of the same Att an Assembly houlden the 10th of Octob^r 1644

John Thetford sonne of ffranc Thetford of Belfast aforesaide was admitted and sworne a ffree merchant Stapler of this said Towne accordinge to the orders & customes of the same at an Assembly houlden the 10th of Octob^r 1644

Roger Leythes sonne of Adam Leythes late of Belfast aforesaide deceased was admitted and sworne a ffree merchant stapler of this saide Towne accordinge to the orders and customes of the same at an Assembly houlden the 10th of Octob^r Anno dni 1644

hee gave 7s to the use of the Towne — James Lynsay merchant uppon his humble Petition unto the Sovraigne and Burgesses of this Towne was admitted and sworne a ffree merchant stapler of the said Towne accordinge to the orders & customes of the same att an assembly houlden the 14th of November 1644

Walter Caruth Chapman uppon his humble petition unto the Sovraigne and Burgesses of this Towne was admitted and sworne a ffree Stapler of the said Towne according to the orders and Customes of the same and gave to the use of the Towne 4s 8d sterl at an Assembly houlden the 14th of Novembr Anno dni 1644

John Miller the younger sonne of John Miller of Antrym uppon his humble petition unto the Sovraigne & Burgesses of this Towne was admitted a free Stapler of this Towne according to the orders & customes of the same and gave to the use of this Towne iiijs viijd the 6th of March 1644

John m'Bryde merchant uppon his humble Petition unto the Sovraigne & Burgesses of this Towne was admitted and sworne a free Stapler & Comoner of this Towne according to the orders & Customes of the same and gave to the use of the Towne 9s 4d the 6th of March

John Miller of Antrym the elder merchant uppon his humble Petition unto the Sovraigne and Burgesses of this Towne was admitted and sworne a merchant Stapler & ffree Comoner of the said Towne and gave to the use of the Towne 9s 4d sterl the 24th of Aprill 1645

Nehemius Richardson Candlemaker uppon his humble Petition unto the Sovraigne & Burgesses of this Towne was admitted and sworne *a merchant Stapler and* ffree Comoner of the said Towne according to the orders & Customes of the same and gave to the use of the Towne iiij^s viij^d the 15th of May 1645

Willm M'Kenna merchant uppon his humble Petition unto the Sovraigne and Burgesses of this Towne *was admitted and sworne* a free merchant Stapler & ffree Comoner of the said Towne according to the Orders and Customes of the saide Towne at an Assembly held the 3 of July 1645

fine 02 00 00

Robte Clugston merchant uppon his humble Petition unto the Soveraigne and Burgesses of this Towne was admitted and sworne a merchant Stapler and free Comoner of the saide Towne accordinge to the Orders and Customes of the same at an Assembly held the 3 of July 1645 and for his ffine he submitted himself to the order of the Bench

John mcDowell merchant uppon his humble Petition unto the Soveraigne and Burgesses of this Towne was admitted and sworne a merchant Stapler & ffree Comoner of the said Towne accordinge to the order & custome of the same at an Assembly held the 3 of July 1645

George Thomson of Belfast Inkeeper uppon his humble Petition unto the Soveraigne and Burgesses of Belfast aforesaid was admitted and sworne a free Comoner of the said Towne according to the order and custome of the same att an Assembly held the 3 of July 1645

Rauffe Hughston of Belfast Taylor upon his humble Petition unto the Soveraigne and Burgesses of Belfast aforesaid was admitted and sworne a ffree Comoner of the said Towne according to the Order and Custom of the same att a Courte houlden the 25th of September 1645

Tempore Willimi Leythes generosi Superior Burgi Sive Ville de Belfast in Com Antrym Anno dni 1645

James fforbus of Belfast in the County of Antrym husbandman uppon his humble Petition [uppon his] unto the Soveraign and Burgesses was admitted and sworne a free Comoner of the said Towne accordinge to the Order and Custome of the said Towne and then toke the oath of a Serg^t of the said Towne at a Courte of Assembly houlden the second day of Octobr 1645

Thomas Garven of Aire merchant uppon his humble Petition unto the Sovraigne and Burgesses of Belfast was admitted and sworne a ffree Stapler of the saide Towne of Belfast accordinge to the ancient use and custome of the said Towne at a Court houlden the 19th of March 1645

non sol ffees

John Gillett of Belfast in the Countye of Antrym Tanner being sonne of a ffree man att his humble Petition unto the Sovraigne and Burgesses of the saide Towne was admitted and sworne a ffree Comoner of the saide Towne accordinge to the ancient use and custome of the same at the Court of Assembly houlden the 8th of Januar 1645

Edward Bell of Malone in the Countye of Antrym was admitted & sworne a free Comoner according to the ancient use and custome of the said Towne

non sol feods

James Martin of Belfast aforesaid Mealeman uppon his humble Petition unto the Sovraigne & Burgesses was admitted & sworne a ffree Comoner of the said Towne accordinge to the ancient use & custome of the same at the Courte of Assembly houlden the 8th of Januar 1646

o   John Marten Merchant att the saide Court of Assemblye was likewise admitted & sworne a ffree Stapler of the said Towne according to the ancient use & custome of the same

non sol feods

John Doake husbandman was admitted & sworne a ffree Comoner of the said Corporacon according to the ancient use and custome of the same at the Court of Assembly houlden at Midsumer 1647

non sol feods

John Kenitye blacksmyth att the same Court of Assembly was admitted a ffree Comoner of the saide Corporacon according to the ancient use and custome of the same

Gilberte Eccles Merchant was admitted a ffree Comon^r of the said Corporacon accordinge to the ancient use and Custome of the same

Willm Cordiner Merchant was admitted & sworne a ffree Comon^r of the said Corporacon according to the ancient use and custome of the same

John Orr Merchant att the Court of Assembly houlden the second day of Appr 1646 was admitted & sworne a ffree Stapler of the said Corporacon according to the use & custome of the same and for his fine submitted himself to the order of the Bench

Willm Richey of Belfast aforesaid Merchant att the saide Court of Assembly was admitted & sworne a ffree Stapler of the said Corporacon according to the ancient use and custome and for his ffine submitted himself to the order of the Bench

ffree Staplers and ffree Comon^{rs} of the Borroughe and Towne of Belfast in the Countye of Antrym admitted and sworne in the tyme of John Ash gen Sovraigne Anno dni 1647

Alexander Sinkler Merchant admitted & sworne a ffree Comoner the 22th of Apprill 1647

non sol feods

Walter Mapus Glover admitted & sworne die & Anno Suprd

non sol feods

Thomas Smyth blacksmyth admitted & sworne a ffree Comon^r the 29th of Apprill 1647

John Harden blacksmyth admitted & sworne die & Anno Suprd

Thomas Quin Corrier admitted & sworne a ffree Comon^r the 12th of August 1647

John fowland Tanner admitted & sworne a ffree Comon^r the second of Septembr 1647

Willm Dawson of Dublin Merchant admitted & sworne a ffree Stapler of this Corporacon the 16th of Septembr 1647

Richard Aspinwall Merchant & Cittizen of London admitted and sworne a ffree Stapler of this Corporacon die & Anno Suprd

non sol feods

Thomas Haslipp Webster admitted & sworne a ffree Comonr the 23th of Septembr 1647

Thomas Marshall shoemaker admitted & sworne die & Anno Suprd

Henrye Wisdome Corrier admitted & sworne die & Anno Suprd

non sol feods

Willm Sym Sadler admitted & sworne a ffree Comon, 28th of Septembr 1647

non sol feods

Roger Tomlinson admitted & sworne a ffree Comon^r 28th of Septembr 1647

Lt Patrick Hepborne an Officer in Col. Maxwells Regmt admitted admitted (*sic*) and sworne a ffree Comon^r of this Corporacon the 29th of Septembr 1647 before the Sovraigne delivred upp his office non sol feods

[Thomas Smyth blacksmyth admitted and sworne a free comoner of the Borrough & Towne of Belfast accordinge to the ancient use & instance of the same]   entered above

Tempore Hugonis Doake gen Superior Burgi
sive Ville de Belfast in Com Antrym 1647: 1648

Att an assembly houlden by the Sovraigne and Burgesses the eight daye of November Anno dni 1647 John Steawarte Merchant was by the genrall assent consent & agreem^t of the saide Sovraigne and Burgesses received again and admitted a ffree Stapler and ffree Comoner of the said Borrough & Towne of Belfast aforesaid according to the ancient libtyes privileidges and ffranchises of the said Towne

Thomas Gill after his disfranchism^t in the tyme of Mr Aysh Sovraigne 1647 uppon his submission & humble Petition unto Mr Doake Sovraigne & the Burgesses of this said Towne was againe readmitted & sworne a free Comoner of the said Towne according to the use & custome of the same

Non sol feods

James Steawart m^t uppon his humble petition unto the Sovraigne and Burgesses of this Corporacon was admitted & sworne a ffree Comoner of the said Towne according to the use & custome thereof the 14th of Octobr 1647

James Maxwell of Carrickfergus m^t uppon his humble Petition unto the Sovraigne & Burgesses was admitted and sworne a ffree Stapler & free Comon^r of the said Towne and submitted himself unto the ancient orders & Bylawes of the said Towne

John Galte husbandman uppon his humble Petition unto the Sovraigne & Burgesses of this said Corporacon was admitted & sworne a ffree Comon^r of the saide Towne according to the according to the (*sic*) use & custome of the said Towne

Tempore Robti ffoster Superior Burgi sive Ville
de Belfast in Com Antrym 1648 1649

ffrancis Thetford sonne of ffrancis Thetford deceased uppon his humble Petition unto the Sovraigne and Burgesses of the said Towne was admitted and sworne a free Comoner of the saide Towne according to the ancient use and custome of the same the 30th of August 1649

Edward Dam Butcher uppon his humble Petition unto the Sovraigne and Burgesses of this Corporacon was admitted a free Comoner of the said Towne and was sworne according to the ancient use and custome of the same the 30th of August 1649

Donnell M'Cormicke Shoemaker uppon his humble petition unto the Sovraigne and Burgesses of this Corporacon was admitted and sworne a ffree Comoner of the said Towne according to the ancient use and custome of the same the 30th daye of August 1649

David Longe Butcher admitted & sworne a free Comoner of Belfast 30 August 1649

James Robinson admitted & sworne a free Comoner at the same

In the tyme of Mr Hanington Sovrane of the Borrough & Towne of Belfast in the County of Antrim 1650 & 1651

The 15th November 1650 these persons hereunder named were admitted & sworne free Comoners of the Borrough aforesaid according to the use and custome of the said Towne and according to the libtyes thereof

∞ 05 ∞
Thomas Gallopp   Smyth   pd

∞ 05 ∞
James Reade   Taylor   pd

∞ 05   o
Mathew Tate   brasier   pd
Thomas Carr   Cooper

∞ 10×∞
George Williamson   Butcher   paid 5s

∞ 05×∞ pd
Robte Jackson   Glover   × pd

∞ 05×∞
William Henderson   Webster   paid
John Thomson   Shoemaker

∞ 05 ∞
George Agnew   Mealeman

∞ 05 ∞
Thomas Lightfoot   Taylor   pd
John Hudlston   Taylor
John Watson   Merchant

∞ 05×∞ pd
Hugh Campbell Merchant admitted & sworne a free Comoner the second day of Januar 1650

The same day Allexander Taylor admitted and sworne a free Comoner

Henrye Morrey Webster admitted & sworne a free Comoner the 10th of Januar 1650

∞ 05 ∞
James Campbell Merchant admitted & sworne a free Comoner the 30th of Octobr 1651

∞ 05 ∞ pd
The same daye Charles Whitlock admitted & sworne a free Comoner

Allexander Reade Merchant admitted & sworne a free Comoner the 29th of Januar 1651

02×∞ ∞
The same daye George M'Cartney merchant admitted & sworne a free Comoner

The 24th of June 1652 Mr Thomas Wareinge was ellected & chosen to bee one of the Burgesses of the saide Towne and then sworne

The last of June 1652 these persons hereunder named were admitted & sworne ffree Comoners of the said Towne

oo o5 oo
Edward Renalls gen

oo✗10✗oo
Mr Robte Brice Clerk. paid by him this 12th of June 1662 yᵉ sume of tenn shills

oo o5 oo
Samuell Harris gen

In the tyme of Mr Thomas Wareing Sovrane of the Borrough & Towne of Belfast in the Countie of Antrim 1653 and 1654

o1✗oo oo pd
The 25th of March 1653 Adam Carnes admitted and sworne a free Comon' and of the staple merchant

oo 10✗oo
John Rodgers Merchant the 16th of September 1653 admitted a free Comon' and of the staple merchant and sworne. This 19th of June 1662 Jo. Rogers tooke his oath that he paid yᵉ above some of 10s to Mr Theaker for ye Townes use

The same daye Peeter Potts admitted & sworne a ffree Comon' and sworne one of the Sergeants of the said Towne

oo 10 oo
Alexander Thomson Cooper admitted & sworne a free Comonr the thertinth of Januar 1652 paid to Mr Willm Leythes Sovrane 1658 10s by Allex Thomson Cooper

The 29th of June 1654 These persons hereunder named were admitted & sworne free Comonrs of the Borrough aforesaid according to the use and custome of the said Towne and according to the libtyes thereof

oo o6✗o8
Arthur Houghton butcher

oo o5 oo
John m'Gowan shoemaker. paid to Mʳ Willm Leythes Sovraign 1658 by John m'Gowan

oo o5 oo
John Kenitye Boatman

oo o5 oo
Mathew ffarra clerk of the parish

oo o5 oo
Willm Burk Mealeman

Thomas Dawson Joyner

The first of July 1654 these persons hereunder written were admitted & sworne free Comoners as aforesaid

o2 oo✗oo
John Corry mᵗ ffree of the staple

oo 10 oo
Josias Marten *m*ᶜ ffree of the Staple

oo 10 oo
Michaell Biggart mᵗ ffree of the Staple merchant

oo 10 oo
John Biggart mᵗ ffree of the Staple merchant
paid to Mr Willm Leythes Sovrane 1658 10s by Jo & Michaell Biggart

oo o5 oo
Henry Thetford Joyner

oo o5 oo
Hugh Golfin Carpenter paid to Mr Willm Leythes Sovrane 1658 5s by Henrye Thetford

In the tyme of Mr Thomas Theaker Sovrane of the Borrough & Towne of Belfast in the Countie of Antrim 1654

oo o2✗oo pd
Archibald Roane admitted & sworne a free Comoner the 28th of Januar 1654

The same daye George ffrissell mealeman admitted and sworne a free Comoner

The 24th of May 1655 John Bratwhat admitted and sworne a ffree Comoner and free from paying anie ffine

The same daye Joh Wheats sworne one of the Sergeants of the Borrough of Belfast

The 17th of September 1655 Mr Edward Denman Merchant admitted and sworne a free Comoner and of the Staple Merchant his ffine or gratuitye for the use of the Towne is referred to his own discretion

The 27th of Septembr 1655 Lewes Thomson Sadler sonne of Leonard Thomson deceased was admitted & swore a ffree Comoner but his ffine was remitted hee servinge his apprentishipp wᵗʰin the Towne and being the sonne of a ffree Com'

Richard Saltus butcher the 27th of Septembr 1655 was admitted & sworne a ffree Comoner his ffine remitted for his manie services don unto the Towne

oo o5 oo—oo o7 oo
John Brookes Slater the 27th of Septembr 1655 was admitted & sworne a ffree Comoner his ffine to bee adjudged by the Sovrane & Burgesses

Tempore Johis Leythes gen qui incipit officium Superior Burgi sive Ville de Belfast 29th September 1655

oo × o4 × o6 pd
Walter Poston glover the 4th of October 1655 admitted and sworne a free Comoner

o1 oo oo
The 11th of Octobr 1655 John Bush Merchant admitted a ffree Comoner

The fees not paid oo o5 oo
The 11th of Octobr 1655 Robte Kitts a Trooper admitted a ffree Comoner

oo o5 oo pd
The 11th of Octobr 1655 John fforguson Owner of the Sara of Belfast admitted a free Com^r and then sworne

pd viiis
The 28th of febr 1655 Chr Monncaster Bricklayer admitted & sworne a free Comoner

oo o4 × o6
The 28th of febr 1655 Daniell Christian Tanner late servant unto Mr Tho Wareinge was admitted a free Comoner of the Borrough of Belfast &c

Jo Leithes Sovraigne o2 oo oo—o3 19 oo
Md   That the ninth of June 1656 Hugh Ecles Merchant at his instant & request by his petition accordinge to the custome of the Borrough by the consent of us the Sovrane & Burgesses now present whose names are hereunder subscribed and by the consent of Mr Willm Leythes & Mr Thomas Wareinge of the number of the saide Burgesses though now absent was admitted a free merchant stapler of the saide Burrough and was sworne accordingly and is to pay for the good of the Corporacon the sum of xl^s sterl

John Aysh   Tho Theaker   Richard × Gately mrk

Edward Evans Taylor the 15th of May 1656 admitted & sworne a free Comoner
The third of July 1656 Thomas ffiner barber Chierurgeon was admitted and sworne a free Comoner

o1 oo oo pd
Willm Moore Merchant the 7th of July 1656 was admitted a free Comoner & Merchant of the Staple wthin this Towne accordinge to the ancient libtyes & privileidges of the saide Towne and was sworne accordinglye

oo 1o oo
John Norvell of Glasgowe Merchant the 7th of July 1656 was admitted a free Comoner and Merchant of the Staple wthin this Towne according to the ancient libtyes and privileidges of the saide Towne and was sworne accordingly

oo o2 o6 pd to Mr Willm Leythes Sovrane 1658 2s 6d Jo Johnston
John Johnston of Belfast aforesaid husbandman the 7th of July 1656 was admitted and sworne a free Comoner of the said Towne

oo o2 o6 pd
Gilberte Wentwith Chapman was admitted and sworne a free Comoner the 14th of August 1658

oo o2 o6
Thomas ffiner barber Chierurgeon was admitted & sworne a ffree Comoner the 17th of July 1656

o1 oo oo
o2 17 o6
Edward Stanton free Grocer of the Citie of the Citie (*sic*) of London the 29th of September 1656 was admitted & sworne a free Comoner and Merchant of the Staple wthin the Towne accordinge to the ancient Libtyes & privileidges thereof

fees not paid
John Leythes sonne of John Leythes Senior one of the Burgesses of this Towne was admitted & sworne a free Comoner the 29th of Septembr 1656

Tempore Tho Wareinge gen Superior in Anno 1656 1657 o2 oo oo
George McCartney surnamed Niger merchant the 13th of No: 1656 was admitted & sworne a free Comoner & Merchant of the Staple wthin this Towne according to the ancient libtyes and privileidges thereof &c and by his owne free consent hee engaged himself to give to the use of the Towne xx^s in hand & twentie shillings when hee is better able

o2 oo oo
Willm Smyth merchant the 13th daye of No: 1656 was admitted & sworne a free Comoner and Merchant of the Staple wthin this Towne according to the ancient libtyes & privileidges thereof and by his owne free consent ingaged himself to give to the use of the Towne xl^s sterl uppon demand

o1 oo oo
[Willm] *Henrye* Litherland Shoemaker the 20th of November 1656 was admitted and sworne a free Comoner of the Corporacon and by his owne free consent engaged himselfe to give for the benefit of the Towne xx^s uppon demand

o2　10　00—07　10　00

Willm Taylor Merchant the 20th of Novembr 1656 was admitted and sworne a free Comoner and Merchant of the Staple w^thin this Towne accordinge to the ancient libtyes & privileidges thereof and by his owne free consent ingaged himselfe to give to the use of the Towne fiftie shillings sterl uppon demand

ffees not paid

John Pegg the 24th of June 1657 was admitted & sworne a free Comoner of the Borrough of Belfast aforesaid

[fees not paid]

Robte Leythes sonne of Willm Leythes one of the Burgesses of Belfast the 24th of June 1657 was admitted a free Comoner of the Borrough aforesaid

o1　00　00

Stephen Clerke Butcher the 17th of September 1657 was admitted & sworne a free Comoner of the Borrough of Belfast & has agreed to pay to the use of the Towne for his ffine xx^s sterl

paid to Mr Willm Leythes Sovrane 1658 5s by Robt Skiner glover　oo　10　oo

Robte Skiner glover the 17th of September 1657 was admitted & sworne a free Comoner of the Borrough of Belfast and was agreed to pay to the use of the Towne for his ffine x^s sterl

paid to Mr Will Leythes Sovrane 1658 10s by David Dowey Cooper　oo　10　oo

David Dowey Cooper the 28th of September 1657 was admitted & sworne a free Comoner of the Borrough of Belfast and was agreed to pay to the use of the Towne for his ffine the sum of x^s sterl

oo　10　oo paid to Mr Willm Leythes Sovrane 1658 10s by John Lenox

John Lenox Cooper the 28th of September 1657 was admitted & sworne a free Comoner of the Borrough of Belfast and was agreed to pay to the use of the Towne for his ffine x^s sterl

oo　10　oo paid to Mr Willm Leythes Sovrane 5s by David Thomson taylor

Tempore Willm Leythes ⎱
gen Superior in Anno ⎰ David Thomson Taylor sonne of David Thomson of
1657 & 1658 ⎰ Belfast aforesaid deceased the fift of No: 1657 was admitted
& *sworne* a free Comoner of the Borrough aforesaid and for his ffine submitted himself to the order of the Court

oo　10　oo

ffrancis Bramston sonne of Thomas Bramston late a Burgess of Belfast deceased the fift of No: 1657 was admitted & sworne a free Comoner of the said Borrough & for his ffine submitteth himself to the order of the Court

paid to Mr Willm Leythes Sovrane 1658 5s by Ja Doogan　oo　10　oo

James Doogan Cooper the fift of No: 1657 was admitted & sworne a free Comoner of the Borrough aforesaid the fift of No: 1657 and for his ffine submitted himself to the order of the Court

oo　05　oo—04　05　oo

Rowland Eyliffe shoemaker the fift of No: 1657 was admitted & sworne a free Comoner of the Borrough and for his ffine submitteth himself to the order of the Courte

oo　10　oo paid to Mr Willm Leythes Sovrane 1658 10s by John M'Cartney Webster

John McCartney Webster the fift of No: 1657 was admitted & sworne a free Comonr of the Borrough aforesaid & for his ffine submitteth himself to the order of the Court

oo　05　oo paid to Mr Willm Leythes Sovrane 1658-59 by Edm Bayley

Edmund Baley [Bayley] Butcher the fift of No: 1657 was admitted and sworne a free Comoner of the Borrough aforesaid and for his ffine submitteth himself to the order of the Court

oo　05　oo paid to Mr Willm Leythes Sovrane 1658 5s by Jo Whitlock

John Whitlock the younger butcher was admitted & sworne a free Comoner of the Borrough aforesaid the 26th of No 1657 and for his ffine submitteth himself to the order of the Court

paid to Mr Willm Leythes Sovrane 1658 5s by Tho Willocks　oo　05　oo—01　05　06

Thomas Willocks shoemaker the second of December 1657 was admitted & sworne a ffree Comoner of the Borrough aforesaid and was agreed to pay to the use of the Towne for his ffine 5s sterl uppon demand

John Williamson the 29th of July 1658 was admitted & sworne a free Comoner of the Borrough aforesaide and for his ffine submitteth himself to the order of the Court

oo　02　06

Willm Roger the 29th of July 1658 was admitted & sworne a free Comoner of the Borrough aforesaid and for his ffine submitteth himself to the order of the Court

oo×06×08 red 1s

Thomas Hardman the first of July 1658 was admitted & sworne a ffree Comoner of the Borrough aforesaid and was agreed to pay [for] *to* the use of the Towne for his *ffine* 5s sterl uppon demande

Robte Nevin merchant upon his Petition the 4th of No 1658 was admitted a free merchant stapler and tooke his oath according to the use & custome of the said Towne

James Kinge merchant [James Kinge] upon his petition the 4th of No: 1658 was admitted a free merchant Stapler and tooke his oath according to the use & custome of the said Towne

John Sleminge Slater upon his Petition the tenth of ffebruar 1658 was admitted and sworne a ffree Comoner of the Corporacon aforesaid and was to give to the use of the Towne three shillings sterl wthin the month of May next.
2s × p

Edward Steawart laborer upon his Petition the tenth of febr^y 1658 was admitted and sworne a free Comoner of the Corporacon aforesaid and is to give to the use of the Towne for his admittance three shill sterl wthin the moneth of May next
o 3 × o

ffrancis Fleminge laborer upon his petition the tenth of februar 1658 was admitted and sworne a free Comoner of the Corporacon aforesaid and is to paye to the use of the Towne for his admittance three shill sterl wthin the moneth of May next
∞ 3   o

Robte McKee laborer upon his petition the tenth of februar 1658 was admitted & sworne a free Comoner of the Corporacon aforesaid and is to pay to the use of the Towne for his admittance 3s sterl wthin the moneth of May next

John Griffith laborer upon his Petition the 10th of ffebr^y 1658 was admitted & sworne a free Comoner of the Corporacon aforesaid and is to give to the use of the Towne for his admittance three shill sterl wthin the moneth of May next
mort ∞ 3   o 26th Sept 1662 he tooke his oath that he wrought out his fine in Mr Will Leathes

John Grahams laborer upon his petition the tenth of februar 1658 was admitted and sworne a ffree Comoner of the Corporacon aforesaid and is to give to the use of the Towne for his admittance three shills sterl wthin the moneth of May next
∞ 3   o pd this 20th August 1662 × pd

George Leister laborer upon his petition the tenth of febr 1658 was admitted and sworne a free Comoner of the Corporation aforesaide and is to give to the use of ye Towne for his admittance three shills sterl wthin the moneth of May next

Allexander McHoole merchant the twelveth of februar 1658 uppon his petition was admitted & sworne a free Comoner and merchant of the Staple wthin the Corporacon aforesaid
∞ 15 ∞ pd

Willm Anderson Merchant uppon his Petition the twelveth of februar 1658 was admitted and sworne a free Comoner and of the Staple within the Corporacon aforesaid
∞ 13 04 pd

Allexander Thomson Merchant uppon his Petition the twelveth febr 1658 was admitted & sworne a free Comoner and of the staple wthin the Corporacon aforesaid this 24th of Novr 1662 claimed by oath that he paid 10s to Mr Wm Leathes & 3s 4d str in money to Mr M'Cartney Sov^r
o 3 o pd

Allexander McCartney Taylor uppon his humble Petition the twelveth of februar 1658 was admitted and sworne a free Comoner of the Corporacon aforesaid
mort o 6 8 pd paid to Mr Rigby this 12th of June 1662

John Loughhead labourer uppon his humble Petition the twelveth of februar 1658 was admitted and sworne a free Comoner of the Corporacon aforesaid
o 6 8 pd

Archibald Moore laborer uppon his humble Petition the twelveth of februar 1658 was admitted and sworne a free Comoner of the Corporacon aforesaide
o 6 8 pd Paid 5s to Mr Wm Leathes Sofferaine 2s 6d to Mr Rigby pd

John Sorbye laborer uppon his humble Petition the seventh of March 1658 was admitted and sworne a free Comoner of the Corporacon aforesaid
o 6 8 pd 5s to Mr Leathes Sofferaine

Thomas Sorbye laborer uppon his humble Petition the seventh of March was admitted and sworne a free Comoner of the Corporacon aforesaid
pd

George Neigus husbandman uppon his humble Petition the tenth daye of March 1658 was admitted & sworne a free Comoner of the Corporacon aforesaid

Ralph Carr shoomaker uppon his humble Peticion the thirteenth day of [March] *October* 1659 was admitted and sworne a free Comoner of the Corporacon aforesd

Thomas Banckes yeoman the 3d day of Novembr 1659 was admitted and sworne a free Comoner of ye Corporation & ye same day swore likewise in ye office of A Sargent to ye said Corporation
∞ 10 ∞ pd 5s

Thomas Hadskinson upon his humble peticion the tenth day of November 1659 was admitted and sworne a free Comoner and marchant of ye Staple within this Towne according to ye ancient libertyes and preveliges thereof
pd 10s pd

John Barton upon his humble peticion the 10th of Novr 1659 was admitted and sworne a free Comoner and Marchant of ye Staple within this Towne according to ye Ancient libertyes and preveleidges thereof
fees paid

John Bayles blacke smith upon his humble peticion the 11th of November 1659 was admitted and sworne a free Comoner [and] of ye towne & Corporacon aforesaid

S

2s. 6d

ffrancis Cockes Tayler upon his humble peticion y* 11th of Novr 1659 was admitted and sworne a free Comoner of the Towne & Corporacon aforesaid

o 2 6

John Crosbey blacksmith upon his humble peticion of ye 14th of November 1659 was admitted and sworne and sworne a free Comoner of this Towne and Corporacon

o 5s o pd

Henry Murdock cooper upon his humble peticion of ye 16th November 1659 was admitted and sworne a free Comoner of this Towne & Corporacon aforesaid

o 10 o pd

James Sparkes marct upon his humble peticion of 7th of December 1659 was admitted and sworne a free Comoner and Marchant Stapler within this Towne according to ye Ancient libertyes and previledges thereof

o 10 o

Henry Tickell marct upon his humble peticion of 7th of December 1659 was admitted and sworne a free Comoner of and Marchant of the Staple within this Towne according to ye Ancient libertyes and previledges thereof

1659

oo o5 oo pd

Richard Westbrooke marc^t upon his humble peticion the 7th of December 1659 was admitted and sworne a free Comoner & Marchant of ye Staple within this Towne according to ye Ancient libertyes and previledges thereof

oo 10 oo pd

Tho Owens marc^t upon his humble Peticion the 7th of Decembr 1659 was admitted and sworne a free Comoner & Marchant of ye Staple within this Towne according to ye Ancient libertyes and previlidges thereof

oo 10 oo pd

Robert Smith marc upon his humble Peticion the 8th of Decembr 1659 was admitted and sworne a free Comoner and Marcht of the Staple within this Towne according to ye ancient libertyes and previledges thereof

oo 10 oo

James Holmes marc & Seafering man upon his humble Peticion ye 15th of Decembr 1659 was admitted and sworne a free Comoner and Marcht of ye Staple within this Towne according to ye Ancient libertyes and previ'edges thereof

1660

mort pd

Mathew Davis gent upon his humble peticion y 16th of Aprill 1660 was admitted and sworne a free Comoner and Marcht of the Staple within this Towne according to ye Ancient libertyes and previledges thereof

oo o2 o6 pd

John McWhirke Shoomaker upon his humble Peticion y 17th of April 1660 was admitted and sworne a free Comoner of this Corporacon afforesaid

o1 oo oo pd 10s

William Warren marc upon his humble peticion ye 17th of Apr 1660 was admitted and sworne a free Comoner and Marcht of ye Staple within this Towne according to ye Ancient libertyes and priviledges thereof

Capt Meeke Sofferaigne after ye intermt of William Leathes was sworne & recd ye rod

Mr Tho Wallcott this 25th of June 1660 was admitted and sworne a free Comoner and Marchant of the Staple within this Towne according to ye Privelidge thereof

fine to ye Towns use is oo o5 oo recd o2 o6

John McCauley this 27th June 1660 was admitted and sworne a free Comoner within this Towne according to ye Prevelidge thereof

fine oo o5 oo

John Nichollson butcher ye 11th October 1660 was admitted and sworne a free Comoner within ye said Towne according to ye prevelidges thereof

no fine because served apprentice in ye towne

the same day Ralph Pitt Butcher was sworne freeman

no fine

the same day Robert Hunter Taylor was admitted and sworne a frēē

oo o5 oo pd

William Persie Shoomaker was admitted ye same day and sworne a frēē

oo o5 oo pd

William George Bricklayer ye same day was sworne a freeman

oo o5 oo

Ralph Jaques Carpinter the same day was sworne a freeman

oo o5 oo pd

George McCartney Millwright ye 12th day of October was admitted and sworne a free Comoner within this Towne according to ye prevelidge thereof

oo o5 oo pd

James Cuningham glover ye same day was sworne a freeman

oo o5 oo pd

John Deane labourer ye same day was sworne a freeman

oo o5 oo
John Dunlop Maltman yᵉ same day was sworne a freeman

oo o5 oo
Andrew Rea Shoomaker yᵉ 18th day of Octʳ 1660 was sworne a freeman

oo o5 oo
Daniell Carrett Weaver yᵉ 25th of Octʳ was sworne a freeman

oo o5 oo
Henry Seaton weaver yᵉ 12th of Novembʳ was sworne a freeman

oo o5 oo pd
James Allen Glaser yᵉ same day was sworne a freeman

oo o5 oo
Henry Wharton Shoomaker yᵉ same day was sworne a freeman

oo o5 oo
John M'Cleland Shoomaker yᵉ same day was sworne a freeman

oo o5 oo fines to ye Towne
James Roch [Shoomaker] *Butcher* yᵉ same day was sworne a freeman

fines to yᵉ Towne oo o5 oo
Thomas ffarmer Taylor yᵉ same day was sworne a freeman

o1 oo oo pd 1o oo
William Spittle marchant yᵉ same day was sworne a free Comoner and Marchant
of ye Staple

oo o2 6 pd
Thomas Becke Baker yᵉ 13th of November was sworne a freeman

mort oo 1o oo pd abated 5s
William Bunnis yᵉ 18th December 1660 was sworne a free Comoner & marcht
of the staple

oo 1o oo pd
[William] *John* Erwin marcht yᵉ same day was sworne a free Comoner & marcht
of the staple

free
William Lesley gentleman yᵉ 19th of January 1660 was sworne Comoner &
Marchant of ye staple

free
Gilbert Wye gentl yᵉ   of   was sworne a free Comoner & Marchant of yᵉ
staple

free
Capt Samuell Blewett yᵉ   of   was sworne a free   and Marcht of yᵉ Staple

free pd
Andrew McCullogh Gold smith yᵉ   of   was sworne a freeman

free pd
James Anderson Stationer yᵉ same day was sworne a freeman

mort oo o5 oo pd
John Stewart Carpinter yᵉ 7th of March was sworne a freeman

1661 free
Coll William Knight Barrester yᵉ 30th 1661 was sworne a free Comoner and
Marcht of ye Staple

oo 1o oo
Allexander M'Kenney Marcht yᵉ 1oth of Aprill was sworne a free Comoner and
Marcht of yᵉ Staple

served his apprent in this Towne
Thomas Stewart Marcht yᵉ same day was sworne a free Comoner & Marcht of yᵉ
Staple

served his apprent in this Towne
John Clughston Junior yᵉ same day was sworne a free Comoner and Marcht
of yᵉ Staple

served prentisᵖ in this Towne
James Chalmers Marcht yᵉ same day was sworne a free Comoner and Marcht of
the Staple yᵉ 1oth of Aprill

served prentisᵖ in this Towne
George Martin yᵉ Younger yᵉ same day was sworne a free Comoner and Marcht
of the Staple

mort served prentisᵖ in this Towne
George Stewart Marcht yᵉ same day was sworne a free Comoner and Marcht of
the Staple

Served prentisᵖ in this Towne
John White Marcht yᵉ same day was sworne a free Comoner and Marcht of yᵉ
Staple

oo o2 o6 pd
William Rochester yeoman yᵉ same day was sworne a freeman

oo o2 o6 pd
John Tavernor yeoman yᵉ same day was sworne a freeman

oo o5 oo pd
Pattrick Corry yeoman yᵉ same day was sworne a freeman

oo o5 oo pd
William M'Clelland Weaver yᵉ same day was sworne a freeman

oo o5 oo pd
James m'Hoole Porter yᵉ same day was sworne a freeman
o1 oo oo [John Porter Labʳ]
John Donnellson Esqr yᵉ 12th of Aprill was sworne a free Comoner and Marchant of yᵉ Staple
o1 oo oo
Hercules Davis gent yᵉ same day was sworne a free Comoner and Marcht of yᵉ Staple
o1 oo oo
Henry Davis gent yᵉ same day was sworne a free Comoner and Marcht of yᵉ Staple
oo o5 oo
Theopholis Taylor marcᵗ yᵉ same day was sworne a free Comoner & Marcht of yᵉ Staple
oo o5 oo
Roger Gravitt marcᵗ yᵉ same day was sworne a free Comoner and Marcht of yᵉ Staple
oo 1o oo
Hugh mᶜManus yᵉ same day was sworne a free Comoner & Marcht of yᵉ Staple
fines to yᵉ Towne oo o5 oo
John Morrisson Pewterer yᵉ same day was sworne a freeman
served his prentisᵖ in this Towne
Marcus Garnett Chanler yᵉ same day was sworne a freeman
served his prentisᵖ in this Towne
Israell Christian Butcher yᵉ 1oth of May was sworne a freeman
oo o2 o6
Lawrance Crosley yᵉ 21st of May was sworne a freeman
served his prentisᵖ in this Towne
William Williamson Butcher yᵉ same day was sworne a freeman
oo o5 oo pd
Michaell Reime yᵉ same day was sworne a free Comoner and Marcht of yᵉ Staple
oo o5 oo pd
Hugh Richardson Slater yᵉ 18th of June was sworne a freeman
oo 1o oo pd
William Orr Apothecary yᵉ 19th of June was sworne a free Comoner of this Towne
oo o5 oo pd
Robert Martin marcᵗ yᵉ 2oth of June was sworne a free Comoner and Marct of yᵉ Staple
served his prentisᵖ in this Towne
Paule Read marcᵗ yᵉ same day was sworne a free Comoner & Marchant of yᵉ Staple
oo o2 o6 pd
James Biggar marcᵗ yᵉ same day was sworne a free Comoner & Marct of yᵉ Staple
pd to Mr le Sovern oo 1o oo
William Erwin marcᵗ yᵉ same day was sworne a free Comoner & Marct of yᵉ Staple
Served his prentice in Towne
Henry Hoole Tanner yᵉ 21th of June was sworne a freeman
oo 1o oo pd
Turlough mᶜGee yeoman yᵉ same day was sworn a freeman
Served his prentisᵖ in Towne
John Drenon ffeltmaker yᵉ 29th of August was sworn a freeman
oo o2 o6
Thomas Rouse Shoomaker yᵉ same day was sworne a freeman
John Rigby Sofferaine   1661
fines to yᵉ Towne oo o5 oo
John ffinch blacksmith yᵉ 1oth of October 1661 was sworne a freeman
oo o5 oo pd
Robert Paver Bricklayer yᵉ same day was sworne a freeman
oo o2 o6 pd
John Horner Butcher yᵉ same day was sworne a freeman
mort   Served his prentisᵖ in this Towne
John Porter Butcher yᵉ   of Novembʳ was sworne a freeman
oo o2 o6 pd
Thomas Waltson shoomaker yᵉ 23rd of January was sworne a freeman
oo o2 o6 pd
Edward Williamson Porter yᵉ 13th of ffebruary was sworne a freeman
oo o2 o6
Andrew M'Hoole Porter yᵉ same day was sworne a freeman
oo o2 o6 pd
James Miller Porter yᵉ same day was sworne a freeman
oo 1o oo
Edward Ellis Apothecary the 24th day of June 1662 was admitted and sworne a free Comoner of yᵉ Borrough afforesaid according to yᵉ previledges thereof

fine paid

Edward Roch y⁰ same day was admitted and sworne a freeman and his fine to y⁰ Towne forgiven him

oo o2 o6 pd

William Van Hovan Gardiner y⁰ 10th of July 1662 was admitted & sworne a free Comoner of this borrough

oo 10 oo pd

Peetter Jones Marchant y⁰ 12th of July 1662 was admitted and sworne a free Stapler of y⁰ Borrough afforesaid

oo 10 oo

Richard Bodkin gent y⁰ same day was admitted and sworne a free Stapler of y Borrough afforesaid

served his prentisᵖ in this Towne

Hugh Breerly Butcher y⁰ 17th of September 1662 was admitted and sworne a free Stapler of the Borrough afforesaid

oo o5 oo pd oo o2 o6

Thomas Gibson Glasier y⁰ 20th of September 1662 was admitted and sworne a free Comoner of the Borrough afforesaid

Towne fine oo o2 o6 pd

William Mickell Shoomaker was admitted and sworne a free Comoner of this Corporacon this 25th of Sepr 1662

Served his Apprentisᵖ in this Towne

Robert Thomson Taylor y⁰ same day was admitted and sworne a free Comoner of this Corporacon

oo o2 o6 pd

Petter Taylor Porter was admitted y⁰ same day and sworne a free Comoner

oo o2 o6 pd

John Reynells Taylor y⁰ same day was admitted and sworne a free Comoner

mort oo o2 o6 pd

the same day Thomas Langsdall Porter was admitted and sworne a free Comoner

oo o2 o6 pd

James Christian Taylor y⁰ same day was admitted and sworne a free Comoner

oo o2 o6 pd

Nicholas Taylor y⁰ same day was admitted and sworne a free Comoner

oo o2 o6 pd

Edward Marshall Taylor this 26th of Sept 1662 was admitted and sworne a free Comoner

mort oo o2 o6 pd

Edward Locher Labʳ y⁰ same day was admitted and sworne a free Comoner

oo o4 o6

Rowland Sharper was admitted and sworne a free Comoner and Marchant Stapler according to y⁰ Ancient custome and previlidge of y⁰ said Towne this 27th of Sept 1662

oo o4 o6 pd

Peirce Wellsh shoomaker y⁰ same day was admitted and sworne a free Commoner of y⁰ said Towne and a Marchant Stapler thereof according to the Ancient previllidge thereof

Served his Apprentisᵖ in this Towne

John Manken Tanner y⁰ same day was admitted & sworne a free Commoner of the sd Towne

oo o2 o6 pd

John Williamson Labʳ was admitted and sworne a free Commoner of the said

oo o2 o6 pd

James Hall Scoolemaster was admitted and sworne y⁰ same day a free Commoner

oo o2 o6

William Cowan Carpenter y⁰ same day was admitted and sworne a free Commoner of y⁰ Borrough afforesaid

oo 10 oo pd

Willfered Bristow of Carlile marcht this 29th of Sept was admitted and sworne a free Commoner [of this] and marchant of y⁰ Staple according to the libertyes and previleidges thereof

oo o5 oo pd o2 o6

Simon Thetford y⁰ same day was admitted and sworne a free Comoner and Marcht of the Staple according to the libertyes and previleidges thereof

oo o5 oo pd

John Christian y⁰ same day was admitted a free Comoner

he served his Apprentisᵖ in y⁰ Towne

Robert Quin *Currier* y⁰ same day was admitted a free Comoner

oo o2 o6 pd

John Shankes *Gardiner* y⁰ same day was admitted a free Comoner

[George Cambell marchᵗ this 13th of January 1662 was admitted and sworn a free comoner and marchᵗ of the staple according to y⁰]

George M'Cartney Soveraigne

mort oo 10 oo paid

John Creichton marchant this 24th day of November 1662 was admitted and sworne a free Comoner and marcht of the Staple of this Borrough according to y⁰ Ancient

Custome and Libertyes thereof & hath paid 10s str to yᵉ use of Towne and tenn shill more he is to pay when he shall become an Inhabitant of of (*sic*) yᵉ said Towne
01　00　00 paid

George Cambell marcᵗ this 13th day of January 1662 was admitted and sworne a free Comoner & marcᵗ of the Staple of this Borrough according to yᵉ Ancient Custome and libertes thereof—hath paid twenty shills to yᵉ use of yᵉ Towne
he sarved his apprentishᵖ in Bellfast

Robert Whitside marchᵗ upon yᵉ humble desire of Hugh Eccles Marcht the 21th of January 1662 was admitted and sworne a free Comoner and marchᵗ of the Staple of this Borrough according to yᵉ Ancient previleges thereof
he sarved his Apprentisᵖ

Tho Roads Butcher upon his peticion *yᵉ 21th May 1663* was admitted and sworne a free Comoner of yᵉ Borrough
00　10　00 paid

George McKnight *Chandler* upon his peticion yᶜ 21th May 1663 was admitted and sworne a free Comoner
00　02　06 pd

George Snowdon made a freeman
this 12th of September 1663

Arthur Ward gent Clarke of yᵉ Crowne for yᵉ North East Circuit of Ulster was admitted and sworne a free Comoner and Marchant of yᵉ Staple of this Borrough according to yᵉ Ancient Priviledges

John Dawson gent was admitted and sworne a free Comoner and Marchant Staple of this Borrough according to yᵉ Ancient previledges
00　10　00 pd

John Agnew Cooper this 1ˢᵗ of October 1663 upon his humble peticion was admitted and sworne a free Comoner of this Borrough &c
00　10　00 pd

John Poole Porter the 1ˢᵗ of October 1663 upon his peticion was admitted and sworne a free Comoner of yᵉ Borrough
he served his apprenticesp in Belfast

David MᶜCullough glover and skiner late apprentice to Robert Skiner was admitted and sworne a free Comoner of this Borrough this 6ᵗʰ of November 1663
he served his apprenticesp in Belfast

Thomas Whittley Tanner late apprentice to Mʳ Thomas Warring was admitted and sworne a free Comoner of this Borrough this 11ᵗʰ of November 1663
fine　00　13　04 paid

James Read of Enniskillin marchᵗ the 21ᵗʰ of November 1663 was admitted and sworne a free Comoner and marchᵗ of yᵉ Staple of this Borrough according to yᵉ Ancient libertyes thereof
fine　00　12　06 paid

William Bickerstafe of Wire Watter Mariner yᵉ 26ᵗʰ Novʳ 1663 was admitted and sworne a free Comoner of this Corporacon
Mort　00　10　00 not paid Sargent Potts deceased yᵉ 3d decr 1663

Allexandʳ Porter shoomaker yᵉ same day was admitted and sworne a free Comoner of this Corporacon
00　10　00 paid

William Gibbs Taylor this 16ᵗʰ Decʳ 1663 was admitted and sworne a free Comoner of this Corporacon
fine　00　07　06 paid

Lᵗ. Thomas Cranston this 17ᵗʰ of Decʳ 1663 was admitted and sworne a free Comoner of this Corporacon
00　10　00 paid

Robert Dowglas Brickmaker this 17ᵗʰ of Decʳ 1663 was admitted and sworne a free Comoner of this Corporacon
00　05　00 paid

Robert Beck Weavour this 7ᵗʰ January 1663 was admitted and sworne a free Comoner of this Corporacon according to yᵉ custome thereof
00　10　00 paid

Daniell Leech Weavor yᵉ same day was admitted and sworne a free Comoner
00　10　00 paid

Daniell ffrissell shoomaker yᵉ same day was admitted and sworne a free Comoner
00　05　00 paid

Michaell Pattridge blacksmith this 7ᵗʰ of January 1663 was admitted and sworne a free Comoner of this Corporacon
00　10　00 paid

Thomas Bell blacksmith yᵉ same day was admitted and sworne a free Comoner of this Corporacon
01　00　00 pd Mr McCartney

Thomas Pottinger Marchᵗ this 23ʳᵈ of January 1663 was admitted and sworne a free Comoner and Marchᵗ of the Staple of this Corporacon
00　05　00 pd Mr McCartney

John Ellison Shipcarpinter yᵉ same day was admitted and sworne a free Comoner

∞ 10 ∞ forgiven
William Oakes Butcher y same day was admitted & sworne a free Comoner

∞ 10 ∞ pd Mr Reynell
Gabriell Holmes Mariner yᵉ 2ᵈ of March 1663 was admitted and sworne a free Comoner of this Corporacon

∞ 10 ∞ paid
James Taylor Mariner yᵉ same day was admitted and sworne a free Comoner

∞ 10 ∞ paid
Gabriell Holmes yᵉ younger yᵉ same day was admitted and sworne a free Comoner

∞ 10 ∞ pd
James Hays Marriner this 1ˢᵗ of Septʳ 1664 was admitted a free Comoner & sworne of this Corporacon

∞ 05 ∞ pd Mr Reynell
James McCaddam Mariner This 15ᵗʰ of Septʳ 1664 upon his humble Peticion was admitted [free] & sworne a free Comoner
he served his prentishp in this Towne

Ric Bourne *Butcher* yᵉ same day was admitted and sworne a free Comoner
he served his prentishp in Bellfast

George Skerris *blacksmith* yᵉ 15ᵗʰ Sepʳ 1664 was admitted & sworne a free Comoner

Henry Dickison Carpinter yᵉ same day was admitted a free Comoner
he made two seales for Leather to yᵉ use of yᵉ Towne

David Scott blacksmith yᵉ same day was admitted a free Comoner

∞ 05 ∞ pd
William Chrighton Taylor yᵉ same day was admitted a free Comoner

∞ 05 ∞ pd
John Corbett Cooper yᵉ same day was admitted & sworne a free Comoner
he served his apprentisp in Towne

David Agnew marchᵗ yᵉ 20ᵗʰ day of Sepʳ 1664 was admitted and sworne a free Comoner & Marchant Stapler of this Borrough

∞ 10 ∞ pd
Hugh White marchᵗ yᵉ same day was sworne a free Comoner and marchᵗ Stapler of this Corporacon

∞ 05 ∞ pd
John Hunter Carpinter yᵉ same day was admitted & sworne a free Comoner

∞ 05 ∞ pd
Robᵗ Taylor Mariner yᵉ same day was admitted & sworne a free Comoner

∞ 10 ∞ pd
Allexandʳ Arthur Tanner yᵉ 22ⁿᵈ day of Sepʳ was admitted and sworne a free Comoner & Marchᵗ stapler of this Corporacon
he served his pentisp

Vallintine Herone Butcher yᵉ same day was admitted and sworne a free Comoner
he sarved his pentisp

George Kennedy weavor yᵉ same day was admitted & sworne a free Comoner

∞ 05 ∞ pd
Robert McCreery Mariner yᵉ same day was sworne & admitted a free Comoner

∞ 04 09 pd
John Worthington yeoman yᵉ same day was sworne a free Comoner

∞ 10 ∞ pd
Hugh Biggar Tanner yᵉ 23ᵈ Sepʳ 1664 was admitted and sworne a free Comoner

∞ 04 09 pd
Andrew Blomfeild Sayler yᵉ 29ᵗʰ of Sepʳ 1664 was admitted and sworne a free Comoner

∞ 05 ∞ forgiven
Joseph Storry Labourer yᵉ same day was admitted & sworne a free Comoner

∞ 02 06 forgiven
John Willson ffeltmaker yᵉ same day was admitted & sworne a free Comoner

∞ 05 ∞
Robert Murrow Labourer yᵉ same day was admitted & sworne a free Comoner

∞ 05 ∞ pd Mr Reynell
Abraham Ponsonbey Joyner yᵉ same day was admitted & swore a free Comoner
he served his apprentisp in this Towne

William Martin Tanner yᵉ sonn of George Martin Burgesse yᵉ same day was admitted & sworne a free Comoner

Tho Warring Esqr Soveraigne   1664

∞ 05 ∞ pd to Mr Warring
George Willis Butcher yᵉ 13ᵗʰ day of October 1664 was admitted & sworne a free Comoner of this Corporacon

∞ 15 ∞ pd to Mr Warring
Richard Hull of Wire Watter Mariner was admitted and sworne a free Comoner yᵉ same day

01 ∞ ∞ pd to Mr Warring
Arthur Smith of Wire Watter Mariner was admitted & sworne a free Comoner & Marchant Stapler

Marcht 01 10 00 pd to Mr Warring

Richard Burrell Merchant this 10th of Janry 1664 wass admited and sworne A ffree [stapler] Comoner and Merch, of ye Staple of this Borrough according to ye antient Custome and Liberties Thereof

sworne Gratuss

Samuell Downes of Belfast *gent* [merch'] wass admited and sworne A ffree Comoner and Mercht Stapler this 10th of Janry 1664

01 00 00 pd to Mr Warring

Mathew [Walter] Rowan of Green Nock in ye Kingdome of Scotland Merchant this 22th of ffebruary 1664 was admitted and sworne a ffree Comr and Merchant of the Staple of the sayd Burrough

00 09 00 to pay 9 more

Ralph Sanderson of Scarburgh in the Kingdome of England Mariner was admitted and sworne ffree Comoner and Merchant of the Staple of the Burrough of Belfast the 31st day of May 1665

5s payd in hand 5s to be pd when able pd Mr Reynell

Andrew Knowes of Belfast Cordwainer was admitted and sworne a ffree Comoner of the Burrough of Belfast the 31st of May 1665

1l 10s 00d for ye use of ye Towne

Richard Page of Westmoreland in the Kingdome of England Merchant was admitted and sworne a ffree Comoner and Merchant of the Staple of the Burrough of Belfast the 14th day of June in the year 1665 according to the custome of the sayd Burrough

promised to pay 10s to the Towne wthin 3 months pd Mr Reynell

Robert Spay of Belfast in the Kingdome of Ireland Cooper was admitted and sworne a ffree Comoner of the sayd Burrough of Belfast the 10th day of August 1665 according to ye custome of ye said Burrough

promised to pay 10s to the Towne wthin 3 months pd Mr Reynell

John Killpatrick of Belfast Merct was admitted and sworne a ffree Comoner and Merct of the Staple of the Burrough aforesayd the 20th day of August 1665 according to the custome of the Burrough

0 05 00 pd Soveraigne

John Speare of Belfast Shooemaker was admitted and sworne a free Comoner of ye Burrough aforesayd the 12th of October 1665

pd 5s to Mr Soveraigne

John King of Belfast Carpenter was admitted and sworne a free Comoner of the sayd Burrough the 12th of October 1665

pd 5s to Mr Soveraigne

Symon Wilson Labourer was admitted and sworne a free Comoner of this Corporacon the 2nd of November 1665

00 10 00 To the Towne pd Mr Warring

William Bagott of Wire Watter in the Kingdome of England Marriner was admitted and sworne a ffree Comoner of this Corporacon the 21th day of November 1665

Sworne gratis

Capt Thomas Beverly Quarter Master to ye Right Honble Arthur Earle of Donegall was admitted and sworne a ffree Comoner and Merchant of the Staple of the sayd Burrough the 22th day of November 1665 Thomas Warring Esqr being then Soveraigne

Sworne gratis

Eodem die William Lorame Quarter Master to Leiftennt Colonell Moses Hill was admitted and sworne a free Comoner and Merchant of the Staple of the Burrough of Belfast Thomas Waring Esqr Soveraigne

00 05 00 pd to Mr

Peter Croft of Stalmin in ye County of Lancaster Marriner was Admitted and sworne a ffree Comoner and Merchant of the Staple of the Burrough of Belfast ye 22th of November 1665

00 05 00 pd to Mr Warring

Eodem die Henry Clarke of Belfast Inholder was admitted and sworne a ffree Comoner and Merchant of the Staple of ye sayd Burrough Thomas Warring Esq Soveraigne

00 05 00 to ye repayre of ye Key pd to Mr Waring

Robert Townson [was Ad] of Leeds in Yorkshire Clothyer was admitted and sworne a free Comoner and Merchant of the Staple of the Burrough of Belfast the 22th day of November 1665. Thomas Warring Esqr then Soveraigne

00 05 00 to ye repayre of ye Key pd to Mr Wm Waring

Allen Burkett of the Grange in Lancashire Marriner was Admitted and sworne a free Comoner and Merchant of the Staple of the Burrough of Belfast the 24th of November 1665 Thomas Waring Esqr Soveraigne

00 05 00 to ye repayre of ye Key pd to Wm Waring

Anthony Wylde of the Isle of ffaney Marriner was admitted and sworne a ffree Comoner and Merchant of the Staple of ye Burrough of Belfast the 22th day of November Thomas Waring Esqr Soveraigne

Tempore Edwardi Reynell Armiger Superior Burgi Sive Ville de Belfast in Comitat Antrim et unus Justiciariorum pacis pro Domino Rege in Comitat pʳdict Communes et liberi homines Burgi Sive Ville pʳdict fact et Admissi Anno Regni Domini nostri Caroli Secundi nunc Angliæ &ᵉ decimo septimo Annoque Domini 1665

ool o5s ood pd for yᵉ use of the Towne

Robert Clarke Sonne of John Clarke having served his Apprentishipp to Hugh Campbell of the same Towne Mercᵗ upon his Peticion was Admitted and Sworne a ffree Comoner and Merchant of the Staple of the sayd Burrough the 14ᵗʰ day of December 1665

oo o5 oo

William Arthur at a Court holden for the sayd Burrough the first day of ffebruary in anno predicto having served his Apprentishipp with William Smith of the same Borough Merchant was admitted and sworne a ffree Comoner and Merchant of the Staple of the sayd Borough Edward Reynell Esqʳ being then Soveraigne

oo o5 oo

Eodem Die John Tofte Taylor having served his time wᵗʰ his father-in law Tho Lightfoote was admitted and sworne a ffree Comoner of the sayd Borough Edward Reynell Esqʳ then Soveraigne ffees unpaid

oo o5 oo

Eodem Die Thomas Barbin ffeltmaker having served his Apprentishipp with Robert Whiteside of the same Towne was Admitted and sworne a ffree Comoner of the sayd Borough Edward Reynell Esqʳ then Soveraigne

to pay 1os to the use of yᵉ Towne

John Hamond the fifteenth day of ffebruary was Admitted and sworne a ffree Comoner and Merchant of the Staple of the sayd Borough Edward Reynell Esqʳ then Soveraigne fees unpayd

o1 oo oo to be payd wthin 3 weekes to yᵉ use of yᵉ Towne Rog Leathes to pay it

John Welsh of Glanavy Tanner was the fifth day of Aprill 1666 admitted and sworne a ffree Comoner and Merchant of the Staple of the Towne and Burrough of Belfast in the time of Edward Reynell Esqr then Soveraigne

he served his Apprentsp in this Towne wᵗʰ Mr Warring

John Roads Tanner was the 3ʳᵈ day of May 1666 admitted and sworne a free Comoner of this Towne

Samson Theaker gent was the fifth day of July 1666 admitted and sworne a ffree Comoner & Mercᵗ of the Staple of the Towne and Burrough of Belfast Edward Reynell Sover

oo 1o oo for yᵉ use of yᵉ Towne pd to Mr Reynell

eodem die James Whyte *Taylor* was admitted a ffree Comoner of the Burrough of Belfast

co 15 oo to yᵉ Towne pd to Mr Reynell

eodem die James Johnston *mercᵗ* was Admitted and sworne a ffree Comoner and Merchant of the Staple for yᵉ Borrough aforesayd

oo 15 oo to yᵉ Towne pd to Mr Reynell

eodem die Henry Taylor was admitted and sworne a ffree Comoner and Merchant of the Staple of the Borrough aforesayd

oo 1o oo pd Mr Reynell

Humfrey Dobbin Mercᵗ was Admitted and sworne a free Comoner and Merchant of the Staple of the sayd Borrough the 12th of July Mr Reynell Soveraigne

oo 1o oo to be paid for yᵉ good of the Towne wᵗʰin a month

Eodem die John Willox Shoomaker was Admitted and Sworne a free Comoner of the Borrough of Belfast

mort sworne gratis

Eodem die [John] *Robert* Jennings Cooke was Admitted and Sworne a free Comoner

sworne gratis

Eodem die John Arbuckles the Earle of Donegalls Gardner was Admitted and sworne a free Comoner

sworne gratis ffees unpᵈ

Mʳ Luke Gould servant to yₑ Earle of Donegall was Admitted and sworne a ffree Comoner and Merchant of the Staple of yᵉ sayd Burrough the 30ᵗʰ of August 1666 ffees unpᵈ

oo 1o oo to yᵉ Towne pd to Mr Sinckler appointed Treasurer for yᵉ Corporacon from this time

eodem die Robert Hutchin shoomaker was admitted and sworne a ffree Comoner of yᵉ Borough fees unpayd

oo 1o oᵊ pd to yᵉ Treasurer Mr Sinckler

eodem die James Tomson was Admitted and sworne a ffree Comoner of the Borrough of Belfast

Sworne gratis

25ᵗʰ October 1666 Robert Clarck Rope Maker was admitted and sworne a free Comoner of the Borrough of Belfast Mʳ Edward Reynell Soveraigne

Served his Apprentiship in Towne

eodem die Richard Curle Butcher was admitted and sworne a free Comoner of this Corporacon

Sworne gratis having served his Apprentishipp wth Tho Waring Esqr

    27th day of November 1666   James Bullar *Tanner* was Admitted and sworne a free Comoner and Merchant of the Staple of the said Corporacon   Edward Reynell Soveraigne

oo   12   o6 pd Mr Sinckler for ye use of ye Towne

    17th January 1666   William Tomson Gray merc^t was Admitted and sworne a free Comoner and merchant of the Staple of the sayd Corporacon   Edward Reynell Soveraigne

oo   10   oo pd to Mr Sinckler for the use of ye Towne

    24th January 1666   John Adam *Taylor* was admitted and sworne a free Comoner of this Corporacon

Sworne gratis having served wth Tho Waring Esqr

    14th ffebruary 1666   John Moore *Tanner* was Admitted and sworne a free Comoner and Merchant of the Staple of sayd Corporacion   Edward Reynell Soveraigne

Sworne gratis having served his time wth Tho Waring Esqr

    Eodem die   Richard Workeman *Tanner* was admitted and sworne as aforesayd fees unpayd

Sworne gratis having served his prentiship wth Joseph Whitlocke deceased

    21th March 1666   Henry Williamson *Butcher* was admitted and sworne a ffree Comoner

Served his apprentishipp wth Robert Skinner

    9th May 1667   Edward Hall *glover* was Admitted and Sworne a free Comoner of this Corporacon

oo   10   oo pd to Mr Sinckler for ye Towne

    30th May 1667   ffrancis Vivian Blacksmith was Admitted and sworne a free Comoner

Sworne gratis having served his Apprentiship wth Alexander Sincklar

    6th of June 1667   William Sincklar *Merch^t* was Admitted and Sworne a ffree Comoner and Merchant of the Staple of the Corporacon

Served his apprentiship as aforesayd

    eodem die   Hugh Speare *Merc^t* was Admitted and Sworne as aforesayd

pd oo   10   oo to ye use of ye Towne to Mr Sincklar

    11th July 1667   John M^cffarran labourer was admitted and sworne a free Comoner of this Corporacon

mort   pd to the use of the Towne   oo   10   oo to Mr Sincklar

    5th September 1667   Thomas Wrench of the Citty of Chester Merchant was Admitted and Sworne a ffree Comoner and Merc^t of the Staple

sworne gratis having served his Apprentiship

    eodem die 1667   Wiliam Karran Blacksmith was Admitted

pd oo   o6   o8 to be pd to Mr to Mr Sincklar by ye Sergeants

    5th September 1667   Andrew Paton Butcher was admitted

Mort   oo   o6   o8 to be payd by the Sergeants to Mr Sincklar for ye use of the Towne

    eodem die 1667   William Coxan Joyner was Admitted

oo   o6   o8 to the Towne to be payd by Robert Martin at All Saints next

    19th September 1667   John Hill *Gray Merc^t* was Admitted and Sworne a ffree Comoner

oo   o6   o8 to the Towne to be payd by John Gryffin at All Saints

    eodem die   John Johnston Taylor was Admitted and Sworne a ffree Comoner

o1   oo   oo pd to Mr Sincklar for ye use of the Towne

    26th September 1667   Tho Tippin was Admitted and Sworne a ffree Comoner

served his Apprentiship in Towne to doe XXs for ye good of ye Towne in worke

    eodem die   Bradshaw Leathes was Admitted and sworne a ffree Comoner and Merc^t of the Staple

oo   10   oo pd to Mr Sincklar for ye Towne

    eodem die   Ennis McAllyster was Admitted and Sworne a free Comoner

oo   10   oo to be payd by Hugh Gollocher

    eodem die   Thomas Richardson Carpenter was Admitted and sworne a ffree Comoner of this Corporacon

oo   10   oo to be payd by Hugh Gollocher

    eodem die   John Gowen Carpenter was Admitted and sworne a ffree Comoner [and] of this Corporacon

mort   Served his time in Towne

    eodem die   Michael Campbell Dyer was Admitted and sworne a ffree Comoner of this Corporacon

oo   10   oo to be payd by Mr Wye

    eodem die   Orlando Ashley *Barber* was admitted and sworne a ffree Comoner

oo   10   oo pd to Mr Sincklar

    eodem die   ffrancis ffisher was Admitted and sworne a ffree Comoner and merchant of the Staple

Served his Apprentishp

    eodem die   Robert Skerris Butcher was Admitted and sworne a ffree Comoner

oo   10   oo to be done in worke

    eodem die   Thomas Orpin Glasier was Admitted and sworne a ffree Comoner

oo   10   oo to be pd in a month

    eodem die   Obadiah Grove Taylor was Admitted a ffree Comoner

sworne gratis
    eodem die   John Bird Clockmaker was Admitted a ffree Comoner
oo 10 oo to be pd in a month
    eodem die   John Brogdon Shoemaker was Admitted a ffree Comoner
Served his Apprentiship in Towne
    eodem die   John Cordiner Chandler was Admitted a ffree Comoner
sworn gratis
    eodem die   Robert Cornwall gent was Admitted and Sworne a ffree Comoner and merchant of the Staple of this Burrough

Tempore Georgii McCartney Armiger tunc Superior Ville Belfast

    24th October 1667   James Burney Merc^t was Admitted and Sworne a ffree Comoner and Merc^t of the Staple served his Apprentishipp wth William Tomb Merc
Twenty shill pd to Mr Sincklar
    eodem die   Lawrence Oram Planter was Admitted and Sworne a ffree Comoner and Merc^t of the Staple
or oo oo to the Town pd to Mr Sincklar
    21th November 1667   Samuel Moore of Ayre Merchant was Admitted and Sworne a ffree Comoner and Merchant of the Staple of this Corporacon
Sworne gratis
    28th November 1667   Capt John Blair Marriner was Admitted and Sworne a ffree Comoner and Merchant of ye Staple of this Corporacon
served his Apprentiship wth George Martin Burgesse
    19th December 1667   George Hardie of Belfast Merc^t was admitted and sworne a ffree Comoner and Merchant of ye Staple
served his Apprentiship wth Arthur Houghton
    2nd January 1667   Thomas Leathes Butcher was Admitted and Sworne a ffree Comoner
served his Apprentiship wth John Herson
    16th January 1667   William Rutcliffe Clothyer was admitted a free Com^r
to pay 10s to ye Towne wthin a month
    eodem die   John Charnley ffeltmaker was Admitted a ffree Comoner
Sworne gratis having served his tyme wth Mr Eccles
    Hugh Lendey Merchant was Admitted and sworne a ffree Comoner and Merchant of ye Staple the 26th of March 1668
oo 15 oo to ye Towne pd to Mr Sinclair
    eodem die   James [A] Egarr Merc^t was Admitted and sworne a free Comoner and Merc^t of the Staple
oo 05 oo to ye Towne to Mr Sincklar
    eodem die   John Smith Glover was Admitted and sworne a ffree Comoner
oo 10 oo to ye Towne pd Mr Sincklar
    Alexander Boyess *Shoomaker* was Admitted and sworne a free Comoner
oo 10 oo to ye Towne pd Mr Sincklar
    9th of Aprill 1668   John Murdough Shoemaker was Admitted and Sworne a ffree Comoner of this Corporacon
Sworne gratis having served his Apprentiship in Towne
    7th of May, 1668   Richard Lam Bricklayer was admitted and Sworne a free Comoner
    14th May 1668   Richard fforester Taylor was Admitted and sworne a ffree Comoner
oo 12 o6
    eodem die   John Adam Merchant was Admitted and Sworne a ffree Comoner and Merchant of the Staple
o 10 oo
    eodem die   Thomas Dunkin was Admitted
Served his Apprentiship in Towne
    eode.n die   Hercules Langtree was Admitted
pd 1 oo oo pd to Mr Sincklar
    9th July 1668   Gilbert Rosse Merchant was admitted & sworne a ffree Comoner of this Borough and Merchant of the Staple
Sworne gratis having served his Apprentiship wth Israel Christian
    eodem die   Patrick Humes Butcher was Admitted
oo 05 oo pd to Mr Sincklar
    23th July 1668   Richard Ashmoore Glover was Admitted and sworne a ffree Comoner
oo 10 oo pd to Mr Sincklar
    eodem die   John Martin Labourer was Admitted & sworne a ffree Comoner of this Borrough
or oo oo to ye Towne pd to Mr Sincklar
    17th September 1668   Monsieur Daniel Mascon *Merchant* was Admitted & sworne a ffree Comoner and merchant of the Staple
Sworne gratis having served his Apprentishipp wth William Thom Merchant
    24th September 1668   Andrew Hutchinson Merchant was Admitted and sworne a ffree Comoner of this Corporacon

oo 10 oo pd to Mr Sincklar
eodem die   ffrancis Mankin Butcher was Admitted and sworne a ffree Comoner
oo 10 oo pd to Mr Sincklar
eodem die   John Brookes Butcher was Admitted and sworne a ffree Comoner
oo 10 oo pd to Mr Sincklar
1ˢᵗ. October 1668   Andrew Keyle Cooper was Admitted & sworne a ffree Comoner
oo 10 oo pd Mr Sincklar
15ᵗʰ October 1668   Thomas Clarck Stone Mason was Admitted and sworne a ffree Comoner of the Borrough of Belfast
oo 10 oo pd Mr Sincklar
eodem die   Thomas Corbitt Taylor was Admitted and sworne a free Comoner
oo 10 oo pd Mr Sincklar
eodem die   William Bryan yᵉ younger weaver was Admitted and sworne a ffree Comoner of yᵉ Borrough
oo 10 oo pd Mr Sincklar
eodem die   John Murrow Carpenter was Admitted and sworne a free Comoner
oo 10 oo pd Mr Sincklar
eodem die   John Tomson Cooper was Admitted & sworne a free Comoner
Gratis
29ᵗʰ October 1668   Sʳ Hercules Langsford Barronett was Admitted and Sworne a ffree Comoner and Merchant of the Staple
Gratis
eodem die   John Chichester Esqʳ sworne ut prius
Gratis
eodem die   Charles Bolton Esqʳ sworne ut prius
Gratis
Arthur Upton Esqʳ sworne ut prius
qy what he pd & to whom—nihil
eodem die   Peter Gubb Vintner was Admitted and Sworne a ffree Comoner & Merchant of the Staple
01 oo oo pd to Mr Sincklar
19ᵗʰ November 1668   Nicholas Cox Merchant was admitted and sworne a free Comoner and Merchant of yᵉ Staple
Sworne Gratis having served his Apprentiship wᵗʰ Peirce Welsh
10ᵗʰ December 1668   William Ogan Shoemaker was admitted and sworne a free Comoner of the Borrough aforesayd
Gratis
eodem die   Alexander ffergason Servant to the Earle of Donegall was admitted & sworne a free Comoner
Gratis
eodem die   Jenkin Jones Servant to yᵉ Earle of Donegall was admitted & sworne a free Comoner
Gratis
eodem die   Robert Stately Servant to yᵉ Earle of Donegall was Admitted & sworne a ffree Comoner
oo 10 oo pd Mr Sincklar
eodem die   William ffulton Shoemaker was Admitted and sworne a ffree Comoner
served his time wᵗʰ his ffather
17ᵗʰ December 1668   ffrancis Ratcliffe yᵉ younger Dyer was Admitted and sworne a ffree Comoner
served his Apprentp wᵗʰ John Hodson
eodem die   Richard Ratcliff Clothyer was Admitted and Sworne a ffree Comoner
oo 10 oo pd Mr Sincklar
eodem die   James English Bricklayer was Admitted and Sworne a ffree Comoner
Towne oo 10 oo Mr Sincklar
17ᵗʰ December 1668   James Ayesdale Slater was Admitted and sworne a free Comoner
oo 10 oo Mr Sincklar
eodem die   John Corsby Mason was Admitted and sworne a ffree Comoner
Gratis
Seaventh of January 1668   Sʳ Arthur Chichester Knight was Admitted and sworne a ffree Comoner and merchant of the Staple of the Borrough of Belfast
Gratis
Eodem die   Richard Coote Esq was *sworne* ut prius
Gratis
eodem die   Conway Hill Esqʳ was sworne ut prius
Gratis
eodem die   Richard Eustace gent was sworne ut prius
Gratis
eodem die   John Chichester gent was sworne ut prius
Gratis
eodem die   Charles Chichester gent was sworne ut prius
Gratis
eodem die   Edward Harrison gent was sworne ut prius

Gratis
    eodem die Chichester Phillipps gent was sworne ut prius

Gratis
    eodem die John Tooley Chirurgeon was sworne ut prius

Gratis
    21th January 1668   Thomas Sandeford servant to the Earle of Donegall was Admitted a ffree Comoner

Gratis
    John Vicar merc^t was admitted and sworne a ffree Comoner & merc^t of the Staple

oo 10 oo pd to Mr Sincklar
    1mo Aprilis 1669 ^no   Andrew Maxwell was Admitted and sworne a ffree Comoner & merc^t of the Staple of this Borrough

Sworne gratis having served his Apprentishipp wth his ffather
    eodem die John Crosley *Blacksmith* was Admitted & sworne a ffree Comoner of this Borrough

Sworne gratis
    William Bigger was Admitted and sworne a ffree Comoner & merc^t of the Staple

oo 10 oo pd Mr Sincklar
    eodem die John Johnston Carpenter was Admitted and sworne a ffree Comoner

oo 15 oo pd Mr Sincklar
    William Rayney was Admitted and sworne a ffree Comoner & marcht of the Staple the day aforesayd

Sworne gratis having served his time wth Mr Eccles merct
    William Dobbin was Admitted and sworne a ffree Comoner & March^t of the Staple the day aforesayd

oo 10 oo on trust
    5th of August 1669 Henry Smith Vintner was admitted and sworne a free Comoner of the Staple the day aforesayd

sworne gratis
    Roger Jonesse Labourer was Admitted and sworne a free Comoner of the Staple the day aforesayd

oo 10 oo pd Mr Sincklar
    26th of August 1669   Archibald McNeall was Admitted and sworne a free Comoner the day aforesayd

oo 10 oo
    David Sharplee was Admitted and sworne a free Comoner & Merch^t of the Staple the day aforesayd

    Simon Sharplee was Admitted and sworne a free Comoner & Merch^t of the Staple of the Staple (*sic*) payd Mr Sincklar oo 10 oo

    Robert Ponge was Admitted and Sworne a free Comoner & Merch^t of the Staple the day aforesayd   payd Mr Sincklar oo 12 06

    Robert Colbert was Admitted and sworne a free Comoner & Merch^t of the Staple the day aforesayd   payd Mr Sincklar oo 12 06

Gratis
    2^d day of September 1669 James McCartney gent was Admitted and Sworne a ffree Comoner and merc^t of the Staple of the Borrough of Belfast

Gratis served his time in Towne
    eodem die William Crawford sworne ut prius

oo 10 oo
    eodem die Hugh Crawford sworne ut prius

oo 10 oo
    eodem die Jonathan Allen Weaver sworne a ffree Comoner

oo 10 oo
    eodem die John McGowan Weaver sworne a ffree Comoner

oo 10 oo
    eodem die John Mercer Butcher sworne a ffree Comoner

oo 12 06
    9th day of September 1669 Alexander Ury Taylor sworne a ffree Comoner

oo 12 06
    eodem die John Hailestones Carpenter

oo 10 oo w^thin a fortnight
    Alexander Spavin Carpenter

oo 12 06
    Archibald Valentine Marriner

oo 10 01½
    James Murray Marriner

oo 10 01½
    John ffarley Porter

01 00 oo
    William Blackstock was Admitted and Sworne a ffree Comoner & Merc^t of the Staple

02 oo oo
    9th day of September 1669 John Waugh Merc^t was Admitted and Sworne a ffree Comoner and Merc^t of the Staple

01 00 00
eodem die   Henry Waugh his Sonn sworne ut prius

Served his time wᵗʰ Nicholas Garnett
eodem die   Mathew Garnett Chandler was Admitted and Sworne a ffree Commoner

00 12 06 Coxan bound to pay it
eodem die   Thomas Hannah Taylor was sworne a ffree Comoner

00 10 00 to be wrought
eodem die   John Bell Carpenter was sworne a ffree Comoner

Gratis
16ᵗʰ September 1669   Hugh Miller Mercᵗ was Admitted and Sworne a ffree Comoner and Mercᵗ of yᵉ Staple

01 00 00
eodem die   Alexander White Mercᵗ was sworne ut prius

00 10 00
eodem die   David Chambers Mercᵗ sworne ut prius

00 10 00
eodem die   James Jackson Yeoman sworne a ffree Comoner

00 10 00
eodem die   Alexander Latimer was Admitted and Sworne a ffree Comoner

Gratis served his time wᵗʰ Mr MᶜCartney
eodem die   John Hamilton Mercᵗ was Admitted and Sworne a ffree Comoner and Mercᵗ of the Staple

00 10 00
16ᵗʰ September 1669   Robert Walker Gray Merchᵗ was Admitted and Sworne a ffree Commoner

00 10 00
eodem die   James Scott Marriner sworne ut prius

00 10 00
eodem die   William Patterson Baker sworne ut prius

Gratis
23ᵗʰ September 1669   Thomas Tompson shipwright was Admitted and Sworne a ffree Comoner

00 10 00
eodem die   Robert White Taylor sworne ut prius

Gratis
eodem die   John Martin sworne ut prius

00 05 00
eodem die   William Nelson Sadler sworne ut prius

00 10 00
eodem die   Thomas Miller Gray Mercᵗ sworne ut prius

00 10 00 Jo: Agnew to pay
eodem die   James Clarck Cooper sworne ut prius
eodem die   John Wyatt Butcher sworne ut prius

Gratis
eodem die   William Taylor Weaver sworne ut prius

00 10 00 to be payd 2 months
eodem die   Alexander MᶜBride Ale seller sworne ut prius

00 10 00
eodem die   John Noble Taylor sworne ut prius
eodem die   William Cowdan Glover sworne ut prius
Tempore Gulielmi Waring Armiger 14ᵗʰ October 1669

00 10 00 Mr Sincklar
Bryan Mercer Butcher was Admitted

00 10 00 pd Mr Sincklar
eodem die   Henry Mercer Butcher was Admitted

0:1 00s 00ᵈ
21ᵗʰ October 1669   Cornelius Van Weedee was Admitted and sworne a ffree Comoner and mercᵗ of the Staple

Gratis
21 January 1669   Sʳ Michael Hicks Knight was Admitted and sworne a ffree Comoner and mercᵗ of the Staple

Gratis
Claudius Gilbert Clerck ut prius

Gratis
Samuel Brian Gent ut prius

Gratis
Hugh Smith Gent ut prius

Gratis
John MᶜIlwaine Chirurgeon ut prius

£0 11s 3d
James Glasco Marriner Admitted and sworne a ffree Comoner

0 10 0
John Kerron Weaver Admitted a ffree Comoner

Gratis
Bartholomew Cade Gent Admitted a ffree Comoner

dead
Hans Hamilton Esqr Admitted a ffree Comoner & merchant of the Staple

Gratis
Dudly Loftus gent ut prius

0 10 0
Thomas Knox merc^t Admitted & sworne a ffree Comoner and merc^t of the Staple

0 10 0
Captaine John Wilson Admitted and sworne a ffree Comoner and merc^t of the Staple

0 15 0
George Chaloner Merc^t Admitted ut prius

0 10 0
Thomas Harper Merc^t Admitted ut prius

Gratis
John Haddock Gent ut prius

Gratis
Gervis Hare Gent ut prius

Gratis
Thomas Bradly Gent ut prius

Served his time wth Charles Whitlock
Edmond Harton Butcher Admitted a ffree Comoner

0 13 6
Henry Chads Admitted a ffree Comoner

Served his time wth Roger Leathes
John McGowan Tanner Admitted a ffree Comoner

Served his time wth Roger Leathes
James Corry Tanner Admitted a ffree Com^r

1 05 0
Thomas Akin Merc^t Admitted a ffree Comoner and Merch^t of the Staple

Served his time wth Arthur Hought
David Ogan Butcher Admitted a ffree Com^r

Served his time w_{th} James Clark
26 May 1670   Robert Murrough Coop^r admitted a ffree Com^r

1 10 0
William Stewart Merc^t Admitted and sworne a ffree Comoner & Merch^t of ye Staple

1 0 0
John White sen Merc^t ut prius

Gratis
William Powell Esqr ut prius

5s in worke
23 June 1670   Thomas Costin Bricklayer Admitted a ffree Comoner

5s in work
Richard Court Glasier ut prius

00 10 0
James Cranston Taylor ut prius

00 10 0
Adam Williamson Tanner Admitted a ffree Comoner

0 15 0
30th June 1670   John Britton Merc^t was Admitted and sworne a ffree Comoner and Merc^t of ye Staple

Served his time wth George Rogers
William Ashmore Glover Admitted a ffree Comoner

Gratis
Henry Earle of Clanbrazill Admitted a ffree Comoner and Merc^t of the Staple

Gratis
William Hill Esqr Admitted ut prius

Gratis
John Lord Butler sonn to the Duke of Ormond Admitted a ffree Comoner and Merchant of the Staple

Gratis
Charles Meredith Esqr ut prius

Gratis
Richard Earle of Arran Admitted and sworne a ffree Comoner and Merc^t of the Staple

Gratis
Peirce Lord Baron of Cayre Admitted ut prius

Gratis
Edmund Butler Esqr Admitted ut prius

Gratis
Major Thomas ffairefax Admitted ut prius

Gratis
eodem die   Anthony Hamilton Esqr Admitted ut prius

Gratis
Collonell William Cecill brother to the Earle of Salusbury Admitted ut prius

Gratis
> Major Samuel Stewart Admitted ut prius

Gratis
> Richard Needham Gent Admitted ut prius

Gratis
> Richard Hutton Gent Admitted ut prius

Gratis
> William Tomson Gent Admitted ut prius

Served his time wth Anderson
> 22th September 1670   Daniel Harper Merc^t was Admitted and sworne a ffree Comoner and Merch^t of the Staple

o 10 o
> Thomas Darby Butcher Admitted a ffree Comoner

Served his time wth Jo Whitlock
> Christopher Pitt Butcher Admitted ut prius

o 10 o
> Alexander McCree Taylor Admitted ut prius

o 10 o
> Thomas Williamson Smith Admitted ut prius

Servant to Michael Bigger
> Alexander Woods Merc^t Admitted a ffree Comoner and Merchant of the Staple

o 10 o
> 13th October 1670   John Bell Weaver Admitted a ffree Comoner

o 10 o
> Robert Adaire Glasier Admitted ut prius

Gratis
> Richard Magee sworne ut prius

Gratis
> Thomas Hurst Gent Admitted ut prius

Served his time wth Jo Hudson
> 27th October 1670   John Symons Clothyer Admitted ut prius

Served his time wth Sanders Sinklar
> 3rd November 1670   John Russell Merc^t was Admitted and sworne a ffree Comoner and Merc^t of ye Staple

Gratis
> William Hinch Joyner Admitted a ffree Comoner

1l 5s od
> 17th November 1670   William Lockart Merc^t was Admitted and sworne a ffree Comoner and Merc^t of the Staple

o 10 o
> Arthur Whiteside [sworn a ff] Gunn Smith sworne a ffree Comoner

o 10 o
> 13th December 1670   John ffisher Taylor Admitted a ffree Comoner

o 10 o
> 12th January 1670   William Ratcliffe Clothyer sworne ut prius

o 10 o
> Alexander Miller sworne a ffree Comoner

o 10 o
> Thomas Hood Shooemaker sworne ut prius

Gratis
> Arthur Haven Gent sworne a ffree Comoner

Gratis
> Lawrence Trent Merc^t sworne ut prius

o 10 o
> William McNeish sworne as afores^d

Gratis
> 22 December 1670   John Williamson Gent sworne ut prius

Served his Apprentiship wth Hugh Gillogh
> Andrew M^cffarran Carpenter Admitted and sworne a ffree Comoner

Served his time wth Robert Quin
> Robert Rowan Curryer sworne ut prius

1os to be payd by Capt Leathes
> Thomas Stalker Joyner sworne ut prius

Gratis
> Thomas Chades Gent sworne ut prius

1os to ye Towne
> 26 January 1670   Andrew Tompson Ale Seller Sworne ut prius

Townes money forgiven
> 26 January 1670   John Beck gent Sworne a ffree Comoner and Merc^t of the Staple

15s to ye Towne
> 16 ffebruary 1670   Archibald Adaire Merc^t Sworne ut prius

Served his time wth And Keyle
> 9 March 1670   Thomas Cranston Cooper sworne a ffree Comoner

Gratis
> John Mercer Gent sworne ut prius

1l to yᵉ Towne
Thomas Taylor Mercᵗ sworne ut prius

Gratis

13ᵗʰ April 1671　William Dobbin Alderman of Carrickfergus sworne a ffree Comoner

Gratis

20ᵗʰ April 1671　Thomas Earle of Ardglas sworne ut

Gratis

Richard Dobb Esquire sworne ut prius

Gratis

Edward Muschamp Esqʳ sworne ut prius

Gratis

Henry Horton Gent sworne ut prius

1os to yᵉ towne

Richard Hodgan Marriner sworne

served his time wᵗʰ Ja Chalmers

18 May 1671　John Chalmers Mercᵗ sworne a ffree Stapler and Comoner

17s 6d to yᵉ Towne

15 June 1671　Richard Slosse Mercᵗ was sworne ut prius

1os to the Towne

Samuel Lennox Mercᵗ sworne ut prius

Gratis

29 June 1671　Nicholas Dowdall Phisitian sworne

1l to the Towne & Sovraigne to be payd in two months

13 July 1671　James Daglish Butcher sworne a ffree Comoner

Gratis

27 July 1671　Sʳ John Rowley Knight sworne ut prius

Gratis

Tristram Berrisford Esq sworne

1os to the Towne

3 August 1671　William McBurney Ship Carpenter sworne a ffree Comoner

Served his time wᵗʰ William Moore

10 August 1671　William Ramsey Mercᵗ a ffree Comoner

1os to the Towne

24 Augᵗ 1671　Robert Humphrey Vintner sworne a ffree Comoner

Gratis

Peter Whyte Soveraignes servant sworne a ffree Comoner

1os to yᵉ Towne

Thomas Lock Cooper sworne ut prius

1os to yᵉ Towne

31 August 1671　Alexander Makay weaver Sworne a ffree Comoner

1os to yᵉ Towne

Mathew Sym mercᵗ sworne ut prius

1os to yᵉ Towne

John Smith Chapman sworne a ffree Comoner

1os to yᵉ Towne

7ᵗʰ September 1671　Mathew King mercᵗ sworne ut prius

1os to yᵉ Towne

James Clarck Chapman sworne ut prius

1os to yᵉ Towne

William Bell weaver sworne ut

Gratis

William Dobson Joyner sworne ut

Gratis

14ᵗʰ September 1671　John Browne Taylor sworne ut

1os to yᵉ Towne

James McCartney weaver sworne ut prius

1os to yᵉ Towne to be payd in a month

Edward McBride Carpenter sworne a ffree Comoner

1os to yᵉ Towne to be pd in a fortnight

John Holmes Sadler sworne ut prius

Gratis

James Jackson Joyner sworne ut

Gratis

William Johnston Tanner sworne

1os to yᵉ Towne

James Rosse mercᵗ sworne ut prius

1os to yᵉ Towne

21 September 1671　Edward Chalkhill Vintner sworne

Served his time wᵗʰ Nich Garnett

John Bell Chandler sworne ut prius

Gratis

28 September 1671　John Lindon Esqʳ sworne ut prius

Gratis

Tho: Rickaby Gent sworne ut prius

T

1os to yͤ Towne
       James Tate Taylor sworne ut prius
1os to yͤ Towne
       George Burton Blacksmith sworne
1os to the Towne
       Thomas Coates shooemaker sworne
1os to the Towne
       William Henderson Butcher sworne
1os to yͤ Towne
       George Lisle Chapman sworne ut prius
1os to yͤ Towne
       Thomas McClunn Taylor sworne
1os to yͤ Towne
       Thomas Chapman Carpenter sworne
1os to yͤ Towne McIlwaine bound
       Charles Toysh Dyer sworne ut prius
17s 6d to yͤ Towne
       Brice Crawford *merchant* sworne ut prius
1o to yͤ Towne John Bell bound
       Hugh Bell Weaver sworne ut prius
Gratis
       28 September 1671 George Waren Gent sworne ut prius
1os to yͤ Towne James Chalmers bound
       William McBlane Mason sworne
Gratis
       Bryan McHenry Aleseller sworne
1os to yͤ Towne Capt Leathes Bayle
       James Holmes Marriner sworne
1os to yͤ Towne Capt Leathes bound
       William Clugston Smith sworne
Gratis
       Thomas Edwards Gent sworne
Gratis
       Capt William Bird sworne ut prius
Gratis
       Richard McGee Merchant sworne ut prius
       Thomas Wallcott Esqr Superr Ville de Belfast
pd oo 1o oo
       19 Ocr 1671 Phiplip Linch sworne a ffree Comoner
Gratis
       Wm Barnett Goldsmith sworne ut pris
pd oo o9 oo
       John Younge marchant sworne
oo 1o oo run away & pd nothing
       Abraham Egerton Butcher sworne ut pr
pd oo 1o oo
       John Willson of Carmoney Butcher sworne
pd oo 1o oo
       John Doake marchant sworne freeman
pd oo 1o oo
       30th of Novr 1671 Phelemon Chamberlin marcht sworne
pd oo 1o oo
       John Gill gent of Lurgan sworne
pd oo 1o oo
       James Stewart of Lurgan gent sworne
oo 1o oo
       John Whinnery Bricklay sworne
Henry Thelford Bayled pd oo 1o oo
       Manns Taylor sworne
Gratis
       James Clifford Parish Clarke
Served his apprentsh
       John Allen Weavour sworne a freeman
apprentice
       Edward Carron shoemaker pprentis & sworne
apprentice
       John Kennedy Carpenter sworne
pd oo 1o oo
       11 January 1671 John Donnellson marchant sworne a ffreeman
oo 1o oo Wm McNeesh Bayle
       James Anderson gray marchant sworne
Served his apprentisp fees gratis
       John McBride marchant sworne ut pris
Gratis
       18 Jany 1671 James Younge marcht served his apprentissp with George McCartney
marcht & sworne a freeman

pd oo o6 o8
John Dowey Cooper sworne a freeman ut prius

pd oo 10 oo
Robt Ranton Baker was sworne a freeman this 1st of ffeby 1671

Gratis
ffra Cary Esqr was admitted and sworne a freeman 16 Nov 1671

served his prent^sp with Mr Smith
Ninian Hill marc^t was sworne and admitted a freeman this 3rd of ffeby 1671

Gratis
this 29 ffeby 1671 William Dean Clothier was admitted and sworne a freeman

served his prentis^p with Jo Bell
Acaias Ratcliffe [was] Carpenter was admitted and sworn a free Comoner

pd oo o5 oo
Hugh m^cCreery Cooper was admitted & sworne a free Comoner

Served his prentisp with Jo Johnston
Brice Boyd was admitted and sworne a free Comoner ut p^r

Gratis
18th of appryle 1672 Andrew McCullogh Bow maker was admitted and sworne a free Comoner

Served his tyme
James Luke Cooper was admitted and sworne a free Comoner

ool 1os ood
Wm Popley Mariner was this 16 of May admitted & sworne a free Comoner of this Corporacon

Gratis
Michael Porter Cooper this 6th of Jun 1672 was Admited & sworne A free Comoner of this Corporation

Graties
Andrew Corsby Carpenter this 6th of Jun 1672 was Admited & sworn A free Comoner of this Corporation

Graties
David Heberon Mariner this 13th of Jun 1672 was Admited & sworn A free Comoner of this Corporation

tenn shill to be pd Wm Ashmor plegd Lamas
July 6th 1672 Wm Ervine this day was admitted a free Comoner of this Corporacon

Gratis
July ye 13th 1672 James Linsey Merch^t was admitted and sworn a free Comoner of this Corporacon and Merch^t of ye Staple

Gratis
David Strange Merch^t was admitted and sworn a free Comoner of this Corporacon & M^cht of ye S^t

1os to ye town
August ye 15th 1672 Peeter Stewart *march^t* was sworne a free Comon^t. & March^t of ye Staple

1os to ye town
Hugh Aspij ut prius

served his tyme wth Ja Martin
George Dumbarre *Sadler* was sworne a free Comoner

served his tyme wth Richar Lemin
Wm Dawsone ut prius

served wth Mr Clugston
Agust 22 Michaell Clugston *march^t* was Admitted and Sworne

1os pd Mr Sov :
Septemb^r ye 12 1672 Wm Collhown *march^t* was admitted and sworn a free Comoner of this Corporacon

1os
Ralph Smith gent ut prius

1os
Allexander Woods *anglus* Merchant ut prius

7s 6d
Brice Smith merch^t was sworne a free Comon^r

1os
Gabriell Throckmorton ut prius

1os
Edward Shewell ut prius

Gratis
Edward Brees was sworn a free Comoner

Gratis
John Sanders ut prius

7s 6d
Septemb^r 19th 1672th James Allexander Taylor was sworn a free Comoner

Gratis
Thomas Gemble Cutler ut prius

1os 2^s 6^d unp^d
Wm Kendall Baker was sworne a free Comon^r

Served his tyme wth Ch Whytlocke

Charles Dobson   ut prius

Septemb^r 26th 1672   William Tuckare Ship Carp^r was sworne a free Comoner of this Corporacon

Served his tyme wth Wm Gibb

William Becke *taylor* ut prius

John Robison gardiner was sworn

William Lockart mason   ut prius

John Drummon   ut prius

Richard Crooke   ut prius

Michael Clugh   ut prius

Mathew Edminston Carp^r was sworn

7s 6d   Wm Husler   ut prius

John Woods   was sworn

Robt Rogerson *Cooke*   ut prius

Tempore Georgij m^cCartneij: n: armiger: superioris Burgi Sive Ville De Belfast in Com Antrim et Unius ex Justiciariis pacis pro Domino rege in Com predict liberi et communes facti ut libertatate Donati sunt sequentes anno Domini Millesimo sexten-tesimo Septuagesimo secundo annoque Caroli Secundi regis anglie scotie ffrancie et hib: Vicesimo quarto

gratis consensu curie

17th of Octob^r 1672   Wm Love gent was admitted and sworn a free Comoner of this Corporacon

10s to be paid to ye Town

Octob^r 31 1672   George Lockart mercht was sworn a free Comon^r & mercht of ye Staple

Quintin Moor was admitted & sworne ut prius

Gratis

November ye 14th 1672   Peter Carteret Esqr was admitted and Sworne a free Comoner and mercht of ye Staple

Gratis

Capt Edward Tarleton *mariner* ut prius

Gratis

Edward Wilson *mariner* ut prius

served his tim wth R Ashmor

Rogger McBurny *skinner* skinner ut prius

oo 10 oo

Andrew Smith   ) Taylor mony pd 20s

oo 10 pd oo   } made freemen 6 Jany 1672

Daniell Christian) Weaver by Daniell Cristian wev to Georg McCartney sover

served his tim wth Wm Keeran

27 of ffebruary 1672   [John] George Kerran Blacksmith was sworn a free Comoner

John McKeown taylor ut prius

10s pd ye Soveraigne

May ye 8th 1673   Allexander Kyle Tanner was sworn a ffree Comoner of this Corporacon p^d

served wth Tho Read

John Sloan Butcher ut prius

10s to be pd to y^e towne

Wm Thompson ut prius unp^d

served wth A Haughton

George Bankes Butcher unp^d

May 15th 1673   John m^cRobts was sworn a free Comoner of this Corporacon unp^d

10s paid

July y^e 3 1673   Robt Hunter ship carpenter was sworne a free Comoner of this Corporacon p_a

10s pd to y^e town

James Campble ship carpenter ut prius

10s to be pd to y^e town

Wm Watson shooemaker ut prius

apprentice

James Coats carpenter sworn before Georg m^cCartney Esqr Sovraigne of y^e said Burrough y^e 13th November 1673

Apprentice

John Buick Blacksmith sworn free man before Georg m^cCartny Esqr Sovraigne of ye said Burrough ye 13th S^bris

Gratis

John Crafford Merchant sworn free Man before Georg m^cCartny Esqr Sovraigne of ye said Burrough ye 20th S^bris

Gratis

James Shonseidegs gent sworn free Comon^r of ye said Burrough before Georg m^cCartny Esqr & other Burgesses ye 27th November

Town Stoke
oo 10 oo

James Read Merchant sworn free Comon^r of ye said Burrough before Georg m^{c}Cartney Esqr Sovraigne & other Burgesses ye 27th November 1673

oo 10 oo

William Woods Admitted & sworn a free Comoner of ye said Burrough befor Georg m^{c}Cartney Esqr Sov^r with ye consent of ye Burgesses ye 11th December 1673

Henery Jacckson Tanner Admitted & sworn a free Comoner befor Georg m^{c}Cartney Esq Sov^r with y^e consent of y^e Burgesses 8th Janry 1673

John Couburn Cooper Admitted & sworn a free Comoner befor Georg m^{c}Cartny Esqr Sovraigne with y^e consent of y* Burgesses y^e 8th Janry 1673

oo 12 o6

James Read Merchant sworn free Comoner of y^e said Burrough befor Georg m$_c$Cartny Esqr Sov^r y$_e$ 26th day of ffebruary

g

Georg Ashmor ffelt maker sworn & admided a free Comoner befor Georg m^{c}Cartny Esqr

gr

John Nessmith merchant sworn & Admitted a free Commoner befor Georg m^{c}Cartny Esq Sovraigne y^e 13th March 1673

oo 10 oo
John ffarran Carpenter

oo 10 oo
James Craiton Tailor

oo 10 oo
John Patterson Tailor

oo 10 oo
William m^{c}Call Tailor

oo 10 oo
John Deevor Tailor

oo 10 oo
William Goodwin barber

} all sworn befor Georg m$_c$Cartny Esqr Sovraigne y^e 21st May 1674

oo 10 oo
Robert Nevin merchant sworn y^e 16th July

oo 10 oo
fh Stuard b

Nathaniell Stuard Masson sworn free Commoner of y^e Burrough y^e 11th June befor Georg m^{c}Cartny Sov^r

John Fletcher merchant sworn y^e 23$_d$ July

Thomas Heslop weavor sworne a free Commoner y^e 23$_d$ July befor Georg m*Cartny Esqr Sov^r

10s
Denis English Tailor

10s
Hugh Wittnell Butcher

Printice
James Pinkerton Weavor

} all Admitted & sworn y$_e$ 30th July befor Georg m^{c}Cartny Esq$_r$ Sovraigne of y^e same

Gratis
Samuell Morgan Mariner

Hugh Doak merchant
John m^{c}Crakin Gardiner

o 10 o
William Miller yeoman

o 10 o
Thomas Read Drover
James m^{c}Cartny Merchant

} all sworn befor Georg m^{c}Cartny Esq$_r$ Sovraigne y^e 3^d S^{bris}

Gratis
Thomas Jacckson merchant of y$_e$ Stapell

Gratis
Georg Theaker merchant Aprentis served wth Hugh Eccles

Apprentice
Thomas Yeoung mrchant

Gratise
John Turner [C] Blockmaker

Apprentice
Allex^r Boccell merchant

Apprentice
Hugh Gilpattrick merch^t

} all sworn befor Georg McCartny Esq$_r$ Sovraigne y^e 10th September 1674

o 10 o
John Craford Carpenter

o 10 o
James Purdy Butcher

o 10 o
Richard Morison Couper

} all sworn befor Georg m$_c$Cartny Esqr Sovraigne of y^e said Burrough y^e 16th S^{bris}

o 10 o	Arthur m c Cann Tanner	all sworn Befor Georg m'Cartney Esqr y^e^ 23^d^ S^bris^ 1674
o 10 o	ffargus Lindsey Tanner	
gr	Thomas Lester Butcher	
gr	James M^c^Guire Butcher	
gr	William Blacck Chapman	
o 10 o	Quartm^r^ Andrew M^c^Ketricck fees [yeoman] p^d^ in wine	
gr	Andrew Agnew Aprentice Couper	
o 10 o	John Edenbury Tailor	
gr	John Sloan Aleseller	

Tempore Hugonis Eccles Armig^r^ Superioris Burgi Sive Ville De Belfast in Com Antrim et unius ex Justiciariis pacis pro Domino Rege in Com predict liberi et Communis facty ut libertate Donati sunt sequentis Anno Domini Milessimo sextentissimo Septuagessimo quarto Annoque Caroli secundi Regis Angle Scotie ffranciæ et Hib [visse] Vicessimo Sexto

	Thomas Leathes Merchant of ye Stapell	Sworn before Hugh Ecckles Esqr Sovraigne ye 1st S^bris^ 1674 gratis
	John Johnston Merchant of ye Stapell	
	Allex^r^ White Merchant of ye Stapell	
	Richard Ld Viscount Ranelagh	Sworn befor Hugh Ecckells Esqr Sovraigne ye 3^d^ of O^tober^ 1674 gratis
	ffrancis Lord Anger	
	John Ld Viscount Massareen	
	Sr William fflower Knight	
	Sr Theophilus Joanes K^t^ & Barronet	
	Sr Arthur Joanes K^t^	
	Georg Tandy gent gratis	
oo 10 oo	John Henderson barber	
	John Quoy Couper sworn ye 4th March Aprentice	
gratis	Edward Stroud Butcher	sworne ye 22^d^ Aprill befor Hugh Ecckels Sovraigne
gratis	William Smith Masson	
gratis	Allex^r^ Hillhouse merchant sworn ye 8th May	
gratis	John Kipton Grosser sworn ye 10th July	
Aprentice	David Christian Butcher sworn ye 12th August	
o 10 oo	John Cambell Baker sworn ye 22^d^ July befor Hugh Ecckells Sovraigne	
1 oo oo	James Stuard Merchant sworn ye 12th August	
o 10 oo	Robert Doake Merch^t^ sworn ye 12 August	
o 10 oo	Thomas Stuard Tobaco Spiner s: 19th August	
gratis	S^r^ ffrancis Blundell sworn a free Commoner befor Hugh Ecckells Esqr Sovraigne &c ye 21th August	
	Leiut John Baserfeild sworn eod	
gratis	John Norrice Esqr sworn eod	
	Mr John Montgomery sworn eod	
	Ensigne Thomas Kittson sworn eod	
gratis	Michell Dawson feltmaker sworn ye 9th 7^bris^	
10s	James Graham Butcher swor ye 16th 7^bris^	
10s	Georg Mankin Chandler	All sworn befor Hugh Ecckels Esqr Sovraigne ye 23rd 7^bris^
gratis	John Blacck Mrch^t^	
gratis	Allex^r^ Spence Mrch^t^	
gratis	David Thomson Sadler	
10s	John Cambell Cordwainer	
gratis	ffrancis Newland Sadler	
gratis	Robert Balantin	
10s	Zakaria Craford Tailor	
10s	James Smith Tanner	
10s	Andrew Cunningham Tailor	

[Cp. William Amos
Edward Williamson } 7 Oct 1675 admitted free]

Tempore Georgi M.Cartney Armig' Superior Burgo de Belfast Michalmas 1675

grat

Capt W Amos

grats

Capt Edward Williamson of Liverpoole } 7th Octo' 1675

admitted and sworne free Commoners & Staplers &c

gra

Ebenezer Winter Gent } 14th Octob' 1675 was admitted free Comoners & March

pd oo 15 oo

Thomas ffletcher march⁴ } Staplers of this Corporacon

gr

Capt Richard Morriss } L⁴

gr

L⁴ Thomas Buckridge } 14th Octob' 1675

gr

En George Stawton } Ensignes

g⁴

Ens Gilbert Butles }

served his appr

ffrancis Johnston marchant } 4th Nov' 1675 admitted a freeman

gratis

William m⁴Kerrell marchant }

served his appr

John Patterson Carpinter 11th Nov' 1675 admitted free

served his apprentiship

Gilbert m⁴Kewne marcht was admitted and sworne y⁴ 25 Nov' 1675

served his apprentisp

Samuell Verner marcht was admitted and sworne y⁴ 25th Nov' 1675

pd oo 10 oo

John Hamillton Taylor was admitted and sworne y⁴ 25th Nov 1675

served his apprent

John Adayre Glayser y⁴ 2d dec' 1675 was admit⁴ & sworn

pd oo 15 oo

John Thomson marcht y⁴ 23 dec' 1674 was sworne & admitted a free man

served as aprentice

David Sim Carpinter y⁴ 23d of dec' 1675 was sworn & admitted a freeman

served as aprentice

John Haslap Carpenter y⁴ 29th of dec' 1675 was admitted and sworne

gratis

Richard Wamsley Baker y⁴ 5th of Jany 1675 was admitted

served appr

Wm Sharpe Carpinter y⁴ 13th Jany 1675 was admitted

pd oo 10 oo

Allexand' Kinge marcht y⁴ 13th Jany 1675 was admitted

Gratis

S' George Maxwell y⁴ 9th March was admitted

pd 10s oo

James Gambell m⁴ 16th March was Admitted

served his Aprentiship

Robert Black Blacksmith [was] admitted and sworne a ffreeman y⁴ 30th day of March 1676

served his apprentiship

John Cooke *Mason* was admitted and sworne a freeman the 6th of Aprill 1676

served his apprentiship

Wm M⁴Crea *shoemaker* was admitted and sworne a freeman of the Burrough of Belfast y⁴ 6th of Aprill 1676

Gratis

Capt Thomas Buckner was Admitted and sworne a free Comoner & *Marchant Stapler* of the Burrough of Belfast y⁴ 21 Aprill 1676

ffra oo 15s pd

Allin Corbitt *merct* was Admitted & sworne a freeman of the Burrough of Belfast the 21st day of Aprill 1676

oo 10 o6 pd

Thomas Martin merct was admited and sworne a ffreeman of the Burrough of Belfast

gratis as apprintis

Hugh M⁴Crea Butcher an apprentice was sworne ut supra

oo 10s oo pd

Wm Gutiher baker was sworne a freecomoner ut supra

oo 10s pd

John Gleane baker was sworne a freecomoner ut supra

served his apprentisp

ffrancis Crumey march⁴ was sworne a free comoner & mearcht Stapler the 28 of Aprill 1676

oo 10 oo
Robert Attkinson blacksmith this 9th of June 1676 was admitted and sworne a free Comoner

oo 10 oo pd
James Adaine Shoomaker admitted free 19th Octr 1676

oo 10 oo pd
John Liggatt Smith admitted 19th Oct, 1676

app^{tis}
James Ramsey m^{rt} admitted ffree 2^d November 1676

pd oo 10 oo
Thomas Sloane butcher admitted y^e 2^d Novr 1676

oo 10 oo
Wm White ship carpinter admitted a freeman 21 Dec 1676

appren^{ts}
John Redagh Joyner admitted a freeman y^e same

gratis
Wm Johnston Carpinter admitted a freeman 4th Jany 1676

apprents
Andrew m_cMullen *march^t* admitted free 11th Jany 1676

apprentis
Allexander Taggart *march^t* admitted free y^e same day

oo 15 oo
Richard Moore march, admitted [free] free y^e 8th ffeby 1676

oo 10 oo
John Gammell Carpenter y^e same day admitted free

app^{sp}
John Hudelston Taylor y^e same day admitted free

app^{sp}
John Bowman Mason admitted ye same day

oo 10 oo
Humphrey Kell shoomaker 15th ffebry 1676 admitted & Henry Thetford ingaged to ye Soveraigne that he nor his family shall be any burden to ye towne

apprentis
Thomas m^cKewan Cooper was admitted ye 21st feby 1676

oo 15 oo
William Kenedy marcht was admitted y^e 1st of March 1676
James Crighton yeoman was admitted y^e 15th March 1676
William Bowston Taylor was admitted y^e 15th March 1676

02 oo oo
Petter Knowles marcht y^e 12th Ap^{rll}. 1677 was admitted a freeman

01 10 oo
James Bodkin marct y_e was admitted free y^e same day

oo 12 o6
[Burnett] William Burnett Chapman was admitted y^e y^e 19th Ap^r 1677

gratis
Anthony Gubb was admitted y^e 3^d May 1677

gratis
Nicholas Redworth y^e same day was admitted

oo 10 o pd
Andrew Donnell Taylor y^e same day

oo 10 oo
David Dog Taylor was admitted ye same day being 3 May 1677

oo 10 oo
Robert Gibb Carpinter was admitted ye same day

oo 10 oo
John Shaw marcht was admitted ye 21 June 1677

app^{tis}
James Martin marcht was admitted ye same day

app^{tis}
Andrew Agnew marcht was admitted ye same day

oo 10 oo
David White marcht was admitted ye same day

oo 10 oo
Robert Holmes Mariner was admitted ye same day

appr^s
William Hatfeild Glover was admitted ye same day

oo 10 oo
David Younge marcht was admitted ye same day

apprentis
Allexand^r Mitchell marcht was admitted ye same day

gratis
Capt Browne marcht was admitted ye same day

aprentis
Oliver Antell marcht was [aditted] was admitted 5th July 1677

aprentis
Andrew Craford marcht was admitted ye same day

oo 15 oo
George Allen Marcht was admitted yᵉ same day
oo 12 o6
James mᶜKewan Malster was admitted yᵉ same day
[Thomas White[field]*side* shipcarpenter yᵉ same day being 30th of August 1677]
oo o4 o9
Thomas Keming Glover being apprentice but sarved not his full time was admitted free 18th July 1677
oo 10 oo
Robert Gentleman Taylor this 18th July 1677 was admitted free
apprentis
John Shearer Taylor was admitted free yᵉ same day
oo 10 oo
Thomas Whiteside Ship Carpinter was admitted yᵉ 30th of August 1677
appr
Allexandᵣ mᶜHoole Slater was admitted yᵉ same day
gratis
Wᵐ Thomson Coper was admitted yᵉ 13 Sepʳ 1677
oo 10 oo
James MᶜTosh Labourer was admitted yᵉ same day
oo 10 oo
John MᶜDowell Taylor was admitted 20th Sepʳ 1677
oo 10 oo
Thomas Orr Smith was admitted yᵉ 20th Sepʳ 1677
James Miller Cooper was admitted yᵉ same day & his fine referred to yᵗ Court
apprent
James Donson Cloyther was admited 4th Octr 1677
oo o5 oo
James Biggar Cutler was admitted yᵉ same day
oo 10 oo
John Allison Weaver was admitted yᵉ same day
gratis
John Munteeth yeoman was admitted yₒ 12th Octobʳ 1677
gratis
Henry Plaskett Butcher was admitted yᵉ same day
oo 15 oo
Thomas Burnett marcht was admitted yᵉ 25th Octʳ 1677
apprentis
John Williams Currier was admitted yᵉ 8th Novʳ 1677
oo 12 o6
William Browne Mariner was admitted yᵉ same day
apprentice
James Mulhollan Smith was admitted yᵉ 29th Novʳ
o1 oo oo
Wᵐ Stewart marct was admitted &ᶜ yᵉ 13th Dec 1677
oo 10 oo
Gabriell Portenfeild Confectioner yᵉ 3 Jany 1677
oo 10 oo
John Lemon Barber was admitted yᵉ same day
oo o7 o6
Robert Hatley Butcher was admitted yᵉ same day
gratis
ffrancis Allen Butcher was admitted yᵉ same day
gratis
Capt James Handyside yᵉ 24 Jany 1677 was admᵈ
gratis
Lᵗ Thomas Hill was admitted yᵉ same day
appr relapsd
George Ogans Butcher yᵉ 31 of Jany 1677 was admitted
appr relapsd
Robert Tusly Butcher yᵉ same day was admitted
gratis
John Logan Tinnman yᵉ same day was admitted
apprᵗˢ
William Burton Chandler yᵉ 14th ffeby 1677 was admited
gratis
Marmaduke Newton marcht was admitted yᵉ same day
apprents
James Morrow Carpinter yᵉ 7th March 1677 was admitted
o1 oo oo
Nathaniell Shannon marcht was admitted yᵉ same day
oo 10 oo
James Mordagh Cobler admitted yᵉ same day
apprents
John Whitehead Butcher admitted yᵉ same day

oo io oo
Henry Coates Grocer yᵉ 21 of March 1677 was admitted

oo io oo
John Scott Taylor yᵉ same day was admitted yᵉ same day

gratis
Thomas Whitlock Butcher 11th Apʳ 1678 was admitted

oi oo oo
Phinley mᶜTeere marcht yᵉ same day admitted

oo io oo
Thomas Willon *Junior* Shoomaker 18th Apʳ 1678 admitted

Andrew Blomfeeld yeoman formerly disfranchised in Mʳ Wᵐ Warrings time now admitted yᵉ 25th of Apʳ 1678 upon his submission

oi oo oo
Archibald Little marcht yᵉ 16th May 1678 admitted

oo io oo
James Cooke Chapman yᵉ same day admitted

gratis
Patrick Hamilton gent 27th June 1678 admitted

gratis
Arthur McCartney marcht yᵉ same day admitted

oo 12 o6
Wᵐ Hunter Taylor yᵉ 4th July 1678 admitted

oo 15 oo
John Parke marcht yᵉ same day admitted

oo io oo
Adam mᶜCragh Carpinter yᵉ same day admitted

oo io oo
Wᵐ Wyely Glover yᵉ 18th July 1678 admitted free

Mansfeild Tucker Chandler 18th July 1678 admitted free

gratis
Robert Harper gent 22ᵈ of August 1678 admitted

gratis
Edward Boyle gent yᵉ same day admitted

apprentis
George McCartney Cooper yᵉ same day admitted

gratis
William Adaine marcht 22 August 1678 admitted

apprentis
Thomas Becke Taylor 5th Sept 1678 admitted

Gratis
Robert Clugston marcht 10th Octoʳ 1678 admitted

apprⁱˢ
William Sloan marcht yᵉ same day admitted

gratis
Robert Cunningham Glover yᵉ same day admitted

gratis
Hugh McGill gent 17 Octoʳ 1678 admitted

gratis
Symond Smith gent yᵉ same day admitted

apprentis
Robert Heslap weaver yᵉ same day admitted

oo io oo
James Gregg Taylor 24th Octobʳ 1678 admitted

oo 15 oo
James Martin marchᵗ yᵉ 17th Novʳ 1678 admitted

gratis
Henry Rankinyore marcᵗ 28 Novʳ 1678 admitted

oo 15 oo
William Younge Chandler yᵉ 9th Jany 1678 admitted

gratis
James Gutter marchᵗ admitted yᵉ same day

oo 15 o
Wᵐ Porter marchᵗ admitted yᵉ same day

oo io oo
George Culbert marchᵗ admitted yᵉ same day

oo 12 o6
John Jowland Tanner admitted yᵉ same day

gratis
John Culbert gent yᵉ same day admitted

oo io oo
Robert Rayne Taylor yᵉ 23ᵈ of Janry 1678 admitted

oo io oo
John Greg weaver admitted yᵉ same day

appᵗˢ
Thomas Carrett dyer admitted yᵉ same day

gratis   Capt Henry Sᵗ George }
gratis   Oliver Sᵗ George Esqʳ } admitted yᵉ 23 Janry 1678

pd 01   00   00

Robert Hamilton marcht yᵉ 17th Apʳ 1679 admitted

gratis

Allexandʳ Leird smith 8th May 1679 admitted

gratis

George Dean Cutler yᵉ same day admitted

appts

Robert Johnston Mason admitted yᵉ same day

00   10   00

James mᶜMurtree Taylor yᵉ 22ᵈ May 1679 admitted

appᵗˢ

Robert Hey shoomaker yᵉ 26 June 1679 admitted

appᵗˢ

John Smith Cooper yᵉ same day admitted

appᵗˢ

Allexandʳ Wright Cooper yᵉ 3ᵈ July 1679 admitted

00   10   00

Thomas Courtney Taylor yᵉ 24 July 1679 admitted

00   10   00

John Dixson Maltman yᵉ same day admitted

01   00   00

Hugh Hannah Linindraper 31 July admitted

00   10   00

Anthony ffowler Butcher admitted yᵉ same day

gratis

Coll John Hill 21 of August 1679 admitted free

00   10   00

John Ramsey Tobacconist yᵉ same day admitted

appᵗˢ

ffrancis Heslap   yᵉ 11th Septʳ 1679 admitted

00   10   00

John Lemon Chandler 18th Septʳ admitted free

00   10   00

Thomas Bell Butcher yᵉ same day admitted free

00   10   00

John Arbuckells yeoman yᵉ 18th Sepʳ 1679 admitted

00   10   00

William Osborne Baker yᵉ 2ᵈ Octobʳ 1679 admitted

gratis

John Hudson Cloither yᵉ 16th Octobʳ 1679 admitted

gratis

Thomas Logan Taylor yᵉ same day admitted

gratis

Robert Willson Tanner yᵉ same day admitted

gratis

Robert Hanskinson gent admitted yᵉ same day

00   15   00

Robert Millin marchᵗ yᵉ 4th Decembr 1679 admitted

00   15   00

John mᶜMun marchᵗ yᵉ same day admitted

00   15   00

Robert Smith blacksmith admitted yₑ same day

gratis

Sʳ. Robert Maxwell Kᵗ & Barronett admitted yᵉ same day

gratis

James Callwell Esqr admitted yᵉ same day

gratis

Cornett Pawlett Phillips admitted yᵉ same day

appts

James Kennedy marcht 15th Jany 1679 admitted

appts

Edward Brice *marchant* yᵉ same day admitted

00   10   00

Pattrick Aitkin marcht admitted yᵉ same day

00   12   06

Thomas mᶜKee marcht admitted yᵉ same day

gratis

Thomas mᶜCune Goldsmith yᵉ 22ⁿᵈ Janry 1679 admitted

apprenᵗˢ

ffrancis ffleminge Taylor 29th Janry 1679 admitted

gratis

William Johnston Butcher 8th July 1680 admitted

gratis

James Allen Butcher yᵉ same day admitted

gratis

George Portis Bricklayer yᵉ same day admitted

oo   10   oo
      Henry Hall dyer y_e same day admitted
      Thomas ffarguson Appothecary 15 July 1680 admitted
      William Browne marcht yᵉ same day admitted
appt⁺
      David Butle marcht yᵉ 15th July 1680 admitted free
gratis
      Wᵐ Ramsey gunsmith yᵉ same day admitted
gratis
      Allgernoone Ouldfeild turner yᵉ same day admitted
oo   10   oo
      James Linn yeoman 6th August 1680 admitted
oo   10   oo
      Henry Hunter Cooper yᵉ same day admitted
oo   10   oo
      John mᶜKnight yeoman yᵉ same day admitted
      James Browne Marriner yᵉ 19th of August 1680 admitted
oo   10   oo
      Daniell Diell Cuttler yᵉ 26th of August admitted
oo   05   oo
      John Henderson Mariner yᵉ same day admitted
      Wᵐ MᶜCoord Joyner yᵉ same day admitted
gratis
      John Hutchinson gent yᵉ 2ᵈ September 1680 was admitted to yᵗ ffreedom &ᶜ
gratis
      Wᵐ Craford marchᵗ was admitted yᵉ same day
apprᵗˢ
      ffrancis Cordiner was admitted yᵉ same day
      Archibald M'Clure Carpinter admitted yᵉ same day
      James Rosse [ye] Smith was admitted yᵉ same day
      William Lowden Cooper admitted yᵉ same day
apptiˢ
      Robert Jordan suggar baker admitted yᵉ same day
apptiˢ
      John Patton Butcher was admitted yᵉ same day
qr   oo   10   oo
      Archibald Todd Porter was admitted yᵉ [16th Sepʳ 1680]
qr   oo   10   oo
      Thomas Wallice Porter yᵉ 16th Sepʳ 1680 admitted
oo   10   oo
      George Moore Porter yᵉ same day admitted
gratis
      Wᵐ Longhead Porter yᵉ same day admitted
oo   10   oo
      John Barber Porter yᵉ 16th of Sepʳ 1680 admitted
oo   10   oo
      John Thompkin Porter admitted yᵉ same day
gratis
      Nathaniell Trimble Marriner admitted yᵉ same day
gratis
      ffrancis Attkinson Weaver admitted yᵉ same day
gratis
      Thomas MᶜIllroy Carman admitted yᵉ same day
apprᵗˢ
      James Whitler bricklayer admitted yᵉ same day
gratis
      William Cambell Tobacco Spiner admitted yᵉ same day
apprᵗˢ
      [Wᵐ Sharper] Rowland Sharper Tanner as admitted yᵉ same day
      John Whitehead Tobacco Spiner was admitted yᵉ same day
            Jo ffletcher to pay
gratis
      Hugh Montgomery gent admitted yᵉ same day
oo   10   oo
      Samuell Wright marchᵗ yᵉ 23th Sepʳ 1680 admited
gratis
      James Patterson Carman admitted yᵉ same day
gratis
      John MᶜIllroy Butcher admitted yᵉ same day
gratis
      Mathew Allexander Shoomaker admitted yᵉ same day
oo   10   oo
      John Tompkin Carman Junior admitted yᵉ same day
gratis
      William Whitler Tobacco Spiner admitted yᵉ same day

apprt̄s
Moses Richardson Watchmaker yᵉ same day admitted

gratis
John Torbourn Carman yᵉ same day admitted

gratis
John mᶜDuffe Carman yᵉ same day admitted

gratis
Wᵐ mᶜCreavy Carman yᵉ same day admitted

gratis
James Rogers Tobacco Spiner yᵉ same day admitted

gratis
Wᵐ Betton Smith yᵉ 23ᵈ Sepʳ 1680 admitted a freeman

gratis
Andrew mᶜGallyard *Yeoman* yᵉ same day admitted a freeman
Henry Ramage Porter yᵉ same day admitted

gratis
Wᵐ Neilson Porter yᵉ same day admitted

gratis
James Cambell Aleseller yᵉ same day admitted
George MᶜCartney Esqʳ High Sheriffe Soveraigne
of yᵉ Borrough of Bellfast 29th Sepʳ 1680

gratis
Roger Warring Cler. yᵉ 30th Septʳ admitted a freeman

gratis
Shelston Theaker Cler yᵉ same day admitted

apprt̄s
John Boyd marchᵗ yᵉ same day admitted

apprt̄s
Lodavick mᶜGowane marchᵗ yᵉ same day admitted

apprt̄s
Gilduffe Gillmore Tanner yᵉ same day admitted

referred to yᵉ bench
Capt Edward Pottinger Marchᵗ admitted yᵉ same day
Anthony Hall marchᵗ admitted yᵉ same day

appt̄s
John Eccles Marchᵗ admitted yᵉ same day

appt̄s
George Wellsh Tanner admitted yᵉ same day

gratis
Quarter Master Thomas Beverley yᵉ 28th day of Apʳ 1681 admitted a freeman

oo 10 oo
John Neile weaver 5th May admitted free

appt̄s
Henry Crossley Shoomaker yᵉ 2ᵈ June 1681 admitted

gratis
Ogan Rush *Yeoman* yᵉ same admitted yᵉ same day

appt̄s
Israell Snowdon marcht yᵉ 14th July 1681 admitted

appt̄s
David Rosse marcht yᵉ 11th August 1681 admitted

oo 09 oo
Robert Younge marcht yᵉ same day admitted

gratis
John Lejey Gent 18th August 1681 admitted

oo 10 oo
Wᵐ Pringle Mariner 1st Septʳ 1681 admitted

oo 10 oo
Wᵐ ffade Chapman 8th Septʳ 1681 admitted

oo 10 oo
ffrancis KinCade Stationer yᵉ same day admitted

appt̄s
George mᶜCartney (Browne) marcht yᵉ same day admtᵈ

gratis
James Callwell bookebinder 15th Sept admitted

appt̄s
Wᵐ Mordagh shoomaker yᵉ same day admitted

appt̄s
Pattrick [Lagan] Loughan Currier yᵉ same day admitted

appt̄s
James Griffeth ffeltmaker yᵉ same day admitted
Charles Coates Chapman yᵉ same day admitted
Wᵐ Biggar marcht yᵉ same day admitted

oo 08 oo
William Johnston Marcht yᵉ 22ᵈ Sepᵗ 1681 admitted

oo 10 oo
James ffife Chandler yᵉ same day admitted

00 10 00
Thomas Lisle Taylor yᵉ same day admitted

00 10 00
William Eglsham Porter yᵉ same day admitted

00 10 00
Thomas Eglsham Weaver yᵉ same day admitted

00 10 00
John Tedford Cooper yᵉ same day admitted

00 04 06
Hugh Smale Taylor yᵉ same day admitted

pd for keepeing Kiles orphants
George Moore Cooper yᵉ same day admitted

22d Sept 1681.   gratis for keepeing his mother and sister from a burden to yᵉ Towne
Thomas Hinch Shoomaker yᵉ same day admitted

These quarrymen made ⎧ Thomas Law quarryman yᵉ same day admitted
free to provide stones ⎪ James Minis quarryman yᵉ same day admitted
to yᵉ comon Kea   ⎨ John Law quarryman yᵉ same day admitted
                       ⎩ Robert Law quarryman yᵉ same day admitted

00 04 06
Thomas Withnell Butcher yᵉ same day admitted

to worke at yᵉ Kea
Archibald mᶜCallister *Labourer* yᵉ same day admitted

to mend ye markett house
John Chruchley plasterer yᵉ same day admitted

gratis
Thomas Quin Currier yᵉ same day admitted

00 04 06
John Patterson Cooper yᵉ 29th Sepᵗ admitted

00 05 00
John Carruthers Cooper yᵉ same day admitted

00 08 00
Bryan mᶜGragh Tobacco Spiner yᵉ same day admitted

gratis
John Adams Aleseller yᵉ same day admitted

00 08 00
George Ramsey Reedmaker yᵉ same day admitted

ffrancis Thetford Esqʳ Soveraigne of Bellfast
29th Sepʳ 1681

apptⁱˢ
John Eccles Junior marchᵗ 13th October 1681 was sworne a free Comoner

00 10 00
ffrancis Lowney Taylor yᵉ 20th Octobʳ 1681 admitted

00 10 00
Robert Storey Shoomaker yᵉ same day admitted
Samuell Hill marchᵗ yᵉ 3ᵈ Novʳ 1681 admitted

apprᵗˢ
Issraell Christian Shoomaker yᵉ same day admitted

apprᵗˢ
John Mitchell Butcher yᵉ 10th Novʳ admitted

apptˢ
Robert fforbus wheelewright or Turner yᵉ 17th Novembʳ admited

00 09 00
William Edgar Taylor yᵉ 17th Novʳ admitted

apptˢ D
Charles McDowell *Marchant* yᵉ yᵉ 24th Novʳ admitted

apptˢ D
Samuell Smith Marchᵗ yᵉ 2ᵈ of ffeby 1681 was admitted

Burg de ⎱ Tempore Georgii Macartney Armiger Junʳ Superioris Ejusdem Ville
Belfast ⎰ Sequentes Municipes facti sunt Ville pʳdict

1723
Novʳ 12ᵗʰ
John Gregg Malster was made free *Dead*

Dead
Do William Matthews Bricklayer was made free

Honʳʸ ffreeman
Do Colonell Robert Ferguson was made Free *Dead*

Honʳʸ ffreeman
Do George Cruming MD made Free *Dead*

Honʳʸ Freeman
Do Captⁿ Christopher Phillips made Free *Dead*

Honʳʸ Freeman
Do Captⁿ Tobias Maloy was made free *Dead*

Honʳʸ Freeman
Do Levᵗ Thomas Ford was made Free *Dead*

Honʳʸ Freeman
Do Ensign Thomas Loyd was made Free *Dead*

Hon^{ry} Freeman

Do Quartermaster Mich^l Phillips was made free *Dead*

Novr 14th

Mr William Simpson *merch^t* was sworn Freeman *Dead*

Do Andrew Ferguson *merch^t* was sworn Freeman *Dead*

Nov 19th

Thomas Johnson was sworn Freeman Wigmaker *Dead*

Novr 21st

John Henning Cooper was sworn ffreeman *Dead*

Nov 25

James Patterson Shooemaker was sworn ffreeman *Dead*

Nov 26

Adam Guttery march^t was sworn ffreeman *Dead*

Do

Gilbert M'Dowell merch^t was sworn freeman *Dead*

Do *Dead*

Geo Macartney merch^t was made free

Dead

John Macartney merch^t was made free

Do

John Houston merch^t was sworn freeman

Do

William Wason merch^t was sworn freeman *Dead*

Nov 27th

James Cormickill Cooper sworn freeman

Decr 5th

The Revr^d Nicholas Thetford was made free *Dead*

Do

Mr William Thetford merch^t was made free *Dead*

Do

Mr Arthur Thetford merch^t was made free *Dead*

Febry 29th

Thomas Gulliland Butcher was made free *Dead*

Do

William Carson Bricklayer was made free *Dead*

Dead

Robert Barry perriwigmaker was sworn Free

1723 March 17th

John Gordon taylor was made free

Do

Alexander Walker was made Free *Dead*

1724 March 31st

Thomas Hunter upholder was made Free *Dead*

May 17th 1724 Gratis

Arthur Clark Carpenter was sworn free

May 21st 1724

Ordered then that James Foreman appear at next court to be held for this Burrough and shew cause why he shall not be Disfranchized

Persons made free Nathl Byrt Esqr Sovrⁿ

[9^{ber} ye 5th **1724** Wm Osborne made free & sworn]
[xb^r 30 Wm Crawford Cordwinder free & sworn]

Nath: Byrtt Esqr Soverⁿ Freemen made in his time

1724 9ber 5th *Dead*

Wm Osburn *butcher* made free and sworn

xbr 30th *Dead*

Wm Craford Cordinder free & sworn

1724/5

Jany 13 *Dead*

James Boyd Taylor free & sworn

-- 15 *D^d*

John fferguson Cooper free & sworn

— 18 *D^d*

David m^cCall Taylor free & sworn

— 20 *D^d*

Wm Carmichell Cooper free & sworn

25 —

D^d John Gregg Junr [m^{ct}] *shopkeeper* free and sworn

D^d John Carnahan [m^{ct}] *shopkeeper* free & sworn

D^d Alex Gilmore [m^{ct}] *shopkeeper* free & sworn

D^d Saml Curry [m^{ct}] *shopkeeper* free & sworn

Robt Bole vintner free & sworn

30 D^d
James Smith weaver free & sworn

D^d
Wm Hamilton Cooper free & sworn

D^d
John m^cKibbin Cooper free & sworn

—
Charles Hamilton Cooper free & sworn

febry 2^d D^d
Alexand^r Mayors Taylor & Impolster free and sworn

4th D^d
James Potter shopkeeper free & sworn

5 D^d
Math Plomer staymaker free & sworn

—
James Davison Taylor free & sworn

11 D^d
John Osburn Baker free & sworn

D^d
John Glen Malster free & sworn

14 D^d
Pat Gibson baker free & sworn

23
Robt Tonragh shumaker free & sworn

1724/5 March 22^d
Leonard Kendal free & sworn D^d

1725 July 31
Gawen Gray Hukster free & sworn fees p^d Ed Hall D^d
John Edgar Smith free & sworn

Augt 5th
Moses Cherry Doctor free & sworn D^d
Robert Snell Doctor free & sworn D^d

Burrough ⎰ Persons admitted and sworn ffree Comon^n of
of Belfast ⎱ s^d Burrough before James Macartney Esqr
⎰ Sov^rn for The Year 1725/6

Tickett
James Chalmers Merch^t D^d
David Lyons Yeo^n Sworn in Curia *dead*

30th Sept^r
Henry M^cffaddan Perrywigmaker *Dead* sworn in Curia

14th Octr 1725
Sam^ll McKelvy Aleseller sworn ffree D^d in Curia

Do 21
Francis Cromey Merch^t D^d Ticket

Do Die
Anthony Thetford Merch^t D^d Ticket

1725 Novemb^r 11th
William Easlake Joyner & Puly Maker D^d sworn in Curia

Decr 11
Hugh Coghran Taylor sworn Freeman D^d

Decr 18
J^no McCreery Taylor sworn Freeman

Decr 18
George Boyd Merc^t sworn ffree D^d

Do 22
James Gallery Carpinter D^d

Do 31st
John Doule Carman sworn free D^d

March 1
Hugh McCaal Taylor sworn free

Do 22
Mr J^no Sharp sworn a free Merch^t D^d

Do Die
Mr Adam McKibbin sworn D^d a free Merch^t

Do Die
Mr Ed^d Mitchel sworn a free Merch^t

28 Martii 1726
Thos Agnew Slater sworn ffree D^d

31 Martii 1726
Henry Varnett Taylor

Do
John Herron Shoemaker sworn ffree D^d

April 1st
Joseph Hughs Merch^t sworn ffree D^d

—
John McKall Aleseller sworn ffree D^d or Malster

James Macartney Butcher sworn ffree *D*ᵈ

John Hughs of Carmony farmer sworn free

Thomas Beaty Inkeepʳ sworn ffree *D*ᵈ

Aprill 6th 1726
William Bigger Carpenter sworn ffree
John Farquhar sworn ffree *D*ᵈ
Aprill 8th **1726** James Hughs ffarmer sworn ffree *Dead*
9th Aprill **1726** John Coleman Merchᵗ sworn ffree *D*ᵈ
James Whitlock Peruck maker sworn ffree *D*ᵈ
John Jackson Butcher *D*ᵈ
Burᵒ de ⎱ Persons sworn & admitted free Comoners of sᵈ Burrough before John
Belfast ⎰ Clugston Esqʳ Sovereign for the year 1726
George Paterson taylor

2 July 1726
George Hunter Wigmʳ sworn free appʳ to Henry East *D*ᵈ

Aug. 6
[James] Robᵗ Watt Merchᵗ sworn free *D*ᵈ
Charles Burn Cooper sworn free *D*ᵈ
Willᵐ English Carpenter sworn free *D*ᵈ

11th Augᵗ
Thomas Gelston Soapboyler sworn free *D*ᵈ

25 Augᵗ
James Montgomery Mariner sworn free *D*ᵈ
Joseph Carswell Mariner sworn free *D*ᵈ

30 Aug
Alexʳ Orr Merchᵗ sworn free *D*ᵈ

1726 July
Robᵗ Coffin smith sworn free *D*₄
Joseph Hall bellfounder sworn free *D*₄
Gilbert Mullygan gunsmith sworn free *D*ᵈ

1726 16 Sepʳ
John ffursythe smith sworn free *D*ᵈ

13 Octʳ
William Burt Slater sworn free *D*ᵈ
Bryan Lenard Slater sworn free *D*ᵈ

Decem 1
James Boyd Carman sworn free *D*ᵈ

ffeby 4th
William McCrea Weaver sworn ffree Gratis for retᵉ a List of fforreigners *Dead*

March 2ᵈ
John Atkinson of Drogheda Tanner sworn ffree

1727 Aprill 27
David Stevenson Carman sworn Free *D*ᵈ
Thomas Collyer Esqʳ Got a Tickett *D*ᵈ
Nathaniell Morrison sworn *D*ᵈ Free
Daniel Kenian sworn free *D*ᵈ
Alexʳ Moorehead sworn free *D*ᵈ
James Murdoch sworn free Cooper *D*ᵈ
Robert Wier Carman sworn free *D*ᵈ

15° die Maij **1727°**
Ticketts ⎧ Benjamin Legg Merchant Admitted ffree *D*ᵈ
⎪ John Stewart Merchant Admitted ffree *D*ᵈ
⎨ Samuell Allen Merchᵗ sworn ffree *D*ᵈ
⎩ James Young Merchᵗ sworn ffree *D*ᵈ
29° die Julij **1727** Hugh McQuoid Gunsmith sworn ffree *D*ᵈ
William Browne was sworn ffree *D*ᵈ
Hugh Spence Taylor was sworn ffree
7° August **1727** Robert Montgomery Merchᵗ got a tickett not sworn *D*ᵈ
James Duggan Butcher sworn ffree *D*ᵈ
26° Augᵗ **1727** Robert Bruce Barber sworn ffree *D*ᵈ
31° Aug **1727** John Smith Merchᵗ got a Tickett *D*ᵈ
Andrew Smith Merchᵗ got a tickett
4th August **1727** William Townsend *Tanner* sworn ffree *D*ᵈ
5th August **1727** Enoch Ball Nailor sworn ffree *D*ᵈ

15th [Aug] Sept 1727
*D*ᵈ Timothy Russell made ffree ⎱ both living at Hollywood
*D*ᵈ James Russell made ffree ⎰
21ˢᵗ September **1727** Charles Walsh Cooper sworn Free *D*ᵈ

U

Robert Gaskin aleseller sworn ffree
Hugh Lowry Cooper sworn Free D^d
Allex^r McReeny Cooper sworn ffree D^d
22^d September 1727   John Flemming an apprentice to James Magee Carpenter
This day was sworn ffree D^d
18th Jany 1727   Henry Hamilton Chapman sworn ffree D^d
29th ffeby 1727   John Peart Butcher was sworn ffree D^d
7th March 1727 William McDowell Fidler was sworn free D^d
21st March 1727   William Munford Blacksmith sworn ffree D^d
John Ratliff [Linen mar] Cloath^r sworn ffree D^d
23 March 1727   John Newman Perukmaker sworn ffree D^d
28° March 1728   Joseph Dingley Taylor sworn ffree D^d
24° Aprill 1728   James Gordon Taylor sworn ffree gratis D^d recomended by
Gen^{ll} Price
gratis D^d
James Adams [farmer] *mariner* [Ballymack] Nock m^a garry
gratis
Allexander Frissall Carman
William Kirk sadler sworn free D^d
D^d
July 16 1728   Samuell Flemin of Hollywood sworn free gratis
D_d
James Heuston Carman sworn free
D^d
John Cudbert Merchant sworn free
The 19th July 1728   Robert Lindsay Farmer sworn Free
Samuel Martin Farmer Got a Tickett
John Lindsay Farmer got Ditto
25th July 1728   John Dayly Butcher sworn ffree D^d
27 Augt 1728   John McMunn Soap Boiler sworn ffree
2^d September 1728   Mathew Craford Huckster sworn ffree D^d
Robert McAllexander Weaver sworn ffree
6th September 1728   John Sloan Apprentice to Tim: Sheilds Baker this day was
sworn ffree
25th September 1728   Mr Nathan Smith Merch^t got a Tickett D^d
Robert Black Shoemaker sworn ffree D^d
26th Jacob Lyon sworn ffree *ffarmer*
Hugh Gibson Glasier sworn ffree D^d
James Arbuckle Junr *merch^t* Got a Tickett D_d
Wm Chalmers merch^t got D° D^d
Hugh Petygrew farmer made free D^d
James Armstrong Linendraper D^d
Michael Whitlock Peruckmaker D^d
Hugh Beggs shoemaker D^d
Hugh McKiterick shoemaker D^d
4th [Marc] Aprill 1728
Robert Smith Marchant sworn ffree D^d
William Rogers sworn ffree D^d
Wm Herron sworn ffree D^d
p^d

28th September 1728 $\left\{ \begin{array}{l} \text{Martin Worthington } D^d \\ \text{Bruen Worthington } D^d \\ \text{W}^m \text{ Worthington } D^d \end{array} \right\}$ Butchers
Hugh Young Merch^t D^d
p^d

Joseph Simpson Merch^t D^d
Hugh Andrew Merch^t D^d
Hans Hutchinson ffarmer D^d
Archibald Hamilton Ballymechen D^d
John Craford D^d } ffarmers
James Craford D^d
Robert Magee D^d } ffarmers
John Kerr D^d
Thomas Curry Hollywood D^d
John Isaac Esqr D^d
James Dunlap Hollywood
p
Wm Stafford marriner D^d
p^d
John Cunningham Carman D^d

p^d

W^m McIllroy Huckster D^d

p^d

Thomas ffife Carpenter

p^d

Robert McDowell ffarmer D^d

p^d

Robert Henderson Watchmaker

p^d

Paul Crutchley Currier D^d

p^d

Wm Maxwell Chapman
[John Lewis carpenter]

p^d

28th Sepr 1728 { John Glover Backer sworn ffree D^d
Victor Touram Peruckmaker sworn ffree D^d
Allex^r Dunlap Peruckmaker sworn ffree D^d

Allex^r Stewart March^t D^d
James Hamilton Gen^t
Richard Joy Chanler
John Jervis Carpenter D^d
John Culbert March^t D^d
Arthur Gear Gen^t D^d
Moses Kinkead
Bryan O'Hamill sworn ffree D^d
John Kinkead

Thomas Banks Esqr Sovr^n 17 October 1728
Willm Miller Shoemaker sworn ffree in Court

1728 Janry 23
Henry Hart of The Citty of Derry Merch^t sworn ffree *Dead*
[John Shanin] George Ewart of The same Merchant sworn ffree *Dead*
John Shannon Taylor sworn ffree

D^d

6 ffebruary 1728 Henry Charley }
Bakers sworn ffree

D^d

John McMeken }

D^d

28 Augt 1729 Kelso of Lisburn Merch^t sworn ffree
11th Septem^r 1729 Neal Patten and }
Wm Johnston } Bakers sworn ffree
John Knox Watchmaker sworn ffree D^d
Andrew Morton Shoem^r sworn ffree

D^d

Abell Bullock smith sworn ffree
Sam^{ll} McWha Taylor
Andrew Joy Mason

D^d

25th Septr 1729 James McQuay Chanler apprentice to Mr Ar: Thetford
sworn ffree

D^d

John Semple malemonger sworn free

D^d

George Long Gardner

D^d

Charles Willson Gardner

D^d

John Charley

D^d

Robert Caulfield shoemaker } Sworn free

D^d

Hugh Martin yeoman

D^d

Wm Montgomery of Whitehouse Marcht

D^d

Hugh Anderson Innkeeper being Sove^{rns} Clke Sworn gratis
Thomas Anderson Sov^{rns} servant sworn gratis

John Duff Esqr Sov^{rn} 24th November 1729

D^d

Daniel McCalister ffarmer sworn ffree

D^d

James Smith Merch^t } sworn ffree Gratis

D^d

Allex. Stewart Merch^t

*D*ᵈ 17 1obʳⁱˢ 1729   William Seeds Merchᵗ sworn free
*D*ᵈ Henery Donlevy ffree Got a Tickett Gratis
*D*ᵈ William Robison Mealman sworn ffree
  January 1ˢᵗ 1729   Robert Blackwood Esqʳ sworne ffree Gratis
*D*ᵈ William McElrath shopkeeper
*D*ᵈ March 5° 1729   James West Taylor from Cumber sworn ffree Gratis
*D*ᵈ Aprill 28° 1730   Thomas Ritchey Shoemaker sworn ffree
*D*ᵈ Hugh Magee porter sworn ffree
*D*ᵈ 1730 June 18th John Miller shoemaker sworn ffree
*D*ᵈ Robert Corbitt shoemaker sworn ffree
*D*ᵈ 1730 June 19th William aDiddell Yarn Merchᵗ son to adam aDidell of The falls
sworn ffree gratis
*D*ᵈ June 20th James Sinklair Taylor Son to Robᵗ Sinklair sworn free Gratis
*D*ᵈ June 25th 1730   John Boyd Merchᵗ Got a Tickett   Gratis
*D*ᵈ 1ˢᵗ July 1730   John Taylor Shoemaker sworn ffree
  23 July 1730   John Satterthwaite Merchᵗ Gott a Tickett   *Dead*
*D*ᵈ William Mankin Silver smith Gott a Tickett
*D*ᵈ Allen McQuerg Merchᵗ sworn free July 25ᵗʰ 1730 & got a Ticket
*D*ᵈ 30 July 1730   Thomas Smallshaw Blockmaker sworn ffree
*D*ᵈ 3ᵈ August 1730   Robert Murray of The City of Dublin Taylor got a Ticket Gratis
*D*ᵈ Thomas Arnold near Dromore gent   Dᵒ   Gratis
*D*ᵈ 5th August 1730   Andrew Campbell Shoemaker sworn free
*D*ᵈ George Ross of Castle Lyons Gent Gott a Tickett Gratis
*D*ᵈ Charles Young Merchant Gott a Tickett
*D*ᵈ Samuel Catherwood Merchant gott a Tickett
  Robert Alexander and   ⎱ Sworn free
*D*ᵈ John Smith Peruckmakers ⎰
*D*ᵈ 19 Augᵗ 1730   Patrick Boyd aleseller sworn free
*D*ᵈ John Shaw Coach Wheel & Carriage Maker Sworn free
  20th Aug 1730   John Brown Chapman   Sworn ffree
*D*ᵈ 25 August 1730   James Boyd Blacksmith sworn ffree   Gratis
  Richard Hoskins Blacksmith sworn free 26 Aug 1730
*D*ᵈ 27 Aug 1730   John Black Shoemaker sworn free
*D*ᵈ 31ˢᵗ John Rodger sworn free Yarn Merchᵗ
*D*ᵈ 14 September 1730   Robert Holms [Wat] of the City of Dublin Watchmaker Gott
a Tickett Gratis
*D*ᵈ John Jelly of Lisbarnett in Com Down Taylor sworn free
*D*ᵈ John Elliot sworn free Gratis
*D*ᵈ 17   George Wealls Chapman sworn free
*D*ᵈ Do   Hans Hamilton of the County of Torone Shoemaker sworn free
*D*ᵈ Do   John Clark Pattin Maker sworn free Gratis
*D*ᵈ Do   George Voughan Esqʳ of the County Donegall got a Tickett Gratis
*D*ᵈ 19 Sepʳ 1730   John Hurd servant to Mʳ Collier sworn free
*D*ᵈ Patrick Kean Servant sworn free ⎱ Gratis
*D*ᵈ Pierce Berry Labourer sworn free ⎰
*D*ᵈ 22 Joⁿ Shannon Taylor sworn free
*D*ᵈ Do   Francis Betty Cooper sworn free Gratis
*D*ᵈ Valentine Thetford Cooper sworn free gratis
*D*ᵈ 23 7ᵇʳⁱˢ 1730   Robert Boyd Shoemaker sworn free gratis
*D*ᵈ 25 7ᵇʳ 1730   John White Carman sworn ffree Gratis
*D*ᵈ John Dornan Servᵗ to Mʳ Isaac McCartney sworn ffree gratis
*D*ᵈ Owen OKennan Servᵗ to the (*sic*) sworn ffree gratis
*D*ᵈ 26th Sbʳ 1730   William Clugston apprentice with Henry Duncan apothecary Got
a Tickett Gratis
*D*ᵈ Arthur McCann Baker sworn ffree Gratis
*D*ᵈ Wᵐ Nutt Hatter sworn ffree
*D*ᵈ Robert Doogan Taylor sworn ffree
*D*ᵈ 28th 7ᵇʳ 1730   Dennis Kinnan Carman sworn ffree
*D*ᵈ William Mankin gent got a Tickett Gratis
*D*ᵈ George Magee at Milewater sworn ffree
*D*ᵈ John Riggs Carman sworn ffree
*D*ᵈ Edward Raa Labourer sworn ffree Gratis
*D*ᵈ Robert Neill appʳntice with James Watt made ffree gratis
*D*ᵈ On the 15th of September 1730 The Sovʳⁿ and Burgesses Did wait on The Right
Honᵇˡᵉ Francis Lord Conway Baron of Ragley In England of Killultagh In Ireland Lord
Lievᵗ & Custos Rottullorum of the County Lord Lievᵗ and Governor of the Town and
County of the Town of Carrickfergus & presented him his Tickett
*D*ᵈ 28 7ᵇʳ 1730 Richard Coleman Yarn Merchᵗ sworn ffree

D^t	Hugh Reilly Clke to Jn° Arnold Att'y	} Got Ticketts gratis
D^t	Allexander Thomas Clke to Collyer & Compy	
D^t	William Teat Taylor sworn ffree	

28th Sbr 1730

Dd	Robert Forsyth of The ffalls	)
Dd	Edward Forsyth of The same	} Sworn ffree
Dd	John Stevenson of The same	)
Dd	William Forbes Wheelwright sworn ffree Gratis	
Dd	William Blain Huester sworn ffree	
D^t	Bryan OHanlan Cutler sworn ffree	

Arthur Byrtt Esqr sworn Sov^rn the 28th September 1730 The undernamed persons made ffree by him

18th February 1730
William Pettygrew Taylor sworn ffree Gratis

19th Ditto 1730
Dd Hugh Beaty Taylor sworn Free Gratis

30 August 1731
Dd Jno McClean Taylor sworn ffree Gratis
Dd William McCleary Baker sworn free
Dd James Granger Baker sworn free
Dd James McDonnell Bricklayer sworn free Gratis
Dd Thomas Kirkpatrick Smith sworn free
Dd Wm Hutchison Shopkeeper sworn free

31st Do Dd
John Barkley   Do   sworn free

Sbr 6 Dd
Wm Kenedy Cooper Sworn free Gratis
George Ainslie Skiner sworn free Gratis

9th Dd
Robt Dickey Cord winer sworn free Gratis   AP

15th Dd
John Potts bookseller sworn free

17th
Thomas Coulter Taylor sworn free Gratis   A.P.

20th
John Boyle Weaver sworn free Gratis
Dd John McKeale Taylor sworn free
Dd James Boyce M^rt free p tickett
Dd Joseph Moorhead Carryer sworn free &
Dd James Young Merc^t free p tickett
Dd
Alex^r McAllister Carryer sworn free gratis

1731 Sepr 25th
Robert Aldridge Staymaker sworn free
John Gabby Taylor sworn free   A.P.

27th
Andrew McCleary Taylor sworn free
Dd George McCuary Mason sworn free Gratis

D 28th
Neill McLaughlin Cooper sworn free Gratis   AP
Dd Robert Anderson merc^t free p tickett
Dd John Burleigh merc^t free p tickett
Dd John Wilson Blacksmith sworn free Gra   A.P.
Dd Robert Thompson Cooper sworn free Gratis   A.P.
Dd John Hackett Blacksmith sworn free Gratis
Dd Francis Hamilton Merch^t free per tickett
Dd John McCraight appothecary free per tickett
Dd Patrick Agnew Merch^t free per tickett
Dd William Shannon Merch^t free per tickett
D
John Pettycrew Merch^t free per tickett

Dd
John Wilson Merch^t free per tickett

1733 Sepr 27 Dd
Joh[a]nnes Fivey Merch^t free per tickett

Dd
James Clark Merch^t free per tickett

Dd
Hugh Kennedy Esqr free per tickett
Arthur Kennedy [merch^t] free per ticket
James Hamilton gentleman free per ticket
James Fivey Merch^t free per ticket

Dd
  Daniel OGillen   free per ticket
Dd
  William Walker Marriner free per ticket
Dd
  Samuel Kirkpatrick Stay Maker sworn free Gratis
          Robert Byrtt Esqr sworn Sov^n 29 Sepr 1733
          The undernamed persons made free by him
  11 of Oct 1733
      Robert Gordon by Ticket   *Dd* gratis
      William Royd Esqr by Ticket   *Dead* gratis
              Margetson Saunders Esqr sworn Sovereign
              29 Sepr 1735
  1736 July 27
      Benjamin Boyd sworn freeman   *Dd*
Dd
  William McClueny sworn free
Sepr 2
  Charles Kennedy Cutler sworn free
  1737 Aug 25
      Hugh McKelvey sworn free (gratis)
      Arch^d Wisely of Bangor free gratis
Dead
  Mr Nathl Byrtt of Carrickf^s free per ticket (gratis)
  Hugh McKelvy of Lairn free — gratis
Dead
  Jas Ross Esqr Portivoe free per ticket gratis
Dd
  Phillip Coats of the Falls free per oath gratis
  Mr Val Jones Junr free per ticket gratis
Dead
  Mr Jo^n Bennet Cooper per ticket free gratis
D
  Wm Hardy Farmer in the Falls sworn free
Dead
  John Paterson Ship ma^r of Erwin free per oath gratis
Dd
  Elias ODidle of the Falls of Belfast made free & sworn
Dead
  Jas Nocher of Belfast Coal Porter sworn free Gratis
  William Kennedy of Knocknagony Farmer sworn free
Dd
  Thomas Stevenson of the Falls of Belfast sworn free
Dead
  James Sommerill porter in town sworn free
Dead
  Hugh Magee porter in town sworn free
  Henry Tisdall son of the rev^d Dr William Tisdall free per Ticket Gratis
  Robt Magee Cooper Belfast sworn free   *Dead* Gratis
Dd
  Thos Cahan Cooper Belfast sworn free Gratis
Dd
  John Fisher porter sworn free gratis
          Robt Byrtt Esqr Sov^n in the year 1739 the
          following persons made free
  7 ffebry 1739
      John Armstrong Merch^t by Tickett the first English Tickett *Dead*
          Persons Made Free by John Duff Sover^n 29
          Septr 1742
  John McClure Carman made free
  John Fisher Sadler made free
          Persons made free by Robt Byrtt Sov^n 30th
          Novr 1742
      John Downey made free   *D*
  2' Decemb^r 1742
      Petter Nuby made free   *D*
  1743 June 15th
      Henry Blair *of* Belfast marchant made Free
      Persons made free by Arthur Byrtt Soveraign
  1744 7th June *Dd*
      Samuel Carson made free *dead* per tickett gratis
      Arthur Byrtt Esqr Sovereign 29th Sepr 1745
  1746 Sep
      John Cartwright of Malone farmer & his two sons

1746 7ᵇʳ 18ᵗʰ
John Shaw & Wᵐ Shaw Tanners per Dᵒ gratis
Wᵐ Stewart wigmaker sworn free gratis *dead*

24
Robᵗ M'Dowell Baker sworn free gratis *Dead*
Hugh Martin Ditto sworn free gratis *Dead*
Tho Sheilds Cooper sworn free Gratis
John Cartwright of Malone farmer free gratis
Wᵐ Cartwright son to Do free gratis
Thoˢ Cartwright son to Do free gratis
John Evans of the Parish of Carmoney sworn free gratis
Andrew McFarran Taylor sworn free gratis

27ᵗʰ
James McWatters Vintner sworn free gratis

Dᵈ
Allexʳ Thompson Malster free per tickett gratis
Wᵐ Polluck shoemaker free per tickett gratis
John Duff Esqᵣ sworn Soverⁿ the 29ᵗʰ Sepʳ 1746 the undernamed persons made free by him
Patrick Hoy Baker made free Dᵈ
xᵇʳ 23ᵈ 1746
Augᵗ 3ᵈ 1747 Joⁿ Minis made free of yᵉ Long Lane sworn this day *dead*
Mʳ Gilbert Orr Merchant made free Augᵗ 5ᵗʰ 1747 Gratis Dᵈ
Andrew Davison of Tullnagee made free Gratis & took yᵉ oath Augᵗ 8ᵗʰ 1747
James Henery of Skegenearl made free Gratis & took yᵉ oath Sepʳ 22ᵈ 1747 Dᵈ
Eccles Woods of the Falls made free Gratis Sepʳ 24 1747 Dᵈ
Wᵐ Allen of Mile Water Gardner made free gratis & took yᵉ oath Sepʳ 26ᵗʰ 1747 Dᵈ

Margetson Saunders Esqʳ Sovⁿ from 29ᵗʰ Septʳ
1747 to 29ᵗʰ 7ᵇᵉʳ 1748
gratis
Brice Blair Baker in Newtown Served his apprenticeship here sworn free
gratis Dᵈ
Thomas Bagley Merchant
William Harrison son to Joⁿ Harrison in Newtⁿ Merchᵗ made free by ticket
James Pinkerton of Belfast Baker served his apprenticeship to his father David Pinkerton sworn free
1748 Sepʳ 26
Wᵐ Coats of the Falls & Townland of Ballymurchy sworn free
27 Dᵈ
James McDougall of Belfast Merchᵗ sworn free
27
Wᵐ Stewart Dealer in North Street sworn free gratis
28
Robᵗ Scott taylor served his time in town sworn free gratis
John Harrison son to Joⁿ Harrison of Newtown sworn free gratis
Burrough } At a Court of Assembly held in the Town Hall of Belfast the 5ᵗʰ March
Belfast } 1752 before Arthur Byrtt Esqʳ Sovⁿ of said Burrough the following
persons were admitted & sworn freemen of said Burrough
James Archbald Merchᵗ Dᵈ
James Pickin Staymaker
Burrough of } At a Court of Assembly held ——
Belfast }
Arthur Byrtt Esqʳ Sovereign
1752 May 22
Michael O'Kenan of Skigin Earle ffree
Dᵈ
Robert Harrison Attorney sworn free gratis
[Aug 4] July 30
Rigby Dobbin *Dead* of Dunean Per Ticket
John Dobbin of Dᵒ Per Ticket
Sep 14 Dᵈ
Richard Tootell of Belfast *Dead* sworn free
Dᵈ
Francis Graham of Belfast Innkeeper sworn free
Dᵈ
John McKerly of Belfast Taylor & Dealer Sworn free
Dᵈ
Charles Macartney Taylor Sworn free
Dᵈ
James Carson Taylor Sworn free
Dᵈ
Patrick Garret Taylor sworn free

D^d

  Daniel McLain of Strandmillis Brickmaker Sworn free

D^d 21

  James Bashford Carpenter Sworn free

D^d

  John Brooks Glassier sworne free
  John Gibson Taylor

21

  Robert Gibson Taylor Sworn free *D^d*

D^d

  Nich Graham Taylor sworn free

D^d

  Thos Orr of Newtown wheel wright sworn free
      Margetson Saunders Esqr Sov^r

  At an assembly the 21st Sepr 1752 the freedom of this Corporation was orderd to
the R^t Honble Lord George Sacville *Principal Secretary of State* To the right Honble
John Ponsonby Esqr The Honble Wm Bristow Esqr the hon^ble Henry Cavendish Esqr the
hon^ble William Champneys Esqr the hon^ble Frederick Frankland Esqr & the hon^ble John
Bourke Esqr Commissioners of the Revenue of Ireland & to the Honble Richard Ponsonby
Esqr their Secretary as a mark of our esteem & affection for them & Hill Wilson Esqr
Coll^r of this Port was requested to present them

    Ent^d by Will Byrtt T.C.   Margetson Saunders Sov^n
  At an Assembly the 23^d Aug 1753
  Mr Bastiaen Molewater merch^t In Rotterdam
  The Revd Ja^s Saurin Vicar of Belfast
  John Balaguier Esqr a Captain in [Genaral] *Coll^l* Poles Regim^t of foot [*Dead*] &
  Arthur Saunders of Trinity College were admitted as freemen by tickets
        Margetson Saunders Sov^n

  20th Sepr 1753 at an assembly the following persons were admitted as freemen
by tickets
  James Crawford merchant *D^d*
  Robert Crawford of Liverpool merchant
  William Brown of Dublin Merchant
  James Brown of ye same Merch^t   M Saunders Sov^n.

  20th Sepr 1753 Fell of Pilafowder merch^t made free by Ticket }p^d for it

10 Jany 1754
  Jo^n Mathews merch^t In town made free by Ticket gratis
1754 10th Jany 1754
  Lewis Jones Attorney in town made free by ticket gratis
1754 May 9
  Jo^n Bruen Taylor sworn free *D^d*
July 20th *D^d*
  [John] *W^m* Richardson Esqr free by ticket *D^d*
  Benjamin Burton of Burtonhall Esqr free by ticket

D^d

  John Arnold Junr Gent Attorney in the Burrough court free by ticket
Sepr 12 *D^d*
  Wm Merryman serv^t to Mr Wm Wilson merch^t in town sworn free gratis

D^d

  Thomas Saunders merch^t Son to ye Sov^n by ticket
  John Dorman mealmonger J.P. Belfast sworn free
  James Blair In Newtown Esqr by ticket gratis
  At an Assembly the 18th Novr 1754
  Mr John Meathers Merch^t in Belfast gratis
  Mr James Lewis Merch^t in Belfast do *Dead*

D^d

  Mr Moses Meathers Carpenter in Belfast do *Dead*
  Mr John B Bradshaw Merch^t in Belfast do *Dead*
  Mr Robt Joy Printer in Belfast do *Dead*

D_d

  Berckley McCleney Farmer in the Falls *Dead*
  admitted as Freemen by   Stewart Banks Sov^n.

  At an Assembly 19th June 1755

D^d

  Mr Thos Sinclaire of Belfast Linendraper

Dead

  Mr John Sinclaire of the same Linendraper were admitted Freemen of this
Burrough

         Stewart Banks Sov^m.

  17th July 1756 Persons admitted to the freedom of the Burrough of Belfast by
George Macartney Esqr Sovereign

D^d The Right Honble Clotworthy Earl of Massereene by Tickett & sworn
D^d The Right Honble Alex^r Earl of Antrim   sworn
D^d William Macartney Merch^t George Macartney & Joseph Macartney Sons of the Sov^r sworn   Geo Macartney Sov^n
1758   Persons admitted to the Freedom of the Borough of Belfast by Stewart Banks Esqr Sov^n

Mr Wm Greg Junr Merch^t in Belfast D^d
Mr John Greg Junr   Do D^d
Mr Wm Stewart   Do
28 Sept 1758   Stewart Banks Sovr^n
Wm Bodle servant to the Sovr^n D^d
Jas McDonald & } Sons of the Serg^t D^d
John McDonald } *Dead*
Hugh Moneypenny } Sons of the Serg^t D^d
Wm Moneypenny }
[George Lindsay of the Hill]
Thos Banks } Sons of the Sovr^n
Robt Banks } D^d Stewart Banks Sovr^n
Wm Atholl smith sworn free D^d
John McDonald mason Do D^d
Wm Johnston Barber Do D^d
Nathl Bodle of the Falls Do   Stewart Banks Sov^n
Persons admitted & sworn Freemen of the Borough of Belfast 27 Sep^t 1760
                                Stephen Haven Esqr Sovereign

William Gordon   } *Dead*
John Alexander   } *dead*
Charles Cuningham } *Dead*
Wm Wilson
Arthur Buntin
Willm Arthurs *Dead*   all of Belfast Merchants
John Campbell
Saml. Mattear Junr D^d
Jasper Curry
John Galt Smith
Willm Haven   } D^d
  son to ye Sovereign
Nathan Armstrong } both of Belfast Carpenters D^d
Robt Miller   }
Henry Kirkpatrick *d* } both of Belfast Mercht^s
Saml Stewart D^d }
Stephen Haven Junr } son to ye Sovereign D^d
Nathl Wilson D^d } } all of Belfast Merch^ts by Ticket
Stephen Wilson   } } Grandsons to ye Sovereign D^d
David Henderson D^d of Belfast Merch^t
Noah McClune D^d of Belfast Barber
John Dunlop D^d of Belfast Butcher
Timothy Burns of Belfast Vintner *Dead*
Geo Ferguson of Belfast Merch^t D^d
John Ferguson D^d of Belfast Merch^t by Tickett
                                Stephen Haven Sovereign
Persons admitted & sworn Freeman of the Borough of Belfast 27th Sept 1760
                                Stephen Haven Esqr Soveraign

James Burns   } D^d
Arthur Goffigan } D^d
William Keas   } D^d all of Belfast Butchers
James Morland   } D^d
Sloan Ogans   } D^d
James McCreary } Disfranchised   Stephen Haven Sov^n
Persons admitted & sworn Freemen of the Borough of Belfast 12th Novr 1761 by Stewart Banks Esqr Sover^n

Mr George Black of Belfast Mercht
Mr Thos Black of Belfast Mercht
Mr Saml Black of Belfast Mercht D^d
Mr Saml Scott of the same Malster D^d
M^r Jno McKelvy of the same Distiller D^d
Mr John Vaght of the same Mercht D^d

Mr Michael Spruson of the same Painter   *Dead*
Mr James Getty of the same Mercht   *D^d*
George Murray of the same Weaver   *Dead*

Stewart Banks Sov^n

On the 1 July 1762 Willes Earl of Hillsborough was admitted a Freeman of this Borough of Belfast by Stewart Banks Sov^n *Died Octr 7 1793*

On the 24 Sept 1762 Wm Stirling of the Falls Farmer *D^d* & Ja^s Stirling of the Falls Farmer were admitted & sworn Free Men of the Borough of Belfast and Elected Serg^{ts} at Mace June 25 1777

Stewart Banks Sov^n

On the 16 Sep^t 1762 Mr Saml Hyde Merch^t was admitted & sworn a Free man of the Borrough of Belfast

Stewart Banks Sov^n

On the 4 Sep^t 1766 John Patterson servant to the Sovereign was admitted a Free man of the Borrough of Belfast

Stewart Banks Sov^n

Persons admitted Freemen of the Borough of Belfast Decr 24 1767
Robt Apsley of Belfast Surgeon   sworn
Henry Fortescue Postmaster
Jno Dunbar Att^{ry} *D^d*
Lieut Thos Saunders made free in 1753 sworn this day
Lieut Jisiea Adair
Revd Wm Tisdall   *dead*
Decr 24 1767   Wm Seed of Belfast Merch^t sworn
Ja^s Armstrong } *D^d*
Thos Neilson { *D^d* Butchers sworn
John Rogers Butcher sworn this 27th Sep^t 1768
    26 Sep^t 1771   Geo Macartney Sov

Adam Coats of the Falls sworn free		*dead*
John Coats of the Falls	do	*dead*
Duke Whiteside of the Falls	do	
Thos Teat of the Falls	do	*D^d*
James [W^m] Teat of	do	
James Woods of	do	*D^d*
Whiteside Woods of	do	
Hill Woods of	Do	*D^d*
John Woods of	Do	*D^d*
Mich^l Woods of	Do	
Wm Kirker of	Do	*dead*
Wm Kirkwood of	Do	*dead*
Wm Kirkwood Junr of	Do	*D^d*
Wm Salters of	Do	*dead*
Fra^s Sergison of	Do	*D^d*
Nevin Williamson of	Do	*dead*
Jam^s Williamson of	D	
S^t. John Main of	D	*dead*
Jam Martin of	D	*dead*
W^m McFarling of	D	
Alex^r Patterson of	D	*D^d*
George Roberts of	D	*D^d*
Jam^s Lowry of	D	*D^d*
Philip Dennis of	D	*D^d*
Wm Coats of	D	*D^d*
John Coats of	D	*D^d*
Whites^d Coats of	D	
Chas Logan of	D	
Henry Gibson of	D	*dead*
Alex^r Boyd of	Do	*D^d*

The above persons sworn free by me   Stewart Banks Sov^{tn}
27 Sept 1771   Thos Bodle son to Sargant Bodle admitted free
John Radclif son to Sergant Radclif   do

Stewart Banks Sov^{tn}

The following person are admitted to the Freedom of the Borough of Belfast
7 October 1772
Shem Thompson Junr } *D^d*
Joseph Thompson   } Sons of the Sovereign
Isaac Thompson   { Admitted free
Richard Thompson *D^d* }

Shem Thompson Sov^n

The following persons were admitted to the Freedom of the Borough of Belfast and sworn the

Robert Gordon of Belfast Esq[r]   *D[d]*
M[r] James Patterson Do   Merch[t]   *D[d]*
William Ferguson   Do   Publican   *D[d]*
Charles Ramadge   Do   Carrier   *Dead*

Shem Thompson Sov[n]

26 July 1773
James Neil of Kilead obtained his Freedom & sworn   *D[d]*

Shem Thompson Sov[n]

25 August 1773
John Gillis of Ballymacarrit obtained his Freedom of this Corporation and sworn

Shem Thompson Sovereign

21 September 1773
The following persons obtained their freedom and sworn

Thomas M[c]Cadam of Belfast Merch[t]   *D[d]*
William Lyons   Do   Linen Draper   *D[d]*
James Taylor   Do   Flax Dresser   *D[d]*
Andrew Hannah   Do   Publican   *D[d]*
Waddell Cuningham Do   Merch[t]   *D[d]*
William Sayers   *D[d]* Do   [Publican] Linen Manufacturer
Hercules M'Comb   Do   Ship Carpenter
John Black   *D[d]*   Do   Cabinett Maker   *D[d]*

Shem Thompson Sovereign

The following persons are admitted to the freedome for the Borough of Belfast
Town Hall 8th Septemb[r] 1774

D[d]

Charles Lewis   } *Dead*
James Lewis   }
Alex[r] Lewis   }   Sons of the Sovereign

Jam[s] Lewis Sov[n]

At the same time were admitted
Robert Simm of Belfast Tanner *dead*
Arthur Simm of the same   *D[d]*
William Irwin of the same   *D[d]*
John Robinson of the same Merch[t]
Hugh Kyle *D[d]* of the same Innkeeper per Ticket
Robert Hathorn   Do   Miller   per Do.   *dead*
John Ewing of the same   Merch[t]
Thomas Beck of the same   Butcher   *D[d]*
James Thompson Ditto   Malster   *D[d]*
Robert Neilson   Ditto   Butcher   *D[d]*
James Ervin   Ditto   Coat Measurer
Rowley Hyland Esq[r]   Longford Lodge   *D[d]*
Samuel Brown of Belfast   Merch[t]
John Henderson of Do   Merch[t]   *D[d]*

Jam[s] Lewis Sov[r].

The following persons obtained their Freedome
Town Hall Septem[r] 16th 1774
Hugh M'Ilwean of Belfast Merch[t]   *D[d]*
Jesse Taylor   of Do   Merch[t]   *D[d]*

Jam[s] Lewis Sov[n]

Borough of }
Belfast   }   The following persons were admitted freemen

1776 Decem[r]	2	Thomas Major Tanner Belfast	
		Hugh Montgomery Belfast Merch[t]	
		Christ[o] Hudson Do Tanner	
	4	William Woodburn Do Cooper	
	6	David Beaty Do Weaver *dead*	
1777	Apr 14	And[w] Allin	*D[d]*
	Sep[r] 4	Tho[s] Hardin } *Dead*	
		Henry Joy Jun[r]. } on the Recommendation of	
		George Joy } M[r] Henry Joy	
	10	Thom[s] Brown *D[d]*	
	13	Andrew Sufferin Taylor *dead*	
		Arch[d] M[c]Clure	
	14	James Hamill Merch[t]	
		Rob[t] Bradshaw Merch[t]	

Elected Serg^t at Mace 19 Richd Moore Tanner
    May 1st 1783 23 John Mathews Merch^t
                   26 James Sufferin Merch^t *D^d*
                   27 Henry McMullan Butcher *D^d*
                      John Fulton Carmony

                                          Jam^s Lewis Sov^n

    Henry Migahan   ) *D^d*
    John Blackwood   } Butchers
    Patrick Moore   } admitted free & appointed overseers
    William Moore   ) *D^d*

                                   J Lewis Sov^n

    Borough of Belfast 27 June 1778 Mr Saml Ferguson Farmer was admitted & sworn a Freeman of this Burrough *dead*

                           Stewart Banks Sov^r

    Borough of Belfast Novr 27 1779 Mr Dav^d Manson of Belfast Scoolmaster was admitted & sworn a freeman of this Borrough *Dead*

                          Saml Black Sov^n

3^d Jany 1781
    Hen Hunter of Belf^t Grocer admitted to the freedom & sworn
    Saml Law dealer   the lyke
    Danl Curry *D^d*)
    Jas Martin   } 24th Apr 1783
    Jo: Blackwood)
Dead Paul Brown   24 Apr 1783
    John Ferguson Farm^r Do
    Hue Graham   Do
    Dav^d Dunn *D^d*   Do Gratis
    John Allen Malone 10 July 1783

    On the 24 Day of November 1796
        John Brown Esqr *being* Sovereign Will Atkinson sworn Clerk of Belfast
    Henry Shaw Moore and Ralph Wilson were admitted and sworn Freemen of the Borough of Belfast

END OF THE TOWN BOOK MSS.

A Perspective View of Belfast from Cromack Paper Mills

HE INCORPORATION of the BOROUGH.

From the commencement of the reign of King James I. it was confidently expected that a Parliament would have been convened in Ireland. The last was held in 1587 by Sir John Perrott, Sir Arthur Chichester's father-in-law. Six years elapsed before the King, anxious to get a Parliamentary recognition of the Ulster Plantation, and to introduce a large scheme of general legislation, sent over the clerk of the Commons to consult with the Lord Deputy Chichester on the method of procedure. In the Chichester papers, preserved in the Carte collection at the Bodleian Library, is the original Journal of the Parliament of 1587, procured no doubt to serve as a precedent for that of 1613. A large number of new boroughs were incorporated principally for the purpose of returning members to this parliament. By a list dated 1st April, 1613 (*Calendar S.P. Ireland, 1611–14*), it appears that there were:—Cities and towns that are counties, 9 ; Shires sending Knights to Parliament, 33 ; Old Boroughs, 31 ; New boroughs, 38 ; The University of Dublin, 1 ; total, 112. To this return Chichester has added in his own hand Catherlagh (Carlow), making the number 113, returning in all 226 members. In August, 1614, the representatives of Tallagh, Lismore, Clonakilty, Carlow, Fethard, Agher, Belfast, and Charlemont, were forbidden by the King to sit in this parliament. The subjoined list of the Irish boroughs incorporated by King James I. has been extracted from the appendices to the *Report on Irish Municipal Corporations, 1835*, with the purpose of showing the variety of titles and the frequent use of that of Sovereign. By the kindness of the librarian of the Bodleian Library, the editor is able to give the following letter [*Carte papers 62, fol. 233*] by an unknown official, which shows that considerable licence was allowed in these details.

"I set downe the Name of Soveraigne upon the occatyon of the Rt. honᵇˡᵉ the Ld. Deputyes Lettres mentyonyng the same name, as also yᵉ name of Provost, &c wishyng us to take yᵉ choyce: wᶜʰ If now my Lᵈ styck at, yee may putt in the warrants the Name of Burgo mayster or Borrough master. I hope yee have Inserted the name of Baptist Hazell instead of Rychard Tyrer: And so I pray set yt onward wᵗʰ such convenyent expedytyon as other the lyke goe on."

(Baptist Hazell was a burgess of Ballinakill for which a fiant of incorporation was drawn 13 Nov. 1612).

As the Charter of James I. is given *in extenso (p. 172)*, a few words of explanation will suffice as to the constitution of the borough. It was entitled, The Sovereign, Free Burgesses, and Commonalty of the borough of Belfast, and consisted of one Sovereign one Lord of the castle, one constable of the castle, twelve other free Burgesses, and Freemen unlimited in number. Six freemen only were known to exist in 1833. A power to have a Merchant Hall was granted by the Charter. This seems to have been acted on, as there are many entries of persons admitted "Merchants of the Staple."

The Sovereign was elected on the feast of St. John the Baptist, the 24th of June, from a leet of 3 names of free burgesses presented to the Sovereign and burgesses then assembled by the Lord of the castle, who was a member of the corporation by tenure of the castle of Belfast.

The charter also granted that all the inhabitants within the borough should be by force thereof freemen. These were represented in early times by a Grand Jury selected from themselves, which, together with the Sovereign and free burgesses, assessed upon the town people sums of money for municipal purposes. Admission was obtained by becoming a "free commoner," a gratuity being usually paid the Corporation. The power of admission seems to have rested with the Sovereign as the chief officer of the Corporation.

List of the Irish Boroughs incorporated by King James I.

Name of Borough	Title of the Corporate body.

ARMAGH. The Sovereign, Free Burgesses, and Commonalty of the Borough of Ardmagh.
ASKEATON. The Provost, Free Burgesses, and Commonalty of the Borough of Askeaton.
ATHLONE. The Sovereign, Bailiffs, Burgesses, and Freemen of the Town of Athlone.
ATHY. The Sovereign, Bailiffs, Free Burgesses, and Commonalty of the Borough of Athy.
AUGHER. The Burgomaster, Free Burgesses, and Commonalty of the Borough of Agher.
BALLINAKILL. The Sovereign, Burgesses, and Freemen of the Borough of Ballinakill.
BALLYSHANNON. The Portreeve, Free Burgesses, and Commonalty of the Borough of Bally-shannon.
BALTIMORE. The Soveraign, Burgesses, and Commonalty.
BANDONBRIDGE. The Provost, Free Burgesses, and Commonalty of the Borough of Bandon Bridge.
BANGOR. The Provost, Free Burgesses, and Commonalty of the Borough of Bangor.
BELFAST. The Sovereign, Free Burgesses, and Commonalty of the Borough of Belfast.
BELTURBET. The Provost, Burgesses, Freemen and Inhabitants of the Borough of Belturbet.
BOYLE. The Borough Master, Free Burgesses, and Commonalty of the Borough of Boyle.
CARRICK ON SHANNON. The Provost, Free Burgesses, and Commonalty of the Borough of Carrickdrumruske.
CASTLEBAR. The Portreeve, Free Burgesses, and Commonalty of the Town of Castlebar.
CAVAN. The Sovereign, Portreeves, Burgesses, and Freemen of the Town and Borough of Cavan.
CHARLEMONT. The Portreeve, Free Burgesses, and Commonalty of the Borough of Charle-mont.
CLOGHER. The Portreeve and Burgesses of the city of Clogher.
CLOUGHNAKILTY. The Sovereign, Free Burgesses, and Commonalty of the Borough of Cloughnakilty.
COLERAINE. The Mayor and Aldermen and Burgesses of the Town of Coleraine.
DUNGANNON. The Provost, Free Burgesses, and Commons of the Borough of Dungannon.
ENNIS. The Provost, Free Burgesses, and Commonalty of the Town of Ennis.
ENNISCORTHY. The Portreeve, Free Burgesses, and Commonalty of the Borough of Ennis-corthy.
ENNISKILLEN. The Provost, Free Burgesses, and Commonalty of the Borough of Iniskillen.
FEATHARD. The Sovereign, Chief Burgesses, Portreeve, and Freemen of the town of Fitherd.
GOREY. The Sovereign, Burgesses, and Free Commons of the Borough and Town of New-borough.
HILLSBOROUGH. The Sovereign, Burgesses, and Free Commons of the Borough and Town of Hillsborough.
JAMESTOWN. The Sovereign, Burgesses, and Free Commons of the Borough and Town of Jamestown.
KILBEGGAN. The Portreeve, Free Burgesses, and Commonalty of the Borough of Kilbeggan.
KILLYBEGS. The Provost, Free Burgesses, and Commonalty of the Borough of Callebegge.
KILLILEAGH. The Provost, Free Burgesses, and Commonalty of the Borough of Killileagh.
LIFFORD. The Warden, Free Burgesses, and Commonalty of the Borough of Liffer.
LIMAVADDY. The Provost, Free Burgesses, and Commonalty of the Borough of Lymavady.
LISMORE. Portreeve and Free Burgesses.
LONDONDERRY. The Mayor and Commonalty and Citizens of the City of Londonderry.
MALLOW. The Provost, Free Burgesses, and Commonalty of the Borough of Mallow.
MONAGHAN. The Provost, Free Burgesses, and Commonalty of the Borough of Monaghan.
NEWRY. The Provost, Free Burgesses, and Commonalty.
NEWTOWNARDS. The Provost, Free Burgesses, and Commonalty of the Borough of Newtoune.
SLIGO. The Provost and Free Burgesses of the Borough of Sligo.
ST. JOHNSTOWN. The Provost and Burgesses.
STRABANE. The Provost, Free Burgesses, and Commonalty of the Borough of Strabane.
TALLAGH. The Suffraine, Free Burgesses, and Commonalty of the Borough of Tallagh.
TRALEE. The Provost, Free Burgesses, and Commonalty of the Borough of Tralee.
TUAM. The Sovereign, Free Burgesses, and Commonalty of the Borough of Tuam.
WICKLOW. The Portreeve, Free Burgesses, and Commonalty.

p. 1.—Payment of Tongues.

The Sovereign of Belfast had but few perquisites of office in comparison, for instance, with the Mayor of Carrickfergus, who claimed the following amongst others :—"In many of the old leases of this place, the tenants were bound to furnish yearly a certain number of fat hens or capons to the Mayor each Christmas, or a specified sum of money in lieu. The owner of the West Mills was also bound to grind all such grain as shall be spent from time to time in the Mayor's house, toll free. As clerk of the market he had also the tongues of all bullocks or cows killed on Fridays, whose flesh was sold in the market on Saturdays" *(McSkimin).* In 1601 it was enacted "that the maior of the Town for the time being shall have towards his Housekeeping the sum of twenty pounds stg per ann, and the third part of her Majesty's Customs and the petty Custom usually belonging to the Town—to the end that no Maior of this Towne hereafter for the time being shall sell either Wine Ale or Aqua Vitae or others either at his Table or in his premises upon forfeiture of his stipend of 20ˡⁱ—payment of the stipend—is to be collected in manner and form following viz. upon every Ton of ffrench Wine four shillings ster Upon every Ton of Spanish Wine six shillings ster, the Ton unloden at the Key of Carrickfergus either by Town or private Bargain." *(Carrickfergus Records MSS.)* Amongst the Duties and perquisites anciently belonging to the Sovereign of Kinsale 1657 are noted—"Imp. Due and payable out of the towne stock or Treasury, 13ˡⁱ. 6s. 8d. It. Out of every beefe slaughtered within the towne or liberties except for burgesses or freemen 3d. It. From every master butcher being a master of a family one stone of tallow about Christmas. It. The Soveraigne is to receive every Royal Fish that is taken in the harbour or precincts thereof, for which he is to pay 12d for each to the taker. It. He is to have the best fish or best sprapp of fish out of any boat paying for same 2d. It. Out of every vessel of pears or apples, for liberty of the market 500." *(Town Book of Kinsale.)*

p. 2. Jo: Vesey.

First Sovereign, and an original leaseholder in the borough.

p. 2. Jo: Ayshe.

The history of the ancient family of Ash, who came from the Isle of Thanet to Ireland in Elizabeth's reign—Thomas Ash, the father of John Ash, being knighted by Sir George Carew in 1603—has been lately published for private circulation, under the able editorship of Rev. E. T. Martin, Dundonald.

p. 2. Henry Upton.

A kinsman of Lord Chichester, and married to a daughter of Sir Hugh Clotworthy. Humphrey Norton, one of the original burgesses of Belfast, settled at Templepatrick, and, incensed at the marriage of his daughter to a Sergeant O'Linn, sold his estate to Captain Henry Upton, who became the founder of the family now ennobled by the title of Viscount Templetown. The wife of Arthur Upton, M.P. for Carrick 1761, introduced crayfish to the Sixmilewater, where they are now plentiful.

p. 2. Walterhouse Crimble.

More properly Waterhouse Crymble, belonged to a family said to have come to Ireland with Sir Edward Waterhouse, secretary to Sir Henry Sidney. Waterhouse settled in Carrickfergus its M.P. in 1585. His account for repairs at the "Pallace," afterwards Lord Chichester's "Joymount," is given in an article on that building. *(Ulster Journal of Archaeology, vol. vii.)* His only child married Roger Crymble, father of the subject of this note. He was one of the first burgesses, and a chief mourner in 1636 at Viscount Montgomery's funeral, Comptroller of Customs at Donaghadee about 1649.

p. 7. Carew Harte.

He was a sheriff of Carrickfergus in 1613. His confession at death, acknowledging his guilt in promising to marry Jane Varey after his wife's death, but denying that he had poisoned her, dated at Carrickfergus 11th April, 1623, is noted. *(Cal. S.P.I. 1615-25.)*

p 3. Absent from Church.

At a Court of the Corporation of Carrickfergus, 4th Sept. 1574, in "le Town House de Knockfergus," the following curious order was passed—"That

Whereas Francis Turner did most slanderously use these unreverent Words following, Viz.: Parson Davye *(sic)* made a Sermon to his parishoners & cried thrice (soho) which he sayed did signify I have found and so sayed he a sort of knaves I have found you, and so I will leave you and so will I sell my House and go my Ways, for the punishment whereof it was ordered that the said Francis shall openly before the Mayor and Aldermen of this Town Say these Words upon his Knee Kneeling Viz. Mr. Maior and the rest of the Aldermen I have slandered your Worships and for the same I ask God and your Worships all forgiveness most heartily and also that the said Francis, shall be committed to the Marshialls Ward and there remain in Bolts so long as it shall please the Mayor and General." *(Carrickfergus Records MSS.)*

p. 5. To sell ale.

As far back as 3rd Feby. 1574—"It was ordered and agreed by the Mayor and the rest of his Brethren that whereas ill measures of Ale was sold within this Town to the great annoyance of the poor and displeasing of God that the said fault should be corrected with punishment according, that is to say for the first fault committed in ill measure by any Man to pay therefore 12^d st^g and the Ale so complained of, and the second time that any man should therein offend 5^s st^g and the Ale complained of, and the third time the whole brewing or the value thereof, the one half of the said fforfeits so taken to belong to the Mayor for the time being and the other half thereof to appertain to his Substitute appointed under him which is appointed under him to Seal the said Cannes and look to the measures thereof. The twenty second day of this month Ralph Crawly for breaking of Crein Duff his head being Sergeant was by the Mayor & the Whole Court condemned to payment of 20^s st^g to the Town & the Bloodshed to the Sheriffs." *(Carrickfergus Records MSS.)*

p. 6. Apprehending anie felons Rouges woodkernes or Craytes.

The *Carrickfergus Records*, under date 8th June, 1624, note this entry—"It was likewise ordered condescended and agreed that Richd Brooke shall have as stipend from this Town for the banishing and driving out of all strong Beggars and other idle and loitering persons both out of the Town and Country the sum of thirty shillings currant money of and in England." A side note adds, "This was likewise the same day with a generall consent also cancelled."

Amongst the Acts propounded for Ireland in 1611 is one against all such as, calling themselves gentlemen, horsemen, or kerne, live loosely and freely, without any certain means or trade of life, as also against rhymers, gamesters, stokeaghes, vagabonds, and beggars. In the same list are acts for the destruction of wolves and sowing flax for making linen cloth. *(Carew MSS.)* By woodkerne are meant the native Irish soldiery, then lingering in such neighbouring fastnesses as the woods of Kilwarlin and the Glynns. John Derrick, in his remarkable rhymed work entitled "The Image of Ireland with a discoverie of Wood Karne wherein is most lively expressed the nature and qualitie of the saied wilde Irish Wood Karne, their notable aptnesse celeritie &c. 1581," gives twelve woodcut illustrations of the Irish wood kerne. Only one perfect copy of the original edition is known. Two of these illustrations are of especial interest, as they portray the Lord Deputy Sidney and his retinue in the North, the background of wooded hills being the first attempt in all likelihood to depict the Belfast mountains. In the eleventh print Rory Oge is shown as a wild Irish kerne shrouded in his mantle in the midst of a desolate wood. From his lips proceed the words, "Ve mihi misere," to which certain prowling wolves make answer, "Ve atque dolor." As a specimen of the author's doggerel these lines are given—

"Their shirtes be very straunge not reachyng paste the thie :
 With pleates on pleates thei pleated are as thick as pleates maie lye
 Whose sleves hang trailing downe almost unto the shoe :
 And with a Mantell commonlie the Irish Karne doe go.
 Now some emongst the reste doe use another weede :
 A coate I meane of strange device which fancie first did breede."

Creaght originally meant wattle or basket work. "The Ulster Irish were a pastoral people. In Fermanagh there was neither town or civil habitation. The chiefs dwelt some of them in clay houses ; others of them, who followed creaghting' or running up and down the country with their cattle, dwelt, like their followers, in booths made of boughs coated with long strips of green turf, instead of canvas run up in a few minutes, for such are the dwellings of the very lords amongst them." (*Preface of Calendar S.P. Ireland, 1611-14.*)

Irish Soldiers, by Albert Dürer.

p. 9.   Henry Le 'Squyre

Henry Le Squire* by his will devised his property at Six Mile Water, County Antrim, to his brother George Squire of Londonderry, with power of appointment among his children.   George conveyed the property to his son William, who served as Sheriff of Londonderry in 1677, and died Mayor of Londonderry in 1692.   His brother was Captain Gervaise Squire, who played such a prominent part in the defence of Derry in 1688 (for an account of whom see Graham's *History of the Siege of Derry*, and his *Ire'and Preserved*, also Hempton's *History of the Siege*).   William was succeeded by his son Alexander, who served as Sheriff of Londonderry in 1709 and in 1713; elected Mayor of the City in 1718 and again in 1721.   He died in 1725, and was succeeded by his only surviving son, James Squire of Rosculbin, Co. Fermanagh, and Manorcunningham, Co. Donegal, who died in 1779.   His only surviving son William died in 1806, having issue who survived infancy one son, William, who died in 1877, and one daughter, Anne, married to her cousin-german, James Chittick, of Manorcunningham, and had issue three sons and two daughters, of whom alone William Gervaise and Erminda had issue.

William Gervaise Chittick, who resides at East Orange, New Jersey, U.S.A., married the eldest daughter of Alexander Lindsay, J.P., of Lisnacrieve House, Co. Tyrone, Alderman of Londonderry, and Mayor in 1847, 1848, 1849, 1863, 1864.   He has by her surviving issue—1, William Gervaise; 2, James; 3, Alice Gertrude.   Erminda married the Rev. Alexander Rentoul, M.D., D.D., of Errity House, Manorcunningham, Co. Donegal, and now resides at The Lodge, Cliftonville.   Her eldest son is Mr. James Alexander Rentoul, LL.D., Barrister-at-Law, County Councillor of London, and M.P. for County Down East.

p. 9.   G. B. Gowen Bolby

The letters G. B. precede the name in the original, and form the trade mark of Bolby or Boultby.   Sometimes it occurs between the names, as at p. 15— John IH Haddocke.   Hugh Doake was erroneously considered unable to write, from his constant use of his mark HD ; he signs in full sometimes.

---

* Descended from the Squires of Essex ; *arms*, three swans' heads, couped at the neck, *or ;* crest, an elephant's head, *ve. ad arg.* ducally gorged.   The name spelled variously—Le Squire, Squier, and Squire.

X

p. 10.

The reduced fac-simile of this page gives a good idea of the appearance of the earlier portions of the original MS. The first signature is that of Lord Edward Chichester, brother of Lord Arthur Chichester, and father of the first Earl of Donegall.

Of in the margin should be printed *ag*[t], viz., against. Similarly on next page *ag*[t] should precede wood chimneys.

p. 11.   A Rate made

This entry is for the first time properly rendered. By mistaking the definite for the indefinite article before Town Hall, Benn was led into the error of supposing that the rate was struck to pay for its erection, whereas it had been in use probably soon after the incorporation of the Borough, and was in fitting up to serve as the Assize Courts next year. Joy evidently read the contracted form of "partitions" as prison, and notes under 1639, "The Corporation fitted up a Courthouse with Bench and Bar, and town prison, and for this purpose an applotment was made on the inhabitants, but only 46 were found able to pay this tax. In the following year the Assizes were held in Belfast." (*Joy's MS.*) In the Charter to Carrickfergus granted by James I. ground for a gaol to be used for Co. Antrim is exempted. The Judges of Assize tried unsuccessfully in 1613 to remove their courts to the town of Antrim, but were prevented by Lord Deputy Chichester. Sir Robert Adair twice petitioned Queen Anne to make Ballymena the assize town, but was defeated by the Corporation of Carrickfergus. Other attempts also proved abortive, and it was not till 1850 that Belfast was adopted. The subjoined is from the *Carrickfergus Records MSS.* "The Grand Jury of the Co Antrim, 13th Aug 1666, passed a presentment empowering Sir George Rawdon, Robert Colville, Michael Harrison, Francis Stafford, and Thaddy O'Hara, to conclude an agreement with the Corporation of Carrick for the sum of seventy pounds per ann. to take upon them the rare charge and pains of repairing and keeping in repair the Session House and Gaol, with the tenements and Rooms thereunto appertaining, and belonging to the County of Antrim." The agreement is a lengthy document; one of the clauses reads, "Whereas the said Sessions House and Gaol are now furnished with Table, Cushions, Carpets, Seats, four long Iron Bolts and twelve Rings or Yokes, Thirty pair of double Iron Bolts and Shackles, four pair of Handcuffs, four Padlocks, Six Horse Locks and three Plate Locks, Forty Rivets of Iron for Bolts, one pair of Stocks, one Iron Grate with a Chain and two great Bolts of Iron at the Door of the said Gaol. The Mayor Burgesses and Commonalty bind themselves if any of the above defray perish or be lost to supply the defect thereof with other utensils and materials of equal value goodness and strength." Some of these fetters and locks are in all probability amongst the large collection from Carrickfergus Gaol presented to the Belfast Museum by the late Dr. James Moore, R.H.A.

p. 13.   Mr. John Arnold

He was attorney in the Borough Court in 1754, and this signature was perhaps made at the instance of Margetson Saunders, then Sovereign.

p. 13.   Winchester measure

Almost identical with the present imperial.

p. 16.   River

This was the stream flowing through the middle of High Street; no portion was arched over at the time.

p. 17.   The charge of Candles for the Army

Additional charges are mentioned at p. 19, with a list of those assessed. This was the army thus referred to in *Adair's Narrative.* "Strafford, by the help of four subsidies from the Parliament in Ireland, raised an army of Irish, and some profane and ignorant of the British, of 8,000 foot and 1,000 horse, and sent them down hither to the North (in order to the invading of Scotland) where the Earl of Antrim had engaged to get them supported. They stayed a considerable time quartered in this country, much oppressing it, and were, both for design and carriage amongst the people, called the Black Band." Benn's

History contains no mention of any part of the army being stationed in Belfast, although this is evident from the list of the officers made freemen in the same year, including Sir Charles Coote, Sir James Dillon, and other distinguished men. Carrickfergus has hitherto been considered the only place they occupied, and from it as head quarters the soldiers were marched to Larne, and exercised in throwing up earthworks at the Curran, of which traces exist close to the present Olderfleet Hotel. As the square earthen redoubt known as Fort William was almost certainly non-existent in Essex's time, and corresponds in plan with another fort having similar small bastions at the four angles to receive cannon, situated immediately under the Cavehill, and called in 1659 the "ditch of Ballyaghagan," there seems a strong probability that these works with that of the Milewater were thrown up to form a continuous line of defence on the North side of the town against any sudden attack of the Scotch from that quarter. *McSkimin's MS.* notes under 1641—"On the breaking out of the rebellion the Kings forces in Ireland amounted to only 2297 foot, and 943, horse and they were greatly despersed."

p. 17.   For ye Bridge at ye Milewater

Mr. John Thompson, City Assessor, Mount Collyer, upon whose property the old bridge till recently stood, has kindly supplied the material for the present note and illustration. The arch of the bridge was so damaged that its original form could not be determined, but was probably semicircular, as the "crown" was much above the ordinary level of the roadway. When the traffic was diverted by the making of the present York Street and the subsequent Cavehill Railway, cottages were built at the north side of the bridge, so as to effectually close up the ancient passage. Adjacent to the north-west side of the bridge, which was evidently erected to allow military stores and artillery to proceed without hindrance between Belfast and Carrickfergus, where Strafford's army lay in quarters, was placed the fort or block-house. This curious little structure had been completely forgotten in recent years ; no historian mentions it. It was circular in shape, with narrow arched apertures for musketry, as shown on the plan. The roof was of domical form, and, like the contemporary bridge, the whole was executed in brickwork, the bricks being about

The Old fort, Mile Water bridge erected 1640.

Plan ¼" scale

8 inches long by 2½ inches thick. The slits were placed at a height of four feet, and were splayed inwards, so as to allow space for aiming. Not far from this Mr. Thompson found a human skull, in a well-made wooden box, greatly decayed. This probably dated from 1798, when the heads of some of Dr. W. H. Drummond's friends were spiked on the old Market-house. He had a school at Mount Collyer about that time, and wrote here his poems of "Trafalgar" and the "Giant's Causeway." It may be of interest to add that the moschatel (*Adoxa Moschatellina*) is recorded by Templeton as growing at the Milewater, its only habitat in Ireland.

p. 17.   Disordered house

"It was ordered and agreed by the whole Court the twenty-ninth day of this month (Oct. 1574) that all manner of Scolds which shall be openly detected of Scolding or evil Words in Manner of Scolding and for the same shall be condemned before the Mayor and his Brethren shall be drawn at the Stern of a Boat in the water from the end of the Weare round About the Queen's Majesty's Castle in manner of Ducking and after when a cage shall be made the party so condemned for a Scold shall be therein punished at the discretion of the Mayor." (*Carrickfergus Records MSS.*)

Mr. John Coates, J.P., late secretary of Antrim Grand Jury, informs the editor that he had in his possession till recently a gag for the mouth which belonged to the Carrickfergus Gaol. From his description it was probably a scold's bridle.

Ancient ironworks, showing a trip hammer.

p. 19.   char Coales

The manufacture of charcoal for the ironworks formerly situated at Strand-millis, Old Forge, Magheralin, and other thickly wooded districts, was very exten-sive.   In the scarce tract entitled *A true relation of several Acts, Passages, done, undertaken, &c., by Captain Robert Lawson, London, 1643,* is the following reference to his father-in-law's (Robert Barr) ironworks at Strandmillis, which were destroyed at that time, traces of which still exist adjoining the first lock of the Lagan Navigation—"The sow-iron unwrought to the quantity of 2,000l. value beside much iron ore, and 1,000 tons of square timber, most burned by the soldiers, 1,000 loads of charcoals burned by the enemy at forge furnace, and in the woods, with three corn mills, and many houses burned, and land laid waste, the land and mills being worth 150l. per annum."   From a copy of Dr. Gerald Boate's *Ireland's Naturall History, 1652,* which has the autograph and motto of John Gorges, Governor of Maine, showing the wide circulation of this valuable work at the time, the following description of these Irish ironworks is taken :—"At the end of a great Barn standeth a huge Furnace, being of the height of a pike and a half or more, and foursquare in figure, but after the manner of a Mault-kiln, that is, narrow below, and by degrees growing wider towards the top, so as the compass of the mouth or the top is of many fathoms.   These ovens are not kindled with wood, nor with sea-cole, but merely with char-coal, whereof they consume a huge quantity.   For the Furnace being once kindled, is never suffered to go out, but is continually kept a burning from the one end of the year to the other.   And the proportion of the coals to the Oare is very great :   For the Mine would not melt without an exceeding hot fire ; the which that it may be the more quick and violent, it is continually blown day and night without ceasing by two Vast pair of bellows, the which rest upon main peeces of timber, and with their pipes placed into one of the sides of the Furnace are perpetually kept in action by the meanes of the great wheel which being driven about by a little brook or water-course maketh them rise and fall by turns.   There is another and lesser sort of Iron works, much different from the former: For instead of a Furnace they use a Hearth therein, altogether of the fashion of a Smith's Hearth, whereon the Oare being layd in a great heap, it is covered over with abundance of Charcoal, the which being kindled is continually blown by Bellows that are moved by wheeles and water courses, in the same manner as in the other works."   Such no doubt were Old and New Forge on the Lagan.   At Randalstown, once called Iron Works, were probably made the nails taken from ancient oak beams in Antrim Castle, and now in the Editor's possession.   They are of singular toughness, resembling the best Swedish iron, and forged with such hammers as Boate describes, "being huge big ones, and never ceasing from knocking day nor night."

p. 19.   For Maces

Benn read "Majesty's" for "maces," and expresses surprise at the cost incurred in such a time for carving his Majesty's arms on the Town Hall.   The mace figured on p. 18 is that bequeathed by Le Squire to the Corporation, and used by him as seneschal of the Manor Court.   His sergeant's gold ring was bequeathed to Robert Foster.   The well-known expert in all such subjects, Mr.

Robert Day, J.P., F.S.A., M.R.I.A., kindly contributes the following description of the Corporation maces :—

"At the reception given by Dr. John Evans, President of the Society of Antiquaries, London, in 1888, there were no less than 130 maces which had been lent for exhibition by the several Mayors and Corporations in the United Kingdom. These were described by Mr. St. John Hope, F.S.A., who was enabled to point out, from their various shapes, the gradual evolution and change of form from the more ancient war-mace. According to the accepted theory, the lower end of a war-mace was first fashioned into a button to receive the Royal Arms. Then the mace was turned upside down, and the flanges were converted into ornaments, and afterwards gradually disappeared. The flanges were finally replaced by a button or boss to counterbalance the weight of the mace-head, which in the meantime had been growing in size.

This occurs in the two city maces of Belfast which I had, through the courtesy of the Town Clerk, Mr. Black, the privilege of examining. The smaller mace terminates at the grip end with a boss, quite plain, and without any engraving of the Corporate arms, which might have been looked for upon its flat, seal-shaped end. The larger mace terminates in a conical foot-knop, chased with lozenges between intersecting bands. *(See p. 231.)* This larger mace is a fine example of the early Stuart period ; it measures seventeen and a-half inches in length ; it has a central knop upon the shaft, and three scroll brackets that support the head, which is in four arched compartments, that are divided one from the other by female term figures with plumed head-gear. These spaces have each the emblems of the Rose, Thistle, Harp, and Fleur-de-lys royally crowned. Above these is an ornamented fillet, which is surmounted by an open-work engrailed ball-top coronet. The head is engraved with the Stuart arms and the letters C.R. It is without hall-mark, but in a maker's stamp are the letters S.G. The smaller mace measures eight inches in length ; it has a perfectly plain and undecorated shaft, with a knop under the head, which is also plain. The coronet exhibits marks of having been entirely broken off, and the head is engraved with the crowned arms of England, but without any supporters. At either side of the crown are the initials of the King, and, below, the date 1639. There is no hall-mark, but in a circular stamp the diphthong Æ between six annulets. This peculiar stamp does not occur in the London makers' list, and, so far as I can ascertain, is unknown. When no hall-mark occurs upon Irish plate of the seventeenth century, we may safely infer that it is of local manufacture. Mr. Young has examined the *Town Book,* and finds among the list of freemen ante 1700—'Andrew McCullogh Goldsmith 19 January 1660 ;' 'Wᵐ Barnett 19 October 1671 ;' 'Thomas mᶜCune 22nd Janry., 1679.' None of these initials, I regret to say, correspond with those upon the maces ; but I am yet inclined to think that they were made, if not in Belfast, in some of the towns of the Pale in Ulster, and I would suggest an examination of the church plate in the diocese of Down, Connor, and Dromore, for the purpose of possibly identifying the initials of these three Belfast goldsmiths with the maker's stamp, which will probably be found upon examples of ecclesiastical plate so preserved. When we have the most conclusive evidence that in the last half of the seventeenth century the manufacture of silver plate existed in Cork, Bandon, and Youghal, in the province of Munster, there is no reason why the same industry should not have flourished in the walled towns of Ulster."

p. 19.   Armes and the Towne Seale for the Towne

The following exhaustive note on the subject has been kindly supplied by Mr. John Vinycomb, F.R.S.A.I. :—

FROM an early period in the history of the Borough a *Town Seal* appears to have been one of the essentials of its corporate existence. In 1612, Sir Arthur Chichester, who may truly be called the founder of the town, was created Baron of Belfast ; and on the 27th April, 1613, the Town was constituted a Corporation by Charter of King James I., to consist of a Sovereign, or chief magistrate, and twelve Burgesses, and Commonalty. In this Charter, which recites the corporate birth of the town, it is stated they may have "one Comon seale in such forme and as shall seem best unto them" (page 177). What may have been the

ARMS OF BELFAST.

special device upon this Seal cannot now be determined, but in the Town Book, under date 1640, we find an entry authorising the payment for what appears to be the insignia of office—"FOR MACES ARMES AND THE TOWNE SEALE FOR THE TOWNE 26*li.*" The Seal here referred to is mentioned in the will of Henry Le Squire, dated 1643—"ITEM :—*I give to the Corporation of Belfast the remainder due upon an account of my disbursements for their Maces, Seale and Coat of Armes, and will that the Mace I have be delivered to the Sufferane for the Townes use.*" "Master Le Squire" was Sovereign of the town in 1635–36 & 39, and was one of the Englishmen who followed the fortunes of the Lord Deputy to Ireland, and settled in Belfast. He was then agent and seneschal to the Lord Edward Chichester.

The Le Squire Seal, until recently almost forgotten, remained the only authoritative source of information as to the correctness of the Town Arms ; various inaccuracies, it was believed, had crept into the Town Seal of 1842. Mr. George Benn, therefore, in preparing his History of Belfast (1877), endeavoured to obtain from Ulster's office information as to what really were the Arms of the Town. The answer returned was—"There is no record in this office when Arms were granted to Belfast. In a MS. book the following Arms appear in the handwriting of the late Sir William Betham, Ulster :—*Per fess argent and azure ; in chief a pile vair, on a canton of the second, a tower of the first : in base a ship with sails set, also of the first. Crest, a sea-horse proper. Supporters—dexter, a wolf rampant proper ; sinister, a sea-horse proper.*" Sir W. Betham must have had an imperfect copy of the Arms before him when he wrote, as there are palpable inaccuracies in his blazon. The blue canton charged with a tower should be "*on a canton gules (red), a bell argent.*" The wolf should be "*ducally gorged and chained or.*"

From various entries in the old Town Book it would almost appear as if the arms upon the old Town Seal had been derived from the properly constituted authority. The composition is the work of a skilled and practised herald, and not that of an amateur. That no entry can be found in the books in Ulster's office may be accounted for by the disorganised condition of the records of the office of arms during the troublous times of James II., when "Athlone," pursuivant, followed his deposed Sovereign to St. Germains, carrying with him many of the books of records, some of which have since found their way to the British Museum, Trinity College, Dublin, and elsewhere. It is not unlikely that in one of these tomes the entry relating to the arms of Belfast may be found.

The fine old Corporate Seal of the Town, which is still in existence (an impression of it appears embossed upon the title-page), is of silver set in a wooden handle : it was in use from Le Squire's time down to the extinction of the old Corporation in 1842, and remains in the possession of an old resident family—Lewis of Nettlefield—descended from one of the Sovereigns of Belfast. It is in very fair preservation, and, though somewhat worn, is in good heraldic character, much superior in this respect to that which superseded it. The Coat of Arms on this Seal reappears, with all its peculiarity of detail, somewhat exaggerated, upon the Map of Belfast, A.D. 1790, a fac-simile of which is in Benn's History (1877).

It will be seen that the Arms upon this Seal, making allowance for the quaintness of the drawing, are precisely the same—heraldically—as those now in use, with the exception of the mural coronet, added by Sir Bernard Burke, Ulster King of Arms, in his recent grant.

Trade Token of John Steward, 1656.

It is a mistake to suppose, as many have done, that the Arms of Belfast were false heraldry. The Bell on the Shield has no reference whatever to the known derivation of the name of the town—*Beul-feirste*, The Mouth of the Ford—but is an instance of what is termed *canting* or *allusive arms*. This manner of playing upon words of similar sound was a prevailing fashion in the heraldry of the time, and to a large extent still continues, of which numberless instances can be given of all periods. The Bell appears upon the earliest Belfast trade tokens of 1656, and continued the most frequent device, together with the ship, used by the early Belfast merchants.

A *wolf gorged and chained* also appears upon a token or coin of Hugh Magarrah, dated 1736; showing clearly that the well-known symbols which form the constituent parts of the Town Arms were taken by the traders of the town as the most appropriate they could devise for their purpose. Two wolves, similarly gorged and chained as that on Magarrah's token, are the supporters of the Chichesters; one such had been adopted as the dexter supporter of the Belfast Shield, probably in honour of the noble patron of the town; while for the sinister supporter and crest, the symbolic creature, the

Reverse of Trade Token of Hugh Magarrah, 1736.

Sea-horse, had been chosen, with true prophetic spirit, to indicate the maritime importance and *fast* progress of the rising town and port; the steeds of Neptune are favourite subjects in ancient poetry and art: many of the maritime states of Greece adopted the sea-horse as their monetary symbol, in allusion to the fleetness of their vessels. The ship in full sail in the base of the Shield has exactly the same significance, and for use upon tokens was a more suitable emblem than the sea-horse, hence its frequent use. The very limited space available upon small coins rendered it impossible that any but the simplest and best understood emblems could be admitted, especially as no rigid heraldic law governed these matters; this will satisfactorily account for the entire coat of arms not appearing on any of the tokens. One of the charges on the Shield, V shape, is, in heraldic parlance, *a pile vair*. The term "pile" has reference to the piles or stakes used to form entrenched camps, while "vair" is a parti-coloured fur used for lining the mantles of noble and official personages of high rank in the middle ages; it is taken from a species of squirrel, bluish-grey on the back and white on the belly, and called in Latin *varrus* on that account.

> "Ferrars his Tabard with rich *verry* spread,
> Well known in many a warlike match before."—DRAYTON's *Barons' Wars*.

"*A chief vair*" forms part of the Chichester Shield, and suggests the source of the adoption of the tincture on the pile. The chained wolf supporter also seems to have been adopted from the Chichester arms, while the motto may have been intended to express the sense of gratitude entertained by the Sovereign and Burgesses towards the founder and benefactor of the young Borough.

On the extinction of the old Corporation in 1842, a new brass Seal was substituted for the old one, of the same size and oval shape. It is very well engraved in modern style. Wings are, however, added to the sea-horse crest and supporters. This new feature has misled many persons, and appears frequently in subsequent

Old Arms used on the heading of the *Belfast News-Letter*, adapted from the Seal of 1842, kindly lent by the proprietors.

representations. This affords a clue to the approximate date of the embroidered cushion in the possession of the Corporation, which has the sea-horse "winged," being evidently modelled on the design upon this Seal.

When the Town Council began to issue bonds in 1874 in connection with the purchase of the Gasworks, the large numbers to be impressed with the Corporate Seal necessitated the adoption of some speedier means of stamping; a steel die and embossing press superseded the old method of sealing on wafers. The design of the Seal, however, remained the same as that of 1842, but a garter was added bearing the words "Belfast Borough Corporate Seal." When Belfast was, by Royal Charter, created a City in 1888, the same Seal was used, changing only "Borough" to "City." In August, 1890, a grant (or confirmation) of Arms was obtained from Sir Bernard Burke, Ulster King of Arms, and a new and larger Corporate Seal was designed in accordance therewith, and executed by Messrs. Marcus Ward & Co., Limited, and is the one now in use. It is in every respect an admirable example of what a Corporate Seal should be. A representation of it will be found on back of the title-page.

ARMS OF THE CITY (according to the grant of 1890).—Per Fess argent and azure, in chief, a pile vair, and on a canton gules, a bell argent; in base, a ship with sails set argent, on waves of the sea, proper. *Supporters*—dexter, a wolf proper, ducally gorged and chained, or; sinister, a sea-horse gorged with a mural crown, proper. *Crest*—a sea-horse gorged with a mural crown, proper.   Motto— PRO TANTO QUID RETRIBUAMUS.

The motto may be freely translated as a question, thus—" *What return shall we make for so much ?*"
In the Latin Vulgate, Psalm cxv. 12, which corresponds to Psalm cxvi. 12 of the authorised version, we read—" QUID RETRIBUAM DOMINO, PRO OMNIBUS QUÆ RETRIBUIT MIHI ?" which in the authorised version stands—" *What shall I render unto the Lord* for *all His benefits toward me ?*"   The prayer-book version (Psalm cxvi. 11) renders it—" *What reward shall I give unto the Lord : for all the benefits that He hath done unto me ?*"   The motto of the Belfast Arms in all probability was suggested by the above passage.

p. 20.   fire and candle-light for the severall Guards
On the night of Saturday, 23rd Oct., 1641, the news of the outbreak of the Rebellion reached the Governor of Carrickfergus, Col. Arthur Chichester, who immediately apprised his father, Lord Edward Chichester, at Belfast.   On Thursday, 28th October, a letter sent by him reached the King at Edinburgh. Little time was lost by the Lord of the Castle in providing means for the defence of the town.   On 6th December a bond was drawn up empowering James Edmondstoune, of Broadisland, to procure arms in Scotland, as the following extract shows :—" We, Edward Viscount Chichester, of Carrickfergus, Captane Arthur Chichester, eldest sone and air apparent of the said Edvard, Sir Arthur Tyringham, Knight, one of his majesties most honorable privie counsell for the Kingdom of Ireland, and Arthur Hill of Killwarlen in the cowntie of Downe, Esquyre, have sent and imployed our trusty and weil belovit friend, James Edmonstoune of Brodeyland in the countie of Antrym, Esquyre, to the citie of Edinburgh, in the Kingdome of Scotland, or to any other part of the said kingdome, to bargane and buy for our use these arms following, that is to say, one thousand muskets with bandeliers [cartridge boxes] two thousand swordis, five hundred and fourtie pickis, fyve hundreth horsemen's peicks with snaphouses [a kind of cavalry firelock] or for want of such, fyve hundreth carbynes, and thrie field peices of thrie or fore pound bullet." (Quoted by *Reid.*)   With these and other assistance the Belfast district was gallantly held till the arrival of the Scotch under General Robert Monro, on 15th April 1642, as described by an

Owen Roe O'Neill.

eye-witness, the original of Scott's Dugald Dalgetty. "We came to the west countrie in 1642, and lay at Irwine, Aire, and Kilmarnock more than a fortnight, waiteing for a faire wind ; which makeing a show to offer itselfe, Monro embarked at the Largs, Home (who had got Cochrans regimint) at Aire, and we at Irwine.   When we were at sea the wind turnd contrarie, and so all of us met at Lamlash, a secure bay on the coast of the Ile of Arran, where we lay a fortnight, if I remember right ; and then the wind againe offering to be favorable, one of the King's ships which was with us shooting a warning peece, all weighd anchor, hoysd saile in ane evening, and nixt day were in Craigfergus loch, and landed that night." (*Sir James Turner's Memoirs.*)   General Robert Monro had seen much service in Flanders and under Gustavus Adolphus, of which he gave an account entitled, *Monro's Expedition with the worthy Scots Regiment called MacKey's Regiment.*

He made several predatory expeditions against the Irish, but was completely
defeated at Benburb by the celebrated Owen Roe O'Neill. His exactions in
Belfast are shown by the constant cesses entered down to the end of 1645.
Scoutbush, two miles from Carrickfergus, was his favourite residence at the
time. He married the widow of the second Viscount Montgomery, and was
living in 1680.

Sir James Turner says—" The officers of this our Scots armie in Ireland
finding themselves ill payd, and which was worse, not knowing in the time of
the civill warre who sould be their paymasters, and reflecting on the success-
full issue of the Nationale Covenant of Scotland, bethought themselves of
makeing one also ; bot they were wise enough to give it ane other name, and
therefore christened it a Mutual Assurance ; wherby upon the matter they
made themselves independent of any except these who would be their actuall
and reall paymasters, with whom, for anything I know, they met not the whole
time of the warre. . . . We fingered but litle moneys, and meale so
sparinglie as seldom we could allow our sogers above a pound a day." This
is borne out by a Commonwealth tract in the Editor's possession entitled
*A Full Relation of the Late Expedition of the Right Honourable the Lord
Monroe, London 1644*, in which it says, "All our Souldiers of the army carried
ten daies victuals in Oatemeale upon their backes, besides their Armes ; and
ten daies more was carried upon baggage horses ; more we could not carry,
nor other shift we could not make, for want of carriage horses, and other
accomodations for a march : and all this twenty daies victuals for the Souldiers
did not exceed 24 pound weight of Oatemeale without any other supply of meat
or drink but Water."

p. 22. Bulworke att the Strande
 By reference to the map of Belfast about this period, on p. 80, it will be
observed that the place where the High Street river falls into the Lagan was
undefended on the Carrickfergus side. It was probably here that the Bulwark
was erected. As the ford across the Lagan almost certainly started close to
this (see p. 63, where "the Strand way over the water" is expressly mentioned),
its defence was of the first importance. Mr. W. J. Doherty, C.E., M.R.I.A.,
informs the Editor that, when making the new quay opposite the Custom House
about 1874, his men had much difficulty in removing the double row of oak stakes
with large stones filled in between them, forming the old ford which crossed the
river diagonally to the ancient road, now called Middlepath Street.

p. 23. for the finishinge of the Rampier
 This was an earthen entrenchment thrown up around the town at this time,
which remained intact in 1685, when Sir Thomas Phillips made his well-
known survey. The course of the Rampart is clearly given in these words—
"The *rampart* ran along the present John'street, from Donegall street, and
round by Hercules S^t where the North gate stood in North S^t then along said
Hercules S^t and Smithfield to the rere of Chapel lane in Castle street, where
it was met by Mill gate, passing from thence to the river Lagan at Cornmarket,
by the Castle gardens (now the White Linen Hall). The north side crossed
from John street, along what is now called the centre of Talbot st. turning east-
ward to the Crooked lane, and so to the sea above the Point feilds, now a part
of the Towne." *(Joy's MS.)* A considerable portion of the bastions and
intervening bulwarks remained till late in last century. In one of the old
books belonging to the 3rd Presbyterian Congregation it gives as a district
"The North street from the north gate both sids to ye Sentry Box at Pitters
hill and from that to Craven Bridge both sids & from Pitters hill to ye
Brewhous one Both sids which bounds is under the Inspection of William
Mitchell and James Chalmers elders," 1725/6. This would tend to show that a
guard was still placed on the rampart, or why the mention of sentry box? In a
similar time of need in Carrickfergus a like defence was thrown up. "Curia
tenta quinta die Octobris A? 1574 coram Guliel Pierse Maiorem et Humfris
Potts et Johan Cockerell Vice com, in le Town House de Knockfergus. This
present day it was Ordered and agreed by the Sheriffs Burgesses and Commonalty that there should be a Vamour (*sic*) of Sodds or Turfs round about the
Town for the Defence or better strengthening of the Inhabitants of the same

which should be finished by the whole Corporation the four mounts at the four corners of the Town Excepted, which was made and compiled at the charge of the Province which Vamour as aforesaid was finished within one month after the Decree was made." In the next year this rampart was supplemented by a wall the cost of which was reckoned as follows. "We the Mayor & Corporation for the better furthering of the walling of this Town took in Bargain of his Honour [Lord Deputy Sydney] to Wall from her Majesty's Castle on the North East unto the Mount of the Mill along by the Sea side at 5ˢ sterl. the foot every foot to be made seven foot in the foundation four foot in the top of the Wall and 16 foot in height as appeareth by the Indentures of the bargain bearing date the 21ˢᵗ of October 1575." (*Carrickfergus Records MSS.*)

p. 25.   for the highe ways

This list contains all the names mentioned in the subsequent lists, which are not printed here, as the names are simply repeated, with slightly varying sums opposite each.

p. 29.   Henrye lord Blaney

He came from Wales in James I.'s reign, settled at Castle Blaney, and was created a baronet in 1621.

p. 29.   Geo: Rawden

The Rawdon family has been described in authentic history as of very ancient lineage. One of the most celebrated of its scions was Sir George Rawdon, who, as diplomatist, senator, commander of troops, and Irish land agent, left many marks of greatness on the age. He was born at Rawdon Hall, near Leeds, in November, 1604. After having received a liberal education, and given evidence of possessing excellent abilities, he was appointed to an important office under Edward, Lord Conway, Chief Secretary of State in the Cabinet of that day.

On the death of his father, the first Lord Conway, which event took place at Lisnegarvy in March, 1630, the noble Secretary and his protégé came over to Ulster, where the new landlord continued to reside for several months every year during the remainder of his life. Young Rawdon, when not otherwise employed, took part in the management of the estate, and having much taste for military affairs, directed the discipline of Lord Conway's Volunteers. In 1639 he was returned to the Irish Parliament as one of the members for Belfast. In the next year Lord Strafford received secret intelligence that some of the deposed chiefs were collecting their forces for an attack on the King's troops. Lord Donegal, Viscount Conway, and Arthur Hill, three of the most extensive landowners in Ulster, added largely to the strength of their respective horse and foot soldiers, and considerable battalions of regular forces were concentrated in Belfast and Lisnegarvy. George Rawdon commanded the Conway troops. He had been over in London on business in October, 1641, when the news arrived that Sir Phelim O'Neill, Sir Con Magennis, and General Plunkett, with a force of seven thousand men, had taken the field, and threatened to drive the loyalists out of Ulster. Rawdon at once set out for Lisnegarvy by way of Scotland. The roads were almost impassable in many of the English shires, and it was nearly three weeks before he reached the Scottish seaport from whence he sailed, and on the 26th of November landed at Bangor. Next evening at a late hour he got to Lisnegarvy, and there found the local and royal troops in hourly expectation of the rebels—who had encamped near Brookhill—making a descent on the town. The story of the sanguinary conflict that took place in the streets of Lisnegarvy on Sunday, the 28th of November, 1641, need only be glanced at here, as the details are pretty well known to readers of Ulster history. General Rawdon, Colonel Chichester, and Sir Arthur Jerningham led the troops with such spirit that the rebels were totally routed, upwards of one thousand of their men having fallen in the conflict, and the dead bodies lay in the market-place and in Bridge Street in confused heaps. The survivors retreated towards Brookhill, but before leaving Lisnegarvy they set fire to the thatched houses, and in some hours the town was one great mass of ruin. On reaching Brookhill the fugitives set it on fire, and a valuable library was consumed, and some thousand ounces of ancient plate belonging to Lord Conway, and which had been placed there for safety, were either stolen or destroyed.

When General Rawdon was thirty-five he married Ursula, widow of Francis Hill, who had erected Hill Hall Fort. That lady bore him a son, but mother and child died soon afterwards. In 1654 he married Dorothy, the handsome and only daughter of his patron Edward, second Viscount Conway, by whom he had seven sons and three daughters. Having displayed the utmost fealty towards the legitimate heir to the Crown during the usurpation of Cromwell, Rawdon was ordered to repair to London in December, 1660, where Charles II. gave him command of a troop of horse, and ordered his appointment to be made out as Governor of Carrickfergus. He was also appointed one of the Commissioners for the Settlement of Ireland, and by royal patent had the grant of several thousand acres of land in Down, within "ye territory of Moyra." He was elected member for Carlingford, and created a Baronet, under the title of Sir George Rawdon, of Moyra House, County of Downe.

p. 30. For Druggs

Apothecaries' Arms.

The following medicines for Cromwell's Troops in Ireland are given in *Ulster Journal of Archæology*—" Powder Sugar, Loaf Sugar, White Candie, Brown Candie, Anniseede, Oyle Olive, Juice of Liquorice, Rubarcke, Sweet Almonds, Almond Cakes, Mannae, Aloes he Pat, Succoritine, Aq. ex. flor. aurant, Sarsaparill."

p. 31. Noiated

Contraction for nominated.

p. 33. Cash of Torfe

Cash is still used in remote districts to indicate a certain measure of turf, made of osiers, equivalent to a small cart load.

p. 33. John Miller

Probably of Antrim, and admitted a merchant stapler 24th April, 1645 *(see p. 251)*. These two entries are partly torn away in the original MS.

p. 34. The Affidavit of Thomas Postley

This entry is also partly destroyed. Major Coughran (Cochrane) was the military governor of the town at the time *(see p. 240)*.

p. 35. John M'Bryd

He was made a freeman on 6th March 1644 *(see p. 251)*. Probably the same person who signed the Solemn League and Covenant at Holywood on 8th April of that year. The original preserved in the Belfast Museum is entitled "A Solemne League and Covenant for Reformation and Defence of Religion, the Honour and Happinesse of the King, and the Peace and Safety of the three Kingdomes of Scotland, England, and Ireland, Edinburgh 1643." On the blank half of p. 6 is written—"At Hollewood the 8 April 1644 and upon the nynth thereof lykewayes After sermon delyvered by Mr. William Adair upon both these dayes the covenant of reformation in religion was explained And Afterwards sworne subscribed and sealed with marks by a number of the inhabitants of the Kingdom of Ireland." Several other Commonwealth tracts are bound up with this unique relic. The Editor has a curious MS. receipt-book, written by Margaret M'Bride, Belfast, 1714, possibly his daughter. It contains, amongst other quaint dishes, the following :—

"To make paist Royall of fflowers, Take cowslip roses and Marygolds and pluck off all the blossoms and beat y^m in a wooden bowl, then put y^m in as much suggar as will make y^m of one collour, w^t 2 or 3 spoonfulls of rose water, and boill it with stirring it untill y^t burn into suggar again, y^n bake it and work it up to paist w^t gumdragon, and strain it w^t rose water, then roll it very thin, and put it in Moulds, and when it is dry, you may serve it up."

p. 36. dockter Nearne

If in practice at the time, he would see much of what Boate called "Leaguer Sicknesses," which he was assured by his brother, then physician general of the English forces, "had their original not from any defect of the climate, but of the cold and other hardships which the soldiers suffered in their marches ; for they many times going to the fields in cold and foul weather, and sometimes marching whole days long, yea several days together, in very dirty and wet ways, where their feet and legs were continually cold and wet, besides that they were sometimes constrained to pass through the water up as high as the knees and waist, and after all that hardship endured in the daytime, to lye in the night upon the wet ground in the open air this caused the above named diseases."

p. 37.   biscet booter and cheese

Fynes Moryson, describing Mountjoy's fight with Tyrone in November, 1600, says, "For the Army had fasted two Days, and after they had eaten but a little Bisket, and Cheese or Butter, never Men went on in a greater Jollity."

p. 39.   Church yard

The Editor has been unable to obtain any earlier information as to the burials than that given in the Parish Register, of which the first volume begins in July, 1745, and continues to June, 1761.   The second volume extends to 9th November, 1766, and is carefully written on parchment ;   the others are on paper, and continue down to the present.   In 1746 138 deaths are registered, of which 22 were buried at Shankhill, the rest in the parish churchyard.   Only a very few are noted as buried at Shankhill after this year.   Five persons were buried in the church from 1745 to 1761, when such entries cease.   Three of these were Byrtts, two Macartneys, and a Widow Hadskinson.   The mortality varied from 71 in 1754 to 209 in 1761 ;   30 deaths are recorded in August of the latter year.   It seems to have been the most fatal month, for in the year 1756, when 193 deaths are entered, 44 deaths occurred in August, 8 being in one day— nearly all children.   In the year 1757, when the first Census of the town was taken, the population being 8,549, there were registered 122 baptisms, 13 marriages, and 130 deaths, of which 69 were females.   In 1780 occurs the entry— "13th Feby Edward Gorman a *Inviled* buried in the churchyard poor."   The old burying-place was of considerable extent, being enclosed by High Street, Church Lane, Ann Street, and Forest Lane, now merged in Victoria Street. Along the walls of the two lanes were ranged the finest monuments, including those of the Pottinger and Collier families.   A venerable relative of the Editor told a curious incident which she witnessed about the commencement of this century in the churchyard, opposite which she then lived.   The parish sexton, in digging a grave, came on a mass of adipocere, which being reported to Dr. Marshall, a leading physician living in High Street, he immediately crossed the street, secured the specimen, which looked like a small cheese, and tasted it with apparent relish, much to her disgust.

p. 40.   Eden Carrick

Properly Edenduffcarrick, now Shane's Castle.   (For a full account of the O'Neills and their castle, see O'Laverty's *Diocese of Down and Connor*, Vol. III.)

p. 42.   laid out for shingles to mend the church w^t

Boate says that besides slates and Dutch tiles "there was another kind of covering in use, both for Churches and houses, to wit, a certain sort of woodden tiles, vulgarly called shingles ; the which are thight enough at the first, but do not many yeares continue so."   The church dedicated to St. Patrick, which occupied the position of the present St. George's Church, was utilised early in 1651 as a citadel, and termed "The Grand Fort" by Venables.   A number of houses were removed to allow of entrenchments being thrown up ; for compensation awarded to the occupiers see p. 69.

Mr. W. E. Armstrong, solicitor, remembers, about the year 1860, seeing a large cannon lying in the excavation made for the sewer in High Street where now stands the Albert Memorial.   Doubtless one of the Commonwealth guns, afterwards thrown into the river, which formed the ditch on that side.

In Fisher's poem, "News from Lough Bagge (Beg) 1643" (*Ulster Journal of Archæology*, vol. 8), a similar sacrilege is thus described—

> "The whole Church wee have overspread
> With shingle-boards in stead of lead ;
> Nor was it truely fitt, or fayre
> We should stand cover'd, and it stand Bare.
> Thus like good tenants wee have cure'd most
> Of these Decays at o^r owne cost

And thoe wee no Churchwardens are
Wee have put the Kirke in good Repayre.
Without we keepe a Guard ; within
The Chancell's made o[r] magazine
Soe that our Church thus arm'd may vaunt
Shee's truly now made Militant."

p. 44.   John Steawart

Several contentions of the kind are given in the *Carrickfergus Records MSS.* In July, 1607, Clement Ford, Burgess, resisted the authority of the Mayor in cessing upon him soldiers, "and in choler swearing by an oath to the Maiors face that he would never attend church or otherwise whilst he was Maior. If he did commit him that should be the *damest* committal that ever he committed."

p. 46.   Captain Roger Lyndon

A son of Robert Lyndon, who came to Carrickfergus with Chichester. His signature as Recorder occurs in *Carrickfergus Records MSS.* Rawdon and himself represented the English as opposed to the Scotch party. The latter were much embittered against the former in 1646, and forced them to leave the town and find quarters elsewhere.

p. 52.   Sovraignes seat

The original corporation pew was no doubt destroyed when the old church was converted into the " Grand Fort." In 1777 St. Anne's parish church was erected at the sole expense of Lord Donegall, and accommodation was then made for the Sovereign and Burgesses in a large square pew about half-way up the main aisle on the north side. It was arranged with the Sovereign's seat and desk opposite the door, so that the burgesses sat in their black and red robes, six on each side. Mr. William Spiller, who was Rev. Dr. Miller's churchwarden in 1870, informs the Editor that " no rent was charged for the pew, it was used to show strangers into, also officers, and barristers on circuit ; the Judges, however, always sat in the Donegall pew. The Donegall family pew was in the front of the gallery, and had a small winding stair from the vestibule. In 1870 the Sovereign's chair and desk were removed to the vestry, where they now remain, and the pew divided into two." The accompanying illustration, from a special photograph kindly made by Mr. Wm. Swanston, F.G S., gives a good idea of the old Spanish mahogany civic chair and desk. The carving is of very fine quality, in the so-called Chippendale style. Mr. James Morrow, one of the Corporation Sergeants-at-Mace from 1864, is represented behind the chair. Born in 1826, he has served, since 1849, 28 different mayors ; and as his father, an old soldier who fought in the Peninsula, died recently at an advanced age, there is every prospect that the popular sergeant will be on duty in the new City Hall.

p. 57.   schole master

In Youghal, under date 1616, 4[li] was yearly paid as a stipend, to teach the petty scholars in the old Lazar House. (*Town Book of Youghal.*)

p. 58.   Captain Robert Lawson

This was the courageous Derry merchant who saved Belfast from the rebels in October, 1641. (*See note on p. 19.*) He was on his way to Dublin, but turned back at Newry on hearing the rebellion had broken out. His own words are : " being Monday went down back again to *great Belfast* where they found most part of the inhabitants fled and flying, and carrying away their goods to Carrickfergus, and the old Lord Chichester shipped aboard in a ship. So Captain Lawson went throughout the town and blamed them for offering to leave the town, and intreated for some arms, either by buying or lending, but could not prevail. At last he found in Master *Lesquire's* house seven muskets, and eight halberts ready in the street to be shipped to Carrickfergus ; which arms he took, and bought a drum, and beating the same about the town raised about twenty men, who came with him again up to the ironworks, having Mr. Forbus and some number with him joined Captain Lawson, where also he gathered in all about 160 horse and foot, who about two of the clock on the same Monday in the afternoon, being the 25th of October, the second day after the rebellion, marched into Lisnegarvy."

Boate describes Londonderry thus :—

"It is nothing big, consisting only of two long streets, the which cut one nother cross-wayes in the midst, but it is very handsome, the streets beeing broad and well paved, the houses some stories high, & built for the most of freestone, with a handsome church, market place, and key : and is inclosed with a thick and very strong stone wall, being one of the principall fortresses of Ireland."

p. 61.   M.ᵈ That the daye and yeare

Rev. G. Hill has kindly supplied the following note :—"As this affair occurred during the struggle in Ulster between the Royalists and Covenanters, it cannot be regarded as an act of piracy on the part of the latter, but rather as a sort of reprisal, or act of justifiable warfare.   The complainants, however, being Royalists, they naturally appealed for protection and redress to the Sovereign of Belfast, who had then recently been appointed to look after the interests of the royal cause in this town.   The 'merchandise and goods,' of which the owners of the 'Katherine of Belfast' had been plundered, consisted, no doubt, in provisions (most probably oatmeal) and perhaps a small supply of ammunition— both of which commodities were in very urgent requisition by the people of the Ards at the date above mentioned.   In the year 1643, General Robert Monro, in the interests of the Parliament and the Covenanters, had seized Belfast by a *coup de main* from the Royalists, and held it—in violation of the original arrangement with the Scottish forces—until June, 1649, when it was retaken from the Presbyterian party by the third Viscount Ards, afterwards created Earl of Mount Alexander."   Bangwell is Bangor, situated two miles from Groomsport, which is a corruption of Graham's port.   In a map of 1693 in the British Museum it is called Grimsport.   Schomberg landed here in 1689.

p. 61.   1649

Under this date *Joy's MS.* states, "About Michaelmas a battle was fought at Bullers feild between the royal army and that of the parliament, in which the former were defeated, the latter was commanded by Col. Venables, who soon after entered the town.   George Martin, sovereign, determined not to give billets, and retired to his country seat near the Whitehouse, in consequence of which his house was given up to be plundered."   The old ruined mansion adjoining Mr. James Thompson's residence at Macedon was probably this country house.   The Editor has a cannon ball made of local basalt, and recently found in excavating for a new building in Corporation Street, opposite the Mariners' Church.   It was probably fired from one of the Scotch four-pounders in lieu of the orthodox missiles then exhausted.

p. 61.

The following deposition, from a copy (believed to be unpublished) preserved by Rev. Classon Porter, is given as an example of the military troubles of the time :—

The examination of Captain Andrew Adare, taken before mee, Captaine John Dallway Maior of Carrickfergus this 12th of May 1653, who for answer saith that about July 1649 the Lord of Montgomerie came and lay close seige to this garrison & was afterwards surrendered unto him.   That the day before the said surrender one Joey Griffin a souldier under his depᵗˢ command raised and made a mutiny within this garrison and gathered to himself severall souldiers in arms under p'tence he wanted his paie.   That notice thereof being given to this depⁿᵗ, as being his captaine, this Depᵗ went and through many good words and speeches p'vailed at p'sent with the sᵈ Griffin and the rest of his confederated mutineers, that he procured a seeming quallification, & soe left him and them for that present.   That soon after this Depᵗ was returned backe to his quarters a suddaine intelligence was brought to this Depᵗ that the said Griffin had deserted his post, and betaken himself to an other place, and in a mutinous manner had procured unto himself five or six files of armed men some with firelocks the rest with musketts and lighted matches and more souldiers gathering together with the said Griffin from all quarters of the said garrison.   That this Depᵗ acquainting the Governor therewith and the said Griffin and the rest of his sᵈ consorte were determined to possess themselves of the keys of the gates by force of armes, this Depᵗ as well as all others the respective officers within the said garrison were forthwith respectively commanded by the said Governor to their respective posts and also sent for and secured the said keys.   That in pursuance of their commands this depᵗ comeing found the said Griffin in a mutinous manner to have deserted his post and retyred to make good another place with the companie of eese.   And this depᵗ soe comeing used all endeavours by persuasion to procure the said Griffin back to his dep[ts] s[d] post, but instead of rendring his submission, or any obedyence to his dep[ts] commands, presented his ffire locke against this dep[ts] breast bidding this dep[t] stand backe and stande of, Where uppon this dep[t] laid fast hould of his bandaliers with intent to secure this dep[ts] life, which breaking this dep[t] by a stumble backwards fell allmost to the ground, and being recovered this dep[t] perceaving the said Griffin to have presented his piece to this dep[ts] breast and discerning nothing less than instant death by the said Griffin's mutinous expressions, to this dep[t], as well to preserve his owne life as all others within the said garrison and the loss thereof, gave unto the said Griffin some small inconsiderable cutt with intent only to force him to obedyence, but he nothing regarding the same nor to render any manner of obedyence but forcibly maintained his said mutinous act, intending hereby nothing less than to surprize the said garrison, Where uppon an other suddaine thrust given the said Griffin he fell downe and dyed, And this dep[t] further answering saith that the same being only asked to qualifie the said mutinous act, and in obedyence to his said command, which in duty he owed to God and which he humbly conceaveth himself no wayes guilty of murther.

Taken before me the day and year said.   JOHN DALLWAY Mayor.

p. 62.   The humble Petition

A similar petition was sent by the Corporation of Youghal.   For this and a large number of Commonwealth proclamations, see *Town Book of Youghal.*

p. 63.   Carrickfergus

The history of this ancient town has been so admirably told by M'Skimin that it would be difficult to add anything of interest.   Till the "Carrickfergus privilege" of retaining one-third of the total duties leviable on all exports and imports was abolished by Wentworth, the Lord Deputy, in 1637, its condition as a trading port was much superior to Belfast.   A copy of the document fraught with so much of future importance for our city is subjoined. Boate, describing the Havens of Ireland, calls what is now Belfast Lough, Knockfergus, and says it grows narrower by degrees "the further it goeth into the land, the which it doth for the space of fifteen miles, as far as to the town of Belfast, where a little river called Lagon (not portable but of small boates) falleth into this Harbour.   In this Bay is a reasonable good Road before the Town of Knockfergus (seated about nine miles within the land) where it is good anchoring in three fathoms."   He puts both Carrickfergus and Belfast far down in his account of the Irish towns.   Describing first Dublin, then Galway, Waterford, Limerick, and Cork, he says—"As for the rest of the Townes, Drogheda, Kilkenny, and Bandonbridge are passable and worthy of some regard both for bigness and handsomeness: But Colrain, Knockfergus, Belfast, Dundalk, Wexford, Youghall and Kinsale are of small moment, the best of all these being hardly comparable to any of those fair market townes which are to be found in almost all parts of England."   The Editor has examined the series of ancient maps of the district preserved in the British Museum, and Record Office, London, in order to ascertain the relative importance of the two towns at various dates.   In some of the early maps, dating from 1558, in the Record Office, which are illuminated in colours, Carrickfergus is shown much larger than its rival, and the Castle enriched with gilding, as if to show its importance. The *Carrickfergus Records MSS.*, from which a number of illustrative extracts are given for the first time, are contained in a large folio of 347 pages of closely-written matter, transcribed at the expense of Dean Dobbs about 1785.   The Irish Municipal Commissioners were informed that the original documents were used by M'Skimin when writing his *History of Carrickfergus,* and never returned.   Dean Dobbs's transcript has been kindly lent to the Editor by Mr. G. M'Auliffe, J.P.   The importance of Carrickfergus as a residence of the gentry continued into this present century.   It was considered on a par with Lisburn in this respect, Belfast being regarded by these towns as merely a mart for trade; but the transfer of the Assizes put an end to their social superiority.   Some of the ancient houses in the town are of much interest.   The former post office contains a room hung with old painted canvas depicting hunting scenes in which the gallant Lord Blakeney, defender of Minorca, and buried in Westminster Abbey, 1761, appears.   Into this room a lady recently deceased was taken as a child to see one of the beautiful Misses Gunning, then on her way to England. In Farquhar's "Twin Rivals," brought out at Drury Lane in 1703, a servant is jocularly asked by his master his opinion of London. "For dear joy," is his reply, "'tis the bravest place I have sheen in my peregrinations exshepting my nown brave shitty of Carrick-Vergus."

BY THE LORD DEPUTY AND COUNCIL

WENTWORTH,
        Whereas Richard Sperpoint Mayor of the Corporation of Knockfergus Edward Johnson and John Hall Sheriffs of the said Corporation and the Burgesses and Commonalty thereof have been humble Suitors unto Us the Lord Deputy and others his Majesty's Committees for his Highnesses Revenues, to accept and take from them for and to the Use of his most Excellent Majesty our Sovereign Lord Charles by the Grace of God of England Scotland ffrance and Ireland King Defender of the ffaith &c his Heirs and Successors a good and Sufficient Surrender to be made in one form of Law of the third part of all and singular the Customs as well great as small to be divided into three parts And all and Singular Sums of Money to them due and payable for and concerning the Customs of any Wares Merchandizes whatsoever from time to time brought or carried into the Port of Knockfergus aforesaid or into any other Port, Bay or Creek belonging or Adjacent to the said Town of Knockfergus and being betwixt the Sound of Faire Furlongs in the County of Antrim and the Beerlomes in the County of Down and of for and concerning the Customs of all Wares and Merchandizes whatsoever from time to time shipped laden or exported or to be shipped laden or exported of from or out of the said Port or Haven of Knockfergus or of or out of any other Haven Bay Creek or any other place within the Sound of ffaire ffurlongs and Beerloomes aforesaid or from any one or any of them And that in consideration of the said Surrender so to be made We the Lord Deputy and Council would be pleased that they the said Mayor Sheriffs Burgesses and Commonalty of Knockfergus aforesaid might have and receive of his Majesty the Sum of three thousand pounds to be bestowed and employed in the purchasing of Lands for and to the Use benefit and behoof of them and their Successors and to none other Use We therefore having taken the premises and the long & faithful Services done to the Crown by the said corporation into consideration and being desirous by all just and honourable ways and means to advance and augment the public Utility profit and Revenues of the said Corporation are contented and pleased And do hereby Order and appoint that the said sum of three thousand pounds shall within two Months next after such Surrender made and perfected be paid unto and deposited in the hands of Arthur Chichester Esqre Arthur Hill Esqre and Roger Lyndon Gent. to be by them disposed of and employed to and for the Use of the said corporation until the said Sum of three thousand pounds shall be disposed of and laid out and employed by the said Mayor Sheriffs Burgesses & Commonalty or the more part of them for the buying purchasing and acquiring Lands for and to the Use of the said Corporation which Lands so to be purchased and acquired We do Ordain and require that   be from time to time employed for the best benefit of the said Corporation without making any Alienation or Estate thereof other than for the Term of one and twenty Years and for Valuable Rents to be reserved to the said Corporation, Except it be by special License from the Lord Deputy or other chief Governor or Governors of this Kingdom and council for the time being   Given at his Majestys Castle of Dublin the first of ffebruary 1637 Adam Loftus Conc^t Adam Loftus G. Lowther Jo: Borlase Geo: Radcliffe Ro: Meredith *(Carrickfergus Records MSS.)*

p. 63.   Mr. Teag O'Hara
        Head of the old Irish family so long resident at Crebilly, Co. Antrim. *(See O'Hart's Irish Pedigrees.)* He died about 1660, leaving four sons, one named Oliver in compliment to the Protector. His grand-nephew, Henry O'Hara, married the daughter of Dr. Hutchison, Bishop of Down and Connor. *Joy's MS.* notes—" 10th Geo. 1st. an act passed to enable Charles O'Hara of Creabilly to sell part of his estate to pay off his debts, and on the 8th April 1733 John O'Neill and Robert Dalway trustees sold off the *Roote* part of said estate to George Macartney, Belfast, who gave them 20 years purchase for them. Part of these lands was called the Castle Quarter of Loughguile. The castle had been the Savages." *(See The Savages of the Ards, 1888.)* Colonel Robert Venables wrote "The experienced Angler; or Angling improved: being a general Discourse of Angling." London, 1662. *(Lowndes, Bib. Man.,* vol. iv. p. 1861.)

p. 65.   Mr. Essex Digby
        Nephew of the Countess of Donegall (Lady Mary Digby), and Incumbent of the parish under the Commonwealth. Afterwards Bishop of Dromore ; died 1683. Dr. Alexander Colville's life is given in Hill's *Montgomery MSS.* He resided at Galgorm Castle, now the property of the Rt. Hon. John Young. For a curious popular tradition of his dealings with the evil one, see *Dublin Penny Journal*, vol. ii. Edmund Yeo was a nephew of Henry Le Squire, and town clerk of Carrickfergus. John Orpin was a pewterer in Carrickfergus "of a mean descent, the way he came to improve his fortune was by being one of the Executors of the Lady Langford, by which he got considerable, but not justly." *(M'Skimin.)*

p. 68.   Sciant presentes et futuri

The original Latin of this and the entries on pp. 108, 156, and 158 is very much contracted. The Rt. Rev. Wm. Reeves, D.D., P.R.I.A., Bishop of Down and Connor and Dromore, has most kindly transcribed them *in extenso*, and supplied the translations.

Be it known to those who are & shall be that we Richard Hunt of Henerichellym, in the County of Surrey, yeoman, and John Hunte, son and next heir of me the said Richard Hunte, have given and granted, and by this our present charter, have confirmed to John Helhows of Walton on Thames in the County of Surrey aforesaid, yeoman, in consideration of a certain sum of money duly paid and satisfied at the sealing of the presents, all that our parcel or piece of ground called Buryguston, lying and being in Walton aforesaid, which parcel or piece of ground to wit, contains as estimated six acres of land be they more or less, and abuts on a certain enclosure of one Richard Bernard on the south side, and on the commons of Walton aforesaid on the east side, to have, hold, and enjoy the said parcel or piece of ground with its appurtenances to the said John Helhowse, his heirs and assigns, to hold for ever of the Lords in Chief the fee thereof by the services thence due, and of right accustomed. And accordingly we, the aforesaid Richard and John Hunt will guarantee for ever, and by these presents will secure the said parcel of land with its appurtenances to the afore named John Helhowse, his heirs and assigns against all folk whatsoever. Be it known moreover that we the aforesaid Richard and John Hunt have made, ordained, constituted, and on our behalf have appointed our beloved in Christ, Thomas Mowld, yeoman, our true, trusty, and lawful attorney to enter, on our behalf, in our stead and names, upon the said parcel or piece of land with its appurtenances, and take lawful and peaceable possession and seizin, thereof, after possession of the same and the seizin thereof thus taken and held, and thereupon for us, in our behalf and names, to deliver full, lawful and peaceable possession and seizin of and in the premises with the appurtenances to the aforesaid John Helhows, his heirs and assigns for ever, according to the force, form, and effect of this our present charter, and to esteem as final and our pleasure all and sundry that our said attorney shall do or cause to be done in the premises. In testimony whereof we have affixed our seal to this our present charter. Given on the 6th day of March in the 3d and 4th years of the reigns of Philip and Mary by the grace of God, of England, Spain, France, both Sicilys and Ireland, King and Queen, Defender of the faith, Archduke of Austria, Duke of Burgundy, Milan, and Brabant, Count of Hapsburg, Flanders, and Tyrol; so that the aforesaid John Helhowse, his heirs, and assigns, do for ever pay or cause to be paid to the aforenamed Richard and John Hunt, their heirs and assigns for ever year by year at the feast of Michael the Archangel on lawful demand.

> The instatement and seizin with the lawful and peaceable possession were taken and delivered the day and year as below, according to the tenor, force, form, and effect of this present charter, in the presence of
>> Richard Woodclerk, Tristram Woodclerk, Thomas Woodclerk, Thomas Dalley, Thomas Greentree, Richard Clerk, John Clerk, and others worthy of credit.

p. 72.   Edw Reynell

The annexed pedigree of the Reynell family has been kindly supplied by Rev. Wm. Reynell, B.D., Henrietta Street, Dublin.

This family, originally of Norman origin, was at first seated in Cambridgeshire, and had estates there, as also in Yorkshire and Somersetshire. During the absence of Richard I. in the Crusades, Sir Richard Reynell, of Pyttney, in Somersetshire, was constituted by that monarch custodian of the castles of Exeter and Launceston. Walter Reynell, seventh in direct descent from Sir Richard, married in 1395 Margery, daughter and heiress of William Stighull, of East Ogwell, County of Devon, by his wife, eldest daughter and heiress of Robert de Malston. The family then migrated into Devonshire, where it flourished for many generations. Prince, in his *Worthies of Devon*, mentions many members of it.

Edmund Reynell, second son of Edmund Reynell, of Malston, by Ann, daughter of Lewis Hatch, of Allan, both in Devonshire, was thirteenth in direct lineal descent from the first-mentioned Sir Richard. He came to Ireland with his kinsman Sir Arthur Chichester, and (with other scions of Devonshire houses) settled at Malone, near Belfast. He married Mary Fortescue, and had, with other children, a son Edward, a Free Burgess and Sovereign of Belfast, who married Katherine ——, and had a son Edmond. Edmond Reynell married Hannah Dobbyn. He was a Sir Clerk in Chancery (Ireland), and acquired estates in Westmeath and other parts of Ireland. He died in February, 1698-9, and was buried in the vaults of St. Michan's, Dublin. Mr. Reynell left, with other children, two sons, Arthur and Richard.

Y

Arthur Reynell was of Castle Reynell, Co. Westmeath, of which county he was sheriff in 1718 and 1727. He married Elizabeth Cooke, of Cookesboro', in the same county, and had issue two sons and nine daughters. He died 1735. Edmond Reynell succeeded. He served sheriff for Westmeath in 1745, and for Longford in 1746. He died unmarried in 1767, and was succeeded by his brother John, who served as sheriff for Westmeath in 1779, and died in 1792. By Catherine, his wife, second daughter and heiress of William Ludlow, he left issue two sons and six daughters. William Reynell, of Castle Reynell, the eldest son, Lieutenant-Colonel Royal Irish Fencibles, married Jane, daughter of Sir William Montgomery, Bart. He died 5th May, 1829, aged 76, having sold Castle Reynell to James Gibbons. Barbara, his third daughter, married John, third Earl of Donoughmore, and had an only son, William, who died unmarried, and three daughters, two of whom still survive.

Richard Reynell, second son of Edmond Reynell, was captain in a regiment of horse. He married Dorcas Cooke, of Cookesboro', Co. Westmeath, and had issue fourteen children. From him descend the families of Reynella, Co. of Westmeath, now represented by Mrs. Balfour, of Townley Hall, Co. Louth ; of Killynon, Co. of Westmeath, now represented by Richard Reynell ; and of Ballinalack, Co. of Westmeath, now represented by Cooke Reynell.

Richard Reynell, of Killynon, married in 1875 Louisa Anna Smyth (she died 1881), and has a son Richard, born 1879.

Arms—Argent, masonry sable, a chief indented of second. Crest—A fox passant, or. Supporters (as antiently borne)—Two foxes. Motto—"Murus aheneus esto," and (over the crest) "Indubitata fides."

p. 77. John Correy

The present Earl of Belmore, G.C.M.G., &c., &c., Castle Coole, County Fermanagh, is the seventh in descent from this former freeman of the town (see p. 254), through his great-granddaughter, Sarah Corry, wife of Galbraith Lowry-Corry, M.P., and mother of Armar, first Earl of Belmore. In the year 1656 John Corry purchased the Manor and Lordship of Castle Coole, where he died about 1681-6. The token issued by him when a merchant in Belfast is described in Vol. iv. of the Proceedings of the Royal Irish Academy, append. iv., p. xxx.; a good example is in the Benn collection, Belfast Museum. It is stated in an old MS. History of Fermanagh, quoted by Lord Belmore in his valuable "Parliamentary Memoirs of Fermanagh and Tyrone," that "the family of Corry was formerly remarkable in Scotland for their vallour by ye frequent warrs which sometimes happened betweene England and Scotland ; and beareth for their Coate of Arms, Argent a saltire Couped Gules, etc." John Corry, Hugh Eccles, and other Belfast merchants were concerned in a Chancery bill anent the will of Archibald Moore, which his mother disputed. She said that John Corry and his wife had been of a long and familiar acquaintance with her son, but his widow successfully proved the will as shown by the entry made by the town clerk (p. 72). John Corry ceased all connection with Belfast in 1656, and was High Sheriff of Fermanagh in 1666. A fine old silver tankard, with the English Hall-mark 1681, belonged to him, and is now preserved at Castle Coole. From photographs kindly sent by Lord Belmore, it appears to be of superior workmanship, with the arms of its original owner engraved on the side in the style of the period.

p. 79. Verses

These doggerel lines are in the autograph of the town clerk of that time. In Anderson's valuable "Catalogue of Early Belfast Printed Books" there is mentioned under date 1795, "Popular Ballads preserved in Memory." This very scarce collection is formed of ballads taken down from local recollection at that time, and composed in the middle of the 17th and beginning of the 18th centuries. One entitled "Kirk and Covenant" bears internal evidence of being written about 1660. It begins thus—

> "Och, and alas, a well a day,
> Sin' now our hands we wring,
> We're slaughtered, murder'd, made a prey,
> A sad and dolefu' thing.
> They who 'tofore, did drone and roar,
> Are now begun to rant,
> And now they pray, the live long day,
> Wae worth the Covenant."

p. 94. Michaell Biggar

THE family of Bigger is one of the few in Belfast of which members still exist after the lapse of 250 years. Three brothers came over from Nithsdale, in Scotland, about the year 1640, and settled in Belfast, and also at Biggerstown, now Hightown, in the parish of Carnmoney. The trade tokens of Michael and James are given herewith. These brothers were "Commissioners" for the old Presbyterian Church adjoining the North Gate. John and Michael Bigger were enrolled as freemen in 1654. Other notices of the family occur through the book. An entry close to the old Market House in High Street was long known as "Bigger's Entry," and had formerly been the entrance to the family residence, which was built at some distance from the street; subsequently premises were added in front, which remained in the occupation of the family till 1830. At Biggerstown the whole district was in their possession at one period, and they still own a considerable portion. The will of Michael Bigger was made at Edinburgh in 1674, and is subjoined as a curious survival of the Scotch element. John Bigger, who had the interesting document on p. 140 recorded, left by his will, in 1721, 20 shillings to the poor of the parish, "to be paid to each of them as yᵉ Rev Mr ffletcher shall think most fitt." The will of Michael Bigger, yeoman, 1718, states—"Imprimis I leave all my body cloaths Linen and wooling except a ticken vest and brickes to—and my chattels to be roped or sold by Publick Cant at a convenient time after may decess at the discretion of my exactᵣ and overseear." James Bigger was one of the earliest volunteers, and a Delegate at Dungannon in 1782. William Bigger and his son Mathew worked a woollen factory at Biggerstown, being subsidised by the Irish Parliament. The latter was a colonel on the Irish side at the Battle of Antrim, and his friends were well represented there. David Bigger started the Carnmoney Cotton Printing Mill about 1800, now the Mossley Mills; he was an original governor of the Academical Institution, and also a founder of the Linen Hall Library. His name is annexed to the Resolutions presented to the Irish Parliament about 1790 in favour of the Roman Catholics, and he was an United Irishman. His son, the late Joseph Bigger, of Ardrie, Belfast, has left the following sons :—H. J. Bigger, Surgeon-Major S. F. Bigger, M.D., India, W. C. Bigger, F. C. Bigger, E. C. Bigger, M.D., and F. J. Bigger, solicitor. The late Joseph Bigger, Trainfield, was a wealthy merchant and chairman of the Ulster Bank; and the recent death of his son, Joseph Gillis Bigger, M.P., was much regretted by his countrymen. W. F. Bigger, J.P., D.L., left Belfast and settled in Derry, his family are—J. Edgar Bigger, W. G. Bigger, M.D., and C. J. Bigger, of the Foyle Shipyard, the late Prof. J. L. Bigger, M.A., was his eldest son. There are also others of the name in and about Belfast.

BADGE OF THE UNITED IRISHMEN.

SEAL OF 1799 — MATᵂ BIGGOR BY CASTON ANTRIM

BRASS SEAL OF MATHEW BIGGER, BALLYVASTON.

WILL OF MICHAEL BIGGER, 1674.

At Edinburgh the Twentie sext day of June, I m v j c'. Three scoir ffouretein yeares. I Michael Bigger of Belfast Merchant—in the keingdome of Ireland. Being for the present seck in body but perfyte in memorie and Judgment. And being most willing to setle my wordlie affaires. Thairfore I nominat and appoynt my weill beloved spouse, Agnes Stewart my only exerix and universal intromissatrix with my haill goods, geir, chattel insight and plennishing debts and sonmes of money adebted and restand att and to me be itsomever maner of way with power to her to give up inventar yᵣ of enter and confirme the same lykas. I leive and appoynt the two third pairts of my free goods and geir more nor payes my just debts to be divydit amongist my children be the advyce of Thomas Stewart of Belfast Merchant my brother-in-law and that my said spouse with his advyce shall proportione and divyde the samyne amongest my said children as they shall find caus and convenient and sichlyke I nominat and appoynt the said Agnes Stewart my said spouse and the said Thomas Stewart her brother Tutors, testamentars to my said children during yr pupillarite and less age and administrators to them for guiding and govering their persones and estaits during the tyme foresaid. This my Letter will and testa to all and sundrie whom it concernes I notifie and make knowin. In Witness yᵗ-of thir putts (wrytten be Andrew Anthone scrivitor to Mr James Weir wrytter to his Maties signet) I have subscrybed the same with my hand and seall Before their witness, Allane Corbet of Hilburrow merchant the said Mr James Weir and the said Andrew Anthone wrytten heirof day moneth and year of God forsaid

Allan Corbett witnes   Andrew Anthone witness

James Weir, witness   Michael Bigger SEAL

p. 100.   Towne Hall

In the view of High Street in 1786, reproduced on p. 100 from the original drawing (and inserted by the courtesy of Mr. Olley), the old building, with its quaint cupola and arched openings, is clearly depicted, standing at the corner of High Street and Corn Market now occupied by Forster Green & Co. Like most market houses of the time, the ground floor or "sellers" was used for store and weigh-house, the upper rooms, to which access was obtained by the "stayres," served as the meeting-place of the old Corporation and for public assemblies in later times. An old lady still living at the age of 104 informs the Editor that she has a distinct recollection of seeing the last blackened heads that were spiked on the parapet of the Market House. They are thus referred to in the *News-Letter* of August 17, 1798 :—" The heads of Dickey, Storey, and Byers have been taken off the market house by order of general Nugent where they were placed on spikes." At this time it was used for the sittings of courts-martial; those arrested for such offences as being found in the streets after nine o'clock p.m. were confined in a basement which extended under the rere portion. Mr. Robert Young, C.E., saw a little Gothic oak window, almost at the ground level, brought to light when Grattan & Co. removed their premises in 1868. Small red bricks similar to those used in the Castle, with some sandstone dressings, formed the walls. "His Majestys arms" gave dignity to the High st front, from which also projected the clock, whose dial fell in 1739, breaking a mans thigh. In the Roll of Freemen under 26 Sept 1667 Thomas Orpin glasier is admitted, the fee of ten shillings to be done in work, no doubt at the market house. On 22 Sept 1681, John Chruchley plasterer was admitted without a fee, but he was "to mend ye markett house." The only relic now existing of its former splendour is the bell, which is of bell metal, with a rough iron clapper, capable, however, of bringing out a fine tone. On an ornamental band is the date 1761 in raised figures. The extreme width and height are the same, viz., 22 inches. After much inquiry it was found and identified at the old Holy-wood Lighthouse, where the Editor saw it by the kindness of the Harbour Commissioners, to whom it was presented by Lord Donegall after the demolition of the market house.

p. 102.   Mallon ffall and dunmury and part of the parish of Coole

These districts were mainly peopled by Lord Chichester's tenants from Devonshire. Mr. W. F. M'Kinney, Sentry Hill, Carnmoney, kindly supplied a copy of the receipt printed herewith.

"Received from the Parish of Carmoney (by the Hand of Mr William Russel) Six Pounds Sixteen Shillings & Six pence Ster: being the contribution of said Parish toward the Expences laid out by me in New Roofing & Repairing the Market House of Belfast. £6 : 16 : 6   Received this 21st Septʳ 1770. Robᵗ Joy.

p. 108.   Omnibus et singulis

To all and singular, Justices, Wards of the peace, and Mayors, Aldermen, Sovereigns, Bailifis, Constables, Officiaries, Ministers, and loyal subjects of the Sovereign Lord that now is, to whom this present writ shall come,—Robert Bindlos, Baronet, Mayor of the borough or town of Lancaster in the county of Lancaster, William Townson and Giles Hoysham, gentlemen, Bailiffs of the same borough or town,—Health in the Lord ever-lasting ; We do you to wit that the town and borough of Lancaster aforesaid is an ancient borough, and that all the Burgesses of that borough have, enjoy, and possess, and as far as the memory of man reaches, have never done otherwise than have, enjoy, and possess, the liberty, privilege and immunity to be relieved and exempt from all toll, passage, pontage, stallage, pannage, tonnage, lastage, as also from all other exactions and demands whatsoever for all their goods, merchandises, bought or sold, through the whole kingdom of England, also through all seaports, and islands, cities, ports, and towns of Ireland, Wales, and Man ; also that the Lord James, late King of England, Scotland, France, and Ireland, by his Letters patents, under his great seal of England, granted and confirmed to his Burgesses and his borough aforesaid, and their successors for ever, the liberties, privileges and immunities aforesaid agreeably to the tenor of divers Charters of the pro-genitors and predecessors of the said Lord the King, and to the same Burgesses and their predecessors granted from the time of King John formerly monarch of this kingdom of England, and lately confirmed by the most excellent prince our Lord, Charles the Second, now King of England, Scotland, France, and Ireland ; and to the same Burgesses and their successors by his Letters Patents, as well under his great seal of England as under the seal of his Duchy of Lancaster, according as in the same Letters Patents and the charters remaining in the possession of the aforesaid Burgesses, more largely is contained and appears. Which things above recited we not only testify to you by the tenor of the presents, and further that one William Yeates was admitted and sworn a Burgess, and for the period of thirteen years now last past has been admitted and sworn to the Liberties of the same borough or town of Lancaster : To wit, he was admitted and sworn as is alleged in and on the ninth day of October in the year one thousand six hundred and fifty-two. Wherefore we the aforesaid Mayor and Bailiffs do in particular ask that when the said William Yeates or his servants shall come to cities, towns, ports or other places within the kingdom of England, or to ports and islands of Ireland, Wales, or Man with their goods or merchandises, they be relieved and free from all Toll, passage (in English through toll), pontage, stallage, pondage, tunnage, lastage, and other exactions and demands whatsoever, according to the grant of said Lord the King and his progenitors as above recited. In testimony whereof we have set the seal of the aforesaid borough or town to these presents the fifth day of February in the eighteenth year of the reign of our Lord Charles the Second, by the grace of God, King of England, Scotland, France, and Ireland, Defender of the faith, in the year of the Lord 1665.

p. 117. The course of the backwater

This was the tail race coming from the Manor Mill across Smithfield, which was probably called so from smithies erected on its course. In 1761 complaints were made of the danger caused by horses sent up to be watered in North Street, no doubt at this conduit. The new plantation was situated at the foot of Waring Street (called after the Sovereign), on the line of Corporation Street. The houses were small, with thatched roofs, and divided into the Fore and Back Plantation in the map of 1788.

p. 121. The new Dock or River up to the sluices

This new Cutt River, as it is termed on Phillips' map, extended from the Lagan to the sea bank, beside the Castle Gardens, and crossed the Blackstaff estuary. Mr. C. H. Brett's valuable " Notes on the Topography of Old Belfast," read before the Belfast Literary Society, describe this fully.

p. 129. Arthur Earle of Donnegall

1st Earl, *see p. 227.* As there was no Registry of Deeds till Queen Anne's reign, Wills, &c., were often enrolled in Town Books for preservation.

p. 134. ye old kea or wharfe be inlarged

On Phillips' map some ships are shown in the lower part of the High Street river, close to two long one-story buildings situated below the church. These were probably the " new stone houses of George Macartney and Henry Thomson," used as warehouses only, as Macartney's dwelling-house, mentioned in his will with garden, meadow, &c., was near his mills.

p. 136. Halberts

The old night watchmen, before 1842, were called by various nicknames— as hornies, bulkies, and charlies, the latter from the reign in which they were introduced. They were armed with halberts, and had a wooden rattle or crake.

p. 138.   yᵉ great bridge

This must have been one of the upper bridges over the High Street river, if the measurement of about 200 Irish perches from the Tuck mill dam be correct. It was the fourth mill ascending the stream, and is now occupied by the Clonard Works. The bridge may have been that opposite the market house, supposed by Benn to be depicted on the famous " Belfast Ticket," of

which the unique original is in the Benn collection, Belfast Museum, but it probably represents the western end of the Long Bridge. The wooden pipes are still occasionally dug up, in fair preservation ; some exhibit the iron ferules inserted at the faucit to prevent the spigot breaking them. The Editor has one about 8 feet long by 9 inches diameter, with a bore of 3 inches.

Belfast Ticket, *c.* 1730, showing market house and bridge.

Native alder and pine were used at first, then Norway poles, whilst square balks were found at Lord Donegall's house, now the Royal Hotel. Cork only got pipe-water in 1761, when Ducart (of canal fame) received £25 "for taking the level of the river Lee and drawing several plans of waterworks." *(Town Book of Cork.)*

p. 138.   Capt Robᵗ Leathes

He was agent to the Donegall estate, and connected with the Lewis family, as shown by the following pedigree, kindly drawn up by Miss Lewis, Nettlefield. Two extracts from his diary, preserved in *Joy's MS.*, are subjoined. "My family and servants with those of another gentleman sailed for Port Glasgow in consequence of the times, 1697, at Pesley (Paisley) saw 3 warlocks and 4 witches burned. 1690. Oct 7. In the morning about a quarter of an hour after seven o'clock, there was an Earth quake in Belfast, shaking houses to the amazement of the Inhabitants, not usual in this place but one above 40 years since. I found it in the lowest room of my house, leaning upon the window at the time. I first believed it to be a giddiness in my head, till comparing with others who fealt the same."   W. Sacheverell notes in 1698—"The new pottery is a pretty curiosity, set up by Mr. Smith the present Sovereign and his predecessor, Captain Leathes, a man of great ingenuity."   The ware was similar to Rouen, of which large quantities were imported here—a shoe in blue and white is at Nettlefield, another dated 1724 is figured. *(Jewett's Ceramic Art, Vol. II.)*

At Nettlefield is still preserved the Oak Punchbowl "presented to Robert Leathes, Sovereign of Belfast and Agent to the Earl of Donegall, in the year 1690, it having been in the Donegall Family for upwards of 100 years previous." His portrait is given on p. 139, reduced from that in MS.

PEDIGREE SHOWING CONNECTIONS OF THE LEWIS FAMILY WITH BELFAST SOVEREIGNS.

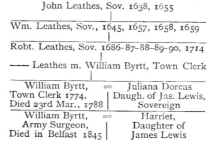

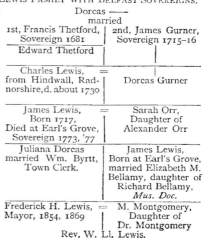

John Leathes, Sov. 1638, 1655

Wm. Leathes, Sov., 1645, 1657, 1658, 1659

Robt. Leathes, Sov. 1686-87-88-89-90, 1714

—— Leathes m. William Byrtt, Town Clerk

| William Byrtt, Town Clerk 1774, Died 23rd Mar., 1788 | = | Juliana Dorcas Daugh. of Jas. Lewis, Sovereign |

| William Byrtt, Army Surgeon, Died in Belfast 1845 | = | Harriet, Daughter of James Lewis |

Dorcas ——
married

| 1st, Francis Thetford, Sovereign 1681 | 2nd, James Gurner, Sovereign 1715-16 |

Edward Thetford

| Charles Lewis, from Hindwall, Radnorshire, d. about 1730 | = | Dorcas Gurner |

| James Lewis, Born 1717, Died at Earl's Grove, Sovereign 1773, '77 | = | Sarah Orr, Daughter of Alexander Orr |

| Juliana Dorcas married Wm. Byrtt, Town Clerk. | James Lewis, Born at Earl's Grove, married Elizabeth M. Bellamy, daughter of Richard Bellamy, *Mus. Doc.* |

| Frederick H. Lewis, Mayor, 1854, 1869 | = | M. Montgomery, Daughter of Dr. Montgomery |

Rev. W. Ll. Lewis.

p. 152. Ad Curiam Publicam

At a Public Court, held on the 20th day of May, in the thirty-fifth year of the reign of His Majesty Charles the Second, and in the year of our Lord [one thousand] six hundred and eighty-three, in presence of Louis Thomson. Sovereign of the aforesaid town, W. E. was elected and constituted [a Burgess] by the general consent of the whole court. In testimony whereof the said Sovereign subscribed these presents, and caused the common seal of the said town to be attached thereto, the day and year above written.

p. 154. Sᵣ William ffrancklin

Of Mavorne, Beds. He married the widow of 1st Earl of Donegall (p. 227).

p. 155. provide a cupple of poles

Fires were numerous in the old boroughs, full of cage-work houses, with thatched roofs. In 1622 nearly 1500 houses were burnt in Cork. where a law was passed to remove all thatch under a penalty of £40 *(Town Book of Cork)*. In one of the thatched cottages still left in Frederic Street, Lord Edward Fitzgerald lay concealed a month in 1798.

p. 156. Jacobus Secundus Dei Gratia

James the Second, by the Grace of God, of England, Scotland, France, and Ireland King, Defender of the Faith, &c. To the Sheriff of Antrim greeting—We command you that you fail not, by reason of liberty in your Bailiwick, to enter the same, and by honest and lawful men, and serve an injunction upon the Sovereign, Free Burgesses, and Common Burgesses of Belfast in the county aforesaid to appear before the Barons of our Exchequer, at the King's Courts, Dublin, on the fifteenth day after Easter next ensuing, to declare to us By what warrant, right, or title they claim to have. use, and enjoy the liberties, privileges, and franchises following,—to wit, that they be of themselves one body corporate and politick in substance, act, and name, under the name of "the Sovereign, Free Burgesses, and Common Burgesses de Belfast," and by said name to plead and implead, to sue and be sued, and to have the power of sending two Burgesses to attend Parliament, and to hold a Court of Record ; which franchises, liberties and privileges it appears the aforesaid Sovereign Free Burgesses and Common Burgesses aforesaid have, for the space of one year now last passed, and longer, usurped and do still usurp, in defiance of Us, and to the grievous injury and manifest hindrance of our Royal prerogative, as in a certain Information against the said Sovereign, Free Burgesses and Common Burgesses of Belfast in the said county, to exhibit by our Attorney-General, who on our behalf sues, more fully is set forth and appears. And further to receive what our Barons thereupon may cause to be done and which of right and agreeably to the laws and customs of our said Kingdom of Ireland ought to be done. And further, that there and then you have the name. and by whom they exercise jurisdiction. and the brief. As witness Henry Hene our Chief Baron of our said Exchequer, at the King's Courts aforesaid, the 12th day of February, the third year of our reign.   Barry

John Nethercott, Deputy Remembrancer of the Treasurer.

As a contemporary writer says—

> "He shall new model all the Nation
> From College unto Corporation ;
> To former plights he shall transplant us,
> By *Mandats, Briefs*, and *Quo Warranto's.*" *(Irish Hudibras, 1689.)*

p. 167. (styl'angl')

The legal year in England began 25th March till 1753. In Scotland it began on 1st January from 1600. The Town Book followed the latter.

p. 168. these things belonging to the Towne

The Charter and Town Seal alone survive. All efforts to trace the old weights and measures proved fruitless. "The great ordinary measure shall be a sive of 24 gallons." *(Town Book of Youghal.)*

p. 170. five dozen of clift boards

The meaning of "clift boards" in this connection is not clear, unless it may be taken as a private term to denote money, known to both parties. The postscript "it would be better yn Irish money" would then be intelligible.

p. 171. the market

As Benn's History treats of the markets, little need be added here. The Countess of Longford was Ann, daughter of 1st Earl of Donegall (pp. 131, 227). The district mentioned includes all Castle Place, into which opened the upper Castle gate, both sides of High Street, as far down as the dock at Skipper Street, and all Bridge Street. The Stone Bridge was opposite Bridge Street, and may have been built by Hugh Eccles in 1664. In 1738, Robert Willis, formerly Latin schoolmaster, intimates that he now keeps shop opposite the Stone Bridge, next door to the Post Office. In 1860, at the making of a new sewer through High Street, the ancient level of the footpath was found to be 3 feet below present surface. By the kindness of Mr. James McGee, the Editor has the large collection of local tokens, &c., acquired by the late J. G. McGee at the time. (*Ulster Jour. Arch.*, ix. p. 113.) In *News-Letter*, Dec. 22, 1761, is the notice, "Next Friday being Christmas Day, the Margymore or great Market of Belfast will be held on Thursday next."

p. 172.   A Coppy of the Charter

The original in Latin is preserved at the Town Hall. This copy was made to precede the recapitulation of all the Corporate bye-laws, which was found necessary at this time, as the originals were difficult to read, full of erasures and interlineations, and scattered. Joseph Smyth published an English version of the Charter in 1812.

p. 187.   ye New Bridge

This was the Long Bridge, which was commenced in 1682, and completed just in time to be seriously damaged by the passage of Schonberg's artillery. Thompson's engraving gives a faithful view of this historic structure in 1823.

```
HENRY
CHADS
IVNIOR
1696
```

In the Belfast Museum are preserved two Scrabo sandstone blocks which were built into the bridge close to each other. Each is about 19 inches high by 11 inches across. One bears a coat of arms,—on a bend, between 3 mullets, 3 cinquefoils ; the other has the annexed inscription sunk in angular letters. If "Mr. Chades bridge" was not one of the small bridges across the High Street river which was to be cleaned to "ye neer mill," viz., the Manor Mill at Millfield, it would appear as if the Long Bridge was called after him as the builder, and perhaps architect. In the *Hibernian Gazetteer*, 1835, the dimensions of the bridge are given. "The whole Bridge is 2562 feet long, of that the 21 arches take up 840, and the dead work 1722, the breadth of the arched part is 22 feet and of the whole 19." It was taken down in 1841.

p. 188.   The humble addresse

It is noted 9th April, 1696—"It. That if the Recorder come not here to draw an Ascotiation (*sic*) for this Corporation (to be presented to his Majʸ) by to-morrow night, that it be drawn up by Mr Harrison." (*Town Book of Youghal.*)

p. 190.   Thomas Knox

He purchased a part of the Donegall estate at Dungannon. An ancestor of Lord Ranfurly.

p. 192.   Warham Jemmett

Formerly collector at Cork, where a bridge was called after him.

p. 193.   whose names follow

These are said by Benn not to have been given.

p. 195.   My Lord Donegall

He was 3rd Earl, and served under Lord Peterborough in Spain (see p. 228). A plan of Barcelona given in *Tindal's Continuation of Rapin's History*, London, 1744, shows Fort Monjuich, or Mount Joie, as close by the sea, and strongly fortified. In the same volume is the map of Belfast about 1660, reproduced on p. 80.

p. 197.   The Corporation of Belfast hath power

The first entry is the same as one supplied to Benn by Rev. Dr. Reeves, with this reference, "A printed Broadsheet bound up in a vol. of old papers in the Primate's Records, and it is endorsed (in Bishop King's handwriting) Belfastes Case, 1703." (*History of Belfast*, p. 475.) It was no doubt cited as part of the case brought against George Macartney, Sovereign, by the widow of 3rd Earl of Donegall, and which he successfully refuted before the House of Commons in 1707. The entry beginning at "Resolved" has reference to this, and is evidently incomplete.

p. 199. Councellor Macartney

This speech seems to be a draft probably composed by the Town Clerk. The reference to Lord Donegall would imply that his death was not known in Belfast, although it occurred on April 10, 1706.

p. 200. Whereas the Key of the Port

The Bill for this improvement was not carried till 1729.

p. 214. Rob.ʳ Green Esq.ʳ Constable of the Castle

He was a lawyer, and the agent for seven years of the Donegall estate, which was managed by Lord Barrymore as trustee. Green Street was named after him. Some of his letters, written about the time he was superseded by the appointment of Thomas Banks early in 1726, contain interesting information as to the state of the town. The following extracts are printed for the first time :—

"Mr Seymer was with me this day desiring to know if yᵗ Lordship (Barrymore) had written anything relating to his searching for Coals, he tells me he hath discovered what looks very like Coals on my Lords Estate at Dunmurry, & doubts not to find them near whitehouse, where they will be of much more value. I hear the lead Ore gott at Innishowen turns to very good acco.ᵗ that M.ʳ Chichester and Mr Jones his nephew have each of them got two hundred guineas to admit a partner to share in their profitt but of this I doubt not butt yᵗ yʳ Lordship hath a better acco.ᵗ from other hands having reason to believe what I write is true. Know it could do no hurt if no good the Merch.ᵗˢ are dayly with me desiring to putt yʳ Lordship in mind of doing something to preserve if not encrease yᵉ remains of their declining trade which cannot be without great encouragem.ᵗ to build conveniencies for trade and to preserve what already built great complaints are made ag.ᵗ the managem.ᵗ of my Lords Courts and not without Cause the exactions are great and delays much greater besides thirty pounds hath been lately levyed of this Mannor to build a Goale by presentments at our sessions at yᵉ instance of Mr Banks who cares not what power he brings into yᵉ Mannor to compass his ends No seneschall or Bailiff ever had a Goale before and in truth it may be rather called a Spunging house being built on a tenem.ᵗ and joining to a tenem.ᵗ that he rents from m.ʳ Macartney the Coll.ʳ with a room to which the Courts & Jurys are to be adjourned his Bailiff keeps the house and sells liquor where many of our Lords Tenants that have anything to do in the Courts are too oft obligd to spend more than they can spare." (Letter of January 29, 1725.)

"My Lord—I have oft writt that the trade of this place decays the inhabitants are moving hence to Dublin & elsewhere and have earnestly recommended yᵉ procuring an Act for setting long leases or for lives renewable, that, woud encourage to build and repair whats most ruinous those whose interest are in houses most sensibly feel the effects of peoples going of with their families. as I do whose study always possible to supply that loss and in order thereto I have long endeavourd to gett a woollen Manufacture sett up here & hope to effect itt if any Encouragement can be on my Lord Donegalls Acco.ᵗ itt will bring many families workmen & artificers here it will keep much money in the town and countrey which is now Annually laid out in Dublin for woollen Manufactures but work houses must be built and for some time little return can be expected from 5 or 6 thousand pounds that must be advanced to carry on the work for the Encouragement whereof and the good of the place I am willing to subscribe 500.ˡⁱ or a greater sum. if your Lordshipp approves the project and thinks itts worth the Encouraging a few lines to that purpose, will soon sett the work on foot. My Lord Donnegall, & his Lordships successors, will gain greatly thereby : and it shall have the best assistance in the power of my Lord your Lordships most obedient Serv.ᵗ Robert Green." (Letter of February 20, 1725.)

His postscript, in a letter to a Dublin friend, adds—

"I would gladly know from him and you what Doctor Tisdall is doing I hope the Church & Dock bill will sleep for ever ! at least till we have another Session or another Parliam.ᵗ."

"Your Lordships of the 12ᵗʰ gave great satisfaction to the Merch.ᵗˢ and chief traders here so soon as rec.ᵈ I communicated what your Lordship had done for the benefit of trade and to free from the great expense and burden that the intended act woud have brought upon them, they then resolvd by a letter to y.ʳ Lordship so far as was possible to express their thanks & acknowledgments, which when our Coll.ʳ heard he gott the Sovereign to assemble yᵉ Inhabitants by Ringing the town bell then read your Lordships letter to him the 27ᵗʰ post Harangued the people to write a letter of thanks. In truth I am informed all but two were against his being named in any letter that they were to sign & earnestly request me to desire No Macartney may have any thing to do in laying out my Lords bounty Most of the poors money is in Isaacs hands already, how or when, it will be gott out of the Lord knows. Our Sovereign it is thought cannot live out his year." (Letter of March 26, 1726.)

"Mr Clugston seems highly delighted to think of his approaching Hon.ʳ all he wants is a book to teach him the law resolving to read much as he hears our Late Sovereign did but he understood not what he read and I believe Mr Clugstons understanding will be abundantly less. I gott not your Lordships Diaper till this week yᵗ order came too late for yᵉ last years whitening. I have bought three sorts for table cloths four of each sort 2 yards & ½ wide. 12 yᵈˢ at 15ˢ pᵉ yard, 12 att 12ˢ 6ᵈ and 12 at 9ˢ 6ᵈ " (Letter of May 7, 1726.)

p. 215.   Candidates

The commonality, with Sovereign and Burgesses, had the right to elect the sergeants at mace by Charter *(p. 177)*. *Joy's MS.* notes—"1824. Only 2 free-men admitted within memory."

p. 219.   The Oath of the Sovraigne

These oaths are placed at the end of the original MS. The two first seem of the time of King Charles I.

p. 220.   Arthur Lord Chichester

The original MS. of Sir Faithful Fortescue's account of his renowned uncle, Lord Deputy of Ireland and real founder of Belfast, is preserved amongst the Fortescue family papers at Ravensdale Park, Newry. It was printed for private circulation by the late Lord Clermont in 1858, and does not contain Bodley's anagram of the King of France's letter at the end of the copy in the Town Book. It is impossible to determine at what time this account was inserted by the Town Clerk, but the accompanying history of the Chichester family seems from internal evidence to be either condensed from Lodge's Peerage of Ireland, 1754, or more likely to have been a portion of a MS. pedigree supplied to Lodge, and which he cites.

Some additional information is here added to Fortescue's narrative, which, however, presents a reasonably accurate portrait of this remarkable man. Arthur Chichester was one of that distinguished company of Devonshire squires, including Raleigh, Drake, and Carew, who shed so much lustre on the closing years of Elizabeth's reign. The second son of Sir John Chichester of Raleigh, by Gertrude, daughter of Sir William Courtenay, he was sent at an early age to Oxford, where his tutor was Alexander Spicer, who afterwards wrote an elegy on him. His youthful rashness consisted in robbing one of the Queen's purveyors—little better than robbers themselves—and he fled into France, not Ireland. As a contemporary notes—

"He was a captaine of the shippe called the Victorie under the command of the Lord Sheffield, employed against the Spanish invasion An. 1587 & 88. Afterwards he was captaine and commander in the Portugal voyage of 200 foot in the Regiment of the General Sir Francis Drake, 88 & 89. He went with Sir Francis Drake to the West Indies, and in Porterico he set fire of the Admiral of the Spanish Frigates, 95 and 96."

He went to Ireland in 1599 to revenge the death of his brother, Sir John, who was killed in a conflict with James MacSorley MacDonnell in 1597 at Ballycarry. Lodge's Peerage contains the anecdote, "In K. James's reign, Mac-Donnell going one day to view the family monument in St. Nicholas's Church at Carrickfergus, and seeing Sir John's statue thereon, asked, *How the de'ell he came to get his head again, for he was sure he had ance ta'en it frae him.*" Pinkerton considered this apocryphal, as before James reigned MacDonnell was dead. *(Ulst. Jour. Arch.,* vol. vii.) It was soon recognised that the most capable man in Ireland was Arthur Chichester ; and after his appointment as Lord Deputy in 1604, the State Paper Calendars of the time show clearly the all-important part he played during his 10 years of office—in one dispatch pleading with the King for an opening of the ports in Ireland ; again, settling the details of the Ulster Plantation, which, unfortunately for the real pacification of the country, were departed from by other statesmen. He was anxious to have arranged the settlement, as if His Majesty were to begin a new plantation in America, disregarding unjust demands for vested rights in land, lest, in the words of Lord Keeper Bacon, addressed to Sir W. Jones, Chief Justice of Ireland in 1617, "Ireland civil be worse to us than Ireland savage." In the four volumes of Irish State Papers now preserved in Philadelphia are many documents concerning Chichester. The following abstract, taken from a letter written to him by King James from Newmarket, March 4th, 1613, sufficiently shows the respect in which his long services were held :—"As his Lordship was first called by his (the King's) election to the high place he fills, the duties of which he has so faithfully discharged, that he has continued him in that employment these many years, beyond the example and custom of former times, so he now of his own mere motion, without any mediation of friends, has advanced him to the degree of a Baron of that kingdom, in acknowledgment of his many acceptable services performed. It was a secret purpose of his long before, and he only deferred it for his Lordship's greater honour, that he might take the opportunity of doing so upon the calling of this his first Parliament. For his Lordship's comfort, he is to know that he serves 'a master with a liberal hand, and one that is so well affected to him,' that this is not the last favour which is intended to him." It is interesting to know that as Lord Deputy he assisted the newly-formed East India Company to build vessels in Ireland, and was at the close of his life Commissioner for the settlement of Virginia with Lord Carew. When ambassador to the Palatinate, being besieged in Mannheim by Count Tilly, he informed him that it was against the law of nations to besiege an ambassador. On Tilly sending word that he took no notice of his having this office, he replied, "Had my master sent me with as many hundred men as he hath sent me on fruitless messages, your General should have known that I had been a soldier as well as an ambassador." As early as 1614 his health gave way, for he had not gone on a regimen like his predecessor Mountjoy, of whom Moryson writes, "Before these Wars he used to have nourishing Breakfasts, as Ponadoes and Broths ; but in the time of the War he used commonly to break his Fast with a dry crust of Bread, and in the Spring Time with Butter and Sage, with a cup of Stale Beer, wherewith sometimes in winter he would have Sugar and Nutmeg mixed. He took Tobacco abundantly, and of the best, which I think preserved him from sickness." His disease recurred again, and as Spicer, his domestic chaplain, says in his elegy, printed in 1625, the year of his death—

> "Lord, what is man? when such a man as he,
> Whose parts excelled in the high'st degree,
> Dies by a plurisie, a corrupted tumour,
> Proceeding from a bad, unhealthful humour."

There is a reference to the death of his wife in the Fee book of the famous Irish physician, Dr. Thomas Arthur :—"1621. I then went to the Lady of Arthur Chichester, the Quaestor or Treasurer of this Kingdom, then living at Carrickfergus, in Ulster, whom, when labouring under dropsy, and forewarning her of her death within a few days after my prognosis, I attended upon : he gave me on the 25th of May £5 . 10 . 0." The tomb, which forms one of the full-page illustrations, was erected during his lifetime, and the kneeling figure (p. 224) of Lord Chichester is no doubt an excellent likeness, as well as that of his wife, which is by the same chisel. The material used for the sculpture, including the small figure of Sir John Chichester, is Derbyshire alabaster. The entire has been richly decorated with colour and gilding, and bears a strong resemblance to the coeval tomb of Lord Cork in St. Patrick's, Dublin.

The Editor, with the permission of the Countess of Shaftesbury, has recently made a careful inspection of the Chichester vault at St. Nicholas, Carrickfergus, of which the following are the particulars :—The vault is twenty feet long by fifteen feet wide, the roof forming a semi-circular arch of cut stone six feet high in centre ; a door, now bricked up, formerly opened into the church. It contains ten lead coffins, which are as follows, beginning with the latest :—1. Sir Arthur Chichester, Baronet, aged 80 years, 1847. 2. Elizabeth, relict of Sir Edward May, Bart., died 26th March, 1823, aged 73 years. 3. Sir Edward May, Bart., died 23rd July, 1814, aged 63. 4. A coffin without inscription, but presumably that of Arthur, 4th Earl Donegall, died 1757. 5. John Chichester, died 1746, brother of the ladies burnt in 1708, and father of 5th Earl. 6. Catherine, Dowager Countess Donegall, widow of 3rd Earl. Her coffin has a finely engraved gilt plate, with coat of arms impaling Chichester and Forbes. An outer wood coffin has been covered with crimson velvet and brass escutcheons. 7. A coffin without inscription, but probably that of Arthur, 2nd or 1st Earl. 8. A child's coffin, shaped, with one handle at the head, and in raised letters, "DEC 3. 1642. E.C." Doubtless Edward Chichester, son of 1st Earl Donegall. Spices have been placed in this coffin, which still emit an agreeable odour. 9. A child's coffin similar to above, but with handle at each end, and in raised letters, " D.C. QUI: OBIIT: 8 IAN 1638." No doubt Digby Chichester, another youthful son of 1st Earl. 10. A small child's coffin, very strongly made, with no inscription, but in which rest the remains of the infant son of the great Lord Deputy, in the words of his epitaph—

"Here lyes the Father's hope and Mother's joy,
Though they seem hapless, happie was the boy;
For of his Life the long and tedious race
He hath despatch'd in less than two moneth's space."

It is strange that the coffin of the infant should remain, when those of his mother and his father, the founders of the vault and sumptuous tomb above it, are alike unknown. In addition to the foregoing coffins, there is a rude lead box, about 12 inches square, containing the *viscera* of Arthur Lord Chichester, Baron of Belfast. (This was a customary usage of the time— see Stanley's *Memorials of Westminster Abbey.*) A wooden coffin, much decayed, holds the bones of four adults; two of the skulls have the upper portion above the orbit removed—one rudely, as if by blows of a sword, the other by a saw. The former may be that of Sir John Chichester, the statement of Lodge that his head was cut off by Sorley Boy being thus restored to credence, as this mutilation would agree with the undoubted fact that he was killed by a shot. Tyrone, to whom the head was sent, may have returned it for interment.

The Editor has carefully examined the site of Lord Chichester's splendid house at Joymount (so called in compliment to Lord Mountjoy), which was completed in 1618, and of which some views may be seen in the British Museum. It is said to have been designed by Inigo Jones, and bore resemblance in the details of its projecting windows and sky-line to his work. Brereton describes it, in 1635, as a "very statelye house or rather like a prince's pallace," but says "the windowes and roomes and whole frame of the house is over large and vast." Anxious to find any traces of his being a "Lover of all civill becoming sports games and recreations," the Editor has discovered an interesting fact not hitherto noticed—viz., that when forming the grounds, Lord Chichester, as an old Devonshireman, and perhaps one of the players at the historic game of bowls in which Raleigh and Drake joined on Plymouth Hoe when the Armada was signalled, had laid out a bowling green, now comprised in Mr. W. Gorman's garden. This gentleman says that in the corner of it beside the town wall a great quantity of bones and bullets were lately dug up, whilst many fragments of deers' horns have been found in the present Joymount garden. Further confirmation of his love of bowling is found in a note on John Cusack, Mayor of Dublin, 1608 :—"This Mayor was a great House Keeper, for, in his Mayoraltie, he invited the Lord Deputie sundrie times. He would make Matches of Bowling and Shooting with the Lord Deputie and Councell." No doubt at Chichester House, which occupied the site of the Irish Houses of Parliament, now the Bank of Ireland, many a return match was played. At Belfast Castle a bowling green was also laid out, which is mentioned in the Charges roll 1666, and in a lease to G. Macartney of a tenement near the Castle it is described as extending backwards to the Bowling Green. It may be added that the old Irish Corporations usually reserved the right of the burgesses to use the green when land was let for that purpose. "3 Feb 1670. It. that Wm Hall shall have a lease of the Bowling-green for 31 years at 20s. for the first year, and 40s. for the remainder, he to fit it and build a house at his own charge ; Burgesses to have the keys." (*Town Book of Kinsale.*) Whether the Bowling Green at the rere of the old Belfast Academy was ever used in this way is uncertain, but it probably dates back to the time of Robert Joy, Town Clerk, who built the house.

p. 225. Chichester Earl of Donegal

The Chichester family, from the time that Belfast was incorporated by the foresight of their great ancestor, have exhibited many substantial proofs of their kindly interest in its welfare, some of which are referred to in the present volume. Carrickfergus, although more centrally situated on the estate, was not fostered at the expense of the more inland town. On the contrary, the 1st Earl of Donegall, in founding his mathematical lectureship at Trinity College, Dublin, expressly stipulates for "such as should be brought up in the school at Belfast erected by him." The poor of Belfast were also remembered in the wills of the family, whilst much employment was found at the large farms and gardens kept up during the 17th century. It is evident, from leases of the time, that rents were very moderate. One instance may suffice, taken from an Indenture dated 1688, in which Francis Thetford (see Lewis's pedigree) conveyed to John Fletcher for £300 his lease of six score and five acres, called the "New Inclosure," adjacent to Oldpark and Skegonearl, for which the rent was £16 13s. 8d. As his lease was dated 1686, and he got such a sum for his interest when civil war was raging, the inference is obvious. A few years after this, Cromac Woods were opened up by wide avenues, called Passes, appropriated to the recreation of the townspeople. In the 18th century the Earls of Donegall improved the town in many respects—a great reclamation was made on the site of Ann Street, and on it the first Linen Hall erected by the estate at a cost of £1,500. Other public buildings succeeded, including the Exchange (now Belfast Bank), which cost £4,000, and the Parish Church and Vicarage, erected at the sole expense of Lord Donegall. There is a large aquatint in the possession of Robert Macadam, showing the Assembly Room over the Exchange as a richly decorated apartment, and the architect's name is given—Sir R. Taylor. The Brown Linen Hall was followed by the generous gift of the site for the White Linen Hall granted in 1787. In this year the Sovereign's gold chain, which is now superseded by the new Mayor's chain, was presented to the Corporation, as the following extract sets forth. (It is worthy of note that this minute, which was found on the books of the Corporation by a committee of the new Corporation, of whom R. S. Lepper was secretary, is the only record known to exist of those contained in the second Town Book, all trace of which is lost):—

Borough of Belfast, March 29th, 1787.

At an assembly of the Sovereign and Burgesses, held this day, the Sovereign informed the Burgesses that Lord Donegall had presented a valuable gold chain to the Corporation, most elegantly executed with a medal appendant, on one side of which are the arms of the Lord of the Castle, on the reverse those of the Corporation of Belfast curiously embossed ; and that his Lordship desired that it may be worn by the Sovereign, for the time being, and delivered to the Sovereigns in succession. That they may be invested with it publickly, upon their being sworn into office, as one of the insignia of their being in full possession of their office.—Resolved, that the warmest and most grateful thanks of the Sovereign and Burgesses be presented to the Earl of Donegall for his magnificent present, and that they trust that this badge of office will be a constant momento (*sic*) of the connection which ought ever to subsist between Lord Donegall's family and the Corporation of Belfast.—Resolved, that, agreeable to his Lordship's desire, the gold chain shall be worn by the Sovereign for the time being, and delivered to the Sovereigns in succession, and that they shall be invested with it publickly, on their being sworn into office, as one of the insignia of their being in full possession of their office. (*News-Letter, 23rd December, 1842.*)

Further proof of this kindly interest is found in "The Journal of Disbursements of the Earl of Donegall's Antrim Estate, from July 1786 to October 1796." "November 28th, 1786. Paid John Knox for a gold box intended to be presented to the Lord Lieutenant with the freedom of this Corporation, £25. March 25th, 1787. Paid the Rev. William Bristow ½ year's salary as Sov^n of Belfast due this day, £50. August 15th, 1787. Paid John Galt Smith account of Sovereign's gown, £7 . 12 . 8."

The Parish Church was also liberally supported. William Ware, the organist, who published a collection of church music, dedicated to the Marchioness of Donegall, is thus mentioned. "W. Ware for instructing singing boys, £30, and providing surplices for ditto, £5 . 13 . 9."

The old Poorhouse, with other charities, such as the Fever Hospital, received large sums. At this same period as much as £70,000 was given to improve the Lagan Navigation. (*Joy's MS.*)

The recent munificent gift of the present noble owner of the estate, made on the occasion of the presentation of the memorial casket containing the address presented to her son, the Rt. Hon. the Earl of Shaftesbury, on his attaining his majority, attests sufficiently to the cordial relations still existing between Town and Castle. The accompanying illustration shows this fine example of modern Celtic art, designed by Marcus Ward & Co., and executed by Sharman D. Neill.

p. 228. Ladys Jane, Frances, & Henrietta were unfortunately burnt

Joy's MS. notes. "April 25th 1708, the Castle of Belfast burned down, and the ladies Jane, Frances, and Heneretta lost their lives. This accident was occasioned by a servant, who left a fire of wood burning in a room which she was airing. A servant woman called Catherine Douglas and a daughter of Parson Berkley perished : Mary Taggart, a servant, made her escape thro' the flames." As the Editor was anxious to verify a note given him by Rev. G. Hill, in which he mentioned that portraits damaged by fire of these unfortunate ladies were preserved by Lord Templetown at Castle Upton, and were called "The Burnt Ladies," and as on enquiry at the Castle only one picture answering to the description was pointed out with the title "The Burnt Lady," he wrote to the Viscountess of Templetown asking for further information, and received the following courteous reply :—"As to the portrait of the Burned Lady, so far as Lady Templetown knows it has nothing to do with the Chichesters, with whom the Uptons are not connected, but is supposed to be the portrait of a Miss Upton married to a local chief of the name of Dunn, who is supposed to have burnt her and her children in front of his own house. This tradition is recorded in a Parochial Survey of Ireland in 1816, page 249, volume 2, by W. Shaw Mason, Sec. to the Board of Public Records." Although the Castle was not rebuilt, it was not entirely deserted till the beginning of this century, when it was finally taken down.

The old lady (see note on p. 100) remembers Montgomery's Market filled with ancient pear trees, and several rooms still inhabited in the Burnt Castle, including a fine parlour with black oak floor, wainscotted walls, and huge chimney-piece. This Market was placed in the Castle yard, as it was exempt from interference by the Corporation.

Amongst the charges entered in the Donegall Journal of Disbursements previously mentioned are several relating to the old castle.

3rd October, 1788. Paid John Bell on account for paving round the Castle, the court, &c., } 6 . 2½

31st Oct. 1788. Received for 2 cows & sundry trees in the Castle Gardens sold by Auction on 22nd Aug. last, } 19 . 18 . 2

13th Jan. 1789. Received from sundries for the old walls } 7 . 1 . 2
& the Pigeon House in that part of the late Castle Garden now }
Arthur St.,

9th April, 1789. Paid one year Hearth Money due on the } 1 . 4 . 0
Castle of Belfast, 12 hearths at 2s., the 21st Nov. 1788, }

John Alexander inhabited the Castle in March, 1789, and county cess paid for him amounted to 5 guineas. The office was built in 1787 : Roger Mulholland was the builder. In 1792 the castle gate was repaired, cost 3s. 3d. 12 hearths are charged at the castle and 4 at the office, showing its occupation still continued in this year.

p. 229. List of the Volunteer Companies

The following extract from the Annals of Kinsale *(Town Book of Kinsale)* sufficiently explains the above :—

"Monday, 21 Feb., 1760. Thurot landed about 1,000 men near Carrickfergus, which he attacked and took, with the Castle, after a brave resistance by Lt.-Col. Jennings with 200 men. The Lord-Lieut., the Duke of Bedford, on receiving the news, sent an express to the Governor of Charles Fort and Kinsale, John Folliot, Esq., to despatch the man-of-war then lying at Kinsale in pursuit of the French. On Sunday morning, Feb. 24, Governor Folliot acquainted Capts. Elliot, Clements, and Logie with the Lord-Lieut'.s orders to proceed to sea, and on Feb. 29 his Maj. ships, Elliot, commodore, came up with the Squadron under M. Thurot off the Isle of Man, and after a sharp engagement of an hour-and-half captured them. Underneath is a statement of the respective force :—Bellisle, 44 guns, 510 men ; Le Blonde, 30 do., 357 do. ; Terpsichore, 24 do., 270 do., com^d. by M. Thurot ; Eolus, 32 guns ; Pallas, 36 do.; Brilliant, 36 do., com^d. by Cap. Elliot."

Mr. F. J. Bigger, Ardrie, Belfast, has two large engravings of that period, one showing the engagement, and the other depicting the French ships as prizes in Douglas Harbour. Lord Charlemont has given a graphic description of the mustering of the volunteers in Belfast, many armed only with a Lochaber axe—a scythe fixed at the end of a pole, but all so impressed with the necessity of regularity, that the crowd was perfectly undisturbed by tumult, riot, or even drunkenness. Two of the commanders named in the list for Co. Down merit a short notice as descendants of the famous William, Baron Savage, who settled in Down in 1177. Henry Savage of Saintfield was head of the Prospect branch of the family. He married Grace, grand-daughter of the Hon. Susan Gillespie, wife of Hugh Gillespie, Cherryvale, daughter of 3rd Baron Rollo, and aunt of Sir Robert Rollo Gillespie, K.C.B., whose statue stands in the Square of Comber. Francis Savage of Ardkeen Castle was High Sheriff of Down in 1732, and the most considerable person in the Ards about 1760. For a fuller account see Prof. G. F. Savage-Armstrong's valuable monograph on *The Savages of the Ards.*

p. 232. Burgess Roll

The first names in black letter were probably entered at the incorporation of Borough.

p. 236. vide page 279

This refers, of course, to original MS. See corresponding page 245.

p. 238. Sir Stephen May, 1815

After this entry is written in pencil on the original, "leave a space for more names." As this list of Sovereigns is incorrect towards the end, and some years not filled in, a list is here subjoined of the names from 1800 to 1842, when the old Corporation ceased. 1800, John Brown ; 1801, same ; 1802, Arthur Chichester ; 1803, Edward May, M.P. ; 1804, same ; 1805, same ; 1806, same ; 1807, Rev. Edward May ; 1808, same ; 1809, Edward May, M.P. ; 1810, same ; 1811, Rev. Edward May ; 1812, Thomas Verner ; 1813, same ; 1814, same, 1815, same ; 1816, Rev. Edward May ; 1817, Thomas Ludford Stewart ; 1818, same ; 1819, Thomas Verner ; 1820, same ; 1821, same ; 1822, same ; 1823, John Agnew, resigned, and Andrew Alexander appointed ; 1824, Andrew Alexander died and John Agnew appointed ; 1825, John Agnew ; 1826, same ; 1827, Rev. Lord E. Chichester ; 1828, Sir Stephen May ; 1829, same ; 1830, same ; 1831, same ; 1832, same ; 1833, same ; 1834, John Agnew ; 1835, same ; 1836, same ; 1837, same ; 1838, same ; 1839, same ; 1840, same ; 1841, Thos Verner, Jr.; 1842, same.

The Town Clerks from 1802, when Wm. Atkinson died, were as follows :—1802-1815, William Byrtt; 1816-1823, Stephen Daniel ; 1824-25, none ; 1826-1836, Henry Ferguson ; 1838-1841, H. C. Clarke ; 1842, Messrs. A. & J. Montgomery.

In 1842 the last list of the old Corporation is thus given :—

CORPORATION OF BELFAST.

Lord of the Castle—George Augustus, Marquis of Donegall.
Constable of the Castle—R. F. Gordon.
Sovereign of Belfast—T. Verner, Jun.

Burgesses.

Sir Arthur Chichester.	John Clarke.
Thomas Ludford Stewart.	Rev. A. C. Macartney.
Thomas Verner.	Sir Stephen May.
Earl of Belfast.	Robert Coulson.
Lord E. Chichester.	John Agnew.
Rev. Samuel Smythe.	Jos. Macartney.

Town Clerks—Messrs. A. & J. Montgomery.
Sergeant at Mace—William Trelford.

The following are the Town Clerks of Belfast since 1842 :—John Bates, 1842-1855 ; J. K. Jackson, 1855-1856 ; James Guthrie, 1856-1878 ; Samuel Black, 1878.

p. 239.   Electio Superiorum

This was the official entry of the election of the Sovereigns.   The swearing in, Juratio Superiorium (*sic*), was alone entered by the Town Clerk after 1644.

p. 241.   and yᶜ two Maces

No doubt those still in the possession of the Corporation.   This notice confirms Mr. Day's opinion that the large mace is of the Stuart period.

p. 242.   thirty five Burgesses

These are given by Benn as thirty-five inclusive of Sovereign, whereas by the terms of the Charter (p. 160) they comprised that number in themselves. The omitted name in his list is that of Toul or Tonˡ O'Neil.   As the more important burgesses are mentioned by Benn, it is only necessary to add a short account of the brothers Dobbin supplied by one of the family, Mr. Leonard Dobbin, Hollymount, Cork.   Humphrey and William Dobbin were the sons of Lieut. James Dobbin, of Duneane, whose name appears on the list of those proposed to be removed to Munster by Cromwell.   He was one of the Carrickfergus Dobbyns who are first mentioned in 1400.   The token of Humphrey Dobbin was issued when he was twenty, and he died 1721.   His son Rigby was Mayor of Carrickfergus, 1724.   William Dobbin was a captain in the siege of Derry, which he assisted to defend, and afterwards resided at Moneyglass. His wife was Mary Eccles.   His daughter married William Morris Jones, Moneyglass.

p. 243.   Kinge William Landed

Several contemporary views exist of this momentous event, and it has also been described by Storey and others (see *Ulst. Jour. Arch. passim*).   The troops landed at Whitehouse, and it has never been explained why the King preferred Carrickfergus, where he only stayed half-an-hour, probably visiting Mountjoy.   He met Schonberg's coach-and-six at Whitehouse, and drove across the Strand to the North Gate.   His Court was held at the Castle, then in possession of Sir W. Franklyn.   Bonivert, a French refugee in the King's service, notes—"We landed at the Whitehouse (five days after the King), where we saw on our arrival a great number of poor people, we went that night to Belfast, which is a large and pretty town ; and all along the road 'you see an arm of the sea on your left, and on the right great high rocky mountains whose tops are often hidden by the clouds, and at the bottom a very pleasant wood, very full of simples of all sorts—The people very civill, and there is also a great house belonging to my Lord Donegall, with very fine gardens and groves of ash trees. The inhabitants speak very good English." There was great mortality in the town from the overcrowded Hospital provided by Thomas Pottinger, and filled with Schonberg's fever-stricken soldiers. Both Shankill and the High St. graveyard were crowded, whilst those dying in the ships were buried at Tillysburn. It is interesting to note that a printing press accompanied the King ; a proclamation issued from it was the first printing in Belfast. The first dated example seems to be, strangely enough, A Coronation Sermon on William and Mary, preached at Dartmouth by Rev. John Flavel, printed by Patrick Neil & Company, Belfast, 1700 ; a copy of it is in the Editor's possession.

In the British Museum an unpublished diary of Lt. Wm. Cramond's is preserved. He went through the Irish Campaign of 1690, and does not mention Belfast at all, although it is difficult to know how he kept out of it in his itinerary. "On 20th April went to Galgorm (coming from the North), 21st to Carrickfergus, 22nd to Newtowne, 25th to Lisburn, 26th to Gilhall, 28th to Newry and part of the way back to Gilhall, 29th to Legacurry, 30th to Dundalk."

p. 246. The Roll of the Freemen

This is particularly valuable as forming a kind of directory for the town at periods where no other information is available. In later times subscribers' lists in Belfast printed books are of importance as a means of determining names and addresses. One of the earliest is to be found in " Dialogues on Education, H. & R. Joy, 1753." From the mention of merchants of the staple it is evident a Guild of Merchants existed in connection with the Corporation. All trading towns of any importance had such bodies. In Stirling a Merchant or Guildry Charter was granted by David II. "We grant also to our said burgesses of Strivelyn that they shall have a merchant guild, except the waulkners and weavers." These latter, with the hammermen, tailors, shoemakers, fleshers, tanners, and bakers constituted in Stirling the incorporated crafts ; outside these was the " Hail Omnigatherum" of callings such as dairymen and porters. Carrickfergus had a guild called free merchants of the staple, no others being allowed to buy or sell under a penalty. The Mayor of the Corporation on retiring was appointed next year " Mayor of the Staple." The staple merchandise of England included wool, wool fells, leather, lead, tin, butter, cheese, and cloth. The guild consisted of a body of persons bound together by laws of their own making, the King's licence being first had to the making thereof. They had thus facilities for collecting accounts and exclusive dealing much like some of the present associations of traders.

All irregularity of dates in the original roll, arising from later lists being carelessly entered by the town clerk, have been preserved. The following notes on some of the freemen are of necessity much abridged :—

P. 247. **John Goye, Joyner.** Some of the oak furniture made by local joiners of the 17th century is occasionally met with. A strong framed press in two heights, for many years in the family of Mr. T. Huston, Ashley, Carnmoney, has on the frieze · JOHN · CLOSH · P · C · 1686 · the letters P. C. = Parish of Carnmoney. Another specimen seen by the Editor had inlaid in holly, BELFAST · 1688. P. 248. **Sir William Wray** married a daughter of Lord Edward Chichester. **Danyell mcNeale** was Daniel O'Neill, son of the unfortunate Con O'Neill of Castlereagh. Born about 1603, he became a protégé of Charles I. Both Laud and Wentworth esteemed him. Charles II. bestowed on him several posts, including that of Postmaster-General. His wife was Countess of Chesterfield. In 1844, a labourer dug up in the fosse of Castlereagh 150 shillings and six-pences of Edward VI. and Elizabeth in a pewter vessel. P. 248. **Sir Charles Coote**, with the other officers, commanded the detachment mentioned on p. 306. He was killed in 1642. His son Charles was created Lord Mountrath. **Theobald Taaffe** became 2nd Viscount Taaffe and 1st Earl Carlingford. There were two **Sir James Dillons** in 1640. P. 253. **George M'Cartney**, called Niger, married the daughter of Quintin Catherwood ; his second wife was Elizabeth Dobbin. His descendant, Earl Macartney, in a MS. pedigree corrected *suâ manu* passes over his position as leading merchant, shipowner, and miller. Portraits of four Georges, commencing with his son, M.P. 1693, are in possession of Dr. H. Hyndman. P. 254. **Robert Brice** Clerk, perhaps grandson of Rev. Edward Brice (first Presbyterian minister in Ireland), of Broadisland. The Editor has a token, found in High Street, of his son Robert, of Castle Chichester, 1671. P. 259. **Gilbert Wye** was steward when **Andrew M'Cullough** made a mustard-pot and silver buckles for Earl Donegall, 1666. P. 261. **William Van Hovan** was

Z

perhaps brought from Holland to lay out the Castle Gardens in the Dutch style. P. 262. **Thomas Pottinger**, ancestor of the family once resident at Mount Pottinger, now represented by Sir Henry Pottinger, Bart. P. 264. **Samuel Downes** was Town Clerk, 1667, perhaps son of Ludovicus Downes, Vicar, 1642. P. 266. **William Tomson Gray** merc⁺· Mr. Hugh M'Call, Lisburn, kindly informs Editor "that the Gray merchant purchased in dull seasons from the Drapers gray or unbleached linen, stored it up, and did large business with bleachers, although not employing weavers, as the Drapers did." In Elizabeth's time they were accused of selling arms, purchased from the soldiers, to the Irish, giving 12d. per lb. for powder, and getting 3s. P. 267. **John Charnley ffeltmaker**, synonymous with hatter; rabbits' skins were the raw material. P. 267. **Monsieur Daniel Mascon.** Probably a wine merchant from Bordeaux, which had much trade here. P. 268. **Sir Hercules Langford.** He is described as of Belfast. Hercules Street was named after him. Married daughter of Henry Upton, sister to Arthur Upton here mentioned. **John Chichester** was a nephew of 1st Earl Donegall; died in William's camp, Dundalk, 1689. **Sir Arthur Chichester** became 2nd Earl Donegall. **John** and **Arthur Chichester** were nephews of 1st Earl. **Conway Hill** was son of Arthur Hill, P. C. Constable of Hillsborough Fort, son of Moyses Hill. P. 269. **Chichester Phillips** was son of Sir Thomas, called by Lord A. Chichester a "discreet and honest servitor." P. 270. **Sir Michael Hicks**, Secretary to 1st Earl Salisbury, ancestor to Sir Michael Hicks-Beach. **Claudius Gilbert**, Vicar, died 1696. For his connection with a ghost story, see *Ulst. Jour. Arch.* iii. P. 271. **Hans Hamilton** was nephew of 1st Viscount Clannaboye. **Dudley Loftus** was Clerk to Lord Mount Alexander, and son of Dr. Dudley Loftus, Vicar-General, whose life has been written by Rev. Dr. Stokes, T.C.D. **Henry, Earl of Clanbrazill**, was 2nd Earl, known as the fat Earl. **William Hill** was son and heir of Arthur Hill (see above). **John, Lord Butler**, 7th son of Great Duke of Ormond, as Earl of Gowran, married Ann, daughter of 1st Earl Donegall. **Charles Meredith**, of Mooretown, married daughter of 2nd Lord Blayney. **Richard, Earl of Arran**, was fifth son of Duke of Ormond; had a lease of the light-house on Island Magee, 1667. **Pierce** was 6th Baron Cahier [Cahir], Tipperary. **Major Samuel Stewart** was lieutenant of Col. Cromwell's troop at Lord Montgomery's funeral in 1663. **Richard Needham** was owner of estates at Newry inherited from Sir Henry Bagnall. The foregoing party were no doubt guests of Earl Donegall. P. 273. **Thomas, Earle of Ardglas**, 1st Earl. James I. granted him Manor of Downpatrick, 1617. **Richard Dobbs'** *Brief Description of the County of Antrim*, 1683, was first printed in Hill's *MacDonnells of Antrim.* Arthur his son was Surveyor-General of Ireland, and on finishing the New Houses of Parliament in 1741 received £250. His descendants still occupy Castle Dobbs. **Edward Muschamp** was of Drumanakelly, Co. Down. **Sir John Rowley** married daughter of Sir Hercules Langford. **Tristram Beresford** had estates at Coleraine. P. 278. **Viscount Ranelagh** was uncle of 2nd Earl Donegall. **Francis, Lord Aungier**, created Viscount Longford, married Anne, daughter of 1st Earl Donegall. **John, Lord Massereene**, as Sir J. Skeffington, married daughter of Sir J. Clotworthy, 1st Lord. The **Joneses**, father and son, were of Osberstown, Meath. **Sir W. Flower's** descendants were ennobled as Viscounts Ashburn. **Sir Francis Blundell** had killed Viscount Taragh on previous 6th July, but received a pardon. P. 282. **Hugh M°Gill**, son of Rev. David Magill, Curate of Greyabbey. The two **St. Georges** were sons of Sir Oliver St. George, Carrick-Drumrusk, Leitrim. P. 283. **Pawlett Phillips** was a brother of Chichester Phillips (see above). **Edward Brice** was a grandson of Rev. E. Brice, Broadisland. A set of silver communion cups was given by him to Ballycarry congregation; they have the Dublin hall mark of 1680. P. 284. **Hugh Montgomery** was of Ballylesson; married widow of 4th Lord Blaney; was Colonel of a regiment routed at Clady Ford by King James, 1689. P. 286. The following names, omitted by a clerical error, should precede 1723:—Wᵐ Scott gener¹ 22 August 1688. Laurance gener¹ 22 August 1688. Wᵐ Leakes march¹ 22 August 1688. Henry Savage march¹ 22 Sepᵗ 1688, made freemen. P. 289. **Joseph Hall**, bellfounder. In 1624 Frederick Rotten was admitted a freeman of Carrickfergus on condition "that he shall cast the first Bell which the town shall have occasion to use. The Town finding and providing the metal wood and fewell." (*Carrickfergus Records MSS.*) P. 292. **William Mankin**, silversmith. Perhaps the silver mounts of "The Psalms, Belfast, 1700" (Gordon's *Historic Memorials of the First Presbyterian Church of Belfast*), were his work; also a silver punch ladle, embossed with vine leaves, without hall mark, for many years in the family of Dr. J. Milford Barnett. P. 292. **Lord Conway** was the nobleman whose huntsman at Portmore, John Stringer, composed "The Experienced Huntsman" (Belfast: James Blow, 1714), the first work of a secular kind printed here. Only one copy of the 2nd edition, 1717, is known to exist. P. 293. **Collyer & Company.** Mount Collyer was named after the family. At the recent demolition of this house and the adjacent Jennymount, Roman objects were discovered in the foundations—at the former a classic head of purple Egyptian porphyry, at the latter a bronze medal of Nero. P. 296. **Lord George Sacville.** This admission of freemen was warmly challenged at the time. **Stewart Banks** was the recipient of a large silver bowl from the weavers of Belfast in 1756. It bears the Dublin hall mark, and is in the possession of his descendant, J. W. E. Macartney, D.L., Clogher Park. P. 298. **Willes Earl of Hillsborough** was created Marquis of Downshire, 1789. He was Secretary of State for the American Department; and the library at Hillsborough Castle contains a number of valuable MSS. relative to his office. P. 300. **Mr. David Manson**, author of English Dictionary (Belfast: Daniel Blow, 1762). In the preface he describes his remarkable system of education which was carried on successfully for many years in Donegall Street. To his ingenuity the cotton manufacture and agriculture owed several improvements. He died at Lilliput, where he had a bowling-green for his pupils' use. (*Dr. Bryce's MS.*) His portrait in oils is in the Royal Academical Institution.

p. 300. A Perspective View of Belfast in 1790

Mrs. T. L'Estrange has kindly allowed this interesting drawing by Mary Patterson to be reproduced here. The Mall which extended from the Paper Mill to the White Linen Hall is partly shown on the map of 1788 in the present volume. It formed the fashionable country promenade at this period. In the Donegall Journal of Disbursements already quoted are the following notices of it in 1788 :—"John Alexander gave his account of making Ditches subdividing the Fields in the Mall—late Mrs. Clarkes, 15 . 16 . 6. Paid John McGain & Partner watching the trees in & near the Mall to prevent their being topped for May-bushes, 2 . 8½." There are two probably unique unfinished proofs of views of Belfast, without title, or painter or engraver's name, in the King's Library, British Museum. They both show the town about 1790 from Co. Down side, and measure 20 inches by 15. At this time "there was in Belfast by calculation, 7 Inhabitants worth £30,000 ; 5 worth from 20 to 29,000 ; 9 worth from 15 to 19,000 ; 14 worth from 10 to 14,000 ; 49 worth from 5 to 9,000." (*Joy's MS.*)

Several art industries were carried on at this period, of which unfortunately very few specimens are now extant. This is particularly the case with respect to the manufacture of fine pottery and faience, which was established in Bally-macarrett by Thomas Greg, John Ashmore, and S. M. Stephenson, M.D. Some pieces of this ware in the form of sauce-boats and quaint jelly-moulds, in the possession of Mrs. T. L'Estrange, show that an imitation of Wedgwood's Queen's ware was aimed at. The glaze used is cream coloured, and the modelling very well done. Volunteer jugs and teapots of Wedgwood's manufacture, which are reputed to be of Belfast make, may yet be seen amongst old family collections of china. Probably the ware was brought over in the "biscuit" state, and the transfer printing put on and burnt in here. The art of glass-making, engraving, and cutting was successfully worked for some years in Ballymacarrett by Edwards and others ; their flint table-glass can be recognised by a peculiar milky opalescence. Notices of employment for glass-cutters occur in old *News-Letters.* The Editor has a well-designed vase in the shape of a classic urn, with cover, cleverly engraved and cut, which shows the perfection attained in this beautiful art. Great skill and taste are also displayed in the contemporary cabinet work executed by John Getty. Some of his inlaid mahogany bookcases, exhibiting the influence of Sheraton, are occasionally met with. His successor, Sloan, although a good workman, yielded to the prevalent taste of the Regency, and inlaying was given up altogether.

For many years after this date the town made but slow progress. The rebuilding of Mulholland's Mill in 1830, and the change from cotton to flax-spinning consequent thereon, may be considered the starting-point of the unexampled development of Belfast from that time. This historic building is shown in the annexed illustration.

As so little is known of our earlier local artists, the Editor has added the following note on the three whose work adorns these pages—viz., Thomas Robinson, painter ; John Thomson, engraver ; and Patrick MacDowell, sculptor. Probably the first notice of the Belfast artists collectively was written by the Editor for the catalogue of the Loan Collection of Works of Art exhibited at the opening of the Belfast Free Library, 1888. In it Thomas Robinson is thus mentioned—"In 1801, Thomas Robinson, a pupil of Romney, settled in Belfast, where he lived till 1808. He was patronised by Dr. Percy, Bishop of Dromore, and painted several of the portraits exhibited.

His finest work, 'The Review of the Volunteers,' or, as it is called in Red-grave's Dictionary, ' Military Procession at Belfast in Honour of Lord Nelson,' is hung in the centre of Room B, and is the most valuable local painting extant, giving portraits of all the prominent citizens at the time, 1804. Thomas Robinson was President of the Society of Artists, Dublin, and died there, 1810." A letter of his, asking for the loan of Boydell's Prints, is given in Anderson's *History of Linen Hall Library.* His son, Dr. T. Romney Robinson, for many years Astronomer at Armagh Observatory, was the author of a volume of poems much praised at the time, although he tried to suppress them afterwards. His likeness by his father on the frontispiece resembles his portrait in the "Review." It was found impracticable to reproduce this fine painting, as the surface is much cracked and the colouring very dark. The Key, which has been substituted for it, is executed in brown ink, and gives the various portraits with all the force of the original, omitting alone the fantastic back-ground—added by the painter, it is said, through chagrin, when the lottery scheme for the disposal of the picture failed.

In this connection an unpublished letter of the artist is given from the original, bound up with a copy of "Juvenile Poems, by Thomas Romney Robinson, London, 1807," in the possession of the Editor.

"Madam, so long a space of time has intervened since I left London that it is probable you may not recollect me : but I shall ever remember with gratitude the attention and kindness I experienced from your good Father, of whome (so many changes have taken place among my Friends in the course of thirteen years,) I am almost afraid to enquire. If as I hope he is still alive, he will feel pleasure to learn that I have a son whose extraordinary poetical talents (which appeared at a very early age) have attracted the notice of the literati of almost every part of Europe ; so much so, that I have consented to publish his Poems as you will see by the enclosed proposals. In this kingdom the proposals have met with un-precedented encouragement, and are patronised by persons of the first consideration. May I request that Mr. White will have the goodness to mention his name amongst the gentlemen who receive subscriptions. I could give you a wonderful account of the amazing Talents of my young Poet, which have been evinced not only in Poetry but in other branches of literature, but you may perhaps conceive the praise of a fond father but a small recommendation, however reference may be had to the Countess of Moira Hastings &c Dr. Percy Bishop of Dromore, William Hayley Esq. Chichester, Professor Stewart or Dr. Anderson Edinburgh. As a tribute due to your own taste for Poetry as well as that of your Brother Mr. T. H. White (to whome and Mr. Harry I beg to be remembered) I have requested the Honble Mrs. Murray Aust to leave with you one of his productions which you will have the goodness to return to her after you have read it, in order that it may be forwarded to my friend Mr. Hayley for whome I have painted a Picture of my Boy strewing Flowers on the tomb of my late Master Mr. Romney : an engraving of which picture, with an Elegy on Mr. Romney's death by my son, you will shortly see in the life of that great Artist, which Mr. Hayley is preparing for the press. With best wishes to you and all your good family, I remain, Madam, your most obedient humble servant, "Thomas Robinson. "Belfast, No. 30, Castle Street, "Sepr. 13, 1805."

John Thomson was not the introducer of engraving here, as in 1753 a copperplate press was set up, and Daniel Pomareda came to the town soon afterwards, when an elaborate book plate for the Belfast Library, 1765, was exe-cuted probably by him. In Mr. Lavens M. Ewart's large collection of Belfast printed books is a volume of poems by M'Williams, with rude etchings, dated 1795. A portrait of Amyas Griffith, by J. Wilson, the Belfast artist, and one or two frontispieces in local books, may also be mentioned. However, such was the difficulty of getting engravings done here so late as 1794, that the United Irishmen had to procure their badge or ticket from Dublin. It was not till the settlement of Thomson that the art was permanently established. Born at Arbroath, he came to Ireland in 1798 as a Tay Fencible, and was first quartered at Ballymena. He there met a soldier, formerly a stamper of the gold embossing seals used by the Linen Board in Dublin, and was led by his advice to commence business in Ann Street as a cutter of these seals. To this was soon added regular engraving, such as book plates, frontispieces, and cards, with some heraldic silver work for the Donegall family and others. In 1805 the caricatures of the famous "Castlereagh" election were produced by him. His attention was also directed to colour printing for bank-notes and cheques. A specimen still preserved shows he had anticipated modern in-vention in this respect. He undertook the series of beautiful plates for A. Mackay, Jun., illustrating Benn's first *Historical Account of Belfast,* 1823. A number of the original copper plates are again used in this work by the kindness of Mr. James Graham, his last surviving pupil, who has successfully carried on the same business till the present time. Amongst these are several which for some reason were never published. Thomson himself was noted for his tasteful ornamental lettering, of which the title-page of the foregoing work is a good example. He also executed a set of copies for the clever writing-master, Thomas Spence. Probably his largest plate is that of which a reduction is here given. It represents a well-known character of old Belfast, *Tantra Barbus*, whose favourite haunt was the Long Bridge, from which he would jump into the Lagan for a "fipenny." Another scarce engraving by him depicts "Cocky Bendy," a bow-legged fiddler. About 1825 Thomson had accumulated a large fortune, which, in an evil hour, he invested in the business of the Oldpark Print Works. The concern, from bad management, soon collapsed, depriving him of all his savings. Undaunted by the disaster, he worked on for many years in his house at the corner of Castle Street and Fountain Street, where he died at Easter, 1847.

**A CELEBRATED
ITINERANT HARDWARE MERCHANT**
of the North of Ireland

Patrick MacDowell was born in Belfast, August, 1799, son of a small tradesman, who lost all his money in a building speculation. His schoolmaster had been an engraver, and encouraged him to draw. Apprenticed to a coach-maker in London, at the end of four years he became the pupil of Peter Chenu, the sculptor, and exhibited a bust in the Royal Academy, 1822. Entering the Academy Schools, he quickly gained a leading position, mainly by the good offices of Sir James Emerson Tennent, who procured for him, amongst others, commissions from Lord Dungannon, R. M'Calmont, and R. Davison. He was elected R.A. in 1846, in which year was completed his noteworthy statue of Viscount Exmouth at Greenwich. In 1856 the fine bronze figure of Frederick Richard, Earl of Belfast (now in the Free Library), was executed. He continued to exhibit at the Royal Academy up to 1869, when he completed his magnificent group of Europe for the Albert Memorial, and died on December 9th, 1870. His noblest work, not even excepting the "Europe," is the exquisite marble group of the Earl of Belfast and his mother in the Memorial Chapel, Belfast Castle. The reproduction, from the fine photograph by W. Swanston, F.G.S., gives its general appearance, but the delicacy of execution can only be appreciated by seeing the original monument, which is most fittingly placed in the midst of the appropriate and richly designed adornments, by which his sister, the present Countess of Shaftesbury, has converted "the Chapel of the Resurrection" into one of the most beautiful ecclesiastical edifices in this country. The inscription on the tomb is as follows :—"Sacred to the Memory of Harriet Anne, wife of George Hamilton, Third Marquis of Donegall, and Daughter of Richard, first Earl of Glengall. Born 3rd January, 1799. Died 14th September, 1860. And Frederick Richard, Earl of Belfast. Their son. Born 25th November, 1827. Died 15th February, 1853."

CHARLES C. CONNOR, Esq., M.A.,
Mayor of Belfast, 1889-90-91.

LIST OF SUBSCRIBERS.

Allen, Robert H., Mus. Bac.,
    College Green, Belfast.
Allen, Robert,
    Old Lodge Road, Belfast.
Allen, Samuel, LL.D.,
    Lisconnan, Dervock.
Allworthy, Edward,
    Royal Avenue, Belfast.
Anderson, John, J.P.,
    Hillbrook, Holywood.
Andrews, George,
    Ardoyne, Belfast.
Andrews, Samuel, J.P.,
    Belfast.
Armstrong, James Moore,
    Craigvarra, Portrush.
Armstrong, W. E.,
    Victoria Street, Belfast.
Armstrong, G. F. Savage, M.A.,
    Sydenham Villas, Bray.
Arnold, Edgar,
    Marino, Co. Down.
Arnold, Rev. R. J., M.A.,
    The Manse, Dunmurry.
Bagwell, R., M.A., D.L., J.P,
    Marlfield, Clonmel.
Barbour, J. M.,
    Hilden, Lisburn.
Barbour, John,
    Marlborough Park.
Barnett, J. Milford, M.D., H.M.I.A.,
    Elmwood Avenue, Belfast.
Barr, James,
    Beechleigh, Windsor Park, Belfast.
Barry, J. B.,
    Donegall Square West, Belfast.
Beck, Fred. E., F.R.C.P.,
    Fitzroy House, Botanic Ave., Belfast.
Beers, J. Leslie, J.P.,
    Leslie Hill, Co. Donegal.
Begley, G. R.,
    Wolfhill Lodge, Belfast.
Belfast City Council,
    Belfast.
Bell, Thomas,
    Linen Hall, Belfast.
Belmore, Rt. Hon. Earl of, G.C.M.G.,
    Castlecoole, Enniskillen.
Beverland, Robert,
    North Street, Belfast.
Bigger, Francis J.,
    Royal Avenue, Belfast
Bigger, W. J., D.L., J.P.,
    Londonderry.
Blackwood, J. Taylor,
    Ulster Bank, Belfast.
Blow, James,
    Mountpleasant, Belfast.
Bole, William, M.A.,
    Granville Villas, Belfast.
Boston Public Library,
    Boston, U.S.A.
Boyd, John,
    Corporation Street, Belfast.

Brett, Charles H.,
    Chichester Street, Belfast.
Brett, John H.,
    Court House, Belfast.
Bristow, Rev. John, M.A.,
    St. James' Parsonage, Cliftonville.
Brown, G. H.,
    Bedford Street, Belfast.
Browne, John, J.P.,
    Ravenhill, Belfast.
Browne, Samuel, R.N., J.P. (the late)
    Lindisferne, Strandtown.
Brown, Thomas,
    Donegall Street, Belfast.
Byers, John,
    Franklin Street, New York.
Byers, Mrs.,
    Victoria College, Belfast.
Cairns, William,
    Glenview, Ligoniel, Belfast.
Campbell, John,
    Rathfern, Whiteabbey.
Carr, James,
    Rathowen, Belfast.
Caruthers, Miss,
    Claremont Street, Belfast.
Cinnamond, Arthur,
    Linenhall Street, Belfast.
Coey, Edward, J.P.,
    Merville, Belfast.
Connor, Charles C., M.A.,
    Mayor of Belfast.
Corporation of London,
    Guildhall, E.C.
Corry, Robert W., J.P.,
    Benvue, Windsor, Belfast.
Corry, T. C. S., M.D.,
    Ormeau Road, Belfast.
Cramsie, John,
    Lisavon, Strandtown.
Crawford, William,
    Mount Randal, Belfast.
Crone, Dr.,
    Kensal Lodge, Kensal Green, London, W.
Curley, Francis,
    High Street, Belfast.
Davidson, S. C.,
    Sirocco Works, Belfast.
Davies, John H.,
    Glenmore Cottage, Lisburn.
Day, Robert, J.P., F.S.A., M.R.I.A.,
    Sidney Place, Cork.
Deramore, Lord (the late),
    Grosvenor Place, London, S.W.
Dick, John C., M.A.,
    Londonderry.
Dickey, E. O'Rorke,
    Donegall Street, Belfast.
Dill, R. F., M.D.,
    Fisherwick Place, Belfast.
Dobbin, Leonard,
    Hollymount, Lee Road, Cork.
Dobbs, Conway E.,
    Dalguise, Monkstown, Co. Dublin.

Douglas, John,
  Donegall Street, Belfast.
Down and Connor and Dromore, His
  Lordship the Bishop of, President
  R.I.A.
  Conway House, Dunmurry.
Drew, Thomas, R.H.A.,
  Clare Street, Dublin.
Duffin, Adam, B.L., LL.D.,
  Waring Street, Belfast.
Dunlop, George,
  Castlereagh Avenue, Belfast.
Dunlop, Robert,
  Chichester Park, Belfast.
Dunlop, James,
  Cambridge Terrace, Belfast.
Edgar, John C.,
  Faulkner Street, Manchester.
Erne, Rt. Hon. the Earl of,
  Crom Castle, Enniskillen.
Ewart, James M.,
  New York.
Ewart, Lavens M., J.P., M.R.I.A.,
  Glenbank House, Ballysillan.
Ewart, Richard Hooker,
  New York.
Ewart, Sir William Q., Bart.,
  Schomberg, Strandtown.
Ferrar, A. M.,
  Torwood, Windsor Avenue, Belfast.
Ferrar, W. A.,
  Osborne Park, Belfast.
Fitchie, James,
  Wellington Place, Belfast.
Filgate, L. G., D.L.,
  Checker Hill, Killagan, Co. Antrim.
Finlay, W. Laird, J.P.,
  Windsor Avenue, Belfast.
Fitzgerald, Maurice F., B.A., C.E.,
  Botanic Avenue.
Gaffikin, William,
  Sandymount.
Gant, S. E.,
  Royal Avenue, Belfast.
Garrett, Mrs. Thomas,
  Wynnstay Gardens, Kensington, W.
Garstin, John Ribton, D.L., M.R.I.A.,
  Bryanstown, Castlebellingham.
Gibson, Andrew,
  Cliftonville Avenue, Belfast.
Gifford, J. G.,
  Loughview, Holywood.
Glendinning, R. G.,
  Wellington Park, Belfast.
Glover, G. T.,
  Hoylake, Cheshire.
Gowan, S. H.,
  Corporation Street, Belfast.
Graham, H. H.,
  Clonlea, Belfast.
Grattan, The Misses,
  Coolgreany, Fortwilliam Park, Belfast.
Gregg, R. P.,
  Coles Park, Buntingford, Herts.
Grogan, Miss Emily,
  College Gardens, Belfast.
Hanna, John,
  Lisanore Villa, Antrim Road.
Hanna, John A.,
  Ann Street, Belfast.
Hanna, John A.,
  Bank Buildings, Belfast.

Hanna, W. W.,
  North Front Street, Philadelphia.
Harbison, M.,
  Ravenhill Terrace, Belfast.
Hardy, Thomas Lee,
  Carramore, Helen's Bay.
Harland, Sir E. J., Bart., M.P.,
  Kensington Palace Gardens, W.
Haslett, Sir J. H., J.P.,
  Princess Gardens, Belfast.
Head, J. Merrick,
  Reigate, Surrey.
Hems, Harry,
  Fair Park, Exeter.
Henderson, James, A.M.,
  Donegall Street, Belfast.
Henry, W. Tennant, C.E., J.P.,
  Hillsborough, Co. Down.
Heyn, James A. M.,
  Ulster Chambers, Belfast.
Heyn, F. L.,
  Ulster Chambers, Belfast.
Hill, Rt. Hon. Lord A., M.P.,
  Hillsborough Castle.
Hodges & Figgis,
  Grafton Street, Dublin.
Hogg, John,
  Academy Street, Belfast.
Hogg, William,
  Beaconsfield Terrace, Belfast.
Houston, J. Blakiston, V.L., J.P.,
  Orangefield, Belfast.
Howden, Charles,
  Invermore, Larne.
Hughes, Edwin, B.A.,
  Lombard Street, Belfast.
Hunter, S. C.,
  Waring Street, Belfast.
Inglis, James, J.P.,
  Eliza Street, Belfast.
Jaffé, Alfred, J.P.,
  Cloona, Dunmurry.
Jaffé, Otto,
  Kinedar, Strandtown.
Johns, Alexander, J.P. (the late),
  Belfast Bank, Belfast.
Johnston, James,
  Seaview, Belfast.
Johnston, W. J., J.P.,
  Dunesk, Belfast.
Johnston, Robert,
  Hughenden Avenue, Belfast.
Johnstone, S. A., J.P.,
  Dalriada, Whiteabbey.
Kennedy, William,
  Kenbella House, Belfast.
Kerr, Samuel P.,
  Seafield, Sydenham.
Kertland, E. H.,
  12, Bedford Street, Belfast.
Kinghan, S., J.P.,
  Glenghanna, Co. Down.
Knowles, W. J., M.R.I.A.,
  Flixton Place, Ballymena.
Kyle, R. A.,
  Donegall Place, Belfast.
Latimer, Rev. W. T., B.A.,
  The Manse, Eglish, Dungannon.
La Touche, J. J., LL.D.,
  Upper Ely Place, Dublin.
Leathem, John G.,
  Northern Bank, Belfast.

Lepper, Alfred J. A., J.P.,
Rhanbuoy, Carrickfergus.
Lepper, F. R.,
Ulster Bank, Belfast.
Lett, Rev. H. W., M.A.,
Aghaderry Glebe, Loughbrickland.
Lewis, Miss,
Nettlefield, Belfast.
Lindsay, David,
Ashburn, Strandtown.
Linen Hall Library,
Belfast.
Liverpool Free Public Library,
Liverpool.
Lowenthal, J.,
Linenhall Street, Belfast.
Lowry, R. W., J.P.,
Pomeroy House, Pomeroy.
Lowson, J. W. B.,
Royal Avenue, Belfast.
Lyons, W. H. H.,
University Square, Belfast.
M'Bretney, W. A. J.,
Haypark Avenue.
M'Caig, G. P.,
Ballysillan, Belfast.
M'Cance, Henry Jones, D.L.,
Larkfield, Dunmurry.
M'Carte, James,
St. George's Hill, Everton, Liverpool.
M'Connell, J. & J., Ltd.,
Tomb Street, Belfast.
M'Cormick, H. M'Neil,
Court House, Belfast.
M'Crea, B.,
Upper Crescent, Belfast.
M'Culloch, James,
Blessington Road, Lee, Kent.
M'Ferran, John,
Barnagheea, Fortwilliam, Belfast.
M'Gee, James,
Holywood.
M'Ilwaine, J. H.,
Queen's Road, Belfast.
M'Kelvey & M'Combe,
Royal Avenue, Belfast.
M'Loughlin, John, J.P.,
Cart Hall, Coleraine.
Macartney, W. E., M.P.,
Clogher Park, Co. Tyrone.
Macauley, John, D.L.,
Red Hall, Ballycarry.
Macauley, A. T.,
Queen's Elms, Belfast.
MacIvor, James,
King's Inns, Dublin.
Macnaughton, J. A.,
Potterswalls, Antrim.
Macnaghten, Rt. Hon. Lord,
Queen's Gate, London.
Macrory, Edmund,
Fig Tree Court, Temple, E.C.
MacTear, Miss,
Ardgreenan, Cave Hill Road, Belfast.
Maguire, Andrew,
North Street, Belfast.
Malcolm, Mrs. J.,
Hughenden Terrace, Belfast.
Malcolm, Bowman,
Richmond, Antrim Road, Belfast.
Malone, John,
Bedford Street, Belfast.

Marsh, John, (the late)
Glenlyon, Holywood.
Matier, Henry, J.P. (the late),
Dunlambert, Belfast.
Meissner, A. L., Ph.D.,
Librarian, Queen's College, Belfast.
Milligan, S. F., M.R.I.A.,
Royal Terrace, Belfast.
Mitchell, W. C., J.P.,
Tomb Street, Belfast.
Mohan, John,
Wellington Place, Belfast.
Monypenny, F. W.,
Templemore Avenue, Belfast.
Montgomery, John,
Ligoniel House, Belfast.
Montgomery, Johnston,
Royal Avenue, Belfast.
Montgomery, W.,
Royal Avenue, Belfast.
Moran, John, A.M., LL.D.,
Trim.
Morrison, Hugh,
Ligoniel.
Mullan, William, & Son,
Donegall Place, Belfast.
Musgrave, James, J.P.,
Drumglass House, Belfast.
Neill, Sharman D.,
Donegall Place, Belfast.
Nettleton, W. J.,
Wellington Place, Belfast.
Newett, B. J.,
Mount Lyons, Belfast.
Newman, S. A.,
Bridge Street, Walsall.
O'Neill, Lord,
Shane's Castle.
O'Hay, James J.,
Ligoniel, Belfast.
O'Laverty, Rev. Jas., P.P., M.R.I.A.,
Holywood.
O'Neill, Rev. James, M.A.,
College Square East, Belfast.
O'Neill, William J., C.E.,
Lurgan.
Park, Rev. W., M.A.,
Alexandra Gardens, Fortwilliam Pk.
Patterson, R. Lloyd, J.P., F.L.S.,
Croft House, Holywood.
Patterson, W. H., M.R.I.A.,
Garranard, Strandtown.
Pinkerton, J. C.,
Victoria Street, Belfast.
Playfair, Charles,
Castle Place, Belfast.
Porter, Hugh,
Hughenden, Fortwilliam, Belfast.
Porter, John B.,
Hughenden Terrace, Belfast.
Preston, Sir John, J.P. (the late),
Dunmore.
Ranfurly, Rt. Hon. Earl of,
Northland House, Dungannon.
Rea, W. R.,
Donegall Quay, Belfast.
Reade, R. H., J.P.,
Wilmont, Dunmurry.
Reed, Talbot B.,
Fann Street, London, E.C.
Reid, James,
Monfode, Greenock.

Reid, John,
　　4, Waring Street, Belfast.
Reid, Joseph,
　　Malone Park, Belfast.
Rentoul, Miss,
　　Cliftonville, Belfast.
Reynell, Rev. W., B.D., M.R.I.A.,
　　Henrietta Street, Dublin.
Richardson, Charles W.,
　　Messrs. Richardson, Sons & Owden.
Riddel, William, J.P.,
　　Beechmount, Belfast.
Ritchie, W. B.,
　　The Grove, Belfast.
Robertson, William, J.P.,
　　Bank Buildings, Belfast.
Robinson, E.,
　　Lismara.
Robinson, Mrs.,
　　Temperance Hotel, Donegall St., Belfast.
Robinson, William A., J.P.,
　　Culloden House, Craigavad.
Rogers, Edgar,
　　Callender Street, Belfast.
Rodman, W.,
　　Riverside, Holywood.
Ross, W. A.,
　　Craigavad.
Shaftesbury, The Rt. Hon. the Countess of
　　Belfast Castle.
Shaw, John G.,
　　67, High Street.
Shillington, T. F.,
　　Dromart, Belfast.
Simpson, W. M.,
　　Hughenden Avenue, Belfast.
Simms, Felix B.,
　　Linen Hall, Belfast.
Sinclair, W. P.,
　　Rivelyn, Princes Park, Liverpool.
Smith, F. W.,
　　Donegall Square, Belfast.
Society of Antiquaries,
　　Burlington House, London, W.
Speers, Adam, B.Sc.,
　　Holywood.
Standfield, T.,
　　Newington Terrace, Belfast.
Stelfox, James,
　　Oakleigh, Ormeau Park.
Stephens, W. H.,
　　Holywood.
Stewart, Rev. Joseph A.,
　　Pond Park, Lisburn.
Swanston, W., F.G.S.,
　　King Street, Belfast.
Templetown, The Viscountess of,
　　Templepatrick.
Thompson, James, J.P.,
　　Macedon, Whitehouse.

Thompson, John,
　　Mount Collyer, Belfast.
Thomson, Sir William, F.R.S.,
　　The University, Glasgow.
Thornton, Francis M.,
　　Benson, Minnesota, U.S.A.
Torrens, John, M.A.,
　　Rosstulla, Whiteabbey.
Torrens, Thomas H., J.P.,
　　Edenmore, Whiteabbey.
Tyler, Henry, J.P.,
　　Limavady.
Valentine, Wm., J.P.,
　　Northern Bank, Belfast.
Vinycomb, John, F.R.S.A.I.,
　　Riverside, Holywood.
Wales, John,
　　Belfast Bank, Belfast.
Walkington, Dolway B.,
　　Thornhill, Malone Road, Belfast.
Walkington, R. B.,
　　Linenhall Street, Belfast.
Ward, Francis D., J.P., M.R.I.A.,
　　F.R.S.A.I., Chevalier Legion
　　d'Honneur,
　　Greenwood, Strandtown.
Ward, F. Edward,
　　Greenwood, Strandtown.
Ward, George G.,
　　Eversleigh, Strandtown.
Ward, John, J.P., F.S.A., F.R.G.S.,
　　Lennoxvale, Belfast.
Ward, J. T.,
　　Cherrykill.
Ward, Robert E., D.L., J.P.,
　　Bangor Castle, Bangor.
Ward, W. H.,
　　Linen Hall, Belfast.
Watson, R., & Sons,
　　Lurgan.
Wilson, James, M.E.,
　　Old Forge, Dunmurry.
Wilson, M.,
　　Sec. Belfast Bank, Belfast.
Wilson, Walter H.,
　　Strandmillis House, Belfast.
Woodside, W. J.,
　　Corporation Street, Belfast.
Workman, John, J.P.,
　　Bedford Street, Belfast.
Workman, Thomas, J.P.,
　　Craigdarragh, Co. Down.
Wright, James,
　　Lauriston, Derryvolgie Ave., Belfast.
Wright, E. Percival, M.D., Sec. R.I.A.,
　　Trinity College, Dublin.
Young, William A., J.P.,
　　Fenaghy, Cullybackey, Co. Antrim.

INDEX.

MARCUS WARD AND CO., LIMITED, PRINTERS, BELFAST.

Royal Arms, engraved by JAMES SMITH, *circa* 1815.